American Indians at the Margins

Racist Stereotypes and Their Impacts on Native Peoples

H. Roy Kaplan

Foreword by Suzan Shown Harjo

McFarland & Company, Inc., Publishers
Jefferson, North Carolina

Library of Congress Cataloguing-in-Publication Data

Names: Kaplan, H. Roy, author. | Harjo, Suzan Shown, writer of foreword.
Title: American Indians at the margins : racist stereotypes and their
impacts on native peoples / H. Roy Kaplan ; foreword by Suzan Shown Harjo.
Description: Jefferson, North Carolina : McFarland & Company, Inc.,
Publishers, 2022 | Includes bibliographical references and index.
Identifiers: LCCN 2022007779 | ISBN 9781476684901 (paperback : acid free paper) ∞
ISBN 9781476645377 (ebook)
Subjects: LCSH: Indians in popular culture—United States. | Indians of North America—Public
opinion. | Indians of North America—Social conditions. | Marginality, Social—United States. |
Racism—United States. | Stereotypes (Social psychology)—United States. | United States—Race
relations. | BISAC: SOCIAL SCIENCE / Ethnic Studies / American / Native American Studies
Classification: LCC E98.P99 K37 2022 | DDC 305.897/073—dc23/eng/20220321
LC record available at https://lccn.loc.gov/2022007779

British Library cataloguing data are available

ISBN (print) 978-1-4766-8490-1
ISBN (ebook) 978-1-4766-4537-7

Front cover images from Library of Congress and Shutterstock

Printed in the United States of America

*McFarland & Company, Inc., Publishers
Box 611, Jefferson, North Carolina 28640
www.mcfarlandpub.com*

This book is dedicated to
the memory of Lee "Jack" Price
and the struggle of Native Americans
for freedom and respect.

We have not asked you to give up your religions for ours.
We have not asked you to give up your ways of life for ours.
We have not asked you to give up your government for ours.
We have not asked you to give up your territories.
Why can you not accord us with the same respect? For your children learn from watching elders, and if you want your children to do what is right, then it is up to you to set the example. That is all we have to say at this moment. Oneh.

—Statement from the Grand Council of Six Nations of the Iroquois Confederacy to the U.S. government in support of the occupation at Wounded Knee, March 19, 1973. Cited in Paul Chaat Smith and Robert Allen Warrior, *Like a Hurricane: The Indian Movement from Alcatraz to Wounded Knee* (New York: The Free Press, 1996), 228.

Table of Contents

Acknowledgments

This book would not have been possible without the assistance of many people who allowed me to interview them in the process of gathering knowledge about this topic. Their hospitality and patience enabled me to pursue a path of discovery that enriched my work. Mario Gonzalez (Lakota) escorted me around South Dakota and introduced me to Tim Giago (Lakota), editor of the *Native Sun News* in Rapid City. Both men were informative as well as committed to obtaining justice and equality for their Lakota brethren. Jennifer Martel, also Lakota, was informative and escorted me around Fort Yates, North Dakota, and the campus of Sitting Bull College. Lynn White (Lakota) of Oglala Lakota College in Kyle, South Dakota, outlined the way discrimination intrudes into the lives of Native Americans today, and Thomas Short Bull (Lakota), president of that college, graciously spoke with me about the issue of assimilation, while Marilyn Pourier (Lakota) escorted me around the campus.

I am indebted to custodians of the archive of the special collections section of the library of the University at Buffalo who helped me locate notes and related materials of Fran Striker, the creator of *The Lone Ranger*. And the librarians at the library of the University of South Florida in Tampa provided me with valuable assistance in obtaining materials from interlibrary loans.

Jacqueline Pata (Tlingit), former executive director of the National Congress of American Indians (NCAI), allowed me to interview her and several members of her staff, including John Dossett, former general counsel at the NCAI, who gave me insight into legal issues concerning Native Americans, and I am grateful to Erin Weldon (Navajo) for arranging this interview.

Eileen Maxwell, in the communications department at the National Museum of the American Indian in Washington, D.C., provided me with important information as well as facilitated interviews I conducted with staff and board members of the museum. Paul Chaat Smith (Comanche), associate curator of the National Museum of the American Indian, gave me a different perspective about the assimilation issue concerning Native Americans, and his books about the politics of Wounded Knee and Native American contributions to culture were invaluable. Suzan Shown Harjo (Cheyenne, Hodulgee Muscogee) generously gave her time and insights into contemporary issues concerning Native Americans, and her contacts with Native Americans on the Pine Ridge Reservation proved invaluable to my research.

Deb DeLone (Menominee) in the Bureau of Indian Affairs provided important information about Native Americans and gaming, and Brian Hallenbeck, a reporter at *The Day*, gave me updates about Indian gaming issues in an interview and insightful articles he wrote. Lori Potter, director of public affairs and communications at the

Mashantucket Pequot Nation, sent me important information about the way revenues are expended by that nation, and her phone conversations on that topic were enlightening. So, too, was the telephone interview I had with Deana Jackson (Navajo) at the National Indian Gaming Commission.

This manuscript benefited from the editorial work of Jennifer Iceton and Michelle Sonnenberg, and it was made possible because of the perspicacity of Charlie Perdue, acquisitions editor at McFarland & Company.

I would like to thank the people who helped me obtain the photos for this book and the permissions for them: Monica Park of the Brooklyn Museum for assistance with Remington's Outlier; Kate Hunzeker, Kim McDonald, and Amanda Allcock for their assistance with a photo of the Crazy Horse Monument; Aaron Carapella for his map of the location of Native American tribes; Daniel Boland and Kim Gatenby of Getty Images; Cody Chapman for securing a photo of the Mohegan Sun Casino; Hannah Elder of the Massachusetts Historical Society; Victoria Lee of the legal department at Marvel Comics; Matthew Cahill of the National Park Service; Sue Garton and Erin Beasley of the Smithsonian Museum; and Melissa Lindberg of the Prints and Photographs Division of the Library of Congress. I would like to thank Liz Dunham (Mi'Kamaq/Abenaki) for her encouragement in the early phase of this project, and my son, Ian, for his technical expertise that enabled me to finish this work. The work of these people greatly facilitated my endeavors, and I hope they are satisfied with the final product, which could not have been completed without the understanding and love of my life partner, Mary.

Foreword
by Suzan Shown Harjo

Native Americans are periodically rediscovered by intellectuals as they become aware of the brutal realities that characterize our lives. We are among the most officially documented of all peoples, and our demographics and our social, psychological, and physiological liabilities are laid bare for the world to see, interpret, and misinterpret. The one consistent conclusion has been that abject poverty and social distress have permeated our lives since we were invaded by Europeans. And like clockwork, the redolent stereotypes that have been used to portray Native Americans reappear as if they are stuck in a time warp. We have been likened to bloodthirsty barbarians, noble savages, drunken illiterates, and, more recently, ascetic mentors attuned to the mysterious links between mind, body, spirit, and the environment.

These characterizations are spurious because, as H. Roy Kaplan submits, they are generalizations borne of racial prejudice that ignore the complex circumstances that contributed to their formation. His book is an attempt to identify the origin of these stereotypes that have been rooted in historical events that shaped the very formation of the United States. From the time of first contact, Europeans have laid claim to land, water, and all other resources they did not own. With technology and, more importantly, foreign diseases, Europeans managed to displace the Indigenous Peoples of this and other continents and, as Kaplan shows, manufacture a cultural worldview and ahistorical record to disguise and justify their theft. The origins of these self-serving stereotypes date back hundreds of years and represent recurring memes in art and literature, government documents, newspapers, and, more recently, motion pictures, radio, television, and the internet.

While many books have been written about Native American Peoples from distinct disciplinary perspectives, this one provides readers with a lucid interdisciplinary analysis that explores the ways in which the arts and communications media have created and reinforced "Indian" stereotypes. By analyzing some of the most impactful sources—such as James Fenimore Cooper, Grey, Faust, L'Amour, and Wilder in literature; Remington, Catlin, and Russell in art; Ford in motion pictures; and Mulford in television—Kaplan provides readers with a summary that shows how these stereotypes continue to impede the status of Native Peoples in American society. More importantly, the author peels away the veneer of bigotry that perpetuates these toxic characterizations. As research shows, the majority of non–Native People in the United States have received inaccurate information about Native Americans.

1

This book provides information that rectifies this situation and should be read by those who care about the conditions faced by Native Peoples today.

The question is not whether the "Indian" stereotypes have been detrimental to actual Native American Peoples—for that, one only has to look at the sordid statistics comparing the health and well-being of Native and non–Native People; rather, the question is what can be done to alter this relationship and correct the imbalance that has been referred to as a "deficit model." The facts are inescapable: poverty, morbidity, and increased mortality are all too often the lot of Native Peoples in the United States, a situation complicated and illuminated by the recent pandemic. The incidence, prevalence, and mortality of Native individuals from COVID-19 has been several times higher than the white population, creating a worst-case scenario that magnifies the systemic and structural inequalities that characterize this nation.

But recent developments threaten to disrupt the centuries-old imbalance predicated on the racial stereotypes that have permeated American society. Native Peoples in the United States (and Indigenous people around the world) are increasing rapidly and are gaining political influence—witness the Native congressional membership that has doubled in recent years and the inclusion of Interior Secretary Deb Haaland (Laguna Pueblo), who became the first Native cabinet member.

Along with the increase in numbers and visibility has been a concomitant increase in awareness of Native Peoples in general American society. Spurred on by our commitments to carry on the old ways, to regain our land, water, and other property, and to use the very court system that was used to wrench us from our homes, we are resisting being erased from history and assimilated into a culture enamored with its own materialism. Respect of our inherent sovereignty, religious freedom, and other civil, human, and treaty rights are not too much to expect from a nation built on stolen land, yet defended by myriad descendants of the very victims and survivors of genocide.

As this book demonstrates, the future of Native Peoples in the United States cannot be predicted by what has happened or even how or why it happened. It is best found in the miracle of what author Gerald Vizenor (White Earth Ojibwe) calls "survivance" and the way songwriter Buffy Sainte Marie (Cree) reflects and compels: "[S]o take heart and take care of your link with Life, Oh carry it on." For many of us, that bright future is assured by carrying on one of the earliest instructions to the Cheyenne People: "The nation shall be strong so long as the hearts of the women are not on the ground."

Aho! Mvto.

Suzan Shown Harjo (Cheyenne & Hodulgee Muscogee) is a writer, curator and policy advocate who has developed landmark laws and led myriad campaigns for Native and Indigenous Peoples' rights; for protection of cultural, historic and sacred places; and for recovery of over one million acres of land. In 2014, President Barack Obama awarded her the Presidential Medal of Freedom.

Preface

The sordid results of the clash between Native Americans and White people reflects the debilitating effects that greed, materialism, and technological chauvinism created during the Native Americans' struggle to maintain hegemony over their resources and freedom. Much has been written about the tribulations of Native Americans, but this book focuses on the origin of racial stereotypes and the impact these stereotypes have had on them. It delineates the sources of misinformation and their effect on relationships between Indians and non–Indians in our society. Interactions between Europeans and Native Americans extends over five hundred years, and the nature of our relationship has taken many twists and turns over the centuries. The ancestors of Native Americans were the first inhabitants of this continent, and even though we periodically rediscovered them over the last hundred years, racist stereotypes about them persist in our society, and new ones that are equally inaccurate and pernicious are supplanting old ones. A recent study of Americans' perceptions about Native Americans, *Reclaiming Native Truth*, concluded that the public is misinformed about the status of Native Americans and "[t]o most Americans, Native peoples are invisible in contemporary daily life." National surveys of people in the United States reveal that half the respondents reported what they were taught about Indians in school was inaccurate, and nearly three-quarters of them thought changes should be made in the public school curriculum about Native American history and culture.[1]

This book focuses on stereotypes because they are endemic to the human condition. The term is derived from old-style printing when a page was set in type and inked, and a run was made, each page identical to the others. The human brain is a complex organ with billions of neural connections governing all sorts of behavior. To simplify predictions, our brains group phenomena and individuals based on common traits and characteristics, hence the application of the term stereotype to people. But people and their motivations are complex, and generalizations about them based on cursory observations can oversimplify human interaction and lead to faulty predictions and prejudice.

Stereotypical thinking may expedite the decision-making process, but the results of generalizations based on this can be flawed and detrimental to the targets of such myopia. Research by Claude Steele and Joshua Aronson on "stereotype threat" revealed the pernicious effects of stereotyping on people of color.[2] In a similar vein, this book traces the evolution of racial stereotypes about Native Americans in our society and links their caustic impact on the lives of Indians to the external *and* internal debilitating effects of prejudice derived from them.

Native Americans' adverse social and economic situation is inextricably linked to the persistence of pejorative depictions of them as inept, inferior, and uncivilized. Even as they win court battles over treaty violations and endeavor to improve their social and political status, they are confronted by implicit biases, which define them for some White people as inferior.

This book is an attempt to reveal the history and contemporary causes of the persisting stigmatization and victimization of Native Americans in our society. There is causality between stereotypical thinking and action, perhaps less overt today than in the past, but still evident in the microaggressions that influence how we treat one another on the job, in school, and in our daily lives. While there is a trend in the social sciences to attribute some portion of our behavior to biology, linking it to genetic predispositions, one fact stands out—humans are capable of rational thought, and because of that we are able to adjust our behavior so that it is humanistic and ethical. We can also make and enforce rules, regulations, and laws to ensure that people behave properly, respecting the rights of others.

The attempt by European/White people to exterminate Native Americans from this land nearly succeeded, drastically reducing their numbers from millions to a few hundred thousand by the turn of the twentieth century. Infectious and communicable diseases spread by explorers and colonists, even intentional attempts at germ warfare and the wanton killing of thousands of peaceful Indigenous people, gradually changed the meme about them. The image of Native Americans evolved from uncivilized, savage barbarians described by early explorers and conquerors like Columbus, to sentimental, romantic, and pitiable misfits. The fantastic success of Longfellow's epic poem "The Song of Hiawatha," published in 1855, reinforced stereotypes about Native Americans as exotic agents at one with nature, but the Plains Indian Wars reinvigorated the earlier stereotypes about Indians as heathen, lusty warmongers bent on the extermination of supposedly peaceful White settlers.

With the near annihilation of Native Americans and their cultures by the end of the nineteenth century, they faded into the shadows of our society, at times becoming cult-like and mystical, as some people paid homage to their reverence for the environment and nature. Yet stereotypes about their supposed predisposition to alcohol and intoxication persist and are linked to their purported slothfulness and unwillingness to accommodate to modern civilization.

Today, the misconception that Native Americans are growing wealthy through gambling in their casinos is an emerging trope that defies logic and the reality of their deprivation. Poverty, unemployment, crime, violence—especially against women—and suicide are endemic to Native American life, on and off reservations. The causes for these social pathologies are deeply ingrained in implicit biases and stereotypes that still influence the dispositions and behavior of non–Native and Native people alike.

This book was written to provide people with an understanding about the causes and consequences of our stereotypical perspectives about Indians in the hope that non–Indigenous people may develop a mature appreciation of the plight of Native Americans and come to terms with the pervasive inequality and blocked mobility that characterize their lives.

Throughout this book terms have been used interchangeably to refer to the Indigenous people who lived on the North American continent prior to and during the invasion of the region by Europeans and subsequent generations of White settlers and prospectors. These terms, including Indians, First Nation, tribes, Aborigines, and Indigenous people, are all recognized and accepted by Native Americans, although the word tribe has a negative and sometimes pejorative connotation, implying uncivilized and primitive.

There is a continuing struggle today over the definition of who is a Native American. I have put the tribal/nation affiliation of persons used as sources of information in the text in parentheses when I was aware of it. As Indians continue to win legal settlements over ownership of land and the distribution of federal funds for health, education, and welfare projects, a different kind of warfare—one fought in the courts of our society—is being waged to resolve the issue of Native American authenticity. Now internecine battles take place between competing groups over the right to collect largesse from the very group that tyrannized and exploited them in the past. How ironic that the victims of exploitation by a dominant and alien civilization find themselves struggling with one another over crumbs while the victors enjoy the spoils of past indecencies.

During the time of this writing the world and our nation were engulfed by the COVID-19 pandemic. Human relationships and the very structure of societies were changed—some forever. In the United States, the disease and reactions to it pointed to deep deficiencies in societal institutions, including the delivery and utilization of health care for millions of people, many deemed "essential workers." The people who care for the sick and elderly, remove refuse, teach our children, police our communities, and grow and serve our food were among groups severely impacted by the halting response to the disease. Nowhere were the effects of COVID-19 felt more adversely than among Native Americans who experienced higher infection and mortality rates than other groups in our society. But throughout the pandemic, Native Americans remained steadfast in their commitment to retain their sovereignty, rekindle interest in their cultures, and strive for the dignity and respect from the dominant White society that eluded them in the past. The people of the United States and the world must take notice that Indigenous people are demanding recognition and equality. Their numbers are increasing, and they will become an inexorable force for social change in the coming years.

Introduction

The Forgotten Minority: How Stereotypes Marginalized the Indians

> We are accidental survivors, unwanted reminders of disagreeable
> events. Indians have to be explained and accounted for, and to fit some-
> how into the creation myth of the most powerful, benevolent nation
> ever, the last, best hope of humankind on earth.
>
> —Paul Chaat Smith (Comanche), *Everything
> You Know about Indians Is Wrong*

On a peaceful day in April 2016 on the windswept countryside of North Dakota, an hour south of the state capital of Bismarck, and half a mile from the Standing Rock Indian Reservation (Sioux), a protest began against the nearly completed thirty-inch pipeline that would carry over five hundred thousand barrels of crude oil per day from the Bakken shale area in Stanley, North Dakota, to Patoka, Illinois. The local Native Americans were soon joined by over a thousand other Indigenous people from around the country and the world. By one account, representatives arrived from over 350 Native American tribes,[1] as well as White supporters, environmentalists, and celebrities such as film stars Leonardo DiCaprio, Susan Sarandon, and Mark Ruffalo. One protester estimated over eight thousand people attended the rallies on a given day,[2] and the landmark study *Reclaiming Native Truth* estimated that twenty thousand people resided in the Oceti Sakowin Camp near the site of the protests, with 360 tribes uniting in their protest against the pipeline.[3]

Over the next year, hundreds of protesters would be gassed, beaten, tasered, and arrested by sheriffs' deputies from Cass and Morton counties and the North Dakota National Guard, as well as set upon by dogs from a private security company retained by Energy Transfer Partners (ETP), the firm attempting to complete the last leg of the $3.8 billion, 1,172-mile project. The abuse of protestors even drew the attention of the United Nations, which noted "inhuman and degrading conditions" for the people arrested by authorities.[4]

The principal areas of contention between the Native Americans and ETP concerned fears that the planned route of the pipeline under the Missouri River near the reservation would endanger the water supply of local residents as well as seventeen million other inhabitants of the region downstream. Native Americans also contended that construction in the area was disturbing sacred burial sites and they had not been adequately consulted about the ramifications of the project. The water protectors raised a rallying cry, *Mni Waconi* (Water is life), and you can still see this message scrawled on garages and sheds in the area.

Tempers flared between law enforcement and the Native Americans and their allies as the number of protestors increased, and tents and teepees dotted the landscape. Unauthorized and illegal incursions onto the right of way and private land precipitated clashes between the parties. A closed metal gate bars access to the area that was the focus of the demonstration, and, until recently, oil flowed silently through the pipes below.

Although the project was initially approved by the U.S. Army Corps of Engineers, the Lakota tribe contended that a leak would jeopardize their existence. (The Pipeline and Hazardous Materials Safety Administration reported more than 3,300 leaks and ruptures in oil and gas pipelines from 2010 to 2016, and in November 2017 the controversial TransCanada Corporation's Keystone Pipeline leaked an estimated 210,000 gallons of oil in northeastern South Dakota.) They further contended that the pipeline was originally intended to cross the Missouri River north of Bismarck but was rerouted because of powerful opposition to the project by residents there.

The Lakota tribe's attorney Dean De Pountis observed, "This pipeline is going through huge swaths of ancestral land. It would be like constructing a pipeline through Arlington Cemetery or under St. Patrick's Cathedral."[5]

Opponents of the project thought they had won when outgoing President Barack Obama halted construction of the pipeline on December 4, 2016. An outraged supporter of incoming President Donald J. Trump, then Republican Congressman Kevin Cramer from North Dakota, now U.S. Senator, labeled the decision as "lawless" and promised that the incoming president would overturn the decision, which is what happened on Tuesday, January 24, 2017, just four days after President Trump took office.[6]

What was overlooked by most media and the despondent Native Americans and their supporters were the extensive ties President Trump had with Energy Transfer Partners and the Phillips 66 petroleum company, which owns 25 percent of the pipeline. Trump owns an estimated $500,000 to $1 million in ETP stock and an equal amount in Phillips 66, and the then CEO of ETP contributed $100,000 to his presidential campaign.

As chagrined David Archambault, then chairman of the Standing Rock Lakota Sioux Tribal Council, noted wryly about the situation: "How do you eliminate a race? That's what the government has been trying to do for 200 years."[7] Lacking political clout, Native Americans once again came out on the short end of the deal, and the oil flowed through the newly constructed pipeline.[8] Today, the fields that were home to thousands of protestors are empty.

It is the twenty-first century and the United States is still struggling with social and political vestiges of racism, and Native Americans remain at the bottom of the socioeconomic ladder—an ethnic group that has, with the passage of time, retreated into the recesses of our mind like the faded Westerns of the late twentieth century. But racism and the efforts of Native Americans to secure social and economic justice periodically intrude into our consciousness despite efforts to suppress it and deny the legacy of slavery and genocide that forged this nation in the crucible of blood, sweat, and tears of millions of people of color denied the rights extolled in our sacred texts.

Despite policies and laws that have been enacted, racial discrimination persists.

Even the most optimistic heralds of the "postracial society" cannot rationalize the killings of people of color by police; the senseless murder of nine members of the Emanuel African Methodist Episcopal Church in Charleston, South Carolina; the White supremacist march in Charlottesville, Virginia, in 2017; the public execution of George Floyd in May 2020; and the continuing struggle of Native Americans against a social and political system that perpetuates poverty, disease, illiteracy, violence, and suicide among them.

This book is about the injustice that was and continues to be perpetrated on Native Americans, a collective of peoples that thrived in the continental United States for thousands of years before the invasion of White Europeans who systematically attempted to expropriate their land and natural resources, misrepresent their culture, and erase their very existence from the collective consciousness of society.

The reader will be taken on a historical tour of the racist stereotypical images that helped create physical and psychological violence against Native Americans—a pattern of actions and ideas that minimized their culture and contributions to contemporary society. Much official U.S. government policy was designed to eliminate the Indian presence from lands coveted by avaricious settlers and politicians. This included genocidal attacks on Indigenous people using superior military technology, even germ warfare, as well as cultural assaults that involved the forced assimilation of Native Americans and their children through relocation to reservations and Indian boarding schools, away from their native habitats and food sources, with the avowed purpose of civilizing and assimilating them into American society and converting them to Christianity.

The English approach to assimilation was large-scale invasion of Indigenous territory and gradual envelopment of Native Americans through the encroachment of successive waves of immigrants (e.g., the Jamestown and Plymouth colonies and the subsequent westward expansion). This differed from the French, Spanish, and Portuguese, who chose the route of intermarriage with Native people and their resulting assimilation and domination through the slow diminution of their cultures, but there is abundant evidence of brutality toward Indigenous people by all the imperialistic powers, including the early European settlers and their posterity.

The remarks by celebrities and violent attacks on ethnic minorities by White supremacist bigots indicate a current of racism that courses beneath the surface of what appears to be our racially integrated society. Great strides have been made over the last half century reversing some of the most egregious violations of civil rights. But the unmistakable stench of racism's putrid odor periodically fills the public's nostrils as gaffes, incivility, and violence intrude into our lives. It is not just perceptual differences over equity between White and non–White people, or even the violent acts of "sovereign citizens" and White supremacists whose crude comments fill the cybersphere and periodically surface in rallies and alt-right manifestos, sometimes resulting in mass shootings and murders as in El Paso, Texas; Gilroy, California; and Pittsburgh, Pennsylvania. The horrific effects of the COVID-19 pandemic in the spring of 2020 revealed the institutional flaws in our social system that led to the unenviable fact that the Navajo Reservation recorded the highest per capita incidences of the coronavirus in the United States, and racism, as we shall see, played a role in that outcome.

The stream of racism runs deep, nurtured by a belief system that light-skinned people are genetically and socially superior to dark-skinned people. There has been a pseudoscientific underpinning of racism that attempts to rationalize discriminatory behavior toward people of color. The level of sophistication of these theories evolved and perverted the accumulation of scientific knowledge. Considerable research has been done to debunk these charlatans (e.g., Stephen Jay Gould's classic *The Mismeasure of Man*).

This book is written to identify the way racial stereotypes about Native Americans became part of our culture and how they permeate our consciousness and perpetuate social inequality by disseminating beliefs that dehumanize and denigrate them. To understand why racism persists, one must comprehend its antecedent conditions (i.e., the nature of the disease that creates the values, beliefs, and behaviors that perpetuate it, even in the face of legal and social sanctions).

This book reveals why racism against Native Americans persists in our society by tracing the origin and evolution of racist thought from antiquity through contemporary society in the United States. It analyzes historical works of fiction and nonfiction and examines their influence on contemporary literature, art, radio, motion pictures, and television.

Half a century after the passage of landmark civil rights legislation, Native Americans are still hampered in their attempt to vote, secure decent housing and health care, and obtain quality education and occupational opportunities. Much has been written about the existence of institutional barriers that prevent them from obtaining economic parity with White people in the United States, but this book addresses the origination of attitudes and beliefs that preceded the construction of racial barriers that make a mockery of the revered words "with liberty and justice for all."

The key to unlocking the code that explains the persistence of the racial animus that permeates our social relations lies within two streams of conscious and, at times, unconscious beliefs about Native Americans. Both stem from the assumption that dark-skinned people are genetically inferior to White people. This belief has been reinforced through the suffusion of our culture with negative stereotypes that denigrate and disparage Native Americans and other people of color through *humor* and *fear*. These primordial emotions distort and attenuate relationships between White and non–White people. The myths that White society created about the inferiority of red and dark-skinned people are the foundation on which institutionalized systems of discrimination were erected. To cleanse our culture of racism, we must be able to identify its *raison d'etre*. That is our mission, and with it rides the hope for a more just and equitable society.

The History of Racism

Racism is a relatively new phenomenon, coming into vogue in the sixteenth and seventeenth centuries as European nations encountered different people and cultures in competition to gain supremacy of land, labor, and capital. Experts concur that prior to these forays there were no calculated philosophical conceptual frameworks that denigrated and disparaged dark-skinned people. The rationalization for the domination and exploitation of Indigenous people in Africa, Asia, and North, Central, and South America by White Europeans was embedded in a belief system that characterized them as genetically inferior to White people and legitimate targets for exploitation.

The origin of stereotypes about people of color, and Native Americans in particular, is present in the ethnocentric ramblings of travelers and writers that found their way into literature and then the mass media, through cartoons, comic books, dime and Western novels, trade cards, radio, television, and motion pictures. For over half a millennium, Indigenous people have been depicted as intellectually inferior, developmentally disabled, subhuman savages. Even as our nation was being established, they were parodied and ridiculed. Words, expressions, and jokes about Native Americans became part of the fabric of our society as elites and, later, working-class White people rationalized discrimination as normal.

The characterization of Native Americans as both wanton barbarians and noble savages was impressed on them from the first European incursions in the New World. These derisive attitudes find contemporary expression in widespread stereotypical depictions of Native Americans that are embraced by decision makers wielding enormous power. Recent studies of diversity in Hollywood and television by the University of Southern California concluded that there is pervasive underrepresentation of women, marginalized groups, and LGBTQ people throughout the industry, describing it as "white-washed" and permeated by an "epidemic of invisibility" for these groups.[9]

Contemporary Racism in America

Prejudicial decisions and actions derive from a base of power. They reflect the higher social status of the group that can define outgroups as oddities, eccentric, and legitimate objects of ridicule and targets for exploitation. White people have infused our culture with derogatory images about people of color that dehumanize and trivialize their existence. These insidious stereotypes are so integrated into our culture that most people, White and dark-skinned alike, often do not recognize their corrosive effect on our attitudes and behavior.

In our increasingly diverse world, we must understand the origin, meaning, and implication of these stereotypes, the implicit biases they convey, and their effects on people who are denigrated by their barbs and dehumanized by their imprecations. In an age of instant communication, where secrets are ephemeral, relationships transient, and cultures regularly collide, knowing the history and intent of racist stereotypes will help readers appreciate the common heritage of humankind and avoid making and approving offensive remarks that perpetuate prejudice. By exposing the history and use of this misinformation, we can break the chains of ignorance that prevent us from interacting on a mature level and become a more equitable society.

A Synopsis of Racism's Origins

Before radio, motion pictures, and television, there was the printed word. From the time of the first modern Western novel, *The Life and Strange Adventures of Robinson Crusoe*, in 1719 by Daniel Defoe, literature was used as an instrument to perpetuate racial myths and stereotypes about Indigenous people. Even supposedly "objective" accounts of Indigenous people by travelers and scholars lent credence to stereotypes about them. The noted English writer Richard Hakluyt (1553–1616) popularized many negative images about Indigenous people, as did the Italian-born historian of Spanish conquests Peter Martyr d'Anghiera's (1457–1526) descriptions of Native people in North, Central, and South America.

Descriptions by explorers to the New World often depicted Native Americans as primitive savages and bloodthirsty cannibals, and early literary compositions by American writers such as James Fenimore Cooper glamorized White settlers' travails in the wilderness and legitimized the sordid treatment of Native Americans. We will examine the evolution of these themes in art, radio, television, and motion pictures, and trace the influence of foundational stereotypical depictions of these stigmatized groups through time.

Upon first contact, Native Americans were cast as savage predators by God-fearing colonists who stole their land and resources. Later, after their removal to wilderness areas referred to as Indian Territory, especially under the policies of President Andrew Jackson, First Americans were stereotyped as lazy, unwilling to work, addicted to alcohol, and incapable of participating fully in the American democratic process. From the late 1800s, following the defeat of the Plains Indians, Wild West Shows toured the United States and Europe popularizing tropes about Native Americans that still exist. These predecessors of radio, motion pictures, and television unleashed a torrent of distorted stereotypes about this continent's Indigenous people that found their way into our culture and distorted relationships between them and the dominant society.

Motion pictures helped diffuse racial stereotypes in a manner unlike print, art, and the more subtle, imaginative radio. Now large White audiences could observe the exaggerated, boorish behavior of Native Americans (often portrayed by White people) and recoil at the sinister implications of their purported inability to coexist and adjust to civilized society. *Birth of a Nation* and the many adaptations of Cooper's *Last of the Mohicans* were milestones in the fledgling cinematic industry. The devastating effects of these early cinematic ventures are reflected in contemporary depictions of non–White ethnic groups on the screen and in White negative perceptions about them.

When television burst on the American scene in the 1940s it brought with it the legacy of racist stereotypes developed and popularized in radio, early motion pictures, and the print media. And what was the fare that it offered? Children were exposed to cartoons based on misinformed, even racist stereotypes derived from Disney's 1946 *Song of the South*. Disney still proffers distorted conceptions of Native Americans and Indigenous people, as in the 1995 animated feature *Pocahontas*.

Then there were the ubiquitous cowboy and Indian shows featuring heroes astride white horses who throttled dastardly villains in black, and savage Indians hell-bent on ravaging White women and stealing cattle from "innocent" settlers. And there was always the faithful Indian sidekick, Tonto, who stuck with the noble masked man, the Lone Ranger, through thick and thin, never disagreeing, raising his voice, or uttering more than monosyllabic "ughs."

Why Read This Book?

Focusing on early landmarks in fiction and nonfiction literature and tracing their imprint on contemporary mass media establishes the pervasive impact these works have on our attitudes, beliefs, and behavior toward Native Americans. Identifying themes that reinforce racist stereotypes and demean Indians helps delineate the consequences of such behavior on political thought and action.

Beyond the social and economic oppression wrought by these conceptions are the adverse psychological impediments imposed on Native Americans who internalize the negative stereotypes about them and in turn delimit their own destinies. This effect is apparent in the high suicide and unemployment rates of Native Americans, and their low level of high school and college graduation. By revealing the underlying processes that led to the formation of racist stereotypes, implicit bias, and discriminatory behavior, this book helps inform White people about the pernicious impact of our racist cultural heritage, and, hopefully, they will correct it.

This book is intended for the general nonfiction-reading audience, people who believe they have reached a level of racial and ethnic sophistication. Their values and traditions perpetuate prejudicial attitudes and behavior toward people of color when they listen to and watch racist comedy and stilted depictions of Native Americans, and repeat words and use symbols that demean them (e.g., Indian mascots).

Reading about the origin of these stereotypes will lead to a cultural transformation, a heightened awareness of the way implicit biases affect Native Americans and people of color in our society. This sensitivity will generate a movement rejecting offensive humor and fostering inclusion of people who have been marginalized and denigrated.

This book is not a call for politically correct speech. *It will promote* understanding of the way White society has marginalized Native Americans for five hundred years. This discussion is indispensable for our future. From the advent of the Red Power movement in the 1960s and '70s, Native Americans have become more vocal about their rights. Recent court decisions and changes in federal policies augur well for their heightened ability to influence and exercise political power, but the Trump administration threatens to reverse hard-won gains.

We owe Native Americans more than passing references to their names on landmarks and sports teams. We must eliminate arcane stereotypical vestiges of racism, become more inclusive, and promote the human potentialities of all people if we wish to survive the coming social challenges of the twenty-first century.

1

Race and Reality

Let the white race perish. They seize your land; they corrupt your women, they trample on the ashes of your dead! Back whence they came, upon a trail of blood, they must be driven.
—Tecumseh (Shawnee chief), 1811

Who Is Native American?

Talking about race and racism in America today in the era of the so-called postracial society is difficult, especially since no one likes to be labeled a racist and branded as a social leper. Many White people steadfastly deny the existence of racism in our society, pointing to the social, economic, and political achievements of people of color as "evidence" that we have attained equality. They drop names like Barack Obama, Colin Powell, Condoleeza Rice, and Clarence Thomas, and remark about the successful careers of Black and Latinx athletes and entertainers such as Oprah Winfrey, Chris Rock, Michael Jordan, LeBron James, and Mark Sanchez.

Rarely is there any mention today of Jim Thorpe, a 6'1", 200-pound Native American (Sac and Fox heritage), born in 1887, who won gold medals in the pentathlon and decathlon in the 1912 Olympic Games in Stockholm. He played professional baseball and football, and was named by an ABC sports poll in 2000 as the greatest athlete of the twentieth century. Nor is the name Will Rogers spoken, one of the nation's most notable humorists and newspaper columnists of the twentieth century. A Cherokee born in Oklahoma in 1879, he was one of the most prominent celebrities of his era.

It is not just the passage of time that has erased these celebrities from our collective consciousness. The contributions that Native Americans have made to our society and culture were ignored and disparaged for centuries, while the dominant White society engaged in expropriating their natural resources, and in the process abrogated hundreds of treaties guaranteeing the sanctity and inviolability of their land. Only recently has the culture and spirituality of Native Americans taken on a positive aura as the insanity of our supercharged materialistic culture presented it as a countercultural alternative.

There are 574 recognized tribes and 326 reservations (see appendix for a list of these), but nearly three-quarters of Native Americans and Alaska Natives live off reservations, mostly in cities, and they comprise nearly two million households (1,792,840). Twenty-one states had populations of one hundred thousand or more in 2015. Alaska had the largest percentage of Indigenous people with nearly 20 percent.

15

Still, with only 6.6 million single-race and combination American Indians and Alaska Natives (AI/AN), they compose only 2 percent of the United States' population. They are not a formidable political bloc, and while they have been winning legal battles over treaty rights in recent years, their collective voice has, with few exceptions, fallen on deaf ears.

The visible accomplishments of successful people of color are noteworthy precisely because they represent a minute segment of the Black, Latinx, and Native American middle and upper class. White ignorance of Native American, Black, and Latinx success in other areas (e.g., business and science) reflects not only indifference, but also White society's unwillingness to recognize accomplishments of people of color.

A list of prominent contemporary Native Americans could be substantial because many people in the United States have some Native American heritage, and more people are proudly claiming it. This is a relatively new phenomenon that developed in the latter part of the twentieth and early twenty-first centuries as the stigma associated with being Native American morphed into a romanticized connection with Indigenous people and their association with sustainable "green" forms of living in accordance with nature.[1]

Although there is a movement among some segments of the Native American population to resist assimilation, they have the highest percentage of people who marry outside of their ethnic group, 58 percent, more than double the next highest group, Asian Americans at 28 percent, with Black people at 19 percent and White people at 7 percent.[2]

Chuck Norris, the motion picture and television martial arts star, is half Cherokee on his father's side. Charlie Parker, the legendary jazz saxophonist, songwriter, and coinventor of bebop, had a mother who was half Native American (Choctaw). Wayne Newton, singer, film, and television star and Las Vegas entertainer extraordinaire, is the son of parents who were Native American—his mother was Cherokee and his father Powhatan, and he claims to be a descendant of Pocahontas. Buffy Saint-Marie, the renowned singer, songwriter, educator, and pacifist, is a Canadian Cree Indian, and Ronnie Spector, the iconic 1960s lead star of the Ronettes ("Be My Baby"), was part Cherokee on her mother's side, as is the multitalented superstar Cher. There are countless other North Americans who knowingly and unknowingly share a genetic link with Indigenous people—a conglomeration of groups, tribes, and nations that has been variously called Indians, Native Americans, First Nation, and Indigenous.[3]

One person who passed himself off as Native American was Espera Oscar de Corti, an Italian American, born in Kaplan (no relation), Louisiana, in 1904. Popularly known (he appeared in two hundred films) as Iron Eyes Cody, de Corti portrayed the "crying Indian" in the iconic public service "Keep America Beautiful" campaign of the early 1970s.

Establishing American Indianness

Some of the confusion surrounding the identity of Native Americans is related to the changing definitions of Indians and their status in the United States. This situation was complicated by the passage of the Dawes Act in 1887 and the policy of termination of Native American tribes that prevailed in this country from the mid–1940s until the mid–1960s. Both of these developments are discussed later. The situation has become even more confused as science helps determine people's genetic links, and political machinations influence laws and public policies that define individual and tribal status as well as ethnicity.

The U.S. government attempts to determine whether a person qualifies as Native American using a form called a Certificate of Degree of Indian or Alaska Native Blood. The form asks applicants to list their lineage and tribal affiliation.[4] Some tribes, as well as the federal government, actively promote the use of the concept of blood quantum, that is, the proportion of genes (blood) contributed to a person through their parental and ancestral lineage. According to sociologist Eva Marie Garroutte (Cherokee), two-thirds of federally recognized tribes specify some measure of blood quantum in their membership criteria, with one-fourth Indian blood being the most common minimum requirement for tribal membership.[5]

Native American scholars like attorney Richard Monette (Chippewa) have contended that the concept of blood quantum is rooted in this country's slave tradition with the notion of hypodescent—the "one drop of blood rule" that was used to prevent non–English people (especially of African descent) from prerogatives of mainstream society such as voting, intermarriage, and property holding.[6] Some Native Americans contend that the federal government's promotion of blood quantum as the method for establishing tribal eligibility is little more than a ruse that will eventually eliminate Native Americans from federally subsidized programs. As Garroutte noted:

> The original, stated intention of blood quantum distinctions was to determine the point at which the various responsibilities of the dominant society to Indian peoples ended. The ultimate and explicit federal intention was to use the blood quantum standard as a means to liquidate tribal lands and to eliminate government trust responsibility to tribes, along with entitlement programs, treaty rights, and reservations. Through intermarriage and application of a biological definition of identity Indians would eventually become citizens indistinguishable from all other citizens.[7]

A similar observation was made by Adrienne Keene (Cherokee): "Notions of 'blood fractions' are colonial constructions, designed to 'breed out' Indians, and now they are being used by our own communities to further restrict not only the futures of our tribes, but our right to love."[8] And Native American activist Suzan Shown Harjo (Cheyenne, Hudulgee Muscogee), the recipient of the Presidential Medal of Freedom in 2014, likened the use of blood quantum standards by Indian tribes to internalized oppression: "We don't need the federal government to breed us out of existence—we are doing it ourselves."[9]

In 1975 Congress passed the Indian Self-Determination and Assistance Act, which allows tribes to set their own standards for eligibility. Establishing tribal membership confers rights like the ability to live on a reservation and receive federal benefits such as education, housing, health care, land inheritance, and, in some cases, payments for land held in federal trust as well as funds that might be distributed from gaming operations or other revenue-generating activities.

Like other Native American critics of biological markers for establishing tribal membership, Garroutte demonstrates the folly of this approach because it ignores the social and cultural components that should also be considered in such momentous decisions, noting wryly that Indians are the only racial group in the United States that are required to document their identity. While illustrating the absurdity of policies that purportedly measure Indianness for tribal membership, she ignored the obvious comparison of this approach with the eugenics movement in the first half of the twentieth century, and the Nazis Nuremberg Laws that used similar methods for establishing Jewishness (Mischling). The implications as well as the methods are at once similar and horrifying.

An excellent anthology about this topic was compiled by Kathleen Ratteree and Norbert Hill (both Oneida). They note that some of the controversy about who qualifies as an Indian goes back to the Indian Reorganization Act of 1934, which stipulated that Indians and their descendants must have resided on a reservation as of June 1, 1934, or have half or more Indian blood. This was the beginning of the federal push to establish Native American eligibility for benefits based on blood quantum.[10]

Some Native Americans question the wisdom and reliability of using blood quantum as the sole or even primary arbiter of tribal eligibility, preferring lineage, reservation residence, parental enrollment, legal adoption of children, marriage, use of Native American language, and cultural traditions. Suzan Shown Harjo contends that "[t]he only way you qualify as a Native American is by being a citizen of your native nation. We have sovereignty. One of the first things a nation does is determine who we are. Nationhood, sovereignty, and citizenship define who we are (e.g., Cheyenne, Cherokee)."[11] From her perspective, it is the responsibility and obligation of each Indian nation to ascertain and define who qualifies for membership within it. Because there are different methods and standards used by the diverse Indian nations, it is difficult to generalize about who qualifies as being Native American. This fact also influences our stereotypical concepts of how Indians should look—something Donald Trump may have been unaware of when he blurted out in a federal hearing on Indian gaming in 1993 (decades before he became president) that the federally recognized tribe of Mashantucket Pequots did not look like real Indians.[12] He was hoping to block their attempt to build a casino in Connecticut but failed.

Genes and Indians

The definition of who qualifies as Native American is a controversial subject precisely because modern scientific techniques can delineate genetic percentages in a person's genome. For less than $100 an individual can find out their genetic heritage and, with some assistance from the many commercial gene-testing companies, trace their lineage. For Native Americans, people of the First Nations who settled this continent, this knowledge can be both enlightening and devastating. Genetic proof that someone is related to distant relatives in Asia may confirm the links between people on these distant continents, but it can also call into question origin stories that emphasize the uniqueness of a tribe and their belief system, which contends they deserve to occupy the land they reside on. A case in point are the Havasupai Indians, who live on a reservation in the Grand Canyon and, through academic deceit and scientific legerdemain, were found to be descendants of Asians who traveled here thousands of years ago.

Conflicts over who qualifies as a Native American have become increasingly divisive and salient in the context of scientific methodologies that can reveal individuals' lineage, but some legal skirmishes may even exceed these perturbations. As Native Americans achieve success in courts, restore abrogated treaties, and receive allocations from federal and state governments for education, housing, health, and welfare, internecine struggles have occurred over the definition of who qualifies as a "legitimate" Indian.

It is perplexing to see the divisions in some tribes as they attempt to finagle their lineage to exclude people from their rolls, even going as far as some Cherokees to advocate for the archaic "hypodescent" rule that was used to relegate people with "one drop of black blood" to an inferior social status. The Cherokee Nation was, until recently, torn apart by earlier court rulings and the Dawes Act that sought to define tribal members and their right to benefits. For decades, members of the Cherokee Nation (about three hundred thousand), the second largest tribe in the United States behind the Navajo, argued over whether to grant tribal citizenship to approximately 2,800 African Americans who they enslaved prior to the Civil War.[13]

In 1860, 11 percent of the Cherokee Nation was composed of Black enslaved people. The head chief of the Cherokees, John Ross, and his brother Lewis, owned five hundred enslaved people, bought to cultivate their land *after* the Trail of Tears.[14] After the Civil War, the Union mandated that enslaved people become members of their owners' tribes. The Cherokees were generally opposed to this order, but acquiesced, infusing more color than some wanted in their communities. In fact, the first law passed by the Cherokee Council after their removal to Indian Territory was titled "An Act to Prevent Amalgamation with Colored Persons."[15] Another act established patrols that roamed the countryside and detained Black people suspected of escaping servitude. Despite being victimized by White people from the inception of European entry into the New World, some Native Americans learned well the rules of racial segregation and racist stereotyping.[16]

This struggle, only recently resolved, will have a significant effect on the lives of approximately forty thousand African Americans, the descendants of the original 2,800 Freedmen who were owned by the Cherokees prior to the Civil War. The Cherokee Nation expelled the descendants of the original Freedmen despite a stipulation in an 1866 treaty with the U.S. government that they and their descendants were entitled to be members of the nation and guaranteed them "all rights of the Native Cherokees."

Some members of the Cherokee Nation were adamantly opposed to extending Cherokee citizenship to the Black Freedmen and their descendants, insinuating that the motivation for desiring tribal citizenship was based on mercenary concerns, but others exhibited traditional racist motives as the email from one agitated member revealed:

> Don't let black freedmen back you into a corner. PROTECT CHEROKEE CULTURE FOR OUR CHILDREN. FOR OUR DAUGHTER[S] … FIGHT AGAINST THE INFILTRATION.

And they demanded tribal rights for only Cherokees by blood. This approach was related to the policies associated with the Dawes Act of 1887 when government census takers determined one's ethnicity by their appearance, considering someone Native American if they looked like an Indian or were white with some Native

American blood, and non–Indian if they had a dark complexion (even though many had mixed lineage).

In 1983 the Cherokee Nation expelled many of the descendants of the Freedmen by requiring them to show a degree of Indian blood through enrollment on the original Dawes Rolls. The issue bounced around in the courts for decades, with the Cherokee Nation spending over $1 million a year by 2008 in a campaign to disenfranchise the Cherokee Freedmen. But under pressure from the Obama administration and Congress, which threatened to withhold $33 million in federal housing funds, the original 2,800 Freedmen were reinstated as Cherokee citizens in 2011. The altercation seemed to conclude with an August 2017 federal district court decision by Judge Thomas Hogan who held: "In accordance with Article 9 of the 1866 Treaty, the Cherokee Freedmen have a present right to citizenship in the Cherokee Nation that is coextensive with the rights of native Cherokees." And while many tribes continue to struggle with the issue of who is a Native American, Bill Barker, former principal chief of the Cherokee Nation, made this prescient observation in 2011: "Now we link arms and march forward. We heal."[17]

In February 2021 the Cherokee Supreme Court unanimously ruled (SC-2017–07) that the words "by blood" are void, were never valid from the inception, and must be removed whenever found throughout tribal law in reference to the Dawes Rolls.

Miscegenation: Myth and Reality

The fact that many people in the United States are of mixed heritage highlights an interesting phenomenon in this country. In the early years of settlement, among some of the principal colonialists, including the French, Spanish, and Portuguese, there was considerable intermixing with Native Americans and other Indigenous people. Offspring of these relationships were often called "half-breeds," a disparaging term among some Europeans, but less significant among Native Americans. Today they are known as *Métis*. Trade in furs by the French, for example, brought them into business and social contact with Indians, and the exploits of Spanish conquistadors are replete with their interactions with Indigenous people as they conquered, enslaved, and interbred.[18]

The high rate of intermarriage and sexual contact between the Spanish and Indigenous people is evident today. A recent study of eight hundred thousand customers of the popular DNA testing company 23andMe found that 18 percent of the genome of Latinx people in the United States was composed of Native American DNA, with another 6.2 percent being African and the rest, 65 percent, European, principally from the Iberian Peninsula.[19] The study found the concentration of DNA was linked to the region where customers lived, with high amounts of Spanish-European DNA in the West and Southwest, and larger amounts of Native American DNA also in these areas because they were historically present there. As previously noted, Native Americans have the highest rate of exogenous marriages of any ethnic group in the United States. Over half of them marry someone outside their group, with women (61 percent) leading men (54 percent).[20]

Obviously, the issue of miscegenation is not currently an issue for Native Americans, but it was for the English in the early days of foreign settlement of this country.

Their culture was steeped in an ideology of White racial superiority, where racial and ethnic intermixing was anathema, taboo, and feared. The story of the most celebrated captive of Native Americans, Mary Rowlandson, is illustrative of this mindset. She lived in her home in Lancaster, Connecticut, in 1675 with her three children and husband, Joseph, who was a Puritan minister at the outbreak of King Philip's War, a bitter conflict fought between the English settlers and the Wampanoag Indians over contested territory and resources. Mrs. Rowlandson was taken captive along with her children and twenty-one others who survived the attack that killed twelve settlers.

For nearly twelve weeks she was led around the region by her captors, constantly roaming from the Connecticut River to what is now New Hampshire, in search of food and asylum from the revengeful British. Her recollections of the ordeal are liberally interspersed with biblical quotes to inform the reader about Divine Intervention, which she believed tested and saved her. Understandably distraught from the violent conflict she had witnessed that resulted in the death of her youngest child within a few days after she was taken captive, her comments are liberally infused with racist stereotypical impressions about her captors: "those black creatures in the night which made the place a lively resemblance of hell," and the "savageness and brutishness of this barbarous enemy." The paucity of food was only surpassed by her impression of its quality; when available, "it was very hard to get down their filthy trash."

Throughout her nightmarish travail, she sought comfort from her Bible that provided solace in the worst of times. Though she was terrified of her captors and initially feared their intentions toward her, she noted that "though I was gone from home, and met with all sorts of Indians, and those I had no knowledge of, and there being no Christian soul near me; yet not one of them offered the least miscarriage to me." And further, "[S]leeping all sorts together, and yet not one of them offered not the least abuse of unchastity to me, in word or action."[21]

Mrs. Rowlandson's ethnocentric ramblings are instructive because they reveal the White Anglo-Saxon racial prejudice that permeated the English culture. Although she was never sexually assaulted, or apparently offended verbally or physically, she retained the most diabolical stereotypes about her captors, even rumors about their purported cannibalism, though from her experience, she knew them to be false. These stereotypical reflections remained with her after her liberation through ransom (20 English pounds) and the freeing of her son and daughter shortly thereafter.[22]

A synopsis of fifteen White captive experiences over a century covering a wide range of tribes and territory in the United States is replete with horrific accounts of Indian cruelties administered to settlers and soldiers. From torture to slavery, readers are led through an assemblage of stories laced with stereotypes about bloodthirsty savages, bereft of civility and remorse. And while the storyline becomes tedious, with Native Americans principally occupying the role of aggressor, there are glimpses within the texts that help explain, if not rationalize, their behavior: theft of their land, violation of treaties, fraudulent negotiations, despoliation of their farming and hunting grounds, debasement of Indigenous women, and disregard for the sanctity of Native American life and lifestyle.[23]

A different type of captive story is that of Mary Jemison, seized by the French and Shawnees in a raid on her home around 1756. A Scotch-Irish girl who was only thirteen years old when taken captive, she was raised by two Seneca Indian women who had recently lost a brother. She lived in western New York among Native Americans for seventy-two years, was married twice to Indian warriors, and raised a family of eight children (one died in infancy), living to the age of ninety-one. Known as "The White Woman of the Genesee," she refused repatriation and is buried in New York's Letchworth State Park.

Herman Lehmann is another case of a White person taken by Indians (Apaches) from his farm in 1870. While some captives were mistreated, tortured, scalped, and killed, others, like Lehmann and Jemison, were adopted into tribes. It was not uncommon for Native Americans to adopt captives to replace children and adults lost through disease, accidents, and combat. Lehmann gained a reputation as a fierce warrior and, like some Christian Janissaries under Muslim control, rose in status. He adamantly resisted concerted attempts to resocialize him into Western culture, preferring the lifestyle of his adopted family.[24]

The experiences of the captive early settlers in Virginia and the Northeast with Native Americans were, at times, horrific in part because both sides were engaged in a terroristic war designed to discourage one another from further encroachments on disputed territory. As vicious as their encounters were with one another (e.g., King Philip's War fought between the colonists in New England and the Narragansett, Pocumtuck, Nipmuck, and Wampanoag Indians in 1675–76, which left many colonial and Native American settlements in ruins), Native Americans in this region of the country refrained from sexually assaulting captive White women. They abided by a code of conduct that, as evidenced by the remarks of Mrs. Rowlandson, respected the personal privacy and integrity of female hostages. This was not the case with some of the Plains Indians and Indians of the southwestern territories.

The Sioux, Cheyenne, Kiowa, Comanche, and Apache garnered the appellation of being ferocious marauders after a series of clashes with White settlers and battles that left federal troops in tatters. Historian Thomas Leonard noted that the war against them intensified following the conclusion of the Civil War. As White settlers and emigrants in search of land and gold invaded Indian Territory and exploited their resources, often in violation of treaties, Native Americans fought back, waging a war of terror to prevent further incursions.

In the last quarter of the nineteenth century, 6.5 million settlers moved west of the Missouri River, swamping the one hundred thousand Native Americans who dwelled in that region. Rail lines were laid across their hunting grounds, and twenty-five thousand soldiers were dispatched to protect the stockmen and miners. But the carnage continued. General Philip Sheridan was appalled by the situation noting: "Since 1862 at least 800 men, women and children have been murdered within the limits of my present command, in the most fiendish manner; the men usually scalped and mutilated, their … cut off and placed in their mouth; women ravished sometimes fifty and sixty times in succession, then killed and scalped, sticks stuck in their persons, before and after death."[25]

Leonard believed that General Sheridan considered Indian fighting the most difficult combat faced by federal troops, and General William Sherman wrote to the secretary of war that "it seems to be impossible to force Indians to fight at a disadvantage in their own country. Their sagacity and skill surpasses that of the white race."[26]

Following the massacre of eighty federal troops and their commander, Lt. Col. William Fetterman, on December 21, 1866, by two thousand Cheyenne and Arapahoe

Indians led by Red Cloud and Crazy Horse (it is said that the Indians loosed forty thousand arrows against the hapless troops who were lured into an ambush), and the decimation of Custer and his contingent of the 7th Calvary at the Little Bighorn ten years later, a series of revenge attacks on Indians culminated in the massacre of Native Americans (Sioux) led by Chief Big Foot at the Pine Ridge Reservation in South Dakota in December 1890. Known as the Wounded Knee massacre, half of the 150–300 Indian victims were women and children. Twenty-five federal troops were lost from the ranks of the ill-fated 7th Calvary. Just two weeks earlier, the famed Chief Sitting Bull was killed by Indian police at the reservation. Tensions were high as federal authorities sought to quell a Native American spiritual resurgence known as the Ghost Dance, predicated on the belief of the inevitable decline of White civilization and the reconquest of plundered Indian lands.[27]

Wounded Knee was the death knell for the Plains Indians, marking the end of their war with the ever-encroaching White civilization. It was not as though they had suffered a string of crushing defeats at the hands of federal troops as much as being overwhelmed by the sheer numbers of White settlers and soldiers and their technological superiority. Deprived of their traditional hunting and farming grounds, some fled north to the inhospitable Canadian climate where leaders like the Chiricahua Apache Chief Geronimo unsuccessfully sought refuge and surrendered with his starving band of just thirty-eight followers in September 1886 to General Nelson Miles. Over five thousand federal troops had been unsuccessfully pursuing him in the United States.[28]

Miscegenation and the Vanishing American

White (predominantly male) fears of miscegenation concerning Indian advances toward White women were resistant to change and resurfaced as pernicious stereotypes in the work of one of the most prolific writers about the American West, Zane Grey (1872–1939). His most famous book, *Riders of the Purple Sage*, was published in 1912 and sold about two million copies, but it was his infatuation with Native Americans of the West that led to his romanticization of the American Indian in *The Vanishing American*.[29]

Initially published in serial form in *The Ladies Home Journal* in 1922–23, with a monthly circulation of 1.9 million copies, it then became a best-selling book by Grosset and Dunlap in 1925. After enduring several rejections by a senior editor at Harper and Brothers, Grey's work became so popular that between 1917 and 1926 his books made the best seller list nine times (each selling over one hundred thousand copies). Publishing eighty-nine novels, half of them about the American West, total sales of Grey's work exceeded forty million copies. They were adapted into 112 films, including over one hundred Western movies, two television episodes, and one television series, *Dick Powell's Zane Grey Theater*, which ran from 1956 to 1961.

Born in Zanesville, Ohio, the fourth of five children, he and his brother Romer longed to be professional baseball players (his brother actually made it). Grey attended the University of Pennsylvania on a baseball scholarship and became a dentist like his father, ultimately forgoing both for writing. Though he suffered from depression and was an avowed philanderer, his wife, Lina Roth, whom he affectionately called Dolly, stuck with him and edited his manuscripts. He was an avid fisherman, frequently catching big game fish in the Florida Keys, New Zealand, and Australia, even holding world records.

One of the first millionaire authors in the United States, and President Dwight Eisenhower's favorite writer, Grey championed the rugged lifestyle of Native Americans and used his novel *The Vanishing American* to dramatize their plight at the hands of unscrupulous missionaries and predatory government officials. The book featured an athletic male Navajo, Nophaie, who bore a striking resemblance to the vaunted Native American athlete Jim Thorpe. Grey was a master at describing Western scenery, but the most compelling parts of the narrative were his criticisms of Christian missionaries who preyed on naive Indians, and the unscrupulous agents of the Bureau of Indian Affairs, who were complicit in their predicament. "How can a man lie to the Indians, cheat them in money deals, steal their water and land, and expect to convert them to Christianity?"[30] And as to the devious missionary, Morgan, Nophaie retorted, "We have no desire to go to your heaven. If there really is such a paradise as you preach about, all the land there will be owned by missionaries. And the Indians would have none to grow their corn and hay."[31]

But Grey went further, indicting the missionaries and federal agents in the corruption of Native American children. Grey initially described Native American girls as occupying a quasi-primitive state:

> The Indian girl of the desert was strangely and pitifully susceptible. She was primitive. She had still the instincts of the savage. Her religion did not make for sophistication—did not invest her with a protection universal in white girls. Her father, perhaps, was a polygamist. Her mother did not teach her to restrain her instincts. There was no strict observance of moral law in the tribe. She did not think evil, because in her creed to think evil was to be evil. She was shy, dreamy, passive, though full of latent fire, innocent as animal, and indeed similar to one. Her mind was a treasure store of legends and lore, of poetry and music, of maiden enchantments, but her blood was red and hot, and she was a child of the elements.[32]

He then alleged that they were being despoiled by unscrupulous predatory White clergy and government employees: "[A]nd the ruin of Indian girls by white men employed on the reservation was the basest crime of the many crimes the white race perpetrated upon the red."[33] Further, "The agent of the government [Blucher] and the missionary of the church [Morgan] were but little miserable destroyers, vermin of the devil, with all their twisted and deformed mentality centered upon itself."[34]

Grey denounced the intentions of the White establishment and its impact on the Indians: "He [Nophaie] saw the incredible brutality and ruthlessness of white men toward his race. He saw that race was vanishing. He was the vanishing American."[35] Further: "The real good to the Indian has been subordinated to the main issue—government employees. This is a waste of money. Actually, most of it is wasted!"[36] These allegations did not sit well with some of his readers who inundated *Ladies Home Journal* with irate denunciations of the work.

Another dominant theme of the novel focused on the love affair between Nophaie and Marian Warner, his blond, White companion who followed him out West to live and work on a reservation where she experienced the duplicity of the authorities firsthand. The original ending finds them marrying, but pressure from the publisher and outraged readers of the *Journal* series caused him to change the ending, where Nophaie dies from exhaustion and influenza after making a pilgrimage to sacred mountains in search of his identity and spirituality.

Through his hero, Nophaie, Grey proposed a solution to the "Indian problem." "Let the Indians marry white women and Indian girls marry white men. It would make a more virile race." And taking a shot at Indian boarding schools: "The Indian children should be educated. Yes! But not taught to despise their parents and forego their religion."[37]

Although Grey was passionate about exposing the adverse situation of Native Americans, the book is suffused with derogatory and outrageous statements about them. He was not above using his considerable wordsmithing to describe Native Americans as "swarthy," "secretive and impassive," with "sloe-black eyes, beady and sharp!"[38] And while his sympathy for Native Americans was real, his prose was suffused with stereotypical descriptions about them. For example, Indians "are not what they appear to most white people. They are children of nature. They have noble hearts and beautiful minds. They have criminals among them, but in much less proportion than the white race. The song of Hiawatha is true—true for all Indians. They live in a mystic world of enchantment peopled by spirits, voices, music, whispers of God, eternal and everlasting immortality. They are as simple as little children. They personify everything. With them all is symbolic."[39] And again: "What did white people realize of the nature and wildness and loneliness that had created these children of the desert? What must dwell in the minds of a race living in this land of enchantment?"[40]

Grey offers ruminations about Indian life through his hero, Nophaie, who had been raised as White and attended a predominantly White university in the East where he was a star football player: "[H]e saw the indolence of this primitive people, their unsanitary ways of living, their absurd reverence for the medicine man, their peculiar lack of chastity, and a thousand other manifestations of ignorance as compared with the evolutionary progress of the white man, Indians were merely closer to the original animal progenitor of human beings."[41]

Somewhat prophetically, Grey concludes, "The Indian deeds are done. His glory and dreams are gone. His sun has set. Those of him who survive the disease and drink and poverty forced upon him must eventually be absorbed by the race that has destroyed him. Red blood into white! It means the white race will gain and the Indian vanish...."[42]

But the White European fear of "the other" blended with racist memes about lustful, predatory Indian warriors in search of White women. This belief persisted despite contradictory evidence that questioned the validity of that assumption, and it found expression in John Ford's masterpiece film *The Searchers*, starring John Wayne and Natalie Wood—a film that explored White male racist repugnance for miscegenation. It was also used, as with the case of Africans and other dark-skinned males, as a cultural club to stigmatize men from other cultures and regions of the globe, denigrating their humanity, reducing them to a level of barbarity and bestiality that assigned them to an inferior social status.

Yet abundant historical evidence reveals rapacious behavior by White male pillagers and conquerors preceding even the Roman Empire. Dark-skinned marauding males never had a monopoly on sexual aggression—historically, it's been a function of power and privilege as can be seen from the behavior of "top dog" White males in our society such as Roger Ailes, Harvey Weinstein, Bill O'Reilly, Jeffrey Epstein, and Donald Trump.

Dark-skinned, powerless males became scapegoats for White Anglo-Saxon repressed sexual fantasies, kindling and perpetuating racist fears of "the other." And while White English colonists recoiled at the prospect of miscegenation, Native Americans tolerated intermixing and marriage with White and Black people from the time of their earliest encounters with these strangers in their land. The Spanish and Portuguese were also agreeable to these interactions, and their legacy is ours today, reflected in the growing numbers of Latinx people that will account for a third of our population before the beginning of the next century. And they, too, are the object of racist attitudes and behavior that prevent them from achieving the promises made in our sacred documents.

2

Why Race Matters

You know the cause of our making war. It is known to all white men. They ought to be ashamed of it. Indians are not deceitful. The white men speak bad of the Indians and look at them spitefully. But the Indian does not tell lies. Indians do not steal. An Indian who is as bad as the white men could not live in our nation; he would be put to death, and eaten by wolves.

—Chief Blackhawk (of the Sac and Fox Nation), 1832

What Is Racism?

Racism is the domination and exploitation of a group based on the color of their skin and associated phenotypical characteristics (e.g., the shape of their nose, eyes, and lips, and hair texture). Along with these overt markers is a racial ideology that depicts dark-skinned people as inferior to White people, labeling them as less intelligent, primitive, lazy, untrustworthy, and incapable of adapting and functioning in civilized society. From the time of the social construction of race in the sixteenth and seventeenth centuries to the present, racism has been used as a justification by light-skinned people (White people) for the mistreatment and subordination of dark-skinned people (Black, Latinx, Asian, and Indigenous populations).

Racism of the most obvious and pernicious form in the United States was represented by the genocidal policies of European colonizing powers (England, France, the Netherlands, Spain, Portugal, Belgium, and Germany), White settlers, and the U.S. government that nearly led to the extinction of Indigenous people on this continent. The systematic displacement of Native Americans through the policy of Indian removal espoused by President Andrew Jackson and later justified by U.S. Supreme Court decisions under the aegis of Chief Justice John Marshall in the early 1800s formed the foundation and legitimization of these policies for decades. Only recently have Indigenous people in North, Central, and South America achieved some semblance of success in reversing them.

The system of chattel slavery, introduced on this continent by the colonizing powers, was responsible for the deaths of millions of kidnapped Africans and physical and social depredations that made the lives of untold millions more wretched. Jim Crow laws enacted after the Civil War in the South systematically deprived Black people of civil rights (e.g., voting and quality educational opportunities) to maintain political and social control over them despite the passage of the Thirteenth, Fourteenth, and Fifteenth amendments to the Constitution.

Blatant racism of the kind symbolized by hooded Klansmen parading before burning crosses represented the traditional visible domination of people of color by White people. With some notorious exceptions, that type of racism has given way to more subtle, tacit, informal methods of dominating and manipulating people of color, what is commonly known as institutional, systemic, or structural racism. While racist behaviors have, for the most part, shifted from overt to covert, the consequences of racism for people of color are apparent in blocked educational and occupational opportunities, pervasive childhood poverty, massive incarceration, high homicide and suicide rates, and shortened life spans.[1]

In all these indices, Native Americans fare worse than other underrepresented groups.[2] Our society ostensibly embraces democracy and human rights while denying the destinies of marginalized groups. A system that prevents the efflorescence of segments of its population must have a rationalization for perpetrating such ignominious beliefs and actions. This book reviews the historical and contemporary role that racist stereotypes play in the continuation of the subordination of Native Americans in the United States, a story as old as this nation, embraced by White and non–White people alike. It is a story with a punch line that keeps hitting and hurting the most exploited and vulnerable people whose immeasurable contributions to the development of this nation were only surpassed by their suffering and immiseration.

Attitudes versus Behavior

Following the acquittal of George Zimmerman of the murder of Trayvon Martin, in July 2013, and the commemoration of the fiftieth anniversary of the March for Jobs and Freedom on Washington, D.C., that year, there were a spate of articles and television reports about the state of race relations in the United States. Most commentators concluded that much progress had been made. The tragic events in Ferguson, Missouri, in August 2014, and soon after in Baltimore, Maryland; Charleston, South Carolina; Pittsburgh, Pennsylvania; El Paso, Texas; Dayton, Ohio; Gilroy, California; and many other locations challenge this conclusion.[3] An objective analysis of the disparities between White people and people of color in educational and occupational attainment, wealth, and health would have revealed this. Yet according to public opinion polls, most White people reject the notion that racism is prevalent in our society and do not believe there is widespread social inequality between White and non–White people. In fact, the popularity of the *Duck Dynasty* show and its memorabilia soared after the homophobic, racist comments made by its iconic leader, Phil Robertson.

Public opinion polls confirm what internet aficionados have known for a long time: prejudicial attitudes toward people of color are rampant in our society. White people's negative attitudes about people of color (e.g., their presumed intellectual inferiority, slothfulness, and criminality), unsaid in public, are often expressed in anonymous conversations, on blogs, and in surveys.[4] Polls also indicate divergent attitudes and beliefs between White people and people of color about critical social issues. The biggest divide concerns assumptions about equity, with White people contending people of color have equal opportunities on a level playing field, and people of color averring the opposite.[5] And while there was a public outpouring of sympathy for the family of George Floyd, and weeks of interracial demonstrations ensued targeting defunding police and attacking systemic racism, a public opinion poll by NPR-IPSOS a few months later revealed that White people's strident attitudes toward these issues appeared to have waned.[6]

A recent poll of Native Americans' perceptions of discrimination against them concluded that "Native Americans report substantial and significant personal experiences of discrimination, across many areas of life." About 30 percent of Native Americans said they have been personally discriminated against in applying for jobs, pay, and promotions, and a similar percentage believe they have been subjected to discriminatory behavior by the police. More than a third (35 percent) reported being subjected to racial or ethnic slurs and people making offensive or insensitive remarks. Fully three-quarters of the respondents believed there is discrimination against Native people in the United States, and four in ten contended that the discrimination is based in laws and government policies.[7]

While rhetoric and practice reveal widescale acts of discrimination and confrontation against Black and Latinx people in our society, offenses against Native Americans are more likely to occur in areas highly populated by Indigenous people, and they believe that some of the most insidious, devastating, and egregious assaults on them have been and continue to be perpetrated by adversarial government policies.[8]

An important dividing line in opinions about race is political affiliation. After the vehicular murder of a civil rights advocate in Charlottesville, Virginia, in August 2017 by a White racist, 58 percent of Americans agreed that racism was a big problem in the United States, up 9 percent from 2015 and 30 percent from 2009. The number of people sensing that racism was an issue grew dramatically during President Obama's tenure, and while the percentage of Democrats who felt that racism was a serious problem (76 percent) was high, the percentage of Republicans exhibiting this sentiment remained fairly constant at around 40 percent. And while 81 percent of Democrats believed that the country needs to do more to combat racism, only 39 percent of Republicans felt that way in a PEW poll conducted in 2017.[9] Nevertheless, there are considerable attitudinal differences between White people and people of color, but the murder of George Floyd by a Minneapolis police officer on May 25, 2020, appears to have had a dramatic effect on the public's perception of race relations as well as justification for police action. In a Monmouth University poll of 807 American adults conducted between May 28 and June 1, 2020, nearly half the White respondents said police were more likely to use excessive force on Black offenders—a stark contrast with the 25 percent of White people who evinced this sentiment in 2016. Even more revealing was the finding that 76 percent of the respondents, including 71 percent of White people and 90 percent of Black people, said that racial and ethnic discrimination was a big problem in the United States, a quarter more than reported this sentiment in 2015. One can only hope that the myriad protests and growth in sympathy for racial and ethnic equality will be sustained in the coming years.[10]

The internet is suffused with racist rhetoric, and much of it was directed at President Obama during his administration. Today, African Americans, Latinx people, Native Americans, Muslim Americans, and immigrants are principal targets. Jewish people are also a favorite of scorn among White supremacists, and hate crimes against them exceed those against all other religious groups. The magnitude of racism on the internet is staggering. Sociologist Jesse Daniels estimated there were over sixty thousand hate websites in 2009, and the number is growing exponentially. Hate groups, estimated to be over one thousand by the Southern Poverty Law Center, White supremacist bloggers, and right-wing radio talk shows bombard our population with a cornucopia of bigotry wrapped in a format of shameless self-indulgent greed,[11] and the inflammatory rhetoric of President Donald Trump incited this behavior. Ruha Benjamin, professor of African American studies at Princeton University, has demonstrated the existence of an insidious form of racism in modern technology—one that is subtly embedded in the very codes and language that perpetuates stereotypes and racial inequality.[12]

Though some racial attitudes have changed over the last century (e.g., the number of White people who accept interracial dating and marriage), others remain firmly contrarian. But there can be little doubt that the populist "America First" movement promulgated by President Donald Trump, replete with its anti–Muslim and anti-immigrant predilections, reflects a bias against people of color. Certainly, his appointment of anti–Indian bureaucrats to the Department of the Interior, persistent denigration of U.S. Senator Elizabeth Warren (D–Mass.) as Pocahontas, and reference to notorious anti–Indian President Andrew Jackson as his idol, did not augur well for the treatment of Native Americans in his administration, which also proposed deep cuts in programs designed to assist them.[13]

Our education system extols the virtues of democracy, justice, and merit, values embraced by White people as endemic to our political and social system, but Black, Native American, and Latinx experiences question the practice of these beliefs. Public opinions and attitudes are ephemeral and quixotic. People do not always level with pollsters and say what they feel. A more innovative and unobtrusive approach for assessing racial prejudice was developed by social psychologists known as the Implicit Association Test. It is a computer-assisted facial recognition exercise designed to assess subliminal affinities for people of different colors. Since its introduction in 1998, almost five million people have taken the test. Many participants are shocked to learn that they are more positively oriented to people of their own color, but that should not be surprising because our society, while increasingly diverse, is de facto segregated.[14] We attend schools, live in neighborhoods, and worship in places that are overwhelmingly monochromatic. For example, about a quarter of the Native Americans in this country live on land designated as "reservations" by the federal government—often isolated and nearly always impoverished. They must contend with rampant poverty, unemployment, blocked educational opportunities, substandard health and inferior health care, and high rates of crime, suicide, drug addiction, and alcohol addiction.

Although there are differences between what people think and say and what they do, there is a connection between our thoughts and actions, otherwise our brains would be merely working to randomly generate ideas. But some highly emotional subjects, and racism is a prime example of this, elicit remarks that are at times superficial or disguise our true feelings. Fear of evoking social opprobrium may mask our attitudes, complicating and confounding the use of attitudinal assessments of racism. Even so, attitudinal surveys on the topic reveal a wide gulf between White people and underrepresented groups in their assessment of racial discrimination and equity in the United States.

Wealth, Real Estate, and Racism

Attitudes are only part of the complex of racial prejudice in this country. Racism today often wears another mask—a less visible but nevertheless insidious, even sinister, barrier to the rights and, more importantly, opportunities of people of color. Dominant White people often unknowingly perpetuate values, beliefs, and behaviors that prevent people of color from obtaining a measure of fairness and equality in their daily lives. The real tragedy of racism is its legacy of dreams deferred and lost, and Native Americans have suffered through generations of destitution and dashed dreams.

Research has determined that Native American tribes that have a high level of self-determination have higher levels of income, employment, and lower poverty.[15] Nevertheless, one-quarter of Native Americans live below the poverty level in the United States; prior to the pandemic of 2020, 12 percent were unemployed (triple the national average), and unemployment rates on some reservations approached 80 percent. Median household income for Native Americans is less than $40,000, slightly above that of African Americans.

Comparison of Median Incomes by Ethnic Groups in the United States, 2016[16]

Ethnic Group	Median Income
Black/African American	$38,555
American Indian/Alaska Native	$39,719
Latinx	$46,882
Two or more ethnic groups	$53,144
Native Hawaiian/Pacific Islander	$57,112
White	$61,349
Asian	$80,720

Source: "Broken Promises", United States Commission on Civil Rights, December, 2018, p. 158.

Currently, 56.2 million acres are held in trust by the U.S. government for Native Americans. The Native American population resides primarily in 187 (5.9 percent) of the 2,237 counties in the United States. Over ninety million acres of Native American land were lost through the allotment process (Dawes Act of 1887). The Indian Reorganization Act of 1934 changed this policy, but only 8 percent of Indian land has been reacquired in trust status, and the Trump administration sought to privatize land ownership on reservations. The federal Land Buy Back program that resulted from a class action suit (*Cobell v. Salazar*, filed in 1996 and settled by the Obama administration in 2009) provided funds to purchase fractionated parcels of land at fair market value to unify sections of Indian land that had been broken up under the allotment policy of the Dawes Act. However, the Trump administration removed fifty tribes from participating in this program and decreased funding for it.

The living conditions of Native Americans on and off reservations are deplorable. This situation is related to the fact that many Native Americans live in rural areas lacking infrastructure and amenities that most Americans take for granted. Fourteen percent of their households have no electricity—ten times the national average. Nearly half of Native American homes do not have access to reliable water sources and clean drinking water. Though water is a sacred and fundamental resource for Native Americans, tribal water systems had 57 percent more water quality violations in the past decade than nontribal water systems, and less than 10 percent of federally recognized tribal governments have water quality standards approved by the federal Environmental Protection Agency.[17]

In 2003, the U.S. Commission on Civil Rights published an important study, *A Quiet Crisis: Federal Funding and Unmet Needs in Indian Country*,[18] that evaluated budgets and spending of federal agencies that support Native American programs. After intensive reviews of the budgets and actions of federal agencies tasked with providing service and assistance to the Native American population in the United States, the commission concluded: "Federal efforts to raise Native American living conditions to the standards of others have long been in motion, but Native Americans still suffer higher rates of poverty, poor educational achievement, substandard housing, and higher rates of disease and illness. Native Americans continue to rank at or near the bottom of nearly every social, health, and economic indicator."[19] And even more damning, "[T]he government's promises to Native Americans go largely unfulfilled."[20] The report noted that funding for the Bureau of Indian Affairs actually declined from 1975 to 2000 by $6 million when adjusted for inflation. Health facilities for Native Americans were frequently inaccessible, and the Indian Health Service was grossly underfunded and consequently unable to meet the health care needs of Native Americans. The housing situation for Native Americans was similarly disadvantaged, and the commission concluded that "[t]he continuously high rates of hunger and poverty in Native communities are the strongest evidence that existing funds are not enough." Further, "[T]he Commission finds evidence of a crisis in the persistence and growth of unmet needs. The conditions in Indian Country could be greatly relieved if the federal government honored its commitment to funding, paid greater attention to building basic infrastructure in Indian Country, and promoted self-determination among tribes."[21]

Fifteen years later, the U.S. Commission on Civil Rights issued another caustic review of the conditions in Indian Country: *Broken Promises: Continuing Federal Funding Shortfall for Native Americans*.[22] The commission concluded that "[d]espite some progress, the crisis the Commission found in 2003 remains, and the federal government continues to fail to support adequately the social and economic well-being of Native Americans." Further, "Native Americans continue to rank near the bottom of all Americans in health, education, and employment outcomes."[23] And, "Federal programs designed to support the social and economic well-being of Native Americans remain chronically underfunded and sometimes inefficiently structured, which leaves many basic needs in the Native American community unmet and contributes to the inequities observed in Native American communities."[24]

Perhaps the most salient contemporary manifestation of the destruction of dreams and lives was the collapse of the real estate market during the Great Recession. Net household worth declined by $16.4 trillion from 2007 to 2009, and real estate values accounted for $6 trillion of that, with housing values declining 30 percent. While people of color managed to overcome past racist exclusionary policies and practices such as redlining, restrictive covenants, and racial steering, institutionalized racism cast a pall over their dreams as mega banks targeted them for high-risk adjustable subprime mortgages that left their homes underwater and foreclosed. The cause for the precipitous decline in the net worth of people of color was attributable to the decline in home equity they experienced, especially in California, Florida,

Nevada, and Arizona—states that experienced some of the most severe reductions in real estate value, and states with high numbers of Native Americans.

The economic status of Native Americans is complicated by the unique housing situation they are in. About a quarter of Native Americans live on reservations and trust lands in the United States. These lands are owned by tribal groups and administered by tribal governments, but they are viewed as wards by the federal government, and the lands are held in trust in Washington, D.C., through the Bureau of Indian Affairs under the authority of the Department of the Interior. While tribal governments are nominally in control of more than fifty-six million acres composing Native American reservations in this country, they are viewed as sovereign nations, and the federal government, through treaties, legal decisions, and contractual arrangements, assists through grants and oversees housing and Native American health and education programs on reservations and tribal lands.

Nearly half (43 percent) of the Native American population resides in the western United States, about a third (31 percent) live in the South, 17 percent live in the Midwest, and 9 percent in the Northeast. The skew in this distribution reflects federal activity and policies that pushed Native Americans further west after settlers took their land. This practice was legitimized by the concept of land acquisition justified under the "right of discovery"—invaders and colonial powers were, under Old English Law, granted authority to claim land they "discovered," regardless of the presence of Indigenous people.

Through treaties and legislation, the federal government promised that it would provide resources to improve housing for Native Americans, but at times the government seized Native American land and even terminated tribes and funding relationships and services. The infamous termination policy during the 1950s was supplanted by a policy that promoted self-determination for Native American tribes. This new approach was bolstered by the civil rights era and culminated in the passage of the Self-Determination and Assistance Act of 1975 that allowed federally recognized tribes to administer housing projects funded by the Bureau of Indian Affairs.

Despite hundreds of millions of dollars that have been allocated to tribes through grants, subsidies, and loan guarantees, the state of housing among Native Americans is wretched. Substandard, overcrowding housing conditions are rampant, and affordable housing is in short supply throughout Indian Country (on or near reservations). A 2017 Housing and Urban Development (HUD) report concluded that "the lack of housing and infrastructure in Indian Country is severe and widespread, and far exceeds the funding currently provided to tribes."[25] The number of Native American households that have inadequate plumbing is ten times the national average, and the number of Native American households with incomplete kitchen facilities is seven times the national average.[26] Nearly three-fourths of Native American homes were estimated to be in need of repair in 2013, and nearly 16 percent of them were overcrowded compared to 2 percent nationally.[27] And the situation is deteriorating. Between 2000 and 2015 the number of overcrowded Native American households and households with inadequate kitchens and plumbing increased by 21 percent.[28]

Slightly more than half (54 percent) of Native Americans own homes compared to nearly three-quarters (65 percent) of the general U.S. population. Much of the household wealth in the United States is related to home ownership. Consequently, average household wealth among Native Americans is considerably below that of the general population, and prior to the COVID-19 pandemic, the average household income of Native Americans living on reservations was $36,486—68 percent below the national average of $53,657 in 2015. Twenty percent of Native American households on reservations earned less than $5,000 annually compared to just 6 percent nationally. Overall, one-quarter of the Native Americans living on reservations exist below the federal poverty level compared to 15 percent nationally.[29]

A study of the housing conditions of Native Americans was funded by HUD in 2016–17 and conducted by the Urban Institute, Econometrica, the National Opinion Research Center of the University of Chicago, and Support Services International. The congressionally mandated study, covering 526 counties and 617 tribal areas in the United States and Hawaii, conducted 1,340 interviews, a telephone survey of tribal departments and other local entities that administer tribal housing activities, and twenty-two site visits. They concluded, "The housing problems of American Indians and Alaska Natives, particularly in reservations and other tribal areas, are extreme by any standard." Living conditions in these areas were described as some of the worst in the entire country.

Forty percent of the reservation housing was considered substandard compared to 6 percent of non–Indian locations. Nearly a quarter of homes in these areas were found to have a serious physical problem compared to 5 percent of the general housing in the nation. One-third of the homes on reservations were found to be over-crowded, and less than half the homes on reservations were connected to public sewer systems with 16 percent lacking indoor plumbing. In some areas, half of Indian homes did not have phone service, and nearly a quarter of Native American households spent 30 percent or more of their household income on housing. Furthermore, the practice of "doubling up" (i.e., having friends and or family members live within a household because they would otherwise be homeless) was a common phenomenon. The report estimated that there are between forty-two thousand and eighty-five thousand homeless Native Americans living in tribal areas.

The squalid living conditions of Native Americans on federally established reservations may be due to the remote location of the reservations and tribal lands, lack of infrastructure to support modernization and development in these areas, and complex legal constraints that impede or prevent significant change. While the Native American Housing Block Grant program and the Indian Community Block Grant and Indian Housing Loan Guarantee Fund provide funding and resources to tribes to meet the needs of Indigenous people, there is still need for improvement.

The HUD report noted that some progress in the housing field has been achieved since the passage of the landmark Native American Housing Assistance and Self-Determination Act (NAHASDA) in 1996, and the Helping Expedite and Advance Responsible Tribal Homeownership (HEARTH) Act in 2012, but much more must be done. The waiting period for new tribal housing can be as long as three years.[30]

A critical impediment to improving housing for Native Americans is their remote location often lacking in necessary infrastructure for housing development like roads, utilities, and sanitary systems. While the Block Grant program, which provides federal funding for housing development to tribes, was established in 1998 by the NAHASDA and is the largest source of funding for Native American housing, enabling the construction of 38,000 affordable housing units and the rehabilitation of 770,000 units, its funding has not kept pace with inflation and the increased demand for Native American housing. Adjusted for inflation, the constant dollar amount for funding for such programs shows a steady decline, and the Trump Administration requested **less** ($54 million in 2018) for this purpose. Although Congress increased the appropriation by $100 million to create approximately 155,000 housing units through Block Grant and Loan Guarantee programs, the need for affordable, safe, and sanitary housing for Native Americans is dire, especially because the Indian population is increasing at twice the rate of the general population.

The 2017 HUD report concluded that federal agencies need to assist tribes to better leverage the assistance they receive, and "tribes have produced and maintained low-income housing much more effectively since the passage of the NAHASDA. Nominal dollars for the Indian Housing Block Grant have not been increased since 1996, however, leading to a substantial decrease in buying power. Limited funding is a key constraint for many tribes who could increase their rate of housing production if they had more funding." Yet a series of investigative reports by Craig Harris and Dennis Wagner in the *Arizona Republic* found widespread malfeasance in the administration and utilization of federal HUD funds by the Navajo Housing Authority (NHA). According to the authors, in 1998 the NHA estimated that 21,000 families on the sprawling 27,413-square-mile reservation, covering parts of New Mexico, Arizona, and Utah, needed new homes. Yet, a decade later, despite receiving enormous amounts of money, the need was up to 31,000 new units, and an additional 34,300 needed to be refurbished.

The need for housing assistance on the reservation is acute. At around 350,000 people, the Navajo Nation is the largest tribal group in the United States. Nearly half the households have annual incomes of less than $25,000. Forty-four percent of adult Navajos have not completed high school, and only 7 percent have college degrees. Less than a quarter of the residents have full-time jobs. Federal housing funds have provided over a billion and a half dollars ($1.66 billion) to the NHA since 1998, but it was sitting on a surplus of $234 million in 2016 despite the desperate need. Half of the existing Navajo homes were in need of repair, yet the authors found that only 543 new houses had been built between 2009 and 2017, with $71.5 million spent on planning and administration alone in 2013 and another $12.6 million to construct NHA offices and a youth club and day care center.[31] Clearly, the housing needs of Native Americans are appalling, and they require more than the liberal application of money to solve them. The situation of Haiti, with its proliferation of nongovernmental organizations (NGOs), comes to mind, where as many as twenty thousand well-intentioned organizations receive the majority of donations yet the island remains impoverished.[32]

Racism in the Corporate Sector

Today, fastidiously dressed businessmen have replaced garish hooded klansmen by promoting systemic racism, and their actions have enormous negative economic consequences for people of color. One of the most visible examples of this type of racism are the settlements concerning misbehavior in the corporate sector. Just two decades ago, many corporations reached landmark agreements with the federal Equal Employment Opportunity Commission. Shoney's settlement in 1992 highlighted racist hiring policies that cost the company $132.8 million, and Denny's 1994 $54.4 million racism settlement followed.[33] The continuation of such behavior has enormous negative impacts on the opportunity structure of our society. Although many White people assume that the United States offers everyone equal opportunities to become successful, 24,600 charges of racial discrimination were filed with the federal Office of Equal Employment Opportunity Commission in 2018, and another 7,106 for discrimination because of national origin.[34]

The color of one's skin continues to have adverse effects on a person's finances. Without admitting it practiced discrimination, American Honda Finance agreed to pay $24 million in relief to thousands of African Americans, Latinx Americans, and Asian and Pacific Islanders in July 2015 as part of a settlement with the U.S. Department of Justice and Consumer Financial Protection Bureau. The corporation was allegedly charging African Americans on the average $250 more than White borrowers, while Hispanic Americans paid an extra $200, and Asian and Pacific Islanders anted up an additional $150 over White customers. The company also agreed to contribute $1 million to fund a consumer education program—perhaps its own agents will enroll. Honda agreed to limit car dealers' discretion to charge interest markups on loans and improve its monitoring compliance.[35]

Native Americans are also victims of institutionalized racism, facing behavior that frequently hurts more than the stereotypical stares and verbal insults hurled in their direction.[36] In the NPR/Harvard/Robert Wood Johnson study of discrimination against Native Americans, about one-third reported being personally discriminated against in pay, promotions, and applying for jobs. Seventeen percent reported discrimination in trying to rent or purchase housing, and 13 percent believed they had been discriminated against when trying to apply to college or attending there. Even more alarming, 38 percent reported they or a family member had actually experienced violence because of their ethnicity.[37]

A recent study of Fortune 500 corporations revealed that just 0.2 percent of senior executive positions in sixteen firms that publicize information on diversity were held by Native Americans and only 0.1 percent were held by Hawaiian or Pacific Islanders. While the sample was small, extrapolating the findings to other large corporations is indicative of the dearth of Indigenous people in the corporate sphere in the United States.[38]

Educational Challenges

Each year about a million students drop out of school in the United States. Research indicates that they and their families will live in the nether world of society, on the margin, barely getting by, making the vaunted American Dream more of a nightmare. In our society, which puts a premium on certification, high school graduates' earnings over a working lifetime of forty years yields $1,200,000; $2,240,000 for people with a bachelor's degree; and just $800,000 for high school dropouts.

The level of academic achievement varies by ethnicity, and the educational attainment of Native Americans is the lowest of all ethnic groups in the United States. Indians have lower test scores in math and reading than all other groups, and disparities between Native Americans and other groups have been growing in recent years. They also have the highest dropout rates in the nation: 13.1 percent for male youth ages sixteen to twenty-four compared to the general male rate of 9.9 percent, and 7.2 percent for Native American females ages sixteen to twenty-four compared to the general female dropout rate of 5.2 percent. Only 17 percent of Native Americans begin college compared to 62 percent of all students in the general population.[39]

Educational attainment among Native Americans lags behind every other ethnic group in this nation. The overall high school graduation rate for Native Americans (the percentage of first-year students who graduate in four years) is 72 percent compared to a national average of 84 percent. This compares with a White high school graduation rate of 88 percent, Asian/Pacific Islanders of 91 percent, Black/African Americans of 76 percent, and Latinx Americans of 79 percent. While 90 percent of Indigenous children attend public schools (1.2 percent of public school students), 8 percent attend schools controlled by tribes under the aegis of the Bureau of Indian Affairs, and their graduation rates are appallingly low: around 60 percent. A Government Accounting Office report found that Indigenous children in schools associated with the Bureau of Indian Affairs scored twenty-two points lower in English proficiency and fourteen points lower in math than Native children attending public schools.[40] In the seven states having the highest percentage of Indigenous students, only about two-thirds of Native American and Alaska Native children graduate from high school in four years. Only 13 percent of Native Americans twenty-five and older have a bachelor's degree compared to 28 percent for other ethnic groups.[41] Only 16 percent of Native American students received a bachelor's degree or higher in 2017 compared to 36 percent for all other groups of students.[42]

Research indicates that early education has an important impact on a child's academic career and later life.[43] Yet nearly half of all Native American children ages three to four **are not** enrolled in a prekindergarten program. And continuing this trend, Native American children are least likely to attend a high school offering advanced placement courses or schools offering a range of math and science courses.[44]

Although the federal government is obligated to provide financial assistance for educational services to Native Americans as part of its trust responsibilities, funding for Bureau of Indian Education (BIE) schools is insufficient to resolve the severe infrastructure and staffing problems many of these schools have, even though the Indian Self-Determination Assistance Act, which was passed in 1975, was supposed to remedy these issues. While approximately 93 percent of Native American children attend public schools operated by state and local authorities, their curricula are often developed without input from Native American sources and perpetuate stereotypical attitudes about them. These schools are often structurally deficient and staffed by inexperienced teachers, with Native children having to endure bullying and microaggressions from staff and peers who are oblivious about their cultural heritage.

Recognizing that BIE schools were underperforming, two-thirds of these schools were placed under tribal educational authorities in 2014, but a year later the General Accounting Office determined that the BIE had not adopted practices that would ensure the success of this realignment.[45] Complicating this problem, President Trump's fiscal 2019 budget called for a $144 million **decrease** in funding for BIE schools, perpetuating a flat level of funding for them between 2007 and 2018. Adjusting for inflation, this **decreased** funding for BIE schools during that decade by 1 percent.

Black, Latinx, and Native American children receive more frequent and severe punishment than their White and Asian peers. Their out-of-school suspensions are longer and their expulsions more frequent, and they are more likely to receive referrals to the office for offenses that their White and Asian peers do not. The situation became so critical that the Obama administration's U.S. Department of Education and U.S. Department of Justice sent a joint "Dear Colleague" letter to every public school in the country on January 8, 2014, to provide guidance and assist schools in meeting federal law regarding student discipline. The letter also included a recent review of racial disparities in delivering student discipline.[46]

Racial Disparities in Health

The Rev. Dr. Martin Luther King, Jr., once said, "Of all the forms of inequality, injustice in health is the most shocking and inhuman." Being of color in the United States not only affects the way you live, but how long you live. Although there has been an increase in the life expectancy of various ethnic groups, Native Americans live 5.5 years less than the national average. Hispanic Americans have a higher life expectancy than Black and White Americans, and Asian Americans lead all groups with a life expectancy of nearly eighty-seven years. Life on Indian reservations is often shortened by poverty and violence (e.g., Native Americans living in South Dakota can expect to live only sixty-eight years).

The health care crisis among people of color was dramatically illustrated by the effects that the highly contagious coronavirus (COVID-19) had on them. As the disease engulfed the United States in the spring of 2020, deaths among Black and Latinx Americans in New York City, the epicenter of the outbreak, were twice that of White people, and in Wisconsin, a state where Black people account for only 6 percent of the population, they comprised 40 percent of the deaths from the disease. In Louisiana, where Black people are about a third of the population, they accounted for three-fifths of the fatalities.[47]

The disproportionate impact of the disease on Black and Latinx Americans was attributable to the confluence of this population being afflicted with multiple preexisting health conditions (e.g., diabetes, obesity, cardiac issues). Likewise, the Native American population was ravaged by COVID-19, which led Congress to appropriate an extra $1 billion for the besieged Indian Health Service to cope with the deadly virus. But the emergency appropriation was too late to assist the nearly 16,000 infected and 645 Indians who already succumbed to the disease by late August 6, 2020. On the Navajo Reservation, which was the site of the highest number of deaths per capita in the country, Dr. Michelle Tom (Diné), a physician who has been working to save her people, likened her frenetic lifestyle to earlier days: "It feels like residency times 10. I've never been challenged this hard spiritually. When we're about to lose one I feel a part of me goes too."[48] She noted that the COVID-19 epidemic in the United States exposed existing inequities in the Indian health care system. In the two communities she served (Winslow, Arizona, and Little Colorado Medical Center), there was no cardiologist or pulmonologist and only four ventilators and twenty-five intensive care unit beds for 170,000 people. It takes a one-and-a-half-hour helicopter ride to a special facility in emergencies.[49] Throughout the tragedy surrounding the

COVID-19 pandemic, the Native Wellness Institute, a 501(c)3 nonprofit organization founded in 2000, provided technical assistance and training to Indigenous people to help them cope with the situation.

To prevent a similar scourge, members of the Oglala and Cheyenne River Sioux tribes established checkpoints at strategic sites around their reservations in early April 2020. Although Governor Kristi Noem of South Dakota threatened to eliminate them, Native American leaders contended that they were exercising their sovereignty to minimize nonessential visitors and monitor who entered and left their reservations.

The literature on race and health disparities is voluminous. It conclusively demonstrates racial prejudice in the utilization and dispensation of health care and, more importantly, different outcomes based on the color of one's skin. The landmark study of this phenomenon, *Unequal Treatment: Confronting Racial and Ethnic Disparities in Health Care*, was published in 2002 and conducted for Congress by the Institute of Medicine of the National Academy of Sciences. Its main conclusion:

> Racial and ethnic minorities tend to receive a lower quality of healthcare than non-minorities, even when access-related factors, such as patients' insurance status and income, are controlled. The sources of these disparities are complex, are rooted in historic and contemporary inequities, and involve many participants at several levels, including health systems, their administrative and bureaucratic processes, utilization managers, health care professionals, and patients.

Further, "Consistent with this charge, the study committee found evidence that *stereotyping, biases, and uncertainty on the part of healthcare providers can all contribute to unequal treatment* (emphasis added)."[50]

What is the net result of such unequal treatment? Pain, suffering, and shorter life expectancy. Epidemiological research is replete with studies showing disparities among and between White, Black, Native, and Latinx Americans from dental to cardiac care and drug prescriptions. One disturbing study revealed Black people were less likely to access painkillers than White people because they were less available in predominantly African American residential areas, even when Black people lived in relatively affluent places.[51]

The health status of American Indian and Alaska Natives (AI/AN) is significantly worse than that of the general public. Through treaties the U.S. government assumed responsibility for the health care of AI/AN people. They are treated under the law as "domestic dependent nations" and have similar status as states in regard to sovereignty. The federal government has a trust obligation in regard to the 574 recognized tribes (there are an additional 265 state or nonfederally recognized tribes).

The Indian Health Service (IHS) was created in 1955 to provide health care to over two million of the nation's 3.7 million AI/AN people, focusing on those living on or near reservations and in rural communities, mostly in the western United States and Alaska. Despite spending over $5 billion in 2019 for the IHS, there is a $450 million backlog for health service facilities construction, and the 2018 federal budget called for a reduction of $300 million in the IHS budget. The agency has consistently received only half of the funds needed and habitually runs out of funding by midyear, leaving patients to fend for themselves.[52]

Although the federal government is committed to provide health care for AI/

AN people, the U.S. Civil Rights Commission recently concluded that "the unmet health needs of the American Indian people are severe and the health status of the Indians is below that of the general population of the United States."[53] The commission attributed this to insufficient funding of the IHS, even with the development of Urban Indian Health Organizations serving many Native Americans who reside off reservations. The Civil Rights Commission noted that only 1 percent of the IHS budget is allocated for urban Indian health care despite the fact that many of the recurring health care problems of Native Americans living in urban areas are more acute than people living on reservations.[54]

The results of this pecuniary policy are evident in the negative health status of AI/AN people. Since a disproportionate amount of funds (99 percent) are allocated for people who reside on reservations, there is a desperate need for health care services for the three-quarters of Native Americans who live off them. The federal government organized the Urban Indian Health Program under the aegis of the Indian Health Service, which is part of the Department of Health and Human Services. It is charged with providing care and services to Indigenous people through a combination of physical, mental, emotional, and spiritual approaches. While funds are annually allocated for the care of Indigenous people in the United States, a report from the Indian Health Service summarized the situation bluntly: American Indian and Alaska Native people have long experienced lower health status when compared with other Americans. Living on average five years less than the non–Indian public, American Indians and Alaska Natives have higher rates of heart, liver, and respiratory diseases. Sixteen percent of the Native American population has been diagnosed with diabetes, twice the national average. They also suffer from higher rates of alcoholism and other forms of substance abuse (twice the national average—18 versus 9.6 percent), and are more often the victims of homicides, suicides, and domestic and sexual violence than the non–Indian population.

Mortality Disparity Rates
of American Indian/Alaska Natives (AI/AN)
in 2009–2011 versus All Other Ethnic Groups in 2010[55]

Cause of Death	Ratio of AI/AN to All Other Groups
Alcohol-induced	6.6
Chronic liver disease and cirrhosis	4.6
Diabetes mellitus	3.2
Accidents	2.5
Homicide	2.1
Influenza and pneumonia	1.8
Drug-induced	1.8
Suicide	1.7
Septicemia	1.6
Kidney disease	1.5
Heart disease	1.1
Chronic lower respiratory disease	1.1
Stroke	1.1
Hypertension	1.1
Cancer	1.0
Alzheimer's disease	0.7

Source: "Broken Promises", United States Commission on Civil Rights, December, 2018, p. 66.

The adverse health status of Indigenous people is compounded by their high rate of poverty (27 percent compared to 14 percent for the non–Indian population), and while some Indigenous people receive health care under the Affordable Care Act, private insurance, Medicare, Medicaid, and the Department of Veterans Affairs (VA), the Indian Health Service remains the most important provider. An analysis of the proposed 2020 federal budget by the National Congress of American Indians revealed that population growth among Native Americans combined with inflation is actually leading to decreased funding for Indian health care. While President Trump's 2020 federal budget would have increased IHS spending by $392 million, the total amount fell a billion dollars short of the $7 billion requested by the Tribal Budget Formulation Workgroup recommended for the IHS.[56]

Being of color in this society not only has negative implications on physical health, but also Black, Latinx, and Native Americans' exposure to daily racial insults and pressures causes mental anguish leading to high rates of anxiety, depression, hypertension, and heart disease. Scientists refer to this phenomenon as *allostatic load*.[57] Experiencing powerlessness just once can leave a scar on one's psyche—a mark of prejudice that many carry deep within. But for marginalized groups—Black, Latinx, and Indigenous people—the frequency and severity of their negative encounters with privileged people serve as constant reminders of their powerlessness, often leading to frustration and despair. As anthropologist Audrey Smedley noted, "A person or group's identity as racially inferior takes precedence over any other qualities that might be present. It evokes attitudes (and behavior) of contempt and disrespect from the white community. This situation imposes enormous stress on low-status people and is a source of much of the feeling of oppression that they experience."[58]

An emerging new line of research called epigenetics poses some startling possibilities in the case of Native Americans. Although the research has not been firmly established, there are indications that trauma can be passed on to future generations through genetic changes made by our neuroendocrine system. According to some studies, our experiences can influence the structure of our genes, enabling them to switch on negative responses to stress and trauma. From this perspective, historical trauma like that experienced by Native Americans not only leads to post-traumatic stress disorder (PTSD), but it can also lead to the development of depression and type 2 diabetes, *and* these ailments may become part of a person's genetic legacy, being passed on to future generations.

The high rates of alcohol and drug addiction, suicide, PTSD, sexual violence, and mental illness among Native Americans and Alaska Natives may, from the epigenetic perspective, be the result of genetic modifications from trauma passed on from previous generations.[59] The National Congress of American Indians (NCAI) has embraced this proposition, which is also associated with pandemic adverse childhood experiences (ACE) among these groups, in part stemming from the horrific experiences their ancestors suffered at the hands of explorers, invaders, government agencies and policies, and Indian boarding schools.[60]

An important caveat here is that heavy reliance on the physiological etiology of social pathologies such as poverty, violence, and PTSD may lend credence to the very systems of prejudice and racist behaviors that Indigenous people and people of color have been fighting against, namely eugenics. Blaming the victims may overlook or minimize the role that societal institutions continue to play in the formation and perpetuation of social pathologies. Overreliance on the purported biological causes of social pathologies may provide an underpinning for the very racism that led to the oppression of religious and ethnic minorities.

Race and Power in America

Imagine a time when you were marginalized because of some characteristic about you (e.g., your gender, stature, age, hair, religion, or skin color). Now consider how your life might be if this happened to you all the time, *or, because of prior experiences, you thought it was occurring on a regular basis.* How ironic that some White males perceive themselves to be the principal victims of discrimination in this society, when power was embedded in institutions designed of, by, and for them to perpetuate their preferential position.[61]

There is a lopsided balance of political power in our society. Only three African Americans and six Latinx Americans currently serve in the U.S. Senate, and only one Native American, Jeanne Shaheen from New Hampshire, was elected in 2009[62] (a twelfth-generation descendant of Pocahontas). There have been only eleven African American, eleven Latinx, and six Native American senators since Reconstruction. Cora Belle Reynolds Anderson became the first Native American woman elected to a state legislature (D–Michigan) and served from 1925 to 1926.

Minority candidates have fared better in the U.S. House of Representatives— there were fifty-four African Americans and forty-six Latinx representatives in the 116th Congress, but only four Native Americans, although their number would increase to six in 2020. All these groups are underrepresented in comparison to their proportion of the population of the country.

African Americans have made tremendous inroads by capturing mayoralty posts. From virtually none in the mid-1960s, there are now over 650 Black mayors. There are currently only four Native American mayors in the United States: Roberta "Birdie" Wilcox Cano (Diné/Pueblo), mayor of Winslow, Arizona; Tasha Cerda (Tohono O'odham), mayor of Gardena, California; Todd Gloria (Tlingit), mayor of San Diego, California; and David Holt (Osage), mayor of Oklahoma City, Oklahoma. But being mayor of a predominantly poor inner city no longer carries the clout these posts commanded decades ago. As sociologist William Julius Wilson noted, the inner cities today have become vast wastelands burdened with debt, unemployment, and the loss of personal and political power.[63]

Hate: The Silent Sickness

This discussion reflects a pattern of discriminatory behavior that clearly disadvantages people of color, especially Native Americans. It is a pattern that social scientists call systemic or institutional racism, which is to say, it is embedded in the very structure and function of our social system. While social scientists often focus on this form of discriminatory behavior, we are concerned here with the underlying social psychological belief system of words and images that provide the rationalization for racism in our culture.

There is a thread, a system of beliefs that justifies the disparagement of dark-skinned people, that is woven through the previous discussion. It draws on centuries-old concepts that depict them as inferior, subhuman, soulless objects, unworthy of respect and undeserving of equal social status in our White-dominated society. This type of thinking originated in the sixteenth and seventeenth centuries in western Europe. It generated a system of perquisites and entitlements that endowed White people with social, economic, and political status, enabling them to maintain hegemony over dark-skinned people in colonized lands.

A belief system about Native Americans and people of color developed that was suffused with innuendo, epithets, sarcasm, ridicule, and deprecation. Negative attitudes toward Native Americans were widespread before the founding of this nation, and they became culturally embedded in White society through the devices we enumerate in the following pages. To the Indians' detriment, they were manifested in federal and state policies that affected treaties with them and their enforcement or, more often, the lack thereof.

Today, these attitudes are often unconscious. Nevertheless, they help perpetuate social inequality by sustaining a system of White privilege and supremacy. Initially, our social institutions were under the exclusive control of a White aristocracy, the "Founding Fathers," who constructed a society that justified their social position and dehumanized people who did not look or act like their dominant group, even poor White people.

Elite White people's domination of Indigenous people through colonization was justified on the basis of their presumed natural physical and moral/spiritual superiority. They were exercising their ability to control other regions and peoples, what is often referred to today as American exceptionalism. This rationalization was bolstered by ideological and theological assumptions about the supportive role that Divine Intervention played in determining the outcome of White expansionism throughout the continent and world.

This reasoning formed the basis for the establishment of White racism and the justification that is still used to demean and disparage Native Americans and other people of color. A mindset arose that assumed non–White people were lower on the phylogenetic scale of evolutionary development, incapable of higher-level reasoning and civilized living. Their "primitive" morphology supposedly enabled them to withstand pain and eschew analgesics.[64] This line of specious reasoning has been used to stigmatize Native Americans and other people of color as unwanted, dangerous denizens who should be caged like beasts, isolated from the dominant "innocent" White society, confined to reservations, and restricted from participating in the political process—sentiments evoked regularly by President Trump's populist followers.

Though often unconscious, and rarely spoken publicly by White people, these attitudes are expressed as rhetorical questions:

If Indigenous and dark-skinned people were not inferior, why were they subjugated by Whites? If everyone has access to free public education, why are Black, Native American, and Latinx children unable to compete with Whites in schools? Isn't their supposed propensity for violence indicative of their incivility and atavism and the reason for their high incarceration rates? Doesn't the Bible indicate that God blessed Whites and cursed the seed of Noah's dark-skinned son, Ham? Doesn't White dominance of our economic institutions demonstrate His favorable intervention on their behalf and, correspondingly, Black, Latinx, and Native American inability to participate in shaping the American Dream?

Practicing Prejudice

The practice of harboring negative attitudes about people because of the color of their skin may be repugnant, but not illegal. Behaviors that prevent people from obtaining equal opportunities are. In contrast to prevalent approaches that link the persistence of racism to institutions that were historically constructed to preserve, promote, and protect the interests of White people, especially males, we focus on the subtle infusion of attitudes and beliefs that suffuse our culture with stereotypical misconceptions about the very nature and ability of dark-skinned people.

Humor and fear exercise insidious, devastating control over our collective patterns of thought, speech, and action. Although these less obvious, even at times inchoate, nuances of language may seem innocent, the collective weight of their impact on our thought processes has had an enduring negative effect on race relations in our society. It continues to prevent the development of human potentialities of dark-skinned people who are stereotyped and stigmatized even through the lens of White, Black, Native American, and Latinx comedians.

Why is there such a visceral dislike of dark-skinned people? What prevents White people from recognizing the persistence of racial oppression that perpetuates social inequality in this society? Our culture is permeated with racist thoughts, images, and symbols; our language laced with racist terms, thick with innuendos that allude to the imputed inferiority of dark-skinned people.

Disparaging terms about Native Americans and other people of color pepper our everyday conversations. The ubiquity of racial slurs and jokes intrude into our consciousness like sugary syrup. They shroud our thoughts with a genteel insulation from accusations of bigotry while permitting the debasement of others deemed less competent, unworthy inhabitants of our country. This racial double entendre gives cover to the users for their bigotry and reinforces stereotypical conceptions of dark-skinned people as subhuman and deficient. Such behavior perpetuates derision and social inequality in a nation ostensibly founded on the principle of justice for all.

As *New York Times* social commentator John Strausbaugh noted, such humor seems to be an integral part of American culture: "Ethnic/identity humor plays a huge role in American culture. It's part of the toughening-up process that leads to mutual tolerance (if not mutual admiration) in America's mongrel culture. Theoretically, all Americans are free to insult all other Americans."[65]

But the centuries of racism that were woven into our culture have left an indelible pattern of prejudice and discrimination in society. Joe Feagin, past president of the American Sociological Association, and a prolific writer on race relations in the United States, refers to the process of embedded racial stereotypes in our society as a *White racial frame* that includes emotions, visual images, even sounds and accents that elicit negative feelings about people of color. These emotions often assert themselves in the form of racial hatred and feelings of White superiority and dominance over people of color, but they can also create fear and anxiety of the very objects of these superior feelings.[66]

When thinking about race and racism we must consider why straight talk about these subjects is avoided while off-handed derisive comments about them are tolerated. It is as if we know or fear the negative implications of intellectualizing the concepts but tolerate and, in some situations, encourage disparaging remarks and references to them. And most often, the "them" or "other" refers to derogatory statements and innuendos about people of color. A look at the historical development of the concepts of race and racism provides some insight into this sociopsychological paradox.

3

The Origin of Race and Racism

As long as water flows, or grass grows upon the earth, or the sun rises to show your pathway, or you kindle your camp fires, so long shall you be protected from your present habitations.
—President James Monroe, to the Cherokee Nation, regarding their land in Arkansas, Georgia, and present-day Mississippi, 1817

A Brief History of the Concept of Race

The process that led to the stigmatization of dark-skinned people was an outgrowth of trends that began in the fourteenth century and reached its height in the 1800s as the United States was wracked by the Civil War. It was a phenomenon invented by dominant White people as they sought to justify their imperialist colonial penetration of non–White regions of the world for the sake of profit and, ostensibly, the glory of King, country, and God. In the final analysis, it was an attempt to justify the domination and exploitation of Indigenous people whose land and resources were stolen.

Scholars concur that the terms *race* and *racism* (i.e., the denigration, stigmatization, and consequent subjugation of dark-skinned people by White people) are a recent phenomenon. The late English historian Ivan Hannaford spent twenty years researching the origin of the concept of race and concluded that race and ethnicity were invented and introduced in modern times.[1]

Thomas Gossett, author of another foundational work on the subject, concurred: These concepts did not exist in antiquity.[2] In his treatise on the historical development of these concepts, Hannaford searched the writing of Greek and Roman scholars for some indication of the existence of what we regard today as the genetic construct of race. From Plato to Aristotle, Virgil to Strabo, he concluded that "there is nothing in this vast literature, which describes the then known world country-by-country, that suggests an idea of race or ethnocentricity."[3]

While the ancients wrestled with the concepts of *gens* (clan) and *polis* (political life), it was within the context of establishing the legitimate role and environment for conducting one's life in accordance with social and ethical behavior that maintained the integrity of the group. What then altered the philosophical landscape? Three trends played a crucial role in the redefinition of the concept of race and the subsequent development of racism.

First, the development of more practical and accurate systems of navigation

46

enabled England and European countries to promote the exploration of lands heretofore beyond their sphere of influence. Prince Henry the Navigator, born in 1394 in Portugal, was responsible for developing a new system of navigation that enabled ships to travel to distant lands, opening up Africa and the New World and expanding trade routes. Second, conquest of new lands and Indigenous people were justified by an ethnocentric European perspective of inherent superiority. Third, enslavement of Indigenous people and exploitation of their lands was justified through Christian beliefs that stigmatized non–Christians as primitive pagans and soulless beings.

Early Encounters with Indigenous People

Explorers initially went in search of spices, silk, and precious metals, and their travels brought them into contact with people whose physical appearance and culture were different from their own. Western science in the fourteenth and fifteenth centuries was heavily infused with religious concepts, permeated with superstition, and anti-intellectual. For example, during the middle of the fourteenth century, nearly a third of the population of Europe was wiped out by the "Black Plague." Much of the blame was placed on women and Jews.[4]

Encounters with Indigenous people in faraway lands fed into the unscientific Eurocentric worldview of Westerners that depicted their culture as superior to all others. Strange tales about curious customs and the "abnormal" physical appearance of Indigenous people emerged from the logs, diaries, and notes of early European travelers. For example, the noted Irish/English author of *The Vicar of Wakefield*, Oliver Goldsmith, attempted to delineate different types of human races much as German biologist Johann Friedrich Blumenbach did in his 1775 treatise, *On the Natural Variety of Mankind*. Unfortunately, many of Goldsmith's conclusions were based on the limited knowledge and hearsay of travelers, and infused with Eurocentric prejudice:

> The first distinct race of men is found round the polar regions. The Laplanders, the Esquimaux Indians[,] the Samoid Tartars, and the inhabitants of Nova Zemela, the Borandians, the Greenlanders, and the natives of Kamtschatka, may be considered as one peculiar race of people, all greatly resembling each other in their statures, their complexion, their customs, and their ignorance. These nations being under rigorous climate, where the productions of Nature are but few, and the provisions coarse and unwholesome, their bodies have shrunk to the nature of their food; and their complexions have suffered, from cold, almost a similar change to what heat is known to produce; their colour being a deep brown, in some places inclining to actual blackness. These, therefore, in general, are found to be a race of short stature and odd shape, with countenances as savage as their manners are barbarous. The visage, in these countries, is large and broad, the nose flat and short, the eyes of a yellowish brown, inclining to blackness, the eye-lids drawn towards the temples, the cheekbones extremely high, the mouth very large, the lips thick, and turned outwards, the voice thin and squaking, the head large, the hair black and straight, the colour of the skin of a dark grayish. They are short in stature, the generality not being above four feet high, the tallest not above five. Among all these nations, the women are as deformed as the men, and resemble them so nearly that one cannot at first distinguish the sexes among them.
>
> These nations not only resemble each other in their deformity, their dwarfishness, the colour of their hair and eyes, but they have, in a great measure, the same inclinations, and the same manners, being all equally rude, superstitious, and stupid. The Danish Laplanders have a large black cat, to which they communicate their secrets, and consult in all their

affairs. Among the Swedish Laplanders there is in every family a drum for consulting the devil; and although these nations are robust and nimble, yet they are so cowardly that they never can be brought into the field.

With regard to their morals, they have all the virtues of simplicity, and all the vices of ignorance. They offer their wives and daughters to strangers; and seem to think it a particular honor if their offer be accepted. They have no idea of religion, or a Supreme Being; the greatest number of them are idolaters; and their superstitions is as profound as their worship is contemptible.

They are, as I am assured, by no means as fruitful as the European women; but they feel the pains of child birth with much less sensibility, and are generally up and well the day following.

The Negroes of Africa ... in general are of a black colour, with a smooth soft skin. Their eyes are generally of a deep hazel, their noses flat and short; their lips thick and tumid; their teeth of an ivory whiteness. This their only beauty, however, is set off by the colour of their skin; the contrast between the black and white being the more observable. It is false to say that their features are deformed by art; since, in the Negro children born in European countries, the same deformities are seen to prevail....

The woman's breasts, after bearing one child, hang down below the navel; and it is customary with them to suckle the child at their backs, by throwing the breast over the shoulder. As their persons are naturally deformed, at least to our imaginations, their minds are equally incapable of strong exertions. The climate seems to relax their mental powers still more than those of the body; they are, therefore, in general, found to be stupid, indolent, and mischievous.[5]

Many travelers and writers in the eighteenth and nineteenth centuries were obsessed with establishing "the Chain of Being," that is, the assumption that God created all animals independently of one another in a hierarchy, with man at the apex. Even after Darwin's foundational work on evolution demonstrated a common human origin, most Europeans still believed in a polygenetic concept of human development that held humans were created in different parts of the world and White Europeans were the most sophisticated and advanced species.[6] "Ironically, today, only a small percent of the population of the United States believes that humans evolved without Divine intervention, and nearly half believe God created humans in their present form."[7] The effect of such rampant anti-intellectualism helps perpetuate negative stereotypes about people of color.

In their search for the so-called missing link, the form of natural man between ape and modern human, philosophers such as Jean-Jacques Rousseau and naturalists like the renowned Georges-Louis Leclerc, Comte de Buffon, contemplated the evolution of man. Too often they relied on faulty, ethnocentric observations of travelers such as Francois Leguat, Daniel Beeckman, and Thomas Herbert,[8] who depicted African and Indigenous people as lower on the phylogenetic scale of development—the great "Chain of Being."

Descriptions of Africans (often called Hottentots, who were actually members of the Khoikhoi or Khoisan ethnic group of southwest Africa related to the Bushmen) characterized them as promiscuous, with the women even mating indiscriminately with apes: "Nature, who does not oppose the Copulation of Horses with Asses, may well admit that of an Ape with a Female-Animal that resembles him, especially where the latter is not restrain'd by any Principle. An Ape and a Negro slave born and brought up out of the knowledge of God, have not less similitude between them than an Ass and a Mare."[9]

Aboriginal and Indigenous people were thought to be immoral, incapable of forming social units as basic as the family, and lacking the ability to make rational decisions. As philosopher Francis Moran concludes, the lines between these so-called natural men were blurred "because Europeans had discovered human beings that looked and acted like animals and animals that looked and acted like human beings."[10] As historian John Friedman noted, "The myths of the monstrous races, though geographically obsolete, were too vital to discard. They provide a ready and familiar way of looking at the native people of the New World."[11]

Racism and the Bible

A more profound developmental influence on our contemporary culture was the fusion of religious teaching that denigrated dark skin and rationalized slavery. Some writers trace this line of thinking to biblical texts referring to Noah's curse on his son Ham's son, Canaan, in Genesis 9:20–27:

> And Noah began to be an husbandman [farmer], and he planted a vineyard. And he drank of the wine, and was drunken; and he was uncovered within his tent. And Ham, the father of Canaan, saw the nakedness of his father, and told his two brethren without. And Shem and Japheth took a garment, and laid it upon both their shoulders, and went backward, and covered the nakedness. And Noah awoke from his wine, and knew what his younger son had done unto him. And he said: Cursed be Canaan; a servant of servants shall he be unto his brethren. And he said, Blessed be the Lord God of Shem; and Canaan shall be his servant. God shall enlarge Japheth, and he shall dwell in the tents of Shem; and Canaan shall be his servant.

How this biblical account of a son's transgression became woven into a belief that provided the foundation for emergent racism in the sixteenth, seventeenth, and eighteenth centuries has been a topic of debate among biblical scholars and philosophers. Historian Hannaford used a slightly different version from the Jewish general and historian Flavius Josephus (Common Era [CE] 37–95), which dramatizes the magnitude of the offense:

> [H]e [Noah] offered sacrifice, and feasted, and, being drunk, fell asleep and lay naked in an unseemly manner. When his youngest son saw this, he came laughing, and showed to him his brethren; but they covered their father's nakedness. And when Noah was made sensible of what had been done, he prayed for prosperity to his other sons; but for Ham, he did not curse him, by reason of his nearness in blood, but cursed his posterity. And when the rest of them escaped that curse, he inflicted it on the children of Canaan.[12]

There is some question about the exact nature of Ham's offense, ranging from this characterization of mockery to allegations that he castrated his father or had sex with his mother.[13] We leave this discussion to theological conjecture. We do know that, according to Hannaford, Josephus divided the world into three parts separately inhabited by Noah's sons after the Great Flood, and this conception remained the orthodox interpretation of the division of mankind through the sixteenth century:

> Japhet and his descendants inhabited Europe. Shem and his progeny dwelt in the region of the Indian Ocean, Persia, Chaldea and Armenia. And Ham and his family occupied Africa.[14]

Who Were the Indians?

Nothing was said in ancient biblical historical writing about who would control North, Central, and South America, leaving European Christians with a dilemma: Who or what were the Indigenous people who became known as Indians? Under biblical teaching, there was no stewardship established for the red men and women who were encountered by the explorers and legions of settlers as they swept across the continents. Sixteenth-century dialogues among clerics such as Bartolomé de Las Casas and Ginés Sepúlveda even considered whether they were human and possessed souls.

The early colonists viewed the inhabitants of the New World as heathens and savages, not unrelated to their negative encounters with them as they encroached on their natural resources. The writing of Cotton Mather and his descendants is filled with denunciations of Native Americans,[15] but gradually the attitude toward Indigenous people on the continent evolved as Catholic and later Protestant missionaries traversed the wilderness to convert heathens, now determined to be human beings, for Christ. Quakers along with Moravians, Mennonites, and Jesuits were early interlopers in the New World, and their ranks were later swelled by missionaries from Protestant denominations (e.g., Episcopalians, Methodists, and Baptists)—the same groups that ran many of the Indian boarding schools in the United States in the nineteenth and twentieth centuries.

A unique interpretation that attempted to explain the presence of Indigenous people was contributed by the Mormons whose theology linked Indians to the ten lost tribes of Israel. The recognition of Indians as possible descendants of wandering Jews from the Diaspora is part of their theological prognostication of the ultimate unification of believers under the dominion of Jesus Christ in the land of Israel when peace and justice will rule the world.[16]

In the sixteenth century, explorer George Best, after traveling to diverse lands around the world, concluded that Black pigmentation was not related to the effects of the sun but the result of a Devil-induced infection derived from Ham's transgression, marking his progeny with the stigma of Blackness and curse to the African continent. Hannaford contended that from the time of Best, the African appeared in literature as someone who "was marked, not with an artificial badge and hideous raiment like the Jews, but with a natural badge of pigmentation understood to be caused by a natural infection brought about by an unnatural act encouraged by an evil spirit."[17]

Historian Nancy Shoemaker contended that Native Americans actually began calling themselves red in the early 1700s, an appellation embraced by White people and imbued with racist overtones in the latter part of the nineteenth century. The Cherokee Nation in particular helped popularize the term "Red Men" based on the red clay where many of them lived, and the red paint that was used to adorn the faces of many Indians. While some Native Americans outwardly acknowledged White dominance, Indians never (to this day) accepted second-class citizenship, and privately scorned and ridiculed White people as late arrivals to a continent they originally inhabited.[18]

Perceptions of Dark Skin

Early Western writers' and travelers' perceptions about Indigenous dark-skinned people were distorted by the combination of their ethnocentric beliefs about the inherent superiority of their own light-skinned people and biblical interpretations of the intellectual deficiency of dark-skinned people who "are not really unlike Monkeys or Baboons in their Gesture and Postures, especially when they sit Sunning themselves."[19]

Even the revered French naturalist Buffon concluded that the Africans of Guiney "appear to be perfectly stupid, not being able to count beyond the number three, that they never think spontaneously; that they have no memory, the past and the future being equally unknown to them."[20]

This quotation demonstrates some critical points about racism. Although the science of anthropology was still in its infancy, one can see the effects of European ethnocentrism infused in the commentary—a perspective that was widely shared by Goldsmith and his contemporaries throughout Europe. In fact, Goldsmith brazenly concluded, "Of all the colours by which mankind is diversified, it is easy to perceive, that ours is not only the most beautiful to the eye, but the most advantageous."[21]

In his *Sketches of the History of Man*, Scottish judge and philosopher Henry Home described Africans in a similar negative vein:

> The inhabitants of the Kingdom of Senaar in Africa are true negroes, a jet-black complexion, thick lips, flat nose, curled woolley hair. The country itself is the hottest in the world. From the report of a late traveller, they are admirably protected by nature against the violence of the heat. Their skin is to the touch remarkably cooler than that of an European; and is so in reality, no less than two degrees on Fahrenheit's thermometer. The young women there are highly prized by the Turks for that quality...[22] The black colour of negroes, thick lips, flat nose, crisped woolley hair, and rank smell, distinguish them from every other race of man.[23]

These writings were representative of the prevalent myopic worldview held by Europeans prior to and during the Enlightenment. Even the work of Darwin, with its evolutionary hypothesis that challenged the polygenetic notion that different species of man had originated around the world, was rejected on religious, philosophical, and scientific grounds.

The arrogance reflected in such accounts, frequently based on hearsay information, might be dismissed for simple naiveté, but that would overlook the pervasive impact they have had on contemporary White people. This orientation influenced the European racist conception of people of color as abnormal, simian, deviant, uncivilized, and heathen. Non–White people were characterized as less than human, and this stereotype has had devastating consequences for dark-skinned and Indigenous people around the world.

Indigenous people were denigrated because of misconceptions about science and evolution derived from stultifying religious precepts and philosophical sophistry. Historian Roxanne Dunbar-Ortiz believes this ethnocentrism led to the Law of Limpieza de Sangre (cleanliness of the blood), which formed the basis of investigations of the Spanish Inquisition, ultimately dooming many Jews and Muslims to the stake and expulsion, laying the foundation for racism and genocide.[24]

Europeans and Christians depicted themselves as the most desirable form of humanity. In fact, as the above quotations demonstrate, so-called other species of people were not only deemed inferior, but deformed. Professor John Block Friedman's classic work, *The Monstrous Races in Medieval Art and Thought*, catalogued fifty distinct medieval "races" of men. These included Greek and Roman depictions of people who inhabited scarcely known regions of the world. They were characterized as headless, one-legged, cannibalistic, speechless people and Straw-Drinkers, and thought to be concentrated in Africa and India and the northern regions near the Caucasus.

Friedman concluded that many of these denominations of men derived from misinformation, misidentification, and misinterpretation of behavior and culture, even misspellings about a group that could be labeled as deviant based on their diet. But one core unifying characteristic among the "monstrous races" was their strangeness. They were viewed as aliens and often denigrated and disparaged by Western ethnocentric observers because they spoke different languages and lived outside of the city, ungoverned by predominate culture and laws. "Monstrous men ordinarily dwell in mountains, caves, deserts, rivers and woods, and cannot truly be understood apart from their barren or savage landscapes."[25] This conclusion, supported by historian James Merrell's work on the founding of Pennsylvania, will be relevant to our discussion of European settlers' perspectives about Native Americans and mythology about their habitat.[26]

Law professor Robert A. Williams, Jr. (Lumbee), traced the origin and evolution of Western perceptions about "the Other," and came to similar conclusions as Friedman after analyzing the writing of the ancients (e.g., Homer, Hesiod, Plutarch, Plato, Aristotle, and Herodotus).[27] People who dwelled in unknown lands were, throughout history, labeled as aliens, monsters, and savages. Likened to wild beasts with horrible deformities, they represented the savage, uncivilized nature of man, more animal than human.

But critics of Greek and Roman society like Ovid and Virgil noted the decadent spiral that appeared to be plunging their society into a morally bankrupt state, without compassion for commoners and lacking man's intimate and harmonious relationship with nature. This sentiment led to a dual perspective about the condition of man among the Classicists—he was perceived by some as wild and savage, yet others believed his relationship with nature was devoid of the financial entanglements and worries associated with civilization, making him free from the chains of modern demands. Longing for the "Golden Age" before society and civilization destroyed natural relationships between men and the environment is a recurrent and even contemporary theme—one that has been expropriated by some White supremacists and survivalists today. It can also be seen in the schizophrenic dichotomy that simultaneously depicts Native Americans as degenerate buffoons and noble savages.

In the Middle Ages, popes and other Christian prelates used the paradigm of the Wild Man/Savage as an instrument for justifying war and military action against Indigenous people in faraway lands. Williams revealed how the policy of Pope Innocent IV (1243–54) reaffirmed the right and responsibility of the Church to exert authority over non–Christians when they did not act in conformity with the Natural Law (i.e., engaged in pagan rituals and violated the human rights of people in territory under their control). "There is only one right way of life for mankind, and ... the papal monopoly of this knowledge makes obedience to the Pope the only means of salvation."[28]

Treatment of Indigenous People

Spanish explorers earned the reputation for being especially cruel to Indigenous people. The Spanish disdain for them was supported by Papal Bull *Inter Caetera* issued by Pope Alexander VI on May 4, 1493, which assigned to Castile the exclusive right to acquire territory in the New World and "barbarous nations be overthrown and brought to the faith itself."[29] The barbaric treatment of Indigenous people in the Americas is recounted in the work of Bartolomé de Las Casas's famous denunciation of the Spaniards' treatment of the Native people in his *A Brief Account of the Destruction of the Indies* and, more recently, David Stannard's *American Holocaust*.[30]

The Catholic Church later adopted a more humane approach to the treatment of Indigenous people; for example, the Papal Bull *Sublimus Dei* issued by Pope Paul III in 1537 admonished faithful Christians to treat Indians humanely, respect their property rights, avoid enslaving them, and convert them by "preaching the word of God and by the example of good and holy living."[31]

Nevertheless, excesses by explorers and colonizers continued. The visceral disdain for people who fell outside the domain of the Europeans, thought to be less important on the "Chain of Being," was reinforced by an important social psychological phenomenon: ridicule differences and marginalize non–White people. From their ethnocentric perspective, Europeans rationalized that they were naturally superior because they assumed:

1. Their species of man was created first and was more God-like and closer to perfection.
2. They were destined to be legitimate conquerors because they possessed the knowledge and ability to travel and dominate Indigenous people.
3. Their culture was innately superior, possessing norms derived from religious beliefs that contained methods for achieving immortality and the means of reproducing their culture through the printed word.[32]

By establishing a norm designating European physiognomy and culture as the standard by which all others would be judged, Europeans constructed a pyramid with themselves at the apex and other peoples and cultures beneath them. Setting standards of beauty that were unobtainable by non–Europeans effectively perpetuated their inferior social status and aided in the transmission of stereotypes about their physical and intellectual inferiority. These stereotypes persist today (not just in the United States, but throughout White-dominated countries), and they are often reinforced without the conscious awareness of their pernicious effect on race relations and the perpetuation of prejudice and inequality.

This philosophy led to the justification for the Crusades and subsequent rationalization for the seizure and exploitation of Native American lands under the Doctrine of Discovery. The Founding Fathers of the United States embraced this doctrine that was initially used by imperialistic colonial powers when they claimed territory that was uninhabited by Europeans. This principle essentially held that lands occupied by non–Christians could be claimed in the name of the sponsoring country by virtue of the presumed inferior status of the inhabitants and the right of the imperial power to exercise its authority and dominion over them. Classical stereotypes about Indigenous people dwelling on this continent arose from this perspective. It depicted them as uncivilized, barbarian, deviant, unchurched, and appropriate targets for domination by the "superior" White Europeans with their formidable technology, Christian theology, and legal system that nurtured and protected private property.

From the outset of their encounters with Indigenous people, White Europeans viewed the world as their own, for they had conquered it. This can be seen in their condescending description of Indigenous cultural practices as well as the people themselves. The distinguished English writer, historian, and geographer of the seventeenth century, Richard Hakluyt, included frequent references about primitive peoples encountered around the world and their propensity for cannibalism.[33]

People living on the coast of Guinea and middle parts of Africa were "a people of beastly living, without God, laws, religion, or commonwealth, and so scorced and vexed with the heat of the sunne, that in many places they curse it when it riseth."[34] Further, "First from Muritania or Barbary toward the South is Getulia, a rough and Savage region, whose inhabitants are wilde and wandering people. After these follow the people called Melanogetuli and Pharusij, which wander in the wildernesse, carrying with them great gourdes of water." And "There are also other people of Libya called Garamantes, whose women are common: for they contract no matrimonie; neither have respect to chastite."

And regarding the people on the east side of Africa:

> About this region inhabite the people called Clodi, Risophagi, Bobylonij, Axiuntae, Molili, and Molibae. After this is the region called Troglodytica, whose inhabitants dwel in caues and dennes: for these are their houses, and the flesh of serpents their meat.[35]

These descriptions were influenced by the writing of Pliny the Elder, the Roman author and naturalist who lived from 23 to 79 AD. His characterizations of scarcely known Indigenous peoples laid the foundation for much misunderstanding and stereotypical conceptions about them in the Middle Ages.

Justification for Exploitation

Writers in the so-called Age of Enlightenment depicted Indigenous cultures as barbaric and childish to justify White conservatorship over them and prevent "backward" people from harming themselves or one another, or from squandering their unappreciated natural resources. Such rationalizations concealed the insidious motive to control, manipulate, and consume natural resources in conquered territories. This approach is enunciated in Sir George Peckham's classic rationalization for English colonization, the use of violence and seizure of Native property:

> [I]t is lawfull and necessarie to trade and traffique with the Sauages.... I say that the Christians may lawfully travel into those countries and abide there: whom Savages may not justly improue and forbidde in respect of the mutuall societies and fellowshipped betweene man and man prescribed by the Law of Nations.
>
> If it were so then, I demaund in what age, and by what law is the same forbidden or denied since? For who doubteth but that it is lawfull for Christians to use thrade and traffique with Infidels or Sauages, carrying thither such commodities as they want, and bringing from thence some part of their plentie?

And regarding Christian explorers:

> [W]hereas the Sauages be fearfull by nature, and fond otherwise, the Christians should doe their best endeavor to take away such feare as may growe vnto them by reason of their strange apparel, Armour, and weapon, or such like, by quiet and peaceable conversation, and letting them live in securitie and keeping a measure of blamelesse defence, with as little discommoditie to the Sauages as may be: for this kind of warre would be onely defensive and not offensive.

To facilitate trade:

> [T]here must be presented vnto them gratis, some kindes of our pettie merchandises and triffle: As looking glasses, Belles, Beades, Bracelets, chains or collers of Bewgle, Chrystall, Amber, Iet or Glassee, etc. For such be the things, though to vs of small value, yet accounted by them of high price and estimation: and soonest will induce their Barbarous natures to a liking and a mutuall societie with us.

As to the nature of Indigenous people:

> [T]he Sauages generally for the most part, are at continuall warres with their next adjonying neighbors and especially the cannibals, being a cruell kinde of people whose food is mans flesh, and have teeth like dogges, and doe pursue them with ravenous minds to eat their flesh, and deuoure them.

And good Christians might take land and crops from Indigenous people because

> the Christians may in this case justly and lawfully ayde the Sauages against the Cannibals. So that is uery likely, that by this meanes we shall not only mightily stirre and inflame their rude minds gladly embrace the louing company of the Christians, proferring vnto them both commodities, succor and kindnesse: But also by their frank consents shall easily enioy such competent quantity of Land, as liuing way shall be correspondent to the Christians effectation and contentation, considering the great abundance they have of Land, and how small account they make thereof, taking no other fruites thereby then such as the ground of it selfe doeth naturally yielde.

If these well-intended overtures are rejected, then,

> in such a case I holde it no breach of equite for the Christians to defend themselues, to pursue reuenge with force, and to doe whatsoeuer is necessarie for the attaining of their saftie: For it is allowable by all Lawes in such distresses, to resist violence with violence: And for their securitie to increase their strength by building Forts for Auoyding the extremitie of iniurious dealing. Wherein if also they shal not be suffered in reasonable quietnesse to continue, there is no basse (as I uidge) but that in stout assemblies the Christians may issue out, and by strong hand pursue togeheir enemies, subdue them, take possession of their Townes, Cities, or Villages, and (in auodying murtherous tyrannie) to vse the law of Armes, as in like case among all Nations at this day is vsed: and most especially to the ende they may with securitie holde their lawful possession, lest happily after the departure of the Christians, such Sauages as have bene conuerted should afterwards through compulsion and enforcement of their widked Rulers returne to their horrible idolatrie (as did the children of Israel, after the decease of Joshua) and continue their wicked custome of most vnnatural sacrifices of humane creatures.[36]

Europeans viewed Indigenous people as racially inferior, stereotyping them as savage, unchurched, and uncivilized, despite the beautiful cities the Spanish found in Central and South America and the agricultural accomplishments of Indians in North America. Nevertheless, from their myopic, ethnocentric, and acquisitive perspective, Indigenous land, and the Native people themselves, were viewed as legitimate targets for domination and exploitation. For example, below is the statement commonly read by Spanish explorers upon claiming territory for their homeland. The practice was referred to as the *requerimiento*, and it was read aloud to Indigenous people who often did not comprehend a word of it:

> I certify to you that, with the help of God, we shall powerfully enter into your country and shall make war against you in all ways and manners that we can, and shall subject you to the yoke and obedience of the Church and of Their Highnesses. We shall take you and your wives and your children, and shall make slaves of them, and as such shall sell and dispose of them as Their Highnesses may command. And we shall take your goods, and shall do you all the mischief and damage that we can, as to vassals that do not obey and refuse to receive their lord and resist and contradict him.[37]

Perhaps it was just as well that the Indigenous people did not understand what the Spanish explorers were saying. The sad fact is that the invading Europeans decimated the peoples they came in contact with. Through the spread of infectious and communicable diseases, war, and genocidal assaults, the number of Indigenous people who populated North, Central, and South America decreased from seventy-two million at the time of first contact with Columbus to approximately four million after just three centuries. In North America, the American Indian population decreased from five million in 1492 to 250,000 by 1890.[38]

Representatives of Catholic countries (France, Spain, and Portugal) had been traveling to the New World before the English and establishing settlements of their own. The harsh treatment of Indigenous people was undergirded by various papal bulls, which were taken as legally binding among Catholic monarchs. These not only relegated Indigenous people and non–Christians around the world to an inferior status, but they also helped establish the Doctrine of Discovery, which "legitimized" the seizure of Indigenous land.

According to Professor Roxanne Dunbar-Ortiz and her coauthor, Dina Gilio-Whitaker (Colville Confederated Tribes), the first papal bull granting European dominion beyond Europe was issued by Pope Nicholas V in 1452. Titled *Dum Diversas*, it authorized Portugal to enslave nonbelievers and helped establish the Portuguese slave trade in West Africa.[39] Other papal bulls like Pope Alexander's *Inter Caetera* issued in 1493 granted newly discovered land in nearly all of the Americas to Ferdinand and Isabella of Spain with "full and free power, authority, and jurisdiction of every kind," and *Romanus Pontifex*, issued in 1455 by Pope Nicholas V, justified the seizure of Indigenous lands and the exploitation of their inhabitants:

> We weighing all and singular the premises with due meditation, and noting that since we had formerly by other letters of ours granted among other things free and ample faculty to the aforesaid King Alfonso [of Portugal]—to invade, search out, capture, vanquish, and subdue all Saracens and pagans whatsoever, and other enemies of Christ wheresoever placed, and the kingdoms, dukedoms, principalities, dominions, possessions, and all movable and immovable goods whatsoever held and possessed by them and to reduce their persons to perpetual slavery, and to apply and appropriate to *himself* and his successors the kingdoms, dukedoms, counties, principalities, dominions, possessions, and goods, and to convert them to his and their use and profit—by having secured the said faculty, the said King Alfonso, or, by his authority, the aforesaid infant, justly and lawfully has acquired and possessed, and doth possesses, these islands, lands, harbors, and seas, and they do of right belong and pertain to the said King Alfonso and his successors.[40]

Such statements leave little to the imagination about Western White attitudes and motivation concerning Indigenous people around the world. Land seizure and exploitation of natural resources for the benefit of the homeland are not only sanctioned, but the decimation of Indigenous people who have the temerity to resist the expropriation of their resources is rationalized in the name of self-defense. And so, the sordid enterprise of imperialism and colonization spread throughout the world under the guise of exploration and gallantry that brought civilization and Christianity to "pagan savages" who were not taking advantage of the munificence the Creator had endowed them with.

Yet, there is evidence that the very first English settlers at the Jamestown colony in the New World recognized Native American land rights and negotiated for parcels. Although some Indian tribes did not have a written language, English settlers bartered goods in exchange for property rights, even though some English businessmen assumed that the Indigenous people had no right to the land. In fact, the original Jamestown colony was established in an area that was deemed to be "waste ground" because it was low and unappealing as a place to plant crops, and, hence, open to anyone who wished to occupy it.[41]

But more often, the prevailing approach that colonial powers took toward Native American land could be described as a grab fest. Take what you can by coercion, fraud, and manipulation, and if that doesn't work, use force to displace the Indigenous inhabitants. This approach became the official U.S. policy advocated by several presidential administrations and, as we will see, most notably enforced by Andrew Jackson in his zealous, mercenary "Indian removal" push to move Indians further and further west to "Indian Country." This policy was legitimized by U.S. Supreme Court decisions in the nineteenth century that justified the "Doctrine of Discovery" concept under the guise that Native Americans were racially inferior and disposed to war with White people.

Dunbar-Ortiz and Gilio-Whitaker present compelling evidence that Supreme Court decisions, many rendered under the aegis of Chief Justice John Marshall, the longest serving chief justice in U.S. history (1801–35), led to the diminution of Native American land rights. Marshall, a Virginian who had served briefly as secretary of state under President John Adams, was a Federalist and believed in a strong central government. Three cases decided by his court, known as the Trilogy (*Johnson v. McIntosh*, 1823; *Cherokee Nation v. Georgia*, 1831; and *Worcester v. Georgia*, 1832), limited Indigenous peoples' rights and led to a decline in their sovereignty. Perhaps the most noteworthy decision was *Johnson v. McIntosh* that established federal primacy over Native American tribal land claims, which created a precedent for the future federal domination and control of Indigenous lands.

Although recognized as one of the preeminent thinkers of his time, Marshall was not averse to stereotyping Native Americans pejoratively as he declared in the *McIntosh* case: "The tribes of Indians inhabiting this country were fierce savages."[42] That stereotype still pervades the thinking of many Americans—with disastrous effects.

The Justification for Slavery and Color Inferiority

In addition to these rationalizations that underlay the foundation for modern racism was the protracted campaign of White southerners to justify the social and economic system of slavery. Prior to the Civil War, scientific discourse about the origin of humans was still in its infancy and hamstrung by obedience to and reverence for biblical dogma that held all humans were descended from a single pair (Adam and Eve). Known as the monogenetic conception of human origin, defense of the biblical perception came increasingly under attack by early ethnologists in the United States and abroad who posited a polygenetic, or diverse, origin of mankind.

The implications of these vastly different perspectives cannot be overstated, because the polygenetic scheme allowed for multiple origins of mankind and held within it the justification for the defense of slavery—a defense that rested on the assumption that God created different races of humans, endowed with different qualities, characteristics, and abilities. Typically, the White race, or what later became known as the Caucasian race, after the work of German scientist Johann Friedrich Blumenbach (1752–1840) in his *On the Natural Varieties of Mankind* (1776), was deemed superior to the others.

Blumenbach's categorization of presumed racial categories of humans included the Caucasian (White) European; Mongoloid (yellow) Asian; Ethiopian (Black) African; North American (red); and Maylay (brown) Philippines, Molucca, Sunda, and the Pacific archipelago including New Zealand and associated islands. Blumenbach believed that humans originated from a single source and there were no significant biological differences among the five groups he enumerated. All had the potential to make important contributions to civilization. Observed variations were the result of differences derived from geography and climate, but these played an insignificant role in the development of civilizations. His enlightened position preceded Darwin by almost a century.

Such early attempts to explain the varieties of humans were, nevertheless, looked on with skepticism by clerics and the majority of the scientific community in the light of biblical assumptions about the oneness of mankind through the Creation narrative. Man was created in God's image—at once nearly perfect and at the highest rung of the Chain of Being. Following biblical imprimatur, humans were of one source, monogenetically created. Evolution was unthinkable.

This perspective did not allow for the polygenetic theory that posited the existence of other races of mankind. The problem for scientists in the 1700s and early 1800s was that early ethnological, anthropological, and biological reports revealed differences among humans who resided in different regions of the planet, and they struggled to resolve the contradictions between these observations (e.g., different skin color, hair texture, eye color and shape, nose, lips) and the biblical monogenetic perspective. Scientists who espoused the polygenetic theory of human diversity borne from multiple creation sites (God created different kinds of humans around the world) risked being ostracized by political and scientific elites, and worse, labeled heretics.

A possible answer to this dilemma resided in the work of some scientists in the United States who, during the middle of the nineteenth century, sought to prove the biological superiority of the White race through a series of experiments designed to measure physiological differences. Foremost among these men was Samuel George Morton (1799–1851), an American physician and naturalist who embarked on a career predicated on measuring the crania of various ethnic groups. His *Crania Americana*, published in 1839, purported to solve the dilemma between the mono and polygenetic positions by demonstrating the larger and, he assumed, superior size of the Caucasian brain cavity.

Morton collected skulls from a variety of Native Americans, White people, and African Americans as well as specimens from other parts of the world (e.g., Egypt). He measured the cranial capacity of skulls by filling them with white pepper seeds and conducting up to thirteen measurements to ascertain the cranial capacity of each skull. He later substituted lead shot for the pepper seed because he believed it was more accurate. Nevertheless, the late biologist Stephen J. Gould replicated his experiments and found them flawed.[43] Morton was convinced that his experiments proved the existence of different races based on cranial capacities. And, low and behold, in the best tradition of popular phrenological thought of the time, which attributed cognitive abilities to the external shape of the skull, he concluded that "those primeval attributes of mind, which, for wise purposes, have given our race [White people] a decided and unquestionable superiority over all nations of the earth."[44]

In the early days of ethnology and anthropology, scientific work was not only encumbered by the domineering obedience to the biblical account of Creation, but also modern techniques of dating archaeological human remains had not been developed. Scientists were left to speculate about human origins without methods to corroborate their suppositions. While ecclesiastical pressure to tow the biblical line weighed heavily on their research and theoretical suppositions, social and political pressure was exerted on them to promote the polygenetic perspective of diverse human origins to undergird the South's social and economic system of slavery.

The proslavery position of southern scientists, one that was also promoted by many clergy at the time, postulated a belief in a monogenetic creation of humans, pegging the age of the Earth at around five thousand years. This theoretical perspective afforded adherents the ability to reconcile God's word in the Genesis Creation story in the Bible with the belief that lesser human beings (dark-skinned people like Black people and Indians) had also been created and they were destined to be servants and slaves of the higher order of humans—White people.

While scientists like Harvard's Louis Agassiz promoted the polygenetic or diverse origin of humans, both perspectives labored under misapprehensions about the age of the Earth and the evolutionary timeline that, in addition to environmental and climatic effects, influenced the distribution and evolution of humans throughout the world. Of course, the justification for slavery and its associated racism fit well with the polygenetic proposition that different races of man had been created by God, and, as Desmond and Moore have shown, southern agents actively propagandized for this position in England and Europe during the Civil War.[45]

Adherents of both positions struggled with a circumscribed timeline that could not encapsulate nascent anthropological and archaeological evidence (e.g., Egyptian monuments that dated back over four thousand years), other than to hold fast to fundamentalist beliefs that humans were indeed only on the Earth for five millennia and the similarities of contemporary people with the ancient Egyptians proved that climate and evolution played an insignificant role in altering the race of man.

Darwin's Contribution

These misguided conceptions were dealt a blow by English naturalist Charles Darwin when he published *On the Origin of the Species* in 1859 followed by *The Descent of Man* in 1871.[46] Aside from demonstrating the effects of natural selection on the evolution of animal and plant species, Darwin's theory established a much broader timeline than the popular fundamentalist biblical perspective, and this lengthier framework allowed for the subtle processes of evolution and migration of species. While it was roundly criticized by staid traditionalists, subsequent scientific research has demonstrated the integrity of his work. Nevertheless, public opinion polls in the United Kingdom and the United States reveal that only a minority of the population believe in Darwin's perspective on evolution.[47] Such attitudes prevail despite subsequent archaeological finds and modern methods of dating ancient artifacts that demonstrate the fundamental role evolution has played in the life of plants and animals on our planet.

The Refinement of European Racism

The year 1848 was a tumultuous, turbulent time. The Industrial Revolution was cranking up, churning workers in factories like disposable parts in children's toys. Class antagonisms were escalating as capitalism accelerated the disparities between the haves and have nots. In the Springtime of Peoples that year, riots and revolutions occurred throughout Europe (e.g., Germany, France, Italy, Poland, Belgium, Sweden, and Denmark) as an unemployed intellectual and his wealthy patron (Karl Marx and Friedrich Engels) exhorted working men around the world to unite and throw off the shackles of capitalism.

The assiduous attempts of scientists in the United States to justify slavery by developing an alternative to the Creation narrative of the Bible occurred simultaneously (mid–1800s) with European White ethnocentrism. The English isles and European continent were a bastion of White ethnic supremacy at this time when a Frenchman, Joseph-Arthur Comte (Count) de Gobineau (1816–82), published his landmark treatise in 1856, *The Moral and Intellectual Diversity of Races*.[48] A French diplomat, writer, and ethnologist, Gobineau promulgated a doctrine of racial determinism that asserted Germanic people (Aryans) represented the apex of civilization and miscegenation diluted the unique creativity of the Germanic racial character leading to stagnation and immorality.

Unlike his American counterparts, Gobineau's theory of racial degeneration was not linked to religious underpinnings but predicated on his assumption that the world was a sullen place, driven by people with a slave mentality. Religion was used by people as a crutch, and coincidentally, like Marx, he believed it gave the masses false values. In the preface to volume one of his *Essay on the Inequality of Human Races*, Gobineau noted, "I was gradually penetrated by the conviction that the racial question overshadows all the other problems of history, that it holds the key to them all, and that the inequality of races from whose fusion a people is formed is enough to explain the whole course of its history."[49]

He further noted, "From the beginning of history, there has been no human society, however small, that has not contained the germ of every vice. And yet, however burdened with this load of depravity, the nations seem to march on very comfortably, and often, in fact, to owe their greatness to their detestable customs."[50] From here he proceeded to lay the foundation for the modern racist position, one adopted by twentieth-century eugenicists and their Nazi followers, that certain civilizations are genetically superior to others.

Asserting that societies perish because they become degenerate through mixing the pure blood of the dominant, superior, conquering race with subjugated inferior stock, he proclaimed:

> The word degenerate, when applied to a people, means (as it ought to mean) that the people has no longer the same intrinsic value as it had before, because it no longer has the same blood in its veins, continual adulterations having gradually affected the quality of the blood. In other words, though the nation bears the name given by its founders, the name no longer connotes the same race; in fact, the degenerate man properly so called, is a different being, from the racial point of view, from the heroes of the greatness. I agree that he still keeps something of their essence; but the more he degenerates the more attenuated does this "something" become. The heterogeneous elements that henceforth prevail in him give him quite a different nationality—a very original one, no doubt, but such originality is not to be envied. He is only a very distant kinsman of those he still calls his ancestors. He and his civilization with him, will certainly die on the day when the primordial race-unit is so broken up and swamped by the influence of foreign elements that its effective qualities have no longer a sufficient freedom of action. It will not, of course, absolutely disappear, but it will in practice be so beaten down and enfeebled, that its power will be felt less and less as time goes on. It is at this point that all results of degeneration will appear, and the process may be considered complete.[51]

Though Gobineau accepted the religious monogenetic scheme of a single human creation by God, he believed that intermixing strains of humans who were offshoots of the original White race led to gradual degradation and eventual extinction of the race, "for no human race can be unfaithful to its instincts, and leave the path that has been marked out for it by God."[52]

While he determined that the White race was superior to the yellow, the Black race was deemed inferior to both:

> Show me rather, among the many regions in which negroes have lived for ages in contact with Europeans, one single place where, in addition to the religious doctrines, the ideas, customs, and institutions of even one European people have been so completely assimilated that progress in them is made as naturally and spontaneously, as among ourselves. Show me a place where the introduction of printing has had results, similar to those in Europe, where our sciences are brought to perfection, where new applications are made of our discoveries, where our philosophies are the parents of other philosophies, of political systems, of literature and art, of books, statues, and pictures![53]

Further, "Ages have passed without their doing anything to improve their condition; they are all equally powerless to mingle act and idea in sufficient strength to burst their prison walls and emerge from their degeneration."[54]

From here he proceeded to draw the link between Black physiognomy and inferiority of intellect to simian-like characteristics: "When we look for a moment at an individual of this type, we are involuntarily reminded of the structure of the monkey, and are inclined to admit that the negro races of West Africa come from a stock that has nothing in common, except the human form, with the Mongolian."[55]

But he reserved his most reviling conclusion about the Native people of Oceania who have "the special privilege of providing the most ugly, degraded, and repulsive specimens of the race, which seem to have been created with the express purpose of forming a link between man and the brute pure and simple."[56]

Considering the plight of Native Americans, he concluded that their genetic inferiority and rejection of superior White customs would ultimately lead to their demise:

> So the brain of a Huron Indian contains in an undeveloped form an intellect which is absolutely the same as that of the Englishman or the Frenchman! Why then, in the course of the ages, has he not invented printing or steam power? I should be quite justified in asking our Huron why, if he is equal to our European peoples, his tribe has never produced a Cesar or a Charlemagne among its warriors, and why his bards and sorcerers have, in some inexplicable way, neglected to become Homers and Galens.[57]

In an attempt to rationalize the mistreatment of Native Americans, he blamed them for their misfortunes at the hand of White people. The European conquerors could not appreciably change the innate blood, culture, and predispositions of the Native Americans, even though, according to his tortured logic, they tried:

> But the redskins of the United States have withered at the touch of the Anglo-Saxon energy. The few who remain are growing less every day; and those few are as uncivilized, and as incapable of civilization, as their forefathers. In Oceania, the facts point to the same conclusions; the natives are dying out everywhere. We sometimes manage to take away their arms, and prevent them from doing harm; but we do not change their nature. Wherever the European rules, they drink brandy instead of eating each other.[58]

He observed: "As for the black and yellow types, they are mere savages in the tertiary stage, and have no history at all."[59] And, "The savage races of today have always been savage, and we are right in concluding, by analogy, that they will continue to be so until the day when they disappear."[60] This is because White Europeans of Anglo-Saxon, Teutonic stock are the most beautiful, intelligent, and genetically superior and "the peoples who are not of white blood approach beauty, but do not attain it."[61] White people

> are gifted with reflexive energy, or rather with an energetic intelligence. They have a feeling for utility, but in a sense for wider and higher, more courageous and ideal, than the yellow races; a perseverance that takes account of obstacles and ultimately finds a means of overcoming them; a greater physical power, an extraordinary instinct for order ... as an indispensable means of self-preservation. At the same time, they have a remarkable, and even extreme, love of liberty, and are openly hostile to the formalism under which the Chinese are glad to vegetate, as well as the strict despotism which is the only way of governing the negro.[62]

And, "The white races are, further, distinguished by an extraordinary attachment to life. They know better how to use it, and so, as it would seem, set a greater price on it…. When things are cruel, they are conscious of their cruelty; it is very doubtful whether such a consciousness exists in the negro."[63]

In his exuberance he concluded that "all civilizations derive from the white race, that none can exist without its help, and that a society is great and brilliant only so far as it preserves the blood of the noble group that created it, provided that this group itself belongs to the most illustrious branch of our species."[64]

The Rise of Eugenics and Working-Class Consciousness

If these sentiments seem familiar, they should be, because they regularly occur in Western culture. They are mouthed by demagogues and fill our airwaves from the internet to Fox News, even President Trump's reference to "shithole countries." And they are the daily fare of rabid, jingoistic radio talk shows. Gobineau's words influenced early twentieth-century racists like Houston Stewart Chamberlain, Madison Grant, and Lothrop Stoddard who, in turn, influenced the eugenics movement, Adolf Hitler, and the Nazis. Some of their most acerbic comments were directed toward immigrants: "Forward-looking minds are coming to realize that social revolutions are really social *breakdowns*, caused in the last analysis by a dual process of racial impoverishment—the elimination of superior strains and the multiplication of degenerates and inferiors. Inexorably the decay of racial values corrodes the proudest civilization, which engenders within itself those forces of chaos that will one day work its ruin."[65]

Or compare another of these writers, Madison Grant: "The great lesson of the science of race is the immutability of somatological or bodily characters, with which is closely associated the immutability of psychical predispositions and impulses ... the folly of the 'Melting Pot,' signified contamination of white Anglos by dark-skinned Alpines and Mediterraneans."[66]

These remarks bear a striking resemblance to that of candidate, and later president, Donald Trump, in a statement he made on June 29, 2015, when he declared his candidacy for president of the United States:

> The US has become a dumping ground for everybody else's problems. When Mexico sends its people, they're not sending their best. They're not sending you. They're not sending you. They're sending people that have lots of problems, and they're bringing those problems with us. They're bringing drugs. They're bringing crime. They're rapists. And some, I assume, are good people.
>
> It's coming from more than Mexico. It's coming from all over South and Latin America, and it's coming probably—probably—from the Middle East. But we don't know. Because we have no protection and we have no competence, we don't know what's happening. And it's got to stop and it's got to stop fast.[67]

The flawed reasoning of early racist theorists may be forgiven because scientific proof about the common origins and DNA of all humans did not then exist, but what excuse could President Trump claim, especially in light of the fact that aspiring Syrian immigrants to the United States are vetted through a twenty-step process?[68]

It was no coincidence that the young social sciences and the so-called scientific approach to understand racial origins and differences sought to rationalize social inequality and occurred almost simultaneously at the middle of the nineteenth century. This was also when the wholesale compartmentalization and fragmentation of work that characterized the Industrial Revolution was proceeding as large numbers of rural agrarian workers were leaving farms and seeking better lives in the cities—only to find they were swapping one form of serfdom for another.

Their negative experiences showed them that the deleterious life of the factories and cities did not provide them solace and salvation, but subordination and immiseration. The inner cities of that time, along with improvements in communication, afforded workers the opportunity to learn about and share their experiences. In the United States, the emergence of nickel and dime novels with their themes of conquest over adversity in the wilderness and urban life was a source of consternation among elites who feared the rise of working-class consciousness and the possible disruption of the existing social order.

The antipathy toward the working class and their cheap entertainment led to campaigns against the proliferation of purported lurid, violent reading material. The movement against such supposedly sordid, salacious materials was led by the youthful reformer Anthony Comstock, who founded the Society for the Suppression of Vice that successfully lobbied for the enactment of the "Comstock Law" in 1873, which prohibited the mailing of obscene materials.[69]

The movement to reform the content of working-class reading tastes received a monumental contribution by industrialist/philanthropist Andrew Carnegie who, in the latter part of the nineteenth century, embarked on a national campaign to promote the construction of public libraries. With the exception of Delaware and Alaska, every state, including the territory of Puerto Rico, received financial grants to build them. By November 1923, 1,419 grants totaling nearly $46 million had been awarded.

The Misuse of Early Social Science

During this time, the newly minted social sciences of sociology and anthropology were gaining prominence through their attempts to apply scientific methods to understanding (and controlling) the rampant social disorganization that was spreading around the world. In France, the science of sociology was founded by a young aristocrat, Auguste Comte, who vowed to use the principles of logical positivism to understand the dynamic processes that were churning social systems, sowing disorder, and threatening societal equilibrium. His work greatly influenced English social scientist Herbert Spencer, who diligently applied Darwin's concepts of natural selection to humans in an attempt to justify social inequality by defining the poor as genetically unfit.[70]

Early anthropologists were preoccupied with publishing and retelling ethnocentric descriptions of travelers that focused on the unorthodox and misunderstood cultural practices of Indigenous people. From their White Eurocentric tradition, these "uncivilized" branches of mankind were barbaric deviations from God's original Adamic creation—long lost evolutionary mistakes with retarded physical and social development. As travel to faraway places became possible, the distorted and misinformed rantings of these visitors spilled over into the writing and conversations of elites and early social scientists who used their descriptions to justify barbaric treatment and exploitation of Indigenous people. While religious salvation (spreading the word of God through conversion) was ostensibly used to justify the (mis)treatment of Indigenous people, lust for natural resources that awaited the European monarchies was a paramount motivator in their quest. The thriving slave trade during the height of Western European expansion in the sixteenth through the eighteenth centuries even used Indigenous people in these lands as natural resources and exploited them as monetary units. And, of course, what better justification could the European conquerors have than the rationalization that the conquered peoples were inferior—lower on the Chain of Being?

Perhaps one of the most pernicious effects of such encounters has been the perpetuation of negative emotions conjured by these distorted ethnocentric descriptions. Take, for example, the recent characterization of former First Lady Michelle Obama by Pamela Ramsey Taylor, director of the city of Clay, West Virginia's Development Corporation, which provides services to low-income people, following Donald Trump's win of the presidency in 2016. She noted on Facebook that she would be happy to see the end of "the ape in high heels" in the White House. To which, the mayor of Clay, Beverly Whaling, replied, "Just made my day Pam." Both of them subsequently resigned, and Taylor was formally removed from her position on December 23, 2016.

The comment of Carl Paladino, a wealthy Buffalo, New York, real estate executive, school board member, and the cochairman of President Donald Trump's New York campaign, was similarly inflammatory. On December 22, 2016, he stated that he hoped President Obama would die of mad cow disease and Michelle Obama should be "let loose in the outback of Zimbabwe." He refused to repudiate his remarks, although his son called the statements "disrespectful and absolutely unnecessary."[71]

Such attitudes persist in our language and are expressed in our art, music, literature, media, and humor. They have become embedded in our culture, resistant to change. This may be why diversity training, which challenges stereotypes about "the Other," is scorned by unwilling participants, its effects transient. It attempts to reverse a lifetime of values, beliefs, and behaviors that have immersed us in attitudes about the supposed natural superiority of White participants and the inferiority of people of color. These perspectives have been reinforced by centuries of de jure and de facto segregation based on naive, racist assumptions. These words and images continue unabated on the internet and find expression in the dramatic increase in hate groups, from 149 in 2008 under President George W. Bush, 892 in 2016 under President Barack Obama, and over 1,000 under President Donald J. Trump.[72]

Racism and the Founding Fathers

The "Founding Fathers" of the United States were products of these warped attitudes, and they harbored racist stereotypes about Black and Indigenous people. Presidents Washington, Jefferson, and Madison recognized that Native Americans had legitimate claims to land coveted by White settlers, and they also discerned that our fledgling country could ill afford to be drawn into conflicts with its Indian neighbors. President Washington declared that a just Indian policy was among his highest priorities: "The Government of the United States are determined that their Administration of Indian affairs shall be directed entirely by the great principles of Justice and humanity."[73]

Early on, the White establishment sought to placate the Indians through a policy designed to "civilize" them. This paternalistic approach attempted to encourage Indians to adopt White European culture and become farmers. In the summer of 1790, twenty-eight Creek chiefs led by a mixed-race chief, Alexander McGillivray, met with President Washington in New York to negotiate a treaty that restored lands in Georgia they had previously ceded to the state. Washington wanted to avoid conflict with the powerful Creek Nation and believed the Indians would eventually disappear through disease, migration west, or assimilation. An oft-cited quote of his in a letter to James Duane on September 9, 1783, has been taken as an indication of his feelings about Native Americans: "Indians and wolves are both beasts of prey, tho they differ in shape."

The learned "father" of the Declaration of Independence, and third president of the United States, Thomas Jefferson, didn't admire Indians, but appreciated aspects of their culture. Nevertheless, he remonstrated, "If ever we are constrained to lift the hatchet against any tribe, we will never lay it down till that tribe is exterminated, or driven beyond the Mississippi ... in war, they will kill some of us; we will destroy them all."[74]

Jefferson was an intellectual tormented by the social and political consequences of race. He was aware of some of the facets of the social and political system of Native Americans, which he described in his *Notes on the State of Virginia* in chapter 11. However, he was disdainful of Black people, noting:

> Are not the fine mixtures of red and white, the expressions of every passion by greater or less suffusions of color in the one, preferable to that eternal monotony which reigns in the countenances, that immovable veil of black which covers all the emotions of the other race? Add to these the flowing hair, a more elegant symmetry of form, their own judgement in favor of the whites, declared by their preference for them, as uniformly as is the preference of the oranootan for the black woman over those of his own species.

Here we see Jefferson's embrace of the racist assumption that Black people were unattractive, primitive beings, barely above apes on the scale of human development and, in some instances, mating with them. And Jefferson also believed Black people were intellectually stunted: "Comparing them by their faculties of memory, reason, and imagination, it appears to me that in memory they are equal to whites; in reason much inferior, as I think one could scarcely be found capable of tracing and comprehending the investigations of Euclid, and that in imagination they are dull, tasteless and anomalous."[75]

Further, "But never yet could I find that a black had uttered a thought above the level of plain narration; never seen even an elementary trait of painting or sculpture."[76]

After pillorying the Black race, Jefferson, who had several children with his slave mistress, Sally Hemings, the half-sister of his wife, concluded:

> I advance it therefore as a suspicion only, that the blacks, whether originally a distinct race, or made distinct by time and circumstances, are inferior to the whites in the endowments both of body and mind. It is not against experience to suppose that different species of the same genus, may possess different qualifications.... This unfortunate difference of color, and perhaps of faculty, is a powerful obstacle to the emancipation of these people. Many of their advocates, while they wish to vindicate the liberty of human nature, are anxious also to preserve its dignity and beauty. Some of these, embarrassed by the question, "What further is to be done with them?" join themselves in opposition with those who are actuated by sordid avarice only. Among the Romans, emancipation required but one effort. The slave, when made free, might mix with, without staining the blood of his master. But with us a second is necessary, unknown to history. When freed, he is to be removed beyond the reach of mixture.[77]

Jefferson was a racial enigma, at various times supporting and then rejecting the institution of slavery. During his lifetime he owned over six hundred slaves who helped organize and operate his magnificent Virginia mansion, Monticello, where, according to historian Henry Wiencek, the plantation operated like a machine "on a carefully calibrated brutality."[78] He died in debt on July 4, 1826. In an effort to retire his liabilities, a lottery was held, and his slaves were sold, unlike the first president of this country, George Washington, who manumitted his slaves.

Jefferson's life as a great statesman, scientist, and writer was strained by his reluctance to fully embrace abolitionism and the racist theories that crept into his writing: "I consider a woman who brings a child every two years as more profitable than the best man on the farm."[79] Yet he noted in his autobiography that the institution of slavery will be dissolved: "Nothing is more certainly written in the book of fate than that these people [Black people] are to be free." But he added, "Nor is it less certain that the two races, equally free, cannot live in the same environment. Nature, habit, opinion has drawn indelible lines of distinction between them."[80]

He was cautious not to offend the Indians who had the potential of delivering punishing attacks against the fledgling states as they had in Virginia and New England. Once he concluded the enormous Louisiana Purchase with the French in 1803 that ceded control of 828,000 square miles to the country, he commissioned his secretary, Meriwether Lewis, along with William Clark to conduct an expedition of the territory to survey the land, identify new plant and animal species, befriend potentially hostile Indigenous people, and find the illusive Northwest Passage that ostensibly linked the Atlantic and Pacific oceans.

The project was greatly facilitated by the addition of a French-Canadian fur trapper, Toussaint Charbonneau, and his wife, a seventeen-year-old Shoshone. She had been captured at the age of twelve by the Hidatsa/Mandan Indians and taken to live in one of their villages near the upper Missouri River near present-day North Dakota, where she was sold to Charbonneau and became one of his wives. Throughout the two-and-a-half-year trek, Sacagawea ("bird woman" or "boat puller") was an indispensable addition to the thirty-three-man party, even though she was nursing her son, Jean Baptiste, who was born just two months before they departed on the eight-thousand-mile journey.

Sacagawea became known for her presence under duress, but more importantly, her demeanor and active role in the expedition signaled to potentially hostile Indigenous people that the party had peaceful intentions. She served as a translator, speaking Shoshone and Hidatsa, and assisted the expedition in identifying three hundred plant and animal species as well as edible and medicinal roots, while helping to navigate through the Rocky Mountains and rivers along the way. When the expedition returned to her Hidatsa/Mandan settlement on April 14, 1806, her husband received 320 acres and $500.33 as compensation for assisting on the project. Sacagawea received nothing, but she became a symbol of women's worth and independence over the decades. William Clark became the legal guardian for her son, Jean Baptiste, and daughter, Lisette, and the boy was sent to a private school in St. Louis and later traveled to Europe in the company of a wealthy German. It is thought the girl died at a young age. Sacagawea died at the age of twenty-four. Numerous books, television shows, and motion pictures used her story, and she has been immortalized in statues around the country. In 2000, a commemorative gold coin was minted in her honor.[81]

Despite the important role that Native American women like Sacagawea played as guides, interpreters, and stateswomen, little space is devoted to them in contemporary history texts. A survey by *Smithsonian* magazine of the guidelines for teaching American history in the fifty states revealed that only 178 of the historic figures were women (1 out of 3), and Sacagawea was one of the most frequently mentioned Native American females. Only 4 percent of the female historical figures referenced were Indians.[82]

Following Jefferson, President James Madison perpetuated the desire of the federal government to goad Indians into relinquishing their nomadic lifestyle and adopt White/European culture. In his address to twenty-nine visiting Sioux, Winnebago, and Iowa Indians at the White House around August 22, 1812, he began, "My Red children," and proceeded to lecture and threaten them:

> I have further advice for my red children. You see how the country of the 18 fires [states] is filled with people. They increase like the corn they put into the ground. They all have good houses to shelter them from all weathers; good clothes suitable to all seasons; and as for food of all sorts, you see they have enough and to spare. No man woman or child of the 18 fires ever perished of hunger. Compare all this with the condition of the red people. They are scattered here and there in handfuls. Their lodges are cold, leaky, and smokey. They have hard fare, and often not eno' of it. Why this mighty difference? The reason my red children, is plain. The white people breed cattle and sheep. They plow the earth and make it give them everything they want. They spin and weave. Their head and their hands make all the elements and productions of nature useful to them. Above all; the people of the 18 fires live in constant peace and friendship.[83]

In his first inaugural address, Madison asserted that it was the federal government's duty to convert American Indians by the "participation of the improvements of which the human mind and manners are susceptible in a civilized state."[84] Although he promised the Indians federal protection against the onslaught of White settlers, the lands of the Northwest Territory were overrun by them. In the Midwest, over four hundred thousand settlers engulfed Ohio by 1815, effectively ending Indians' land rights there.

For most of the Founding Fathers, Native Americans were at first an oddity, then an inconvenience, and finally a menace that had to be removed. Encounters with Indians, misnamed by Columbus because he thought he was in Asia, were initially characterized by White people as quaint and even comical from their ethnocentric perspective. The Indigenous people of the New World, scantily clad and illiterate by White European standards[85] of "civilization," were viewed as heathens and savages by the God-fearing Christians who did not understand or appreciate their semi-nomadic communal societies.

Indigenous people were cast as impediments to White endeavors to exploit the natural resources on the land they occupied. Indian resistance to White encroachment helped solidify White/European stereotypes about them as barbaric savages creating a self-fulfilling prophesy that was used by the invaders to justify the removal and extermination of Native Americans.

The Spanish earned the designation of being cruel and despotic overlords as they ruthlessly crushed Indigenous resistance in their expansionist push to secure land and resources for the Crown.[86] The French pursued another tactic, trading with the Indians, to pacify them through the exchange of goods and connubial relations. The development of a thriving fur trade in North America and the sexual liaisons between the French and Indians helped solidify commercial and social bonds between them that endured through the Seven Years' War (French and Indian War from 1754 to 1763).

Alternatively, the British, fortified with their racist ethnocentric orientation, embarked on a strategy designed to conquer and crush Native American opposition to attempts to seize their land and natural resources. From their inception, the fledgling colonies viewed Native Americans as a threat and potentially hostile to White people. This position was even enunciated by Jefferson in the Declaration of Independence as a grievance against King George III for his purported incitement of the Indians against the colonists: "He has excited domestic insurrections amongst us, and has endeavored to bring on the inhabitants of our frontiers, the merciless Indian Savages whose known rule of warfare, is an undistinguished destruction of all ages, sexes and conditions."

Jefferson began promoting the removal of Native Americans in 1776, before he became president, when he recommended forcing Cherokees and Shawnees out of their ancestral lands to territory west of the Mississippi River. He believed this policy was the only way to ensure their survival in the face of the onslaught of White settlers. And while his rhetoric and that of President Washington seemed to confirm their recognition of the Indians as deserving respect and equity, their policies and the actions of their successors were predatory and detrimental to the welfare of Native Americans.

More than any of his predecessors, President Andrew Jackson promoted the removal of Native Americans west to Indian Country, noting:

> My original convictions upon this subject have been confirmed by the course of events for several years, and experience is every day adding to their strength. That those tribes cannot exist surrounded by our settlements and in continual contact with our citizens is certain. They have neither the intelligence; the industry; the moral habits, nor the desire of improvement which are essential to any favorable change in their condition. Established in the midst of another and superior race, and without appreciating the causes of their inferiority or seeking to control them, they must necessarily yield to the force of circumstances, and ere long disappear.[87]

Federal policies traditionally leaned in favor of White settlement and the control of Native American resources, to the detriment of Indians. The perspectives of leaders of our nation have, despite remarks sometimes to the contrary, reflected a condescending approach to relationships with Indigenous people, tinged with the assumption that they are naive and unable to manage their own resources without the aid, intervention, and even control of White people. Although Jefferson respected Indians, he and his successors were desirous of their land. He even floated the idea of wooing them by encouraging them to increase commerce with White people and expand their agricultural endeavors. He believed this would increase their indebtedness, creating a dependence on the White power structure eventuating in their assimilation into White/European customs and ultimately submission to White authority and control.

Historian Ibram X. Kendi suggests that southern segregationists' belief in the innate inferiority of people of color, popularly depicted as savages and barbarians, and their supposed inability to assimilate into White civilization, influenced Jefferson and many of his contemporaries. But this does not absolve them from their complicity in perpetuating a depraved and inhuman institution whose legacy still impacts our society and the world. Kendi painstakingly demonstrates that even abolitionists like the renowned William Lloyd Garrison and Harriet Beecher Stowe conceptualized

Black people as docile, feminine, malleable, and willing to accommodate to White society. This biologically deterministic perception of Black people and other people of color ignored their desire for equality and self-sufficiency. By assuming that White leadership was the preferred method for eliminating slavery, their paternalistic assimilationist perception of Black people and the South perpetuated negative Black and Indian stereotypes, even as they sought to restore justice and equality to these beleaguered minorities.[88]

Even the "Great Emancipator," Abraham Lincoln, harbored doubts about the ability of Black people to coexist with White people in the United States. In an 1858 debate with Stephen Douglas, Lincoln remarked:

> I will say then that I am not, nor ever have been in favor of bringing about in any way the social and political equality of the white and black races—that I am not nor ever have been in favor of making voters or jurors of negroes, nor of qualifying them to hold office, nor to intermarry with white people; and I will say in addition to this that there is a physical difference between white and black races which I believe will forever forbid the two races living together on terms of social and political equality. And inasmuch as they cannot so live, while they do remain together there must be the position of superior and inferior, and I, as much as any other man, am in favor of having the superior position assigned to the white race. I say upon this occasion I do not perceive that because the white man is to have the superior position the negro should be denied everything.[89]

Apparently, Lincoln shared these sentiments with many of his predecessors—twelve of the first eighteen presidents of the United States were slave owners, and eight owned slaves while they were in office. Lincoln's attitudes toward Indians were ambivalent and influenced by his preoccupation with the Civil War. Prior to the outbreak of hostilities with the Confederacy, Lincoln was thrust into a decision that challenged his erudition and fairness. In the face of broken treaty promises, Sioux warriors left their reservation in 1862 and proceeded to slaughter White women, children, and male settlers along the Minnesota River in the new state of Minnesota. The Indians were initially protesting late and insufficient annuity payments, insufficient food, and unscrupulous federal Indian agents who misappropriated resources ostensibly meant for them. The Dakota War resulted in the deaths of approximately eight hundred people according to a statement Lincoln made in his second inaugural address.

The U.S. Army, under orders from the Lincoln administration, succeeded in quelling the disturbance and capturing over a thousand Sioux. Over three hundred Sioux warriors were tried, found guilty of serious crimes, and sentenced to hang. Lincoln commuted the sentences of all but thirty-eight of the men, who were hung in the largest mass execution in this country's history on December 26, 1862, for attacking White settlements with "extreme ferocity." Five days later Lincoln signed the Emancipation Proclamation.[90]

According to historian Christopher Anderson, Lincoln viewed Native Americans simultaneously as foreign and respectable, but certainly people who would need to be removed through purchase and conquest.[91] His early childhood was influenced by the violent murder of his grandfather and namesake, who was killed by an Indian while farming in Kentucky in 1786, but as he matured, he assuaged his negative impressions of Native Americans in his characteristic desire to treat people fairly.

During his stint as an enlisted soldier in the Illinois militia in 1832, though he never personally fought the insurgent Indians in the Blackfoot and Sauk War, he witnessed the grisly results of the combat. Yet he intervened to prevent the lynching of a Native American at the hands of other soldiers when the Indian entered their encampment with the intent of disclosing intelligence about their adversaries.

While in the presidency, Lincoln followed his predecessors' policies, viewing Indians as wards of the government while negotiating with them as sovereigns. Historian W. Dale Mason contended that Lincoln made no dramatic changes in Indian–White relations, and though he called for reform of the way Native Americans were treated, Indians, during his term in office, were still placed on reservations,[92] and he praised General Winfield Scott's removal of the Cherokees during the "Trail of Tears."

Significantly, during Lincoln's administration the notorious "Long Walk" of the Navajos and Mescalero Apaches was conducted, which led to the death of two hundred people as they were forcibly evicted from their homes in eastern Arizona and western New Mexico to the arid Bosque Redondo in New Mexico. Another feature of his administration was the passage of the Homestead Act in May 1862. Predecessors of the act were opposed by southern states because they feared that the expansion of the western territory would diminish the power of slave states.

The Homestead Act opened up settlement in the western territory already occupied by Native Americans who hunted, fished, and farmed in the region. By the end of the Civil War, 15,000 claims were made for the 160 acres of federal land offered by the act. Settlers could pay $1.25 an acre and obtain the land in six months or live continuously on the land for five years. Eventually, 1.6 million claims were approved covering 420,000 square miles.

Another problematic action of the Lincoln administration that adversely affected Native Americans was Lincoln's decision to use federal funds for the construction of a transcontinental railroad that cut a swath across the country through Indian territories. Lincoln didn't live to see the conclusion of the project on May 10, 1869, when the last spike was laid at Promontory Summit, Utah, uniting the Union Pacific and Central Pacific railroads (who had been receiving $32,000 per mile of rail laid from the federal government). The project was opposed by many Native American tribes (e.g., the Sioux, Cheyenne, and Arapaho), who harassed the workers, stole equipment, and attempted to destroy the rails. Once completed, the transcontinental railroad provided a safe and relatively inexpensive avenue allowing settlers into the western territories in unprecedented numbers. In search of land, gold, and silver, they flooded the region and precipitated further clashes with the Indigenous inhabitants.[93]

Perpetuation of Non–White Stereotypes

Bolstering eighteenth- and nineteenth-century pseudoscientific theories were cultural depictions of people of color and Indigenous people that characterized them as ugly, ape-like creatures with big lips, frizzy hair, exaggerated breasts, buttocks, and libidos. These characteristics became the foundation on which modern racist symbolism evolved, and it has been perpetuated through humorous depictions embedded in our culture. Satirical lampoons and scathing caricatures of Black people and Native Americans blended with comedic characterizations of racially marginalized groups performed by minstrels in the antebellum and postbellum eras.

But these attitudes are also perpetuated by contemporary self-deprecating assaults on the physical and psychological integrity of Black, Latinx, and Indigenous peoples by members of their own groups. Today, racist barbs delivered by comedic cultural assassins create an unremitting diffusion of these stereotypes in our culture. They contaminate our collective psyche through the stigmatization of "the Other" as physically and culturally inferior. Distorted characterizations of dark-skinned and Indigenous people portray them in unflattering ways, indicative of Western ethnocentric attempts to depersonalize and dehumanize "the Other." These anomalies are injected into White-dominated society, often accompanied by textual material that belittles their intellectual capacity and denigrates their culture.

4

In the Beginning

> Throughout American history the perception of Native Americans
> changed in response to the Native's usefulness to Whites. When the
> early colonists needed them to stay alive or help fight a war, the Indians
> were thought of as brave and noble savages. When the Indians got in
> the way and threatened the White Man's plans, they became animalis-
> tic and bloodthirsty savages. The Indian, who had been important when
> trade and explorations were the keys to overseas involvement, became
> an inconvenient obstacle to settlement of the lands to the West.
> —Redface! The History of Racist American
> Indian Stereotypes (www.red-face.us).

The origin legend of the Havasupai Indians (Havasu Baaja), a group of around seven hundred people who reside at the bottom of the Grand Canyon in Arizona, holds that the Great Spirit created them thousands of years ago and gave them dominion over the region where they live. Although many modern scientists believe that Native Americans are the descendants of Asians known as Clovis people (for the shape of their tools), who migrated across a trans–Siberian land bridge that spanned the Bering Sea some sixteen thousand years ago, the Havasupai legend remained intact until the mid–1990s when an anthropologist from Arizona State University subjected blood samples from the group, ostensibly gathered to detect genetic mark-ers for diabetes, to DNA analysis and discovered that they were indeed descendants of migratory Asians.[1]

Aside from the obvious ethical and trust violations associated with this behav-ior (the Havasupai successfully sued the university and regained the genetic material they donated as well as $700,000), this incident highlights other salient issues, such as who is a "legitimate" Native American and whether or not the science of genetics should be used to ascertain this and related issues. The status of Native Americans and their lands was complicated by the passage of the Dawes Act (also known as the General Allotment Act) in 1887 that divided Indian lands into parcels and awarded them to individuals if they promised to become "civilized" and relinquish their sur-plus land to White settlers. In the following half century, until President Franklin Del-ano Roosevelt signed the Indian Reorganization Act (Wheeler-Howard Act) in 1934, which ended the allotment practice and restored Indian rights to reorganize and form self-governments, over ninety million acres of Native American land were sold to mostly White settlers.[2]

Native Americans not only lost their land during this time, but in the years fol-lowing the Dawes Act, successive administrations also embarked on policies that promoted the assimilation of Native Americans and the termination of over one hundred tribal organizations. These actions also led to the diminution of Native American control over their lands. The Kennedy and Johnson administrations launched policies to reverse this trend, and President Richard Nixon formally initiated the policy of Native American self-determination in 1970.

Serious damage had been done to Native Americans' confidence in the political process. Today, there are 574 officially recognized Native American tribes, but there is disagreement among Native Americans over who qualifies as a legitimate tribal member and the use of DNA testing to confirm this. There is an ongoing debate among Native Americans over the efficacy of the use of DNA and other modern scientific methods for studying Indigenous people. Writing in *The Atlantic*, Rose Eveleth summarized Native American concerns: "Who will be using this data, and for what?"[3]

Among the concerns of Native Americans is a taboo against tampering with or removing a piece of a deceased ancestor. As Nick Tipon, vice chairman of the Sacred Sites Committee of the Federated Indians of Graton Rancheria, an organization that represents Native Americans in northern California, noted, "Rest in peace means forever, not to be disturbed, not to be studied, unless they consented to that."[4] Additionally, scientific attempts to ascertain the origin of a tribe may create conflict and ambiguity with their historical traditions. As Kim Tallbear, a member of the Sisseton-Wahpeton Oyate tribe, contends, "We know who we are as a people, as an Indigenous people, why would we be so interested in where scientists think our genetic ancestors came from?"[5] This perspective can be better understood in light of historical interactions between White colonizers of this continent and the Indigenous people who lived here when they arrived.

First Contacts

The late author and lecturer on Native Americans Stan Steiner observed that Native Americans openly welcomed Europeans when they landed in the New World. They were so hospitable that Columbus thought he had found a new Garden of Eden. The Indians were "so entirely our friends it is a wonder to see. Anything they have, if it be asked for they never say no, but rather invite the person to accept it, and show so much lovingness as though they would give their hearts."[6] Similarly, the intrepid explorer of North America Amerigo Vespucci concluded that the Indians were "so giving that it is an exception when they deny you anything.... They showed themselves very desirous of copulating with Christians."[7]

From these and other written accounts of early interactions between Europeans and Indigenous people, it is obvious that they approached the European interlopers with equal measures of curiosity, wonder, and generosity. But their benevolence was not always reciprocated. Whether by happenstance or intention, encounters between Native inhabitants of lands "discovered" by European explorers often turned deadly, and the preponderance of casualties were among Indigenous people. Estimates of the number of Aboriginal people inhabiting North America at the time of Columbus's arrival vary between 2.1 million and 18 million with a consensus around 7 million. The estimated total number of Indigenous people inhabiting North, Central, and

South America probably surpassed fifty million and might have been as high as one hundred million in pre–Columbian times.[8] A recent study by Alexander Koch, Chris Brienley, Mark M. Maslin, and Simon Lewis reviewed 119 population studies of the Americas prior to contact with Columbus in 1492, and concluded that the population of the Americas was then around 60.5 million people, and nearly 55 million of them died within a century of contact with Europeans. Known as the Great Dying, this 95 percent depopulation of North, Central, and South America resulted in the decrease of fifty-six million hectares of arable land (1 percent of the land mass of the Americas) that had been devoted to cultivation. Consequently, there was a significant amount of carbon dioxide that was retained in new growth forests and not released into the atmosphere, which resulted in global cooling known as the Little Ice Age, bringing the temperature of the Earth down by 0.15 degrees Celsius.[9]

Lately, there has been a reevaluation of the mythology surrounding the heroic figure Christopher Columbus. Many cities have decided to either forego Columbus Day celebrations or recast them. In New York City, Mayor Bill de Blasio was enmeshed in a controversy with various Italian American organizations over the possible removal of an iconic statue of Christopher Columbus, while cities like Los Angeles, Austin, Bangor, and Burbank have opted for turning the day into a commemoration of "Indigenous peoples' celebration."[10] In 2019, Vermont and Maine joined South Dakota and New Mexico in renaming Columbus Day to reflect the sanctity of the Indigenous peoples' diaspora in the New World.[11]

Many myths surround the early encounters Europeans had with Indigenous people in North America. We have seen how early travelers' descriptions of them were gross distortions of reality. Consequently, some Europeans who reached the shores of North America were apprehensive about their interactions with Native Americans based on preconceptions they had about the uncivilized, unchurched, "savages" who dwelled there.

Mythical Foundations of the New World: Jamestown

Ironically, the mythology that developed around Europeans' encounters with Native Americans in North America depicted them favorably, at least initially. For example, every American school child can recall the romantic encounter between the English Captain John Smith and the Indian princess Pocahontas that ostensibly occurred near the first English settlement in Jamestown, Virginia, in 1607. Chartered by King James I in 1606, and sponsored by the Virginia Company of London, the objective of the project was to find a northwest passage to eastern Asia to connect England to other countries, exploit the resources of the new land, and convert Indigenous people to Christianity.

Decades of internecine warfare involving England, France, Spain, Portugal, the Netherlands, and other European nations had forced them to seek new sources of wealth to replenish their treasuries. The development of mercantilism fueled by the improvement of navigational techniques, along with the avaricious motives of wealthy capitalists, encouraged exploration in the New World.

Three ships, the *Godspeed, Susan Constant*, and *Discovery*, left England on December 20, 1606, with 105 passengers. They landed on the Virginia coast in April

1607, and an expedition led by Captain Christopher Newport made its way to a site on the James River on May 13 where it began the famous Jamestown settlement.

What school children often fail to learn is that the colonists were surrounded by fourteen thousand Algonquian Indians, members of some thirty tribes ruled by Mamanatowick (Chief of Chiefs) Wahunsenacawh, or, as the English referred to him, Powhatan. In 1608, Captain John Smith became the colony's leader. His elevation to this position was based on his prior experiences as a soldier and leadership ability, but his petulant, and at times abrasive, behavior led to his arrest and confinement on board the *Susan Constant* from which he saw the land that would become the first English settlement in the New World.[12]

Smith was a tenacious defender of the settlers who were liberally sprinkled with upper-class Englishmen lacking survival skills as farmers and laborers. To avoid starvation, Smith, a tough negotiator on behalf of the colony, was known to barge into Indian villages and hold a pistol to the head of inhabitants demanding food. This behavior did not endear him to the Indians, and in 1609 Powhatan laid siege to James Fort, leading to the death of several hundred colonists by starvation,[13] and the first Anglo-Powhatan War.

Smith and Powhatan, both strong personalities, squared off many times. Powhatan, a wizened sixty-year-old with reportedly over a hundred wives, was understandably suspicious about the colonists' intentions. What was their purpose? How many would be coming? How did these naive interlopers plan to survive? And, importantly, did they plan to use and share their superior technology with his people?

The Pocahontas incident stems from Smith's capture by Opechancanough, Powhatan's younger brother and chief of the Youghtanund, a nation related to Powhatan's, as Smith was exploring the Chickahominy River. Under Powhatan's control, Smith was, according to popular mythology, saved by Powhatan's daughter, Pocahontas, who supposedly threw herself between him and an executioner. To spice the tale a bit, legend has it that there was a romantic relationship between them.

The facts are somewhat at odds with this story. Pocahontas (her Indian name was Matoaka, which means "flower between two streams") was born in 1595 to one of Powhatan's favorite wives who died giving birth to her. Nothing about the incident is recorded in Smith's earlier writings, but the event is described in his book *The General Historie of Virginia, New England, and the Summer Isles ...* published in London in 1624. It is true that Pocahontas was a favorite of Chief Powhatan, but her young age may have excluded her from the ritual that enveloped Smith at Powhatan's village—a ritual that may have simulated his rebirth into the Algonquian community. In his own words:

> At last they brought him to Meronocomoco, where was Powhatan their Emperour. Here more than two hundred of those grim Courtiers stood wondering at him, as he had been a monster, till Powhatan and his trayne had put themselues in their greatest braveries. Before a fire upon a seat like a bedsted, he sat covered with a great robe, made of Rarowcun skinnes, and all the tayles hanging by ... having feasted after their best barbarous manner they could, a long consultation was held, but the conclusion was, two great stones were brought before Powhatan: then as many as could layd hands on him, dragged him to them, and theron laid his head, and being ready with their clubs, to beate out his braines, Pochontas the Kings dearest daughter, when no intreaty could prevaile, got his head in her armes, and laid her own upon his to saue him from death: whereat the Emperour was contented he should live to make him hatchets, and her bells, and copper, for they thought him as well of all occupations as themselues.[14]

While there is some doubt about Smith's interpretation of the event and his recollection of Pocahontas's role in it, the facts about her life are depressingly clear. She was only ten years old at the time of this incident. At the age of fourteen she married an Algonquian warrior, Kocum, brother of a Potowmac chief, Japazaw. She became pregnant and gave birth to a child. Kocum was killed by an English captain, Samuel Argall, two years later in a kidnapping plot in the hope of deterring future Indian aggression against the colonists.

In an attempt to free English hostages taken by the Algonquians, Pocahontas was lured aboard a ship captained by Argall on April 13, 1613, and was held hostage for a year. There she was taught English and converted to Christianity by an English minister, Alexander Whitaker, and christened Rebecca. Her treatment by the English was less than commendable. She was reportedly raped, and her conversion may not have been volitional. Though she was known to be kindly disposed to the English colonists in Jamestown, at times providing them with food, it is doubtful she and her retinue regularly visited the English encampment, and she never saw her Indian child again.

On April 5, 1614, Pocahontas was married to Englishman John Rolfe. His English wife and child had died on the voyage over, and he and his new bride farmed in the Virginia countryside for two years, where she gave birth to a son, Thomas. They and a dozen Indians left for England in 1616 where she was presented as an Indian princess—a model of how "savages" could be civilized and Christianized. She did have a chance encounter with Smith, who had returned to England for medical treatment, and reportedly shunned him.

Although she was apparently in good health, she became ill following dinner on board a ship that was bound for Virginia and died at the age of twenty-one. Some historians attribute the cause of her death to tuberculosis or some other infectious disease, but there is suspicion that she was poisoned. The ship was captained by the same man, Samuel Argall, who had kidnapped and imprisoned her before her trip to England. She was buried at Gravesend, England, on March 21, 1617. Many of the Indians accompanying her were sold as servants or used as carnival attractions. Some were sent as slaves to Bermuda. Rolfe returned to the colony and became a prominent tobacco farmer after learning the Indians' secret of curing tobacco—a sacred process only revealed to him because of his marriage to Pocahontas. This endeavor helped save the Jamestown colony.[15]

The union between Rolfe and Powhatan's daughter, Pocahontas, smoothed relations between the colonists and the Indians for several years after their marriage in 1614. Pocahontas's death in 1617 was followed by that of her father, Powhatan, within the year. This led to unstable relationships between the two groups as Opechancanough assumed the mantle of emperor. Resentful of the increased English presence in his territory (there were over 1,200 settlers and 15 plantations strewn around Jamestown), Opechancanough resorted to various tactics to dislodge and then eliminate the settlers.

His patience with the English intruders came to an end on March 22, 1622, when an all-out surprise assault was waged against them, resulting in the deaths of 347 men, women, and children, one-third of their number. But this assault only stiffened English opposition to the Native Americans. The English King James and private donors sent prodigious armaments and gunpowder to be used against them in a vengeful series of attacks that claimed hundreds of Indians, all in accordance with the

Perspectives about immigrants: Pocahontas being baptized and Capitol Police arresting protestors from the Poor People's Campaign, 2018 (Chip Somodevilla, Getty Images).

admonition of the directors of the Virginia Company to undertake "perpetual warre without peace or truce."[16]

Settlers continued to perish from disease, malnutrition, and Indian attacks, and the toll of English retaliatory attacks on Indians and their crops ultimately led to an unsteady truce until the flood of Europeans enveloped the Indians and pushed them into oblivion. How ironic that a protest for poor people in May 2018 in the nation's capitol would be staged in front of a painting of Pocahontas being baptized.

The Facts about the Plymouth Colony

The practice of English and other early explorers to capture Indigenous people and sell them into slavery or put them on exhibition in the Old World understandably made the Indians suspicious of intruders. And well they should have been, because their world was not only subjected to the predations of these men and the settlers who followed them, but their very existence was also threatened by the germs they spread. A case in point involved the two Native Americans who made contact with the Pilgrims thirteen years later and 620 miles north of the Jamestown settlement in what is now Plymouth, Massachusetts.

In a desperate attempt to obtain religious freedom, 105 people left England in

September 1620 and sailed across the Atlantic Ocean, making landfall on the coast of Massachusetts at Cape Cod on November 11, 1620. The expedition had originally intended to land in Virginia, but bad weather forced them to the Cape.

As with their predecessors in Virginia, the settlers were unprepared for the harsh climate they encountered. Despite an abundance of fish and game, they lost half of their party during their first winter to infectious diseases. All the while, they lived in fear of the Indigenous people who lingered barely in sight but remained as a constant reminder that they were not alone.

Though the Pilgrims had some provisions, they were insufficient, and their seeds did not adapt to the soil and climate in the New World. When an expeditionary party came upon an abandoned Indigenous village, they excavated mounds and took varieties of corn, beans, and burial artifacts, desecrating the sites. While this did not ingratiate them with the area's Native Americans, members of the Wampanoag Nation (meaning "people of the light"), it assisted their survival, and they vowed to compensate the owners in the future (which in fact they did six months later).

Native Americans, consistently referred to as savages by the colonists, were frequently sighted, much to the dismay of the settlers whose precarious situation caused them to post sentries and build fortifications in fear of an imminent attack. One can only imagine their demeanor when a tall, half-naked Indian, Samoset ("he who walks over much"), strode purposefully through their encampment on March 16, 1621. This Sagamore, or subordinate chief, of an eastern Abenaki tribe ("people of the eastern dawn") in what is now Maine, welcomed the settlers and asked for a beer. "Welcome! Welcome Englishmen!" he exclaimed, and as one observer described it, "He very boldly came all alone, and along the houses, straight to the rendezvous; where we intercepted him, not suffering him to go in, as undoubtedly he would out of his boldness."

Samoset had learned English from sailors and fishermen who frequented the coast of his native land. The startled settlers offered him food and whiskey and, as the weather grew colder, gave him a blanket. He would become an important liaison between them and the great Chief Massasoit, the leader of the Wampanoag Nation. More importantly, Samoset introduced the Pilgrims to an English-speaking Native American, Squanto or Tisquantum, who taught the settlers how to cultivate crops, fish, and survive the arduous conditions that threatened their existence. As William Bradford, governor of the colony, recounted, "[we were] [s]hort of supplies, unprepared for a winter much colder than in England or Leiden," and they were afflicted by the diseases that come from being shipbound in those times; they endured brutal conditions in "a hideous and desolate wilderness."

Squanto was, in many ways, the savior of the Plymouth colony. His contributions to the Pilgrims were described by Bradford as a divine gift, "a special instrument sent by God for their good, beyond expectations." Squanto was the sole survivor of his tribe, the Pautext, who had inhabited the area where the Pilgrims established their settlement. In an ironic twist of fate, he was abducted by English Captain Thomas Hunt in 1614, who was a member of the expedition of the same Captain John Smith who helped settle Jamestown seven years before. Hunt captured Squanto and twenty-six other Native Americans and sold them as slaves in Malaga, Spain. Squanto was rescued by Friars and managed to escape to England where he lived with John Slaney who had an investment in Newfoundland where Squanto was sent as an interpreter and expert on North American natural resources.

In Newfoundland, Squanto met English explorer Thomas Dermer, and he returned with him to the New World in 1619 only to find that his entire village had been wiped out by an epidemic (probably the plague). Squanto's captivity had saved his life, and with his assistance, the English colony in Massachusetts survived the harsh conditions of its early years. He died of a fever on November 30, 1622, in the care and presence of William Bradford while on a trading expedition.[17]

"I'll Take Manhattan"

Another popular myth that helped build stereotypes about Native Americans as dim-witted savages concerns the "sale" of Manhattan Island by a group of Indians to the Dutch West India Company in 1626. Although a legal document or deed concerning this transaction does not exist, the Dutch National Archives (the Rijksarchief) has a primary reference for the transaction. Pieter Schaghen, a Dutch merchant employed by the Dutch West India Company, made reference to the sale in a November 5, 1626, letter to the directors of the company: "They have purchased the Island of Manhattees from the savages for the value of 60 guilders [$24]."

There is some confusion about which group of Indians "sold" the property to the Dutchman, Peter Minuit, a man in his early thirties who represented the company as

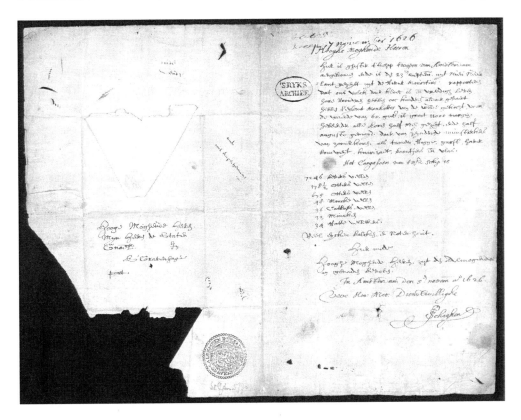

The sale of Manhattan (National Archives of the Netherlands, 5751B Schaghenbrief, November 5, 1626).

a director in New Amsterdam. The land in question probably belonged to the Wappinger Confederacy, Lenape Indians also known as Delawares. While most of the island was inhabited by the Weckquaesgeeks (Wappingers and also Delawares), some historians believe that the sellers of the property were Canarsie Indians who actually lived in what is now Brooklyn and Long Island. Another possible seller were the Raritans, who lived on what is now Staten Island.

An even larger issue concerns whether the property was actually sold, or, as some experts believe, loaned or granted to the Dutch so they could exercise hunting, fishing, and trapping rights, while the Indians retained permanent property rights for themselves. A primary objective of the West India Company was the exploitation of land to maximize investment income. Fur trapping, especially beaver, otter, and mink, were commonly traded and bartered with the Indians for Western technological implements like axes, adzes, awls, and muskets.

Much derision has been heaped on Native Americans over the centuries for selling prime real estate for the paltry sum of $24. A copy of an internal communication sent by Schaghen to the directors of the West India Company details the terms of the transaction. But in view of the confusion over the seller of the property and the fact that it may have been sold to naive settlers multiple times, it is conceivable that the Indians had the last laugh.[18]

5

Conquistadors and Cannibals

The Indians were "so giving that it is an exception when they deny you anything. They showed themselves very desirous of copulating with Christians."

—Amerigo Vespucci

To the Victor...

The earliest interactions between Western European explorers and Indigenous people in the New World were characterized by domination, exploitation, and brutality. Indigenous people were easily subdued by Europeans with their technological advantage of modern weapons, armor, and military tactics. Geographer Jared Diamond recounts the slaughter of thousands of Incans by a band of 168 Spanish soldiers led by Francisco Pizarro on November 16, 1532, in the Peruvian town of Cajamarca. The Indians vainly tried to defend their king, Atahualpa, who was captured. Although they paid a ransom of gold worth millions, the Spaniards executed him anyway after imprisoning him for eight months.[1]

The Spanish obtained the first foothold in North America, establishing St. Augustine in 1565, under the leadership of Pedro Menendez de Aviles, following the landing of Ponce de Leon in the region in 1513. They drove north and south in their ravenous quest for resources to fill the coffers of their rulers. They gained a reputation among the Native people as ruthless predators, an appellation that was reinforced by their seeming indifference to the humanity of the Indigenous people they came in contact with.

One of the earliest descriptions of Spanish cruelty toward Indigenous people was written by the first ordained Catholic priest in the New World, Bartolomé de Las Casas, in 1542. Having served with Spanish explorers in the Caribbean, Las Casas witnessed widespread mistreatment of the Native people and wrote his famous treatise, *A Brief Account of the Destruction of the Indies*, more popularly known as *Tears of the Indians*, in which he described the inhumane torture, mutilation, and murder of the Indians of the Caribbean and the near destruction of the Indigenous Taino Nation. The Spaniards "spar'd no Age, or Sex, nay not so much as Women and Child, but ripping up their Bellies, tore them alive in pieces."[2] He noted that the Spanish conquest of the Caribbean had decimated the Indigenous population: "[O]f the Three Millions of Persons, which lived in Hispaniola itself, there is at present but the inconsiderable remnant of scarce Three Hundred." And, "[T]he Spaniards by their barbarous and execrable Actions have absolutely depopulated Ten Kingdoms, of greater extent than all Spain, together with the Kingdoms of Arragon and Portugal."[3]

Historian David Stannard estimated that the Spanish were directly or indirectly responsible for the deaths of between sixty and eighty million people by the end of the sixteenth century.[4] Las Casas was so moved by these early depredations that he pleaded his case for humane treatment of the Indians before the Spanish Parliament in 1519. Years later, in 1550–51, he debated his antagonist, the Catholic theologian Juan Gaines Sepúlveda, before the Council of Valladolid in Spain. Sepúlveda argued that Indigenous people and their resources could be treated as the normal spoils of war, entitlements belonging to the conquerors. Even more insidious was the assumption that Indigenous people were not the equal of Europeans; they were lower on the Chain of Being, primitive, and even devoid of souls. As Sepúlveda noted in his *Democrates II*, "Concerning the Just Cause of the War Against the Indians," the Indians "are inferior to the Spaniards just as children are to adults, women to men and, indeed, one might even say, as apes are to men."[5]

If the Spanish and other colonizers like the English, French, Dutch, Germans, and Portuguese were cruel exploiters of Indigenous people, their callous depredations paled in comparison to the havoc wrought by the transmission of infectious and communicable diseases that Indigenous people had little immunity to. Within forty years of Columbus's landing in Hispaniola in 1492, nearly all of the three hundred thousand to four hundred thousand Arawak and Taino Indians who had inhabited the region were gone. Geographer Diamond estimates that diseases spread by Europeans killed 95 percent of the pre–Columbian Indigenous population.[6]

It has been estimated that Indigenous people suffered as much as 90 percent mortality from infectious and communicable diseases after contact with Europeans. Between 1616 and 1619 almost all the Native Americans in New England were wiped out by diseases brought by the English and French. Smallpox, influenza, yellow fever, the plague, and leptospirosis were the principal culprits. Although many thousands of Native people were slaughtered by the invading explorers and settlers, the principal culprit in the demise of millions of Indigenous people were the diseases carried by the Europeans.

Natural selection had whittled down European genetic stocks through epidemics, enabling survivors to develop some measure of immunity to infectious and communicable diseases. The most notorious event was the infamous Black Death (bubonic plague transmitted by fleas who bit infected rats) that killed an estimated twenty million people, one-third of Europe's population, from 1347 to 1352. Though they were oblivious about germ theory, they surmised that it was dangerous to come into contact with sick people. There is evidence that during the Middle Ages, Europeans hurled corpses infected with communicable diseases over the walls of besieged fortresses.[7]

Captain John Smith noted in his journal that in three successive years "neere two hundred miles along the Sea Coast, that in some places there scarce remained five of a hundred."[8]

Thomas Morton, an early American colonist who founded what is now Quincy, Massachusetts, observed that the forests around Boston Harbor, which had been populated by Native Americans, "there hath been one [Indian] left a live, to tell what became of the rest, the living being (as it seems) not able to bury the dead, they were left for the crowes, Kites and vermin to prey upon. And the bones and skulls upon the several places of their habitations, made such a spectacle after my coming into those partes, that, as I travailed in the forest nere the Massachusetts, it seemed to me a new found Golgotha."[9]

While most transmission of disease was incidental and unintentional, European disdain for Indigenous people and the desire for their land led Jeffrey Amherst (later Lord for his service in the French and Indian War) to order the distribution of blankets infected with smallpox to the Indians in upstate New York to "Extirpate this Execrable Race."[10]

The Cannibal Connection

One of the most pernicious stereotypes that plagues Indigenous people is the association of their ancestors with cannibalism. It is difficult to pinpoint the exact origin of this stereotype, but it is safe to say that the publication of Daniel Defoe's *The Life and Strange Adventures of Robinson Crusoe* in 1719 in England helped weave it into the fabric of Western culture.

Born in London in 1660 into a working-class family, Daniel Defoe added the prefix De to the family name to convey an air of gentility. After failing as an entrepreneur and going bankrupt in 1692, Defoe dedicated himself to writing and became an indefatigable political pamphleteer. His jibes landed him in the pillory on several occasions. Defoe initially wrote against racial prejudice in England, even defending King William III (William Henry of Orange) who was ridiculed by some as a foreigner and outsider, having come from the Netherlands.

Robinson Crusoe, Defoe's first novel, was likely influenced by the true experiences of European castaways of that time and was an instant success. It went through six printings in the first four months and was translated into many languages and adapted for the stage, earning Defoe the reputation as the preeminent popularizer of the English novel. By 1895 there were 196 editions and 110 translations. One writer contends there are now over seven hundred editions with more than three dozen films based on the novel.[11] Today, the story has been popularized by the mass media, has been spun off in a multitude of popular television productions ranging from *Gilligan's Island* to *Survivor*, and is packaged as a children's book. Its racial stereotypes of Indigenous people as cannibals remains an integral part of Western culture.

Essays on the capitalistic, colonial, and Puritanical myths propagated by the novel are critical of Defoe's sentimental portrayal of Crusoe's domination and exploitation of his "Island of Despair," master/slave relationship to his "Man Friday," and revulsion toward Indigenous people who visited the island.[12] Examples of his Puritan upbringing permeate the story, as in Crusoe's mastery over the environment (which was not particularly adversarial) through English ingenuity, perseverance, and initiative. Philosopher Jean-Jacques Rousseau, author of *The Social Contract*, wrote that the novel "furnished the finest of treatises on education according to nature," and Edgar Allan Poe contended that *Robinson Crusoe* "has become a household thing in nearly every family in Christendom."[13] Critic Ian Watt countered that the book was a testament to capitalism and the self-made man—"homo economicus."[14]

Aside from frequent references to the virtues of industriousness and Christian piety, which saw Crusoe through twenty-eight years on his island, a lingering gift to posterity can be found in Defoe's ubiquitous references that denigrate and disparage Indigenous people and stereotype them as abominable heathens. His habit of referring to the people who live in the territory as savages is coupled with the assertion that they are all cannibals: "I concluded by all my observations, [I] must be near the Spanish dominions, and perhaps was all inhabited by savages, where if I landed, I had been in a worse condition than I was now...."[15] Further, "[T]he savage coast between the Spanish country and Brazils, where are found the worst savages, for they are cannibals or men-eaters, and fail not to murder and devour all the human bodies that fall into their hands."[16]

Crusoe's fear was reinforced when he stumbled upon the Native people's gathering place:

> When I was come down the hill to the shore ... I was perfectly confounded and amazed; nor is it possible for me to express the horror of my mind at seeing the shore spread with skulls, hands, feet, and other bones of human bodies; and particularly I observed a place where there had been a fire made, and a circle dug in the earth, like a cockpit, where I supposed the savage wretches had sat down to their human feastings upon the bodies of their fellow-creatures.

This struck him as "a pitch of inhuman, hellish brutality, and the horror of the degeneracy of human nature."[17]

The thought of falling into the hands of such "hellish wretches" tormented Crusoe, and "for night and day I could think of nothing but how I might destroy some of the monsters in their cruel bloody entertainment, and if possible save the victim they should bring hither to destroy."[18]

But there was still room for compassion in Crusoe's musings, which gives us insight into Defoe's Christian upbringing. Despite his initial assumption that they were abandoned by God, Crusoe reconsidered slaughtering the Native people:

> I began, with cooler and calmer thoughts, to consider what I was going to engage in, what authority or call I had to pretend to be judge and executioner upon these men as criminals, whom Heaven had thought but for so many ages to suffer unpunished to go on, and to be as it were the executioners of His judgments upon another; how far these people were offenders against me, and what right I had to engage in the quarrel of that blood which they shed promiscuously upon one another.[19]

And he continued:

> When I considered this a little, it followed necessarily that I was certainly in the wrong; that these people were not murderers, in the sense that I had before condemned them in my thoughts, any more than those Christians were murderers who often put to death the prisoners taken in battle; or more frequently, upon many occasions, put whole troops of men to the sword, without giving quarter, though they threw down their arms and submitted.[20]

He concluded that "these people had done nothing to me." And, "[I]t could not be just for me to fall upon them; that this would justify the conduct of the Spaniards in all their barbarities practiced in America, where they destroyed millions of people."[21]

Nevertheless, upon seeing a party of Native people preparing to eat their human captives, Defoe lets Crusoe explode on the scene, wreaking havoc on them with his superior weapons. This eventuates in the rescue of one of the captives whom Crusoe calls "Man Friday." Shortly before he took custody of Friday, Crusoe "fancied myself able to manage one, nay, two or three savages, if I had them, so as to make them entirely slaves to me, to do whatever I should direct them, and to prevent their being able at any time to do me any hurt."[22]

His description of Friday reflects common Western stereotypes about Indigenous dark-skinned people, prevalent to this day[23]: "His hair was long and black, not curled like wool.... The colour of his skin was not quite black, but very tawny; and yet not an ugly, yellow, nauseous tawny, as the Brazilians and Virginians, and other natives of America are...."[24]

One of the unforgettable scenes of the book, reprised in the movies, was Friday's invitation to Crusoe to exhume the bodies of his vanquished captors and devour them: "[Friday] showed me the marks that he had made to find them again, making signs to me that we should dig them up again and eat them."[25]

Defoe spared no verbiage in driving home the fiendish nature of these Indigenous people:

> The place [where the Native people killed and ate their captives] was covered with human bones, the ground dyed with their blood, and great pieces of flesh left here and there, half-eaten, mangled, and scorched; and, in short, all the tokens of the triumphant feast they had been making there, after a victory over their enemies. I saw three skulls, five hands, and the bones of three or four legs and feet, and abundance of other parts of the bodies.[26]

Friday and his compatriots had a prodigious appetite: "[He] told me he was once there [on the island] when they ate up twenty men, two women, and one child."[27]

Despite his predilection for portraying Indigenous people in the most nefarious manner, in the end, Defoe admits of their capacity for humanity:

> This frequently gave me occasion to observe, and that with wonder, that however it pleased God in his providence, and in the government of the works of his hands, to take from so great a part of the world of His creatures the best uses to which their faculties and the powers of their souls are adapted, yet that He has bestowed upon them the same powers, the same reason, the same affections, the same sentiments of kindness and obligation, the same passions and resentments of wrongs, the same sense of gratitude, sincerity, fidelity, and all the capacities of doing good and receiving good that He has given to us; and that when He pleases to offer them occasions of exerting these, they are as ready, nay, more ready, to apply them to the right uses for which they were bestowed, than we are.[28]

He added, "[W]e did not know by what light and law these should be condemned."[29]

Unfortunately, his negative characterization of Indigenous dark-skinned people persisted beyond his humanistic demurral, tainting the perceptions of generations. But Defoe was not alone in the propagation of this myth. Peter Martyr d'Anghiera, the foremost chronicler of Spanish explorations in the New World, wrote of Columbus's first encounter with Indigenous people on the Island of Hispaniola:

> The Spaniards learned that there were other islands not far distant, inhabited by fierce peoples who live on human flesh; this explained why the natives of Hispaniola fled so promptly on their arrival. They told the Spaniards later that they had taken them for cannibals which is the name they give to those barbarians. They also call them *Caribes*. The islands inhabited by these monsters lie towards the south, and at half-way to the other islands. The inhabitants of Hispaniola, who are mild people, complained that they were exposed to frequent attacks from the cannibals who landed amongst them and pursued them through the forests like hunters chasing wild beasts. The cannibals captured children, whom they castrated, just as we do chicken and pigs we wish to fatten for the table, and when they were grown and became fat they ate them. Older persons, who fell into their power, were killed

and cut into pieces for food; they also ate the intestines and the extremities, which they salted, just as we do hams. They did not eat women, as this would be considered a crime and an infamy. If they captured any women, they kept them and cared for them in order that they may produce children; just as we do with hens, sheep, mares, and other animals. Old women when captured, were made slaves. The inhabitants of these islands (which from now on we may consider ours), women and men, have no other means of escaping capture by the cannibals, than by flight. Although they use wooden arrows with sharpened points, they are aware that these arms are of little use against the fury, and admit that ten cannibals could easily overcome a hundred of their own men in a pitched battle.[30]

Despite popular assumptions about the practice of cannibalism (anthropophagy), anthropologist William Arens systematically debunked the assumption that it was widespread and culturally relevant to Indigenous people throughout the world, concluding that "the available evidence does not permit the facile assumption that the act was or has ever been a prevalent cultural feature."[31] Arens was especially critical of Western anthropological reports of cannibalism based on hearsay information and ethnocentric myths. He noted that

all cultures, subcultures, religions, sects, secret societies and every other possible human association have been labeled anthropophagic by someone. In this light, the contemporary, though neglected, anthropological problem emerges more clearly. The idea of "others" as cannibals, rather than the act, is the universal phenomenon. The significant question is not why people eat human flesh, but why one group invariably assumes that others do.[32]

How ironic that the stereotypical portrayal of Carib Indians[33] as bloodthirsty cannibals was false. According to Professor Basil A. Reid of the University of the West Indies, there is "[n]o evidence, either archaeological or from firsthand observations by Europeans [that] conclusively proves that Island-Caribs ever consumed human flesh."[34] Reid contends that the Indigenous people of the Caribbean were labeled savage cannibals because they resisted the intrusion of Europeans, who then created stereotypes about them as uncivilized and barbaric.

Cannibalism has, however, occurred in various places and times around the world and was practiced for centuries by Europeans through the Middle Ages. Sarah Everts, writing in *Smithsonian* magazine, reported fossil evidence of European cannibalism dating back one hundred thousand years to bones of Neanderthals found in a French cave. She noted that the world's first documented incident of cannibalism occurred during the Crusades in 1098 when Christian soldiers captured the Syrian city of Ma'arra and ate the flesh of local Muslims.[35] She points out that English markets in the eleventh century sold cooked human flesh in times of famine, and as late as the sixteenth century, Spain and England used flesh, skin, bones, blood, fat, and urine of cadavers as well as the bodies of recently executed criminals for medicines. Somewhat facetiously she adds, "While Indigenous people were being described as cannibals, Europeans were imbibing in human flesh."

The label of cannibalism was used as a stereotypical tool of White imperialistic peoples as they sought to denigrate dark-skinned and Indigenous inhabitants in lands they desired. Labeling adversaries with an abhorrent appellation not only stigmatized the victimized group, it also exonerated the oppressors and rationalized their behavior, justifying their own depredations. Claiming the moral high ground, they deflected accusations of predatory, even rapacious behavior by justifying their actions as legitimate, even noble excursions against purportedly barbaric, bloodthirsty savages who

The European market for human flesh, by Theodor de Bry, sixteenth century (Historical Picture Archive, Getty Images).

engaged in the heinous activity of eating their own kind. This is a recurrent theme in Western historical and fictional accounts of encounters with ethnic "Others," including Native Americans.

A recent treatise on the scope and functions of cannibalism by zoology professor Bill Schutt of Long Island University, who is also a research associate at the American Museum of Natural History, demonstrates that the phenomenon was practiced by humans around the world, but there is scant evidence of it in the Caribbean. It seems that the Spanish explorers' lust for gold and silver were bolstered by edicts from Queen Isabella and papal bulls that legitimized the destruction of Indigenous populations presumed to be cannibalistic. In reality, Schutt points out, people were often labeled man-eaters and their societies decimated if they were bereft of the precious metals—they were regarded as expendable. Land and other resources, including the people, were taken as substitutes. Native peoples were sold as slaves in the fever to generate wealth for greedy monarchs and capitalists. "In the end, tall tales, especially those with bestial or cannibalistic angles, effectively dehumanized the islanders. Not only did they serve to justify Spain's rapidly evolving slave-raiding agenda, but it also established a mindset toward the locals that came to resemble pest control."[36]

Schutt concludes, as did Professor Reid: "As for the claims of Caribbean cannibalism, though, the fact remains that beyond the second—and third—hand accounts, there isn't a shred of physical evidence, nor is there any indication that Columbus or his men ever witnessed man-eating firsthand."[37] In effect, Schutt concurs with Arens that the appellation of the term "cannibal" was often given to cultural groups "discovered" by European explorers as a method for rationalizing their marauding and racism. But the allegation that Native Americans were unrepentant cannibals periodically resurfaces, and we will revisit this issue.

6

The Lasting Testament
of *The Last of the Mohicans*

The English who came first to this country were but a handful of people, forlorn, poor and distressed. My father did all in his power to serve them. Others came. Their numbers increased. My father's counselors were alarmed. They urged him to destroy the English before they became strong enough to give law to the Indians and take away their country.

But a small part of the dominion of my ancestors remains. I am determined not to live till I have no country.

—King Philip (Metacom), 1676

Early Impressions of Native Americans

To early explorers and colonists who "discovered" North America, Indigenous people who inhabited the land were variously viewed as quaint, eccentric, and uncivilized. Their culture, with its emphasis on reverence for nature, parsimonious use of natural resources, communal collaboration and cooperation, and nomadism, was antithetical to the expansionist, acquisitive, capitalist, individualistic, and exploitative ethic of the waves of European immigrants who came to the Americas in search of fame, fortune, and a better life. Racist theorists like Gobineau tried to rationalize their mistreatment by blaming them for rejecting invaders' values:

Consider the position of the American Indians at the present day. They live side by side with a people which always wishes to increase in numbers, to strengthen its power. They see thousands of ships passing up and down their waterways. They know the strength of their masters is irresistible. They have no hope whatever of seeing their native land one day delivered from the conqueror; their whole continent is henceforth as they all know, the inheritance of the European. A glance is enough to convince them of the tenacity of those foreign institutions under which human life ceases to depend, for its continuance, on the abundance of game and fish. From their purchases of brandy, guns, and blankets, they know that even their own coarse tastes would be more easily satisfied in the midst of such society, which is always inviting them to come in, and which seeks by bribes and flattery, to obtain their consent. It is always refused. They prefer to flee from one lonely spot to another; they bury themselves more and more in the heart of the country, abandoning all, even the bones of their fathers. They will die out, as they know well; but they are kept, by a mysterious feeling of horror, under the yoke of their unconquerable repulsion from the white race, and although they admire its strength and general superiority, their conscience and their whole nature, in a word, their blood, revolts from the mere thought of having anything in common with it.[1]

Being unaware of the function of Indigenous customs, Europeans, like Gobineau, recoiled at Indians' quest for survival through subsistence, in contrast to their own competitive, religiously inspired work ethic with its capitalistic profit motive. Nomadism and ritualistic feasts like potlatch, practiced by Indigenous people of the Pacific Northwest (e.g., the Kwakiutl), where participants gave away many of their material possessions, were anathema to the stoic Christians schooled in the virtues of Calvinism and Wesley.

Indians, at least those who survived the depredations wrought by the introduction of European-borne diseases, were unceremoniously pushed off their land in what became the doctrine of Manifest Destiny. Christianity provided the rationale for depicting Indigenous people as ungodly, heathen savages. Following the pattern established by other explorers toward Indigenous people, Indians were viewed as subhuman objects whose land and very persons were subordinated to the noble expansionary goals of King, country, and God.

The late historian Robert Berkhofer, Jr., provided an erudite exposition about the origin of White conceptions about Native Americans. The three principal colonizers of the Americas—Spain, France, and England—depicted Indigenous people as wild savages and cannibals, without a semblance of the accouterments of civilization (e.g., clothes, government, and religion). These sentiments were apparent in the writing of the earliest explorers. For example, Columbus noted:

> In these islands I have so far found no human monstrosities, as many expected, but on the contrary the whole population is very well formed.... Thus I have found no monsters, nor had a report of any, except in an island "Carib," which is at the second of the coming into the Indies, and which is inhabited by a people who are regarded in all the islands as very fierce and who eat human flesh. They have many canoes which they range through all the islands of India and pillage and take whatever they can. They are ferocious among these other people who are cowardly to an excessive degree, but I make no more account of them than of the rest.[2]

Likewise, Amerigo Vespucci, for whom the continent of North America was named, characterized the Indigenous dwellers of the New World thusly: "First then as to the people. We found in those parts such a multitude of people as nobody could enumerate (as we read in the Apocalypse), a race I say gentle and amenable. All of both sexes go about naked, covering no part of their bodies; and just as they spring from their mothers' wombs so they go until death."

After discussing the Native people's affinity for piercing their bodies, he continued:

> They have another custom, very shameful and beyond all human belief. For their women, being very lustful, cause the private parts of their husbands to swell up to such a huge size that they appear deformed and disgusting; and this is accomplished by a certain device of theirs, the biting of certain poisonous animals. And in consequence of this many lose their organs which break through lack of attention, and they remain eunuchs.

He further elaborated on their supposed propensity to cannibalism: "I knew a man whom I also spoke to who was reputed to have eaten more than three hundred human bodies. And I likewise remained twenty-seven days in a certain city where I saw salted human flesh suspended from beams between houses, just as with us it is the custom to hang bacon and pork. I say further: they themselves wonder why we do not eat our enemies and do not use as food their flesh which they say is most savory."[3]

First published representation of supposed cannibalism in America, German woodcutting, ca. 1497–1504 (Universal History Archive, Getty Images).

Such accounts were infused with misunderstandings about Indigenous culture and full of ethnocentric distortions and stereotypes. The early colonizing nations and their settlers variously referred to Indigenous people in the Americas as Natives, savages, wild men, pagans, barbarians, and heathens. But there was a duality to their portrayal of the Native peoples that contained positive as well as negative impressions, hence, the description of Indigenous people as noble savages who lived vicariously off the land, struggling to survive against the elements, in harmony with nature, and, simultaneously, bloodthirsty cannibals at war among themselves and with White settlers who ostensibly desired to live in peace.

Much of the colonizers' ambiguity can be attributed to what Berkhofer described as their religious orthodoxy, which depicted Native Americans as corrupt descendants of the more noble and civilized White Europeans. From this perspective, they were, in the final analysis, degenerate creatures who strayed from the true faith and practices.[4] "Whether evaluated as noble or ignoble, whether seen as exotic or degraded, the Indian as an image was always alien to the white."[5]

Anthropologist Audrey Smedley contends that the English were primarily responsible for the virulent racism that characterized their interactions with Native Americans and, later, Africans. The negative stereotypes that permeated their perceptions of these groups were derived from centuries of English interaction with the Irish—a group who resisted their attempts at colonization and domination. According to Smedley, English ethnocentricity about their culture led them to conceptualize all other people and religions as inferior. References to the Irish as uncivilized savages emerged from their unsuccessful attempts to subjugate them. Facets of their culture were antithetical to English Anglo-Saxon morality (e.g., Irish pastoral life, plural mates, and nudity). "The English were frustrated in their inability to establish complete suzerainty over Irish lands ... or to transform the natives and absorb them into English culture."[6]

The English transferred this sentiment about the brutish, savage Irish to all other groups they encountered in their attempt to repress and exploit Indigenous people around the world, and Smedley noted:

> It was the invention in the English mind of the Irish "savage" that made possible the development of policies and practices that could be perpetuated for gain, unencumbered by reflections on any ethnical or moral considerations. The savage was first of all a "heathen," a godless and immoral creature "wicked, barbarous and uncivil." He was lazy, filthy, evil and superstitious; he worshipped idols and was given to lying, stealing and murdering, double-dealing, and committing treachery.[7]

Smedley contended that these negative stereotypes about the Irish were woven into the fabric of early American settlements by some of the same English imperialists (e.g., more than forty members of the Virginia Company had interests in the colonization of Ireland).

Cooper's Legacy

These sentiments surfaced in the literature that captivated the imagination of White civilization and influenced subsequent generations through the mass media. One of the earliest and most influential North American writers who focused on pioneers and their interaction with Native Americans was James Fenimore Cooper (1789–1851). Born in Burlington, New Jersey, the eleventh of twelve children, his father, William, founded Cooperstown, New York, where James lived for many years with his wife and seven children. Expelled from Yale because of a prank (he blew up another student's door), he became a merchant seaman and later joined the U.S. Navy. He wrote his first novel, *Precaution*, in 1820 after his wife wagered that he could write a better book than the one she was reading. This launched him on a new career that produced nearly three dozen novels and seven works of nonfiction, among them the definitive *The History of the Navy of the United States* (1839).

Cooper is best known for his five-volume *Leatherstocking Tales* series published from 1823 to 1841. He is often acknowledged as one of the creators of the American novel, and though his books are not as widely read as in previous generations, his stereotypical depiction of Native Americans has been embedded in our culture through adaptations of his works in television and motion pictures. Zane Grey, one of the most widely read Western novelists of the twentieth century, was influenced by the *Leatherstocking Tales*.

Victor Hugo, renowned author of *Les Miserables*, considered Cooper a master of modern romance, but Mark Twain thought he was an incompetent pedant,[8] and literary critic Leslie Fiedler concluded that the *Leatherstocking Tales* "on all counts, if judged by critical standards—[are] bad books: ineptly structured, shamelessly periphrastic, euphemistic and verbose; at last, unforgivably boring."[9] Yet Cooper was extremely successful in his time and even honored with a U.S. commemorative stamp in 1940. But as with Defoe's *Robinson Crusoe*, his fictional expositions propounded distorted perceptions of Indigenous people that persist to this day.

Fiedler contended Cooper's writing tells us much about our values and motives, our ambivalence to non–White people who live in America:

> The attitudes and assumptions embodied in the *Leather-Stocking Tales ...* are regressive, reactionary, downright wicked in terms of the enlightened moral consensus of the late twentieth century. They are ... racist, sexist and anti-democratic; based on an ethnocentric, culturally imperialist and hierarchical view of society which serves to perpetuate, indeed celebrates the subservience of Red and Black men to white ones, of females to males, and of the uncultivated poor to the lettered rich.[10]

Much of Cooper's writing about early America develops themes that are still prominent in our society: materialism, classism, despoliation of the environment, and the desire to be at one with nature. Cooper developed these themes through a romanticized portrayal of the demise of Indigenous people (viz., the Delaware Nation), using a precursor to James Bond in the form of a multi-talented frontiersman, Natty Bumppo (also referred to as Deerslayer, Hawkeye, Long Rifle a.k.a. La Longue Carabine, the Scout, the Guide, the Trapper, and Leatherstocking).

Nick of the Woods, written by physician Robert M. Bird and published in 1837, was also widely read, and it portrayed Native Americans negatively, referring to them over 110 times as savages and more than 30 times as barbarians. Bird left little to the imagination of nineteenth-century readers about Indians' purported lack of humanity, incessantly referring to them as cannibalistic, bloodthirsty, and uncompassionate: "[W]e know of no instance where an Indian, torturing a prisoner at the stake, the torture once begun, has ever been moved to compassionate, to regard with any feelings but those of exultation and joy, the agonies of the thrice-wretched victim."[11]

Bird's novel went through twenty-three English editions and four translations, with the German version reportedly selling over ten thousand copies. Three theater adaptations were also made, but unlike Cooper's stylized serialization of his hero, Natty Bumppo, *Nick of the Woods* lacked the staying power of the *Leatherstocking Tales*. Nevertheless, the negative stereotypes and sentiment about Native Americans is strikingly similar in these works and helped lay the foundation that contributed to hostile feelings about Indians in the United States.

Historian Richard Slotkin traced the origin of the Natty Bumppo literary character to the real-life outdoorsman Captain Benjamin Church in the eighteenth century in the early American colonies—a figure that was later developed by the nineteenth-century entrepreneur and writer John Filson, who was responsible for popularizing the mythical status of Daniel Boone.[12] These outdoorsmen were the foundation for a mythical American lifestyle that reflected Puritan values of independence, frugality, reverence for nature, industriousness, and fidelity to family and friends.

In a way, Cooper preceded contemporary environmentalists in his flowery depiction of our pristine wilderness and its degradation wrought through population growth and accompanying despoliation of the environment.[13] Although he commiserated with the plight of Native Americans whose lands were being destroyed through the onslaught of European immigrants, his romanticized tales contributed to the distortion of their culture.

For example, in referring to an attempt to heal a sick Indian woman in *The Last of the Mohicans*, "[H]e prepared to commence that species of incantation, and those uncouth rites, under which the Indian conjurers are accustomed to conceal their ignorance and impotency."[14]

His style of writing predated what may be labeled historical fiction—an increasingly popular genre akin to the docudrama. It is a literary technique that combines fact and fiction into a tale that leaves readers wondering about the veracity of the tome. Cooper lent credibility to the underlying negative stereotypes about Native Americans by fusing presumably authentic footnotes and asides to actual historical events in the text. This practice reinforced the believability of the stereotypes he created in readers' minds by making the fictional side of his work plausible, linking them to factual events in his narrative. *The Last of the Mohicans* was, according to one scholar, "the most thorough blending of factual history with romantic fiction Cooper was to write."[15]

One of the most egregious illustrations of this technique concerns Cooper's gruesome account of the surrender of the British Fort William Henry during the French and Indian conflict (Seven Years' War, 1754–63) at the conclusion of a siege from August 3 to 9, 1757, by the French and a number of Native American tribes. Being hopelessly outmanned without a chance of reinforcements, the English Lt. Col. George Munro agreed to generous terms offered by French General Marquis de Montcalm. As the besieged remnants of the fort departed, they were attacked by Indians who disregarded the terms of surrender.

> More than two thousand raging savages broke from the forest at the signal [from Magua], and threw themselves across the fatal plain with instinctive alacrity. We shall not dwell on the revolting horrors that succeeded. Death was everywhere, and in his most terrific and disgusting aspects. Resistance only served to inflame the murderers, who inflicted their furious blows long after their victims were beyond the power of their resentment. The flow of blood might be likened to the outbreaking of a torrent; and as the natives became heated and maddened by the sight, many among them even kneeled to the earth, and drank freely, exultingly, hellishly, of the crimson tide.[16]

Cooper's version of the massacre at Fort William Henry paints a horrific description of the event, which, according to his reckoning, included the massacre of three thousand English soldiers and their families. He castigated the French soldiers and their leader, General Montcalm, for not intervening.

In reality, there was an Indian attack on the retreating English following the surrender of the fort. Reports vary, but estimates of English losses range from 69 to 185 people. French soldiers actually intervened to prevent further carnage. The surviving column of English men, women, and children arrived under Lt. Col. Munro at Fort Edward with a French guard on August 14, 1757.

Historian Thomas Philbrick believed Cooper wrote the book hurriedly in four months after visiting the site. He may have obtained some of his background information from written descriptions of the incident in Benjamin Trumbull's *A General History of the United States of America*[17] and from Jonathan Carver's *Travels Through the Interior Parts of North America in the Years 1766–1767.*[18] Carver claimed to be an eyewitness to the incident, serving as a volunteer under Col. Munro. His description of the "massacre" was vivid and similar to Cooper's: "By this time the war hoop was given, and the Indians began to murder those that were nearest to them without distinction. It is not in the power of words to give any tolerance idea of the horrid scene that now ensued. Men, women and children were dispatched in the most wanton and cruel manner, and immediately scalped. Many of the savages drank the blood of their victims, as it flowed warm from the fatal wound."[19]

After criticizing the French for not intervening and stopping the carnage, he continued: "But whatever was the cause from which it arose, the consequences of it were dreadful, and not to be paralleled in modern history."[20] By his account, "It was computed that fifteen hundred persons were killed or made prisoners by these savages during this fatal day. Many of the latter were carried off by them and never returned."[21] A fascinating account that no doubt greatly influenced Cooper, but one that is not corroborated by other witnesses and the facts about the survivors who reached the British Fort Edward. Nevertheless, it made for good reading, motion pictures, and television.

It is conceivable that Cooper also perused the journal of a high-ranking French officer, Louis Antoine de Bougainville, who served with the French army during the French and Indian War. Bougainville was very critical of the French conduct during the war and the widespread corruption among French military and civilian authorities in the French colonies in North America. From his journal, it was evident that the French had successfully cultivated their contacts with many Indian nations in North America and subsidized them with food, arms, beads, and alcohol. One reason the French enjoyed more success in recruiting Indians was because the English had hanged some Indian chiefs.

It is also clear that the French sought to convert the Indians to Christianity and had a condescending view of their culture. Numerous negative, facetious comments about their lifestyle appear throughout his work, including references to their supposed penchant for mutilating their victims and occasional cannibalism. In a letter to his brother dated June 30, 1757, he noted:

> We have nearly 8,000 men, 1,800 of whom are Indians, naked, black, red, howling, bellowing, dancing, singing the war song, getting drunk, yelling for "broth," that is to say blood, drawn from 500 leagues by the smell of human flesh and the chance to teach their young men how one carves up a human being destined for the pot. Behold our comrades who, night and day are our shadows. I shiver at the frightful spectacles which they are preparing for us.

His manuscript contains seven distinct references to cannibalism, but not one can be corroborated from his own eyewitness account. For example, the journal entry for July 6, 1757, states:

> Courier from Carillon. Extract from letter M. de Bourlamaque, dated the second. "Our detachment of 200 Indians, to which I added 25 Abnakis or Iroquois, left on June 30 with 3 colony officers and 6 cadets, in all 235 men. The Iroquois, with whom was Kametagon [Kanectagon?], lead the march. They took the road to the place where they usually hid their canoes, but upon entering the Chicot River, which is narrow and bordered with rocks, they were saluted by a volley of musketry which killed a cadet and mortally wounded several Indians. They could not get ashore on the enemy's side. It was necessary to pass the night with the river between them. At daybreak they crossed. The English were dislodged. They took up their trail and captured two Mahicans and a wounded Englishman. The Indians brought two of them to me and tore the other apart, and, as he was good, they ate him up."[22]

Historian James Merrell refers to such accounts as little more than mythological—the imaginary postulations of lurid tales that settlers *and* Indians had of one another in the context of the unknown and hostile woods of early North America.[23]

While Bougainville was present at the early part of the siege of Fort William Henry, he left to carry the message of the English capitulation to senior commanders in Montreal and was absent at the time of the supposed massacre of English soldiers and civilians. He did note that the Indians were intoxicated from rum they were given by the French and English soldiers.

Although the French forbid the Indians from plundering the retreating English, some of them did because they expected to receive booty as payment for their service. Hundreds of English soldiers were taken prisoners by the Indians against the terms established by Montcalm and Munro, but Bougainville noted that most of them were released one or two days later. According to his account, the "drunken Indians killed some dozen soldiers."

Even more revealing is his letter to Madame Herault, dated September 1757, where he attributes some of the blame for the Indians' behavior to "accomplices among people who call themselves Frenchmen; that greed for gain, the certainty of getting very cheaply from the Indians all the goods they had pillaged, are the primary causes of a horror for which England will not fail to reproach us for a long time to come."[24]

Like Bougainville, Cooper was fond of using inflammatory prose and terminology (e.g., frequent references to Indians as savages—not less than ninety-eight times in *The Prairie* where he dismissed the Sioux Nation as "[a] band of beings, who resembled demons rather than men," and "a treacherous and dangerous race" where "few white men trusting themselves in the remote and unprotected region where so false a tribe was known to dwell." Such commentary, along with frequent references to Native American women as squaws (a Mohawk term for vagina), reverberated through our culture and gained traction in a society at once fascinated and repulsed by the culture of Indigenous people.

The Fear of Miscegenation

Interspersed in Cooper's novels lie the seeds of an ignominious stereotype: that Indian men lust after White women. This theme is interwoven in *The Last of the Mohicans* as the villainous Magua pursues Cora Munro, and recurs in *The Prairie* with the Sioux Chief Mahotree and his Pawnee counterpart, Hard-Heart, lusting after Inez: "Nothing so fair, so ideal, so every way worthy to reward the courage and self-devotion of a warrior, had ever before been encountered on the prairies, and the young brave appeared to be deeply and intuitively sensible to the influence of so rare a model of the loveliness of the sex."[25] It also recurs in *The Pathfinder*, as the chief, Arrowhead, lusts after the heroine, Mabel.

Miscegenation has, for centuries, triggered the basest reactions among White men who have held dominion over virtually all females, White and ethnic alike. By stoking White fears through the infusion of the miscegenation theme, Cooper was playing on the White supremacist ideology that characteristically placed White females above (but not beyond) the reach of non–White people, adversaries as well as allies. "The Anglo American is apt to boast, and not without reason, that his nation may claim a descent more truly honorable than that of any other people whose history is to be credited."[26]

The theme that White women were more beautiful and desirable than Native American women resurfaces in his depiction of the Sioux Chief Mahotree's lust for Inez and loss of interest in his third, and most recent, young wife, Tachechana: "Her charms had not been without the most powerful attraction in the eyes of her husband, until they had so unexpectedly opened on the surpassing loveliness of a woman of the Palefaces. From that hapless moment the graces, the attachment, the fidelity of the young Indian, had lost their power to please."[27]

And the Sioux chief confides to Natty Bumppo: "Sing in the ears of the dark-eye [Inez]. Tell her that the lodge of Mahtoree is very large, and that it is not full. She shall find room in it; and none shall be greater than she. Tell the light-hair [Ellen, the other captive White female], that she too may stay in the lodge of a brave, and eat of his venison. Mahtoree is a great chief. His hand is never shut."[28]

The assumption that White women were the epitome of beauty and sought by men of color was one of the most insidious and pernicious themes infused in Cooper's work—one that fuels racist White supremacist ideology to this day. It was not only used against Native Americans, but also evoked rage and internecine war between White and Black people, and was the soil from which lynching grew into "Strange Fruit," the allusion to Black people hanging from trees in the South in Billie Holiday's notable song.

True, Natty Bumppo, the hero of his *Leatherstocking Tales*, is the vehicle through which Cooper infuses a reconciliation between men and nature and a romantic bond among men from different cultures. But his prose is suffused with stereotypes and inaccurate references to Native American cultural practices that, as in the case of scalping, were popularized by Europeans. Unfortunately, these stereotypes have endured.

"Strange fruit": Black lynching in America. Photograph by Lawrence Beitler, August 7, 1930, Marion, Indiana, lynching of Thomas Shipp and Abram Smith (Division of Rare and Manuscript Collections, Cornell University Library, Stephan Loewentheil Photograph Collection).

Throughout his works, Cooper conveys the impression that Native Americans are noble savages—uncivilized, though possessing admirable traits. For example, Chingachgook, Natty Bumppo's ally in the struggle against social and environmental injustice, was baptized John Mohegan by the Moravians. We learn that "[f]rom his long association with white-men, the habits of Mohegan, were a mixture of the civilized and savage states, though there was certainly a strong preponderance in favour of the latter."[29]

In his first installment of the *Leatherstocking Tales, The Pioneers*, Cooper lays the foundation for what became a prevalent stereotype about Native American rage and impetuosity: "You are but little acquainted with this peculiar people, Miss Grant," he said, "or you would know that revenge is a virtue with an Indian. They are taught, from infancy upward, to believe it a duty, never to allow an injury to pass unrevenged; and nothing but the stronger claims of hospitality, can guard one against their resentments, where they have power."[30]

Despite Cooper's inclination to humanize Chingachgook, his tale is filled with innuendos that lead readers to doubt the outcome: "[F]or I seen him next day [Chingachgook] with thirteen scalps on his pole. And I will say this for the 'Big Snake' [Chingachgook], that he always dealt fair, and never scalped any that he didn't kill with his own hands."[31]

Cooper endows Chingachgook and other Native Americans with the propensity to rage as a consequence of their "hot blood," something that is biologically predetermined. "'It is the hereditary violence of a native's passion, my child,' said [Minister] Grant, in a low tone to his affrighted daughter, who was clinging, in terror, to his arm. 'He is mixed with the blood of the Indians, you have heard; and neither the refinements of education, nor the advantages of our excellent liturgy, have been able entirely to eradicate the evil. But care and time will do much for him yet.'"[32] To which, Oliver Edwards, the "Young Hunter," replied: "Be not alarmed, Miss Grant, at either the wildness of my manner, or that of my dress. I have been carried away by passions, that I should struggle to repress. I must attribute it, with your father, to the blood in my veins, although I would not impeach my lineage willingly, for it is all that is left me to boast of."[33]

Racial stereotypes are liberally sprinkled throughout the novel about the supposed interracial lineage of "the Young Hunter," Oliver Edwards, and its detrimental effect on his temperament: "This, you see, cousin Bess, is the natural reluctance of a half-breed to leave the savage state. Their attachment to a wandering life is, I verily believe, unconquerable."[34]

Further, "But when did you ever know a half-breed, 'duke,' who could bear civilization? for that matter, they are worse than the savages themselves. Did you notice how knock-kneed he stood, Elizabeth, and what a wild look he had in his eyes?"[35]

Nor can the "stain" of race be removed, even with the civilizing intentions of Christianity. As Indian John (Mohegan, Chingachgook) lays dying, Cooper has him revert to his "savage" customs, forsaking Christianity and yearning for peace and eternal youth with his long-departed Delawares, much to the horror of Minister Grant who observes his death throes along with Natty Bumppo.[36]

The novel also contains degrading references about Black people. They appear in servile jobs and seem inept, superstitious, incompetent, and silly.[37] Cooper even alludes to racial antagonisms between Native Americans and Black people when the sheriff (Richard) comments about Oliver Edwards's supposed antipathy toward Black people: "He is part Indian, it is true, but the natives hold the negroes in great contempt. No, no, he would starve before he would break a crust with the negroes."[38]

Cooper was not above infusing a bit of White privilege into his hero, the Leatherstocking (a.k.a. Natty Bumppo): "The Leather-stocking, who had imbibed, unconsciously, many of the Indian qualities, though he always thought of himself, as of a civilized being, compared with even the Delawares...."[39] This Anglo-Saxon ethnocentric jibe is a recurrent phenomenon that, as we will see, wends its way through literature and the mass media of our culture, defaming and deprecating Indigenous people, providing the rationale for centuries of domination, exploitation, and neglect.

7

Native Americans and Atrocities: Scalping, Raping, and Pillaging

There is a soul and heart, under that red skin, rely on it, although they are a soul and a heart with gifts different from our own.
—Natty Bumppo in *The Pathfinder*[1]

Numerous allusions to the practice of scalping are made in the *Leatherstocking* series, especially the last work, *The Deerslayer*, published in 1841 as a prequel to the preceding volumes, leading the reader to believe that it was a common Indian custom.[2] As Natty Bumppo proclaims in *The Pathfinder*, "We are white men, and cannot mangle a dead enemy; but it is honor in the eyes of a red-skin to do so." Further, "Christians they are not, and do not pretend to be, and do not wish to be, and in calling them devils you have scarcely misnamed them."[3] Later, the heroine, Mabel, exclaims to Natty Bumppo (*The Pathfinder*), "And yet they scalp, and slay young and old women and children!" To which he replies: "They have their gifts, Mabel, and are not to be blamed for following them, Natur' is natur', though the different tribes have different ways of showing it. For my part, I am white, and endeavor to maintain white feelings."[4]

Cooper's later description of alleged Indian atrocities did not leave much to the reader's imagination: "The terrific war-whoop arose out of the covers of the island, and some twenty savages, horrible in their paint and other devices of Indian ingenuity, rushed forward, eager to secure the coveted scalps. Arrowhead was foremost, and it was his tomahawk that brained the insensible Jennie, and her reeking hair was hanging at his girdle, as a trophy, in less than two minutes after she had acquitted the blockhouse."[5]

In *The Deerslayer*, he conveys the impression that Indians reveled in hacking Europeans apart when one of the leading characters is found clinging to life "simply scalped to secure the usual trophy, and was left to die by inches, as has been done in a thousand similar instances by the ruthless warriors of this part of the American continent."[6]

European opinions about Native Americans' supposed penchant for scalping were popularized during the settlement/invasion of the New World. Descriptions of the practice among different tribes of Native Americans are ubiquitous in the recollections of former Indian captives.[7] While the practice existed among some Native groups prior to the arrival of Europeans on the North American continent, scalping and beheading had been done centuries before in Europe, even, according to Greek historian Herodotus, by Scythians in the fifth century BCE. Scalping in North

America was escalated by the introduction of bounties offered by the French and then adopted by the governors of Massachusetts and Pennsylvania. Cooper knew and acknowledged this in *The Deerslayer*, a novel developed around the greedy, bloodthirsty attempt of two White men to obtain bounties for Indian scalps.

Professor Juha Hiltunen, of the University of Oulu in Finland, concluded that the evidence clearly demonstrates that torture and scalping were practiced by Indigenous people in North, Central, and South America centuries before Columbus arrived. Matrilineal societies were more heavily involved in these practices—for example, the Iroquois. The function of torture and scalping varied according to the ethnic group and its culture. For example, scalping one's enemy could be viewed as a trophy of war, the bestowal of supernatural powers on the scalper, or the belief that the soul or essence of the victim would not be able to enter the Happy Hunting Ground (heaven) and would be unable to fight again in the afterlife.[8]

But similar practices were also utilized by Europeans, and they promoted it in the colonies. Professor Roxanne Dunbar-Ortiz linked the practice of beheading, scalping, and bounties to the English who used it against the Irish in the early 1600s.[9] During the French and Indian War (1754–63) bounties were placed on French and Englishmen's scalps, but it was the Indians who were blamed as well as victimized for this activity. They were even targeted by White settlers earlier when, for example, Samuel Shuttle, governor of Massachusetts in 1722, declared war on the Abenaki Indians. A bounty was placed on them and proof of kills by bounty hunters was affirmed by scalps. Bounties set by the English for adult males often brought in twice that of females and children. The bounty for such fiendish activities in the Massachusetts colony in 1755 was put at 40 pounds for Indian adult males and 20 pounds for females and children under the age of twelve.[10] Then Governor Spencer Phips was responsible for this atrocity.

The practice of paying a bounty for Native American scalps was also used by Mexican governors between 1835 and 1880, with the bloodied scalp serving as a receipt of the kill. The price was initially $100 for braves, but by 1847 it had risen to $200.[11] Historian George Franklin Feldman provides grisly details of two notorious American scalpers, James Kirker and John Joel Glanton, who sold their services to Mexican authorities in the mid–1800s in an attempt to eradicate the Apache Nation.[12]

By linking Indigenous and dark-skinned people to heinous depraved affronts to ostensibly civilized Europeans, the pattern of denigrating and disparaging non–European culture became institutionalized in the mythological landscape that formed the basis of Western conceptions of "the Other," automatically rendering non–Western cultures alien, degenerate, and uncivilized. As the late literary critic Leslie Fiedler put it:

> Most of Cooper's admirers have been the literate sons of fathers who, if not successful, have been at least white and, preferably, Anglo-Saxon: a race, according to Cooper, just a little whiter than any other. Not all of them by any means have confessed even to themselves that they shared the doctrine implicit in his fiction: that Western Culture, i.e., White European Christian Civilization was destined to conquer not only dark-skinned America, but all the non–White world; and that those born to other cultures have the choice of accommodating to it, or disavowing it to die in a genocidal war which they have no chance of winning. In their secret hearts, however, such readers respond to that message; thrilling to a vision of the vanishing Other embodied in the image of the noble Mohicans, whose ultimate nobility is proved by a willingness to immolate themselves, like Chingachgook, in order to make way for the higher civilization which the Christian God, in his inscrutable wisdom,

By His HONOUR

SPENCER PHIPS, Efq;

Lieutenant-Governour and Commander in Chief, in and over His Majefty's Province of the *Maffachufetts-Bay* in *New-England.*

A PROCLAMATION.

WHEREAS the Tribe of *Penobfcot* Indians have repeatedly in a perfidious Manner acted contrary to their folemn Submiffion unto His Majefty long fince made and frequently renewed;

I have therefore, at the Defire of the Houfe of Reprefentatives, with the Advice of His Majefty's Council, thought fit to iffue this Proclamation, and to declare the Penobfcot Tribe of Indians to be Enemies, Rebels and Traitors to His Majefty King GEORGE the Second: And I do hereby require His Majefty's Subjects of this Province to embrace all Opportunities of purfuing, captivating, killing and deftroying all and every of the aforefaid Indians.

AND WHEREAS the General Court of this Province have voted that a Bounty or Incouragement be granted and allowed to be paid out of the Publick Treafury, to the marching Forces that fhall have been employed for the Defence of the *Eaftern* and *Weftern* Frontiers, from the *Firft* to the *Twenty-fifth* of this Inftant *November*;

I have thought fit to publifh the fame; and I do hereby promife, That there fhall be paid out of the Province-Treafury to all and any of the faid Forces, over and above their Bounty upon Inlifment, their Wages and Subfiftence, the Premiums or Bounty following, viz.

For every Male *Penobfcot* Indian above the Age of Twelve Years, that fhall be taken within the Time aforefaid and brought to *Bofton, Fifty Pounds.*

For every Scalp of a Male *Penobfcot* Indian above the Age aforefaid, brought in as Evidence of their being killed as aforefaid, *Forty Pounds.*

For every Female *Penobfcot* Indian taken and brought in as aforefaid, and for every Male Indian Prifoner under the Age of Twelve Years, taken and brought in as aforefaid, *Twenty-five Pounds.*

For every Scalp of fuch Female Indian or Male Indian under the Age of Twelve Years, that fhall be killed and brought in as Evidence of their being killed as aforefaid, *Twenty Pounds.*

Given at the Council-Chamber in *Bofton,* this Third Day of *November* 1755, and in the Twenty-ninth Year of the Reign of our Sovereign Lord GEORGE the Second, by the Grace of GOD of *Great-Britain, France* and *Ireland,* KING, Defender of the Faith, *&c.*

By His Honour's Command,
J. Willard, Secr.·

S. Phips.

GOD Save the KING.

BOSTON: Printed by *John Draper,* Printer to His Honour the Lieutenant-Governour and Council. *1755.*

Early attempts to place bounties on Indian scalps, 1755 (Massachusetts Historical Society).

has destined to replace theirs. It did not bother Cooper that his God operated through the agency of dedicated chivalric (and, of course white) warriors, who made the New World safe for the Christian virtues of charity and forgiveness, not by practicing them—but by shooting straighter, fighting harder, killing more efficiently than their pagan enemies.[13]

Historian Slotkin concurred that the "myth of America," the propounding of a romanticized conception of the colonization and civilization of North America, was facilitated by writers such as Cooper: "Through repeated appearances and re-castings in the literary marketplace, a narrative which proved viable as a bestseller or a vehicle for religious or commercial persuasions would be imitated by more or less professional writers (where such existed) or those emulous or literary or ecclesiastical reputation. Thus the experience would be reduced to an imitable formula, a literary convention, a romantic version of the myth."[14]

In their analysis of the long-term success of Cooper's work, British academics Martin Barker and Roger Sabin similarly conclude that *The Last of the Mohicans* resonated with White affluent American readers who were captivated by the mythological representations within it about land, the frontier, the concept of the wilderness, and virtue embodied in the text.[15] The situations and characters developed in Cooper's works enunciated a White populist conception of manifest destiny: "[T]he [American] Dream implied that this was God's will: it was predestined that the natives would vanish before the onset of civilization, ordained as the natural progression of evolution."[16] They concluded, "So, if for whites the American Dream meant a new beginning, for Native Americans it meant the beginning of the end."[17]

But for all these failings, there was an air of transcendence, of spirituality in Cooper's writing that revealed at times an inner awareness about the sacredness of the environment and the uniqueness of human diversity:

> Look about you, at mankind, and tell me why you see a red warrior here, a black one there, and white armies in another place? All this, and a great deal more of the same kind, that I could point out, has been ordered for some "special" purpose; and it is not for us to fly in the face of facts, and deny their truth. No—no—each colour has its gifts, and its laws, and its traditions; and one is not to condemn another because he does not exactly comprehend it.[18]

Regrettably, this message did not have the same impact as Cooper's negative portrayal of Native Americans. In subsequent treatments of his work on television and in motion pictures, the bloodlust and depravity of Indians was exaggerated while White excesses were minimized. Slotkin believes colonists' fears and negative depictions of Native Americans devolved from their religious assumptions about the origin and status of Indians. "In Europe all men were under authority; in America all men dreamed they had the power to become authority."[19] The way to promulgate this value system was to depict Native Americans and the wilderness as disciples of the devil, hellish agents dwelling in an inhospitable threatening environment.

In a later analysis, Slotkin identified the themes developed by authors in contemporary literature and motion pictures as reconceptualizations of Cooper's works: incidents and heroes whose names change, but the underlying concepts surrounding what he characterized as the Frontier Myth, with men fighting the wilderness employing White character exceptionality in opposition to Black, Red, and Yellow inferiority, remain the same.[20]

The Puritans and later settlers took Indian lands because they wanted or needed them. They rationalized that God would look favorably on this if they were pious. Cultivating the land, farming, and domestication of livestock was their civilized response to the Indians' hunter/nomadic unregimented lifestyle. The land had to be wrested from the devil's agents—Indians. "The implication is that 'here,' the New World, has in fact been part of the devil's kingdom and, in its natural wild state, remains Satan's."[21] Such sentiments were embedded in our hypocritical treaties with

Native Americans—sentiments like those expressed in the Northwest Ordinance of 1787 that declared:

> [T]he utmost good faith shall always be observed towards the Indians; their lands and property shall never be taken from them without their consent; and in their property rights and liberty, they shall never be invaded or disturbed, unless in just and lawful wars authorized by Congress; but laws founded in justice and humanity, shall from time to time be made for preventing wrongs being done to them, and for preserving peace and friendship with them.[22]

The Curse of Cannibalism

The colonists' ignorance of Indian culture fueled irrational fears that evolved into their belief in the demonic powers of Native Americans. Paramount among their fears was their characterization of Indians as cannibals. Stories about cannibalistic rituals among Native Americans were common in the narratives of rescued captives and became part of the colonists' belief system.[23] Slotkin, tongue in cheek, refers to the purported Indian ritual of eating the heart of an adversary as a "wilderness Euchrist."[24] But he generally accepts the premise that "cannibalism played an important role in Indian ritual," despite acknowledging that "the Puritans not only massacred their captives but also lynched friendly Indians and went back on Church's promise of mercy to sell their captives into West Indian slavery."[25]

There can be little doubt that cannibalism and the ritualistic eating of animal and human body parts was occasionally practiced by some Native Americans. Whether from hunger, self-preservation, vengeance, or terroristic intentions, there is no evidence that cannibalism was a regular, institutionalized phenomenon among Native Americans despite mythologically scandalous claims to the contrary. It is ironic that Slotkin, despite his painstaking scholarship, doesn't question the veracity of the writers he cites and the possible exaggerations of their claims about Native American cannibalism, yet his work is devoted to exploring the mythological treatment of colonists and Indians on the American frontier.

No doubt much of the narrative concerning cannibalism among Native Americans is laced with innuendo, exaggerations, and distortions, but contemporary scientific analyses of Native American mummies and entrails of cadavers do substantiate the fact that cannibalism was practiced by some Native American groups.[26] While it is probable that prehistoric ancestors of contemporary Native Americans imbibed in human flesh to stave off famine and hunger, the ritualistic motivation for engaging in such behavior, namely, institutionalized human sacrifice, headhunting, and cannibalism, was not as widespread as secondhand reports indicated.[27] Still, the image of the Indian as an uncivilized savage predator persists, as well as stories about Plains Indians dining on the hearts of their adversaries and unlucky White settlers. The contemporary depiction of this stereotype can be seen in the 2016 movie version of *The Magnificent Seven* in a scene where a Native American played by Martin Sensmeier, himself an Alaskan Indigenous person, shares the heart of a deer he killed with a chagrined Denzel Washington.

8

Barbarians, Savages, Braves, Warriors, Statesmen, and Heroes

I am tired of fighting. Our chiefs are killed. Looking Glass is dead. Too-hullulsote is dead. The old men are all dead. It is the young men who say no and yes. He who led the young men is dead. It is cold and we have no blankets. The little children are freezing to death. My people, some of them, have run away to the hills and have no blankets, no food. No one knows where they are. Perhaps they are freezing to death. I want to have time to look for my children and see how many of them I can find. Maybe I shall find them among the dead. Hear me my chiefs, I am tired. My heart is sad and sick. From where the sun now stands I will fight no more forever.
    —Chief Joseph (Hinmaton-Yalaktit) of the Nez Perce (Idaho), 1877

The mythology and stereotypes about Native Americans evolved as the invading Europeans became familiar with them. First contacts were fraught with anxiety and trepidation as explorers expectantly observed the scantily clad Indigenous people, unsure about how they would be treated. Upon encountering Indigenous people for the first time, Columbus noted in his log entry of October 11, 1492:

As I saw they were very friendly to us, and perceived that they could be much more easily converted to our holy faith by gentle means than by force, I presented them with some red caps, and strings of beads to wear upon the neck, and many other trifles of small value, wherewith they were much delighted, and became wonderfully attached to us. Afterwards, they came swimming to the boats, bringing parrots, balls of cotton thread, javelins and many other things which were exchanged for articles we gave them, such as glass beads, and hawk's bells; which trade was carried on with the utmost good will.[1]

This encounter eventually led to the enslavement and death of tens of thousands of Taino Indians in the West Indies. Within four years, most of them were dead, and those who weren't suffered terribly under the yoke of Spanish conquistadors.[2]

First encounters with North American Indians by the English did not go smoothly, and the results were tragically the same for the Indigenous residents. The immigrants' lust for land and natural resources led them deeper into tribal territories inhabited by Indigenous people. Various wars spurred on by settlers' acquisitiveness and government policies eventuated between White Europeans and Native Americans. These were fueled by immigrants' and traders' indiscriminate use of alcohol to inebriate Indians for the purpose of stealing their land and natural resources, and the ever-westward push by settlers, with the tacit encouragement and assistance of government entities, to pursue land and resources, especially furs, gold, and silver.

Just as significant was the federal government's abrogation of treaties with Native Americans. It has been estimated that over five hundred of them were broken. Promises of lifetime annuities, food, clothing, and tools were disregarded or attenuated, leaving Indians, who acquiesced to federal terms, without living essentials, trying to survive on isolated reservations. This practice became a self-fulfilling prophesy, forcing Indians to bolt from reservations in search of food and more advantageous accommodations, followed by authorities subduing and compelling them to return to reservations, imposing penalties for *their* violation of treaties. A lengthy succession of such activity reads like a list of federal atrocities, with isolated skirmishes won by Native Americans, but in the end, White people winning the wars.[3]

One of the first, and perhaps most devastating, wars against White encroachment into Native land is known as King Philip's War, waged between the New England colonists and Indians principally from the Wampanoag and Narragansett tribes. The Native Americans were led by Metacomet, a son of renowned Chief Massasoit, who had maintained amiable relations with the settlers until their mistreatment of Indigenous people strained relationships. Forced to sign a humiliating treaty with the colonists in 1671 that required him to relinquish his arms, and after the hanging of three of his warriors in 1675, Metacomet (a.k.a. Prince Philip), now the *sachem* of his nation, led a coalition of Algonquian tribes against the colonists throughout New England from 1675 to 1676. It is estimated that 1,200 homes were burned and 8,000 cattle were lost. Half of all the New England towns were attacked, and twelve were destroyed. The death rate of male colonists who fought the Indians was twice that of the Civil War and seven times higher than World War II. With six hundred to eight hundred of the males of military age killed, the nascent colonial economy was ruined.

While the colonists suffered from the onslaught of the Indians, they fought back and inflicted heavy losses on their adversaries. Approximately three thousand Indians were killed, leading to the end of their prominence in southern New England and the rise of colonial settlements as new waves of European immigrants arrived. Their success was facilitated by the prevalence of communicable diseases such as smallpox, measles, and typhoid that took a huge toll on the Indigenous population. Metacomet once stated, "I am determined not to live until I have no country." His remark was prescient. When he was killed by an Indian on August 12, 1676, his corpse was drawn and quartered and hung in trees for the birds to pluck, and his decapitated head hung from a pike in Plymouth for twenty-five years. One of his hands was given as a trophy to the Indian who killed him, and he occasionally displayed it in local bars to obtain free drinks.[4]

A remarkable departure from these conflicts occurred in Pennsylvania in the late seventeenth century. When King Charles II of England gave a 45,000-square-mile land grant to William Penn, he wisely sought to cultivate relationships with the Lenni-Lenape (Delaware) Nation and entered into a series of agreements with one of their leaders, Tamanend (1625–98). King Charles haughtily proclaimed that the Indigenous "savages" had no more right to the land than the squirrels and rabbits, but Penn astutely sought to establish amicable relationships with the Indians, even offering to purchase their land.

The problem with land purchases from Native Americans was that the concept was alien to them. As historian Gus Wiencke noted, "To sell land was as incomprehensible to Tamanend as it would be to sell a bushel of tomorrow's sunshine."[5] Eight separate documents between the Indians and Penn were executed in the late 1600s, affirming amity and cooperation between them, even demarcating boundaries for the land that was purchased by the English, for a paltry array of weapons, blankets, and foodstuffs. But Tamanend was a visionary, and like Penn, who was a Quaker, he believed in the value of peaceful cooperation between the two parties. He reportedly said that the Lenapi and English colonists would "live in peace as long as the waters run in the rivers and creeks and as long as the stars and moon endure." In fact, peace reigned between the two parties for seventy years—long past his demise.

As a tribute to his wisdom and achievements, festivities and monuments were created across the country, and abridgements of his name (Tammany) were appended to public buildings and festivals. A hundred years after his passing a revival occurred, and even Cooper resurrected him for a part in his *Leatherstocking Tale, The Last of the Mohicans*. Unfortunately, relationships between Native Americans and European settlers were not always amicable.[6]

PHILLIP alias METACOMET of Pokanoket.
Engraved from the original as Published by Church.

Artist's rendering of Metacomet (King Philip), ca. 1600s (Library of Congress).

The history of Native American resistance to European intrusion into their territory is replete with warriors who fought to preserve the integrity of their land and people. Some of the most distinguished leaders are enumerated below, but many others could have been included. Note the prominence of western Native Americans as White settlers encroached into their territory in an attempt to gain hegemony over Indian land. The facility of Native Americans as statesmen and stateswomen became prominent as the White threat to Indians' survival became more realistic.

The invasion and subjugation of eastern North American Indigenous people was abetted by the British colonists' victory over the French and Indians (1754–63), primarily the Algonquians and Shawnees, but relationships and affiliations among the

French and British shifted as the Native Americans sought to ally themselves with the victorious side. For example, the Algonquians fought against the British during the French and Indian War, but with the British and against the American colonists in the Revolution. The Lenape mostly supported the French during the French and Indian (Seven Years' War), but some sided with the British, and the group supported the American revolutionaries against them.

Chief Pontiac (Obwandiyag) of the Odawa (Ottawa) tribe (circa 1714–69), born in the Great Lakes region, was an opponent of the British and unsuccessfully laid siege to Fort Detroit in 1763. Although he managed to unify disparate groups of Indians in their desire to rid the region of the British and resume cordial relationships with the French, which led to Pontiac's War from 1763 to 1766, his stature among Native Americans declined after his abortive assault on the British fort, and he was assassinated in 1769 by a Peoria warrior who sought revenge for Pontiac's assault on a relative.

At the Battle of Oriskany (upstate New York), the Oneida Nation fought alongside the Continental Army against the British on August 6, 1777. Two hundred Continental soldiers were killed along with thirty-six Seneca Indians, including six chiefs. The Oneida were joined by the Tuscarora Nation as allies of the colonists in their struggle for freedom from British domination, but the other four nations in the Iroquois Confederation (Mohawk, Cayuga, Onondaga, and Seneca) allied with the British, believing that colonial settlements would be prohibited if the British won the war.[7]

Though Cooper's work focused primarily on the eastern Native American nations, much extant folklore in American culture revolves around the Plains Indians and their leaders, some of whom have become mythological. No doubt the artistic works of Russell, Curtis, and Remington, as well as the ubiquitous Wild West shows of Buffalo Bill and the innumerable motion pictures and television shows that pervaded North American culture during the nineteenth and most of the twentieth centuries helped create cults of personality around some of the Native American leaders. For example, Tecumseh (1768–1813) was a visionary Shawnee leader (his name meant shooting star, or panther across the sky, or blazing comet). He developed an aversion to White people early in his life when his father was killed by settlers who seized Indian land in violation of a treaty. His brother, Tenskwatawa, became known as a prophet among the Shawnees and nearby tribes. Together they sought to create a confederation of Native Americans united in their mission to dislodge White settlers from their land.

Tenskwatawa predicted an apocalyptic destruction of the White community, and with the unification of Native American tribes in the confederation advocated by his brother, Tecumseh, Indians would regain their lost land and heritage. Under the leadership of Tecumseh and Tenskwatawa, the Shawnees established their headquarters in Prophetstown (now in Indiana) and challenged the authority of White incursion into their land. Tecumseh refused to sign the Treaty of Fort Wayne in 1809 that ceded nearly three million acres to the federal government (in latter-day Illinois and Indiana) in exchange for promised subsidies and liquor, retorting: "Sell a country! Why not sell the air, the great sea, as well as the earth? Did not the Great Spirit make them all for the use of his children? How can we have confidence in the white people?"[8]

His antipathy toward White people led him into many skirmishes with the U.S. military. Despite his brother's contention that the Indians under his command would be impervious to the bullets and knives of the White soldiers, Tecumseh's forces suffered a major defeat by General William Henry Harrison, later to become the ninth president of the United States, if only for a month, at the Battle of Tippecanoe in 1811. Tecumseh was not present at this battle, but the losses suffered by his warriors

TECUMSEH.

Shawnee Warrior Chief Tecumseh, 1768–1813 (Library of Congress).

shook the foundation of his fledgling Indian confederacy. The coup de grâce came two years later at the Battle of the Thames (near present-day Chatham, Ontario) when an American force led by General Harrison routed the forces of British Major General Henry Proctor and decimated his Indian allies, killing Tecumseh in the fight and thereby spelling the end of his vaunted Indian confederacy.[9]

The spirit of Tecumseh and his rejection of White land acquisition and culture would be reborn time and again as the invasion of White settlers spread ceaselessly across the land, pushing Indigenous people further and further west, away from their sacred land and resources that provided them with solace and nourishment. One of the most notable opponents of the incursions made into Indian lands by Spanish and American settlers was Cochise (1805–74) (Cheis, meaning "having the quality of hard wood"). Originally a peaceful inhabitant of the Southwest, Cochise was a Chiricahua Apache who led his warriors in relentless attacks on Mexican and American settlers and outposts during the 1860s. Much of his antipathy toward the U.S. government stemmed from a calumnious meeting between his band of Apaches and Lt. George Bascom in 1861. Cochise and his followers were accused of raiding a ranch owned by John Ward and kidnapping his adopted son, twelve-year-old Felix Tellez. Cochise and several members of his family were deceived and captured by Lt. Bascom, who was intent on gaining the release of the stolen child. He managed to escape by cutting through a tent. Shortly thereafter he captured some Americans in a raid with the hope of exchanging them for his family members. Bascom rejected the proposal. Cochise killed three of the captured Americans, and Bascom retaliated by hanging Cochise's brother and two of his nephews, but he later released Cochise's wife and son. Years later, the kidnapped boy became a scout for the U.S. Army and revealed that Cochise and his band were not the group that had taken him.

Cochise's enmity was further piqued when his father-in-law, Mangas Coloradas, a notable chief and warrior, and ally of Cochise, was duped into attending a bogus peace conference and executed. During the 1860s Cochise, known for his physical prowess and bravery, raided settlers in the Southwest and fought American troops in a ceaseless attempt to avenge the deaths of his tribal and family members and preserve his ancestral lands. As the Civil War waned, more federal resources were allocated to pacifying the Native Americans in his region, and technological innovations gave the American soldiers a clear advantage on the battlefield. Howitzers were employed to barrage the Indians in their mountain redoubts, and resistance became futile.

When President Ulysses Grant sent General Oliver Howard to establish a peace with Cochise in 1872, the warrior-statesman seized the opportunity to end hostilities. One of his allies in the struggle against the White interlopers was Geronimo, who may have served as a Spanish interpreter during the peace negotiations. Initially, Cochise and his followers were allowed to remain in their coveted Dragoon Mountains in Arizona, but he died two years later (probably of abdominal cancer), and the Chiricahuas were dispersed to eastern reservations where most of them died. Today, there are only a few remaining descendants of this tribe, and, according to historian Kathy Weiser, none live on their original land.[10]

As White settlers and prospectors fanned out over Native American territory in search of land and gold, they pushed the original inhabitants further and further to the fringes of their homelands. Some, like Cochise, initially resisted the incursion, while others agreed to removal to reservations with the promise of annual stipends, food, clothing, and tools to supplement the meager resources on their reservations. These promises were often broken, forcing starving Indians to leave their reservations in search of food.

The Plains Indian Wars were among the most cruel and protracted conflicts between the invading White population and the Native Americans who farmed, hunted, and inhabited the American Midwest and Southwest in the middle and latter part of the nineteenth century. The warrior that exemplified the spirit of Native American defiance and aggression, the man whose name struck fear into the hearts of settlers and soldiers, was Geronimo (1829–1909).

Born in the upper Gila River country of Arizona, Geronimo, like Cochise, his father-in-law, was a Chiricahua Apache. He developed a resolute hatred of Mexicans after his mother, wife, and three small children were murdered by Mexican soldiers in 1851 while he was away from his village. He and two hundred of his followers avenged their deaths, tracking down and killing the soldiers. The Treaty of Guadalupe Hildago of 1848 that ended the

Bust of Chiricahua Apache Warrior Chief Cochise, 1805–74, by Betty Butts, Fort Bowie National Historic Site (National Park Service).

Mexican-American War expanded U.S. territory to include half of New Mexico, most of Arizona, Nevada, and Utah, and parts of Colorado and Wyoming—the ancestral lands of the Apache. New acquisitive interlopers replaced their Mexican predecessors. One group of exploiters was removed, but to Geronimo and his followers, the avaricious intentions of the settlers was the same, and they were not welcome.

As the White tide surged over the Apache land, the Indians were forced to retreat in the face of formidable numbers and superior technology. Initially, they were allowed to remain on a restricted portion of their homeland, but they were gradually forced onto the San Carlos Reservation in the mid–1870s where Geronimo remained for four years. Disillusioned with and distraught over White misrepresentations and promises, he and a small band of his followers repeatedly fled the reservation to live in parts of Mexico and the U.S. Southwest, constantly pursued by Mexicans and, at one time, five thousand U.S. troops. Eluding the authorities for five years, while conducting raids against settlers and government troops, he eventually recognized the futility of trying to evade the government forces and surrendered to Lt. Charles B. Gatewood and Captain Henry Lawton, under the command of General Nelson Miles in Skeleton Canyon, Arizona (north of the Mexican border), on September 4, 1886.

In the last five months of his war, his meager band of sixteen warriors were reputed to have killed five hundred to six hundred Mexicans.

Geronimo and his band of about four hundred people were sent, along with the Apache scouts who helped track him down in the service of the U.S. military, by train to Fort Sam Houston in Texas, then to Fort Marion in St. Augustine, Florida, and, in 1894, to Fort Sill in Lawton, Oklahoma. Hundreds of their children were sent to the Carlisle Indian School in Pennsylvania where a third of them perished from tuberculosis.

Geronimo spent fourteen years at Fort Sill, but was periodically released to appear at social gatherings, including a brief stint with Buffalo Bill's Wild West Show where he was accompanied by federal agents because he was still viewed as a prisoner of war; the 1901 American Exposition in Buffalo, New York; and the 1904 World's Fair in St. Louis. He even rode horseback in President Teddy Roosevelt's inaugural parade in 1905.

Some White people at the time called Geronimo "the worst Indian who ever lived." He and his followers spent twenty-seven years as prisoners of war, and though he personally beseeched President Roosevelt for the return of his people to their land in Arizona in 1905, his request was denied. He died in 1909 after being thrown from a horse and reportedly said from his deathbed, "I should never have surrendered. I should have fought until I was the last man alive."[11]

While the Apache, Comanche, and other tribes were fighting White encroachment in the Southwest and West, the northern Plains Indians were engaged in fending off territorial assaults by avaricious settlers and prospectors. The Sioux, Cheyenne, and Arapaho bore the brunt of the struggle against White people in the northern Great Plains, and one of the most formidable adversaries the government troops had to contend with was Thathanka Lyotake or, as White people knew him, Sitting Bull.

Born in 1831 by the Yellow River near what is now Miles City, Montana, this Hunkpapa Lakota Sioux chief was originally named Jumping Badger, but his name was changed to Sitting Bull after he killed his first buffalo at the age of ten and distinguished himself in battle against the Crow at fourteen. He became a renowned warrior and, throughout his life, fiercely resisted White encroachment of traditional Indian territory, conducting raids against settlers and soldiers in retaliation for transgressions against his people, and to discourage future White settlements.

Chiricahua Apache Warrior Chief Geronimo, 1829–1909 (Library of Congress).

Sitting Bull was the first Lakota chief to unite the disparate Lakota Sioux tribes, and his reputation as a prophetic spiritual holy man (Wichasa Wakan) even attracted Cheyenne and Arapaho Native Americans to ally with him. One of his most impressive visions emanated from his spiritual experience during a Sun Dance ceremony in June 1876 when, in a trance-like state, he visualized a great military victory over U.S. government soldiers by the Sioux. During this experience he inflicted one hundred sacrificial cuts to his arms as a symbol of his commitment to his visionary spirituality. Within weeks, a coalition of Sioux, Cheyenne, and Arapaho Indians annihilated a two-hundred-man contingent of the 7th Calvary of U.S. soldiers led by Lt. Col. George Armstrong Custer at the Battle of the Little Big Horn.

The discovery of gold in the sacred Black Hills of the Lakota brought more prospectors and settlers to their territory, and the end of the Civil War enabled the federal government to devote more resources and attention to repressing the Sioux. Sitting Bull resolutely resisted White incursions into Lakota territory and rebelled at the violation of treaties that ostensibly traded Indian lands for the safety, security, and resources of reservations. He was especially incensed at the violation of the 1868 Fort Laramie Treaty that granted Sioux control of the Black Hills as part of a larger reservation. When Sitting Bull refused to accept modifications to the treaty, the U.S. government declared war on the Native tribes who occupied the desired territory.

Custer's defeat at the Battle of the Little Big Horn spurred the determination of the federal government to punish and subdue the Sioux. Thousands of soldiers were enlisted to defeat them. Realizing the futility of fighting the onslaught of soldiers with their superior technology and resources (in 1864 he witnessed the effects of artillery used by General Alfred Sully against Teton Sioux at Killdeer Mountain in North Dakota), Sitting Bull and five thousand of his followers sought refuge across the border in Canada where they remained for four years. But the harshness of the Canadian winter and the paucity of game led to their near starvation, and he decided to return to the United States where he and 185 other Sioux surrendered in 1881. He was held as a prisoner of war at Fort Randall in South Dakota Territory (near Pickstown, South Dakota) from 1881 to 1883, and then returned to the Standing Rock Reservation.

In 1885 he joined the famous Wild West Show of Buffalo Bill Cody, earning $50 a week and charging $2 for autographed photos of himself. He befriended the famed markswoman Annie Oakley in 1884 and was so enamored with her that he symbolically adopted her as a daughter, naming her "Little Sure Shot." But after four months he became disillusioned with the show and left, giving most of his money away to the homeless. The racist jeers he encountered and poverty he witnessed in the cities the show visited confirmed his intention to return to his people, noting, "I would rather die an Indian than live a white man."

In the late 1880s, a Native American Paiute mystic named Wovoka began the Ghost Dance movement that foretold the demise of the White race and the restoration of Indians to their relationship with nature. The movement enticed Indians to dance and chant for the rising of their deceased relatives, the return of the buffalo, and the restoration of their land. It may have arisen out of their desperation over the loss of their way of life at the hands of their White conquerors. Sitting Bull became an advocate of the Ghost Dance and came under suspicion by federal authorities who were fearful that the spread of such a messianic movement might inflame Native Americans and ignite the Plains once again. On December 15, 1890, he was killed during a skirmish with Indian police on the Standing Rock Reservation in North Dakota.[12]

Chief Red Cloud (Mahpiya-Luta) (1822–1909) was another Plains Indian leader who was known for his steadfast opposition to the incursion of White settlers and prospectors on Native American lands. Born near the Platte River (the present-day city of North Platte, Nebraska), his mother was an Oglala Lakota Sioux and his father a member of the Broule' Lakota Sioux. Following the predominant Native American tradition of matrilineal descent, when his parents died, he was raised by his maternal uncle, Old Chief Smoke.

He distinguished himself as a youth for his bravery in fighting against the Pawnee and Crow and rose to become a leader in the war against the U.S. Army in what became known as Red Cloud's War between 1866 and 1868 that included the massacre of the eighty-one-man Fetterman detachment outside of Fort Phil Kearny in 1866 near present-day Story, Wyoming.

Red Cloud's ire against White people was raised following their continuous incursions into Native American hunting lands. Although the White establishment had promised that Native lands would remain sacrosanct, settlers in search of land and prospectors were encouraged by the discovery of gold by the ill-fated Lt. Col. George Armstrong Custer's expedition in 1874. The Black Hills of South Dakota were flooded by White people and so was the Bozeman Trail that bisected Indian territory as it linked Montana and Wyoming on its way to Oregon. This trail became the primary conduit for White settlers as they traveled from east to west and traversed Indian Country.

The Fort Laramie Treaty of 1851 guaranteed that Indians would be able to continue hunting in their territory but allowed the military to construct roads and forts in return for recognition that Indians from eight affected tribes (Sioux, Cheyenne, Crow, Arapaho, Assiniboine, Mandan, Hidatsa, and Arikara) owned the land and would receive an

Hunkpapa Lakota Chief Sitting Bull, 1831–90 (Library of Congress).

annual annuity of $50,000 for fifty years. But the treaty was violated by White settlers and miners.

Red Cloud and his followers maintained pressure on the U.S. military through a series of attacks on forts and detachments of soldiers, and actually forced the U.S. Army into peace negotiations that left sections of the Bozeman Trail from the North Platte River to the gold fields in Montana in Native American control. A second Fort Laramie Treaty of 1868 was obtusely worded, and Red Cloud didn't fully comprehend its implications. It mandated that the Bozeman Trail would be closed and present-day South Dakota west of the Missouri River would become the Great Sioux Reservation, and it bestowed Indian hunting rights above the North Platte River (the northern half of Nebraska) and along the Republican River in northwestern Kansas. Indians were expected to become "civilized" and take up farming. White settlers would not be able to occupy present-day northeastern Wyoming and southeastern Montana without permission from the Native Americans who occupied these lands. In return for abandoning their war with the White settlers, the Indians were promised goods and annuities for thirty years, and the U.S. government agreed to build schools while holding Indian lands inviolate and the peace permanent.

President Grant and his generals were weary of conflict following the Civil War. It had become difficult to recruit and retain soldiers, and so the U.S. government was eager to end hostilities with Red Cloud and his people. Upon conclusion of the treaty, Red Cloud's followers burned Forts Kearny and Smith, but he did not realize that it was a Pyrrhic victory because the nebulous terms of the treaty allowed the U.S. government to take control of unceded lands at any time. When hostilities erupted again between the Native Americans and the encroaching White settlers and prospectors in 1876–77, Red Cloud chose not to join Crazy Horse and Sitting Bull in rebellion against the White people, remaining instead on what became known as the Pine Ridge Reservation where he died at age eighty-seven.

Throughout his life, Red Cloud supported Native American rights and land claims. He waged the most successful Native American war against the U.S. government, and twice traveled to Washington, D.C., to meet with presidents to present the Native American perspective about their plight and rights. He was an avid opponent of the 1887 Dawes Act that guaranteed land allotments to Indians who promised to become "civilized" and farm, and he is reported to have said: "They [U.S. government] made us many promises, more than I can remember. But they kept but one. They promised to take our land and they took it."[13]

The struggle between the White settlers and the U.S. government versus the Indigenous Native Americans occupying the Plains created many unforgettable characters. One of the most notable ones, remembered for his steadfast opposition to White encroachment, was the Lakota Sioux chief known as Crazy Horse (Tashunka Witko, 1842?– 77). The exact year of his birth is in question, but scholars agree that it was in the early 1840s. He was born near Bear Butte on the Belle Fourche River in South Dakota near present-day Rapid City.

His father was an Oglala Sioux, and his mother was a member of the Broule' Sioux. He shared the same name as his father, although he had the appellation of Curley as a child because of his wavy hair and fair skin that distinguished him from his peers. There are no known pictures of Crazy Horse—he refused to be photographed (in contrast to Red Cloud who was reputed to be the most photographed

Oglala leader Red Cloud, 1822–1909 (Library of Congress).

Native American in history), and he also refused to sign treaties and other official documents. It is said that he thought taking his picture would shorten his life by taking his soul, reportedly asking, "Would you imprison my shadow too?"

Crazy Horse became known as a fearless Native American leader who risked his life in many battles against the U.S. Army. Believing he was invincible to enemy bullets, he acted as a decoy in the famous ambush that led to the Fetterman massacre of 1866 near Fort Phil Kearny (known among the Native Americans as the Battle of the Hundred in the Hands). In 1876 he conducted a successful campaign against General George Crook at Rosebud Creek on June 17, and on June 25 he led a combined force of Native Americans from the Sioux, Cheyenne, and Arapaho nations against Lt. Col. George Armstrong Custer in the Battle of the Little Big Horn.

Although his enmity against White people was no doubt related to their intrusion into and desecration of Native American land, and the abrogation of treaties they made with his people, some of his ire could be traced to a childhood incident. When he was an adolescent, he witnessed a small contingent of U.S. soldiers, under command of Lt. John Grattan, enter a Sioux village in search of an Indian accused of killing a settler's cow. When Chief Conquering Bear did not comply with their demands, he was killed in an ensuing scuffle. In retaliation, the Sioux warriors killed Grattan and his thirty-man detachment.

Rumors circulating after the massacre by Custer and his men accused Crazy Horse of personally killing him. There is no solid evidence of this, but Crazy Horse continued his fight against White incursion and the U.S. Army. When Sitting Bull fled north into Canada with some of his followers, Crazy Horse stayed behind and fought on for another year, but the relentless pursuit by the army and dwindling food and resources led him and a small band of his followers to surrender on May 6, 1877. They spent that summer near Fort Robinson close to the Pine Ridge region, northwest of Nebraska.

Crazy Horse was killed by a U.S. soldier who thrust a bayonet into his back while he was resisting arrest at Fort Robinson on September 5, 1877.[14] Though he reputedly never lost a battle with U.S. government forces, his petulance earned him respect and enmity among American soldiers who resented the slaughter of Custer and his men at the Battle of the Little Big Horn. While he was often reviled during his lifetime, his likeness is being preserved for posterity in the Crazy Horse Memorial, a gigantic sculpture carved into the Black Hills of South Dakota, just seventeen miles from the iconic busts of Washington, Jefferson, Lincoln, and Theodore Roosevelt carved into Mt. Rushmore.

Begun by sculptor Korczak Ziolkowski in 1947, the work is still unfinished, but the magnitude of the project is breathtaking. When completed, it will stand 567 feet tall and be 641 feet long, and it will be the largest monument of its kind in the world. The Ziolkowski family are diligently working to finish the project, which carries a $7 million annual budget that supports the excavation along with a Native American museum. While they are exuberant about the impending completion of the project, not everyone is so sanguine. "They were for us [the Black Hills] to enjoy and they were there for us to pray. But it wasn't meant to be carved into images, which is very wrong for all of us. The more I think about it, the more it's a desecration of our Indian culture, not just Crazy Horse, but all of us," said Elaine Quiver, a descendant of the warrior.[15]

Perhaps a more fitting memorial to the chief was the issuance of a U.S. Postal Service 13-cent stamp in 1982 in the Great Americans series. Although we have no definitive likeness of the great warrior, his response to a cavalryman's sarcastic quip, "Where are your lands now?," "My lands are where my dead are buried," reverberate through time.[16]

Chief Joseph (Hin-mah-too-yah-lal-kekt) (Thunder Rolling Down a Mountain) was born into the Nez Perce Nation in the Wallowa Valley in Oregon Territory in 1840. He died in 1904 after an illustrious life as a leader of his people in their journey to escape U.S. government troops that included a flight to seek refuge in Canada. By all accounts, he was an eloquent orator, although he did not speak English.

©Crazy Horse Memorial Fnd.
Korczak, sc.
1/34th scale model

Crazy Horse Memorial Foundation

Crazy Horse Monument in the Black Hills of South Dakota (Crazy Horse Memorial Foundation).

Nevertheless, he was able to communicate his disdain for warfare. Despite a solemn promise to his dying father, Elder Joseph (he had been baptized with this name when he converted to Christianity in 1838), that he would never give up the beautiful land of the Wallowa Valley ("This country holds your father's body. Never sell the bones of your father and your mother," to which he replied, "I clasped my father's hand and promised to do as he asked. A man that would not defend his father's grave is worse than a wild beast"), he reluctantly acquiesced to U.S. government demands to remove his followers to a small reservation in Idaho.

The story of Chief Joseph and his Nez Perce followers is complicated by U.S. government deception and perfidy. His father had negotiated a treaty with the U.S. government in 1855 (the Treaty of Walla Walla) that established a reservation of 7,700,000 acres, but when gold was discovered on the property the government renegotiated the treaty, cutting the size of the territory to 760,000 acres, excluding the entire Wallowa Valley. Despite the government's offer of financial compensation and establishing schools and a hospital for the Indians, Elder Joseph and other chiefs refused to sign the amended treaty.

While some of the Nez Perce moved to the new reservation, Chief Joseph and his followers tried valiantly to remain in the Wallowa Valley after the passing of their patriarch, but they were given an ultimatum to leave within thirty days and relocate to a smaller reservation in Lapwai, Idaho, far from the Wallowa Valley in Oregon. Recognizing the futility in fighting the government soldiers with their superior numbers and armaments,[17] Chief Joseph led his band of 700 people, including 200 warriors, on a harrowing 1,170-mile journey across treacherous mountains and cliffs of the Lolo Trail and into the Bitterroot Valley in Montana.

They eluded the U.S. Army for three months as they traveled across Oregon, Washington, Idaho, Wyoming, and Montana. Originally, they hoped to receive aid from the Crow Nation, but when that didn't materialize, they sought to join Sitting Bull's Lakota contingent in Canada. Pursued relentlessly by General Oliver Otis Howard, Chief Joseph's band intermittently engaged in skirmishes with the U.S. Army. At the Battle of the Big Hole in a high mountain meadow in Montana, Colonel John Gibbon attacked the Nez Perce and killed eighty people, including fifty women and children, while losing twenty-nine of his soldiers.

Throughout their desperate dash for the Canadian border, Chief Joseph and his followers outmaneuvered the military by doing the unpredictable—crossing supposedly impassable territory. Ultimately, they succumbed to exhaustion, starvation, and disease. Just a two days' ride from the Canadian border, the weary chief surrendered to General Nelson A. Miles in the Bear Paw Mountains of Montana on October 5, 1877. Along the way, Chief Joseph lost five of his children; his brother, Olikut; and two prominent Indians, Chief Looking Glass, and a holy man, Toohoolhoolzote, respected by Joseph for his vision that foretold of the eventual triumph of the Indians over the White people.

While the Indians evaded the pursuing troops, people across the nation read of their plight. Chief Joseph was referred to as the Red Napoleon and the ill-fated escape as one of the greatest military retreats in history. He is known for his eloquent statement at the time of his surrender: "I am tired. My heart is sick and sad. From where the sun now stands, I will fight no more forever."

Chief Joseph and his surviving followers, numbering under four hundred people with just eighty-seven warriors, were, under orders from General William T. Sherman, transported in unheated rail cars to Fort Leavenworth, Kansas, and held as prisoners of war for eight months. Ravaged by disease and neglect, the survivors were taken by rail that summer to Oklahoma (Indian Territory) where they lived for seven years, with disease claiming more victims.

The chief never relinquished his claim on the Wallowa Valley or gave up his dream of returning there with his people. In 1879 he met President Rutherford B. Hayes in Washington, D.C., to plead for their return to Oregon, but to no avail. He made numerous public appearances, including riding with Buffalo Bill Cody in a New York City parade honoring former President Ulysses S. Grant, and in 1903 met with President Theodore Roosevelt in a vain effort to plead for the return of his people to Wallowa. Although Joseph and some of his followers were allowed to move west in 1885, they never inhabited their beloved Wallowa Valley again. He died on the Colville Indian Reservation in the state of Washington on September 1, 1904.[18]

Quanah Parker (1850?–1911) was the son of a White woman, Cynthia Ann Parker, who was captured in 1836 when she was nine years old by Comanches in a raid on her family's residence near present-day Groesbeck, Texas. She married Quanah's father, Peta Nocona, a respected Comanche chief, and bore him another son, Pecos, and a daughter, Topsana.

Quanah was a leader of the Comanche resistance to White incursion into their territory, and although he was never elected a chief of his tribe, his leadership abilities and reasoning about Native American assimilation led the U.S. government to select him as a chief for all Comanches around 1875, a position he held for over twenty-five years.

The threat posed by widespread killing of buffalo, the Plains Indians' staple for food and other necessities, alarmed Parker and led to a famous assault on Adobe Walls where twenty-eight seasoned buffalo hunters held off a combined force of seven hundred Native Americans. The superior weaponry of the buffalo hunters contributed to their success, but the outcome of previous skirmishes with U.S. soldiers under command of Colonel Ranald Mackenzie was different, and led to the Red River War (1874–75) pitting Comanches, Southern Cheyenne, Kiowas, and Arapahos against poorly trained soldiers.

The Red River War between Mackenzie's soldiers and Parker's Comanches and allies culminated in the Battle of Palo Duro Canyon on September 28, 1874, when Mackenzie's forces destroyed the Comanche village there and his

Chief Joseph of the Nez Perce, 1840–1904 (Library of Congress).

troops killed 1,500 of their horses. (The earlier practice of seizing Indian horses was abandoned after Indians recovered them.)

Parker helped negotiate the surrender of the Comanches to Mackenzie in 1875, which led to the settlement of the Kiowa, Comanche, and Apache Indians on a reservation in Indian Territory, now present-day southwestern Oklahoma. When Parker surrendered, he was taken to Fort Sill, Oklahoma, where he served as the leader of the Native Americans there.

Although he initially opposed leasing Indian land to White settlers, Parker changed his mind and became a wealthy entrepreneur, perhaps the wealthiest Native American in the country. His money came from investments in land, cattle ranching, and grazing contracts with other ranchers. He even went hunting with President Teddy Roosevelt and unsuccessfully tried to convince him to allow the Comanches to retain four hundred thousand acres that were eventually sold to homesteaders. He lived in an ostentatious two-story home called the Star House, which he built in Cache, Oklahoma.

In addition to being known for his good looks, accommodation to Western civilization, and business acumen, Parker helped establish the Native American Church Movement that rejected traditional Protestantism in favor of a spiritual faith that embraced elements of Christianity coupled with the use of the mind-altering drug peyote, which was used during the communion ceremony. One of his sons (he had eight wives and twenty-five children), White Parker, became a Methodist minister. He once noted, "The White Man goes into his church house and talks about Jesus, but the Indian goes into his tipi and talks to Jesus." Although he opposed the spread of the Ghost Dance, both traditions had a messianic, somewhat apocalyptic thread—no doubt related to the declining status of Native Americans and the theft of their resources by White people.[19]

Another notable Native American who resisted the efforts of the federal government to forcibly relocate his people was Manuelito (1818–93), a leader of the Diné or Navajo people of the Southwest. Primarily living in eastern Arizona and western New Mexico, this Indigenous group, for the most part peaceful, were forcibly marched in what became known as the "Long Walk," a three-hundred-mile trek from their homeland in the midst of four sacred mountains to an arid encampment near Fort Sumner, known as the Bosque Redondo.

The plan was devised by Major General James H. Carleton and executed by none other than the storied Indian hunter Colonel Kit Carson in 1864. Little, if any, assistance was given to the eight thousand to nine thousand Navajos on the arduous trip, and two hundred people perished along the way. Living on the forty-square-mile inhospitable reservation was a hardship, and their numbers steadily declined. In 1868 Manuelito and his activist wife, Juanita, traveled to Washington to plead for the return of the Navajos to their ancestral lands among the four mountains, and, for one of the few times, a Native American group was allowed to return. "The Long Walk Home" began on June 18, 1868. They were granted 3.8 million acres. Today the Navajo Reservation encompasses nearly twenty-five thousand square miles across Arizona, New Mexico, and Utah, the largest Indian reservation in the United States. But an awful toll was taken on the young Navajos. As the number of childbearing couples declined through the enforced movement of the group, genetic abnormalities arose, possibly due to overexposure to uranium in the area, contributing to the misery of

Comanche Nation leader Quanah Parker, 1845–1911 (Library of Congress).

the people. Yet they survived and endured, and today the Navajo Nation is the largest Native American group.[20]

Sequoyah (1775–1843), also known as George Gist or Guest, became legendary for his invention of the Cherokee syllabary—a method for conveying the spoken Cherokee language through eighty-five symbols representing unique Cherokee sounds. Born in the Cherokee town of Tuskegee (now in east Tennessee) to a White

Photograph of Diné (Navajo) leader Manuelito, 1818–93 (Library of Congress).

father and Cherokee mother, he became a skilled silversmith and blacksmith. Although he was illiterate and could not speak or write English, he was fascinated by the way White people communicated through written expression and decided to create a mechanism through which Cherokees could send and preserve their thoughts and ideas by adapting letters and symbols from other languages.

He began this project in 1809, but it was interrupted by a stint in the U.S. Army where he fought against the British in the War of 1812. He also participated in the victorious Battle of Horseshoe Bend against the Creek Red Sticks with General Andrew Jackson on March 27, 1814. By 1821 Sequoyah had developed his syllabary, and, despite some opposition from tribal members who thought writing was a form of witchcraft, he persevered, teaching his daughter to use the technique that employed vowels and consonants and convincing his people to adopt it. The syllabary was embraced by the Cherokee Nation and found expression in the publication of the first Native American newspaper, the *Cherokee Phoenix*, which began publishing in English and Cherokee on February 21, 1828. He desired to unite the eastern and western factions of the Cherokee Nation through his syllabary and written language.

Thanks to the efforts of Sequoyah, the Cherokees had the first printing press and first written characters of any Indigenous group in North America. He was the first person in history to create a written language while being illiterate. Sequoyah hoped that the widespread literacy among the Cherokees would signify the civilized nature of his people to the White establishment. He traveled to Washington to negotiate for land and aid for displaced Cherokees. Unfortunately, some Cherokee leaders agreed to voluntary resettlement and removal,[21] signing a treaty with the federal government that ceded all their land east of the Mississippi River in exchange for land in Oklahoma. This disputed settlement eventuated in the forcible removal of Cherokees in the infamous Trail of Tears.

But Sequoyah was immortalized by the designation of giant redwood trees in his name and the following statement by the Cherokee Nation: "He accomplished a

SE-QUO-YAH
Inventor of the Cherokee Alphabet

Courtesy Bureau of American Ethnology, Smithsonian Institution

"By cloud-capped summits in the boundless West,
  Or mighty river rolling to the sea,
 Where'er thy footsteps led thee on thy quest
  Unknown, rest thee, illustrious Cherokee."

Cherokee leader Sequoyah, ca. 1775–1845, and his syllabary (Library of Congress).

feat, no other person in history has done single-handedly ... he brought our people literacy and a gift of communicating through distance and ages. This one person brought to his people this great gift without hired educators, no books and no cost." He died in New Mexico searching for other members of the scattered Cherokee Nation.[22]

Native American resistance to the incursion of White people in the Southeast was linked to the ghastly treatment of Indians on the infamous Trail of Tears, but Indians under the leadership of a young Seminole warrior, born to a Creek mother and Scottish father, rallied to preserve their autonomy and Native lands even before this atrocity. Born in Alabama in 1804 with a given name of Billy Powell, Osceola earned the respect and admiration of his ardent followers, including many runaway African American slaves who joined forces with him against the White intruders. Some Native Americans who refused to move west to Indian Country (Oklahoma) in the Trail of Tears following President Jackson's signing of the Indian Removal Act of 1830 sought refuge in the untamed land of Florida, then principally under control of the Spanish.

The Seminole Nation (the word *Seminole* is Muskogee meaning wild) was composed of a diverse group of tribes and individuals including, among others, Creek, Hitchiti, Muskogee, Cherokee, and Miccosukee as well as ex–African American slaves, including one of Osceola's wives, who bore him four children. He fought against the enslavement of his people and refused to surrender his wife for repatriation to her owners at one peace negotiation, leading to further conflict between his followers and federal forces.

Osceola gained prominence in the first Seminole War (1817–18), opposing then General Andrew Jackson's bid to resettle eastern Indians to Indian Country. While Jackson and other federal commanders managed to secure Florida from the Spanish by successfully attacking their settlements and forts, leading to the ceding of the Florida territory to the United States in the Adams-Onis Treaty of 1819, Osceola and his followers resisted White incursions and led the attack on a detachment of federal soldiers commanded by Major Francis Dade in 1835 in what is now Bushnell, Florida, which left Dade and 107 other soldiers killed—only two surviving.

Osceola was a trusted adviser to Micanopy, the principal chief of the Seminole Nation. Fiercely independent, Osceola rejected federal attempts to secure peace through treaties that would require Indians to relinquish their land and move west. Ironically, Osceola met an untimely end after being tricked into peace negotiations on October 31, 1837, by General Joseph Hernandez, under orders from General Thomas Jessup, at Fort Peyton (near St. Augustine). Osceola was seized, despite meeting under a white flag of truce, perhaps attesting to the frustration federal authorities were experiencing because of his intransigence. He became ill from a throat infection and malaria while imprisoned at Fort Moultrie (South Carolina) and died within a few months. A number of well-known personalities visited him while he was there, including George Catlin, who painted the portrait of him below. Upon his death, Dr. Frederick Weedon removed his head, perpetuating the stereotype about Native Americans as a scientific curiosity and unique species of subhumans.[23]

The westward expansion of settlers and prospectors continued unabated, reaching the shores of the Pacific Ocean in the mid–1800s. Spurred on by the lure of gold, silver, and fertile land, White settlers poured into Native American territory, pushing

Seminole leader Osceola, 1804–38, by George Catlin (Library of Congress).

them into enclaves of resistance and inducing the federal government to herd Indians like cattle onto reservations. The Indians of California suffered the most of any group at the hands of the Spanish and, later, other European intruders. From the infamous mission system established under the tutelage of Father Junipero Serra in the eighteenth century, to the invasion of Indian land sparked by the discovery of gold in Sutter's mill a century later, Indians were treated as interlopers on their own land—obstacles to White conceptions of progress.

Some of the tribes, like the Modocs, were rounded up and sent to live in inhospitable surroundings, with hostile neighbors from another Klamath tribe. Longing for their treasured homeland bordered by the Tule, Lower Klamath, and Clear lakes with abundant fish, waterfowl, and other game, some of them followed the rebellious young warrior Kintpuash, or as White people referred to him, Captain Jack.

Born near Tule Lake in 1837 near what is now the California and Oregon border, Kintpuash, the chief of the Modoc tribe in this area, led some of his people away from the Klamath Reservation to their prior land. When the U.S. Army sought their return to the reservation, they resisted by fleeing into nearby lava beds where they hid. When the Modocs refused federal offers of safe passage back to their reservation, three hundred troops launched an unsuccessful assault on their redoubt.

After months of stalemate, peace negotiations were begun between the warring parties. Kintpuash was advised by tribal members that the federal troops would abandon their mission if their leader was killed. On April 11, 1863, Kintpuash and some of his followers killed General Edward Canby, the Rev. Eleazar Thomas, and several other peace negotiators, earning him the distinction of being the only Native American ever charged with war crimes.

A massive assault with over one thousand soldiers conducted by General Jefferson Davis (not the same person who later headed the Confederacy) took three months, but ultimately Kintpuash was captured and hanged with three other accomplices on October 3, 1873, at Fort Klamath. As with Chief Osceola, their heads were severed and sent by train to the Army Medical Museum in Washington, D.C., for study, continuing a bizarre tradition of using the heads, scalps, and skins of Native Americans as bounty, souvenirs, and objects of curiosity. Kintpuash's skull was returned to his family by the Smithsonian Institution in 1984, but his followers did not fare much better. Approximately 150 of them were sent by rail over 2,000 miles to the Quapaw Reservation in

Photograph of Kintpuash (Captain Jack), 1837–73 (National Archives).

Oklahoma where they had difficulty adapting to the climate and terrain. By the turn of the twentieth century, only fifty survived.[24]

Technological Innovation and the Indian Wars

The Plains Indian Wars between the 1850s and 1870s that the U.S. government waged for control of the West were facilitated with the help of intrepid Native American allies who lent their knowledge of traditional adversaries and the local geography to the soldiers. Following the Civil War, the military was frequently hamstrung by inept leadership, plagued by desertions, and initially replete with men of questionable character. The federal effort was, in the early years of this campaign, outmatched and overwhelmed by their Indian adversaries who had superior numbers and warriors with the fortitude and commitment to a cause—the preservation of their land and people.[25]

No doubt the federal troops would have been severely disadvantaged without the assistance of Crow and Pawnee scouts. Even the pursuit of Cochise and Sitting Bull was assisted by Apaches who signed on with the cavalry only to be ignominiously stripped of their weapons and shipped off to prison along with the survivors of the ill-fated campaigns. Racism against Native Americans permeated the ranks of commanders and soldiers,[26] and, despite their sacrifices, scouts could not overcome the prejudice White people evinced toward them and the vengeance they harbored for the Fetterman debacle and Custer's defeat.

In the end, the Indians were overwhelmed by superior numbers of troops sent by President Grant and led by determined officers like Generals Sherman and Sheridan. Perhaps more decisive in the struggle for the West was the utilization of advanced technology by the federal troops. The use of the 1873 model Winchester lever-action repeating rifle, developed by Oliver Winchester in 1866, enabled soldiers to replace their cumbersome single-shot muzzle-loading arms with fast-action rapid-fire weapons that discharged many rounds before reloading. About fifty thousand of these weapons were purchased by the Turks and successfully used in their war with the Russians in 1877. The U.S. Cavalry had similar success using it against the Indians, earning it the sobriquet, "The gun that won the West."[27]

Along with these rifles came the feared Gatling gun, invented by Richard Gatling in 1861, and used by Union troops in the Civil War. Hand cranked and multibarrel, it was cooled and synchronized and capable of firing two hundred rounds per minute. It was a precursor to the vaunted Hotchkiss gun, invented by Benjamin Hotchkiss in 1872. This relatively light weapon could easily be packed on two mules and transported into battle and replaced the heavier but equally devastating mountain Howitzers that had previously been used. The rapid-fire version of these guns took the form of revolving canons that could fire sixty-eight rounds per minute and were accurate to two thousand yards. They were used against the Nez Perce in 1877, and at the Battle of Wounded Knee in 1890 when hundreds of Sioux Indians, many of them women and children, were slaughtered by remnants of Custer's 7th Cavalry, and at the Battle of San Juan Hill in Cuba in 1898, during the Spanish-American War.

Though not always outmaneuvered, facing the rising tide of settlers and prospectors, and a reinvigorated U.S. Army following the end of the Civil War, Native Americans were clearly outnumbered and outgunned. Many of their leaders realized that and negotiated settlements that initially promised them some of the land and resources they had claim to, but these treaties were abrogated as White people descended on their territory like a swarm of hungry locusts. Some Native American leaders were transported east to Washington, D.C., and other cities to meet with federal officials, even presidents. Lincoln, Grant, and later, Theodore Roosevelt received delegations of Native Americans, ostensibly to lay the foundation for subsequent peace negotiations, but also to persuade Indigenous leaders that resistance to the material and technological onslaught of the White man was futile. Indians' plaintive requests for the White establishment to respect their territorial integrity fell on deaf ears.

When Cheyenne Chief Lean Bear and a contingent of other peace-minded Cheyenne chiefs met President Abraham Lincoln on March 27, 1863, he was given a bronzed-copper peace medal and papers signed by Lincoln attesting to their friendship. He was wearing the medal and clutching the peace papers a year later when he rode out to meet a unit of the U.S. Army, the 1st Colorado under command of Lt. George Eayre, who killed him on the spot. Eayre had been operating under orders from Col. John Chivington to "kill Cheyennes whenever and wherever found."[28]

Pursuing the Military Mission: Massacres

While it is true that Native Americans committed offenses against White people, so-called massacres were also perpetrated against them. Aside from the storied massacre of Sioux in 1890 at the infamous Wounded Knee location on what is today the Pine Ridge Reservation, a series of assaults against different Indian tribes occurred throughout the mid- to latter part of the nineteenth century. A common characteristic that precipitated these conflicts was the increasing presence of White settlers and gold miners who encroached on Indian hunting grounds, seized their land, and impoverished the Indians by despoiling their natural resources and killing their game.

Perhaps the deadliest of these confrontations was the Bear River Massacre that occurred on January 29, 1863, near what is now Preston, Idaho, in the Cache Valley. Although few people know of this conflict, probably because the American Civil War was raging at the time, as many as five hundred Northwestern Shoshone were killed by a force of the 3rd California Volunteer Infantry Regiment commanded by Col. Patrick Edward Connor who was dispatched to "make clean work of the savages." An additional 160 women and children were captured, while the U.S. soldiers sustained 21 fatalities and 42 wounded. Chief Sagwitch survived and, along with other members of his tribe, became allies and converts to the LDS Church (Mormons).[29]

One of the most infamous conflicts between U.S. forces and Native Americans is known as the Sand Creek Massacre. It occurred on November 29, 1864, when a peaceful band of Cheyenne and Arapaho Indians were ruthlessly attacked by nearly

700 Colorado volunteers commanded by Col. John Chivington as they encamped at the site that is approximately 170 miles southeast of Denver. The government attack was, like many others, provoked by incessant Indian raids on White settlers who encroached on their land. Although they were guaranteed considerable property in the First Treaty of Fort Laramie in 1851, the Treaty of Fort Wise ten years later reduced their holding to one-thirteenth of its original size.

Even though Chivington was a Methodist preacher, this did not deter him and his men from the wonton killing and mutilation of the Indians they attacked. Two dozen soldiers were killed and fifty-two were wounded. Estimates of Native American casualties range from sixty to two hundred fatalities, with more than half of them women and children. When factual circumstances about the slaughter of the Indians came to light,[30] Chivington resigned, but he remained a hero to the White settlers in the Denver area. Black Kettle, the leader of the ravished Indian band, took survivors to a new reservation in Indian Territory (Oklahoma).[31]

The Washita River Massacre, near present-day Cheyenne, Oklahoma, was committed by the 7th U.S. Cavalry commanded by Lt. Colonel George Armstrong Custer on November 27, 1868. It involved a band of peaceful Cheyenne led by Chief Black Kettle (who had escaped the attack on his people in the earlier Sand Creek conflict), except he and his wife, Medicine Woman, perished in this onslaught along with 102 other Southern Cheyenne warriors from Custer's account, compared to 21 soldiers killed and 14 wounded. Other estimates put the number of Indian dead at fifty along with fifty wounded. In addition, Custer seized fifty-three women and children as hostages to protect his escape. Custer had recently been reinstated by General Philip Sheridan after being disciplined for desertion and mistreating his soldiers. He resolved to make an example of the Cheyenne who had a habit of making peace in the winter and waging war in summer. "I want no peace until the Indians suffer more.... I fear the agent of the Indian Department will be ready to make presents too soon.... No peace must be made without my direction."[32] The Indians were reportedly flying American and white flags from their encampment before they were attacked.

On January 23, 1870, a band of peaceful Blackfeet Indians were attacked by a contingent of federal troops under the command of Col. Eugene Baker as they encamped by the Marias River in northern Montana. When warned by his scout Joe Kipp that the group was not the Indians they were pursuing, Baker replied, "That makes no difference, one band or another of them; they are all Piegans [Blackfeet] and we will attack them." Indiscriminate shooting by the soldiers left thirty-seven Native American men, ninety women, and fifty children dead. Another 140 women and children were seized and were to be taken back to the soldiers' base at Fort Ellis, but they were found to be infected with smallpox and were abandoned. The details of this conflict so affected President Grant that he changed government policy regarding Indian agents, appointing clergy to those positions, and kept the Bureau of Indian Affairs in the Department of the Interior.[33]

Aside from retaliation for Native American transgressions against White people, albeit with provocation at times, the ruthlessness and cavalier attitude of the commanders and their soldiers toward Indians was no doubt fueled by stereotypical preconceptions they held about them. Indians were often viewed as irritants, criminals, vagrants, and vermin—standing in the way of progress, fit only for extermination or removal to reservations where they could be monitored and kept in check.

Fighting for Our Freedom

Yet the campaigns waged against Native Americans benefited from the assistance of Indian scouts. Some of them lent their knowledge about other tribes to federal troops because of long-standing feuds that existed between their clans as with the Pawnees and Crows versus the Cheyenne, Kiowa, and Chippewa (Anishnabe). In the Northeast, there was strife between the Iroquois tribes and the Algonquians in the sixteenth and seventeenth centuries.

Besides blood feuds and revenge, some Native Americans aligned themselves with U.S. forces because they needed a job, and fighting as scouts, while it didn't pay well, was preferable to starving on reservations. Native Americans have had a long and illustrious history of serving this country's military—even when they weren't recognized or accepted as citizens or equals. As far back as the American Revolution, Native Americans fought on the side of the fledgling United States. While four of the famous Six Nations of the Iroquois Confederacy fought with the British (Mohawk, Onondaga, Cayuga, and Seneca), two (Oneida and Tuscarora) aligned with the colonists. In the South, the Cherokees sided with the British but were defeated by the rebels, and the western tribes of the Shawnee and Wyandot (Huron) remained neutral. (The Plains, southwestern, and western Indian nations then existed beyond the locus of control and interest of the White establishment.)

Even prior to the Revolution, Native Americans were choosing sides in the Seven Years' War (French and Indian War) that pitted the British and their colonial subjects against the French and much of the Iroquois Nation, culminating in the Treaty of Paris of 1763 that gave control of much of present-day Ohio, eastern Indiana, western Pennsylvania, and northwestern West Virginia to the British.

By the time of the Civil War, White expansionism encompassed vast areas previously populated by Native American tribes, and although some were openly hostile to White settlers and prospectors, an estimated twenty thousand Native Americans joined the Union side, perhaps in the false hope of ending discrimination and westward expansion. The Delaware Nation was the first Native American group to proclaim support for the Union in October 1861. Indians fought bravely for the Army of the Potomac and were represented by members of the Creek, Seminole, Kickapoo, Seneca, Osage, Shawnee, Choctaw, and Chickasaw tribes in the 1st and 2nd Indian Home Guard created in 1862.

One of the most distinguished predominantly Native American units was Company K of the 1st Michigan Sharpshooters, composed of Ottawa, Delaware, Huron, Oneida, Potawatomi, and Ojibwa Indians. They fought in the Battle of the Wilderness and Spotsylvania and captured six hundred Confederate troops at Shand House near Petersburg.

The Cherokee Nation initially supported the Confederate side under the leadership of John Ross, but after the Battle of Pea Ridge in Arkansas in March 1862, many defected to the Union. Ross was captured that summer and proclaimed his loyalty to the Union, but his successor, Colonel Stand Waite, took command of the remaining

Cherokee troops and led them to many victories over Union forces. He was promoted to brigadier general in 1864 and was the last Confederate military leader to surrender—two months after General Lee signed the Articles of Surrender at the Appomattox Court House on April 4, 1865. The articles had been drawn up by General Ely S. Parker, a Seneca Indian, who was trained as an attorney and on the staff of General Ulysses S. Grant. Grant and Parker were close friends, and Grant served as best man at Parker's wedding to Minnie Sackett, a White woman.

As president, Grant appointed Parker as the commissioner of Indian affairs, the first non–White person to hold that position, which he later relinquished after a congressional investigation into alleged irregularities he purportedly committed. Despite no findings of wrongdoing, Parker left Washington under a cloud and died destitute in 1895. It is said that at the famous courthouse, on noticing Parker was a Native American, General Lee commented to him, "I am glad to see one real American here." To which Parker replied, "We are all Americans."[34]

Although federal troops had more resources and sophisticated weapons than their Native American adversaries, they did not know the terrain they occupied. Realizing this, Congress authorized the U.S. Army to form a corps of one thousand Indian scouts on August 1, 1866. The work they performed for the army was inestimable. As one of the most well-known Indian fighters, General George Crook, noted, "Without reserve or qualification of any nature.... I assert that the scouts did excellent service, and were of more value in hunting down and compelling the surrender of the renegades than all other troops engaged in operations against them combined."[35] Ten Indian scouts under Crook's command received Congressional Medals of Honor "for gallant conduct during campaigns and engagements with Apaches."[36]

After Geronimo's surrender in 1886, the Indian Wars were de facto finished. By 1924 only eight Indian scouts remained, and the last four Native American scouts were retired in 1947. One of these men was Staff Sergeant Sinew Riley who later commented:

> We were recruited from the warriors from many famous nations. We are the last of the Army's Indian scouts. In a few years we shall be gone to join our comrades in the great hunting grounds beyond the sunset, for our need here is no more. There we shall always remain very proud of our Indian people and of the United States Army, for we were truly the first Americans and you in the Army are now our warriors. To you who will keep the Army's campfires bright, we extend our hands, and to you we will our fighting hearts.[37]

Code Talkers

Despite their commitment and battlefield successes, Indians were relegated to "colored troop" units along with Black soldiers in the Civil War. This practice was discontinued in World War I, when ten thousand Native Americans served alongside White soldiers, although African Americans were still confined to segregated units. No one disputes the dedication of Native Americans in our military and to our society. Approximately thirty of them have received our nation's highest military award, the Congressional Medal of Honor.

One of the most intriguing roles Native Americans played in World Wars I and

II, and to a lesser extent in the Korean conflict and Vietnam, was as transmitters of secret information, or commonly referred to as code talkers. A wide variety of languages were spoken by Native Americans, many of them unintelligible to one another, and much to the pleasure of U.S. military intelligence and the Signal Corps, our enemies could not decipher them either.

Among the first code talkers were Cherokee and Choctaw Indians serving in the U.S. military in World War I. They had responsibility for transmitting secret tactical messages over military phones and radios. They were initially used in the American 30th Infantry Division in the Second Battle of the Somme in September 1918. A second unit consisting of fourteen Choctaw men in the U.S. Army's 36th Infantry Division also used Native American language as code. The efforts of these soldiers helped the American Expeditionary Force win battles in the Meuse-Argonne offensive in France from September to November 1918.

The Germans were so curious about the code talkers that they sent a contingent of anthropologists to the United States to learn Native languages before World War II, but they were not assisted, and the project failed. At the beginning of World War II, fewer than thirty non–Navajo people understood the language, but knowing about the German initiative, the U.S. military confined most of the code talkers, now principally Navajo, to the Pacific theater. However, fourteen Comanche code talkers served at the invasion of Normandy in the 4th Infantry Division at Utah Beach. The French government awarded Comanche code talkers in World War II the Chevalier of the National Order of Merit for their service in 1989. Ten years later, the U.S. Department of Defense presented Charles Chibitty, a Comanche, the Knowlton Award for outstanding military intelligence as a code talker in the European theater.

The Navajo code was modeled on the Joint Army/Navy phonetic alphabet that uses English words to represent letters. The Navajos, who were mostly enlisted as Marines, were able to decipher and transmit codes faster than machines (e.g., a three-line English message could be transmitted or deciphered in twenty seconds compared to thirty minutes by machines). Howard Connor, the signal officer of the 5th Marine Signal Division at Iwo Jima, said, "Were it not for the Navajos, the Marines would have never taken Iwo Jima."[38]

Like the Germans before them, the Japanese never broke the Native American codes, and though the Indians were indispensable to the Allies, they did not receive recognition for their contribution until President Ronald Reagan conferred on them a Certificate of Recognition for their work and named August 14, 1982, as "Navajo Code Talkers Day."

On December 21, 2000, President Bill Clinton signed Public Law 106-554, awarding Congressional Gold Medals to the original twenty-nine World War II Navajo code talkers and Silver Medals to nearly three hundred other Navajo code talkers. On November 5, 2008, President George W. Bush signed into law the Code Talkers Recognition Act (Public Law 110-420) that recognized every Native American code talker who served in the U.S. military during World Wars I and II with Congressional Gold Medals. To date, thirty-three tribes have been identified and honored.[39]

Racial slurs and stereotypes persist even at the highest level of our society. At a ceremony honoring Native American code talkers from World War II at the White House on November 27, 2017, President Donald J. Trump could not refrain from disparagingly referring to Senator Elizabeth Warren (D–MA) as Pocahontas while he stood alongside three World War II Native American heroes who helped the Allies transmit messages that couldn't be understood by opposing forces during the war. He was in front of a large portrait of President Andrew Jackson, the orchestrator of the infamous "Trail of Tears" that resulted in the expulsion of fifteen thousand Indians (primarily Cherokee, Creek, Chickasaw, Choctaw, and Seminole) from Georgia, Alabama, Tennessee, and North Carolina to Oklahoma in 1838, and the death of four thousand to eight thousand of them from inclement weather, disease, exhaustion, and starvation. "But you know what I like about you. You are special people," intoned the president, although he averred that President Jackson was his hero.

Then Navajo Nation President Russell Begaye noted the incident demonstrated that "all tribal nations still battle insensitive references to our people. The prejudice that Native American people face is an unfortunate historical legacy. As Native Americans, we are proud people who have taken care of this land long before there was the United States of America and we will continue to fight for this Nation."

The Warrior Tradition

Native Americans distinguished themselves on many fronts in World War II. The vaunted 45th Infantry Division, established as the National Guard for Oklahoma in 1923, became known as the Thunderbird Division during the war. Seeing combat in Sicily, Italy, France, and Germany, the unit was laced with Native Americans. General George S. Patton considered it one of the best fighting units in the entire army. Three soldiers in the unit received the Congressional Medal of Honor, including Ernest Childers, the first Native American to receive that honor in the war. It was also the division that liberated the Nazi concentration camp Dachau on April 29, 1945.[40] Native Americans have the highest record of military service per capita of any ethnic group in the United States—22 percent of all Native American men eighteen years or older are veterans.

On Veterans Day 2020, a $15 million war memorial honoring the 156,000 Native Americans and Alaska Natives who served in the U.S. military opened after two decades of planning. The "Warrior's Circle of Honor" will stand outside of the Smithsonian's National Museum of the American Indian in Washington, D.C.[41]

9

Cooper's
Enduring Influence

I admit that there are good white men, but they bear no proportion to the bad; the bad must be the strongest, for they rule. They do what they please. They enslave those who are not of their color, although created by the same Great Spirit who created them. They would make slaves of us if they could; but as they cannot do it, they kill us. There is no faith to be placed in their words. They are not like the Indians, who are only enemies while at war, and are friends in peace. They will say to an Indian, "My friend; my brother!" They will take him by the hand, and, at the same moment, destroy him.
—Pachgantschilias, Great Chief of the Delawares, 1787[1]

Notwithstanding the military heroics of Native Americans in service to this country, the popularity of Cooper's work and themes permeated American culture through the twentieth century and persist to this day. In their analysis of Cooper's most enduring work, *The Last of the Mohicans*, Barker and Sabin identified thirteen English-language film versions,[2] including five feature motion pictures and one twelve-part serial (1932), starring Harry Carey as Hawkeye. From D. W. Griffith's one-reeler in 1909 and the 1920 silent version featuring a svelte Wallace Beery as the ignominious Magua, to the much-heralded 1936 version starring Randolph Scott as Hawkeye and culminating in the $40 million blockbuster starring Daniel Day-Lewis directed by Michael Mann in 1992, audiences in the United States and around the world have been seduced by Cooper's stereotypical themes about Native Americans. With the exception of the latest motion picture version, all roles of Native Americans were played by White people, and the theme of miscegenation was prominent throughout. As one reviewer noted of the 1936 film, "Racism immediately arises in the form of Captain Randolph, who censures Cora for daring to respect a mere savage." And, "Ethnic authenticity is obviously scarce in a picture where the most dramatic Indian character is played by a highly un–Indian-like actor [Wallace Beery] covered in makeup."[3]

In addition to the prodigious motion picture and television market for Cooper's works, over two million copies of *The Last of the Mohicans* were published by 1940, and a lively dime novel and later comic book trade were based on his works.[4]

Although the 1936 version of the film attempted to be historically accurate, with Ed Lambert, the principal researcher for the film, reportedly studying the Remington Schuyler painting, *Custer's Last Stand*, depicting scalping in progressive stages as well as interviewing descendants of "this country's outstanding scalpers,"[5] the dominant message conveyed about Native Americans was one of savagery and cruelty.

Michael Mann, the director of the 1992 version, attempted to invest the events depicted in the novel with historical accuracy. In an interview twenty years after the release of his film he noted Cooper's bias: "Cooper had vast real estate holdings in 1825 when he wrote the book. So the novel is almost a justification for a massive land grab ... that the Euro-Americans will be a better steward of the riches that God bestowed upon American Indians. And that, of course, was not the perspective of American Indians. So the revision of history was one of the things I didn't care for in the novel."[6]

Unfortunately, audiences in the United States and elsewhere have been consistently misled by the predominant negative depiction of Native American culture displayed in the films and numerous television spinoffs. Commencing with the 1957 television series *Hawkeye and the Last of the Mohicans*, a thirty-nine-episode series originated in the United States, followed by television shows like the 1969 German mini-series *Die Lederstrumpferzahlungen*, based on the novel, and the television series *Hawkeye* that ran from 1994 to 1995 begun in the United States and later released in Germany, Finland, France, Italy, and Canada, there has been an unremitting scramble to capitalize on the heroic adventures of Hawkeye and the somewhat warped romantic image of Native Americans.

At the Tenth Cooper Seminar, Jeffrey Walker, professor of English at Oklahoma State University, opined that the Hollywood film industry consistently misrepresented Cooper's script and intention: "In their versions of *The Last of the Mohicans*, filmmakers have rewritten Cooper's plot, miscast and mislabeled his characters, modernized his dialogue, misunderstood his themes, and misrepresented history."[7] By all accounts, the blame for this must be shared by the author as well as his admirers and replicators to the detriment of our society.

Devastating Effects

From Las Casas's lamentations about the Spaniards' cruelty toward Indians, to the scathing indictment by Vine Deloria, Jr., of their exploitation in the United States during the nineteenth and twentieth centuries, and the condemnation of American domestic policies that decimated and exploited Native Americans by historian Dee Brown,[8] there has been a cascade of indignant prose exposing the duplicity and rapaciousness of White attitudes and government policies toward Native Americans.[9]

Indian culture and values were anathema to capitalism, and White politicians and clergy sought to change them: "As soon as the Indian is taught to toil for his daily bread, and realize the sense of proprietorship in the results of his labor, it cannot but be further to his advantage to be able to appreciate that his labor is expended upon his individual possessions and his personal benefit."[10]

One of the most devastating accounts of our government's abrogation of treaties with Native Americans is Helen Hunt Jackson's *A Century of Dishonor*. She documented specific cases where treaties were broken or ignored resulting in the confiscation and dispersal of Native American land and resources. Realizing the futility of their situation, faced with overwhelming numbers of White people and their superior technology, most Native American nations sought to reach an accommodation with the invading hordes of White settlers and their government.

Historian Dee Brown's review of the theft of Native American land by state and federal governments confirms Jackson's analysis. Time after time Indians were forced off their land by settlers, government officials, and speculators, and removed to less desirable and unfamiliar territory. Pressured to sell their land for a pittance of its worth, deceived about annual annuities, and given inadequate provisions to sustain them, many Indians succumbed in the harsh climate they were exposed to. For those who bolted or remained steadfast, they were forced to fight the "bluecoats" with their greater numbers and modern weapons. There never was a doubt about the outcome.

Facing the onslaught of the White military might, Cheyenne Chief Lean Bear exclaimed, "The Indians are not to blame for the fighting. The white men are foxes and peace cannot be brought with them; the only thing the Indians can do is fight."[11]

Despite stereotypical depictions of Indians as hostile, aggressive, uncivilized savages, Jackson presents them as pragmatic, even willing and eager to accommodate to Western ways. They became successful cultivators of the land they were relegated to, raising crops and livestock, running sawmills, and developing crafts. They recognized the necessity for education and sent their children to school; and they adopted prevalent American lifestyles, built homes, wore conventional clothes, converted to Christianity, and tried to assimilate into society.

The Trail of Tears

The White man's greed, exemplified by the continuous invasion of Indian lands by avaricious settlers and speculators, led to a pattern of confiscation of their property and their removal to less desirable territory. Monies allocated for their children's education, the building of schools, health care facilities, food, farm implements, and other provisions promised to them in ostensibly binding treaties, were not provided or reduced to paltry sums insufficient to meet their needs. Indian agents described the most humiliating, neglectful, and abusive treatment of Native Americans. Starving and brutalized by force and circumstance, even Nature seemed to conspire against them in their attempt to survive.

> It is a matter of astonishment to me that the Government should have ordered the removal of the Ponca Indians from Dakota to Indian Territory without having first made some provision for their settlement and comfort.... [N]o appropriation has been made by Congress except of a sum a little more than sufficient to remove them; and the result is that these people have been placed on an uncultivated reservation, to live in their tents as best they may, and await further legislative action.[12]

An 1869 Commission on Indian Affairs appointed by President Grant concluded: "To assert that 'the Indian will not work' is as true as it would be to say that the white man will not work. Why should the Indian be expected to plant corn, fence lands, build houses, or do anything but get food from day to day, when experience has taught him that the product of his labor will be seized by the white man tomorrow?"[13]

Under these conditions, some Native Americans rebelled and attempted to resist the forces that were aligned against them, even in the face of adverse publicity that distorted their situation. But the struggles of iconic Native American heroes like Sitting Bull, Geronimo, and Chief Joseph were doomed from the start. As the renowned Indian-fighter and later sympathizer with their plight, General George Crook, observed:

> It is too often the case that border newspapers ... disseminate all sorts of exaggerations and falsehoods about the Indians, which are copied in papers of high character and wide circulation, in other parts of the country, while the Indian's side of the case is rarely ever heard. In this way the people at large get false ideas with reference to the matter. Then when the outbreak does come public attention is turned to the Indians, their crimes and atrocities are also condemned, while the persons whose injustice has driven them to this course escape scot-free and are the loudest in their denunciations. No one knows this fact better than the Indian, therefore he is excusable in seeing no justice in a government which only punishes him, while it allows the white man to plunder him as he pleases.[14]

Perhaps the most ignominious chapter in the maltreatment of Native Americans is known today as "The Trail of Tears." In the early 1800s, Cherokee Territory was larger than the combined states of Massachusetts, Connecticut, and Rhode Island. It included the northwestern part of Georgia, northeast Alabama, and parts of Tennessee and North Carolina. Much of their land was devoted to farming, and they were successful at it. Even after they were displaced from their homeland, the Cherokees retained their commitment to agriculture and Western mannerisms.

Throughout the early 1800s there was an unremitting assault by White settlers and governments on the Cherokee Nation with the purpose of dispossessing them from their land. White settlers made repeated incursions into their territory and pressured the federal and state governments to abrogate treaties with them. Ultimately, the federal government was persuaded to remove the Cherokees to Indian Territory, a region created in 1834 by Congress through legislation titled "An Act to Regulate Trade and Intercourse with the Indian Tribes and to Preserve Peace on the Frontiers."

Indian Territory's original borders included all of the United States west of the Mississippi River and "not within the States of Missouri and Louisiana or the Territory of Arkansas." But as historian Brown noted, before the law could be put into effect, a wave of White settlers swept into the region and formed what became Wisconsin and Iowa, and the boundaries of Indian Territory were shifted from the Mississippi to the ninety-fifth meridian. Within twenty-five years, White settlers in search of gold and land penetrated further into their territory, resulting in further reductions of their land, depriving Plains tribes of their entitlement as Kansas, Nebraska, and Minnesota became states.[15] Indian Territory shrank from 138 million acres in 1887 to 3 million in 1951.[16]

Increasing pressure on the Cherokees to sell their land met with limited success. Some tribal members adamantly refused, and as historian Helen Hunt Jackson concluded more than a century ago, "The doom of the Cherokees was sealed on the day when they declared, once and for all, officially as a nation, they would not sell another foot of land."[17] Journalist Steve Inskeep makes the case that General, and later president, Andrew Jackson had personal and political designs on Indian land for decades, including their confiscation and purchase at fire-sale prices, with profits accruing to himself, friends, and White settlers.[18] Jackson, like many other White people, lobbied for a policy of removing Native Americans from the East to the West. "The object of the Government," noted Jackson, "is to bring into market this land and have it populated."[19]

According to Inskeep, "[R]ecords that survive show that after 1816 the names of Andrew Jackson, his relatives, and his two closest business associates appeared on the titles to more than forty-five thousand acres of newly opened Alabama land."[20]

This policy was not unique to Jackson, as Inskeep noted, because President Jefferson, in an 1803 letter advised, "We shall push our trading houses and be glad to see the good and influential individuals among them [Indians] run in debt, because we observe that when these debts get beyond what the individuals can pay, they become willing to lop them off by a cession of lands."[21] And Jackson himself contended, "We must address ourselves to their fears and indulge their avarice."[22]

By 1835, after intense prodding and pressure, the Cherokees relinquished all their land east of the Mississippi River—seven million acres, though some members of the Cherokee Nation rejected the Treaty of 1835 with the federal government and spurned assistance. Then, in 1838, General Winfield Scott was ordered to forcibly remove them. Reluctantly, Scott noted: "The full moon of May is already on the wane, and before another shall have passed away, every Cherokee man, woman, and child in those states [Georgia, North Carolina, Tennessee, and Alabama] must be in motion to join their brethren in the West."[23]

Fifteen thousand people—men, women, and children—were forced to march about a thousand miles from June to December. Between four thousand and eight thousand people died on the journey from disease, starvation, and inclement weather. Known among the Cherokee Nation as Nunahi-duna-dlo-hilu-I, "The Trail Where They Cried,"[24] to this day, the Trail of Tears represents an ignominious chapter in the sordid history of White treatment of Native Americans in the United States.

Even more disconcerting is the fact that many Cherokees attempted to assimilate into White society before and after their displacement. Aside from learning English and sending their children to school, they were assiduous farmers and ran democratic governing councils in their towns and communities. They adopted American clothes and customs and were punctilious about their work.

After being forcibly removed, many Cherokees remained loyal to the Union. "Upon the first appearance of United States forces in their country an entire regiment of Indian troops, raised ostensibly for service in the rebel army, deserted and came over to [the Union side]."[25] But six to seven thousand Cherokees fought for the Confederacy, an act that did not endear them to the victors. This no doubt heightened tensions between the Cherokees and White people who already coveted their land and held prejudicial attitudes toward them. Despite their attempts at assimilation, the Cherokees were rebuffed and continually harassed even after their removal to Indian Territory.

Presidents Jefferson and Jackson referred to Native Americans as savages, and their views were epitomized by the comments of national leaders like Henry Clay, speaker of the House of Representatives and candidate for the presidency in 1824. These comments are taken from a speech he made to the Colonization Society of Kentucky: "We are enjoined by every duty of religion, humanity and magnanimity to treat them [Indians] with kindness and justice, and recall them, if we can, from their savage to a better condition."[26] Upon retiring and perceiving that his Indian removal policy was about to be implemented, President Jackson commented, "The States which had so long been retarded in their improvement by the Indian tribes residing in the midst of them are at length relieved from the evil."[27]

As the intrusion of White settlers into Native American land increased so did the pressure to remove them further west to Indian Country where the land was barren and inhospitable. Pushed further from their ancestral lands as White people invaded, the process of making Indians into "vanishing Americans" was finalized and their fate sealed with the advent of the railroad. Settlers now poured into their territory, and they were tricked, pressured, and coerced into treaties that deeded their lands to the federal government and unscrupulous, avaricious businessmen. Life on reservations in inhospitable environments took a heavy toll on Native Americans as they languished waiting for promised seeds, tools, food, clothes, and money that never came or arrived too late to prevent starvation. Faced with the choice of starvation or extermination, some Native Americans fled the reservations and offered resistance to federal authorities.

Armed conflicts erupted, and between 1866 and 1886 wars were fought with the Teton Sioux, Cheyennes, and Arapahos in Wyoming and Montana; the Paiutes in Oregon and Idaho; on the Central Plains with the Cheyennes, Arapahos, Sioux, Comanches, and Kiowas; the Modocs in California; the Lakota Sioux, Cheyennes, and Arapahos in Montana and Wyoming; the Nez Perce in the Northwest; the Bannocks, Paiutes, and Cayuses in Idaho and Oregon; the Utes in Colorado; and the Apaches in the Southwest.[28]

Custer's Last Stand

One battle between Native Americans and federal government forces had a lingering effect on the tenor of Indian relations in the country—the ill-fated conflict between the American 7th Calvary and a gathering of Lakota Sioux, Northern Cheyenne, and Arapaho warriors on June 25, 1876, at the Little Big Horn River in Montana. The defeat of Custer led to heightened tension between White people and Indians and the passage of regressive legislation that further encroached on the resources of Native Americans.

The Sioux, who inhabited the region, then known as Montana Territory, had been given exclusive rights to the Black Hills, but when gold was discovered miners and settlers invaded the area. To protect the White settlers, the federal authorities ordered the Indians to stay on their reservations, but they resisted.

Custer, born in Rumley, Ohio, and a graduate of West Point (he finished last in his class of thirty-four cadets in 1861), rose to prominence as a dashing young commander during the Civil War, where he received battlefield promotions and rose to the rank of major general, though still in his twenties. At the First Battle of Bull Run and in subsequent conflicts he distinguished himself as a capable field commander. At the Battle of Gettysburg, he assisted in preventing Confederate General J. E. B. Stuart from attacking the Union rear, and he played a major role in defeating Confederate General Jubal Early's army at Third Winchester and Cedar Creek. The cavalry unit he commanded blocked General Robert E. Lee's retreat and hastened his surrender at Appomattox on April 9, 1865.

Custer was at times arrogant, brash, flamboyant, and impetuous. He was even suspended for a year in 1867 for leaving his command on the Kansas frontier and returning, without orders, to Fort Riley to be with his wife, Libbie. General Sheridan reinstated him after ten months so he could lead a campaign against the Cheyenne. Custer had a reputation as being a risk taker and gallant commander—and until the Little Big Horn, he led a charmed life, having sustained minimal wounds in battle. But he made a monumental miscalculation on his last assignment when he disregarded orders and engaged what he presumed to be a small band of Indians encamped at the mouth of the Little Big Horn River, also known to the Indians as the Greasy Grass.

Although General Alfred Terry had ordered Custer and his 7th Calvary to scout the enemy, Custer pressed ahead with the six hundred men under his command. Custer planned to attack the Indian camp from three sides, but two of his units led by Captain Frederick Benteen and Major Marcus Reno were forced to retreat to one side of the river because of superior Native American forces. Custer and his 275 men engaged the Indians, who were led by Sitting Bull, Crazy Horse, and an estimated 3,000 warriors.

The battle lasted less than an hour. Custer and all his soldiers were killed while the Indians lost about one hundred men. It was the worst U.S. Calvary defeat in the Plains Indian Wars. The Indians stripped the dead soldiers' bodies and mutilated them in the belief that the souls of mutilated bodies would be forced to walk the earth eternally. Custer's body was not mutilated, perhaps because he was wearing buck-skins and the Indians thought he wasn't a soldier.[29] More than a century later, Professor C. Richard King noted that the federal memorial on the site of the battlefield contained negative stereotypical imagery and artifacts that perpetuate the image of Native Americans as degenerate savages: "[T]he site works to erode Native American subjectivities as well as their victory, dissolving in many ways both the conflict and its historicity."[30] And further, "[T]he exhibit fashions Native Americans as people without history, mired in superstition, possessing a culture now extinct but observable in interesting, didactic, and ultimately flat objects."[31]

The Indians retreated two days later when federal troops arrived in the Black Hills. After eluding the troops for nearly a year, Sitting Bull led a small band of Indians to Canada but returned five years later and was eventually settled on the Standing Rock Reservation in South Dakota where he was killed by Indian police on December 15, 1890. Two weeks later, on December 29, 1890, the massacre of 150–300 Sioux Indians occurred at Wounded Knee on the Pine Ridge Indian Reservation in South Dakota. A gun discharged while government troops were trying to disarm the peaceful Indians. The soldiers unleashed a fusillade killing and wounding most of them. Half of the victims were women and children, many hunted down like animals and killed in the snow, including their leader, Spotted Elk. Several babies were later found alive lying under their deceased mothers, and one was reportedly buried alive in a mass grave with many of the other victims. The assault was carried out by none other than the U.S. 7th Calvary, part of the same unit that was wiped out along with Custer, fourteen years earlier. The encircling force of five hundred soldiers commanded by Colonel James Forsythe destroyed the ill-fated Native Americans (Miniconjou and Hunkpapa Lakota) using four Hotchkiss guns to dispatch them. Twenty-nine government soldiers were killed in the event, many by friendly fire. Twenty Congressional Medals of Honor, some to Indian scouts from other tribes, were awarded to the soldiers.[32]

I visited the scene of the event in September 2018. I was struck by the desolation of the area. A nondescript sign on an open field beside a highway marked the site of the massacre. Nearby was a lean-to where Native American trinkets were being hawked. Across the sandy street, on top of a low hill, encased by a chain-link fence was the rectangular common burial site where over 150 of the victims were buried shortly after the massacre. A simple gate with a yellow ribbon guarded the entrance to the hallowed ground.

For more than fifteen years, attorney Mario Gonzalez (Lakota) tried unsuccessfully to secure funding to erect a monument to the fallen Indians.[33] Wounded Knee was also the site of a seventy-one-day siege (February 27–May 6) in 1973 begun by members of the American Indian Movement (AIM) and two hundred Oglala Lakota Native Americans in pursuit of recognition of Indian issues by the U.S. government.[34]

The Black Hills dispute led to the redrawing of the boundary of their reservation, with the sacred Black Hills outside of it, leaving their land open to White settlers. Public sentiment also turned against Native Americans. In 1887, the infamous General Allotment Act, also known as the Dawes Severalty Act after Senator Henry Dawes from Massachusetts who authored it, was passed by Congress. This legislation authorized the president of the United States to survey Indian tribal land and divide it into allotments for individual Indians. Ostensibly designed to alleviate poverty among Native Americans and help them assimilate into White society, the act broke up tribal lands because those individuals who accepted allotments and lived separately from the tribe were given citizenship. The federal government then classified as "excess" Indian reservation lands remaining after the allotments and sold them on the open market to non–Native Americans.

In 1893, Senator Dawes also chaired a commission that decided who was legally an Indian. He once noted:

> The head chief [of the Cherokees] told us that there was not a family in the whole nation that had not a home of its own. There is not a pauper in that nation, and the nation does not

The death of Spotted Elk at Wounded Knee, December 29, 1890 (Library of Congress).

owe a dollar. It built its own capitol ... and built its schools and hospitals. Yet the defect of the system was apparent. They have got as far as they can go, because they hold their land in common. It is Henry George's system, and under that there is no enterprise to make your house any better than that of your neighbors. There is no selfishness, which is at the bottom of civilization. Till these people will consent to give up their lands, and divide them among their citizens so that each can own the land he cultivates, they will not make much progress.[35]

Even more damning is the following statement from an 1869 report of the Board of Indian Commissioners, appointed by President Grant:

The history of the border white man's connection with the Indians is a sickening record of murder, outrage, robbery, and wrongs committed by the former as the rule, and occasional savage outbreaks and unspeakably barbarous deeds of retaliation by the latter as the exception.... The testimony of some of the highest military officers of the United States is on the record to the effect that, in our Indian wars, almost without exception, the first aggressions have been made by the white man, and the assertion is supported by every civilian of reputation who has studied the subject.[36]

Negative generalizations about Native Americans as savages and uncivilized fueled White political sentiment against them. A recurrent stereotypical theme tainting White perceptions about Indians was their presumed inability and unwillingness to accept White cultural and economic principles—to become civilized. The essential problem with Native Americans, from the dominant White cultural perspective, was their reluctance to embrace White, Christian customs that promoted individualism and capitalist morality—both antithetical to Native American customs of communalism and parsimonious relationships with nature.

10

Compulsory Assimilation:
Indian Boarding Schools

> Several of our young people were formerly brought up at the colleges
> of the northern provinces; they were instructed in all your sciences;
> but when they came back to us, they were bad runners; ignorant of
> every means of living in the woods; unable to bear either cold or hun-
> ger; knew neither how to build a cabin, take a deer, or kill an enemy;
> spoke our language imperfectly; were therefore neither fit for hunters,
> warriors, or counsellors; they were totally good for nothing. We are,
> however, not the less obliged by your kind offer [to provide college edu-
> cations to some young Iroquois men] though we decline accepting it:
> and to show our grateful sense of it, if the gentlemen of Virginia will
> send us a dozen of their sons, we will take great care of their education,
> instruct them in all we know, and make men of them.
> —Anonymous Iroquois spokesman, 1744

Dawes's sentiments exemplify the White repugnance for Native Americans and help explain the disdain many Westerners had for their collectivist values. Aside from the ubiquitous White ethnocentric bias settlers and governments had for people of color, Western Europeans could not fathom Indigenous people who lived vicariously off the land, freely collaborated with one another in the conscientious conservation of the environment, and rejected capitalism.

To reprogram Native Americans so they'd espouse competitive capitalist val-ues, the U.S. government embarked on an education program designed to socialize Indian children so they would embrace the American Way. As Richard Henry Pratt, the founder of the Carlisle (Pennsylvania) Indian School and champion of the forced assimilation policy, noted: "[A]ll the Indian there is in the race should be dead. Kill the Indian in him, and save the man."[1]

The instrument of this plan was the Indian boarding school. The project was launched in 1860 under the Bureau of Indian Affairs at Yakima, Washington, and devised by two well-intentioned eastern reformers, Herbert Welsh and Henry Pan-coast. At their zenith, there were 153 Indian boarding schools, and as late as 1973, 60,000 Indian children resided in them. The schools were based on the premise of replacing Indian culture with American capitalist values, essentially promoting the assimilation of Indians into the "American Way of Life." In actuality, the schools were committing cultural genocide, and their methods were cruel and perverse.

The methodology of the schools was to remove Indian children from their homes and communities so they could learn White, Western ways, and become assimilated into the dominant culture. The schools were highly regimented and focused on teaching English, farming, and industrial arts for the boys, and cleaning, sewing, cooking, and laundering for the girls. Meant to be self-sufficient, the schools raised much of their own food, though Indian food was largely forbidden and replaced by standard White fare.

Perhaps the cruelest indictment of the boarding schools was the virtual kidnapping of students who were often forcibly taken from their parents on reservations. Once on campus they lived highly regimented lives with strict discipline. Boys' long braids were cut, and the children were given Anglo names and uniforms. The overriding philosophy was to eradicate vestiges of Indian culture and substitute dominant American (White) values of thrift, industriousness, individual initiative, and self-restraint.

After reviewing eighty-five interviews, memoirs, and autobiographies of Canadian and American individuals who underwent the boarding school experience from 1819 to 1934, Professor Maureen Smith concluded, "It is clear that the experience thoroughly altered their lives. The educational system brought changes not only to individual American Indians, but also to whole tribal communities."[2] Indian children were forbidden to speak their native languages by the Commissioner of Indian Affairs in 1886, and some students who violated this injunction had sewing needles pushed through their tongues.[3]

Many of the schools were also religiously based, emphasizing Christianity over Native American spirituality. The Catholic, Presbyterian, United, and the Episcopal churches were prominent influences, and, not surprisingly, they focused on the virtues of the Ten Commandments, the Beatitudes, and the Psalms.

The children were taught to venerate American leaders like George Washington, "The Great White Father." Holidays were underscored with perverse significance; for example, Thanksgiving was a celebration of "good Indians" who aided the brave Pilgrims, and they were taught that Columbus Day marked the beginning of the Native Americans' ascent to civilization. "On Memorial Day, some students at off-reservation schools were made to decorate the graves of soldiers sent to kill their fathers."[4]

In the summers, students were often placed with White families to further assist in their assimilation and indoctrination. This "Placing Out System" was designed to prevent them from interacting with their families and communities in a further attempt to extinguish their ties to Indigenous culture. It was also hoped that Native American children raised as White people might not only become socially assimilated but also physiologically amalgamated through intermarriage, leading to a "Whitening" of their skin and further destruction of their "Indianness," a policy that was also attempted by the White Australian government in regard to the Aboriginal population in that country.[5]

Discipline at the schools was severe, ranging from deprivation of privileges, to confinement, diet restrictions, and corporal punishment. Some students were sexually abused, and disease was rampant, especially infectious and communicable disorders like measles, tuberculosis, and trachoma. At the Phoenix Indian School, in a ten-day period in 1899, there were 325 cases of measles, 60 cases of pneumonia, and 9 deaths.[6]

In 1928, the Meriam Report (named after the chief of staff of the investigating committee of the Institute for Government Research, later known as the Brookings Institution) was issued based on a survey of the social and economic conditions of Native Americans. After seven months of investigation that included visiting ninety-five jurisdictions, it concluded: "An overwhelming majority of the Indians [in the United States] are poor, even extremely poor, and they are not adjusted to the economic and social system of the dominant White civilization." Further, "The health of the Indians as compared with that of the general population is bad." And, "The prevailing living conditions among the great majority of the Indians are conducive to the development and spread of disease."[7]

Indian boarding schools received a scathing review. The committee found

deplorable health conditions at most of the schools. Old buildings, often kept in use long after they have been pulled down, and ultimately bad fire-risks in many instances; crowded dormitories; conditions of sanitation that are usually as good as can be under the circumstances, but certainly below accepted standards; boilers and machinery out-of-date and in some instances unsafe, to the point of having long since been condemned, but never replaced; many medical officers who are of low standards of training and relatively unacquainted with the methods of modern medicine, to say nothing of health education for children ... serious malnutrition, due to the lack of food and use of wrong foods; schoolrooms seldom showing knowledge of modern principles of lighting and ventilating; lack of recreational opportunities ... an abnormally long day ... the generally routinized nature of institutional life with its formalism in classrooms, its marching and dress parades, its annihilation of initiative, its lack of beauty, its almost complete negation of normal family life, all of which have disastrous effects upon mental health and the development of wholesome personality.[8]

Although the Committee found a few exceptions to these conditions it concluded, "In almost no case, however, could a reasonably clean bill of health be given to any one school."[9] The abuse and neglect documented in the Meriam Report eventuated in the Wheeler-Howard Act of 1934, also known as the Indian Reorganization Act.[10]

The physical and emotional trauma that Native Americans sustained in Indian boarding schools was reflected in dramatic accounts about life there by survivors. As one former resident of a boarding school recounted: "The Sister School [Catholic] was a place where the very fact of being Indian was wrong, something to be corrected. My mother held on to the details of those cruel corrective measures until she died. Like an awful looping spirit that wouldn't let go, those experiences permeated her life, filling her with fear and anger."[11]

Historian Brian Dippie presented a more sympathetic portrayal of Pratt and his contemporaries' motives for establishing the boarding schools. Dippie attributed their zeal to assimilate Native American children to an altruistic motivation to prevent the annihilation of Indians during the clash between their way of life and the dominant White culture that threatened to engulf them.[12] Still, contemporary social scientists and Native Americans are appalled at the seeming callousness of the effects of their policies, and the incontrovertible fact remains that the system was designed to extinguish every vestige of Native American culture by Anglicizing Indian children so they fit into White society. Yet not all of Pratt's charges viewed him and the process negatively. Upon his death in 1924, some of his former students contributed funds to establish a memorial in his name at Arlington National Cemetery with the inscription "In Loving Memory" of the "Friend and Counsellor of the Indians."[13]

Abuses were curtailed over the years, but a startling recent report by the American Civil Liberties Union detailed extensive abrogation of Native American custody rights for thousands of children who are summarily placed with foster parents, ignoring due process. The practice is widespread in South Dakota where Indian children compose just 13 percent of the total number of children in the state but represent 53 percent of the children in foster care.[14]

In October 2018 the U.S. District Court for the Northern District of Texas declared (*Brackeen v. Zinke*) that the Indian Child Welfare Act (ICWA) was unconstitutional. The court's action reversed forty years of policies and practices designed to preserve Native American sovereignty and the welfare of tribal children. The Association on American Indian Affairs, begun in 1922, was instrumental in the passage of the ICWA, and along with the National Congress of American Indians, the National Indian Child Welfare Organization, and the Native American Rights Fund vowed to contest this decision. The court decision was overturned on August 9, 2019, by the Fifth Circuit Court of Appeals (*Brackeen v. Bernhardt*), which affirmed the constitutionality of the ICWA.

Canada and Australia used similar methods (i.e., taking Indigenous children from their parents and homes and placing them in boarding schools to destroy their native culture and force them to assimilate). Canada's first prime minister, John A. MacDonald, justified the practice of forcibly resocializing Aboriginal children in a speech before Parliament in 1883 when he noted that assimilation could only be accomplished this way, otherwise an Aboriginal child would only be "a savage who can read and write."

On June 11, 2008, then Canadian Prime Minister Stephen Harper gave a public apology for the Canadian government's cultural genocidal policies "causing great harm that has lasted for generations." In Canada, it is estimated that 150,000 Indigenous children were taken to 139 federally funded schools in all but three provinces (Newfoundland, New Brunswick, and Prince Edward Island). The schools were joint ventures with the Anglican, Catholic, Presbyterian, and United churches.[15] Controversy about his statement and the Truth and Reconciliation Commission that was established to investigate the abuses, as well as a recent voluminous report on the use of boarding schools to assimilate Aboriginal children, is still raging in Canada.[16]

On February 13, 2008, then Australian Prime Minister Kevin Rudd made a formal apology to Aboriginal people in his country for similar offenses. Estimates of the number of children forcibly taken from their Aboriginal parents vary greatly, though Prime Minister Rudd mentioned the figure of fifty thousand. The Australian government report about the sordid affair, *Bringing Them Home*, noted, "Most families [of Aboriginal people] have been affected, in one or more generations, by the forcible removal of one or more children."[17]

On December 9, 2009, former President Barack Obama gave a similar apology to Native Americans after the U.S. Congress passed the Native American Apology Resolution, acknowledging "a long history of official depredations and ill-conceived policies by the Federal Government regarding Indian tribes." However, this statement was appended to a sixty-seven-page Defense Appropriations Act (HR 3326), and his apology was given behind closed doors, unlike the other two that were publicly televised. No reference was made to the Trail of Tears, the Long Walk, Sand Creek, or Wounded Knee massacres.

The Obama administration attempted to streamline and improve Native American schools and turn them over to tribes. But present-day Native American schools are, for the most part, inferior to their public counterparts. Although per pupil spending in Native American schools in 2014 was $15,391 compared to an average of $9,896 in public schools, Native American students score far lower than their White peers in reading, math, and science. In 2013, 52 percent of the 14,217 Native American students who took the ACT college qualifying exam met *none* of its four college readiness benchmarks that try to predict a student's chance of getting a C or higher in English, reading, math, and science. Although 86 percent of Native American students said they wanted to pursue some type of postsecondary education, the percentage of them who completed the ACT-recommended core curriculum was lower than any other racial or ethnic group. In fact, Native Americans were the only group to experience a decline in the ACT benchmarks since 2009.[18]

Even though financial resources have been directed to the schools, results have not been encouraging. Perhaps mismanagement plays a role in their lack of student achievement. A report by the General Accounting Office found $13.8 million in unallowable spending at the schools. There are approximately 180 of them today with 41,000 students, mostly on reservations and in remote areas. The GAO admitted that it was inadequately monitoring the schools because of high staff turnover, reductions in the number of education line office administrators, and lack of expertise and training among its staff.[19]

Changing Orientations

John Collier, commissioner of Indian affairs under President Franklin Delano Roosevelt, was a guiding force behind the Wheeler-Howard Act of 1934 that changed national policy toward Native Americans. A strong proponent of Indian self-rule, he advocated for the reinvigoration of Indian culture. The act reversed the previous policy that promoted the total assimilation of Native Americans and curtailed the land allotment system promoted by the Dawes General Allotment Act of 1887 that led to White ownership of two-thirds of Indian land by 1932. Not all First Nations accepted the terms of the act, especially tribes in the Pacific Northwest not primarily engaged in farming.[20]

But the status of Native Americans remained perilous, and official U.S. policy changed once again. Under President Truman an Indian Relocation Program was begun, headed by Dillon Myer, the man who oversaw the internment of Japanese in the United States during World War II. The 1950s saw a renewed effort to assimilate Native Americans with the legal standing of more than one hundred tribes terminated.

As the plight of Native Americans and the perfidious relationship they had endured with the federal government became publicized, more progressive policies were implemented. In 1968, the Indian Civil Rights Act was passed by Congress, guaranteeing much of the Bill of Rights in Indian Country, that is, all federal trust lands held for Native Americans (reservations and allotments).

On July 8, 1970, President Richard Nixon recommended self-determination for Native American tribes, and this sentiment led to the Indian Self-Determination and

Education Assistance Act of 1975 (Public Law 93-638). This law authorized the Secretary of the Interior and the Secretary of Health, Education, and Welfare (now Health and Human Services) to enter into contracts with and make grants to federally recognized Indian tribes.

As Native American agitation for civil rights increased during the 1970s with the occupation of the former federal Alcatraz prison and the political work of organizations like the National Congress of American Indians (NCAI) and the American Indian Movement (AIM), federal and state policies became more benevolent toward them. But it should be noted, Native Americans born in the United States were not granted citizenship until June 2, 1924, and they did not have the right to vote in New Mexico and Arizona until 1948, Maine in 1956, and Utah in 1957. To this day, some Native Americans have difficulty voting because of limited voting sites, requirements that necessitate leaving reservations to register, bans on roving registrars, and elections held in places hostile to Indians. Still, there are about one million Native American voters, enough to solidify the victory of some candidates in states and locales with high proportions of Indians. In fact, there are over eighty Native Americans holding elective offices in the United States today.[21]

An indication of the lack of political clout of Native Americans and other Indigenous people in the Americas was delivered by Pope Francis on his trip to the United States in September 2015. While celebrating his first mass in the United States, the pope canonized the eighteenth-century missionary Father Junipero Serra. A Spanish Franciscan friar known as the "apostle of California," Serra is believed by some Native Americans to be a villainous malevolent tyrant who forced Indigenous people into servitude and harsh lives in the missionary system he established.

After arriving in California in 1769, Serra worked indefatigably to create nine Catholic missions to bring unchurched Native people to the Catholic faith. While his motives may have been benevolent, his missions were characterized by oppression and cruelty, where Native people were ruthlessly subjugated and, at times, tortured, imprisoned, and forced to labor to secure his objectives. He is credited with converting between five thousand and six thousand Indians while enduring enormous self-sacrifice and mortifications of the flesh. (He wore heavy shirts with sharp wires pointed inward for self-flagellation and walked hundreds of miles in dangerous terrain to convey the tenets of the faith.) The Spanish and Serra are held responsible for reducing the Indian population in California from three hundred thousand in 1769 to two hundred thousand by 1821 (largely through the transmission of diseases). Mission Indians suffered during this time. They were legally under the total control of the Franciscans and were whipped, shackled, and imprisoned—even hunted if they fled.

Indians were often forced to convert at gunpoint, and their life expectancy in the mission was just ten years.[22] The pope defended his action by declaring that Serra "sought to defend the dignity of the native community, to protect it from those who had mistreated and abused it," and he "sowed the seeds of Christian faith amid the momentous changes wrought by the arrival of European settlers in the New World."[23] Some may think that the climate in the Indian boarding schools was more civilized than the brutal actions of the conquistadors, but survivors note that the schools took more than hands and feet—they destroyed lives.

In June 2021, Deb Haaland, the Secretary of the Interior, announced that the United States Department of the Interior will investigate federal Indian boarding schools. This announcement was made after the discovery of the graves of 215 children who attended a Roman Catholic Indian boarding school in Kamloops, British Columbia. At the height of the Indian boarding school movement in the United States, there were 350 Indian boarding schools. The National Native American Boarding School Healing Coalition is working on this project, but at the time of this writing, they did not know how many Indigenous children had perished in the system.

11

The Drunken Indian Stereotype

The white people buy and sell false rights to our lands, and your employers have, you say, paid a great price for their rights. They must have a
plenty of money to spend it in buying false rights to lands belonging to
Indians.

—Red Jacket (Seneca), 1811

From the earliest interaction with Native Americans, Europeans coveted their
land and resources. Through warfare and Indian boarding schools' forcible assimilation, White people's orientation to Native Americans can be characterized as genocidal because they attempted to destroy their culture and traditions as well as the
Indians themselves.

The collective social, political, and health status of Native Americans in the
United States today is appalling, and one of the most devastating, enduring stereotypes about them is their propensity to abuse alcohol. The U.S. Indian Health Service has declared that alcohol along with tobacco and drug dependence constitute
an urgent health problem for Native Americans. In a given year, approximately 12
percent of the deaths among Native Americans are alcohol related. This rate is four
times higher than the general population. Alcoholism is more common among Native
American men than women, and the Northern Plains Indians have higher rates than
other tribes. In some tribes, fetal alcohol syndrome among live births is seven times
the national average.

Traditional mythology about Native Americans holds that Indians have a biological predisposition to alcoholism—they can't hold their liquor. It was this "drunken
Indian" stereotype that was used to deceive and manipulate them. Colonists tried to
depopulate Indian lands by plying Native Americans with alcohol so they could steal
their resources. Benjamin Franklin observed in his *Autobiography*: "And, indeed, if it
be the design of Providence to extirpate these Savages in order to make room for cultivators of the earth, it seems not improbable that rum may be the appointed means.
It had already annihilated all the tribes who formerly inhabited the sea-coast."[1]

The strategy of utilizing alcohol as a trading commodity with Indians was
embarked on by English and French explorers and traders—men like Henry Hudson
and Jacques Cartier, and, later, the famous Captain James Cook who explored Canada
and the Pacific Ocean. Bonnie Duran, a public health professor, traced the evolution
of the "drunken Indian" stereotype of Native Americans as violent, lawless, impetuous, and genetically incapable of handling alcoholic beverages to fourteenth- and

PUCK.

THE HOSTILES ON THE TRAIL.

"President Arthur, on his trip to the Yellowstone region, will join one of Gen. Sheridan's 'Military Exploring Parties.' There is a tradition among the Indians that you can always identify the trail of 'Little Phil's' exploring parties by the empty whiskey bottles, etc., scattered along the line of march."—*Brooklyn Eagle*.

The drunken Indian stereotype, in *Puck Magazine*, January 1, 1883 (Transcendental Graphics, Getty Images).

fifteenth-century European themes about "wild men,"[2] but it came into prominence in the United States in the late seventeenth and eighteenth centuries with the influx of European settlers in North America.[3] The noted "father of American psychiatry," Dr. Benjamin Rush, depicted Native Americans as constitutionally prone to slothfulness and drunkenness, perpetuating the prevailing stereotype about their genetic inferiority and inability to become civilized and participate in White society.

In their classic analysis of Native American inebriation, anthropologists Craig Mac Andrew and Robert Edgerton documented early interactions between Whites and Indians with regard to trading and the use of alcohol.[4] Negative stereotypical comments about Indian abuses of alcohol were rampant, e.g., Father Chrestien Le Clereq's late seventeenth century characterization was not unique: "Lewdness, adulteries, incests, and several crimes which decency keeps me from naming, are the usual disorders which are committed through the trade in brandy, of which some traders make use in order to abuse the Indian women, who yield themselves readily during their drunkenness to all kinds of indecency.... Injuries, quarrels, homicides, murders, parricides are to this day the sad consequences of the trade in brandy; and one sees with grief Indians dying in their drunkenness."[5]

Looking between the lines of this negative characterization, one apprehends what Mac Andrew and Edgerton conclude—it was the practice of traders and some merchants to intoxicate Indians and manipulate them into disadvantageous agreements that were detrimental to their well-being for the purpose of obtaining their resources, most notably, land. As Duran concluded, "Native drinking, despite all statements to the contrary, was encouraged in order to increase trade profit, induce concessions, and sap the strength of the tribes."[6]

Alcoholic drinks were known to some Native groups in North and South America prior to the influx of European settlers in the seventeenth, eighteenth, and nineteenth centuries, but many groups of Indigenous people were unfamiliar with the rum, brandy, and wine that traders and merchants proffered to them. The strategy of disempowering and destabilizing Native American societies by introducing alcohol was effective. In fact, the dissipation and disintegration of Native American society through alcohol abuse had progressed to such an extent that a federal law was passed in 1832 making it illegal to provide alcohol to Indians throughout the United States and its territories—a law that was often flouted but not officially abandoned until 1953.[7]

While the stereotypical conception of intoxicated, violent, aggressive, and socially inept Indians pervades the public consciousness, a meticulous review of historical documents dating back to initial contacts with Europeans by MacAndrew and Edgerton demonstrated the fallacy of such conclusions. In fact, reports of interactions between European explorers and naive Indians revealed their passive, nonviolent reactions to alcoholic drinks when they became inebriated, and they concluded that "when the North American Indians' initial experience with alcohol was untutored by expectations to the contrary, the result was neither the development of an all-consuming craving nor an epic of drunken mayhem and debauchery."[8] This conclusion is supported by the historical fact that leading Native American prophets like the Seneca Nation's Handsome Lake (circa 1800 and the Shawnee leader Tenskwatawa (circa 1800), advised their followers to be judicious in the use of alcohol.[9]

If, as the observations of some Jesuits and traders suggest, Native Americans often avoided alcohol and comported themselves civilly when intoxicated, what accounts for documented observations depicting them as wild drunken barbarians? While the stereotype of the "drunken Indian" was an accurate description of *some* inebriated Native Americans, it was not an accurate generalization of the behavior of *all* intoxicated Indians. Not having experience with the disinhibiting effects of alcohol, Indians learned from observing intoxicated White people the violent and uncivilized behavior that might accompany the abuse of alcohol.

There is reason to believe that the behavior of drunken White people often terrified Native Americans. As the English trader Alexander Henry noted in 1809, "My hunters and other men have been drinking and rioting since yesterday; they make more d---d noise and trouble than a hundred Blackfeet."[10] Similarly, trader Daniel Harmon noted that the French Canadians were more violent and barbarian than the Indians when intoxicated: "Of all the people in the world, I think the Canadians, when drunk, are the most disagreeable; for excessive drinking generally causes them to quarrel and fight, among themselves. Indeed, I had rather have fifty drunken Indians in the fort, than five drunken Canadians."[11]

Sufficient reports contradicting the "drunken Indian" stereotype caused MacAndrew and Edgerton to conclude: "So, in account after account we are informed of the whimsical effects that alcohol had upon the Indians of North America. Sometimes the changes in comportment that accompanied drunkenness were highly dramatic, and sometimes they were virtually nonexistent; moreover, when changes did occur, while the typical transformation was from sober tranquility to drunken hostility and violence, exactly the opposite order was not infrequently observed."[12]

Further challenging the "drunken Indian" stereotype is the fact that some Native Americans mimicked White people, feigning drunkenness as an excuse for otherwise illegal or morally reprehensible behavior. Perhaps the most devastating repercussion of the contact and manipulation experienced by Native Americans in White society was the replacement of their culture with European White values. Some feigned obeisance, others attempted to assimilate, but by and large, Native American attempts at assimilation led to pain and dysfunction. In time, as Duran noted, "[A]lcohol was associated with assimilation and, like other white cultural artifacts, such as food and clothing, was condemned as a threat to Native identity."[13]

In fact, MacAndrew and Edgerton provide abundant evidence that prereservation Indians *did not* indiscriminately misbehave violently when drunk, and they were no more likely than White people to evince uncivilized behavior. Accounts of misbehaving drunken Indians were not infrequently based on exaggerated stereotypical ethnocentric ramblings of White people, most often French clergy and fur traders, concluding that "when writers subjected the severity of drunken changes-for-the-worse [after drinking] to specific comparisons of white versus Indian, the Indian not infrequently had to settle for second place."[14] Indignation about the drunken Indian stereotype even led authors Roxanne Dunbar-Ortiz and Dina Gilio-Whitaker to conclude, "To even suggest that Indians are simply more prone to alcohol abuse than non–Natives implicitly makes assumptions about the superiority of the dominant white society and thus the inferiority of Native peoples."[15]

Though early anthropologists like A. I. Hallowell[16] subscribed to the genetic explanation that attributed Native American antisocial behavior to their constitutional inability to reasonably manage alcohol, modern scientific genetic research disproves this widely held assumption. But despite the popularity of such viewpoints, researchers like MacAndrew and Edgerton, half a century ago, realized the importance of learning and situational norms as primary determinants of the way people behave while consuming alcohol. To assume that Native Americans have a physiological flaw predisposing them to alcoholism is tantamount to the racism of eugenicists who opposed the influx of immigrants from Eastern and Southern Europe in the early twentieth century under the assumption they would pollute the gene pool in the United States. Such backward views are not only unscientific, but they also ignore the negative effects of centuries of White domination and exploitation of Native Americans—the theft of land, desecration of their habitat and resources, destruction of their families through forced displacement, removal to reservations and boarding schools, and genocidal policies that led to the abrogation of hundreds of treaties by the U.S. government.

Modern science has helped dispel the fallacious genetic drunken Indian stereotype. A national study comparing the drinking behavior of 171, 858 White people and 4,201 Native Americans during the years 2009–13 found that *more* Native Americans abstained from drinking in a month's time than White people (60 percent compared to 43 percent), and more than twice as many White people as Native Americans were light to moderate drinkers (33 percent compared to 15 percent). No significant differences between the two groups were found in the number of people who were classified as binge drinkers (approximately 17 percent) and heavy drinkers (approximately

8 percent). The scientists concluded that Native Americans had lower or comparable rates of alcohol consumption across a range of alcohol consumption measures.[17]

An analysis of genetic studies of Native American substance abuse issues in the *American Journal of Psychiatry* stated: "The high rates of substance dependence seen in some tribes is likely a combination of a lack of genetic protective factors (metabolizing enzyme variants) combined with genetically mediated risk factors (externalizing traits, consumption drive, and drug sensitivity tolerance) that combine with key environmental factors (trauma exposure, early age at onset use, and environmental hardship) to produce an elevated risk for the disorder." The authors concluded that "these studies suggest that the regions of the genome that influence externalizing disorders and substance dependence in Native Americans are most likely similar to those found in the general population." And there is "little overall evidence to support a genetic association specific to a Native American tribal group or to the Native American population as a whole."[18]

Dysfunction and Death

Essentially, the researchers concluded that there are biological markers present in Native Americans that predispose them to substance abuse, **but** these markers are also present in the general non–Native American population. In other words, no significant genetic differences have been found between Native Americans and non–Native Americans in their propensity for substance abuse. The explanation for their extraordinarily high rates of abuse lies elsewhere.

One cannot ignore the experiences of Indians in pre- and post-reservation living and their effects on alcohol use and abuse—their displacement from their land and resources, their immiseration, and the associated social and psychological trauma eventuated in substance abuse, destitution, emotional disorders, and suicide. These factors all contribute to the social, emotional, and cultural influences that predispose some Native Americans to abuse alcohol as Fred Beauvais, a psychologist who has researched the issue of Native Americans and alcoholism, concluded: "So far the evidence seems to indicate that although some proportion of alcoholism risk may be heritable, this trait varies more within population groups than between them."[19]

Just how devastating life can be for Native Americans is glimpsed in their outsized rates of poverty, unemployment, and suicide. A report by the National Center for Health Statistics in 2016 found that the suicide rate for Native American males and females evidenced the most dramatic increase of any ethnic group over the last thirty years—rates rose by 89 percent for Native American women and 38 percent for Native American men. In the eighteen-to-twenty-four-year age group, Native American males were more likely to commit suicide than females (34.9 per 100,000 versus 9.9 female deaths per 100,000 people), which was twice the rate of other racial and gender subgroups in the population of the United States. Even more disturbing, the government report noted that suicides among Native Americans and Alaska Natives are underreported by as much as 30 percent.[20]

The suicide rate of Native Americans ages fifteen to thirty-four is four times higher than the national rate, and on selected reservations it reaches astounding and shocking levels. For example, eleven people between the ages of twelve and twenty-four took their own lives during the first half of 2015 on the Oglala Sioux Pine Ridge Reservation in South Dakota.[21]

The reservation covers two million acres and is home to a transient population of sixteen thousand to forty thousand Indians. The site of the Wounded Knee Massacre in 1890, today's life expectancy for men is less than fifty years (the lowest in the Western Hemisphere). The county where the reservation is located has the highest poverty in the United States and contains high rates of alcoholism, drug abuse, violence, and unemployment. There were nearly one thousand suicide attempts on the reservation between 2004 and 2013. Said Erin Bailey, executive director of the Center for Native American Youth at the Aspen Institute: "This is the result of historical trauma, chronically underfunded health care services, education, roads, water."[22]

On the Gila River Indian Reservation in central Arizona, home of the O'odham and Pee Posh peoples, eight young people committed suicide in 2014. There, one-fourth of Indian children live in poverty amid what has been described as "historical trauma," "crushing hopelessness," and "despair." Children are twice as likely to die before the age of twenty-four than the rest of the nation.[23]

The alarming rate of Native American youth suicide prompted a call for a federal study of the problem by U.S. Senator John Thune (R–South Dakota) in 2015. A year earlier, former U.S. Senator Byron Dorgan (D–North Dakota), who cochaired the Attorney General's Advisory Committee on American Indian and Alaska Native Children Exposed to Violence, noted that the high suicide rate among Native American youth is linked to a "trail of broken promises to American Indians" going back to treaties of the nineteenth century that guaranteed but didn't deliver health care, education, and housing.[24] The committee found rampant violence perpetrated on Native American and Alaska Native children and concluded that the rates for post-traumatic stress disorder among them was the same as veterans returning from Afghanistan and Iraq—triple the rate for the general population—and cautioned service providers and policy makers that they "should assume that *all* AI and AN children have been exposed to violence."[25]

Joe Flood, a *New York Times* reporter, speculated that the high suicide rate among Native American youth might be related to the problem of sexual abuse experienced by many Native American children. For example, a teacher on the Pine Ridge Lakota Sioux Reservation was told by a veteran teacher shortly after starting work there that most of the girls and many of the boys had been molested or raped by the time they reached high school.[26]

The extent of violence and sexual violence committed against Native Americans and Alaska Natives is staggering. As of 2016, 5,712 missing Native American women were reported to the National Crime Information Center. More than half of Native American women have been sexually assaulted, one in three are raped during their lifetimes, and 60 percent (three in five) are physically assaulted. The rate of sexual assaults against Native American women is 2.5 times that of White women. Native women are twice as likely as non–Native women to be stalked, and their murder rate is ten times the national average.

The most comprehensive survey ever conducted on the extent of violence among Native Americans, *Violence Against American Indian and Alaska Native Women and Men*, done by the National Institute of Justice for the U.S. Department of Justice, was based on interviews with 2,473 adult Native women and 1,505 adult Native men who self-identified as Indigenous people alone or in combination with another racial group. More than four in five Native women (84.3 percent) and men (81.6 percent) reported experiencing violence in their lifetimes. Over half the women (56.1 percent) and more than a quarter (27.5 percent) of the men had experienced sexual violence, and over half (55.5 percent) of the women and nearly half (43.2 percent) of the men had experienced physical violence by an intimate partner. Two-thirds (66.4 percent) of the women reported experiencing psychological aggression as did nearly three-quarters (73 percent) of the men.[27]

Extrapolating these figures to the total Native American and Alaska Native population means that over 1.5 million Native women and 1.4 million Native men have experienced violence in their lives. Interestingly, Native American and Alaska Native men and women are victimized disproportionately by an interracial perpetrator—not another Native person. And although many victims needed services (e.g., medical and legal), over a third (38 percent) of the women and 17 percent of the men were unable to obtain them.[28]

Native American communities in the region of the Bakken oil fields (North Dakota, Montana, Saskatchewan, and Manitoba) were bracing for a new wave of violence against Indian women as the demand for oil brought a new cadre of shiftless predatory laborers into their homelands. Some of these men hold stereotypes about Native American women as hypersexualized objects. As Lisa Brunner, codirector of the Indigenous Women's Human Rights Collective and professor and cultural coordinator at the White Earth Tribal and Community College in Mahnomen, Minnesota, remarked: "We as Native women are hunted. We are deliberately sought after by sexual predators."[29]

One of the most perplexing findings from this report concerns the high incidence of violence committed against Native people by non–Native perpetrators. Until recently, Native Americans were impeded in their quest for justice because Indians did not have criminal authority over non–Indians—the group that perpetrates 88 percent of the violent crimes against Native women and men. More than three-quarters of the people on tribal lands and 68 percent of the people in Alaska Native villages are non–Indians. Between 2005 and 2009 U.S. attorneys declined to prosecute over two-thirds of Indian Country sexual abuse cases, let alone investigate them.[30]

A report released by the Urban Indian Health Institute (UIHI) revealed that thousands of Indigenous women have disappeared in urban areas of this country and *most* of them were unaccounted for in law enforcement files. Only 116 Indigenous women and girls out of 5,712 who were missing in 2017 were found in the U.S. Department of Justice files, yet the Centers for Disease Control and Prevention lists murder as the third leading cause of death among American Indian and Alaska Native women, with rates of violence on reservations as much as ten times higher than the national average. The UIHI received minimal assistance from many law enforcement agencies in the seventy-one cities it surveyed. Most of the Indigenous girls and women (80 percent), with an average age of twenty-nine, had gone missing since the year 2000.

The lack of support the UIHI received from law enforcement agencies around the country is reflected in the fact that only forty agencies (56 percent) provided some level of assistance to their research. Many of the missing girls and women were presumed murdered based on UIHI's review and analysis of available information, yet more than 95 percent of the cases in the study were never reported in national or international media. The researchers concluded that the lack of quality data about these girls and women was the result of underreporting, racial misclassification, poor record keeping, institutionalized racism in the media, and the lack of substantive relationships between journalists, law enforcement agencies, and Indigenous communities, noting: "If this report demonstrates one powerful conclusion, it is that if we rely solely on law enforcement or media for an awareness or understanding of this issue, we will have a deeply inaccurate picture of the realities, minimizing the extent to which our urban American Indian and Alaska Native sisters experience this violence."[31]

Despite some changes in laws pertaining to crimes committed on reservations, a 2016 report by the U.S. Department of Justice revealed that 680 cases of crimes on Indian reservations were closed without referral for prosecution—most for insufficient evidence.[32] Decisions to forgo prosecution of cases on reservations stem from a 1978 U.S. Supreme Court decision (*Oliphant v. Suquamish Indian Tribe*), which banned tribes from prosecuting non–Indians. This position held until a Special Domestic Violence Criminal Jurisdiction Statute was added to the reauthorization of the Violence Against Women Act (VAWA) in 2013. This statute gave tribes jurisdiction over non–Indians in cases of domestic violence, dating violence, and violations of protective orders that occur in Indian Country if the victim is a Native American and the perpetrator is non–Indian and works, lives, or has an intimate relation on tribal lands. This change gives Indigenous people an important option in their quest for justice, but many tribes have yet to comply with federal regulations such as guaranteeing diverse juries for the accused, and so the injustice continues and with it the insecurity and fear that provide fertile ground for the social and psychological trauma that pervades Native American and Alaska Natives' lives.[33]

In his book about the history of Illinois, James Gray discussed the culture and temperament of the now extinct Illinois Indian tribe, drawing a profound conclusion about Native Americans: "It has ever been the way of the white man in his relation with the Indian, first to sentimentalize him as a monster until he has been killed off or conquered and, second, to sentimentalize him in retrospect as the 'noble' savage."[34]

In many ways, our discussion about Native Americans has led us to a similar conclusion: The presence of Indigenous people in North, Central, and South America, indeed throughout the world, represented at first a curiosity to Europeans, and then an encumbrance as the invading/colonizing/imperialistic and exploitative designs of the visitors became paramount. Initially, as we have seen, Indigenous people were depicted as strange, even alien beings, lacking European moral and ethical values and behavior. Stereotypes such as subhuman, barbaric, scalping, man-eating savages facilitated the treatment of Indians and other Indigenous people as uncivilized, soulless heathens at once childlike in their natural state, but fearsome, even loathsome, when aroused or intoxicated. These stereotypes continue to adversely influence the lives of Indigenous people and distort the perspectives of the dominant White society about them.

12

Indian Casinos:
Winners and Losers
in the Game of Life

> The economic world of many tribes has been turned upside down, and
> there is not a welcome prospect of any stability in the immediate future.
> —Vine Deloria, Jr., "Anthros, Indians, and Planetary Reality"

Indian gaming is a misunderstood phenomenon in our society. A stereotype gaining popularity is that Native Americans are becoming wealthy from their casinos, yet the reality is quite different. From the first Indian gaming venture in 1979 that became known as "high stakes bingo" in Florida, the evolution of gambling on Native American reservations has grown into a multibillion-dollar industry, but with a few exceptions, Native Americans are not reaping the benefits of these endeavors, despite their seeming success.

Indian lands are sovereign territory, but they must comply with the Indian Gaming Regulatory Act of 1988 and other relevant state and federal laws. The growth of gaming on Indian tribal lands has been phenomenal. About half (244) of the federally recognized tribes, operating in twenty-eight states, had gaming revenues that accounted for $33.8 billion in 2018—a sum representing about a quarter of all legal gambling receipts in the United States. Another $5.3 billion was generated in ancillary revenue.

Tribal gaming ranked eighty-eight by economic impact among all 538 industry sectors in the United States in 2018, ahead of "bottle and soft drinks," "gasoline stores," "furniture and home finishing stores," and "retail sporting goods, hobby and musical instruments."[1] The industry is expanding rapidly with an increase in gaming revenues of 4.28 percent in 2018 over 2017 and ancillary revenues increasing 9.63 percent.

There are three major classifications of Indian gaming. Class I falls under the purview of tribal regulations and includes Indian gaming that may be part of tribal ceremonies and celebrations as well as social gaming for minimal prizes. Class II gaming includes bingo, pull tabs, and similar games as well as nonbanked card games where players compete against one another—not the house. Tribes can license and regulate Class II games if the tribe is in a state that permits such gaming and the tribal government adopts a gaming ordinance approved by the National Indian Gaming Commission (NIGC). Tribal governments regulate Class II gaming with oversight from the NIGC.

Class III includes all forms of gaming not in Classes I and II and pertains to casino style games (e.g., slot machines, blackjack, roulette, craps, and other wagering games of chance). The types of gaming in Indian casinos must already be permitted by the state where the tribe is located, and tribes must negotiate a compact with the state that must be approved by the Secretary of the Interior. The chairman of the NIGC must also approve the tribal gaming ordinance.

The U.S. government delegates to state governments the right to negotiate compacts with tribes seeking to establish Indian gaming operations (e.g., casinos). For this imprimatur, states take a percentage of casino revenues, usually between 10 and 25 percent. The agreed-upon sum can be vital to the integrity of the operation where margins between success and failure hang in the balance. At times, the Seminole Tribe and the state of Florida cannot agree on the fee or conditions; Florida was without an executed compact for six years. A new compact was reached in May 2021, giving the Indians a percentage of sports betting wagers and the right to expand existing games and casinos, but the deal is being challenged in the courts.

There are signs of unrest in other states, too. Governor Ned Lamont of Connecticut is embroiled in a compact dispute with Native Americans who own the two casinos in his state, and so is Governor Kevin Stitt in Oklahoma who is seeking to renegotiate that state's Indian Gaming Compact with thirty-five participating tribes. Apparently, all three states are resisting granting Indians exclusivity rights to sports betting, and they are having second thoughts about the size of fees being received by the states from Indian gaming operations. More dissension among states can be expected as laws and technology impact Indian gaming operations.

The 506 Indian gaming operations[2] run by 252 tribes in 28 states generated 766,000 direct and indirect jobs in 2018, but over half of them were filled by non–Indian employees. The overall economic output of the Indian gaming industry in 2018 was $87,023,847,012, with $17,243,917,654 generated for federal and state governments. Over $90 billion from 2013 to 2018 plus an additional $20 billion was contributed to Social Security and Medicare through employers and employees.[3]

While tribal gaming ranks twelfth among the top employers in the United States, ahead of Walgreens and Starbucks, not all Native Americans are benefiting from this enterprise.

Nationwide, prior to the COVID-19 pandemic, the unemployment rate among Native Americans was twice that of White people and has remained at double digit levels for more than five years. Although 39 percent of tribes have casinos, only 12 percent generate 68 percent of Indian gaming revenue. The top five states generating jobs, labor income, economic output, and taxes (California, Oklahoma, Florida, Washington, and Arizona) dwarf the other twenty-three states in these categories (e.g., generating 55 percent of the jobs). Only a quarter of tribes with gaming operations issue a per capita check to tribal members, which is subject to federal taxes. Less than 9 percent of Native Americans profit from gaming, and much of this is the result of tribal government expenditures on services, and economic and community development.

Indian casinos in just three states with less than 3 percent of the total Native American population account for nearly half (44 percent) of total Indian casino revenue, whereas casinos in five states with more than half of the Native American population account for less than 3 percent of total Indian casino revenue. Since most tribes require their members to live on reservations to receive distributions from profits, and about three-quarters of Native Americans live off them, most tribal members do not receive gaming revenue payments.

A related phenomenon is the matter of who runs Indian gaming operations. Although some tribes maintain managerial control over casinos on their land, others have arrangements with for-profit corporations that provide managerial expertise for a fee. But there is growing interest among Native Americans in the management of gaming operations, and extensive training opportunities are promoted by the National Indian Gaming Association.[4]

Although revenues to Indians and states can be substantial, there have been instances of abuse and outright fraud concerning funds generated by Indian gaming. For example, Washington, D.C., lobbyist Jack Abramoff charged Indian tribes $85 million between 1995 and 2004 to promote and protect their gaming interests while *lobbying against them*. He served forty-three months in prison for fraud and corruption. More recently, the long-time chair of the Seminole Nation in Florida, Chief Jim Billie, was recalled by a unanimous vote in September 2016, and Marcellus Osceola, Jr., was elected the seventh tribal council president. Billie had a checkered career as the head of the Seminole Nation and had been suspended without pay in 2001 after it was revealed that he moved $60 million in tribal funds to a brokerage account and funneled tribal funds into a secret offshore internet gambling venture. It was discovered that he had also invested in an airplane manufacturing plant, made a down payment on a $30 million luxury jet, and started a cattle operation in Nicaragua. Despite these contretemps, he received $600,000 in a legal settlement with the tribe and was reelected chair in 2011 and 2015.[5]

While net revenues from Indian gaming may be distributed to members of individual tribes, the proceeds are often far less than the public's assumption: Per capita income among Native Americans is less than half of the national average, and the median household income of Native Americans was only about 70 percent of the national average ($38,530 versus $55, 775) in 2015.

The amount of money distributed to individual tribal members varies based on a number of considerations. Paramount among them is the tribe's Revenue Allocation Plan, which is its specific policy for the use of gaming revenues. These plans are filed annually with the U.S. government and must be approved by the Bureau of Indian Affairs (BIA), which resides in the U.S. Department of the Interior.

Before funds can be spent, a tribe's Revenue Allocation Plan must be approved by the secretary for the Department of the Interior. Many tribes do not distribute funds directly to their members because they fear adverse effects on them (e.g., dependence on tribal governments, lowered work ethic, and decreased motivation for educational advancement).[6] Some nations, like the Navajo, designate gaming revenues for the construction and maintenance of schools, infrastructure (building and maintaining roads) on reservations, cultural and athletic activities, and health care initiatives (e.g., to supplement BIA health programs).

Gaming net profits can only be used to fund tribal government operations or programs, provide for the general welfare of tribe members, promote tribal economic development, donate to charitable organizations, and help fund local government operations. Consequently, most of the profit is not distributed to individuals. About seventy-five tribes make per capita payments, but few disburse large sums of money.

The amount distributed per capita also depends on the number of people who receive it, the amount of gaming revenue available for disbursement at the end of the year, the locale and magnitude of the gaming industry on the reservation, as well as management fees that may be paid by the tribe to the company running the gambling establishments, and the fees paid to the host state in their compact. Felons are not eligible to receive shares of net gambling revenues.

The Blue Lake Rancheria tribe in northern California illustrates how gaming revenues can improve a tribe's quality of life. Located on ninety-one acres five miles from the Pacific coast, it is partnering with the state of California, private industry, academia, and the federal government to develop clean, renewable energy. Recently, the tribe installed solar panels and reduced energy costs on the reservation by $250,000 a year. The tribe is one of the largest employers in Humboldt County and has infused over $60 million from gaming revenues into the local economy. By March 2017, the tribe's contributions to education exceeded $1.5 million that went to a local school, scholarships, and community workforce development.[7]

A wide variation in per capita distribution exists among the tribes. For example, the Shakopee Mdewakanton (Lakota) tribe outside the Twin Cities in Minnesota may be the richest tribe in the nation, distributing over a million dollars per person per annum from casino revenues from their two casinos. But the tribe is small (around five hundred people), and it donates more money to charity than wealthy Minnesota businesses like the 3M Corporation.[8]

Alternatively, the 286,000 Navajos (the largest Native American nation) decided against per capita payments more than half a century ago in favor of distributing revenues for community services.[9] The Navajo gaming enterprise is small compared to some Native American gaming initiatives. The practice of receiving federal and gaming funds has led to internecine struggles between full-blooded and partial-blooded Native Americans over who is eligible to receive stipends, at times leading to the termination of tribes.[10]

Just 12 percent of Native American gaming establishments generate about two-thirds of Indian gaming revenues. About 175 Indian gaming establishments are marginal enterprises. Many Indian casinos are in rural areas like the ones I observed on the Oglala Lakota Pine Ridge Reservation in South Dakota (Prairie Wind Casino and Hotel) and the Standing Rock casino near Fort Yates, North Dakota (Prairie Knights Casino and Resort). Research indicates that a casino needs to be within fifty miles of a metropolitan area with at least ten thousand people to be highly profitable, therefore, the majority of Native American casinos are not doing well financially because they are in rural areas. The most successful growth in the industry has occurred in populous areas of the West Coast, especially California.

Two of the largest Indian casinos, Mashantucket Pequot, known popularly as Foxwoods, in Ledyard, Connecticut, and the Mohegan Sun casino in Uncasville, Connecticut (Cooper would be smiling), have racked up enormous debts totaling nearly $3.3 billion. The accounting firm of Deloitte and Touche noted, "These matters raise a substantial doubt about the enterprise's [Foxwoods] ability to continue as a going concern."[11] Some of the problems for these casinos were related to their expansion immediately prior to the severe economic downturn in our economy beginning in 2007. Then, too, there has been a proliferation of other Native American and state casinos following their opening, further eroding their economic base. Lori Potter, director of communications for Foxwoods, assured me that the casino operation was again on solid ground. "In 1992 when we opened Foxwoods, the only gaming jurisdictions in the United States were Atlantic City, the State of Nevada, and the Mashantucket Pequot Indian Reservation. Back then we had a monopoly on gaming in the Northeast and since we were in the most populated corridor of the country, Foxwoods Resort Casino was an overnight success, bringing in over $1 billion a year in revenue. Our strategy ... is to continue enhancing our resort and attract both local and travel destination clientele."[12] This includes building championship golf courses and bringing in celebrity talent to entertain patrons.

Although there is some controversy surrounding the lineage of some current members of the Mashantucket Pequot tribe, there can be little doubt that the man who created the concept of gaming on the Pequot Reservation, Skip Hayward, was a visionary. Rising above the hills of eastern Connecticut, the resort is a conglomeration of buildings composed of nine million square feet. When I visited the facility on October 5, 2018, I began by going through the cavernous 308,000-square-foot Mashantucket Pequot Museum and Research Center, which cost $193.4 million and opened in 1998. It is flanked by an enormous 185-foot-tall observation tower and an accompanying zip line that runs from the museum to the casino.

After paying my senior admission fee of $15, I entered and was struck by the sheer size of the building and how empty it was. I could count the number of visitors on one hand. Immediately, I was confronted by two life-size dugout canoes occupied by realistic-looking models of Pequot Indians from four hundred years ago. The other exhibits featured a variety of scenes from the Ice Age and what life was like for members of this tribe hundreds of years ago. There are dazzling displays of Native American art, and life-like mannequins in a variety of scenes growing and harvesting food and hunting.

One of the most interesting exhibits is a room dedicated to displaying portraits and photographs of current tribal members. A background recording broadcasts over the loudspeaker that one should not dwell on the apparent discrepancy between the public's stereotypical conception of what Indians should look like (an observation reinforced by the mannequins liberally dispersed throughout the museum) and the smiling faces of Black and White tribal members.

A short distance from the museum is the casino complex—a sprawling group of buildings that stands out against the wooded hills of the reservation. The nearly full parking garage adjacent to the casino held vehicles with license plates from around the region, but mostly Connecticut. Inside, the cavernous rooms are, like most casinos, dimly lit except for the flashing slot machines with their garish colors and sounds designed to lure customers. It was midafternoon on a Friday, and many of the tables were active, although the facility was operating at much less than capacity. Still the clank of the slots and the fast pace and smiling faces of the crowds in the halls gave the impression that patrons were enjoying their experience.

Less than ten miles away stands the ultramodern competition: Mohegan Sun, a casino complex made of glass and metal with names on the high-rise parking garage like Indian Summer and Autumn, controlled by the Mohegan tribe of approximately two thousand people. A visitor is immediately alerted to performances by celebrities on flashing signs surrounding the complex. The hustle and bustle inside were accentuated by an ongoing slot machine tournament that pitted female and male contestants against one another for a $50,000 prize held in a hallway adjacent to larger rooms (e.g., Hall of Lost Tribes) containing the ubiquitous and (profitable) slot machines. A large number of Asian people thronged around a roulette wheel and nearby black-jack and baccarat tables. In the hall I spoke briefly with an Asian marketing manager responsible for recruiting them. I complimented him on his success and made for the nearest exit, past the themed restaurants, Starbucks, and candy shops, past the throngs of prospective winners, to the serenity of my Subaru, and I headed home.

No one disputes that Indian casino gambling is a big business and a winner for states in some locations. The largest Native American casino, WinStar World Casino in Thackerville, Oklahoma, near the border with Texas, controlled by the Chickasaw Nation, has contributed over $1 billion to the state of Oklahoma since 2006. But for many tribes, deficits are a reality. Foxwood's Resort Casino experienced a 28 percent decline in revenue in the first quarter of 2017 compared to the same quarter in 2016. Gaming revenues accounted for 78.3 percent of overall revenues of the casino's gross—virtually unchanged from the previous year. Some savings were derived from cutting some of the 4,800 full-time workforce, but the Mashantucket Pequot Gaming Enterprise continues to operate under the terms of a forbearance agreement it reached with senior tribal leaders in 2014 after it was found to be in violation of a 2013 debt-restructuring agreement. The financial distress of the organization continues. Foxwoods' revenues were down nearly 8 percent in the third quarter of 2019 compared to the previous year.[13] Nevertheless, the enterprise was planning to build a Foxwoods-branded casino in Biloxi, Mississippi, but according to Brian Hallenbeck, a reporter who covers Indian gaming for *The Day*, the project may have been scrapped.[14] Another project with the Mohegan tribe, to develop a casino in East Windsor, Connecticut, which the tribes have already spent $20 million on, has encountered opposition from the MGM Resorts International group that recently built a casino in nearby Springfield, Massachusetts, and proposed building a casino in Bridgeport,[15] and the Trump Administration was stonewalling their application. Yet financial contributions from Native American casinos to the state of Connecticut have been considerable. The Foxwoods Casino, the first Native American casino in the United States, and one of the largest in North America, contributed over $4 billion from slot machine revenue to the state between the years 1993 and 2017.

Obviously, Foxwoods and Mohegan Sun are challenged by the saturation of the gaming market and are trying to reinvent themselves to maintain a competitive edge.[16] Communications Director Potter at the Mashantucket casino (Foxwoods) noted that in the early 2000s some of the revenue from the casino was distributed to tribal members, but this practice was discontinued. Gaming revenues are now used for a wide variety of purposes in addition to expanding the operation and making it "a fully integrated resort experience offering something exciting for everyone." Revenues go to operate police and fire departments, 911 dispatch and emergency medical services, security and surveillance, a natural gas power facility, water and sewage treatment plants, waste removal and recycling, education from preschool through college for tribal members, a child development center, youth programs, child protective and other social services, a pharmacy, the Pequot Native American museum, regulatory oversight bodies for gaming and natural resources protection and preservation, and inspections for food, safety, and employment.[17]

Mohegan Sun Casino, Uncasville, Connecticut (Mohegan Sun).

While some tribes and their members may benefit from the proceeds of legal gambling, the data consistently indicate that the legalization of gambling on Indian land has not appreciably improved the lot of the Native American population. One exception might be the members of the Seminole tribe in Florida, but a series by the *St. Petersburg Times* in 1997 (now the *Tampa Bay Times*) revealed widespread fraud and misuse of federal funds received for children in its Headstart program and questionable housing subsidies from the federal Department of Housing and Urban Development.[18]

In the final analysis, Indian gaming is no more a panacea for Native American social problems than legalized gambling is for states' financial woes. The ebb and flow of the economy creates large fluctuations in gaming revenue (e.g., the Great Recession of 2007–09 had a devastating impact on gaming revenues, especially in Las Vegas, which saw unemployment and housing foreclosures skyrocket).[19] It became painfully obvious that the Las Vegas economy had to diversify and increase the level of education of residents if the city and state were to become competitive in the future.

Although the gaming industry has increased employment in construction and service industries, these jobs are insufficient for creating a stable flourishing economy. With 27 percent of Native Americans living below the poverty level, they remain the most impoverished ethnic group in the nation,[20] often untouched by the development of the gaming industry and its illusionary rags to riches cachet. Yet research by professors Celeste Lacroix and Jeffrey Hawkins[21] indicates that Native Americans are increasingly being stereotyped as wealthy beneficiaries of the gaming industry. A recent study about the public's perception of Native Americans revealed that one of the most common and pernicious myths about Indians is that they are being enriched through the casino industry.[22]

Ironically, according to an article in the *Washington Post*, some of the responsibility for this stereotype can be traced to the behavior of none other than President Donald Trump, who spread such attitudes about Native Americans while he was actively trying to secure managerial contracts with tribes about to commence casino projects. His vitriolic language attempted to link Native American casinos with organized crime. Speaking on the *Don Imus Radio Show* on June 18, 1993, Trump lambasted the competition: "A lot of these reservations are being, in some people's opinion, at least to a certain extent, run by organized crime and organized crime elements. There's no protection. There's no anything. And it's become a joke."[23]

The *Washington Post* analysis demonstrated Trump's duplicitous machinations and racist attitudes toward Native Americans because some of their casino operations were in competition with his organization. It is likely that some responsibility for the "rich Indian" casino stereotype can be traced to Trump and other White casino industry moguls who covet their operations.

Just as some Native American casinos appeared to be snagging a portion of the nation's nearly $90 billion in gambling revenue in 2019, Social Casinos, which allow people to wager online in casino style games such as blackjack and slots from their phones and computers in the privacy of their homes, soared in popularity. Now estimated to be generating over $5 billion annually for the budding industry, according to a joint exposé by Reveal News and PBS,[24] the industry is targeting potential problem gamblers and luring them into wagering large sums of money with the help of social media corporations like Facebook.

The May 14, 2018, U.S. Supreme Court decision *Murphy v. National Collegiate Athletic Association* (No. 16-476), which overturned the federal law that restricted sports betting to Nevada (the Professional and Amateur Sports Protection Act of 1992 Pub. L. 102-559), has allowed the expansion of the lucrative sports betting industry, which experienced a 65 percent increase in revenues from 2017 to 2018. Now, over half the population of the nation resides in states allowing sports betting, and wagers can be tendered in a variety of venues, including on phones and home computers.

The once burgeoning Indian gaming industry is facing competition from a variety of technologies that may siphon away an increasing amount of funds as well as gamblers. This phenomenon has led many large Indian casinos like Mohegan Sun and Foxwoods to promote their properties as family resorts, much as large casinos do in Nevada, offering a variety of activities from gambling to golf, with options for the whole family, including blockbuster entertainers. In December 2019 Mohegan Sun hosted the Miss America pageant, but times are changing, and the COVID-19 pandemic threatened the very existence of Native American casinos as states impose social distance requirements and enforce stay-at-home policies. It seems that no matter what they do, Indians haven't been able to win in the long-term game of life, but as we will see, their future appears brighter.

13

Making Stereotypes Stick:
Indians as Cultural Artifacts

The Great Spirit made us both. He gave us lands and He gave you lands. You came here and we received you as brothers. When the Almighty made you, He made you all white and clothed you. When He made us He made us with red skins and poor. When you first came we were many and you were few. Now you are many and we are few. You do not know who appears before you to speak. He is a representative of the original American race, the first people of this continent. We are good, and not bad. The reports which you get about us are all on one side.

—Red Cloud, chief of Oglala Sioux, 1870

Native Americans in Newspapers

The role that newspapers have played in the stigmatization of Native Americans has varied since the inception of this nation, rising and falling with events (e.g., the Fetterman and Custer massacres), as well as the distribution of publications. While the distribution of newspapers and periodicals was limited in the early years of the fledgling nation, settlers were exposed to a negative portrayal of Indians in the first newspaper in the English colonies, *Publick Occurrences, Both Foreign and Domestick*, which was filled with news about Indians as enemies in the French and Indian War. Subsequent colonial newspapers printed information about Indians that emphasized their savagery in attacks on White people, a situation that was, in fact, precipitated by White transgressions as well as Native Americans' attempt to terrorize invaders and dissuade them from settling on their land and stealing their resources. Widely circulated accounts of captives were sensationalized in early writing (e.g., the experience of Mary Rowlandson), providing a formula that gripped readers in a timeless stereotypical drama that would be exploited over the next two centuries, replete with negative stereotypes about Indians and their supposed lust for White women and penchant for violence.

The stereotypical depiction of Indians in the press has come under scrutiny, and two analyses of this phenomenon do an admirable job of following the evolution of popular reportage through the nineteenth and twentieth centuries. Nineteenth-century newspaper stories were focused on the western tribes (e.g., the Sioux and Cheyenne), who waged wars of resistance to White incursions. A fascinating exposition of the role played by newspapers in nineteenth-century America is presented in communication Professor John Coward's *The Newspaper Indian*. His meticulous analysis of the press during the pre– and post–Civil War era reveals a pervasive bias against Native Americans that fed into negative popular stereotypes about them. Coward demonstrated the press's habit of dramatizing the plight of "innocent" settlers and exaggerating the bellicosity and viciousness of Indians in conflict with White people. Common themes emphasized wanton violence, bloodlust, carnage (frequently labeled as massacres), torture, mutilation, and murder, but frequently details were absent or even contrived.

Indians were often portrayed as subhuman, without morals and values—uncivilized and incapable of being civilized. Their actions were sensationalized to elicit racial bigotry and hatred toward them. They were labeled ruthless, untrustworthy, and portrayed in unflattering terms with recurrent disparaging adjectives such as heathen, wild, cruel, violent, bloodthirsty, savage, barbarian, evil, murderers, marauders, brutal, ferocious, warlike, treacherous, criminals, hostile, demons, lazy, petty thieves, red devils, and red skins.

The juxtaposition between many of these terms and the prevailing ideological and political climate was anything but accidental. The press largely ignored the forced removal of southern tribes to Indian Territory (Oklahoma), overlooking the pathos and tragedy of the Trail of Tears. Some papers took up the diaspora of the Poncas, who had been displaced from their land through deception by the Bureau of Indian Affairs in the latter part of the nineteenth century. But much of the reporting about Indians in the early decades of that century revolved around a theme that is still operant today: violence sells. This theme, coupled with self-serving political and economic motives of publishers and politicians with vested interests in promoting the displacement of Indians from lands they coveted, was linked with a religious, Christian belief in the moral and racial superiority of White people. Together they helped rationalize the ideology of Manifest Destiny, which provided a multipronged approach that eventually overwhelmed Native Americans in a White invasion. As Coward noted: "Even in the 1830s, violence, not tranquility, was the stuff of news."[1]

The news media often used what Coward termed an "Indian news frame" (i.e., a stereotypical way of reporting about Indians that focused on their unprovoked violence and savagery). Rarely did reporters develop in-depth analyses of Indians' motivation for engaging in conflict, preferring instead to glorify retaliation by troops for depredations ostensibly perpetrated against "innocent" settlers. This process was aided and abetted through telegraphy, which expedited the transmission of bits of news that accentuated the sensational at the expense of in-depth reporting. Combined with the creation of the Associated Press and the use of war correspondents, reporting about Native Americans became increasingly standardized and contained "a limited range of ideas about their lives, their cultures, and their relations with whites in the American West."[2]

In the middle of the century the illustrated press arose, most notably *Frank Leslie's Illustrated Newspaper* (1855) and *Harper's Weekly* (1857). With wide circulations (*Harper's* had a circulation over 120,000 during the Civil War) and lavish illustrations, readers' imaginations were captivated by stereotypical descriptions of Native Americans in wanton acts of savagery that were frequently attributed to the recollections of military men in the field, but, in actuality, were created by artists and writers in New York City. "The myth, after all, was what sold papers."[3]

After Custer's defeat at the Little Bighorn, the anti–Indian rhetoric accelerated in the press, and it was especially deprecating in regions with a salient Indian presence. For example, the Bismarck *Tribune* published this gem on July 12, 1876:

> Let that christian [*sic*] philanthropy which weeps over the death of a lazy, lousy, lying and stealing red skin, whose hands are still reeking with the blood of defenceless [*sic*] women and children, slain on the frontier, and who are ever ready to apologize for these murderers, take a back seat. Invite the soldier to the front and sustain him while he causes the Indians to realize the power, and those that still live to respect the white man. Wipe out all treaties, rub out all agencies and reservations, and treat the Indians as they are, criminals and paupers.[4]

Even news stalwarts like the *New York Times* were not above reinforcing stereotypes about Indians (e.g., references to them as savages were common), especially in relation to the Custer debacle, which may explain the following jaundiced description of murdered Indian Chief Sitting Bull in the paper: "[O]f all the Indians, [Sitting Bull] was the most unrelenting, the most hostile, the most sagacious, the most cruel, and the most desperate foe of any chief of modern times."[5] Not to be outdone, the Boston *Daily Globe* declared, "If Sitting Bull is really dead the impossible has come to pass. He has become a good Indian." The next day the paper stated: "If the parents of SITTING BULL had named him LYING BULL they would have hit nearer the mark. There is no authentic record of any occasion on which the late distinguished Sioux statesman ever told the truth if he was sober."[6]

When the Poncas were illegally forced from their land in the Dakotas in 1877 to Oklahoma by the federal government, more than eighty of them perished along the way. Following a court ruling, which held that they had legal recourse to their original land granted to them by treaty, the *Chicago Tribune* ruefully noted: "Such Indians have laid aside their savage instincts and customs, and they are now law-abiding, frugal, and industrious."[7] Such comments reflect the reality that newspapers' support of Indians was often related to their willingness to adapt to White demands and become "civilized," eschewing their culture and, sometimes, their habitat. While the Poncas earned the reputation of "good" Indians, the Sioux did not acquiesce and were labeled "savages."

Despite a landmark court ruling in favor of the Poncas (*Standing Bear vs. Crook*, May 12, 1879), when Judge Elmer S. Dundy ruled that "an Indian is a person the same as a white man and similarly entitled to the protection of the constitution," the *Daily Rocky Mountain News*, a staunch opponent of Indian rights commented: "War with the Indians is cheaper than peace with them. Powder and shot makes a bad red man a quiet and inexpensive reminiscence. It would be cheaper to board them at first class hotels, than it is to feed and protect them on reservations."[8]

Through their biased, stereotypical coverage of Indians, newspapers stoked White fears about them, inordinately focusing on violence. They were often replete with stereotypical adjectives to denigrate and demean them. Indians were portrayed as impediments to progress and their communal cultures as obstacles to economic growth. Such depictions demonstrated the lack of understanding reporters had about Indian cultures as well as the political and ideological intent of newspapers that routinely reinforced the theme of Indian inferiority while reinforcing the concept of Manifest Destiny.

Although Coward included information demonstrating the presence of humanistic perceptions about Native Americans in newspapers, the overwhelming portrayal of them in the nineteenth-century press can be characterized as superficial, with Indians depicted as uncivilized obstacles to progress. He concluded, "Nineteenth-century journalists could be sympathetic to Indians from time to time, but they could not render Native Americans as fully realized individuals from cultures as valuable and as important as their own."[9]

An equally scholarly analysis of the stereotypical treatment of Native Americans in newspapers and other written mass media was conducted by communications professor Mary Ann Weston, but she focused on the twentieth century.[10] Weston found that the dominant themes about Native Americans during the early decades of the last century reflected the clash between the political policies of the old Bureau of Indian Affairs that advocated assimilation of Indians into mainstream society, as in compulsory boarding schools, and the cultural pluralist perspective of reformers such as John Collier, who would head the agency during FDR's New Deal. Collier advocated for the freedom of expression and cultural practices of the diverse Native American tribes in contrast to the previous government policy of neglect and enforced assimilation. His supporters included such luminaries as Zane Grey, Mary Austin, D. H. Lawrence, Carl Sandburg, Edward Markham, and Elsie Clews Parsons.[11]

One primary focus of newspaper reporting during this time period was the fate of the Bursum Bill, a controversy precipitated by the introduction of a bill in 1922 by U.S. Senator Holm Olaf Bursum of New Mexico (Republican). The bill would have deprived Indigenous Pueblo Indians of the ownership of arable land in New Mexico by disallowing their claims and ceding their land to White Spanish-American settlers, and it threatened the Indians' sovereignty by proposing to assign internal Native American disputes in the area to federal court jurisdiction. The U.S. Senate initially passed the bill without debate as an "administrative measure," but the controversy it created resulted in the passage of a compromise bill in 1924. Weston found that the Bursum Bill controversy was reported in forty-nine newspapers and magazines as well as on wire services and syndicated stories between 1922 and 1923. The Pueblos were portrayed as "good Indians" and "noble savages." Most important, they were assumed to be inclined to assimilation and the adoption of dominant White values as opposed to "bad Indians" like the Sioux who resisted assimilation.

A recurrent theme in Weston's analysis is the depiction of Native Americans as exotic and spiritual, with a culture unchanged through time. In the case of the Pueblos, the press habitually described them physically, noting their stature, clothes and jewelry (e.g., "[T]he Indians appeared in full regalia, feathered head-dress, blue and red blankets and beaded moccasins").[12]

Another dominant theme about the Pueblos and other Native Americans during this time frame was the portrayal of Indians as anachronistic—out of place in modern society. Their embrace of a lifestyle that was devoid of materialism was at once repellant and alluring to White people who labored under the excesses of industrialism. Weston concluded, "These erroneous descriptions, while certainly less egregious than the generic Indian images often depicted in Western movies and fiction, still indicated that in the press, as in popular culture, Indian traits were sometimes generalized and little distinction made from one aboriginal culture to another."[13]

While the Pueblos' situation became a *cause celebre* during the 1920s, the image the press painted about Indians persists to this day. Popular stereotypes produced by the press then as now often depict them as exotic, unusual, separate, and distinct from White society. They are portrayed as outsiders or "Others," not part of our general social system. This makes it easier to avoid, ignore, and stigmatize them. For some, Indians are lower on the "Chain of Being." To prove their inferiority, Indians are often portrayed as innocent and childlike, incapable of comprehending modern behavior and customs. An article written for the *Saturday Evening Post* in 1924 by then Secretary of the Interior Hubert Work blithely described Indians as "instinctively trusting and confiding.... His childlike faith is racial, but his confidence has been constantly abused."[14]

Condescension toward Native Americans and other Indigenous people has been a persistent theme in White relationships and views toward non–White people over the last four hundred years. It has been used to justify a stereotypical characterization of them as well as abusive treatment and attempts at enforced assimilation. In the latter part of the nineteenth century, the federal government prohibited some Native American dances (e.g., the Sun Dance, which involved the ritualistic piercing of the chests or backs of dancers who were then tethered to a pole, which they danced around until their flesh tore, releasing them). This annual activity was viewed as an important demonstration of renewal and rebirth among Plains Indians, but it was banned by the government.

The Ghost Dance, which reached its zenith among Indians around 1890, was also forbidden. The Native American prophet Wovoka was a Paiute religious leader who founded the second and most ambitious invocation and propagation of the dance that reached into the Plains and Navajo tribes. Practitioners believed that the Ghost Dance would raise Native American dead and hasten the demise of White culture and society while restoring Indian resources and ways of life. Wearing sacred Ghost Shirts would make them invincible to their enemies' bullets. Fear of the implications of this phenomenon and stereotypical misperceptions about Ghost Dance practitioners contributed to the massacre at Wounded Knee, South Dakota, by the 7th Cavalry in 1890.[15] Even more discomfiting was the lack of reportorial attention devoted to explaining the origin, meaning, and function of these rites that were tied to Native American cultures and had profound significance for their ways of life.

Though both dances were prohibited by the federal government, vestiges remained into the twentieth century, and some Native Americans have resurrected them today. Their practices are protected by the American Indian Religious Freedom Act of 1978, later amended and expanded in 1994 to allow Indians to practice their religion, including the use of peyote. However, obstacles still prevent the free and unfettered practice of Native American religious and spiritual customs.[16]

But newspaper and mass media stereotypes have a long shelf life, and the desire to Christianize Indians, force them to assimilate, and gain control over their resources have been enduring themes of the mass media in this society. Attempts to make farmers out of hunters might work with some tribes already engaging in agricultural pursuits, but it proved to be less successful with nomadic tribes like the Sioux and Cheyenne. Summing up her analysis of the 1920s, Professor Weston concluded: "In virtually all articles examined, Indian people themselves were treated in stereotypical ways. The images varied according to the type and viewpoint of the article, but few of them could be labeled accurate."[17]

Even when infusing the ideology of cultural pluralism, she found newspapers frequently evinced White ethnocentric bias, which depicted Native Americans as "good Indians" and romantic child-like purveyors of a wistful culture at peace with the environment. If this sounds familiar, it should, because contemporary mass media, from newspapers to television and the cinema frequently convey similar images about Native Americans. Weston's analysis of the 1930s revealed a preoccupation with the reforms generated under the leadership of John Collier, including the passage of the Indian Reorganization Act of 1934 that ended allotments, provided for Native American self-government, and rejected forced assimilation, but Collier became a lightning rod that drew the ire of some Christian missionaries who viewed the promotion of Native American cultures as a move toward paganism.

Among Weston's insights was the conclusion that the nature of reporting about Native Americans was directly correlated with the proximity of the Indian group to the press. "The more distant a native person or group, the more likely was the story to engage in sweeping generalizations that amounted to stereotyping."[18] While newspapers and reporters were grappling with new styles of reportage attempting to interpret as well as report the news, biases and stereotypes remained and permeated national magazines such as *Time, Newsweek, Collier's, Reader's Digest,* and the *Literary Digest.* For example, *Time* magazine, reporting on John Collier's attempt to persuade Indians to accept the Indian Reorganization Act, stated that he "had to hold many a powwow to persuade braves and squaws that his plan is good."[19]

Another theme that arose about Native Americans during the decade of the 1930s was the portrayal of Indians as concerned citizens who were avidly involved in determining their own destiny. This theme surfaced in reporting Native American perspectives about the Wheeler-Howard Act of 1934 (Indian Reorganization Act) and, according to Weston, had a profound influence on the public's perception about Indians that "connoted social separation and inferiority."[20]

When *Scientific American* proclaimed that "the Indian is now a creature of the past, who can be studied mostly in books and museums,"[21] it fed into another trope that recurs today, "the vanishing American," except then, as now, it was false. As we will see in our final chapter, the Native American population is growing and experiencing a cultural, political, and social efflorescence that puts the lie to naive assumptions about their demise and assimilation into mainstream White society.

Much of the reporting during the decade of the 1940s was consumed with events surrounding World War II and its aftermath. Over twenty-five thousand Native Americans actively fought against fascism and for the United States in the Second World War, but it didn't prevent the press from purveying stereotypes about them, praising them for their valor, but more often reinforcing the stereotype about noble and brave warriors possessing skills that purportedly made them suited for combat (e.g., endurance, daring, and physicality). Then, in the 1950s, when the Bureau of Indian Affairs embarked on a mean-spirited and miserly attempt to limit federal expenditures on Native Americans by terminating tribes (108 were initially cut loose from federal subsidies; many, like the Menominees were reinstated later), the tenor of reporting often revolved around the theme of what is referred to as a "deficit model" that exaggerates Native American deficiencies in health, education, employment, housing, violence (especially suicide rates), and sexual violence. Although some Indian activists contend that this approach distorts non–Native perceptions about Indians, it does serve to promote the plight of many Native Americans, and it has led to increased discussions and research about their status. Unfortunately, in 2018 Native Americans lost two important allies with the passing of Senator John McCain (R–Arizona) and the electoral defeat of Senator Heidi Heitkamp (D–North Dakota) who advocated for Indian issues. The fact remains, then as now, Indians' social, health, and economic status lags far behind other ethnic groups in our society. Nevertheless, relying solely on such characterizations can lead to a distorted stereotypical view of Native Americans, as the recent report *Reclaiming Native Truth* cautions.[22]

According to Professor Weston, from 1952 and 1957, between seventeen thousand and twenty thousand Indians were relocated with federal assistance to urban areas in the United States. This concerted program included free one-way transportation from reservations as well as assistance with housing, employment, and groceries—all in an attempt to hasten the removal of Indians from reservations. However, 75 percent more Native Americans *left* reservations between the end of World War II and 1952! And Weston cites articles that described the negative effects of Indian relocation in addition to the theft of their land (e.g., mental health issues such as hopelessness, isolation, and depression among the transplants). "Two months ago Little Light, her husband Leonard Bear, and their five children were persons of standing in a Creek Indian community in Oklahoma. They had only eighty acres of poor land and a modest cabin, but except for the hungry seasons they understood their way of life; they were at peace. Today they are slum dwellers in Los Angeles, without land or home or culture or peace."[23]

Although Weston noted an increase in reporting about Native Americans during the 1950s and 1960s, no doubt related to the rise of Indian civil rights activities known as the Red Power movement, she caustically concluded that the press "still, on occasion, found Indian subjects to trivialize and demean."[24] When Native Americans occupied Alcatraz, initial reports were suffused with stereotypes about "noble savages" seizing their ancestral land, living close to nature in the exotic ancient Indian way. As the months passed the tone of the press became sinister depicting the occupiers as uncivilized, savage vandals who wantonly destroyed government property and resisted authorities who sought to regain control of the aged facility.

Overall, press coverage of Indians in the '60s and '70s was characterized by longer and more supportive pieces, at times written by Indians such as Vine Deloria, Jr., and Richard Oakes. These articles emphasized self-determination, the restoration of Native American tribal lands, and the recognition of Native American cultural identities. Still, articles appeared that characterized Indians who occupied Wounded Knee, Alcatraz, and the Bureau of Indian Affairs in Washington, D.C., as uncivilized, bloodthirsty savages.

Despite a more friendly and evenhanded treatment of Indians by the press in the '80s and '90s, Weston discerned the continued presence of negative stereotypes about them that resurrected images of Indians as inept, uncivilized, and poverty ridden—misfits who cannot or will not adapt to modern civilization.

The first two decades of the twenty-first century have witnessed an increase in reporting about Native American issues with a number of articles written by Indigenous people. A paramount topic is the issue of sovereignty and self-determination. In the face of diminishing resources and policy changes implemented by a hostile administration in Washington, Native Americans became increasingly concerned and outspoken about treaty rights and violations that affect their entitlement to subsidies, land, and natural resources (e.g., fishing and mining rights), as well as having a strident voice in self-governance, and opposition to federal and private intrusion on Indian lands (e.g., the Dakota Access Pipeline incident at the Lakota Reservation in Standing Rock, North Dakota).[25]

The issue of assimilation also ranks high on the list of Indian concerns as well as who qualifies as a Native American and is eligible to receive federal benefits and, in some cases, proceeds from Indian gaming ventures.[26] In recent years, as Indian gaming revenues have exceeded $30 billion, a profusion of articles have appeared in the mass media alleging fraud, abuse, and disputes over control and disbursement of the assets and revenue.[27]

Of course, the perennial topics that depict Native Americans as impoverished victims of decadent and deceitful White society—low educational attainment, poor health status (especially high rates of diabetes, alcoholism, drug abuse, suicides, and violence), deficient housing, and high unemployment—are common themes in the popular press. But a backlash to this "deficit model" has emerged that cautions readers to avoid stereotypical reporting that promotes outmoded memes that seek to encapsulate all Indians as their numbers exceed five million reflecting diverse lifestyles and cultures.

As contemporary reporters become more sensitive to Native American issues, we can expect a wider variety of features and stories about Indians, but readers must be vigilant about the continued presence of timeworn images of Native Americans as "braves," "warriors," "exotic," "ancient," and "natural." A majority of pieces written about Indians still accentuate life on reservations, yet less than a quarter of Native Americans reside there, and while a majority of Indians still endure health and economic hardships, one would hope to encounter more articles in the mass media about Native American successes in law, science, and the humanities. The search for authenticity in reporting should include more incisive attempts to uncover the reasons for Native Americans' disadvantageous situations and disclose the origin of the myths and stereotypes that continue to stigmatize Indians as "outsiders." Perhaps then a majority of the population will reverse its Neanderthal perspective about Native Americans as mascots. As Professor Weston concluded: "Too seldom did journalists look beyond the loud voices to investigate independently. Often they failed to add the layers of historical and cultural content that would truly explain the meanings of events."[28]

The real (and underreported) story about Indians in the United States is that they are not a vanishing group of savages, but a growing, diverse ethnic constituency with increasing self-awareness that is demanding recognition of their rights and privileges as American citizens.

The Dime Novel

In addition to the popular press, the emergence of inexpensive mass production fiction in mid–nineteenth-century America helped diffuse stereotypes about Native Americans. The proliferation of these "dime novels" and their successors in what became known as "pulp fiction" (because of the cheap stock used in the production of this genre of American literature in books and magazines) played a significant role in the perception of the White public of the supposed savage and uncivilized nature of Indigenous Americans. The most influential publisher of the new genre of American literature was the publishing house of Beadle and Adams.

Begun after a succession of struggling businesses by brothers Irwin and Erastus Beadle, a publishing partnership was formed with a young Irishman, Robert Adams, first located in Buffalo, New York, and then in New York City. The founders hit on the idea of glorifying the American Frontier using heroes in a readable, inexpensive format. Most of the stories released in the early years (mid–1800s) focused on the frontier. As historian Albert Johannsen, the leading authority on the Beadles, noted, "[T] his type of fiction was our very own. It had never belonged to another nation, and in no sense could it be called a reflection; it was the literary outcropping of a pioneering people."[29]

Irwin Beadle was the prime force behind the scene that launched a literary frenzy, which permeated the homes and offices of the nation. Although the dime, half-dime, and fifteen-cent novels were looked on derisively by some segments of the population, millions of children and youth, and multitudes of adults pored over this literature to vicariously experience the adventures with the real and fictional heroes of past and present generations.

Historian Michael Denning traced the emergence of the dime novel phenomenon in the United States to the success of the story paper, an eight-page weekly newspaper, which appeared in the 1830s and '40s that cost about five to eight cents. It offered readers serialized stories about adventures and romances, and they also contained correspondence, sermons, humor, advice about fashion, and bits of arcane knowledge. Originally published in New York and Philadelphia, the story paper was followed by the publication of a fifty-page pamphlet novel that sold for thirteen cents in 1842. These "shilling novelettes" were widely imitated until postal rate increases put them out of business in 1845. Denning linked the trends of success and failure in the cheap publishing industry to fluctuations in the postal rates.[30]

Dime novels often drew aspersions about upper-class society because of their popularity among the working class. They had wide appeal, and Denning concluded that young workers, especially Irish and Germans in cities and mill towns of the North and West, were among the most avid readers. Their topics were not salacious but evocative and provocative—filled with hyperbole though often drawn from factual situations as with the ubiquitous dramatized accounts of Indian encounters and battles on the frontier and well-known exploits of pioneers and explorers.

According to Denning, a struggle emerged over access and content of the genre because upper-class affluent members of society wanted to influence what the working class read to restrain their radicalism and gain their allegiance to the status quo. This strategy met with limited success; even children and young adults in the privileged class were known to imbibe in the genre.

It is difficult to estimate the number of novels sold by the firm of Beadle and Adams because different author names were sometimes used for the same novels. Some were pen names and others used to snare gullible readers. Likewise, different names were sometimes used for the same novels as well as material reprinted from magazines and other books as well as condensations that altered the original material. Denning estimated that 3,158 separate titles were published by the firm, which was smaller than competitors such as Street and Smith, and the enterprises of George and Norman Munro.

A content analysis of the 321 original titles in the first series of Beadle and Adams dime novels revealed that half (157) had Indian themes. These themes continued to dominate the works of this publishing house and its many rivals for the next several decades.

Originally printed on plain paper in black and white, the publishers soon adopted a dark yellow color and utilized evocative artwork depicting the travail of heroes by skilled artists and engravers such as George White and John Karst. Especially in the early decades of the dime novel genre, the works were presented as quasi-fictional accounts of heroism and adventure, most focusing on the American western frontier, although few of the writers had ever visited the region or locations they shared with their readers. Some well-known authors wrote these manuscripts, but it was not uncommon for writers (and the publishing staff) to use pseudonyms. Authors would be paid between $75 and $150 for a novel, but some received as much as $700 for their work. Many of the writers were successful professionals, artists, teachers, and businessmen and women. In fact, the first dime novel, *Malaeska; The Indian Wife of the White Hunter*, was issued in June 1860, and was written by Ann Stephens and originally published in *The Ladies' Companion* in 1839.

The authors developed a formulaic approach in their writing, and, with some guidelines and suggestions from publishers, they sought to involve readers in the experience, capturing their attention and creating a form of interaction predating contemporary social media events.

The number of pages in these tomes ranged from 96 to 130. The instant success of *Malaeska* led these entrepreneurs to release a rash of other pieces within three months, followed by their first original blockbuster novel, *Seth Jones*, about the adventures of a fictional American frontiersman. Written by a twenty-year-old New Jersey schoolteacher, Edward Ellis, who submitted the manuscript on a lark, his prose and timing were right on target. The canny publishing trio seized the opportunity and with an avalanche of advertising sold forty thousand copies within a few weeks. Estimates put the total number of sales as high as six hundred thousand.[31] Ellis's work was favorably reviewed, and the public's enthusiasm for the theme and format helped him secure an exclusive multibook contract with Beadle and Adams. It was the beginning of a phenomenon that permeated American culture for more than half a century. Many other publishing houses, some much larger than Beadle and Adams, like Street and Smith also of New York City, accounted for thousands of novels that extolled, exaggerated, and distorted the exploits of American heroes such as Buffalo Bill, Kit Carson, and Daniel Boone and infused stereotypes about Native Americans throughout American society. In 1861, the Beadles began publishing dime novels in England, with a total of sixty books by 1866, when the enterprise was bought and continued by Routledge, perpetuating stereotypes about minorities there, too.

During the Civil War, the Beadles varied their publishing schedule from twice a month (on the first and fifteenth) to every three weeks and sometimes even semi-monthly. According to Johannsen, the size of the novels increased, and thousands of them were distributed to soldiers. By July 1, 1865, American sales of the first twenty dime novels was 4,352,000, and by January 1, 1864, sales in England were 1,223,000 copies, and many of the early works featured conflicts between settlers and frontiersmen against Indian "savages."

The dime novels (and early cinema as we shall see) played on Cooper's theme that emphasized White dominance over Native Americans and developed the frontier, cowboy genre that featured the domination of opponents of civilization by subduing outlaws and Indians. As the late Native American historian Vine Deloria, Jr., noted, "There is little doubt in anyone's mind that the dime novel used the Indian as the villain and relied heavily upon racial slurs and derogatory stereotypes to support most of the plots. Dime novels attributed evil and savage motives to the Indians so that the white hero would be seen in a favorable light."[32]

As the western frontier was settled and its Native American inhabitants conquered, the themes of these little tomes took on another caste. Cooper's influence was still prevalent, but twentieth-century American mythology now focused on heroes fighting on behalf of the underdogs, against "the system." Now there were demonstrations of class warfare where colonists and homesteaders were supplanted by working men, farmers, and unionists of the new Industrial Age, all allied against capitalist robber barons, banks, and utilities. While Indians were no longer depicted as a threat (the Plains Wars had left them without their land and defeated), new heroes and villains emerged to fight against avaricious industrialists who were taking advantage of "the little guy," and cops and robbers tales featuring crusading law enforcement agents and "private eyes" fighting for the "American way."[33]

The public's taste for heroes underwent this evolution, and with the development of new publishing technologies as well as the advent of motion pictures and radio, interest in dime novels waned. Denning attributed their demise to the failure of John Lovell's U.S. Book Company trust in 1893, which had purchased the rights to many titles, as well as the

Kit Carson as a dime novel hero. (Albert Johannsen, *The House of Beadle and Adams,* **University of Oklahoma Press, 1950).**

establishment of the International Copyright Agreement in 1891 that prevented the dime novel publishing houses from further pirating British and European fiction. The development of the Sunday newspaper and the blossoming of the pulp magazine revolution that brought fiction to a wide reading audience in the 1890s also played a role in their decline. Despite the pejorative appellation they acquired, dime novels and their literary successor, pulp fiction, left an indelible imprint on the American psyche about Native Americans.

The "King of Pulp Fiction"

When Owen Wister's *The Virginian* was published in 1902,[34] it helped create a burgeoning market for Western novels and stories that captivated readers for nearly four decades. Authors found a ready audience for their formulaic prose that presented cowboys as moral and physical superheroes seeking revenge in a struggle between good and evil—a struggle that extolled the virtue of Manifest Destiny and escapism from the monotony of readers' lives in a quest for sexual conquests with beautiful women. Indians were viewed as irksome barbarians whose presence was incidental to plots. They were invariably depicted as aggressive, illiterate, uncivilized, unwanted interlopers. The enormous output of one man often reinforced these stereotypes but at times countered prevailing perceptions about Indians.

Born Frederick Schiller Faust, in Seattle, Washington, in 1892, he became the most prolific and widely read author of works in the Western genre in the United States and Europe in the early decades of the twentieth century. Yet, many of his readers were unaware that the author they idolized as Max Brand, or the other twenty pen names he used, was one and the same man. In a frenetic writing career that spanned little more than a quarter of a century, Faust published thirty million words, equivalent to more than five hundred books each of sixty thousand words. A new Faust book was published every four months from 1919 to 1985, yet only half of his magazine work has been converted into book format.[35]

Although some critics of Faust disparagingly referred to him as a pulp hack, his creative genius, manifested in the sheer volume and variety of his stories, contradicts such criticism, although he, himself, was not fulfilled by his commercial writing. He aspired to be a poet.

Faust published over 400 articles in the Western genre, and authored 220 books in that vein, many derived from hundreds of his serials and novelettes in pulp magazines like *Western Story Magazine* and slicker products like *Argosy, Harper's, Colliers*, and the *Saturday Evening Post* under pen names such as George Owen Baxter, Evan Evans, and George Challis, sometimes in the same issue. Incredibly, Faust wrote another two hundred books on medicine, and a series based on his college friend George Fish that became the popular Dr. Kildare television show starring Richard Chamberlain, which ran from 1961 to 1966 on NBC.

One of Faust's biographers calculated that he wrote over five million words in the early 1930s—equivalent to seventy-five novels. Working furiously at his typewriter in a hunt-and-peck mode, without the aid of a secretary, he could produce a book-length manuscript in four days, a fifty-page novelette in one evening, and an average-length short story in one hour.[36]

His official website reads "The World's Most Celebrated Writer!" This statement may surprise people who never heard of him, and it certainly doesn't reflect his humble beginnings. As a child, his parents moved to the San Joaquin Valley in California. They were very poor, and although his father was a lawyer, he never managed to make ends meet. Faust was orphaned when he was thirteen and lived for a time with a distant relative, Thomas Downey, who was the principal of Modesto High School, which he attended. Downey, a disciplinarian, stressed the classics, and Faust took to them, later infusing his works with heroic and mythological themes.

Faust began writing as a poet but never achieved notoriety for his verse despite a lifelong pursuit of it. He attended the University of California at Berkeley and became a regular contributor to university periodicals such as *The University of California Chronicle*, and editor of the yearbook, *The Blue and Gold*, as well as publishing articles for the school's newspaper, *The Daily Californian*. Despite winning accolades from professors and students, the unconventional Faust managed to alienate the president of the university, Benjamin Wheeler, who prevented him from graduating.

Faust married his college sweetheart, Dorothy Schillig, and they had three children. Their marriage was complicated by his heavy drinking, long work hours, extraordinary energy, propensity for spending more than he earned, and affairs with other women. The Faust family lived in splendor in a rented estate in Florence, Italy, for many years, which he remodeled to suit his sumptuous needs.

Although he was being paid four or five cents a word for his stories, and at the height of his career in the mid–1920s and 1930s he earned around $100,000 a year (equivalent to nearly $1,500,000 today), Faust and his family were always living on the edge of insolvency thanks to his profligate spending, generosity, and extravagant tastes.

Perhaps economic concerns were a primary motivation for his indefatigable lifestyle. His hard-driven work schedule, heavy smoking and drinking, and passion for excitement and the opposite sex exacerbated a heart defect (a form of arrhythmia), which periodically disabled him. Despite this condition, and warnings from physicians in the United States and England to adopt a more sedentary lifestyle, he continued working and playing as if he were immune to the disease.

His prodigious production benefited from the advice of close confidants and literary agents as well as editors at leading Western pulp magazines, publishing houses, and motion picture companies. Literally hundreds of his stories, serials, and novelettes were repackaged and republished as novels, many under the pen name Max Brand. When Faust signed on with MGM Studios as a screenwriter in 1938, he began a new career that provided a steady income at the rate of $1,500 a week. Some of his fellow screenwriters were envious of his high level of productivity—being able to turn out scripts and stories in a fraction of the time they did. Faust became a celebrated screenwriter, and over eighty major motion pictures were produced based on his scripts, stories, and novels, six films in 1939–40 alone. The scope of his talent and imagination were unparalleled. In addition to Westerns, he wrote spy and crime thrillers, urban romances, historical adventures, and, of course, the very successful motion pictures and television series centered around Dr. Kildare.

Many leading actors and actress from the 1930s to the 1960s starred in his films, including such luminaries as Tom Mix, Errol Flynn, Randolph Scott, Glenn Ford, Humphrey Bogart, Lionel Barrymore, George O'Brien, Joel McCrea, Victor

McLaglen, Paul Henreid, Roy Rogers, Vaughn Monroe, Alan Ladd, Mickey Rooney, Audie Murphy, Lew Ayres, Robert Young, Van Johnson, Ava Gardner, Gloria de Haven, Lana Turner, and Laraine Day. His 1930 Western novel, *Destry Rides Again*, was made into a movie twice and featured Andy Griffith and Delores Gray in a Broadway play that ran for 472 performances between 1959 and 1960. The 1939 film version starred James Stewart and Marlene Dietrich.

Although Faust and his family lived luxuriously in Italy and Brentwood, California, they were often nearly broke, but he always managed to tap his creative juices to avert financial disaster. While he worked assiduously to produce millions of words for the pulps, slicks, and motion pictures, his first and most endearing love was poetry, "the God of my worship."[37] From letters to his wife there are indications that he abhorred the writing that made him comfortable and famous. "Daily I thank God in three languages that I write under a pen name."[38] And though he would have preferred to become an established poet, he could not forsake his gift of creativity and energy that made an indelible mark on the psyche of millions of readers around the world.

Faust's perception of Indians was influenced no doubt by the writings of Cooper, but the more contemporary work of Owen Wister and Zane Grey also impressed him. According to English professor and former president of Augusta State University in Atlanta, Georgia, William A. Bloodworth, Jr., his first Western novel, *The Untamed*, marked a change in course for him as he developed his own unique style. Like Grey and Wister, Faust seemed to abhor modernity and often used Indians as props to develop his Western dramas. Bloodworth contends that Faust was criticized for basing his images of Indians on the stilted romantic accounts of them by James Willard Schultz and George Bird Grinnell, two nineteenth- and early twentieth-century writers. Early in his career he took a sympathetic view of Native Americans, especially the Cheyenne, but overlooked White racism and Indians' depredations against White people. In his later writing he explored the theme of White greed, treachery, and racism toward Indians. As author Edgar Chapman noted, "Brand [Faust] had a remarkable talent, and his treatment of the Indian in his Western fiction was strikingly fair and truthful, given the time when he wrote, and the sources he used."[39]

One astounding fact about Faust was that he did relatively little research for his writing. A voracious reader, he often integrated classical themes into his stories and allowed his imagination to write the ending for him. As Bloodworth noted, he might read a story halfway through, imagine how it would end, and then create a new beginning to fashion a different story.

Bob Davis, one of Faust's earliest editors at Munsey Publications, who published much of his earliest work, encouraged him to travel to El Paso to observe how a working ranch operated, but he knew Faust generated his work from his vivid imagination rather than from observations and advised him, "It is easier to dream fiction than to fake facts."[40] Unlike Grey (and L'Amour who followed him), Faust eschewed researching western life. His disdain for this is apparent in his communication with his wife, Dorothy: "Lord, how I hate the prospect [of staying on a ranch]. It's worse than the army, in a way. I'd rather have my teeth pulled, one a day. Stinking cowpunchers—rides in all sorts of weather—all stuff that a hundred other men have done before me."[41]

Faust made an imposing figure of a man. At 6'3" he was tall and robust, but his heart condition periodically disabled him. As a teenager he worked in various menial jobs to survive, had a reputation as a local tough, and was not averse to fighting. This macho strain in his personality, combined with the adversity he faced growing up, no doubt influenced his perspective on writing, which was augmented by his reading of Greek, Roman, and Arthurian mythology as well as other classics. It is said that he even memorized the works of Shakespeare.

He desperately tried to join the military to fight Germany in World War I, but after enlisting in the U.S. Army in 1918 he was assigned to dig latrines at Camp Humphreys in Virginia (now Fort Belvoir) near D.C. Believing that "a man's chief business was in fighting of one kind or another and that to die in battle was the best kind of death,"[42] he became distraught, especially when some of his friends were actively engaged in the war. He then enlisted in the Canadian army hoping to fight abroad, only to be assigned to noncombat roles in Canada, and he deserted.

It was his pursuit of the heroic myth that eventually led to his demise. At the age of fifty-one, he managed to inveigle a war correspondent's position with *Harper's Magazine*. Despite his age and infirm heart, he valiantly tagged along with GIs in their assault on the German stronghold near Monte Cassino, where the Allies launched a withering barrage on the German defense of the Gustav Line during the night of May 11, 1944. That fateful evening found Faust among the first wave of soldiers storming German defenses where he was wounded in the chest by shrapnel. He exhorted the troops to leave him and attend to others. When they returned, he was dead. It was May 12, 1944, just eleven days short of his fifty-second birthday.

Faust's prodigious reading and classical training, along with his creative genius, enthralled pulp fiction readers and, later, movie goers and the general reading public. Despite what gradually developed into a sympathetic portrayal of Native Americans, his work reinforced stereotypes about Indians in the United States and abroad. Like his contemporary Zane Grey, Faust projected the image of Indians as backward, warlike, and unpredictable. For example, his series about the adventures of *Thunder Moon*, written in the late 1920s, is replete with the subject of scalping, as is *The Rescue of Broken Arrow*.[43] There are passages in Faust's voluminous works that evoke the age-old stereotypes of Indians as cruel savages engaged in wanton murder and destruction.[44] Yet the stoic Indian, at one with nature and at risk of being enveloped by a materialistic White society, became a common theme of both writers.

The *Thunder Moon* serials, originally published as magazine articles and subsequently as books, are based on a heroic figure, William Sutton, a White man who was kidnapped as an infant by Big Hard Face and raised by the Cheyenne. The final piece, initially published in *Western Story Magazine* on November 3, 1928, under the pen name of George Baxter as "Thunder Moon Goes White," is predicated on a theme not unlike Edgar Rice Burroughs's *Tarzan*, who lived as the "Great White Hero" among African Native people. The two authors were contemporaries, and key components of their plots are strikingly similar. In the final installment of the *Thunder Moon* saga, the reader is reminded that William Sutton, acknowledged as a great Indian warrior among the Cheyenne, with near superhuman physical attributes ("among the Cheyennes he was a force. He was like a king of the body and the spirit. There were other chiefs who led them, nominally, in war. But to Thunder Moon they turned as to a prophet and a preserver in times of evil. In peace they surrounded him with their adulation and their homage."),[45] is still at a disadvantage to pure bred Indians: "Even an Indian woman, even an Indian child, had sharper eyes than his, had quicker senses to note the changes upon the grass, the leaves, the ground, which indicated that other life stirred nearby. By the flight of the very birds, they could read what was passing along the surface of the earth, many miles away, and yet all of these abilities were quite beyond the talents of Thunder Moon."[46] And we learn that "Thunder Moon was full of the white man's fighting madness such as never comes over a savage brain."[47] The preoccupation of scalping one's enemies and throwaway references about the character of Indians ("Courage is great in the heart of every worthy Indian,"[48] "Any Indian would bet up to his last penny with a cheerful countenance,"[49] and, condescendingly, "[A]mong the frontiersmen, the red man was looked upon as a sort of hybrid species—a little above the snake and a good deal below the wolf"[50]) appealed to Faust's wide readership, and reinforced stereotypes about Native Americans as spirit-like, wild, and naturalistic—recurrent themes found in the work of other Western writers for stage, screen, and television.

Faust's writing about Indians is suffused with stereotypes depicting them as superstitious savages, barbarians, primitive, ignorant, and warlike. His characters often refer to Indians pejoratively as fools, animals, and infantile: "[T]he prairies, infested as these are by wild Indians!"[51]; "[I]t's not a bad thing to be a king even of a pack of red wolves"[52]; "[B]ut the rest of the Cheyennes seemed to take this nonsense [referring to a medicine dance] in the most serious way"[53]; and, "These fellows [Indian villagers] were like children grown big in body but not in mind"[54]; or, "Do any of these staring fools understand English?"[55] For good measure a reference to cannibalism was included: "[T]hen slidin' in amongst a couple of thousand man-eatin' Pawnees and snatchin' off scalps and stealin' magic hosses as you go!"[56]

It is difficult to encapsulate all of Faust's myriad writing into a one-dimensional framework about Native Americans. Nevertheless, it can be said that the "King of pulp fiction" played an important role in shaping the stereotypical views of the White reading and moving-going public. The sheer weight of his work in this regard should not be minimized. As Bloodworth wryly noted, Faust may have squandered a great literary gift on pulp writing, but he managed to tell Americans about the conflicts between White people and Indians, and in the final analysis, " [His work] was popular entertainment, for its own times, presented in an engaging style and offering its readers a view of human life inspired 'by love and high aspiration.' At its best, Max Brand [Faust] was a means of tapping into rich veins of human fantasy."[57]

Native Americans in Comic Books

One of the most iconic media used for stereotyping Native Americans continues to be comic books. These relatively inexpensive paper presentations have, for decades, purveyed representations of Indians as an extinct or near extinct form of humanity, one lower on the Chain of Being than the White Europeans who invaded their territory and nearly drove them into oblivion. Although there has been an evolution in the short scripts devoted to Native Americans in comic books in recent times, many of the images used, as well as the plots and language, still convey images of Indigenous people who dwelled in the Old West, the past, as if there were no contemporary Native Americans.

Professor Michael Sheyahshe, a member of the Caddo Nation of Oklahoma, provided a detailed analysis of the themes and stereotypes about Indians employed in comic books, past and present. As with other forms of literature and the mass media (e.g., motion pictures and television), Native Americans are predominantly portrayed as wearing buckskins and feathers, riding horses, and wearing war paint. They are often devoid of an intellectual bearing and speak in choppy sentences often punctuated by monosyllabic "Ughs."[58]

Sheyahshe was particularly disturbed by the habit of comic book writers to depict Native Americans as extinct, or nearly so, instead of a diverse conglomeration of hundreds of tribes or nations, often with different cultures, customs, and languages.[59] Comic books also stereotype Indians as sidekicks to White heroes, the Mohican Syndrome employed by James Fenimore Cooper, with the White hero outperforming Indians in their proclivities to survive in natural settings. Similarly, the Lone Ranger's pal and sidekick, Tonto, became the overused model for many comic books with an Indian theme in the 1950s, '60s, '70s, and '80s, where the Indian played second fiddle to the White hero, always obeisant, never speaking from an intellectual perspective, grunting approval, and never taking an independent position. (Jay Silverheels must have suffered mightily through his many roles as an ignorant, subordinate Indian, but through his civic actions and charitable contributions he helped pave the way for generations of Native Americans who followed him—hopefully not in his footsteps.)

Sheyahshe demonstrated how modern writers who are more culturally sensitive to Native American cultures were overruled by ostensibly media-savvy publishers in their attempt to depict Indians more progressively as complex intellectual human beings. Instead, Indians are depicted in stereotypical costumes wearing and using artifacts and other appendages that, from their perspective, will make the piece more marketable (e.g., the use of moccasins, fringed clothing, wearing of feathers, the use of shamans, and spiritual powers that purportedly link Indian characters with nature). Even the names of Indian comic book characters exude stereotypical archetypes like Raven, Scout, Stalking Wolf, Red Wolf, Thunderbird, Warpath, Coyote, Turok, Scalphunter, and Straight Arrow.

Infused into many of the modern comic book treatments of Native Americans is what Sheyahshe terms "instant shamanism"—the conflation of spiritual and supernatural powers conferred on Native American sidekicks and heroes in the stereotypical assumption that all Indians are stoic and capable of communing with Mother Nature, Manitou, or, as we knew it years ago, "The Great Spirit." And while Sheyahshe demonstrates that the trend among young modern comic book writers is to make their Native American subjects more articulate, reflective, and intelligent, much of the comic book world is still locked in the past, reinforcing the subordinate role that Native Americans play as appendages to White heroes, lower on the scale of humanity. As Jon Proudstar, Native American actor, writer, and creator of the comic book mutant hero bearing his own name, reminds us:

> [W]e are a people not a decoration. That we love, hate, live and die. That we are plagued by the by product of sins and atrocities committed by the American forefathers. That the blood of our people stripe the American flag. These facts are constants to our people. And true that some of us are not the best representations of what has survived. But survive we did. The country scorns our existence because we are a constant reminder of a terrible act that was committed by the Americans. And until that sin or atrocity is acknowledged and the treaties are honored this country will never know solace.[60]

A fascinating development in the comic book genre has been the linkage between Native American mythology and superheroes. A recent public exhibition by S'Klallam (Pacific Northwest) artist Jeffrey Veregge, at New York's National Museum of the American Indian, featured contemporary Native American icons, like the resurrected Red Wolf, ensconced in the universe of Marvel Superheroes. Veregge has managed to fuse his modern Native American images with transcendental colors that leap out at onlookers. More importantly, he appears to be successfully fusing Native American traditions with Marvel concepts to promote understanding and appreciation of Native American art and traditions.[61] And Michael Sheyahshe is leading a coalition of Native American artists and writers in the development of comics that emphasize Indian heritage as related through the words of Indigenous storytellers.[62] He is also engaged in the Indigenous Narrative Collective, the INC Universe, which features Native American artists and writers as well as other creative people, in the production of comic books and characters that defy traditional stereotypes about Indians.

Other Native American artists and writers are engaged in developing ethnic pride through their emphasis on the spiritual and historical facts about Indian lives. The Winter 2019 edition of the *National Museum of the American Indian*[63] presents a number of Native American artists and their works. And a compelling discussion is also presented in this issue about the rise of award-winning Native American science fiction writers such as Rebecca Roanhorse (Ohkay Owingeh Pueblo) who penned a recent *Star Wars* novel that was used in the blockbuster film *The Rise of Skywalker*. However, she has encountered some opposition from Diné people because of her alleged cultural appropriation of their spiritual beliefs. She counters, "We are rising from the apocalypse, folding the past into our present and writing a future that is decidedly Indigenous."[64]

Even more enthusiasm has been generated among budding Native American artists through the development and evolution of a new wave of Indigenous comics promoted by Lee Francis IV (Laguna Pueblo), the founder of Indigenous Comic Con, now known as Indigenous Pop X or IndigiPopX. He is also head of Native Realities and Indigenerd as well as Red Planet Books and Comics. What has become an annual celebration of Native American comic book media, IndigiPopX was supposed to run from March 20 to 29, 2020, in Albuquerque, New Mexico, featuring comic artists, fashion, music, and Indigenous food, but it was moved to a virtual format because of the COVID-19 pandemic. Such events have also been produced in Australia, New Zealand, and Canada as well as other parts of the United States.

While promoting Indigenous artists is important, Francis asserts that dispelling historical stereotypical depictions about Indigenous people is paramount. In his quest for Native understanding and entrepreneurship, he acknowledges that having a large audience has been difficult for Indigenous artists and writers who encounter reticence in the Big Media that is still enmeshed in traditional stereotypes about Indigenous people. His goal is to convince the Big Media industry that there is a market for authentic, nonstereotypical work about Indigenous people. "We can showcase, we can pull the blanket off of the structural prejudice, and that's what we're trying to do."[65]

Left and right: **The evolution of an American comic book hero, Red Wolf. By Neal Adams, 1971, and Jeffrey Veregge, 2015 (© 2021 Marvel).**

Indians in Advertising Cards

Although he doesn't devote much space to the topic of video games, Sheyahshe notes that many of the stereotypes about Native Americans appear in them, burdening yet another generation with outmoded generalizations and preconceptions about a complex group of nations that defies generalizations. Yet another practice of the past was recounted by English professor Jeffrey Steele, who traced the proliferation and impact of Indians as symbols in advertising trade cards that were freely and widely distributed during the nineteenth and early twentieth centuries. Steele noted that the use of such symbols helped market products to consumers by creating "fetishized images that satisfied the hunger for entertainment and disposable commodities."[66] Then, as now, some corporations and entrepreneurs found that the commercialization of Native Americans was profitable (e.g., Land O'Lakes products and Indians as athletic team mascots). Steele concluded that "nineteenth century trade cards remain to this day the most graphic examples of racial and ethnic stereotypes being used as marketing tools."[67]

Cigar Store Indians

The foundation of racist stereotypes is built on imagery. Conceptions of Native Americans and other oppressed ethnic groups are imbedded in our psyches, stamped on our conscious and unconscious minds, diffused in our White–dominated culture. Even though most Americans living today have never read Defoe or Cooper's works or seen films based on them, stereotypical imagery about Native Americans and Indigenous people have been inculcated into our perceptions about them. While few people today have ever seen a wooden or metallic representation of a Native American standing outside of a smoke shop, the practice of marketing tobacco this way was prevalent from the late nineteenth century through World War II when the wood and metal used to create these statues became more desirable than the artifacts themselves.

The practice of positioning a stoic or menacing Indian brave holding a spear or tomahawk outside a tobacconist was commonplace in Europe and America, although early European representations of Native Americans looked more like Black slaves because many Europeans didn't have a good idea about the appearance of Indians. These early representations were called "Black Boys" or "Virginians." Because Indians were presumed to have introduced Europeans to tobacco, they were immortalized as purveyors of tobacco products.

In time, warlike braves were replaced by comely Indian princesses with thin lips, smiling faces, and inviting curves designed to lure White males into tobacco stores. But the demand for the raw materials

— No. 70 —

CAPTAIN JOHN SMITH

A rugged, fearless soul was CAPTAIN JOHN SMITH. Made prisoner on shipboard on his way to America, he rose to be "the man of the hour" when death, sickness, and food shortage confronted the settlers at Jamestown. Captured by the Indian Chief, Powhatan, he was condemned to die but was saved by the beautiful, tender-hearted, gentle Pocahontas, daughter of Powhatan.

This is one of a series of ninety-six cards. More cards illustrating romantic America to follow

INDIAN GUM
The World's Greatest Penny Value

Goudey Gum Co.　　　　　Boston

Native American myths in advertising cards (Kronozio).

Perpetuating Native American stereotypes through cigar store Indians (Library of Congress).

found in these artifacts outweighed their commercial value. However, some statues command as much as $500,000 today in the burgeoning world of folk art.[68]

Native Americans as Mascots

Once the invading avalanche of Western White humanity with its superior numbers and technology gained a foothold, another prominent theme about Indigenous people emerged—their representation as inept, inconsequential buffoons. In the United States, the transformation of Indian stereotypes from fierce, warlike, bloodthirsty savages to lazy profligates took less than a century, and the negative characterization of Native Americans persists today. It is apparent in the popular conception of Indians as shiftless drunks and unemployed vagrants and finds expression in their depiction as mascots for sports teams—a practice that is subsiding in the face of Native American objections, but is, nevertheless, still embraced by a majority of the White population. Although the National Collegiate Athletic Association (NCAA) banned the use of "hostile or abusive" nicknames and mascots on team uniforms and other clothing on February 1, 2006, and many colleges and universities complied, public and private schools throughout the country still use them despite opposition from Native American organizations and professional associations.[69]

One of the most offensive sports mascot names is the Washington Redskins professional football team. Some critics of this franchise even refuse to use the name. Among them is humanities professor C. Richard King of Washington State University, who has written extensively on the subject. He likened Native American mascots to trophy "remnants from a kill, longingly kept reminders of past glory, and continuing signs of prowess and superiority through which Euro-Americans channel the strength and energy of those they (or, better said, their forebearers) have vanquished."[70] King acerbically compared the White European penchant for Indian mascots to a process of disfigurement and dehumanization reducing Native Americans to a conquered people while promoting White masculinity and camaraderie among fans.

There is abundant social science research indicating Native American mascots have negative effects on Indian children in the United States. After reviewing the literature and conducting studies on the effects of stereotypes on Native American students, psychologist Stephanie Fryberg (Tulalip) and her colleagues concluded that "American Indian mascot images have a negative impact on American Indian high school and college students' feelings of personal and community worth and achievement-related possible selves." Their research suggested that the mascots and caricatures lack positive images of Indians in American society and they are not relevant or useful for students' identity construction. Their studies suggested that "American Indian mascot images have harmful psychological consequences for the group that is caricaturized by the mascots."[71]

One of the pioneers against the use of Native Americans as mascots is Tim Giago (Lakota), the crusading editor of *Native Sun*, a Rapid City, South Dakota, newspaper that, under his tutelage, has been fighting for Native American rights for decades. An outspoken opponent of some of the tactics of the American Indian Movement, he was nearly assassinated one evening as he sat in his pickup truck and a bullet whizzed by his head.

In an interview, Giago recounted growing up on the nearby Lakota Reservation and playing football against a predominantly White high school: "We were booed and made to run through a corridor as the crowd jeered us. It was like being in a cattle car. They threw rocks at us as we went through. After that, they quit having the game for ten years."[72]

Despite overt racism and hostility toward Indians engendered by mascots, and in the face of evidence demonstrating the negative impact they have on Native Americans, especially children, owner of the Washington football franchise, Daniel Snyder, adamantly refused to change the name of his team. President of the team, Bruce Allen, said, "There is nothing that we feel is offensive. And we're proud of our history." Even commissioner of the National Football League, Roger Goodell, backed the team's stance, and a public opinion poll by the Associated Press-Gfk in 2013 of 1,004 adults found 79 percent *in favor* of keeping the name (down 10 percent from a similar survey in 1992). Only 11 percent of football fans in the survey thought the name should be changed. "This is a really good example of why you never put racism up to a popular vote, because racism will win every time," said Suzan Shown Harjo (Cheyenne and Hodulgee Muscogee), plaintiff in the case to revoke the Redskins' trademark protection.[73] Perhaps Professor King's remarks sum up the situation: "The willingness of so many to continue to believe a lie communicates something very deep about settler society, namely the lasting force, value, and utility of stereotypes about Native Americans and the power and privilege non–Indians have enjoyed to use those stereotypes to stage themselves for the world."[74]

On July 9, 2015, Federal District Judge Gerald Bruce Lee ruled that the Redskins' trademarks are offensive, upholding a similar ruling by the Federal Trademark and Appeal Board in 2014, which was later overturned by the U.S. Court of Appeals for the Federal Circuit in 2015. The team could still use these materials pending a lengthy appeals process. According to Allen, "We are convinced that we will win on appeal as the facts are on the side of our franchise that has proudly used the name Washington Redskins for more than 80 years."[75] And indeed he did—and perhaps permanently, as far as the legal argument surrounding the use of the team's trademark, when the Supreme Court of the United States ruled 8–0 in June 2017 that Section 2(a) of the Lanham Act, known as the disparagement clause, was unconstitutional, allowing the use of the derogatory name to stand under the guise of free speech.

In a case involving the Asian rock band the Slants, the Supreme Court determined that private speech cannot be used for denying or canceling a trademark even if it disparages a substantial percentage of a distinct group of people, be it racial, ethnic, religious, or political, because it violated the free speech clause of the First Amendment. In effect, the Court ruled that the government should not decide which trademarks are offensive and which aren't. The ruling then led the U.S. Court of Appeals for the Fourth District on January 18, 2018, to overturn Judge Gerald Bruce Lee's 2015 decision to sustain the Patent and Trade Office's planned cancellation of the Redskin's trademark.[76]

A *Washington Post* public opinion poll of 504 Native American adults in all 50 states revealed how insensitive even some Native Americans are. Ninety percent of the randomly selected respondents were not offended by the football team's name and logo—a finding that hasn't changed in over a decade since the Annenberg Public Policy Center polled on the same question. Owner Snyder was heartened by the findings: "The Washington Redskins team, our fans and community have always believed our name represents honor, respect and pride. Today's *Washington Post* polling shows Native Americans agree. We are gratified by this overwhelming support from the Native American community, and the team will proudly carry the Redskins name."[77]

But there is still a chance that ethics and veracity will win out. On May 2, 2018, Richard E. Besser, president and CEO of the prestigious Robert Wood Johnson Foundation, the world's largest health-related philanthropic organization, announced in an op-ed for *USA Today* that his organization would no longer be involved with entities that use a "name, brand or practices [that] denigrates, harms or discriminates against a racial or ethnic group." Besser apologized for his organization's selection of professional sports teams that use Native American mascots and concluded that progressive organizations should abandon them: "It requires all of us to keep listening, learning and looking in the mirror."[78] Despite the indifference and fog that obfuscates reality, rays of light shine through, and the power of corporate prestige and, ultimately, investment, may reveal the truth and change that calumny. Sure enough, in the midst of the COVID-19 pandemic and national protests over systemic racism and police brutality following the brutal televised police murder of George Floyd in May 2020, sponsors of the Washington team (e.g., Fed Ex, PepsiCo, and Nike) exerted pressure on Daniel Snyder, the owner of the Washington football team, who swore he would never change the franchise name, and Roger Goodell, the chairman of the National Football League, to reevaluate their position. The team began to be referred to as the Washington Football Team. The reluctant Snyder stands to reap a bonanza from the sale of new team merchandise. And in December 2020, the Cleveland baseball team announced that it would no longer be called the Indians. The new name for the Cleveland baseball team is the Guardians, and on February 2, 2022, the Washington football team was re-named the Commanders.

14

The Contemporary Western Novel and Native Americans

> Who of us can believe that you can love a people of a different color
> from your own, better than those who have a white skin, like yourselves?
> —Captain Pipe (Delaware), 1781

In the last half of the twentieth century, the medium of television gained prominence as the principal vehicle for proffering stereotypes about Native Americans. The home screen supplanted the movie theater as couch potatoes of all ages were exposed to timeworn reruns of "shootum ups" between "innocent" struggling settlers and ferocious, predatory, lustful "Injuns." One man, more than any other in the latter part of the twentieth century, is responsible for promulgating stereotypes about Native Americans in literature, on television, and in film—Louis L'Amour. His work was prodigious. He wrote three books a year from 1955 until his death in 1988, most for Bantam Press, nearly all in the Western genre, and many of them contained stereotypes about Indians. Even today, more than two hundred million copies of his eighty-nine novels are in circulation in the United States, and another hundred million are circulating worldwide. He also authored over four hundred short stories, mostly about the West. One of his most popular books was based on a short story, *The Gift of Cochise*, originally run in *Collier's* in 1952. The following year it was published as *Hondo* and sold over 1.5 million copies, solidifying his success. John Wayne purchased the rights to it and starred in the movie, just one of numerous Hollywood films and television productions based on his writing. Sales for some of his most popular novels (e.g., *Flint, Bendigo Shafter, The Lonesome Gods, The Walking Drum, The Burning Hills, The Daybreakers, Mojave Crossing, The First Fast Draw, Lando, Silver Canyon, The Sackett Brand*, and *Last of the Breed*) each exceeded two million copies.

Audio cassettes have been made for dozens of his novels, and his works have been translated into more than twenty languages including Chinese, Danish, Dutch, Finnish, French, German, Greek, Italian, Japanese, Norwegian, Polynesian, Portuguese, Spanish, Swedish, and Serbo-Croatian.

American literature professor emeritus Robert Gale reported that each of L'Amour's eighty-seven novels topped one million in sales, and his books in the late 1980s and early 1990s were selling at the rate of fifteen thousand to twenty thousand **a day,** seven days a week. In fact, Gale calculated that if you stacked all of L'Amour's books in print, they would reach 1,500 miles into space.[1]

Born in Jamestown, North Dakota, in 1908, the son of a veterinarian and the youngest of seven children, L'Amour (his family name had been Americanized and changed to La Moore from the original French L'Amour) spent hours as a child reading at a public library where one of his sisters worked. He dropped out of school when he was fifteen, in the tenth grade, and worked in a variety of jobs that paid little but contributed to a wealth of experiences that nourished his imagination and writing. Most of all, he read. "There was no plan, nor at the time could there be. One had to read what was available, and it had been so from the beginning."[2]

As a young man he earned extra money by boxing and won fifty-one of fifty-nine bouts, and pugilistic encounters are prominent in many of his books. His first love was writing poetry, but in the midst of the Great Depression, that didn't provide enough compensation. His professional writing career began in 1938 when his short stories began appearing in books and magazines. He even continued writing when he was a merchant seaman and later when he served in the U.S. Army during World War II as a quartermaster in a truck company.

L'Amour toured the world working as a laborer in jobs as varied as a fruit picker, gold prospector, lumber jack, cattle skinner, and elephant handler in a circus. He even hung out with a group of bandits in Tibet and sailed on an East African schooner. Meeting people from diverse backgrounds along with the stories his mother related to him about his Irish and French ancestors traversing the American frontier spurred his creative imagination. His grandfather fought in the Civil War, and his great-grandfather was reportedly scalped by the Sioux, a bit of family history that undoubtedly influenced his perspective about Indians. He once said, "I write my books to be read aloud and I think of myself in that oral tradition." Thirty-three of his relatives had been writers and he noted, "I wanted to write from the time I could walk."[3]

His autobiography, *Education of a Wandering Man*, published posthumously by his family, was a recollection of his experiences as a traveler and laborer, but most of all, it is a description of the many books he read that contributed to his erudition and shaped his writing. Possessing a personal library of over ten thousand copies, L'Amour drew on the accumulated wisdom of the ages, voraciously consuming literary classics and lesser known gems that figured into his prodigious writing. When he kept records, we see, for example, that in the 1930s, he averaged reading over one hundred books a year **in addition to writing short stories, novels, and reviewing books.** He incessantly reminded the reader to engage in conversations with local characters who possessed firsthand information about historical events that can provide grist for the writers' mill.

L'Amour was a meticulous researcher, often traveling to the location where the novel was set, living there, and interviewing people in the vicinity—learning about their culture and lifestyles before integrating these experiences into his books. "I go to an area I'm interested in and I try to find a guy who knows it better than anyone else. Usually, it's a broken-down cowboy."[4] L'Amour's works reflected traditional values and moral absolutes of right and wrong. He even dressed like the cowboys he lionized, wearing ten-gallon hats, hand-tooled boots, and braided-leather bolo ties.

Professor Gale characterized his work as melodramatic. His heroes always survived with a happy, almost fairy tale ending. L'Amour even admitted that he never outlined his novels or knew how they would end. He wrote only one draft off the top of his head and never rewrote his work. He is undeniably the most widely read contemporary author of fiction about the American West, and he had plans to write dozens more books prior to his death from lung cancer (he was not a smoker) in 1988.

L'Amour, like Zane Grey, was a master with words and an eloquent painter of western scenery. Among his millions of fans were Presidents Eisenhower, Johnson, Ford, Carter, and Reagan. He is the only U.S. novelist to receive both the Congressional Gold Medal (1984) and the Medal of Freedom (1988). From 1983 to 1987, two or more of his books were simultaneously on the best seller list. His books still annually sell in the millions, and the Western Writers of America rated *Hondo* (1953) and *Flint* (1960) among the top twenty-five Western novels of all time.[5]

Some of L'Amour's other popular Western novels were *Catlow* (1963) and *Down the Long Hills* (1968). He is also known for creating the *Sackett Family Series* (seventeen novels and an accompanying guide),[6] which was adapted for television in 1979. Among the more memorable motion pictures based on his work are *Stranger on Horseback* starring Joel McCrea (1955), *The Burning Hills* starring Tab Hunter and Natalie Wood (1956), and *Shalako* featuring Brigitte Bardot and Sean Connery (1968).

L'Amour's writing often included a hero resembling that of his own youthful days when he was a roustabout. There is a definite theme in many of his novels that reflects rugged individualism, even social Darwinism, and the belief that White people are entitled to the land they took from Native Americans—Manifest Destiny. "When a man can settle down to do what he does best, he's happier, and his work is better. I guess that's where civilization began, with people getting together in a town, sharing the work, and having a chance to talk together."[7] And, "[A] man should be strict with himself."[8] Or, from his autobiography, "There is no reason why anyone cannot get an education if he or she wants it badly enough and is persistent."[9] Later, in his autobiography, he cited the Chinese adage, "A journey of a thousand miles begins with one step," but, "One just has to keep taking that one step over and over again. There is no easy way; there are no shortcuts."[10] And further, "I believe that creativity and inventiveness are there for anybody willing to apply himself."[11]

His writing often contains an element of aggression and a rationalization for violence. "Men strive for peace, but it is their enemies that give them strength, and I think if man no longer had enemies, he would have to invent them, for his strength only grows from struggle."[12] From his perspective, our constitutional right to keep and bear arms was sacrosanct: "We have a militia of a sort, but our greatest strength lies in the fact that so many of our people not only possess weapons but also understand their use, and above all, they are prepared to defend themselves against any sudden attack by an enemy."[13] This passage could have come out of a flyer for the National Rifle Association, but it was an aside spoken by a heroine of his *Lonesome Gods* story to the hero, Johannes Verne.

In his autobiography, as in his novels, L'Amour extolled the virtue of hard work, individual initiative, courage, and honor. The Sackett stories were designed to relate the story of a family settling the American frontier. "Story by story, generation by generation, these families are moving westward. When the journeys are ended and the forty-odd books are completed, the reader should have a fairly true sense of what happened on the American frontier."[14]

L'Amour was a staunch patriot, and according to Gale (and it's apparent in L'Amour's writing), Indians of the American West could call the land their own only as long as they could defend it against intruders—a sentiment shared by one of his admirers and the star of *Hondo*, John Wayne. In L'Amour's stories Native Americans are habitually referred to as savages, rapacious, killers, scalpers, and brigands. They are depicted as marauders infatuated with scalping White people and cast as red bogeymen in relentless pursuit of White settlers. They are characterized like the Apache chief, Cochise, as villains with "malevolent black eyes," and with "eyes black with hatred" and "black-faced Apaches" in his famous short story "The Gift of Cochise" that later became the blockbuster 1953 film, *Hondo*.

The reader is presented with the stereotype of Indians (frequently disparaged as Injuns or Red Injuns or Redskins) as malicious and malevolent without any meaningful discussion of *why* they are angry at the intruders who stole their land and despoiled their resources. Time and again scenes are skillfully described in his inimitable style: the Comanche war party "swept through the small camp, knifing and killing."[15] They are pictured as half-naked, pitiless vagabonds only concerned with the satisfaction of their personal needs and desires. "Ashawakie was no more concerned with the feelings of the children then he would be with those of wolf cubs."[16]

Plains Indians like the Apache, Comanche, and Kiowa often bore the brunt of his vilification. L'Amour described them as innately hostile to White people: "[E]ach time [they] had come upon the sort of hell that only an Apache could leave behind. Lonely ranch houses burned, the stock run off, the dead and mutilated bodies left behind in the sun."[17] To drive the point home, the hero of the *Kiowa Trail* novel, Conn Drury, described the Apache attack that killed his mother: "[T]here was another bang and the *whiff* of an arrow ... and Ma was dead. Afterward, learning what I did learn, I was glad it happened that way."[18]

Native Americans are described as backward and uncivilized. "The big Indian, Ashawakie, was curious, as any wild thing is curious."[19] And their logic is unknowable to Western, civilized people: "Who knows how much an Indian knows? No Indian feels it necessary to tell what he knows about anything. They are good people, most of them, but they think differently than we do."[20] Later in the novel, "Who knows what an Indian is thinking but another Indian? Who knows what they believe? I've known men who claimed they knew Indians ... they were talking through their hats. Nobody does."[21]

We are informed that "Apaches favor mule meat"[22] and have little use for canned goods apparently because they were not sure what they were.[23] This image bolsters the stereotype of Native Americans as disposable commodities, appendages to an increasingly modern society that is making their lifestyle and very existence obsolete. They are seen as obstacles to progress, pests, and vermin. "In the mind of Aaron McDonald that rates him a mite lower than a red Indian."[24]

Readers are seldom given a glimpse of the causes for the hostility among Native Americans—the wholesale trespass of White settlers and prospectors on their traditional hunting and fishing grounds, the theft of their land and abuse of their natural resources, and the resulting impoverishment of their communities. Although L'Amour seldom offers an explanation for Indians' hatred of White people, halfway through one of his last novels, *Last of the Breed* (1987), a contemporary struggle between the forces of evil (the Soviet Union) and a downed test pilot, Major Joseph Makatozi, referred to throughout the book as Joe Mack, who is part Sioux and Cheyenne Indian and represents the force of good (capitalism, rugged individualism, and freedom), L'Amour acknowledges, "His people had no way of gauging the power behind the westward movement or the white man's drive to own land, to live on the land. Only the first men to come had been rovers like the Indian; the rest had been settlers who came and built cabins, who plowed up the grass and planted corn. Not until too late did the Indian realize what was happening to his country. He and many of the white men, too, bewailed the killing of the vast herds of buffalo," but in a tip of the hat to Manifest Destiny and the belief in inevitable White progress, he rationalizes the destruction of the Indians' way of life by noting, "[B]ut where millions of buffalo roamed there were now farms that could feed half the world; there were hospitals, universities, and the homes of men."[25]

The story enumerates the travail of the fiercely independent airman as he eludes capture by the Russians for a year in the Siberian wilderness, tapping into his Native American ancestry as he becomes one with nature and an Indian warrior. "I may be the last Indian who will live in the old way, think the old thoughts," he says stoically.[26] L'Amour wrote, "He has gone to the forest and his natural home is the forest."[27] Joe Mack acknowledged that he was comfortable enduring hardship and suffering because "I am a Sioux. At heart I am a savage. The forest is my home. I am a part of it, just as are the tiger, the bear, and the wolf. I belong here and have always known it."[28] Further, "I walk in the shoes of the men of today. I fly their planes. I eat their food, but my heart is in the wilderness with feathers in my hair."[29] To justify Joe Mack's violence, L'Amour declares, "He was what a Sioux had been bred to be, a warrior."[30] Such pronouncements help perpetuate stereotypes about Native Americans as socially and biologically inferior and incompatible with Western (White) civilization.

The book makes for a good read, as do many of L'Amour's stories. It might easily have served as a template for Sylvester Stallone's *Rambo* movies that appeared around the time of its publication. L'Amour's work had an enormous impact on the motion picture industry and the emerging mass television market. Over forty-five of his books and stories were produced as Hollywood films or wormed their way into television stories and series. But despite his apparent profundity and consummate storytelling, he conveyed a flawed stereotypical message about Native Americans to his readers. A passage from his book, *The Sackett Companion: A Personal Guide to the Sackett Novels*,[31] is revealing: "Very few Indians fought for their land. The idea that they might lose it was beyond their conception. Indians fought for scalps, for loot, for any one of a dozen reasons, just as white men did."[32] And further, "From my personal study, reading of reports, diaries, and early newspapers, my impression is that for every Indian who died in the settling of the West at least ten white people died. Not necessarily in fighting, though by one means or another."[33] That's one reason why his work is classified as historical fiction. Despite L'Amour's painstaking research, listening to and reading biased accounts about the "settling of the West" by White people does little to peel the fog and deception away from centuries of White rationalizations about Native American rights and behavior. It merely reinforces stereotypical impressions and prejudices he, and many of his readers, already had. An entertainer at heart, perhaps he knew that as he spun his engaging stories about the Old West.

But many contemporary historians and the courts take a different approach to the rights of Native Americans. They point to the theft of Indian land and resources and the abrogation of hundreds of treaties by the U.S. government. L'Amour's jaundiced depiction of Indians are out of step with the current view of Native Americans. Even Gale, a fan of L'Amour, referred to his references about them as "gross generalizations that among other things, do not recognize differences in customs and character among tribes and individuals."[34] Essentially, L'Amour viewed Indians as a hindrance to White civilization, an obstacle that could and would be removed through the "superior" values and technology of White people as they spread inexorably across the West. This is a very different perspective from his predecessor Zane Grey. Judging by L'Amour's popularity, his stereotypical depiction of Indians has had a lasting impact on the White American psyche.

Western novels and films often captivated readers and audiences by providing them with an escape from the reality of their lives—opportunities to embark on dreams about the triumph of good over evil, revenge for immoral and unethical assaults perpetrated against them, sexual escapades, American morality exemplified through virtuous heroes who were physically and morally superior to their adversaries, and the American dream of Manifest Destiny captured through the wanderlust of the free spirits of inquisitive young men and women in search of freedom.

In addition to writing about unscrupulous cattle ranchers and bankers, L'Amour often stereotyped Native Americans as irksome barbarians, and they were incidental to many of his plots. As impositions they were often depicted as illiterate, unpredictable, and untrustworthy. His disdain for them may stem in part from the childhood stories he heard from his mother about marauding Indians terrorizing his Irish and French ancestors.

The similarities between L'Amour and Faust are striking. Although they lived around the same time, Faust was older. Both read and were influenced by Cooper and Grey, and appreciated the negative impact that modernization was having on traditional Native American habitats and lifestyles, although they frequently stereotyped Indians as uncivilized and aggressive. They were voracious readers and drew on that for creative themes and stories. Yet Faust relied almost exclusively on his imagination for plots while L'Amour traveled to most of his western locations and interviewed people there for research about his stories.

Despite their prodigious writing in the Western genre, they were both aspiring but rather unsuccessful poets. They were large (over six feet tall), pugilistic, and worked in varied menial jobs early in their lives to stave off poverty. This macho image pervades much of their Western writing as do the themes of good versus evil and the embellishment of Manifest Destiny, American exceptionalism, and rugged individualism. "We ask of our children virtue, for ourselves strength," wrote Faust. "Strength is never contemptible."[35]

15

Television, Cowboys, and Indians

Some trails are happy ones, others are blue. It's the way you ride the trail that counts, here's a happy one for you.
—Dale Evans and Roy Rogers theme song "Happy Trails"

The proliferation of Western novels provided an enormous resource that the technological innovation television could draw on. Milking the works of Grey, Faust, and L'Amour, media entrepreneurs introduced masses of people to the visual spectacle of seeing Indians act and dress in stereotypical ways that the masters conjured in their literary genre. While the profusion of Hollywood (and later Italian) Western motion pictures emanating from the works of these writers flooded theaters around the world, the work of Clarence E. Mulford made a significant impression on the American psyche through Big Screen and television adaptations of his wildly popular novels about Hopalong Cassidy.

Mulford was born in Streator, Illinois, in 1883 and died in Portland, Maine, in 1956. Like his contemporaries, he was a prolific writer, but like Faust, he derived most of his ideas and descriptions about the West from his imagination and library research. He visited the West only once (1924) and disliked his excursion, preferring to toil as a city clerk in New York during the day and write late into the night at his home in Brooklyn.

At the height of his writing career he wrote at a furious pace, often at the rate of 1,200 words a day. Mulford's short stories, many of which were serialized in magazines (e.g., *Outing Magazine*, *West* magazine) and later published as novels by McClurg and then Doubleday, trace the life of fictional Western characters. His biographer, Francis Nevins, Jr., contended that he was one of the best action scene writers of Western novels. His first Hopalong Cassidy novel was *Bar-20*, named for the ranch where young Hopalong supposedly worked.

After Mulford achieved some success, he moved with his mother to Fryeburg, Maine, where he later hired a housekeeper and settled with his wife, Eva, who passed away from heart disease in 1933 at the age of forty-eight. This event devastated Mulford, and he drastically curtailed his writing for many years. But it did not prevent him from indulging in creating models of machines and collecting guns, purportedly including the Sharp's rifle that was used to kill Sitting Bull.[1]

According to Nevins, Mulford initially received $2,500 for each Hoppy television episode.[2] When he created the character of Hopalong Cassidy (so named because of a gunshot wound he sustained to his thigh that resulted in a limp—but which was jettisoned in the television portrayal of the character by William Boyd), he never dreamed of the fantastic success that his hero would generate. In 118 films and television episodes, the character of Hopalong Cassidy helped make Mulford and William Boyd, who bought the rights to the Cassidy enterprise for $350,000, wealthy, and created a cult of followers who devoured hats, shirts, holsters, toy guns, lunch boxes, and assorted icons of the popular all-American hero. Dressed in black, with silver hair, flashy nickel-plated six-shooters, and riding a white horse named Topper, Boyd's motion picture and television version of Cassidy was a far cry from Mulford's red-haired, foul-mouthed, roustabout cowpuncher who faced adversity, bad guys, Mexicans, and renegade Indians (usually Apaches) on the western range.

When Boyd bought the television rights to Hopalong Cassidy from Mulford in 1948, he proceeded to show weekly edited one-hour (fifty-four-minute) versions of the feature films. Despite the heavy-handed editing, the films became a smashing success, making Boyd a wealthy star. There ensued the first successful commercialization of a television entity, and Hoppy products became a runaway sensation with children in the United States.

Boyd eventually sold all the Cassidy assets to William Boyd Enterprises for $8 million and retired to live with his fifth wife in Palm Desert, California. He died from a combination of cancer, congestive heart failure, and Parkinson's disease in 1972. Prior to that, he and his third wife bequeathed all rights in the Hoppy films to the Children's Hospital in Los Angeles. Although he had a reputation as a heavy drinker earlier in his career, no doubt exacerbated by an unfortunate newspaper story that incorrectly confused him with another actor with the same name who had been involved in a scandal, he limited his alcoholic intake as the persona of the gentlemanly Cassidy soared.

Besides losing the limp, Boyd and his media compatriots burnished the image of Cassidy, making him more like the American idol than a swarthy ranch hand. Mulford lived to see Boyd's incarnation of Cassidy and was so taken aback by the whitewashed depiction of his character that he fainted in the theater and had to be revived with smelling salts.[3]

First drawing large audiences on radio, and then in sixty-six films and television episodes running from 1949 to 1951, Boyd managed to parlay the image of Hopalong Cassidy into a money-making icon that brought him millions of dollars in return for his initial investment. He was even featured on the cover of *Life* magazine (June 12, 1950). The films, comic books, newspaper comic strip, and television show (the first television Western series) created a massive audience. In 1950, *Hopalong Cassidy* was rated as the seventh most popular television show in the United States, and the phenomenal success of the show and its lucrative spinoffs in merchandise and feature films led to a proliferation of other Western motion pictures. By 1959, seven of the top ten television shows in the United States were Westerns (e.g., *Rawhide*, *The Rifleman*, and *Maverick*).

Mulford, like L'Amour and Faust (and, as we will see, Laura Ingalls Wilder, another widely read author at this time), was a staunch libertarian. He denigrated the concept of "Big Government" and was an avowed critic of FDR and the New Deal. A social Darwinist at heart, Mulford, like Faust, Grey, and L'Amour, created fictional characters and situations that dramatized the struggle between good and evil, parlaying the American obsession with rugged individualism and an idealized perception of freedom in the West into a formulaic model that often denigrated Native Americans for the sake of inflating the heroic persona of their all-American characters. Rather than risk paying taxes, which he abhorred, Mulford bequeathed nearly all his personal wealth and his copyrights to the Clarence E. Mulford Trust he created in 1950.[4] Much of this money was used to fund education for needy students in the Fryeburg, Maine, area, and in 1952 he donated his manuscripts and large personal library on western American life to the Library of Congress.[5]

The *Hopalong Cassidy* phenomenon flourished, making Mulford and Boyd wealthy. Reprints of Mulford's articles and books were published by Doubleday, and when he retired, he recommended that the then struggling Louis L'Amour succeed him as author of new Hoppy novels. L'Amour turned out four Hoppy books for Doubleday in 1950 under the pen name Tex Burns, but for most of his life he denied writing them, finally admitting, "A long time ago I wrote some books, I just did it for the money, and my name didn't go on them. So now, when people ask me if they were mine, I say no."[6] According to his son Beau L'Amour, Louis L'Amour once said, "I don't care for the books, and I don't care for the whole situation. Those books have no relationship to the work I'm doing now. They agreed I could write them one way but they went back on their deal."[7]

The success of *Hopalong Cassidy* on television led to a proliferation of other shows in the same genre and the "singing cowboys" like the husband and wife combo of Roy Rogers and Dale Evans. They, along with Gene Autry and others, splashed on the television screens in the '40s, and '50s, feeding the public's seeming insatiable desire for nostalgia riddled with myths and stereotypes about the Old West. Western television shows transfixed the nation through the decades of the '50s, '60s, and '70s—even into the '80s. Repeats still appear including blockbuster shows like *The Virginian*, starring Doug McClure, James Drury, and Lee J. Cobb, which initially ran from 1962 to 1971 on NBC; *The Rifleman*, starring Chuck Connors, which ran from 1958 to 1962 on ABC; *Rawhide*, starring Eric Flemming and, among others, the illustrious hard-nosed cowboy, Clint Eastwood, running on CBS from 1959 to 1965; *Wagon Train*, starring Frank McGrath, Terry Wilson, Robert Horton, and Ward Bond, which initially ran on NBC and then moved to ABC from 1957 to 1965; *Bonanza*, starring Lorne Greene, Dan Blocker, Pernell Roberts, and Michael Landon (who later starred on *Little House on the Prairie*), which ran on NBC from 1959 to 1973; *Have Gun, Will Travel*, starring Richard Boone, which aired on CBS from 1957 to 1963; *Maverick*, which aired on ABC from 1957 to 1962 starring James Garner and Jack Kelly; and the granddaddy of them all, *Gunsmoke*, starring James Arness, which was televised from 1955 to 1975 on CBS, the longest running Western show. Reruns of these shows can still be found on contemporary television.

Romance on the Frontier

Women also had a hand in extolling the virtues of meritocracy, rugged individualism, Manifest Destiny, and American exceptionalism. Willa Cather (1873–1947) devoted a trilogy of novels[8] to frontier life on the Great Plains. Though her works are long on romance and somewhat short on the toil and drudgery facing settlers in Nebraska and Colorado where they were set, and references to Native Americans are seldom found in them, except for an occasional remark about their color or state of mind, her exquisite style and meticulous character development led the acerbic literary and social critic H. L. Mencken to boldly assert, "There is no other author of her sex, now in view, whose future promises so much."[9] His words were prophetic, with Cather winning the Pulitzer Prize in 1923 for her novel *One of Ours* (1922) set in World War I.

Cather herself was something of an enigma. Though she was born in Virginia and lived on a farm from 1883 to 1896 in Nebraska, she resided in New York City from 1906 until her death in 1947, most of the time with female companions in Greenwich Village. Though some chroniclers of her career considered her a lesbian, there is no definitive evidence of this, and it does not appear to have influenced her writing. Her early childhood experiences on the Great Plains left an indelible mark on her work, which is characterized by mature social and psychological insights into human relationships that shaped frontier life and interactions among Swedes, Bohemians, Norwegians, and French immigrants. Despite considerable interest in her life and writing, her influence on Native American stereotypes was infinitesimal compared to the work of a true Western pioneer who has influenced the lives of millions of readers and television viewers, Laura Ingalls Wilder.

The Little House Phenomenon

Perhaps the most influential fusion of literature and television that perpetuated stereotypes about Native Americans was the adaptation of the work of a genuine frontierswoman, Laura Ingalls Wilder, who was born in Wisconsin in 1867 and died in Missouri in 1957. She was the author of eight children's books that have sold over sixty million copies in forty-five languages in over one hundred countries. Two of her books, *Little House in the Big Woods* and *Little House on the Prairie*, are ranked by *Publishers Weekly* in the top twenty best-selling children's books of all time. Wilder's books became the basis for one of the most successful television programs (*Little House on the Prairie*) during the 1970s and 1980s in the United States, and her book, *The Long Winter*, was one of one hundred English-language books approved by General Headquarters for reading by the Japanese at the end of World War II because its message of forbearance was thought to resonate with them, and General MacArthur was a fan of hers.

The key to Wilder's success was the glorification of themes that personified the American Dream of the pursuit of happiness, Manifest Destiny, and American exceptionalism. Her works were imbued with the ethic of rugged individualism, thrift, independence, industriousness, and stoicism in the face of calamity. Wilder didn't begin her writing career until she was fifty-seven, and there is speculation whether her daughter, Rose Wilder Lane, an established writer in her own right, played a pivotal role in her mother's works,[10] and how accurate her accounts were of past experiences. One of her biographers concluded that in her "autobiographical work, 'truth' would become a battlefield."[11] Another biographer noted: "From the beginning, she was more concerned with fitting her family's story into a larger pioneering experience."[12]

Despite the widespread belief that Wilder's books were accurate representations of her family's experiences, her works are what is commonly referred to today as historical fiction. As biographer Hill explained: "[T]he greater truth of fiction, the satisfying arc of a good story, ultimately interested Wilder far more than the precise details of her own past."[13] Wilder even acknowledged that she used creative license in her work, noting that an incident in her book *By the Shores of Silver Lake* was invented, rationalizing, "The book is not a history but true story founded on historical fact."[14] This explanation might just as easily have been proffered by President Trump's adviser Kellyanne Conway, an advocate of "alternative facts," and fake news.

In one of her most engaging books, *The Long Winter*, Wilder omitted reference to other dwellers in her household, later acknowledging that it detracted from the storyline about the hardship her family endured. "The point of the situation would be blunted, the family must be alone," she wrote her daughter.[15]

Biographer Hill provides ample evidence demonstrating the collaborative arrangement between Wilder and her daughter, who critiqued and edited her mother's manuscripts and, at times, was condescending about her mother's prose. Lane was also known to stretch facts in pursuit of a more compelling story—a technique that generated criticism from some of the objects of her biographical writing (e.g., the family of writer Jack London, Charlie Chaplin, and Herbert Hoover).

Self-educated, Laura Ingalls Wilder did not graduate from high school. The largely autobiographical books, begun in the spring of 1930 and completed in 1943, are based on her recollection of experiences growing up as the child of an itinerant homesteader, Charles Ingalls, who worked tirelessly to establish a home and livelihood for his wife, Caroline, and their five children, as well as her own life on the western frontier as the dutiful wife of Almanzo (Manly), her husband of sixty-four years. In her writing she also used family lore, letters, hymnals, and artifacts from her past. In addition to her daughter, she was assisted by an aunt, Martha Carpenter, and two of her sisters who shared their recollections with her.

Wilder approached her writing by developing themes linked to the seasons, and she managed to enthrall youngsters by inculcating her family's infatuation with a search for freedom and beauty in the West. Wilder admitted that she wrote the eight *Little House* books because "I wanted the children to now understand more about the beginning of things—to know what is behind the things they see—what it is that made America as they know it."[16]

Biographer Hill contends, "This thematic emphasis—always looking west, never turning back—is the spine, the rigid, inflexible backbone of the entire series."[17] But Wilder chronicles many instances when adversity compelled her family to reverse course, even retreat to their previous home in Wisconsin. Throughout her writing, Wilder focused on her family's courage in the face of adversity and created a heroic and nostalgic reverence for her main characters and the American infatuation with Manifest Destiny and the past.

Wilder, married at eighteen and a mother at nineteen, still has a huge following among youthful readers in the United States, and her books are routinely recommended and read to children by teachers and librarians. Her stoic vision about the pioneer struggles of her family and friends has produced "scores of adaptations in print, on stage and on screen—including a Japanese anime version—and a website of song books, cookbooks, sequels, and chat sites. There are licensed dolls, clothes, fabrics and, inevitably, sunbonnets."[18] Indeed, "She has become one of the national figures by which we take the measure of pioneer women."[19] As she once stated, "I realized that I had seen it all—all the successive phases of the frontier, first the frontiersman, then the pioneer, then the farmers, and the towns."[20] Many of her books received highly favorable reviews in the *New York Times* and *Kirkus*, a publishing industry guidepost, and several of them were nominated as Newbery Honor Books for children.

The books dramatize the struggle of the Ingalls and later, Laura's life with her husband, Almanzo, as they tried to survive against the ravages of inhospitable climate (drought, hail, tornadoes, searing heat, prairie fires, and blizzards); locusts that devoured their crops of wheat and corn; economic and political calamities (the depressions of the 1870s, 1890s, and 1930s); state and federal government interventions to attenuate the plight of settlers by implementing legislation that at times alleviated their hardship and at other times aggravated it; as well as her jaundiced perception about the Native Americans who inhabited the land that her family settled on.

The *Little House* monographs are a testimonial to the infatuation of Americans with the western frontier, and they perpetuate mythology about the virtues of hard work, meritocracy, and self-sufficiency. Wilder's children's books read like they could have been written by Cotton Mather himself and reinforce the thesis of German social scientist Max Weber about the driving ethos in Western society that fused ascetic Protestantism and work.[21] Wilder once poetically advised her youthful readers, "If you've anything to do, do it with all your might. Don't let trifles hinder you if you're sure you're right. Work away, work away. Do it with all your might."[22] Aphoristic lessons, like "Laura worked hard, but she knew that hard work never hurt anyone" and "From sunrise to sunset each day, Laura was busy,"[23] are liberally sprinkled throughout her books, exhorting children to adopt the mythological philosophy of the American Dream and accept adversity stoically, as when her sister, Mary, became blind. "Throughout her illness, Mary had not complained. When she became blind, Mary did not mourn. She was patient and accepting, and thankful for Pa and Ma and her sisters." Further, "Laura learned much from Mary. She practiced patience and cheerfulness and kindness, inspired by Mary's example. Laura was growing up."[24] These illustrations appear in a biography of Wilder that was written for children, and they convey the same message that hard work and individual initiative will overcome even the most onerous obstacles put in one's path—the kind of rationalization that is still being used to denigrate Native Americans and less fortunate people in our society.

Wilder's lesson for children about forbearance and stoically accepting one's situation is captured by her observation, "They were lucky little girls, to have a good house to live in, and a warm fire to sit by, and such a turkey for their Christmas dinner."[25] After all, her father once observed, "There's no great loss without some small pain,"[26] after deciding to leave their homestead under threat of eviction by the federal government.

Here, in her own words, we find similar pronouncements: Mary and Laura drank water because "They could not drink coffee until they grew up."[27] And, "Laura swallowed hard, to keep from crying. She knew it was shameful to cry, but there was crying inside her."[28] Referring to her father's effort to build their house, "It would never do to lose or waste a nail."[29] And Wilder's writing reinforced still prevalent characterizations of women as subordinate to men: "Now we must get dinner. Pa will be here soon and we must have dinner ready for him."[30] Readers are also told constantly, "It isn't nice to contradict,"[31] and "It was not polite for little girls to interrupt."[32]

Living occasionally in eight "frontier" states (Wisconsin, Minnesota, Missouri, Kansas, Nebraska, Florida, Iowa, settling in De Smet, South Dakota, and winding up in Mansfield, Missouri), the Ingalls', and later Wilder's, lives were characterized by harrowing experiences that often left the family destitute and food insecure—not knowing where their next meal would come from. But to the reader, her parents and husband were saints—unselfish, creative, resourceful—able to cope with the elements, to construct dwellings that withstood the onslaught of nature, till and harvest fields, build and repair furniture, hunt and fish, and prepare a variety of wild and domestic fare for dinner.

But the Ingalls knew that the land they squatted on belonged to the Osage Indians. Her father even admitted this in *Little House on the Prairie*: "If some blasted politician in Washington hadn't sent out word it would be all right to settle here, I'd never have been three miles over the line into Indian territory."[33]

For all their disdain of Big Government and charity, the family was not averse to taking advantage of Uncle Sam's largesse and rationalized the theft of Native American land, as when her father supposedly told Laura, "When white settlers come into a country, the Indians have to move on. The government is going to move these Indians farther west, any time now. That's why we're here, Laura. White people are going to settle all this country, and we get the best land because we got here first and take our pick."[34]

The books were supposedly based on Wilder's recollections of life on the western prairie as well as stories told to her by her peripatetic settler father whose memory was also influenced by the passage of time and his own stereotypical impressions of events. And although Indians were sometimes treated kindly in her spotty recollections, such as when they shared food with the starving interlopers, she was never able to forget the trauma of the Dakota uprising of 1862 in Minnesota (five years before she was born) when a group of Dakota Indians conducted a series of raids against White settlers in the region, brutally torturing, raping, and ultimately killing 500–600 White people, including 70 soldiers, and losing 150 of warriors.

The so-called Great Sioux Uprising of 1862 was precipitated by the poor treatment of the Indians by the U.S. government, which signed treaties (Traverse des Sioux and Mendota) in 1851 that ceded twenty-four million acres of the Indian land to the federal government for as little as 30 cents an acre, leaving the Indians on two narrow reservations each twenty-two miles wide and seventy miles long. The Indians were also guaranteed annual stipends and food, but these were often late in arriving. Traders would routinely grant the Indians credit and claim their stipends, at times inflating their indebtedness and leaving the Indians without food and funds. Their land was reduced by another one million acres in 1857.

Tensions between the White settlers and the Native Americans were already high when, on May 17, 1862, four young Dakota Indians killed five White settlers near present-day Grove City, Minnesota. Returning to their village and revealing the incident, their tribe, under the leadership of Chief Little Crow (Taoyateduta), decided to go to war, attacking White settlements along the Minnesota River. The Dakota destroyed the predominantly German town of New Ulm and attacked other settlements before a force of troops under command of General John Pope and Colonel

Henry Sibley (the first governor of Minnesota and originally married to a Dakota woman, Red Blanket) subdued them. When dispatched by President Lincoln to quell the uprising, General Pope's state of mind was revealed in this letter to Colonel Sibley:

> The horrible massacres of women and children and the outrageous abuse of female prisoners, still alive, call for punishment beyond human power to inflict. There will be no peace in this region by virtue of treaties and Indian faith. It is my purpose utterly to exterminate the Sioux if I have the power to do so and even if it requires a campaign lasting the whole of next year. Destroy everything belonging to them and force them out of the plains, unless, as I suggest, you can capture them. They are to be treated as maniacs or wild beasts, and by no means as people with whom treaties or compromise can be made.[35]

Over 2,000 Indians were rounded up, and 392 people were hastily tried under the supervision of Sibley. Cultural and language differences between the accused and accusers made a mockery of the trials, and when 303 Indians were sentenced to death, President Lincoln reviewed their cases and noted, "Anxious to not act with so much clemency as to encourage another outbreak on one hand, nor with so much severity as to be real cruelty on the other, I ordered careful examination of the records of the trials to be made, in view of final orders, the execution of such as has been proved guilty of violating females."[36]

Notice the repugnance in these letters of White men toward assumed Indian sexual assaults against White women. When only two Indians were found guilty of rape, Lincoln expanded the criteria for capital punishment to include those who had participated in civilian massacres. He then recommended thirty-nine Indians be executed. Sibley complied, and on December 26, 1862, all but one of them were publicly hung in front of a crowd of four thousand people in Mankato, Minnesota. (One Indian received a last-minute reprieve.) Sixteen other Indians were given prison sentences. The executed Indians hung there for half an hour and were then buried in a mass grave. Many bodies were immediately exhumed and used by physicians as cadavers for their research.[37] This event remains the largest mass execution ever conducted in the United States.

Following the surrender of the Dakota on September 26, 1862, 285 hostages were released. During their imprisonment in Davenport, Iowa, that winter, 120 Dakota Indians died. Additionally, 1,700 Dakotas (mostly women and children) were marched to Fort Snelling, Minnesota, and were set upon by a riotous crowd of settlers in Henderson, Minnesota. During the winter of 1862–63, another one hundred to three hundred Indians perished from diseases such as measles.[38]

Spurred on by the prospect of cheap and even free land ($1.25 an acre in some instances) through the Homestead Act of 1862 that granted families 160 acres of surveyed land for a $10 filing fee for the promise of five years of continuous residence, and unscrupulous railroad and real estate agents who touted the virtues, beauty, and lifestyles awaiting settlers in this region, tens of thousands of would-be farmers flocked to the then western fringe of the United States determined to seek their fortune by eviscerating the vast plains and prairies that were the home of Native Americans who farmed, hunted, and fished there before them.[39] Ironically, plowing the lush prairie grass, tilling the sod (hence the nickname "sod busters"), and planting huge expanses of wheat and corn contributed to the aridity and heat of the region's climate, just as the die-off of Indigenous people in North, Central, and South America had precipitated a decrease in the region's temperature in the seventeenth and eighteenth centuries when they no longer cultivated their fields. Now, with vast expanses of prairie cultivated, disturbing the natural environment, the region experienced warming temperatures and drought that devastated crops and created the "dust bowl" conditions of the late 1800s through the 1930s.[40]

The homesteaders at times encountered hostile Indians who were upset over the land grab that left them without resources, often starving as their annual allotments of food and money were late or disregarded by a federal government engaged in the Civil War. The buffalo, one of their principal sources of food and clothing, was nearly exterminated by hunters for the burgeoning railroads, and the proliferation of horses among the Indians further facilitated their decimation through improved hunting techniques.

Life for most people, settlers and Indians, on the western frontier was inhospitable. Freezing winters and scorching summers made living a challenge, and Wilder's books combine factual incidents with homespun allegories that serve to reinforce the narrative that American exceptionalism and Manifest Destiny could overcome adversity.[41] The land, according to Wilder's father, Charles, belonged to Uncle Sam who generously offered it to homesteaders. Wilder recalled one of the cheerful songs he sang while he played his fiddle: "Uncle Sam is rich enough to give us all a farm."[42]

Other squatters like the Ingalls' neighbors, the Scotts, also harbored condescending attitudes toward the Indigenous people. "Mrs. Scott said she hoped to goodness they would have no trouble with Indians. She said, 'Land knows, they'd never do anything with this country themselves, all they do is roam around over it like wild animals. Treaties or no treaties, the land belongs to folks that'll farm it. That's only common sense and justice.' She did not know why the government made treaties with Indians. The only good Indian was a dead Indian. The very thought of Indians made her [Laura's] blood run cold."[43]

Yet the land Charles Ingalls settled on belonged, by treaty, to the Osage Indians. In fact, there was a well-used trail not far from their house, and they observed frequent Indian traffic on it. Although the Osage were not around when the Ingalls arrived, apparently away on a seasonal hunt, they were entitled to rent from settlers, which might explain their uninvited appearances and penchant for handouts of food. Throughout these and other incidents it is apparent that Laura was terrified of them.

Little House on the Prairie contains numerous descriptions of the Indians as "wild men" and savages.[44] Some of her negative views of Native Americans were undoubtedly derived from her mother, Caroline. For example, when she asked her, "Why don't you like Indians, Ma?" she replied, "I just don't like them, and don't lick your fingers." To which Laura queried, "This is Indian country, isn't it? What did we come to their country for if you don't like them?"[45]

Although Laura saw Indians frequently, she was obsessed with thoughts of them as uncivilized, dangerous barbarians: "Laura knew they were wild men with red skins, and their hatchets were called tomahawks."[46]

Here's how she described the first Indians who visited their new home: "[S]he saw two naked wild men coming, one behind the other, on the Indian trail. They were tall, thin, fierce-looking men. Their skin was brownish-red. Their heads seemed to go up to a peak, and the peak was a tuft of hair that stood straight up and ended in feathers. Their eyes were black and still glittering, like snake's eyes." When they disappeared Laura and her sister, Mary, "looked at the place where those terrible men would appear when they came past the house." And when they entered her home, Mary whispered, "'They are in the house with Ma and [baby] Carrie.' Then Laura began to shake all over. She knew she must do something. She did not know what those Indians were doing to Ma and Baby Carrie."[47]

After noting that their visitors smelled horribly, probably because their breech cloths were made of recently killed skunks, she recapitulated the stereotype of them as fierce-looking wild men with glittering black eyes making "harsh sounds in their throat," who ate every crumb of cornbread her mother gave them. After they left, she asked her mother, "Do you feel sick, Ma?" "No," she replied. "I'm just thankful they're gone."[48] Later, her father averred that they had done the right thing by feeding them and giving them some of his tobacco: "The main thing is to be on good terms with the Indians. We don't want to wake up some night with a band of the screeching dev...."[49] Although he didn't finish his sentence, Laura knew exactly what he was going to say, and that sentiment influenced her later perception of Indians during a critical incident in their life in Indian Territory.

The Ingalls lived in Kansas, then Indian Territory, from 1869 to 1870. Most of the time the Osage Indians were unobtrusive, living near a creek in a hollow surrounded by stone bluffs. But one evening Laura was startled by "a wild, fierce sound, but it didn't seem angry."[50] Mr. Scott, their neighbor, did not know why a large group of Indians were congregating, but some of the settlers assumed they were preparing for war with other tribes. Although Charles Ingalls believed the Indians were peaceful, he remained vigilant because he knew that some of them were unhappy about being moved further west by the government, and some "naturally hated white folks. But an Indian ought to have sense enough to know when he was licked."[51] But there was an uneasiness among the Indians that night as the Ingalls listened to the "savage voices shouting."[52] Laura was petrified by the sounds: "Night crept toward the little house, and the darkness was frightening. It yelped with Indian yells, and one night it began to throb with Indian drums. In her sleep Laura heard all the time that savage yipping and the wild, throbbing drums."[53]

Her father tried to assuage her fear by reminding her that soldiers were nearby at Forts Gibson and Dodge, but she was "horribly afraid." When the sound of their voices rose even higher, she went to the doorway and observed a long line of Indians making their way south. Later in the day, "As far as she could see to the west and as far as she could see to the east there were Indians. There was no end to that long, long line."[54]

Her father noted that earlier that day two other parties of Indians had gone west. He mistakenly thought that their dislodging was the result of a quarrel among them, when, in actuality, their chanting and departure were because of their displacement from land granted to them in federal treaties. The supposed war cries that had terrified young Laura, were, in all probability, mournful dirges uttered by Osage who were once again victimized by a White civilization focused on the acquisition of their land and resources.

To rationalize the mistreatment of the Osage, Wilder concocted a story about an Indian chief, Soldat du Chene, who ostensibly convinced his brethren to abandon their plans to massacre the White squatters. A fascinating and very readable story, but English professor Frances W. Kaye could find no evidence corroborating this event, and the very existence of du Chene at this time was doubtful.[55]

Aside from her abhorrence of Indians, Wilder also harbored negative impressions about Black people. For example, when her entire family became ill, they were treated by a Black physician, Dr. Tan, who served the Indians nearby. Recognizing that he saved their lives, Laura recounted her first interaction with him: "Then the doctor came. And he was the black man. Laura had never seen a black man before and she could not take her eyes off Dr. Tan. He was so very black. She would have been afraid of him if she had not liked him so much. He smiled at her with all his white teeth."[56]

Wilder's apprehension about people of color is even reflected in her self-concept. Her older sister, Mary, had blue eyes, and "Mary's hair was beautifully golden, but Laura's was only a dirt-colored brown."[57] And, "Laura's throat swelled tight, and she could not speak. She knew golden hair was prettier than brown."[58] Her preference for Aryan features was evidenced in the numerous references she made in her books about Pa's "blue eyes" that sparkled and twinkled as he played the fiddle in the evenings to entertain her family. Such attitudes reflect deep-rooted, negative, dominant societal perceptions of "the Other," namely Native Americans and African Americans. Although her legion of followers was predisposed to give her a pass on her racist observations, accolades for her work evolved into scorn and even contempt as societal standards of acceptable racial attitudes and sentiments changed.

Wilder and her daughter, Rose, were critical of FDR's New Deal, yet their family was not averse to taking advantage of the government's largesse and social supports when they were in need. Laura's father, Charles, joined the Farmer's Alliance, which became the Populist Party that demanded government takeover of the railroads and the establishment of federal warehouses for farm produce to ensure price stability.[59] Laura herself worked for many years in the Federal Farm Loan program, and her family received land under the Homestead Act.

Her books have been successful partly because of their nostalgic portrayal of the American West and the mythological characteristics of American settlers who persevered in the face of overwhelming obstacles—poverty, inclement weather, hostile Indians. But, as biographer Fraser points out, she and her daughter blamed Big Government for the failures of the settlers, overlooking their poor decision making, violation of the region's ecology, insufficient capitalization, and the gullibility of homesteaders who believed the extravagant claims of railroads and realtors hawking the land to entice naive settlers by the lure of wealth and natural resources that did not belong to them.

In her later years, Rose Wilder Lane became a staunch libertarian and friend of Ayn Rand (*The Fountainhead, Atlas Shrugged*), and helped launch the movement that developed into the contemporary Libertarian Party. How ironic that these women, raised in poverty, who extolled the virtues of thrift, deferred gratification, and stoicism, became wealthy. As biographer Fraser wryly noted, "Showing American children how to be poor without shame, she herself grew rich."[60]

Wilder's readers and the viewers of the *Little House* television show did not know that seven Native American tribes (loosely called Sioux, a term they dislike to this day because it overlooks the ethnic uniqueness of each group and derogatorily meant "little snakes" when used by their adversaries, the Ojibwe) inhabited the land prior to her family and others squatting on it. In 1851, approximately 6,000 Dakota Indians were forced to live on a reservation that was 140 miles long and 10 miles wide bordering the Minnesota River. A series of treaties between the Dakota tribes and the U.S. government supposedly ensured specific rights and payments to the Indians for the land (530 million acres) that was acquired under the auspices of President Jefferson through the Louisiana Purchase in 1803 from the French.

The ambiguous treaties were disregarded by settlers and later homesteaders who coveted the territory. According to biographer Fraser, in 1840 there were only a few hundred White people in the territory and twenty-five thousand Native Americans, but those numbers changed dramatically. By 1858 there were 150,000 White people seizing land and building a variety of structures from roads to sawmills and in the process destroying the Indians' way of life.[61]

Wilder's recollections of her encounters with Indians must be viewed from the perspective that the Indians had been forced to relinquish large tracts of land and were destitute. Her father's first homestead in "Indian Territory" was, as previously noted, illegally developed well within the official boundary of the Osage tribe in Kansas (what is referred to as the Diminished Reserve of 1870). Although she was only four years old at the time, Wilder recalled hearing the chants of the Osage and watched them file past her house as they once again were forced to vacate the land they called home. What she described as menacing war hoops and chants might well have been the mournful cries of these forlorn dispossessed Indians.[62] Yet, she recognized the beauty of the lands her family occupied and noted in her diary about her family's trip from South Dakota to Mansfield, Ohio, "If I had been the Indians I would have scalped more white folks before I ever would have left it."[63]

Professor Kaye referred to Wilder's literary façade as a litany of human rights violations, an ethnic cleansing of the Great Plains leaving her legions of youthful readers oblivious about the culpability of White settlers in the displacement and demise of the Indians.[64] By 1865 more than ten thousand Native Americans had been removed from eastern Kansas and the lands they had been promised in perpetuity, and she noted: "Wilder and her readers accept that loss as virtually inevitable in the clash of two cultures, of two peoples equally determined to find homes and sustenance for their children. Like the treaty makers, Wilder and her readers see the story of the Ingalls family in Kansas in a light that valorizes the settlers and makes the removal of the Osages emotionally quite bearable. The sadness readers feel is ennobling, not wrenching. A friendly and respectful expulsion from one's homeland, however, is still expulsion, and by definition, neither friendly nor respectful."[65]

While there is some question about whether Wilder was a racist, sometimes her words belied her denials. For example, on page two of *Little House on the Prairie*, she described how isolated their family was when they traveled west: "[A]nd there were no settlers. Only Indians lived there." The original version of the book read, "[A]nd there were no people. Only Indians lived there." This statement was changed after the mother of a youthful reader pointed out the implication of the passage. Wilder and her editor apologized, but the passage is representative of the implicit stereotypical prejudice that becomes embedded in our culture about Indians and other people of color.

An obvious discordant point between Wilder's portrayal of White settlers and Indians is reflected in her values of piety, stoicism, and industriousness. Historically, White stereotypes about Native Americans (and other Indigenous people) have characterized them as indolent and dissolute, inhabitants who occupied the land that God gave them. But it took the intellect, sedulousness, and moral superiority of White people to properly develop the natural resources according to God's Plan. Pity that Wilder and her avid followers do not recall the eighth and tenth commandments.[66]

Some readers of Wilder's novels began having second thoughts about her work, including the Association for Library Service to Children (ALSC), which began bestowing an annual award in her name in 1954 for contributions to children's literature. Not surprisingly, Wilder was the first recipient. But her work was reevaluated as societal values changed, and in 2018 the association changed the name of the award to the Children's Literature Legacy Award because of her use of pejorative stereotypes about people of color. In doing this the organization, a subsection of the American Library Association, noted:

> Laura Ingalls Wilder's books have been and continue to be deeply meaningful to many readers. Although Wilder's work holds a significant place in the history of children's literature and continues to be read today, ALSC has had to grapple with the inconsistency between Wilder's legacy and its core values of inclusiveness, integrity and respect, and responsiveness through an award that bears Wilder's name. Wilder's books are a product of her life experiences and perspective as a settler in America's 1880s. Her works reflect dated cultural attitudes toward Indigenous people and people of color that contradict modern acceptance, celebration, and understanding of diverse communities.[67]

Wilder's books continue to sell prolifically and have become a model of Manifest Destiny and American exceptionalism. Generations of children, even today, have been exposed to her stereotypes about people of color and shibboleths about the "proper" way for "good" children to behave. But the story doesn't end here, because the National Broadcasting Company adapted Wilder's work into a television series, *Little House on the Prairie,* starring Michael Landon (playing Laura's father, Charles), Karen Grassle (playing Laura's mother, Caroline), and Melissa Gilbert as young Laura. The series ran from 1974 to 1983 and was consistently ranked among the top thirty television shows in the United States. In 1997, *TV Guide* ranked one of the episodes, "I'll be Waving as You Drive Away," among the top one hundred greatest episodes of all time.

Although the show was canceled, it garnered four Emmys for music and cinematography, and reruns are standard fare on cable networks. Three post-series television movies were made in the early 1980s, and the show, which was often written and directed by Michael Landon, who died of cancer in 1991, is still popular as it spins its aphorisms and nostalgic lessons about life on the western frontier. One saving grace, Native Americans are notably absent from its scripts.[68] Still, in 2014 a new annotated edition of Wilder's *Pioneer Girl* was published by the South Dakota Historical Society and quickly became a best seller, demonstrating her continuing popularity and the endurance of her stereotypical messages.

Though few millennials have seen or are aware of these books and shows, their contribution to our culture, like that of radio, motion pictures, art, and other literature has indelibly woven stereotypes about Native Americans into the fabric of our society. It is not just place names and mascots, but the very images that are conjured up when we hear the word "Indian" testifies to the massive infusion of stilted conceptions Americans, and people around the world, have about Native Americans. One television show, perhaps more than any other, has contributed to the misinformation about people of the First Nation—*The Lone Ranger.*

The Lone Ranger Rides Again

The popular television series *The Lone Ranger* featured one of the most iconic and stereotypical portrayals of Native Americans in the person of "Tonto," the faithful sidekick of the heroic masked man who was the perennial hero of the show. The project began as a radio program on station WXYZ in Detroit in 1933. It was created by prolific script writer Fran Striker (1903–62), who worked for then radio station WEBR in Buffalo, New York. Striker wrote 156 *Lone Ranger* scripts a year, as well as scripts for *The Green Hornet*, Lone Ranger comic scripts, and, eventually, two novels.

Actor Clayton Moore starred in 169 half-hour television segments and two feature Lone Ranger films in 1956 and 1958. The aging actor fought to preserve his role in the franchise late into his life, wearing a white hat and making public appearances around the country as the masked hero. Moore, who died in 1999, was predeceased by his famous sidekick, Jay Silverheels, the first Native American actor to have a star on Hollywood's Walk of Fame.

Born Harold John Smith on the Six Nations of the Grand River First Nation Indian Reservation near Brantford, Ontario, in 1912, he changed his name as he became typecast in numerous films and television appearances as a Native American. An outstanding athlete who played lacrosse at a high amateur level, he was also a serious Golden Glove middleweight contender. Silverheels's character was selflessly and slavishly devoted to his White role model as they fought the forces of evil in the Old West. Yet Silverheels recognized the importance of assisting his fellow Native Americans in television and motion pictures and helped found the Indians Actors Guild and Indian Actors' Workshop in Los Angeles in 1966 to promote the training and use of Indian actors.[69]

The Lone Ranger was one of the most widely viewed shows on television during the early 1950s, creating the first series hit for the ABC television network. Of the 221 episodes produced, Moore and Silverheels's characters and Striker's scripts sought to embody principles that extolled the virtues of good human beings and citizens of the United States including being friendly, promoting equality, preserving the environment, and being self-sufficient, truthful, and morally upstanding in relationships with one another.

The Lone Ranger's credo appears to be a combination of utilitarianism, AA, and a self-help book. Yet in their zeal to portray the masked hero as a true humanitarian, Striker and George Trendle, WXYZ radio

The Lone Ranger (Clayton Moore) and Tonto (Jay Silverheels) (Library of Congress).

station owner in Detroit at the inception of the series, had the two sidekicks address one another in peculiar appellations: the Lone Ranger referred to his Indian pal as Tonto, and he, admiringly, addressed the Ranger as Kemo Sabe. The origin of these terms is still a mystery, but speculation about what they mean rages to this day. One possible explanation lies in the Spanish translation for Sabe, which is derived from the word wise. The Spanish word *Tonto* means fool. It is conceivable that the originators of the series played a prank on the unsuspecting public by having the trustworthy pals affectionately addressing one another this way and, in the process, violating most of the Ranger's sacred creed. Perhaps the writers of the 2013 motion picture remake starring Armie Hammer as the Lone Ranger and Johnny Depp as a deranged, comical version of Tonto believed this. As they rode off into the sunset together, the Ranger chided his sidekick, "Do you know what Tonto means in Spanish?"[70]

Contemporary Television

Throughout the history of television, Native Americans have been featured as the lead characters in less than half a dozen series. Two of these, *Northern Exposure* and *Doctor Quinn, Medicine Woman*, had five-year runs in the 1990s. Although the shows attempted to dispel stereotypes about Native Americans, both fell short by projecting images of Indigenous people as indistinct generalized groups, ignoring the web of unique, intricate customs, traditions, and ethnic distinctions. It is likely that few Hollywood or television executives knew about the richness of Native American cultures and languages—that North American Indigenous people spoke from fifty-six distinct language families with two thousand distinct dialects.[71]

Stereotypes about Indians are especially unfortunate and inopportune in the case of northern Indigenous people (e.g., Athabaskans, Tlingits, Haidas, and Aleuts), leading one critic to conclude that the show *Northern Exposure* "celebrates the composite, but ends up co-opting native culture."[72] Another critic, S. Elizabeth Bird, a retired anthropology professor, criticized *Dr. Quinn, Medicine Woman* for proffering a distorted image of Plains Indians that likewise ignored the distinct attributes of their many nations (e.g., Sioux and Cheyenne).

Although it is unlikely contemporary children have seen any of these episodes, the negative mythology about Indigenous people continues. For example, the highly successful Disney film *Pocahontas* (1995) reflected derogatory stereotypes about Native Americans in the song "Savages" that describes Pocahontas's people as worse than vermin, "filthy little heathens," whose "skins are a hellish red," as a cursed and disgusting race, as evil, "barely human," and "only good when dead." (The last line was no doubt a reference to the oft-cited comment made by Civil War hero General Philip Sheridan and later modified by Teddy Roosevelt: "I don't go so far as to think that the only good Indians are dead Indians, but I believe nine out of ten are, and I shouldn't like to inquire too closely into the case of the tenth.") One wonders how many Americans subscribe to such sentiments, especially in view of public opinion polling about the use of Indians as sports team mascots.

We have seen how television and literature were suffused with distortions about Native Americans.[73] Yet even the new generation of supposedly enlightened representations of Native Americans have not been able to eradicate the damage perpetrated by decades of historical malfeasance. Although the threadbare misrepresentations about Indians have decreased over the last few decades, the theme of American exceptionalism along with its mythological trope of good versus evil persists, though often in the contemporary scientific meme of humans versus aliens or zombies, or contemporary combat movies pitting U.S. soldiers against radical Islamists.[74]

While films and television programs about Indians diminished in the latter part of the twentieth century and the early decades of the twenty-first, Native American stories that were produced featured subdued characters, often with a nihilistic bent, but not infrequently tending toward exculpatory themes for Native American predations on White people as the tone shifted from savage marauders to displaced victims and stoic environmentalists. Today, few films and television programs with distorted stereotypical depictions of Native Americans are found in the mass media. They were displaced by high-budget projects that focused on the wars in Vietnam, Iraq, and Afghanistan, and high-tech science fiction blockbusters like the *Star Wars* features now being developed by Disney Studios after purchasing the rights from George Lucas's Lucasfilms for $4 billion in 2012. Now, abductions of "innocent" White settlers by savage arrow-shooting Indians have been supplanted by intergalactic boogeymen with ray guns, lasers, and force fields. The trusty horses of the heralded Plains Indians have been replaced by warp-bending spaceships traveling faster than the speed of light. Yet the ineluctable good versus evil trope that depicts White people in the former role and Indians in the latter persists. Doubting readers need look no further than *Avatar*, the 2009 James Cameron blockbuster film that featured White spacemen waging war against Indigenous bow and arrow Native people over rare natural resources on a planet in another solar system—except in the first installment, the Indigenous folk won, but the story goes on, resistant to time and space (and Native American sensitivities), just as its earlier American counterparts. However, a new generation of Indigenous writers, directors and actors is gaining prominence in television and motion pictures, as noted by Valerie Taliman in *The American Indian* magazine (Winter 2021). Leading the way are the award-winning television series *Reservation Dogs*, *Rutherford Falls*, and *Resident Alien*. Tatanka Means (Oglala Lakota, Omaha, Diné) has had acting stints in the HBO series *I Know This Much Is True* and the feature film *Once Upon a River* which helped solidify his status as a rising star along with Sterling Harjo (Seminole Nation and Muskogee) and Taiki Waititi (Maori) as Indigenous writers and directors.

16

Buffalo Bill, Art, and Indians

> It is a fact that admits of no question that Eastern people have formed
> their conceptions of what the Far-Western life is like, more from what
> they have seen in Mr. Remington's pictures than from any other source.
> —William Coffin, 1892

Buffalo Bill and the Wild West

Indians lack the political clout derived from numbers and wealth that has insulated some ethnic minorities (e.g., Jewish and Asian Americans) against obtrusive public depredations. The downward stereotypical spiral of Native Americans, their descent from noble savages to derelicts and buffoons, was accentuated through popular American culture, most notably film and television portrayals. As film critic John O'Connor observed, Indians were originally cast as villains and heavies because they were not able to influence Hollywood decisions—there was no one to advocate for them. "Perhaps the ultimate irony is that in Western films, where Indians most often appear, producers have always had to consider the demands of the American Humane Society about the treatment of horses—yet the Native Americans are not treated with nearly as much politesse."[1]

Our perspective about Native Americans was indelibly influenced, as we have seen, by the writing of Cooper, which found its way into our mythological culture, with all of its imperfections and deleterious stereotypes. Though the novel by Robert Montgomery Bird, *Nick of the Woods*, published in 1837, was widely read and also presented Native Americans in a negative light, Cooper's works gained more traction among the public. This was not the case with theatrical presentations with a Native American theme during this era. Of the dozens of plays that dwelled on Native American issues during the early to mid–1800s, only one, *Metamora or the Last of the Wampanoags*, was a box office smash. It drew throngs of theatergoers to see the performance of the leading man, Edwin Forrest, who played an ill-fated Indian modeled after King Philip (Metacom), the leader of the Wampanoags in a bloody and destructive war against White settlers between 1675 and 1676 in New England.

It is said that Forrest so relished the role he played for more than forty years that he included makeup and affectations that convinced many theatergoers he was an Indian. Strong, handsome, and a consummate actor, he embellished the role that brought him fame and fortune. The play, a melodrama about the White invasion of Native American territory, was the winning entry in a contest designed by Forrest that specified it must be original and about Aboriginal people in this country. The $500 prize was claimed by author John Augustus Stone. Set in New England in the seventeenth century with the arrival of the Puritans, it opened one year before President Andrew Jackson signed the Indian Removal Act.[2]

Later in the nineteenth and early twentieth centuries, there arose an entertainment genre that created an international fixation on the West and Native Americans—Wild West shows. Paramount among them were those of William Frederick "Buffalo Bill" Cody (1846–1917). Cody, a Medal of Honor winner for his gallant service as a civilian scout in 1872 to the 3rd Calvary in action against Sioux Indians at Loupe Forke on the Platte River in Nebraska, was a master showman who founded a troupe known as Buffalo Bill's Wild West and Congress of Rough Riders of the World in 1883.

Drawing on his experiences and contacts with other notable western historical figures, Cody parlayed his troupe into a traveling organization that achieved international fame. Cody got his nickname, Buffalo Bill, after the Civil War when he contracted to supply workers with the Kansas Pacific Railroad with buffalo meat. In one 18-month period, he is reported to have killed 4,282 bison, an act that hardly endeared him to Plains Indians who relied on the animals for sustenance.

His shows featured reenactments of Custer's Last Stand, the massacre of Sioux at Wounded Knee, settlers' cabins and stagecoaches under Indian attack, and the Battle of Summit Springs where Cody allegedly killed Cheyenne Chief Tall Bull. He used actual Native Americans, cowboys, and elite horsemen from France, Russia, Great Britain, Mexico, Germany, and the Middle East, and United States cavalrymen in his expositions.

Historian Richard Slotkin perceived a strain of social Darwinism in Cody's lavish reenactments of struggles between Indians, settlers, cowboys, and the U.S. Cavalry. The Indians' inevitable defeat was seen as emblematic of the concept of the survival of the fittest, which rationalized the Anglo-Saxon right to control their lands.[3] Native American historian Vine Deloria, Jr., theorized that the legend about Cody emerged because Americans needed a folk hero—a mythical figure who risked life in pursuit of freedom to live on a vanishing frontier. Cody exemplified someone who challenged the wilderness and fought bravely to preserve American values, even though his exploits were exaggerated.[4] Nevertheless, after examining Cody's exploits and interaction with Native Americans, Deloria concluded, "When all the evidence is considered, Buffalo Bill seems to have been a kindly, decent person who treated everyone with dignity and respect."[5]

Although Cody fought Indians, he respected them and their culture. He invited the families of Indians in his troupe to live on the campgrounds to accurately portray their lifestyle for patrons. His retinue included lawmen, gunslingers, and gamblers like James Butler "Wild Bill" Hickok, sharpshooter Annie Oakley, and the spiritual leader of the Sioux who defeated Custer at the Little Bighorn, Sitting Bull, along with twenty of his braves. Even the famous Apache warrior Geronimo was briefly a member of his troupe.

While Sitting Bull, the Hunkpapa Lakota Sioux chief, remained with Cody for only four months in 1885, the organization regularly featured orchestrated clashes between Native Americans, cowboys, and settlers in what was billed as an authentic depiction of the Wild West. The show had a tremendous following in the United

William "Buffalo Bill" Cody, 1846–1917 (Library of Congress).

The cast of Buffalo Bill's Wild West and Congress of the Rough Riders of the World (Buffalo Bill Center of the West, Cody, Wyoming; McCracken Research Library; MS 006-William F. Cody Collection; P.6.0205).

States through the turn of the twentieth century. Even more astounding was the attendance abroad. Tours in England (where command performances were given for Queen Victoria and other royalty and dignitaries) were attended by over 2.5 million people. The troupe performed in Paris at the Exposition of 1889, Barcelona, Italy (where Pope Leo XIII received a delegation from them), Austria-Hungary, Germany, Belgium, the Netherlands, the Balkans, Poland, Ukraine, Romania, and Bohemia.

Cody's fame in the United States was enormous. According to David Katzive, former director of the DeCordova and Dana Museum and Park, over a *billion* words were published about him before the turn of the twentieth century.[6] Undoubtedly, many appeared in the 550 dime novels about him, originating with Ned Buntline's 1869 *Buffalo Bill, the King of the Border Men.*

The size of the touring group was prodigious. An 1887 troupe that gave a command performance at Queen Victoria's Golden Jubilee at Windsor Palace consisted of 200 stage hands, performers, and assistants, 97 Indians, 18 buffalo, 181 horses, 10 elk, 4 donkeys, 5 Texas longhorns, 2 deer, and 10 mules.[7] Afterward, the Queen described the experience in her diary: "Wild painted Indians from America, on their wild bare backed horses, of different tribes.... The cowboys are fine looking people, but the painted Indians, with their feathers and wild dress (very little of it) were rather alarming looking & they have cruel faces.... Their war dances, to a wild drum and pipe, was quite fearful, with all their contorsions [*sic*] and shrieks, & they come so close."[8]

Cody was one of the most recognized celebrities at the turn of the twentieth century. The portrayal of Native Americans as warring, bloodthirsty savages was sown like weeds throughout the Western world. Yet Cody acknowledged, "Every Indian outbreak that I have ever known has resulted from broken promises and broken treaties by the government."[9] Nevertheless, the stereotypes promulgated by the Wild West show resonated with the gawking masses who devoured the distorted sensationalist performances, further solidifying the prejudicial foundation from which sprang a deluge of motion pictures and television shows during the 1950s and '60s. As historian Vine Deloria, Jr., observed: "[T]he authors of these fictional pulp stories were generally Easterners who had never been in the West and who committed to paper fantasies and stereotypes that no self-respecting, experienced Westerner would have tolerated for a moment. Then, like today, the credibility of the story depended almost wholly on its popularity and commercial success—not upon any relationship to historical or geographical reality."[10]

Historian Slotkin credits Cody's shows with cementing the Frontier Myth in America, transmitting this message to the waves of immigrants arriving between 1885 and 1905, at the height of Cody's popularity. The Wild West was the source of some of the most vivid images and expectations immigrants had of their new land. His shows invented and tested the images, staging, and themes that also provided much of the personnel for the motion picture genre Western. By 1981 more than thirty Hollywood films had been released in which he was a character.

The profusion of paintings, lithographs, photographs, dime novels, and illustrated magazines, along with the works of writers such as Frederick Schiller Faust, Louis L'Amour, Zane Grey, Laura Ingalls Wilder, and cowboy idols like William Hart, Hoot Gibson, Tim McCoy, Ken Maynard, Hopalong Cassidy, Gene Autry, Roy Rogers, and Tom Mix, solidified the image of the "Wild West" as synonymous with a battle of good (White culture and values) versus evil (Native American culture and anticivilization), and this found expression in art.

Art as Propaganda

The list of notable American artists enamored of Cody and the West contains the names of mythical greatness: Alfred Jacob Miller, Albert Bierstadt, John Mix Stanley, and N. C. Wyeth. But one of the earliest and most prolific artists and writers about Native Americans was George Catlin (1796–1872) who traveled over eight thousand miles sketching and painting Indigenous people and publishing several books about his exploits. His most famous exposition on Native Americans, based on his travels throughout the West, is a two-volume compilation of letters, sketches, and paintings of Indians that he developed along the way.

Catlin provides us with an interesting example of good intentions gone awry. His books are suffused with beautiful portraits of Native Americans he met on his excursions, primarily with a military escort (he had a letter of introduction and assistance from the secretary of war), and serene landscapes inhabited by Indigenous people. Reared in the East, he attended law school and began practicing in Pennsylvania, but turned to portraiture around 1821, earnestly pursued it, and developed a reputation as a budding artist.

Catlin, the fifth of fourteen children, was a self-taught artist. His fascination with Indians was partly the result of stories told to him about his mother and grandmother's brief abduction by Iroquois Indians in 1778 along the Susquehanna River. As a young man, he saw a delegation of Indians, "noble and dignified-looking … from the wilds of the 'Far West,'" who had journeyed to Philadelphia where he resided. He became obsessed with painting them and telling their story. In 1830 he moved to St. Louis, where he met General William Clark, one half of the team (with Meriwether Lewis) who led the famous Corps of Discovery eight-thousand-mile expedition from 1804 to 1806 of the Louisiana Territory. Clark was then the superintendent for Indian affairs for western tribes, and he accompanied Catlin on a four-hundred-mile trip up the Mississippi to observe and paint Native Americans from the Sauk, Fox, and Sioux nations.

Catlin sensed that the Indian's day was sunsetting. Before they vanished, he committed himself to painting them and telling their stories. Traveling from 1832 to 1839, he visited about fifty tribes, sketched and painted their chiefs, warriors, women, and children, and collected artifacts including costumes, headdresses, and tools to create a "museum" to educate the public about this "vanishing race." The collection included over six hundred paintings and thousands of artifacts, and accompanied his prodigious two-volume exposition, *Letters and Notes on the Manners, Customs, and Conditions of the North American Indians*.[11] He maintained that he traveled to the Far West of North America to create a "literal and geographic delineation of the living manners, customs, and character of an interesting race of people who are rapidly passing away from the face of the earth—lending a hand to a dying nation, who have no historians or biographers of their own to portray with fidelity their native looks and history; thus snatching from a hasty oblivion what could be saved for the benefit of posterity, and perpetuating it, as a fair and just monument, to the memory of a truly lofty and noble race."[12] He affirmed, "I will do all I can, however, to make their looks and customs known to the world."[13] Further, "[T]here is no subject that I know of, within the scope and reach of human wisdom, on which the civilized world in this enlightened age are more incorrectly informed, than upon that of the true manners and customs, and moral condition, rights and abuses, of the North American Indians."[14]

His intentions were noble. His tomes were suffused with criticisms of the negative effects of White/Western civilization on Native Americans and their innocence: "They live in a country and communities where it is not customary to look forward into the future with concern, for they live without incurring the expenses of life, which are absolutely necessary and unavoidable in the enlightened world."[15] He wanted non–Indians to gain a mature, objective understanding of them through his work: "I find that the principal cause why we underrate and despise the savage, is generally because we do not understand him; and the reason why we are ignorant of him and his modes, is that we do not stop to investigate—the world have been too much in the habit of looking at him as altogether inferior—as a beast, a brute; and unworthy of more than a passing notice."[16]

While his artwork was impressive (although art critics of his time considered him a B talent), the volumes are filled with ethnocentric and myopic generalizations about Indigenous behavior, not the least of which is the profusion of the word "savage" throughout the text, despite an early disclaimer that cautioned against its use. "The very use of the word savage, as it is applied in its general sense, I am inclined to believe is an abuse of the word, and the people to whom it is applied."[17]

To be fair, one has to view the work as a product of its time, when the science of anthropology with its ethnomethodological orientation had not yet emerged. That would not occur until the turn of the twentieth century under the design and tutelage of Franz Boas and the Columbia University school that produced stellar humanistic anthropologists. This also helps explain his continual references to the pseudosciences of phrenology and physiognomy to link human visages with tribal behavior.

Some of his generalizations are outright wrong, as when he emphatically stated that all Indians practiced polygamy, or that the wives of Indian chiefs and warriors were "slaves" whose main function is to perform household drudgery for their husbands. This conclusion revealed his naiveté about the structure and function of Native American families and the important role that women played in many tribes that were actually matriarchal.

Even more exasperating are his frequent references to Native American medicine as hocus pocus, or when he naively started a fight in a Sioux tribe when he painted a well-known warrior from the side, showing only part of his countenance and causing some of his peers to call him "good for nothing." The ensuing fight led to the death of the warrior and the hasty departure of Catlin and his two guides. (The warrior was avenged by his brother a year later.)

Catlin continually reminds the reader about the importance of preserving the environment, but his books contain many accounts of the wanton destruction of animals, sometimes by his own hand. For example, buffalo were relied on by the Indians for food, clothing, and a host of other indispensable necessities, yet there are numerous accounts of his participation in their slaughter. One chilling account placed blame on the military. "From morning until night, the [Army] camp has been daily almost deserted; the men have dispersed in little squads in all directions, and are dealing death to these poor creatures to a most cruel and wanton extent, merely for the pleasure of *destroying*, generally without stopping to cut out the meat. During yesterday and this day hundreds have undoubtedly been killed, and not so much as the flesh of half a dozen used."[18]

On one occasion he participated in killing seventy-five grouse for sport—the birds were fleeing a prairie fire and alighted in nearby trees where they were shot. He somewhat nostalgically noted, "We murdered the poor birds in this way." Yet he knew that Indian lands and resources should be protected from avaricious White settlers and unscrupulous traders and businessmen. "This picturesque of 200 miles, over which we have passed, belongs to the Creeks and Choctaws, and affords one of the richest and most desirable countries in the world for agricultural pursuits."[19]

He was especially critical of fur traders and trappers he accused of cheating the Indians by trading inferior goods, giving them liquor, debauching their women, and introducing diseases that decimated the Indigenous population—even extorting them by threatening to release smallpox from a bottle. Some of his material is informative and illustrative, and his explanations of some of the functions of customs and ceremonies are fairly accurate. But he unknowingly participated in the desecration of an Indian gravesite by taking a buried skull.[20] And his affinity for the Mandans smacked of Eurocentrism. The diversity of this tribe's complexions, hair and eye colors, language, and peculiarity of their customs indicated to him that they were more "civilized" than other Indians and "sprang from some other origin than that of other North American tribes, or that they are an amalgam of natives in some civilized race."[21]

Perhaps one of his most important contributions was to attempt to convey the fact that Indians were not intrinsically prone to violence. Although he emphatically stated that a main preoccupation of the tribes was to engage in internecine conflict among themselves, numerous passages contain illustrations of Catlin, soldiers, and White people being welcomed and treated cordially. Unfortunately, this was contradicted by his frequent statements concerning the "wild" and "savage" life of Indians. Perhaps, more importantly, the latter impression was even more widely conveyed by one of his contemporaries, James Fenimore Cooper, whose *Leatherstocking Tales* cast Native Americans in a very different light.

Catlin actually embarked on a mission to educate the public about what he considered to be the Native Americans' impending demise. In 1837 he tried to sell his collection to the United States, but Congress did not oblige him, so he took his accumulated "museum" of paintings and artifacts and displayed them from 1837 to 1839 in communities along the Ohio River, visiting cities such as Pittsburgh and Cincinnati, and on the East Coast (e.g., New York City). Following that, he brought his collection to Europe where it was exhibited for five years in London, Brussels, and even the Louvre where it drew large crowds. By this time Catlin's exhibition included three dozen Ojibwe and Iowa Indians as a tantalizing promotional lure. While the crowds were initially large, the project ended in failure.

By 1852, at the age of fifty-six, he was destitute and thrown into debtor's prison in London. He tried unsuccessfully once again to sell the collection to the United States, reducing the price from $65,000 to $25,000. Then a wealthy Pennsylvania railroad tycoon, Joseph Harrison, who knew him, purchased the collection for $20,000 and paid off his debts. Despite Catlin's wish that the gallery be used to educate the public about the grandeur and plight of Native Americans, the collection gathered dust in the boiler room of one of Harrison's buildings. In 1879, Harrison's widow donated the collection to the Smithsonian, and despite the belief that Catlin's work was an American treasure, it received little notoriety until it was displayed in the Renwick Gallery of the Smithsonian American Art Museum in Washington, D.C., in 2002–03.

As for Catlin, he embarked on travels to explore the habitat of Indigenous people in Central and South America, painting people as he had in North America to inform the public. He recreated most of his original Native American paintings, which he referred to as his "cartoon collection," although he never achieved the notoriety and wealth he sought. Catlin's life was like a double-edged sword, it cut two ways. One side represented the noble, sincere educator who longed to inform the public about the perilous condition of Native Americans, and the other contained elements of a garish promoter who sought to benefit from his adventures. W. Richard West (Cheyenne and Arapaho), the founding director of the Smithsonian's National Museum of the American Indian, recognized this when he praised him for his defense of Indians but criticized him for exploiting them.[22]

An unfortunate illustration of his promotional exploits was recounted by historian Richard Ribb. It seems that Catlin lent his name to a British firm that was selling land in Texas to speculators in Europe. Catlin even gave promotional speeches about the virtue of living in the American West, but the deal ended with investors bereft of land and their money.[23]

The next generation produced one of the most heralded artists of the Old West and Native Americans, Frederic Remington (1861–1909), who achieved the success in his short life that eluded Catlin. Remington displayed an interest in art as a child. His father was a career military man and died at the age of fifty from tuberculosis. He moved to Montana in 1881 where he fell in love with the Old West—nature, cowboys, the topography, and Indians. He tried his hand at sheep ranching but failed, and invested his energy in his paintings and sketches, and later sculpture.

Although his early works were unimpressive, he received a commission from *Harper's Weekly* when he was just twenty-five to do a work on the Apache Chief Geronimo (although he never met him). He later signed an agreement with *Harper's* that catapulted him

A masterpiece: George Catlin, *Stu-mick-o-súcks, Buffalo Bull's Back Fat, Head Chief, Blood Tribe,* 1832, oil on canvas (Smithsonian American Art Museum, Gift of Mrs. Joseph Harrison, Jr., 1985.66.149 418).

to fame generating a large audience of admirers. His first one-man show in 1890 was well received and facilitated his fame, which was reinforced by his frequent publications in popular magazines of the times (e.g., *Harper's Weekly*, *Outing*, and *Collier's*).

Along the way he became a friend of Teddy Roosevelt—a friendship that would last through his life—when he was retained to illustrate Roosevelt's book *Ranch Life and the Hunting-Trail* in 1887. Both young men had suffered financial setbacks in ranching ventures, and both utilized their western experiences to promote themselves as rugged western outdoorsmen.

Remington produced a prodigious amount of work including sketches for 142 books and 41 magazines, most utilizing a Western theme. He created twenty-five thousand paintings and epic bronze statues that immortalized the West and Native Americans. He also wrote Western stories like *Pony Track* (1895), *Crooked Trails* (1898), and *Sundown Le Flare* (1899).

Remington later became a favorite portrait painter of American Army officers who were fighting Native Americans in the Plains Indian Wars (e.g., General Nelson Miles). He thought Native Americans were "unfathomable, superstitious, ignorant, and pitiless," while White people were often depicted in his paintings as brave and noble. Nevertheless, many of his paintings represent Indians in a nostalgic, even manner, and they evoke some of the same feelings evinced by Catlin about the imminent end of the lifestyle of Native Americans.

His style was naturalistic and sometimes impressionistic, developed from his extensive travels in the West. He shunned the use of a camera in his work, preferring to paint from memory. Commenting about him, Teddy Roosevelt observed, "The soldier, the cowboy and rancher, the Indian ... will live in his pictures and bronzes, I verily believe all time."[24]

It's difficult, unfair, and probably unwise to attempt comparisons among gifted artists of the Old West, but no one would deny that Charles Marion Russell (1864–1926) deserves a place among them. A contemporary of Remington, Russell, born in Oak Hill, Missouri (near St. Louis), shared the sentiment about the West and Native Americans that pervaded the works of Catlin and his successors. His paintings and later sculptures are suffused with the romantic images of Indians as a vanishing bulwark against the ever encroaching White civilization that eviscerates man and nature with "progress."

First devoting his career to the subject of cowboys and the Old West, Russell became enamored with Native Americans after spending six months with a Canadian Native American tribe called the "Bloods" during the winter of 1888–89, who named him Ah-wah-cous (the antelope). His affinity for Native Americans was focused primarily on the Plains Indians, no doubt because of his eleven-year career as a cowboy in Montana and the conflict between the U.S. Army and the Plains Indians during his lifetime. Though he often portrayed confrontations between White people and Indians, his paintings showed partiality toward the latter because he admired their way of life.[25]

One of the most renowned observers of Native American traditions was Edward S. Curtis, who spent thirty years photographing and describing Indians in North America. He was born in 1868 in Whitewater, Wisconsin, and his family moved to Seattle. A chance encounter with prominent scientists on Mt. Rainier in 1898 led to a lifelong infatuation with the study of Native Americans. The life similarities between Curtis

A masterpiece: Frederic Sackrider Remington (American, 1861–1909), *The Outlier*, 1909, oil on canvas, frame: 51½ × 38½ × 2 in. (130.8 cm × 97.8 × 5.1 cm (Brooklyn Museum, Bequest of Charlotte R. Stillman, 55.43).

and Catlin are ironic. Both attempted to delineate the lives and traditions of Indians to preserve knowledge of their existence before White civilization destroyed it. Both of their masterworks were largely ignored during their lifetimes, and they lived on the edge of poverty. Both men tried various schemes to promote their work to the general public, and their collections laid unattended in storage rooms for many years before being "rediscovered." And both men died in relative obscurity.

The first volume of Curtis's twenty-volume magnum opus was lauded by Theodore Roosevelt: "The Indian as he has hitherto been is on the point of passing away," but Mr. Curtis "is an artist who works out of doors and not in the closet. He is a close observer, whose qualities of mind and body fit him to make his observations out in the field, surrounded by the wildlife he commemorates. He has caught glimpses, such as few white men ever catch, into their strange spiritual and mental life ... from whose innermost recesses all white men are forever barred."[26]

Although he had a photographic studio in Seattle, Curtis did not have sufficient funds to pursue his mission of documenting Native Americans before their assumed extinction. He ultimately succeeded in convincing the wealthy industrialist J. P. Morgan to bankroll his expeditions into Native American territory. Morgan gave him $75,000 over five years for twenty-five sets of his volumes and five hundred original prints, and with that money he purchased equipment and hired interpreters and researchers to accompany him on his photographic journeys. Unfortunately, when Morgan died in 1913, his son did not fund the project at the same level, and Curtis abandoned his field research for six years. Only eleven of the contemplated twenty volumes had been produced by the outbreak of World War I, and in 1935 Curtis's materials were sold by the Morgan estate to the Charles Lauriat Company, including nineteen complete sets, thousands of prints and unbound papers, and glass-plate negatives, and they sat, like Catlin's works, in the basement of a building (in Boston) until they were rediscovered in 1972, long after his death.

After a bitter divorce in 1916 (he had four children with his wife, Clara), Curtis searched for ways of making ends meet, including producing a film, *In the Land of the Head Hunters*, about the Kwakiutl Indians on Vancouver Island. The staged film included Indigenous men with fake nose rings and shaved faces. It was a box office flop, costing him $75,000. He then went to Hollywood and worked for well-known producers like Cecil B. DeMille.

After improving his financial situation, he ventured once again into Native American homelands, only to find that the tribes he had visited earlier had been decimated by U.S. government policies and relocation. Indian children had been taken to boarding schools, many tribes had been forced onto reservations, and some of their religious practices and traditions were forbidden (e.g., the Sun and Ghost dances). This situation challenged his attempt to depict Native Americans in their authentic garb engaged in actual ceremonies.

Curtis was eager to document ideal images of Native American culture and noted in the Introduction of the first volume of his work, "The value of such a work, in great measure, will be in the breadth of its treatment, in its wealth of illustration, and in the fact that it represents the result of personal study of a people who are rapidly losing the traces of their aboriginal character and who are destined ultimately to become assimilated with the 'superior race.'"

But Curtis was forced, in some situations, to recreate traditions that were no longer practiced by some Indian groups. His effort to depict Native American culture occasionally included retouched scenes to eliminate modern artifacts (e.g., a clock), reenacting battles, wearing of period clothes that were no longer used, and the staging of ceremonies. He also was, at times, misled by Indians about the authenticity of his observations. For example, he paid three Navajo men to perform a Yei be Chei healing dance, but they performed the ceremony backward and omitted the most sacred parts. Like Catlin, Curtis did not have formal anthropological training, and his work reflected that. And neither did he devote space in his works to criticizing the adverse relationship between the U.S. government, White people, and Native Americans.

Nevertheless, his work, though it was flawed and helped perpetuate stereotypical perceptions of Native Americans, was well intentioned and prodigious. Photographs are accompanied by articulate explanations of the individuals, traditions, and ceremonies. The reader is overwhelmed with his methodical observations, the result of years of patience and persistence (e.g., he waited for six years to gain the cooperation of a Hopi Snake chief to allow him to participate in a ceremonial snake hunt).

Upon the publication of the first volume, the *New York Herald* proclaimed that it was the most ambitious enterprise in publishing since the King James Bible. But his arduous travel and calamitous personal life left him physically and emotionally drained. He spent his last days living with one of his daughters, Beth, in Los Angeles where he died of a heart attack, in relative obscurity, in 1952. It would take two decades before his work would be resurrected and reach the status of masterpiece. Today, one can find copies of his work for sale on the internet in excess of $30,000.[27] An exhibit containing 723 of his photographs was displayed in the Muskegon Museum of Art in 2017–18.

Edward Curtis photograph of Weasel Tail (Library of Congress).

Remington's works and that of other painters like George Catlin and Charles Russell, and photographer Edward Curtis, left indelible stereotypical impressions on millions of White people about the looks and lifestyles of Native Americans. Romanticizing and exoticizing their life and surroundings, at times staging poses and scenes, their works seeped into the fabric of White society, staining it with mythology and misinformation that led to misunderstandings that persist to this day.[28]

Even though they attempted to depict Native Americans in a positive light, their works often

A Charles Russell masterpiece, *When Sioux and Blackfeet Met,* **1902 (Library of Congress).**

reinforced pejorative stereotypes about them. Simultaneously, Americans and Europeans were being exposed to the writing of Cooper and his contemporaries as well as stereotypical images of Native Americans, especially Plains Indians, that distorted their lives and very existence. While art and literature were exploited for the purpose of dramatizing the plight of Indians by some writers and artists, dime novelists were busy plying their trade in a frantic attempt to deceive Americans into believing the worst stereotypes about Indians and their bloodlust for settlers and White women.

As this artistic onslaught was occurring in print, live entertainers were plying their trade in the towns and cities of North America and across the Atlantic depicting Indians and Black people in stereotypically backward, violent, and misanthropic conditions through minstrel and Wild West shows. Along the banks of the Erie Canal, throughout the East and Midwest as well as Europe and the British Isles, people who had never been exposed to Black people and Indians received a grotesque, hideous, distorted impression of them and their culture that reinforced the foundation of racist beliefs harbored by the White majority—a set of values, beliefs, and associated behaviors that persist to this day.

17

Native Americans
in the Modern Media

> Illusion came to matter more than authenticity—and illusion proved
> to be one of the great aesthetic joys of both film production and film
> viewing.
>
> —Philip Deloria (Standing Rock Sioux),
> *Indians in Unexpected Places*

One of the most insidious and devastating assaults on the representation of Native Americans and Indigenous people has been conducted through the mass media, and the motion picture industry, from silent films to today's blockbuster cinematic extravaganzas, has contributed to a vast stereotypical morass, perpetuating them in the most unfavorable, myopic, and hackneyed form. English professor Michelle Raheja (Seneca) of the University of California at Riverside summed the situation thusly:

> Native American involvement in both mainstream film and independent media production has been marginalized at best and completely elided at worst. This condition reveals much about film historiography, racial politics in the United States and Canada, and competing discourses around the concept of the nation and liberal white manifestations of guilt and its attendant forms of identity, belonging, and what [cultural anthropologist] Renato Rosaldo has termed "imperialist nostalgia."[1]

Jacquelyn Kilpatrick (Choctaw, Cherokee), film critic and English professor, noted wryly at the conclusion of her perceptive book, *Celluloid Indians*: "The [motion picture] industry must therefore accept the responsibility of clearing away the cobwebs of misinformation it has strung throughout the last century, webs that have wrapped the American Indian in a cocoon of misunderstanding, derision, hatred, and nostalgic guilt."[2] Her words are supported by meticulous research that traced the treatment of Native Americans in the early and mature stages of the United States' cinematic industry.

From its beginning at the dawn of the twentieth century, Kilpatrick contended, the American cinematic industry used three stereotypes to depict Native Americans: mental, sexual, and spiritual. Native Americans were first, and most significantly, cast as less intelligent and civilized than European invaders. Initially depicted as bloodthirsty barbarians, they were also represented as innocent, childlike casualties of advancing civilization. Europeans' early ambivalence toward Indians was gradually transformed into antipathy and animosity as the battle for land and resources led to confrontations and calamities leaving Native Americans living on reservations and sardonically characterized as inebriated fools.

The prohibition against miscegenation that proscribed sexual relations between Indians and White people, especially Indian males and White women, hung like a pall over interactions between them, replete with fears, mythical misconceptions, and distortions about Native American intentions toward White women. The early works of film directors like D. W. Griffith, Cecil B. DeMille, and Thomas Ince perpetuated these stereotypes.

As the film industry developed in the latter part of the twentieth century, an evolution in the portrayal of Native Americans occurred that depicted them as sagacious custodians of a planet in need of restorative balance with nature through the spirituality of their traditions that fostered oneness and harmony with Mother Earth.

First Impressions

Early cinematic endeavors in the United States featured Native Americans as uncivilized, bloodthirsty savages wreaking havoc on "innocent" White settlers. Producers and directors cast Indians in the role of villains in search of scalps and White women. As Professors Gretchen Bataille and Charles Silet note, works like Edison's peep shows, where White cowboys were cast as heroes and Indians as villains, were replete with cultural distortions and stereotypes about Native Americans. "The white heroes got the billing, and the Indians got the pratfall."[3]

Early films about Native Americans dwelled on the struggle between White people and Indians and often pitted two women (one White and the other Indian) against one another for the affections of a White male. The White male seldom died in these potboilers, but the Indian woman usually did after betraying her people so the White lovers could unite in a blissful future together.[4]

While some early filmmakers like Joseph Dixon attempted to portray Indians as a unique cultural group, they often staged footage to achieve the desired effect and perpetuated stereotypes about them. This practice, coupled with the prevalent use of White actors to play Indians, distorted public perceptions of Native American culture by dramatizing the exotic and eccentric to attract and captivate White audiences. This so infuriated Native Americans that a delegation of them traveled to Washington, D.C., in 1911 to urge Congress to regulate the moving picture industry. They contended that moving picture promoters, "in order to get thrilling pictures of the Indians have used white men costumed as Indians in depicting scenes that are not true pictures of the Indian and are in fact grossly libelous."[5]

Critics of Hollywood's stereotypical depiction of Native Americans castigated the industry for misleading the public by oversimplifying and generalizing their web of complex cultures and focusing on some of the more aggressive horse-riding tribes of Plains Indians (e.g., the Sioux and Apache). As a matter of fact, horses were reintroduced to Native Americans by the Spaniards in the 1600s, but the unknowing public was fed this stereotypical generalization because violence sells at the box office. It has been observed that "Native people were broken upon the wheel of an alien culture superior in terms of numerical population, weapons technology, and mental aptitude for total war. Of the last, the abilities to reduce one's opponents to nonhuman terms and to miscategorize diverse opposing groups into homogenous lumps are paramount."[6]

There is a historical truism that governs relations between the victor and vanquished in the clash of civilizations: The victor has the prerogative to interpret and write history, and the history revolving around interactions between Native Americans and White people is replete with stereotypes and misinformation about Native Americans and their cultures. The practice of mixing Native American cultural groups typifies this criticism. It was not uncommon for filmmakers to combine stereotypical Indian garb in ludicrous, even outrageous ways. As Kilpatrick noted: "A man described as a Sioux might have been found wearing a Navajo blanket over his chest plate, carrying weapons from a northeastern tribe, wearing an Apache bandanna, and standing in front of a northwestern tribe's totem pole."[7] These stereotypical messages are still conveyed in the cinema and find expression in reproductions of "authentic" Native American culture depicted in sport teams' mascots (e.g., Florida State Seminoles' use of a horse and a flaming war spear).

The late author and social critic Leslie Fiedler referred to Native Americans as historyless antiquities with no concrete ties to the past.[8] The significance of this statement cannot be overstated. This condition not only facilitated the seizure of their land and resources because they could not, by European standards, prove ownership, but it also enabled the early film industry to portray Native Americans in a way that perpetuated what historian Richard Slotkin called the Frontier Myth—a dramatization that extolled the heroic hordes of European interlopers, touting American exceptionalism, while denigrating the people of the First Nations.

The practice of stereotyping Indians became commonplace, and, as media studies expert Allison Griffiths noted, it was defended by distinguished motion picture educator Ernest Alfred Dench in his famous 1915 treatise, *Making the Movies*. He contended that it was preferable to employ White actors over Indians because Indians were lazy, undependable, and treacherous. Dench concluded, with good makeup, White actors are indistinguishable from Native Americans.[9]

Bataille and Silet demonstrated that the American film industry continued to purvey stereotypical images of Native Americans through the 1940s: "Hollywood produced the homogenized Native American, devoid of tribal characteristics or regional differences. As long as an actor wore fringed pants and spoke with a halting accent he was an Indian."

"*The Indian* [had] no tribe, no identity, almost always a male—was either noble (still savage, but noble nevertheless) or bloodthirsty and vicious."[10] While audiences may have believed they were seeing authentic Native Americans, they were actually seeing what film critic Kilpatrick termed a "new tribe of Hollywood Indians."[11]

The proliferation of Westerns that featured the domination of the western frontier and occupation of Native American lands through the efforts of the U.S. military and carefree cowboys peppered the screens of movie houses throughout the nation in the first half of the twentieth century. While Kilpatrick estimated that over a hundred silent movies with Indian themes were produced between 1910 and 1913, thousands of films with these themes followed in subsequent decades. It is estimated that at least eighty-six Indian versus the U.S. Army themed films were produced between 1950 and 1970.[12] As Bataille and Silet noted, "[B]y and large the Indian of the film exists in a world somewhere between the landing of the Pilgrims and the end of the nineteenth century, the primary focus being on the period between 1850 and 1900, the time when Indian people were desperately trying to hold on to their land and were fighting for their lives."[13]

Hollywood's preference for using White actors in leading Native American roles saw stars such as Rock Hudson, Jeff Chandler, and Paul Newman splashing on tanning lotion (sometimes wearing bandannas and loin cloths) to conceal their White identity. Indians were relegated to simplistic lines often punctuated by the guttural utterance—ugh! The practice of using non–Indians for leading roles in motion pictures continues even today. A female leading role in the 2018 feature film *Woman Walks Ahead* was played by Rulan Tangen, an Asian American.[14] Although the film, directed by Susana White, about the relationship between Sitting Bull and New York artist Catherine Weldon (Jessica Chastain) was more balanced in the portrayal of Native Americans at the end of the Plains Wars, one wonders why a Native American wasn't cast in this role.

The late film critic and Indian historian Raymond William Stedman chided the television industry, film industry, and eighteenth- and nineteenth-century literary works for portraying Native Americans as using stilted dialogue to convey their supposedly inferior and infantile culture. This custom created a dilemma for writers who tried to convey Indians' mature thoughts while utilizing stereotypes that presupposed their inability to reason rationally. The result was the prevalence of the "silent" Indian and the use of clichés.[15]

Though today it is unseemly to perform in blackface, it is, as film critics Ralph and Natasha Friar note sarcastically, still acceptable to perform in redface.[16] They wryly speculate that if Indians had been employed to play themselves in the thousands of themed Indian films and television shows produced in the twentieth century, there wouldn't be Native American poverty.

But Native Americans did manage to resist some of the profane attacks on their culture. Raheja's theoretical paradigm of Native American reactions to White domination and exploitation in the film industry involved, from her perspective, "redfacing" (i.e., the process of "playing Indian" by Native American actors who sought to lend credibility to the stereotypical roles prescribed for them). Some Indians rebelled against the dominant distorted tropes and embraced the role of "tricksters" to disguise their true identities and allegiances to confuse and confound the dominant White society. By intentionally shielding their true selves from motion picture studio staff and the public, they were able to retain some semblance of their integrity. The extent of their rejection and rebellion even went as far as Indians refusing to play dead in movie scenes and purportedly substituting live ammunition for blanks on the set.[17]

Another technique used by Native Americans to resist White stereotypical dominance of them was the creation of more relevant depictions of Indigenous culture through "visual sovereignty," that is, the construction of meaningful and culturally accurate representations of Indians not reflected in the dominant White mythological stereotypical depictions of them. Unfortunately, as we noted, Hollywood and the television industry are still controlled by the dominant White culture, and leaders in this industry have been reluctant to use authentic representations of Native Americans. Bound by tradition and formulaic practices, Indians (and other ethnic, religious, and cultural minorities) remain outside the Hollywood mainstream. While there is a growing, vibrant counterculture of Native American filmmaking in the documentary genre, general audiences have not been exposed to this unique niche. The attention span of the moviegoing public remains captivated by the blockbuster, and Native American artistic cinematic endeavors remain largely unnoticed.

Modern Film Representations

In films prior to the middle of the twentieth century, Indians were presented as violent by nature, whereas White people were represented as virtuous and civilized with the occasional nefarious individual. Today, modern writers and filmmakers use Indians less frequently, and when they do, they are often used to show the villainy and futility of postindustrialism and materialism. In general, the portrayal of Native Americans on the big screen has been less than flattering.

Representations of Indians, especially in the Western genre, perpetuated images of them as savage, warlike, sadistic, and uncivilized. From the outset of the motion picture industry in the early decades of the twentieth century, Westerns gained a stranglehold on Hollywood and the American public. From 1914 to 1920, one man, William S. Hart, captivated American viewing audiences until the film industry declined along with the general economy during the Great Depression. But a plethora of so-called B Westerns, emanating, according to historian Slotkin, from an article by Howard Mumford Jones in a 1938 issue of *The Atlantic Monthly*, led to the resurrection of the Western genre.

Taking a cue from Jones's piece, Hollywood began to invest resources into Westerns, which in turn led to a renewed distortion of Native Americans. An important ingredient in the success of the Western genre was the reconceptualization of the format as an epic and the emergence of a cult of Hollywood stars (e.g., John Wayne, Ronald Reagan, and, later, Clint Eastwood) leading a legion of adoring fans that catapulted their movies into box office successes.

The modern Western was suffused with the Frontier Mythology that extolled the virtue of American exceptionalism and Manifest Destiny, both reflecting strong overtones of White Anglo-Saxon Protestant racial superiority, invariably set as a counterpoint to savage warlike Indians, swarthy Mexican criminals, and nefarious greedy city-slickers (most often bankers), intent on immiserating industrious farmers and ranchers. The racial overtones of these portrayals were calculated to strike a chord with dominant anti–Indian and anti-immigrant sympathies among the masses.[18]

Over a quarter of all Hollywood films from 1930 to 1960 were Westerns.[19] This phenomenon increased, and, according to film historian Frank Manchel, there were two thousand Westerns produced by the turn of the twenty-first century.[20] Most of these were Indian themed. Despite the trend toward realistic representations of Indians and their social and cultural issues within the dominant White society, the overwhelming portrayal of Native Americans on the screen and television was one of Indians as miscreants standing in the way of White western expansion. As English professor and film historian Ken Nolley observed, "The particular conventions of the genre, [Westerns] then equate progress in the West with the destruction of Indigenous cultures, and studio imperatives did not see an honest contemplation of that destruction as marketable."[21]

Film historian John O'Connor echoes this sentiment, contending that Hollywood portrayals of Indians reflect business decisions, and political and dramatic considerations: "[L]ittle time has been spent in developing the screen personalities of Indians. They become flat characters, relatively nondescript evil forces that help establish an atmosphere of tension within which the cattle ranchers, the townspeople, the stagecoach riders, the outlaws, the sheepherders, the cavalry officers, the schoolmarms, and the barmaids can relate to one another."[22]

From the outset, Native Americans were cast in a racist stereotypical frame as reflected in the words of Louis Reeves Harrison, a reviewer for *Moving Picture World* in 1912:

> The Indian, however, remains one of the most interesting and picturesque elements of our national history. He is almost typical of the fighting male, a restless, dominating, ever-struggling human creature, principally engaged in works of destruction, but representative of the ancestral strain that conquered all the other creatures delivered from the fertile womb of Mother Earth. He was essentially a man of physical action, using only that part of his brain which enabled him to be crafty in the hunt for food, though he had vague poetic ideals and nebulous dreams of barbaric splendor. Mentally he was far below the Egyptian of 6,000 years ago, but he was the physical superior of any man on earth except the strong-armed European who cultivated brain along with brawn.[23]

In Westerns of the mid–twentieth century, the Indian was often depicted as the supreme enemy of American values. Even as the thematic focus of Westerns morphed into a more salubrious trope that portrayed Indians in a sympathetic light as in *Broken Arrow*, released by 20th Century Fox in 1950, Native Americans were still stereotyped. Jeff Chandler, cast as the Apache Chief Cochise, looked and acted White to give the audience the impression that he could be trusted. As historian Slotkin noted, "Thus the racism that the film banishes on one level returns on another. We can trust the Indians to make peace with them because they are 'just like us,' but to demonstrate that 'truth' we have to transform them into Whites and expel or suppress the ethnic Indian from the picture."[24]

The production and dissemination of racist images in Hollywood and on television about Native Americans (and other Indigenous people) has occurred because these groups have limited political power. Native American and Indigenous people have had, until recently, limited access to and interaction with screenwriters, producers, and directors, allowing distorted images of them to proliferate, as Professor Amanda Cobb (Chickasaw) has noted.[25]

There has been a massive infusion of the popular media with images of Native Americans as stereotypical savages with cultures inferior to Western White civilization, and television has played a major role in purveying them. Journalism professor Annette Taylor estimated that in the late 1950s and 1960s, during the heyday of Westerns on television, as many as twenty-eight Westerns ran each week including *Cheyenne*, *Wagon Train*, and *Gunsmoke*.[26] As with Hollywood feature films, Indians were often portrayed as intellectually backward and their culture irrelevant to modern American society. Native American languages were rarely used in the film industry, and, as Kilpatrick pointed out, the 1939 film *Scouts to the Rescue* ran the English dialogue backward as the purported genuine Native American dialect.[27] Even when authentic language was used, as in Kevin Costner's 1990 film *Dances with Wolves*, which Kilpatrick termed a decent attempt to depict the Sioux as "wholly realized human beings," the male actors were inadvertently using a feminine inflection.[28]

The theme surrounding Native Americans in the film industry began to change in the middle of the twentieth century when the preeminent director of Westerns, John Ford, began to present a more complex and nuanced visage of Native Americans in his works. His trilogy, *Fort Apache* (1948), *She Wore a Yellow Ribbon* (1949), and *Rio Grande* (1950), depicted Native Americans from the perspective of sympathetic White people, as anthropologist John Price noted.[29] Yet some of Ford's works were replete with negative stereotypes about Native Americans as seen in his 1956 film *The Searchers*, which focused on Ethan Edwards's (John Wayne's) relentless search for his niece (played by Natalie Wood) who had been kidnapped by Comanches. The film, set in Ford's beloved Monument Valley, Utah, is characterized by unsurpassed videography. A visual feast for the eye, it is suffused with White fear, anger, and racism toward a band of hostile Comanches led by a renegade chief, Scar. Throughout the five-year search for the kidnapped niece, viewers are exposed to the basest primal prejudices toward Indians as they are reminded of the violent acts some of their brethren perpetrated against "innocent" White settlers. Murder, rape, mutilation, and the "scourge" of miscegenation are the driving force behind Ethan Edwards's pursuit of Scar, to the point that he nearly kills his long-lost niece because she had been living with the Comanches. The themes of White antipathy about miscegenation and racism toward Indians are particularly prevalent in the movie, which grossed nearly $170 million on a budget of $3.7 million. Fortunately, Ford traveled from this macabre orientation in later films, but still, as film critic Stedman noted:

> The relief that is shown to a theater audience—hardly justifies the jarringly racist tones that have set it up. With its climax the film says only that at the moment of truth John Wayne cannot murder a white girl who also is a close relative. Toward the Comanches themselves *The Searchers* displays not a grain of understanding in word or action, except as it grows from audience distaste for writing and directorial bias in an otherwise well-made film.[30]

Ford's last Western about Native Americans, *Cheyenne Autumn*, released in 1964, was an epic (two hours and thirty-four minutes long) designed to elicit sympathy for the very Indians that he had denigrated in earlier works. Filmed mostly in his favorite location, Monument Valley on the Navajo Indian Reservation, the story was based on the actual 1878–79 flight of 286 Cheyenne Indians from their enforced reservation in Oklahoma (then known as Indian Territory) where three-quarters of them perished from disease and starvation, to their homeland, 1,500 miles away, in Wyoming.[31]

The film is unsurpassed in its cinematic beauty. More importantly, it was a calculated attempt to demonstrate the degradation and futility of Indian life on reservations and the duplicity of U.S. government officials who reneged on treaties, and avaricious businessmen who coveted Native American ancestral lands. The movie is laced with instances of official Army malfeasance and mistreatment of the Native Americans as they battle starvation and the elements in the quest for their homeland.

Ford was sixty-nine when he directed this motion picture, and his fascination with valorizing and exoticizing Native Americans is evident throughout, as are the stereotypes that still permeate the work. For example, early in the film Captain Archer, played by Richard Widmark, a sympathetic advocate of the fleeing Indians, attempts to instruct a Quaker schoolteacher, played by Carroll Baker, on the realities of the group she is enamored of: "They're [Cheyennes] the greatest fighters in the world.... A Cheyenne is a soldier from the first slap on his butt. War is his life. He's fierce, he's smart, and he's meaner than sin."

The film is laced with other stereotypes about Native Americans—peace pipes and medicine bags are prominent as well as numerous scenes of stoic Braves and fawning, subservient Indian women. Although Ford used Navajos as extras, all leading roles were played by non–Indians (e.g., Gilbert Roland, Ricardo Montalban, Sal

Mineo, and Victor Jory). Although the language was Native American, it was Navajo, not Cheyenne, and unbeknownst to the director, vulgarities were inserted by extras in scenes to poke fun at White culture. Ford was able to sell the project to Warner Brothers, but despite its large budget (over $4 million), it was not successful at the box office.

As the Vietnam War churned on, directors and writers eschewed Native Americans and turned to more contemporary political and economic depredations. But despite the diminution of Native American–themed projects, one can still recognize many of the following stereotypes about Native Americans in motion pictures and on television:

> Riding horses, hunting buffalo with bows and arrows, wearing tailored leather clothes, having feathers in their hair or headdresses, persistently in warfare, fighting as a tribal unit under a chief, scalping, pursuing White women, constantly being cheated by Whites, drunken, taciturn, humorless, and speaking in simple monosyllabic phrases.[32]

Modern writers and filmmakers often use the Indian as a countercultural hero. This trend began with the depiction of Native Americans as victims and survivors during the anti–Vietnam War movement of the '70s. Beginning with the film *Little Big Man* in 1970, starring Dustin Hoffman, a kinder, gentler portrayal of Native Americans began to emanate from Hollywood, culminating with Kevin Costner's Academy Award–winning 1990 film, *Dances with Wolves*. But some contemporary films in the Western genre are riddled with stereotypes about Native Americans and cowboys such as the box office debacle farces *Cowboys and Aliens* (2011) and *The Lone Ranger* (2013). Even the 2015 blockbuster Academy Award–nominated film *The Revenant*, directed by Alejandro Inarritu and starring Leonardo DiCaprio, depicted Native Americans as White-hating savages feasting on raw meat—a theme repeated in the 2016 remake of *The Magnificent Seven*. And the 2017 Scott Cooper film *Hostiles*, about the journey of a military detachment to return a dying Apache chief (played by veteran Native American [Cherokee] actor Wes Studi) to his homeland in Montana, while empathetic, stereotyped Comanches as shiftless, vicious marauders.

The damage to the American psyche has been done, and stereotypical conceptions about the social and economic status of Native Americans remain embedded in the dominant culture of our society. As historian Stedman observed, the dark visage of Indians was carefully lighted in close-ups to assume a "demonical countenance that has by now been securely locked in the memories of veteran moviegoers—and may never be fully erasable."[33]

One of the most erudite analyses of the evolution of stereotypes about Native Americans in motion pictures was done by Harvard historian Philip J. Deloria (Dakota). He traced the roles that were available to Native American actors in Wild West shows like Buffalo Bill Cody's and in motion pictures. Cody attempted to recreate events (e.g., Custer's Last Stand and Indian attacks on stagecoaches) using people who participated in the original event. This strategy worked well for the shows for a number of years, but it failed to enthrall audiences drawn to the new cinematic medium.

Cody even made movies of the events using some of the actual Indians who participated in the battles, but actors and the dramatization of the incidents captured viewing audiences more than his turbid recreations. It was during these motion picture recreations that some of the Indians' animosity was evinced toward authority figures like General Nelson Miles, a combatant in the Plains Indian Wars and an adviser to the productions. Deloria linked the rumor of Indians threatening to use live ammunition on the set to this circumstance, but he discounted it.[34]

One fact is clear, motion pictures drew heavily on the exoticized representation of Native Americans. Producers and directors eagerly provided viewing audiences with dramatic representations that utilized White actors playing Indians in roles and events that often exaggerated and distorted interactions between the Native American and White society. Despite initial attempts to use Indian actors by Cody and Thomas Ince, producers like Cecil B. DeMille relied more heavily on White actors to play Indians in melodramatic encounters between the civilizations. The clash left little to the imagination of viewers who were fed a large and distorted dose of violence and maudlin themes that pitted Native American savagery against innocent White settlers and women—highlighting the age-old miscegenation theme. As Deloria noted, "With the retirement of Cody's cohort, the reenacting of Miles, Schunk, Red Shirt, Black Elk, Standing Bear, and others—based (at least in theory) on history as authentic memory—would give way to the imaginative acting of those who had *not* been there, whose loyalty was as much to the audience as it was to the self or the past."[35] This trend reached its zenith in the videography of John Ford in the middle of the twentieth century, and in television series that captivated a generation of children, such as *Hopalong Cassidy*, *Roy Rogers*, and *The Lone Ranger*.

18

Proselytizers, Do-Gooders, Voyeurs, and Exploiters

> It is [anthropology], and continues to be, a deeply colonial academic discipline, founded in the days when it was doctrine that the colonial races of the world would be enslaved by Europeans, and the tribal peoples would vanish from the planet.
> —Vine Deloria, Jr., "Authors, Indians, and Planetary Reality"

Our discussion of the nature and origin of stereotypes about Indigenous people, especially Native Americans, has dwelt on the role that literature, art, and the media have played in defining and relegating them to second-class status in our society. We would be remiss if we did not attempt to place some of the blame for their victimization on the four groups that occupy the title of this chapter, for they have, by accident or design, contributed to the stigmatization of Indigenous people around the world.

Proselytizers

The role that Christianity played in motivating, organizing, and extirpating Indigenous people was, sadly, monumental. From the earliest days of conquest in the fifteenth and sixteenth centuries, the primary exploratory goals of European nation-states were to increase the wealth and status of the homeland and harvest heathens for Christ. Explorers were not only overwhelmed by the abundant natural resources they beheld in the New World, they were also captivated by the Indigenous people they observed, and recognized the possibility of satisfying their sponsor's desire to increase their material fortune as well as bringing large numbers of unbaptized Aboriginal people into the fold of Christianity.

The writing of early explorers is replete with comments about the Indigenous people they encountered. While some Native people were hostile, most were friendly. Early colonizers, encountering Indigenous people of color for the first time, were ignorant about their culture, often dismissive of their customs. Possessing superior technology and imbued with ethnocentric notions about their moral and cultural superiority, they disdainfully characterized Native people as heathen and pagan, referring to them as wild, savage, and barbarian—a representation that ostensibly rationalized their mistreatment of Indigenous people who they denigrated as subhuman.

We have seen how Indigenous people, including Native Americans, were relegated to inferior social status by labeling them cannibals, despite evidence that revealed the absence of institutionalized cannibalistic behavior among their societies. Another pejorative reference to Indigenous people was their nakedness or seeming disdain for clothing, especially of the type worn by Europeans. This situation, along with the customs of some Indigenous societies to flaunt their sexuality, starkly contrasted with stolid European conceptions of social interactions (at least enunciated in religious and cultural texts).

Some explorers even wondered whether the "heathen" Native people were human and possessed souls. Such attitudes unfortunately found expression in the brutality of explorers, colonizers, and settlers, and threaded their way into the social fabric of our contemporary society. Bartolomé de Las Casas, the first priest ordained by the Catholic Church in the New World, provided a heart-wrenching description of the cruelty Spanish conquistadors exhibited toward Indigenous people. The full title of his tome, *A Brief Account on the Destruction of the Indies*, with the subtitle *Or a faithful Narrative of The Horrid and Unexampled Massacres, Butcheries, and all manner of Cruelties, that Hell and Malice could invent, committed by the Popish Spanish Party on the inhabitants of West-India, TOGETHER with the Devastations of several Kingdoms in America by Fire and Sword, for the space of Forty and Two Years, from the time of its first Discovery by them*, left little to the imagination, but a quotation from the work illustrates the cruelty inflicted on Indigenous people by the invading Spanish in the name of King, country, and God:

> [The Spaniards] ... spar'd no Age, or Sex, nay not so much as Women and Child, but ripping up their Bellies, tore them alive in pieces. They laid Wagers among themselves, who should with a Sword at one blow cut, or divide a Man in two; oar which of them should decollate or behead a Man, with the greatest dexterity; nay farther, which should sheath his Sword in the Bowels of a Man with the quickest dispatch and expedition. They snatcht young Babes from the Mothers Breasts, and dasht out the brains of those innocents against Rocks; others they cast into Rivers scoffing and jeering them, and called upon their bodies when falling with derision, the true testimony of their cruelty, to come to them, and inhumanely exposing others to their Merciless Swords, together with the Mothers that gave them Life. They erected certain Gibbets, large, but low made, so that their feet almost reacht the ground, every one of which was so ordered as to bear Thirteen Persons in Honour and Reverance (as they said blasphemously) of our Reedemer and his Twelve Apostles, under which they made a Fire to burn Ashes whilst hanging on them.[1]

Las Casas became a defender of Indigenous people and importuned Spanish King Ferdinand II to restrain the excesses of his conquistadors, noting that the Indigenous people were peaceable and their population had been decimated (e.g., the island of Hispaniola's population of nearly three million had been reduced to three hundred, and "the Spaniards by their barbarous and execrable Actions have absolutely depopulated Ten Kingdoms, of greater extent than all of Spain, together with the Kingdoms of Arragon and Portugal").[2]

The carnage perpetrated against Indians in the name of God continued with the dispersion of Catholic and Protestant missionaries who spread the word of the Gospel as well as infectious and communicable diseases that decimated Indigenous populations in the Americas. The treatment of Native Americans in North America at the hands of these proselytizers was, at times, compassionate, but historical records are replete with the brutality they inflicted on Indians that came under their purview.

As we noted, the establishment of the Catholic Franciscan mission system in California in the latter 1700s under the direction of Father Junipero Serra is a case in point.[3]

We must also not forget that many of the Indian boarding schools were run by religious organizations to Christianize Native Americans while destroying their Indigenous culture and transforming them into little capitalists. Cutting their hair, forbidding them to speak their native languages, banishing cultural adornments, and farming them out on vacations and during summers to work with locals was part of the strategy to "humanize" savages and turn them into God-fearing Christians. While missionaries touted noble goals associated with their work, Vine Deloria, Jr., was not being facetious when he noted that when they arrived they had the prayers and the Indians had the land, but when they left it was the other way around.

From the writing of Cotton Mather and Jonathan Edwards's famous sermon "Sinners in the Hands of an Angry God," preached to his congregation in Northampton, Massachusetts, in 1741, to contemporary evangelical pastors who denigrate the concept of interracial intermarriage, there has been an unbroken thread of misinformation and bigotry woven into the fabric of our society—a thread that reeks of the cultural and social superiority of White supremacy that has led to the stigmatization and decimation of non–White Indigenous people in the Americas.[4]

Do-Gooders

The decimation and mistreatment that has afflicted Native Americans for four hundred years has been characterized by some observers as genocide (i.e., the intentional attempt to destroy a people and their culture). Whoever said that "the road to Hell is paved with good intentions" may have been thinking about the behavior of some "advocates" for Native Americans, because the policies and actions that emanated from their advocacy not only perpetuated stereotypes about Indians, but they also nearly led to their extinction.

From the bucolic paintings and photographs of Catlin, Remington, Curtis, Russell, and other artists, to the heroic depictions of Indians living in harmony with nature found in the work of writers such as Zane Grey, the public's attitudes toward Native Americans began to change around the turn of the twentieth century. Perhaps the stark reality that Indians were disappearing from those beautiful landscapes motivated the White majority to develop a more benevolent attitude about them. Their numbers had dwindled to a few hundred thousand by 1900.

Indian resistance to White incursions onto their lands had been attenuated with the end of the Plains Indian Wars in 1890. Compelled to live on inhospitable reservations, often far removed from their homelands, frequently (or so White politicians initially believed) bereft of natural resources to sustain them, remnants of Native Americans' eastern tribes were pushed farther and farther west into Indian Territory (Oklahoma), while Indigenous people in the West and Southwest saw their territory sliced into fragmentary parcels a fraction of their original size. To this day, Native Americans are contesting the abrogation of treaties and federal policies that deprived them of their land and natural resources.[5]

Without doubt, the motivation of some religious emissaries was benevolent. Although strings were often attached to promises and largesse, the years since early interventions by missionaries have produced a fair share of mea culpas and compensatory sympathetic policies, pronouncements, and activities. Even more impressive has been the creation of museums dedicated to Native Americans containing precious artifacts representing the diversity of their cultures. The most renowned of these was founded by an ex–Wall Street investment banker, George Gustav Heye, who began collecting Indian artifacts in 1897 when he purchased a Navajo deerskin shirt in Arizona. He then purchased items from other collectors and museums. Heye even commissioned anthropological expeditions to secure artifacts in his quest to determine the origin of Native Americans, and his collection of nearly one million objects was the largest of one person.

Heye originally kept his relics in his apartment on Madison Avenue in New York and then loaned items to the University of Pennsylvania. In 1916 he established the Museum of the American Indian–Heye Foundation, and the collection was opened to the public in 1922 at its home then on 155th Street and Broadway. It moved later to the historic Alexander Hamilton U.S. Custom Office near Battery Park in New York City where it now resides. In 1989 parts of the Heye collection were transferred to the National Museum of the American Indian, keeping the location in New York City, with some artifacts sent to the Smithsonian's National Museum of the American Indian on the Mall in Washington, D.C.

The philanthropy and largess of Heye should not be understated, however, some Native Americans are displeased with activities that produce artifacts from theft, scavenging, and the hoarding of sacred and secular relics that belonged to them. Although such collections have preserved a record of antiquity and may contribute to our understanding of Indigenous peoples' culture, we should be circumspect about the way they were obtained. Objections are often couched as opposition to securing items that were obtained through indiscriminate poaching of sacred and/or historical sites, much as some aficionados of Egyptology disdain the way ancient artifacts were secured by raiding tombs and unearthing remains of long-buried individuals and their property. Recall the words of Nick Tipon, vice chairman of the Sacred Sites Committee of Federated Indians of Graton Rancheria in northern California: "Rest in peace means forever, not to be disturbed, not to be studied, unless they consented to that."[6] Such sentiments find expression in the reticence of some Native Americans to contribute specimens for DNA research. There is also Native American opposition to the indiscriminate "collection" of Indian artifacts. Since the passage of the Native American Graves Protection and Repatriation Act of 1990, the U.S. Park Service estimates that the remains of nearly 58,000 Indians along with 1.5 million funerary objects as well as 241,000 nonfunerary Native American objects have been repatriated along with 5,136 sacred Indian objects.[7]

Another category of do-gooders are people who are supposedly considerate of the interests of Indians and want to have a role in improving their lot. Their actions may have an impact on the status of Indians in our society through the passage of laws or implementation of public policies. Anthropologist David Treuer (Ojibwe) recalled the antics of Dr. Joseph Kossuth Dixon, a graduate of Rochester Theological Seminary, photographer of Native Americans, film producer (along with Rodman Wanamaker, scion of the Wanamaker department store family), and, notably, author of *The Vanishing Race* (1913), which lamented the demise of Native Americans and their culture as depicted through photographs of Native Americans and their "Last Great

Indian Council," which he and Wanamaker had orchestrated.[8] An unsuccessful advocate for all–Indian regiments in World War I, Dixon made presentations before more than four hundred thousand people around the country about Native Americans based on the film *Song of Hiawatha* that he produced with Wanamaker.

One of the most important figures affecting the revamping of federal policies toward Native Americans was John Collier (1884–1968), Columbia University graduate (sociology) who also studied at the College of France in Paris. He served as the commissioner of Indian affairs under FDR from 1933 to 1945. He was born in Atlanta, Georgia, and his father was mayor there from 1897 to 1899. He was orphaned at sixteen, his mother having died from pneumonia and his father from an accident or possible suicide.

Collier was an indefatigable advocate for Indian self-determination and freedom of religious expression. From 1907 to 1919 he worked for the People's Institute in New York City developing programs for immigrants that emphasized their traditions and political awareness. He recognized the role that social institutions played in influencing self-esteem and the development of personality.

Collier spent 1920 living in Taos, New Mexico, working with the Pueblo Indians, studying their life and culture. He then became the research agent for the General Federation of Women's Clubs in 1922, where he advocated for policies against assimilation of Native Americans and for the return of Indian lands. He was a proponent of cultural pluralism before it became fashionable to espouse cultural diversity.

A severe critic of the Bureau of Indian Affairs, Collier believed that their policies were wrong-headed. A 1932 press release from the U.S. Department of the Interior called him a "fanatical Indian enthusiast with good intentions, but so charged with personal bias and the desire to get a victim every so often, that he does much more harm than good … his statements cannot be depended upon to be either fair, factual or complete."[9] Ironically, three years later, at the urging of Harold Ickes, secretary of the interior under FDR, Collier was appointed the thirty-third U.S. commissioner of Indian affairs.

While Collier worked to end the Dawes Act with its onerous allotment policies that led to the loss of millions of acres of Indian land (from 138 million to 48 million), and he was an outspoken advocate for Native American culture and freedom of religious expression, his enforcement of some New Deal initiatives that sought to stabilize the economy were viewed by some Indians and their supporters as repressive. He enforced the Navajo Livestock Reduction Program in the 1930s during the Great Depression, which resulted in the elimination of half the livestock (mostly sheep) of the Navajo Nation. He even had opponents of his policy jailed. The Indian Rights Association called him a dictator, while the American Indian Federation tried to have him removed from office. To this day, according to anthropologist Treuer, many Navajo (Diné) view him as a tyrant.[10]

Collier's efforts led to what is termed "the Indian New Deal." Although his policies met with mixed success, his ideas were reflected in the American Indian Religious Freedom Act of 1978. His emphasis on self-government, improved Indian education, appreciation of Native American culture, and tribal autonomy promoted through democratic reforms among Native American tribes met with mixed support among Indians. While 172 tribes voted for his Indian Reorganization Act (IRA), which passed in 1934, 73 opposed it. Some criticism of the IRA was leveled at

Federal Indian conclave opened with John Collier and Indian chiefs, 1934 (Library of Congress).

Collier's promotion of constitutional reforms that were modeled after the Pueblo he lived with in Taos, New Mexico. This approach wasn't appealing or appropriate for many other tribes with different cultures and organizations, especially in regard to disputes among tribal members and between Native Americans and White people.[11]

Voyeurs and Exploiters

The long and sometimes sordid history of interaction between Indigenous people and Europeans began with early contacts among explorers and Native people. From their Eurocentric perspective, explorers and colonizers believed in the genetic superiority of White people and the corresponding inferiority of people of color who were initially viewed as novelties and later exploited as human capital (slaves). Recall Friedman's[12] treatise on the "monster races," which were thought to inhabit unchartered "wild" territories. Encounters between naked and scantily clad Indigenous people and Christian emissaries of royal families and aristocrats often resulted in the seizure and exploitation of Aborigines for the curiosity and pleasure of the invaders. From Columbus's first encounters with the Taino, when he brought back six of them to show Spanish Queen Isabella and King Ferdinand, to the kidnapping of Pocahontas and Squanto, Indigenous people of the Americas were viewed as oddities, soulless beings, morally depraved, easily subjugated, and suitable for exhibition and servitude to White people. This perspective was successfully propounded in Wild West shows, which featured similar exploitation of Indians (e.g., William Cody, a.k.a. Buffalo Bill), and of course, television and motion pictures.

One of the most sordid examples of the exploitation of Indigenous people was the exhibition of Sarah Baartman who was of Khoi Khoi descent living in South Africa in the late 1700s. "Discovered" by a British ship's doctor when she was a slave in the Cape Colony, her unusually large breasts, buttocks, and labia resulted from a genetic condition known as steatopygia found among Indigenous people in the region she came from. It facilitates the dispersion of body heat and the storage of fat. This condition made her an object of Eurocentric curiosity in England and France where she was displayed for gawking audiences. When the public lost interest in her she became a prostitute and died at the age of twenty-five, possibly from syphilis. But Baartman was not laid to rest. Noted French zoologist George Cuvier made a plaster cast of her body and removed her skeleton, brain, and genitals, which were preserved in bottles that were displayed in French museums for 160 years until they were taken from the Musee de L'Homme in Paris and interred in South Africa in 1994 at the request of the public and Nelson Mandela.

In the case of Native Americans, early stereotypes that depicted them as savages facilitated the conceptions of colonizers and clerics who, on encountering them, calculated the ways they could be subjugated and exploited. These chauvinistic characterizations were, as we have seen, embedded in the Eurocentric literature and found expression in the mass media, which large numbers of people are still exposed to today. But it may come as a surprise to some readers that the early social sciences, notably anthropology, helped reinforce such stereotypical images of Indigenous people.

Early anthropologists who engaged in observations of Indigenous people were often unable or unwilling to separate their ethnocentric interpretations of them from reality. Consequently, some of their observations were distortions of the cultures they recorded. Lacking professional detachment, their observations and writing often ignored the unique cultural relativism and diversity exhibited by the people they studied. It remained for the German immigrant Franz Boas to inject a modicum of professional dispassion in research involving Indigenous people. Ironically, Boas, who taught at Columbia University and whose namesake was responsible for the extermination of millions of Indigenous people, became known as "the father of cultural anthropology." Boas taught budding anthropologists about the importance of objectivity and integrity in research, and was active from 1896 until his death in 1942. His protégés included such luminaries as Margaret Mead, Ruth Benedict, Edward Sapir, and Alfred Kroeber.

But they were not immune from making ethnocentric judgments about their observations. For example, Margaret Mead's much heralded observations of Indigenous youth in *Coming of Age in Samoa: A Psychological Study of Primitive Youth for Western Civilization*, first published in 1928, was castigated by anthropologist Derek Freeman in his 1983 book *The Making of an Anthropological Myth*,[13] which criticized her for lack of objectivity and misunderstanding of Indigenous culture. Later, she deceived Omaha Indians to facilitate her data collection,[14] and as anthropologists Thomas Biolsi and Larry Zimmerman sanctimoniously conclude: "Such a procedure, let alone the attitude behind it, would be unthinkable in the 1990s if for no other reason than the existence of institutional review boards."[15] Yet we have seen how the privacy and creation legend of the Havasupai Indians were disregarded by an anthropologist at Arizona State University as late as 1994 (the case was settled in 2010).

From the inception of the social sciences in the nineteenth century, practitioners recognized the peculiarities and challenges associated with trying to explain human behavior. The first psychological laboratory, founded by Wilhelm Wundt at the University of Leipzig in Germany in 1879, established the scientific bona fides of psychology qua science, to demonstrate the inviolability of psychology as a legitimate form of scientific inquiry based on the scientific method of experimentation and objectivity. And the founder of modern sociology, Frenchman Auguste Comte, was said to practice cerebral hygiene to avoid the intrusion of societal influences and subjectivity in his work.

Scholarly notables such as the German social scientists Max Weber and Karl Mannheim urged their followers to be objective in their interpretations of human behavior and consider the totality of the environment in which it occurred. I can recall one of my early sociology instructors, Glenn Vernon, insisting that the discipline must be value-free to promote objectivity. Of course, studying human beings is fraught with challenges. Even the topic of one's research depends on a value decision—a choice to study one phenomenon over another. As we previously mentioned, human variability and multiple causality frequently complicate our attempts to differentiate fact from fiction. The arbitrary and capricious nature of humans makes research on them difficult and often problematic.

Unethical behavior by researchers has led to some glaring misadventures. For example, the infamous Alabama Tuskegee experiment conducted by the U.S. Public Health Service from 1939 to 1972 (when it was exposed) destroyed the lives of the 399 African American men who had syphilis and were intentionally left untreated without their knowledge. One hundred and twenty-eight of them died, and forty of their wives and nineteen of their children were infected.[16]

Strict requirements for researchers interacting with human subjects were subsequently implemented. Among the new guidelines was the requirement for obtaining informed consent of potential human subjects—they must know the purpose of the study and agree to participate in it. (For children under the age of eighteen, written parental consent must be secured by the researcher after full disclosure is made about the purpose and methods of the study.) Additionally, universities throughout the nation established institutional review boards (IRBs) usually staffed by volunteer faculty to review proposals and determine whether adequate protections would be used and ethical standards maintained by researchers in a proposed study.

Although the thrust of the IRB process and the emphasis on treating humans ethically was to avoid mistreatment of human research subjects, to social science researchers, whose work often focuses on values and attitudes along with human behavior, the process often seems more like institutional overkill than oversight. Nevertheless, social science research benefits from such strictures. Native Americans have been the targets of "hit and run" studies by aggressive and upwardly mobile researchers for over a hundred years.

There was consternation among Native Americans about the use and abuse of their trust and privacy prior to the research reforms. In his iconic condemnation of White society, *Custer Died for Your Sins: An Indian Manifesto*, lawyer and philosopher Vine Deloria, Jr., excoriated academics, especially anthropologists, for exploiting

Native Americans, and violating their trust and privacy for personal gain. Deloria enumerated unprofessional and inauthentic behavior then commonly found among academics in his grievances about their naive and, at times, exploitative behavior. Although he acknowledged some of their well-intentioned motives, he believed some of them were intentionally misguided by Indians to conceal sacrosanct rituals and the true meaning of Native American rites (e.g., the Hopi Snake Dance).

In his inimitable style, the late scholar noted: "Indians have been cursed above all other people in history. Indians have anthropologists."[17] Furthermore, they come from their schools for their "great summer adventures" descending on Indian Country to conduct their questionable, irrelevant research. "Indians are equally certain that Columbus brought anthropologists on his ships when he came to the New World. How else could he have made so many wrong deductions about where he was?"[18]

Deloria accused social scientists, especially anthropologists, of bias and reinforcing stereotypes about Native Americans in their work. According to him, "Pure research" is "an abstraction of scholarly suspicions concerning some obscure theory originally expounded in pre–Revolutionary days and systematically checked each summer since then." Applied anthropologists were accused of using their field observations to justify their preconceived suspicions about Indians, noting that the difference between pure and applied anthropology was, from his perspective, dependent on the number of footnotes used in "professional" journal articles (pure used more than applied).

Toward the end of his life, Deloria tempered some of his animosity toward the discipline of anthropology, but in his earlier treatise he condemned anthropological methods and objectives: "The fundamental thesis of the anthropologist is that people are objects for observation, people are then considered objects for experimentation, for manipulation, and for eventual extinction."[19] And "behind each policy and program with which Indians are plagued, if traced completely back to its origin, stands the anthropologist."[20]

What most irked Deloria was the stultifying effect that social science, especially anthropological research, was having on Native Americans. The litany of societal and tribal failures that supposedly caused high rates of poverty and disorganization among Indians was, he thought, attributable to the crescendo of negativity heaped on Indians by self-seeking and naive social scientists. Their theories and slogans came to be "excuses for Indian failures."

Yet as we shall see in the next chapter, there has been a resurgence in Native American life from art and music to respect for the environment and asceticism among Indians, and the non–Indian population is developing respect for the "old ways" of life and Native American culture. Paramount among the interests of Native Americans is their insistence on maintaining tribal sovereignty and resisting assimilation—two challenging objectives given the current political climate in the United States and the size and reach of the dominant materialistic American culture.

Trends have occurred that have mitigated the adverse influences of previous decades of exploitative academic intrusion into Native American life. As the social sciences have matured and research methods evolved, these disciplines have developed more sophisticated and relevant codes of ethics governing the treatment of human subjects and data collection. No doubt much of the impetus for this trend emanated from the revelation of previous aberrations (e.g., the Tuskegee experiment), but the maturation and evolution of these relatively young disciplines has also led to a more respectful, realistic, and useful collaboration between academics and Indians. Deloria himself acknowledged this phenomenon in a later observation, noting some of the benefits derived from academic assistance.[21] The creation of comprehensive ethical codes of conduct by the American Anthropological Association and associated disciplines has also contributed to the professionalization and quality of social science research related to the study and interpretation of Native American behavior.[22]

A second trend has been the increasing introduction of Native Americans into the social sciences, especially anthropology. At the time of this writing there were 213 members of the Association of Indigenous Anthropologists, a subsection of the American Anthropological Association, formed in 2008 by JoAllyn Archambault (Standing Rock Sioux). In addition to mentoring budding Native American anthropologists, the organization promotes the study of Indian cultures in the past and present, encourages the professional development of Native American scholars, provides a network for Indigenous students, facilitates intellectual exchange among practitioners through workshops and seminars, and encourages professional work among scholars that has a tangible benefit for the discipline of anthropology and Indigenous communities.[23]

In 2018, there were approximately ninety-five Native American members of the American Anthropological Association. A 2017 analysis revealed that Native Americans were more likely to study anthropology relative to other academic disciplines—126 percent of Native Americans received their associate of arts degrees, 153 percent earned their bachelor's degrees, 368 percent obtained their master's degrees, and 203 percent received their doctoral degrees in the discipline of anthropology compared to the rates expected in overall degree attainment.[24] The percentages about the number of Native Americans enrolled in various higher education programs were higher than expected by the amounts shown, e.g. 26% higher in AA degrees, 53% higher in bachelor's degrees, 268% higher in master's degree programs, and 103% higher in doctoral degrees. That is to say, there was an excess of Native American students studying in anthropology at each one of these levels. Today, there are numerous scholarly journals and professional archives dedicated to the study of Native Americans and other Indigenous people.[25]

The passage of legislation to protect Native American sacred and religious sites, relics, and activities (e.g., the Native American Graves and Repatriation Act passed by Congress in 1990[26]), as well as lawyers, law firms, and law journals dedicated to pursuing justice and ensuring compliance to such legislation, helps promote Native American interests in the face of lax federal policies. Deloria recognized the potential for positive outcomes based on ethical social science research: "If, however, anthropologists and other social scientists begin to speak critically of the shortcomings of their own society using the knowledge which they claim to have derived from observation of the tribal peoples, that will be a signal that something of real value is contained within the tribal context."[27]

Although significant ethical and methodological changes in the social science approach to studying Native Americans (and other human subjects) have been made since Deloria's caustic assessment, problems still emerge (e.g., DNA and the Havasupai, exploitation of the Hopi,[28] and conflict over interpretations of Iroquois traditions[29]). The contemporary struggle over who qualifies as a "legitimate" member of a tribe, often for the purpose of entitlement to tribal and government largesse, at times devolves on the use of social science as well as medical research, challenging ethics, and integrity.

In the final analysis, not too much has changed in our materialistic age from the time Deloria penned his sarcastic words. When one's academic standing depends on research funding and publishing, the incentive to misinterpret and misrepresent Native American art, religious symbols, and lifestyle remains tantalizing. The issue of who has the power to initiate research and what topics are legitimate foci for study (or exploitation) remain cogent and unresolved, although Native Americans are demanding more input into processes that affect their lives. As the stakes grow larger in terms of financial and academic career payoffs, the prospects for beneficial outcomes derived from scholarly research on Native Americans and other Indigenous people remain problematic, and the perpetuation of stereotypes becomes conditional in part on the good will and integrity of researchers (institutional review boards notwithstanding). Recent advances in ethical and methodological studies of Indigenous people point to a noble but still skeptical path to enlightenment.

19

The Final Fight?

Now we're on the other side of the Apocalypse.
—Chief Nephi Craig (White Mountain Apache/Navajo)

Bears Ears is a sacred Native American region in southern Utah encompassing 1.5 million acres. It is named for two nine-thousand-foot buttes and was designated as a National Monument by outgoing President Barack Obama under the federal Antiquities Act. A preliminary report issued in June 2017 by Ryan Zinke, then interior secretary under President Donald Trump, said serious consideration was being given to cutting the monument down to 160,000 acres. In his words, "right-sizing it." A monument that "encompasses almost 1.5 million acres where multiple-use management is hindered or prohibited is not the best use of the land and is not in accordance with the intention of the Antiquities Act."[1] And on December 4, 2017, President Trump issued an executive order reducing the Bears Ears and Grand Staircase–Escalante area by two million acres.

A coalition of Native American tribes (Hopi, Zuni, Ute Mountain, and Navajo) vowed to sue the federal government to prevent a reduction in the size of the monument. "There was nothing wrong in the way it was established; only Congress has the power to change or reduce a monument," said Natalie Landreth, an attorney for the Native American tribal coalition. "Every eighth of an inch has [cultural] objects. There aren't any unused or extra pieces—any reduction of it is illegal." This was done, she contended "for purely political reasons."[2] The monument is thought to contain over one hundred thousand cultural and archeological sites, but the Trump administration wasn't satisfied with this action. On August 2, 2019, it announced its intention to open up the remaining 15 percent of the Bears Ears National Monument and Wilderness Area (approximately eighty thousand acres), signaling that economic priorities take precedence over social and cultural considerations. That is the climate that Native Americans must contend with as they seek to regain control over their lands.

But an even larger issue facing Native Americans concerns their presence in a White-dominated society that uses many of the stereotypes we have discussed to define them. In such a perverse social climate, where do Native Americans fit? What is their role in a postindustrial society? How do they perceive themselves, and how do they wish White-dominated society to view them?

Contemporary discussions about the status, interests, and behavior of Native Americans in our society can be couched in the following words: erasure, assimilation, sovereignty, resiliency, and sustainability. Native Americans are emphatic about having the truth told about their interactions with Euro-Americans. The prospect

247

of denying the facts about the colonization of this continent along with the theft of Native land and resources, their mistreatment at the hands of White settlers, the abrogation of hundreds of treaties, the forcible removal of Indians from their land to reservations and then urban areas, the theft of Indigenous children and their enforced education in boarding schools, and attempts to characterize Native Americans as historical artifacts representative of extinct cultures are viewed as anathema by Indians—and in light of developments discussed below, out of touch with Indigenous movements that are becoming ascendant as Indians strive to rejuvenate their culture and secure rights to land and customs previously denied them.

Efforts to compel Native Americans to forego their history and culture and assimilate into the dominant White Euro-American culture are also eschewed by Native Americans and many White people who believe in the sanctity of Indigenous customs and traditions and the benefits of Indigenous lifestyles that elevate the community and environment above the individual and competition. This perspective finds expression in the multitude of Indigenous cultural endeavors (art, music, and literature) as well as the profusion and reintroduction of Native American customs (e.g., powwows) and languages. No doubt assimilation of Native Americans has occurred, but present trends put the lie to assumptions about "vanishing Americans."

Along with the rekindling of Native American culture and traditions is their incessant and unremitting claim for sovereignty. The 574 tribes want to be recognized as independent sovereign nations—peoples who have independent voices with differing hopes, aspirations, and needs. People who have the right, by treaties with our federal government, to express their concerns and lend their wisdom to issues relevant to them. They want a voice in determining their own destiny—a voice promised to them through treaties that pledged to respect and recognize their land, resources, and honor. And while attempts are continuously being made to erode these promises, Native Americans continue to promote their desire for autonomy and recognition, and as we will see, this is being undergirded by court decisions in their favor.

The following discussion provides a brief glimpse of current Native American activities that demonstrate their resiliency and attempt to sustain their diverse cultures in the face of the Euro-American cultural juggernaut that threatens to envelop and negate them. Here are some activities of Native Americans intended to revitalize their ancient cultures and challenge negative stereotypes about them. First, we turn to a brief synopsis of the conditions they must address before they embark on their voyage for recognition and equality.

Disastrous Consequences Persist

Looking at indices pertaining to the physical and mental health of Native Americans, it is difficult not to assume what the report *Reclaiming Native Truth*[3] pejoratively refers to as a "deficit" orientation, but the facts clearly demonstrate multiple social, economic, and political challenges Native Americans endure. Perhaps the most devastating consequence of the dominant culture's assault on Native Americans is their high suicide rate, especially among the young. Suicide is the second leading cause of death among Native Americans ages ten to twenty-four. But the legacy of White domination and exploitation has also contributed to a panoply of social pathologies including poverty, domestic violence, rape, human trafficking, substance abuse, and despair. Paramount among the social maladies confronting Native Americans is their high unemployment rate—a perennial problem even before the COVID-19 pandemic, and it is especially troublesome on Native American reservations. Even in affluent times, Native American unemployment was widespread. A survey conducted in 2005 found fifteen Indian reservations with unemployment rates over 80 percent. One of the most distressed sites was that of the Oglala Sioux Reservation in Pine Ridge, South Dakota, where 89 percent (26,408) of the 29,539 eligible workers were out of work.[4]

When I visited the Pine Ridge Reservation in September 2018, I was struck by the enormous expanse of territory, the sparsely populated rolling hills, and the lack of resources and infrastructure to employ people. Outside of farming and ranching, there are few tangible opportunities to support residents, and the hills and valleys were dotted with trailers and junk cars reminiscent of the Dust Bowl era of the Great Depression.

Three-quarters of Native Americans do not live on reservations, and they are not faring well either. According to a report by the Economic Policy Institute, there is only a 2.5 percent difference in the employment rate between Indians living on the reservation and those living off. (Indians living on reservations had lower employment rates.) Native Americans experienced four times the decline in employment as White people during the Great Recession. An examination of thirty-four states containing the majority of Native Americans in the United States revealed that between 2009 and 2011, Native Americans had an employment rate over 13 percent lower than White people. More relevant to our discussion of discrimination was the conclusion that "[e]ven when Native Americans are the same age, sex, have the same educational level and marital status, reside in the same city and the same state, and are similar to whites on all of the other variables in the analysis, Native Americans still have 31 percent lower odds of being employed than whites."[5]

The factor that had the most important effect on the rate of employment was education. The higher the education, the higher the rate of employment. Native Americans with a GED had a 50 percent higher rate than dropouts, a high school diploma increased employability by 108 percent, an associate's degree by 269 percent, a bachelor's degree by 427 percent, and an advanced degree by a whopping 607 percent, or seven times the odds of being employed as Indians without a high school diploma. Unfortunately, the educational attainment of Native Americans lags considerably behind the White population, but this is not because of genetic deficiencies or the will to work. It is the result of a cascade of social, psychological, and political decisions that have perpetuated the immiseration of Native Americans that, until the latter part of the twentieth century, kept them dependent on and alienated from the dominant White society.

One hopeful sign is the growth in higher education attainment among Native Americans. Still lagging behind the non–Native population, there are bright and promising spots. For example, Oglala Lakota College, founded in 1971, functions on nine campuses throughout the sprawling Pine Ridge Reservation in South Dakota, with a total enrollment of 1,300. Over half of these students come from families living below the poverty level, and a quarter of them are the first generation attending college. Nearly nine out of ten entering first-year students need remedial help in math, and nearly three-quarters need remedial English instruction, but these young men and women are graduating each year from this fully accredited institution and entering diverse occupations and professions—doctors, lawyers, teachers, social workers, nurses, and a rich panoply of trades and specialties that are not only financially rewarding, but also contribute to Native American and the dominant White society. Sadly, the graduation rate is abysmally low, only 8 out of 147 students in 2017 at the campus in Kyle, South Dakota (which I visited in September 2018), despite remedial and financial support.

Positive changes in the lives of Native Americans have ensued because of successes achieved on the legal and cultural fronts, and we now turn to a review of progress in these areas.

Legal Gains and Losses

Most legal experts on Native American jurisprudence would agree that the U.S. Supreme Court decision tendered by Chief Justice John Marshall in 1823 (*Johnson v. McIntosh*, 21 U.S. 543) was the most backward legal ruling affecting Indigenous people in the United States and around the world, because it served as a template for other colonial governments. In his zeal to legitimize the rights of invading European nations, Justice Marshall delivered a justification for the Doctrine of Discovery. Essentially, Marshall and the Court concluded that colonizing nations could legitimately claim ownership of Indigenous lands by merely possessing them, thereby extinguishing the title to land and self-determination rights of Native Americans and other Indigenous people with the stroke of a pen.[6]

Since that time the legal status of Native Americans has undergone many changes, but the fact remains that the reservation system still occupies a special place in the United States. Native Americans are still viewed as wards of the federal government, and a morass of contradictory laws and policies affecting Indians and non–Indians who commit crimes on reservation land continues to impede and, at times, prevent Indians from receiving equal justice in our society. As we have seen, this is especially problematic in cases involving violence committed against Native Americans, especially women, by non–Native people on reservations.

Law professor Robert A. Williams, Jr. (Lumbee), does an admirable job of demonstrating that the U.S. Supreme Court has, from the time of Chief Justice John Marshall in the 1800s, employed racist stereotypical language about Native Americans, viewing them as uncivilized, savage, and incapable of governing and protecting themselves. Professor Williams shows how, during the nineteenth and twentieth centuries, the Supreme Court continually upheld White rights and U.S. territorial claims against Indians to their detriment, justified seizure of their lands under the Doctrine of Discovery (*Johnson v. McIntosh*, 1823), and established in *Cherokee Nation v. Georgia* (1831) and *Worcester v. Georgia* (1832) the legitimatization of the "trust doctrine" that viewed Indians as wards of the federal government and gave federal law priority over state laws concerning Native Americans, with the federal government having exclusive control over most Indian affairs.

These nineteenth-century rulings, referred to as the *Marshall Trilogy*, are still used by the U.S. Supreme Court to justify the treatment of Native Americans and circumscribe their rights. While there have been some Native American court victories in recent years (e.g., land disputes and fishing rights and control of other resources), for the most part, our government has pursued the policy of "might makes right" using racist stereotypical imagery of Indians to justify decisions against them, and rationalize the denial of their claims to land, resources, and compensation for them. For example, in the infamous *Tee-Hit-Ton v. United States* (348 U.S. 272, 1955) case, the U.S. Supreme Court denied a claim for compensation of land by a group of Alaskan Indigenous people that would have cost the federal government $1 billion to $9 billion (depending on whose estimate was used).

Williams notes that the Supreme Court reversed the racist orientation and implications of the *Dred Scott* (1856) and *Plessy v. Ferguson* (1896) cases in the *Brown* (1954) decision, but it has not done the same to rectify the situation of Native Americans. He contends that modern legal decisions are still based on racist stereotypical portraits of Indians, noting that the famous *Oliphant v. Suquamish Indian Tribe* (435 U.S. 191, 1978) decision rendered by Chief Justice William Rehnquist relied on the *Marshall Trilogy*'s racist stereotypes to deprive Native Americans of the right to enforce laws against non–Native Americans on their reservations. The Supreme Court's 2004 ruling delivered by Justice Stephen Breyer in *U.S. v. Lara* (541 U.S.193) seemingly affirmed Native Americans' tribal sovereignty and allowed them to prosecute criminal offenders on reservations. John Dawson, former legal adviser for the National Congress on American Indians, contended this was a landmark decision,[7] but Professor Williams regards the ruling as yet another decision steeped in Marshall's racist, anti–Indian ideology, reinforcing the plenary power of the Court to decide if and when Indian sovereignty can be applied.[8]

If legal progress has been slow on the criminal front, civil decisions affecting Native American land, resources, and general treaty rights that were violated by local, state, and federal governments have, at times, been significant. Since equity in our legal system is associated with the ability to afford competent representation, some major Native American legal victories may owe their success to the passage of the Gambling Regulatory Act of 1988, which gave Native American tribes the right to conduct gaming activities on their land. Although this act has yielded mixed economic returns for the many tribes that have attempted to capitalize on the situation, some of the more successful and affluent groups have used the resources garnered from gaming revenues to retain high-powered legal assistance in the struggle to regain land and resources taken from them in the past. A case in point is the Oneida Nation that brought suit against the state of New York to regain 250,000 acres in New York and Wisconsin. In 2000, the federal government and New York offered to give them $500 million, but they declined the offer.

Ten years later, the Second U.S. Court of Appeals in Manhattan ruled 2–1 that the Oneida Nation cannot reclaim ancient lands and the state does not have to pay anything for the 250,000 acres taken from them centuries ago. In a similar case, the same court threw out a land claim by the Cayuga Indian Nation in 2005, and the U.S. Supreme Court refused to hear their appeal, effectively ending similar attempts by Native Americans to regain lost land and resources and receive fair compensation for them.

When the Oneida Nation first filed their claim in 1970, they were impoverished and owned only thirty-two acres. At the time of the ruling they had amassed seventeen thousand acres, a chain of gas stations, and owned the lucrative Turning Stone Resort and Casino in Verona, New York, which generated $500 million annually.

According to Native American anthropologist David Treuer, the U.S. Supreme Court ruled in favor of Indian rights 120 times between 1950 and 2006, including affirming, in 1979, Federal District Court Judge George Boldt's 1974 decision, which awarded 50 percent of the Washington state salmon catch to Indians with treaty fishing rights.[9] A subsequent U.S. Supreme Court decision mandated that the state of Washington must replace nine hundred culverts that obstruct the migration of salmon at a projected cost of $3.7 billion.[10]

Despite some gains, Native Americans are still viewed as second-class citizens by some in the White majority, and, as Williams deftly illustrates, federal and state laws frequently treat them that way. His solution is to rely more heavily on international law, which promotes the rights of Indigenous people and equitable treatment of them around the world. While this is admirable, in view of the current toxic relationship between the U.S. government and the International Criminal Court (former National Security Adviser John Bolton indicated in an address on September 10, 2018, that the ICC was "dead to us"), his idealism may be laced with naiveté. For the foreseeable future, the struggle for Native American and Indigenous rights will continue to be waged in state and federal courts, with an ebb and flow of decisions reflecting the changing public mood.

Political Pressure

Native Americans have become increasingly sophisticated about the political processes in this country, and while they have experienced mixed success in their attempt to change public policy at the state and federal levels, they have made significant inroads into the consciousness of the public and some legislators in our society. Testing the legitimacy and durability of treaties, demanding access and control over natural resources on their present and former land, exercising control over people who commit felonies on reservations, and a host of other issues about Native resources and the environment continue to be addressed by Native American organizations that lobby local, state, and federal agencies to recognize the rights bestowed by government entities on Native Americans.

One of the most important cases concerning the land and resource rights of Native Americans was launched by Elouise Cobell (Blackfoot) on June 10, 1996. It was the largest class action suit at the time lodged against the federal government (*Cobell v. Salazar*). It alleged mismanagement of Native American trust funds. The suit contended that corporations were destroying Native American natural resources such as water and vegetation and inaccurately reporting the profits generated from them. Trust funds couldn't be traced because of improperly kept records and lost or destroyed files.

Cobell contended that Native Americans were owed $27.5 billion by the federal government. On February 1, 2001, a U.S. court of appeals ruled against the federal government finding that the Indian Trust Fund had indeed been misused. In hearings led by senators John McCain and Byron Dorgan, a settlement with the Indians was reached for $8 billion, but the deal was canceled a day before it was finalized by the George W. Bush administration.

In the long acrimonious litigation that marked the suit, U.S. District Court Judge Royce Lamberth was removed from the case. The Obama administration later settled the suit for $3.4 billion plus a $60 million scholarship fund for Native Americans and Alaska Natives—fourteen years after the suit began. Cobell died four months later, before any checks were paid to plaintiffs. She received the Presidential Medal of Freedom posthumously in November 2016.[11]

The National Congress of American Indians (NCAI) is the oldest and most recognized advocacy group on behalf of Native Americans and Alaska Natives in the United States. Its power has waned and revived over the last decades, and it has emerged as the preeminent voice for the rights of Indigenous people in this country. At the celebration of its seventy-fifth anniversary in Denver, Colorado, in October 2018, Indian representatives from across the country heard presentations about Medicaid, voting power among Native Americans, accurate counting of the Native American population in the 2020 Census, ending violence against Native American women, climate action across tribal nations, building sustainable tribal economies, Native American home ownership issues, and strategies for preventing substance abuse. The NCAI also conducted seminars and workshops throughout 2018 on transportation issues, child welfare, tribal judicial courts, self-governance, water resources, youth activities, public health, and gaming issues.

On September 12, 2018, the NCAI sponsored "Tribal Unity Impact Days" on Capitol Hill to inform Congress about issues and concerns of Indians such as the 2018 Farm Bill, reorganization of the Department of the Interior under the Trump administration, reauthorization of the Violence Against Women Act, cultural protections of Native Americans, water resources, and self-governance. Delegates from the Affiliated Tribes of the Northwest Indians, Alaska Federation of Natives, the California Association of Tribal Governments, the Great Plains Tribal Chairman's Association, the Inter-Tribal Association of Arizona, the Rocky Mountain Tribal Leaders Council, the United South and Eastern Tribes Sovereignty Protection Fund, and the United Tribes of Michigan met legislators at the Dirksen Senate Office Building and exchanged views about these and other issues related to Indigenous people in this country.

The Native American pursuit of political progress has gone far beyond the sensationalist days of the Red Power movement that emerged in the 1970s under the charismatic leadership of Russell Means (Oglala Lakota) and Dennis Banks (Chippewa), founders of the American Indian Movement along with Clyde and Vern Bellecourt (Ojibwe) and Richard Oakes (Mohawk). In their perceptive analysis of the rise and fall of AIM and the Red Power movement, Paul Chaat Smith (Comanche) and Robert Allen Warrior (Osage) chronicled the tortured twists and turns that characterized the machinations of this nascent Indigenous movement from the abortive seizure of Alcatraz from November 20, 1969, to June 11, 1971, to the ransacking of the Bureau of Indian Affairs in Washington, D.C., in November 1972, and the catastrophic showdown between Native Americans and federal agents at Wounded Knee on the Oglala Lakota Reservation in South Dakota in 1973.

The demise of AIM did not spell the destruction of Native American involvement in the larger society and their commitment to rectifying social inequality in the treatment of Indians and Alaska Natives. A cadre of new Native leaders has emerged, educated and skilled in the use of policies and laws created by the very system that subjugated them in the past. One of the stars of the contemporary Indian civil rights movement was the well-known and respected Cherokee leader, the first woman elected as the principal chief of the Cherokee Nation, Wilma Mankiller. Born in 1945 in Tahlequah, Oklahoma, the capital of the Cherokee Nation, Mankiller devoted her life to advocating for women's and Native American causes. She was inducted into the Women's Hall of Fame in New York City in 1994 and presented with the Medal of Freedom by President Bill Clinton in 1998.

Her passing in 2010 ignited the passion to serve among other Indigenous people, led by the indefatigable Suzan Shown Harjo (Cheyenne and Hodulgee Muscogee). She received the Medal of Freedom from President Barack Obama in 2014 and is responsible for the return of over a million acres to Native Americans. She also founded the Morning Star Institute in 1984 to promote sacred Native American land claims and the protection of cultural rights and artistic expression. One of her and the institute's primary objectives is the elimination of Native American sports mascots.

A record number of Indigenous people ran for office in the 2020 elections nationwide. The field was led by U.S. Representatives Deb Haaland (Laguna Pueblo–New Mexico) and Sharice Davids (Ho Chunk–Kansas) as well as Markwayne Mullin (Cherokee–Oklahoma) and Tom Cole (Chickasaw–Oklahoma) who were reelected, along with newcomers Yvette Herrell (Cherokee–New Mexico) and Kai Kahele (Indigenous Hawaiian).

Contemporary politicians are becoming aware of the growing Native American influence in our society. On August 19–20, 2019, a presidential candidate forum devoted exclusively to Native American issues was held in Sioux City, Iowa. It was attended by many of the candidates for the Democratic Party's nomination who discussed their plans for Indian rights and concerns,

Wilma Mankiller (1945–2010), Presidential Medal of Freedom recipient, activist, and principal chief of the Cherokee Nation, with President Bill Clinton (Paul J. Richards, AFP/Getty Images).

and a NCAI national program, *Native Vote Taking Action Virtual Rally*, was held on May 28, 2020, with a lineup of Native American stars to encourage the Native American vote.

Winona La Duke (Anishinaabe), former Green Party vice presidential candidate with former presidential candidate Ralph Nader, remains committed to pursuing equity in Native American land and environmental rights, as does Oren Lyons (Onondaga), who is also concerned with securing equity in treaty rights with the United States and is a leader of the Iroquois Confederacy. Tom Goldtooth (Navajo/Dakota), an environmentalist, directs the Indigenous Environmental Network that seeks environmental protection through spiritual activism. Ray Halbritter (Oneida) is a wealthy businessman who was the publisher of *Indian Country Today* and a steadfast opponent of the use of Indians as mascots.[12]

Nick Tilsen (Oglala Lakota) founded the NDN Collective, headquartered in Rapid City, South Dakota. The collective pursues equity and justice for Indigenous people by promoting self-determination and collaboration. Similarly, IllumiNative is a Native American–led nonprofit organization that challenges stereotypes about Indians and seeks to ensure accurate portrayals of them and their communities. Both are youth oriented, designed to appeal to future Native American leaders, and represent a new wave of activism among Native Americans.

A sign of increasing Native American political influence was seen in the 2020 election when Every Native Vote Counts boosted turnout in swing states such as Arizona and Wisconsin, bringing the Native American vote into the Democratic Party and helping assure the election of Joe Biden.

Suzan Shown Harjo, activist and Presidential Medal of Freedom recipient (Mandel Ngan, AFP/Getty Images).

Our treatment of Native Americans has been, as historian Berkhofer noted, based on our imaginary perception of them:

> For most Whites throughout the past five centuries, the Indian of imagination and ideology has been as real, perhaps more real, than the Native American of actual existence and contact. As preconception became conception and conception became fact, the Indian was used for the ends of argument, art, and entertainment by White painters, philosophers, poets, novelists, and movie makers among many. Although each succeeding generation presumed its imagery based more upon the Native American of observation and report, the Indian of imagination and ideology continued to be derived as much from the polemical and creative needs of Whites as from what they heard and read of actual Native Americans or even at times experienced.[13]

We have seen that the legacy of this tradition has had devastating effects on the social, psychological, and physiological condition of Native Americans, and the media bear much responsibility for perpetuating stereotypes about them. As film historian Kilpatrick concluded: "The film industry and television have spun cobwebs of misinformation, misunderstanding, derision, hatred and guilt about Native Americans."[14] From barbaric, bloodthirsty demons to noble savages, from fearsome warriors to pathetic, marginalized buffoons, racist stereotypes continue to exact a toll on Native Americans calculated in heartbreak, disease, and death. Throughout this book we have seen that it has been the prerogative of the dominant White/European culture to define Native Americans and perpetuate stereotypical racist impressions of them. The result of the "clash of civilizations" that occurred on this continent was preordained based on differences in technology and demography.

The descent of the Native American image from fearsome, noble warrior to unemployed, homeless, substance-abusing derelict was a path dictated by the same genocidal policies and practices that nearly led to their extinction. At base, it was and is a matter of power. As Paul Chaat Smith (Comanche), associate curator of the National Museum of the American Indian, put it, "In the final analysis, Indians are unimportant, and not a subject for serious people."[15] As Indians relinquished their land and declined in numbers, they became victims of an avaricious society that regarded them with disdain, even contempt. The words of L. Frank Baum, author of *The Wonderful Wizard of Oz*, typified this attitude in an editorial in his newspaper, the *Aberdeen* (South Dakota) *Saturday Pioneer*, on December 20, 1890 following the killing of Sitting Bull: "With his fall the nobility of the Redskin is extinguished, and what few are left are a pack of whining curs who lick the hand that smites them. The Whites, by law of conquest, by justice of civilization, are masters of the American continent, and the best safety of the frontier settlements will be secured by the total annihilation of the few remaining Indians."

American studies professor Joel Martin captured the essence of White America's depredation of Indians in his essay on the changing perceptions of southerners toward them compared to Black people. As wave on wave of White settlers and prospectors encroached on and stole their land, Indians were initially respected by White society for resisting the onslaught. Their names became symbolic labels representing freedom and romanticism and functioned like trophies to justify White domination of their resources. While "[t]he actual living Indian had been exiled; the fictive dead Indian was romanticized. The former was the precondition for the latter, if not the cause."[16]

The sordid history of the evolution of White people's perception of the Native American from noble savage to drunken derelict resulted from a confluence of events and trends that began with the White man's covetousness of their lands from the time of first encounter, the provocations that precipitated Native American retaliation, the abnegation of treaties and promises by the federal government, the genocidal slaughter, forced removal, and sequestration of Indians, and their inevitable immiseration.

Fleeting Wealth But Resilient

Even now, with the discovery of valuable resources on what was previously deemed worthless Native American land, there is discussion about property and mineral rights. According to the Council of Energy Resource Tribes, Indian energy resources may be worth $1.5 trillion, but a study of Indian land resources concluded that the federal government "deprives tribes of the opportunity to benefit from such wealth" by stifling bureaucratic regulations and policies that impede resource development.[17] Ironically, much of the buried Indian wealth is in the form of coal, a carbon-rich pollutant that is losing favor as an energy source in this country even as the Trump administration was opposed to such settlements and sought to cut funds for the Bureau of Indian Affairs.

Yet the Obama administration acknowledged responsibility for the mishandling of Native American resources when it agreed to pay $490 million in October 2016 for mismanagement of Native tribal lands dating back to the nineteenth century. The Department of the Interior currently manages 55 million acres for 250 tribes incorporating over 100,000 leases for a variety of purposes ranging from commercial housing and agriculture to mineral and gas extraction. At the time of this settlement, suits brought against the federal government by Native Americans totaled over $3 billion.[18] Whether they will be successful in their litigations is becoming increasingly problematic because the Trump Administration was opposed to such settlements and cut funds for this program and the Bureau of Indian Affairs.

Paralleling the social and economic impoverishment of Native Americans was an unremitting barrage of propaganda that depicted them negatively. As the late Native American historian Vine Deloria, Jr., noted, Indians were seen as un–American by White people and relegated to "a picturesque species of wildlife."[19] But it was the Indians' rejection of White culture that sealed their fate. As Deloria observed, Black people were denied rights by White people to deprive them, but White rules and laws were pressed on Indians to force them to become like White people. "The white man preached that it was good to help the poor, yet he did nothing to assist the poor in his society. Instead, he put pressure on the Indian people to hoard their worldly goods, and when they failed to accumulate capital but freely gave to the poor, the white man reacted violently."[20]

Deloria was especially bitter about the negative role that Christian churches played in the relationship between Indians and the federal government: "Much of the problem was caused by the agitation of the churches for franchises to hunt souls on the reservations. This demand created the feeling that Indians were pawns in the great experiment of civilizing a savage people."[21]

Suzan Shown Harjo, the Indian activist, contends that Native Americans defy generalizations about them. Their many languages and customs make unique contributions to our country. Contrary to the common belief that Indians have been assimilated into the larger White society, she believes it's the other way around: "We're distinct peoples and we want to maintain that. We don't want to be separate. We have sovereignty. Indians are in the American psyche. Look at all the Indian names of things—locations, concepts. You could say Americans have assimilated to Indians."[22] This observation might seem overly optimistic, but she harbors no illusions about the deleterious effects the dominant White culture inflicted on Indigenous people in this country: "We're the poorest people in the richest country in the world, and that has never changed since records were kept on this." Yet she is sanguine about the future of Native Americans as they endeavor to rejuvenate nearly lost languages, develop an appreciation of their culture, and improve their educational, housing, and health status.

Cultural Efflorescence

Despite the sordid history of federal duplicity, indifference, and genocide directed at Native Americans, they have survived. Although their nations were decimated, and some groups became extinct, there is growing interest by non–Native and Indigenous people in the cultural traditions that make them unique and distinct from White American society. The profusion of Native American cultural activities reflects the desire of Indians to reclaim their traditions—in opposition to the overwhelming pressure of the dominant White society to assimilate. The list of insults perpetrated against Native Americans by White society, the clash between the Aboriginal and dominant civilizations, includes the abrogation of hundreds of treaties by the federal government with Indians nations, the splitting up of Native American tribal lands and the forced relocation of Indians to disparate parts of the country (Indian Territory), the termination of tribal status and property rights, the reallocation of tribal land under the Dawes Act, the theft and compulsory reeducation of Native American children in Indian boarding schools, and the forced resettlement of Native Americans from reservations to urban areas. Yet Native Americans, with the help of changing public opinion about them, some favorable court decisions, and emerging political participation in state and federal venues, are undergoing a cultural regeneration.

This phenomenon is exemplified by the profusion of museums dedicated to educating the public about their history and cultural traditions. Some of the most expansive ventures were the recipients of Native American casino revenue like the Mashantucket Pequot Museum and Research Center adjacent to the sprawling Foxwoods Casino at that location in Ledyard, Connecticut. In one of the last hard-copy issues of *Indian Country Today*, a series of articles highlighted the emergence of these museums around the country.[23] Four of the gems that I've visited and highly recommend are the National Museum of the American Indian in Washington, D.C. (4th Street SW and Independence Avenue SW); the Museum of the American Revolution, financed in part with a $10 million gift from the Oneida Nation (101 S. 3rd St., Philadelphia); the Crazy Horse Museum (12151 Avenue of the Chiefs, Crazy Horse, South Dakota); and the National Museum of the American Indian (1 Bowling Green, New York City), whose artifacts were donated by the late wealthy collector, George Gustav Heye.

Another sign of the revitalization and resurrection of Native American culture is the growth in courses designed to teach Native American languages. While many people may be familiar with the vital role Native Americans played in World Wars I and II as code talkers, using indecipherable Indian languages to communicate secret logistical information, relatively few Native American children (and adults) are able to speak their native tongue. This is an understandable situation given past pressure exerted on Indians to abandon their language and culture, and their forced regimentation in Indian boarding schools that promoted their assimilation into the dominant White society.

The resurgence of interest in Native American languages—they are many and varied (over three hundred) with few cognates, making it difficult to transfer from on to the other—is another attempt to spur interest in the culture and traditions of ancient Native American civilizations. When I visited the Oglala Lakota College in Kyle, South Dakota, several courses featuring instruction in the native Lakota language were highlighted on the bulletin board. In conversations with Lakota administrators at that school and Sitting Bull College in Fort Yates, North Dakota, I learned that Native American staff were enthusiastic about trying to master their native language and some were enrolled in these courses.

When Native American elders realized that few of the younger members of their communities could speak their language, they began to mobilize efforts to preserve their cultural heritage. While the Navajo Nation has the most speakers of their native language (about half their people), other groups of Native Americans are down to a few elders, with the possibility of cultural extinction looming. Now new and innovative strategies are being utilized to appeal to younger students to preserve the cultural identity of tribal members and increase the self-esteem of young Native Americans.[24]

In 2006 Congress passed H.R. 4766, the Ester Martinez Native American Languages Preservation Act, which provides three-year grants to educational groups to teach native languages to children, staff, and parents. Grants require that students receive a minimum of five hundred hours in native language instruction, and teachers are schooled in their native language so they can share it with their students. Unfortunately, the dearth of instructors in native languages, their complexity, and the volume of other mandated educational requirements impedes progress in these programs.

Renaissance in Native American Art

The public's interest in Native American arts and crafts, especially painting, sculpture, and jewelry, has been increasing dramatically in recent years. Native American artists display their works in a wide array of public and private venues, from the National Museum of the American Indian in Washington, D.C., to the Santa Fe Indian Market in New Mexico, the largest outdoor juried Native art market in the world. There, handmade crafts from across the nation, such as jewelry, weavings, drums, bead work, pottery, leather goods, painted hides, metal and wood sculptures, paintings, prints, and photographs, are on display and for sale. They represent the works of over a thousand Native American artists in over six hundred booths. Held every third weekend in August, there is also a Native American Cinema Showcase and a clothing contest as well as a modern fashion show.[25]

Many groups are promoting Native American art and culture. In addition to the annual Native American art festival in Santa Fe, the Redhawk Native American Arts Council in Brooklyn, New York, annually hosts four art festivals, the largest in the Northeast, and diverse museums and arts councils such as those found at Yale University in New Haven, Connecticut, and Portland, Oregon, are the home of Native American art and cultural artifacts that educate the public.[26]

The popularity of Native American art led to an increase in fakes and forgeries, with Indians as well as White patrons being ripped off. Consequently, in 1935, Congress passed the Indian Arts and Crafts Act, which was overhauled in 1990. But it wasn't until 2018 that Nael Ali, an offender, was sentenced to a six-month term in prison and fined $9,048.78, although the law provides for fines up to $250,000 and five years in prison. This light sentence was given despite the fact that federal agents uncovered a vast conspiracy to defraud the public and deprive Native American artisans of needed income. The fake jewelry and Indian artifacts, estimated to be sold for tens of millions of dollars in the United States, were being manufactured in the Philippines and distributed throughout this country by two Palestinian families.[27] The Native American art and jewelry industry is estimated to gross a billion dollars a year in the United States.[28]

Native American Music

A number of Native Americans have been making major contributions to the world of music. For half a century, Buffy Sainte-Marie (Cree) has been combining music with social action to improve understanding and tolerance about Native Americans. Through singing, songwriting, and the visual arts, she has spread knowledge and goodwill across North America. In 1997 she founded the Cradleboard Teaching Project, an educational curriculum to further these goals.

One of the earliest and best-known bands composed of Native Americans was Redbone, a group founded in California by Patrick and Candido (Lolly) Vasquez-Vegas. Although the brothers performed for more than a decade prior to 1970, when the band was formally organized, the group became widely known after the release of the single "Come and Get Your Love," which brought them international fame. A mix of rock and Cajun sounds, the group got its name, Redbone, from the Cajun term, which means mixed blood, like the members who were part Latino, Cherokee, Yaqui, Apache, and Shoshone. It was the first Native American band to go mainstream in the United States.

A popular contemporary group of Native American musicians is the Dream Warriors who play a variety of hip-hop mixed with Indigenous sounds. Formed in 2015, they embarked on a nationwide Heal It tour with stops at many colleges and universities. Through talks, performances, and workshops, they focus on creating sustainable family and community relationships and advocate for mature male and female roles. Another rising contemporary pop Native American musician is Taboo (Shoshone and Hopi) from the Grammy–winning group, the Black Eyed Peas.[29]

Professor Philip Deloria provides a fascinating analysis of Native American music, demonstrating its unique rhythms and percussive nuances, citing leading scholars and performers who are trying to educate the public about the authentic way Native Americans use music to communicate thoughts and feelings about the world.[30] Contemporary Native American musicians cover the gamut of music from heavy metal to classical. They defy generalization and challenge narrow perceptions of Indigenous people as primitive and uncivilized.[31]

A growing trend among Native American musicians and composers is to combine classical/European music with Indigenous sounds, producing a unique blend of both traditions (e.g., Cellist Dawn Avery [Mohawk] and composer Steven Alvarez [Mescalero Apache]). For Native Americans trained in the classical tradition, it sometimes challenges their allegiances, causing them to question their commitment to the dominant exploitative culture that nearly extinguished their own. Yet there is evidence that the new blend is rewarding for Native American performers as well as the listening public.[32]

Literature

Perhaps the dean of Native American writers is N. Scott Momaday (Kiowa), a novelist, essayist, and poet who was born in Lawton, Oklahoma, in 1934. His first novel, *House Made of Dawn*, won the Pulitzer Prize for fiction in 1969. The author of numerous books of poetry and novels, he earned a doctor of philosophy degree in English from Stanford University and holds a dozen honorary degrees from universities such as Yale, the University of Massachusetts, and the University of Wisconsin. He is the recipient of numerous literary awards including the Academy of American Poets Prize, the Golden Plate Award from the American Academy of Achievement, an award from the National Institutes of Arts and Letters, and Italy's highest literary award, the Premio Letterario Internationale "Mondello." He is credited with leading the renaissance of Native Americans in contemporary American literature that began in the late 1960s.

Noted Native American literary figure N. Scott Momaday (Robin Marchant, Getty Images Entertainment).

Certainly, Gerald Vizenor (Ojibwe/Chippewa), also born in 1934, deserves mention for his enormous literary and philosophical contributions to our understanding and appreciation of Native Americans. As the former director of Native American studies at the University of California at Berkeley and the holder of numerous other teaching and administrative positions at leading universities around the nation, Vizenor, whose Native American father was murdered when he was only two years old, has written many award-winning novels and nonfiction books that explore the nature of relationships between Native Americans and the dominant White society. Though his mother was Swedish, and many of his ancestors were of mixed blood, he is gratified that the Ojibwe people accepted them. He is more concerned with adherence to Native American values than blood quantum, believing that the imagination of tribal people is more important than the documentation of anthropologists and historians.[33]

Vizenor coined the term *cultural schizophrenia* to refer to the strain experienced by Native Americans as they grapple with pressures to assimilate to the dominant White culture.[34] From 1964 to 1968 he worked in Minneapolis for an employment organization and gained firsthand knowledge about Native American unemployment, in addition to racial and alcoholism issues. As a reporter and editor for the *Minneapolis Tribune*, he managed to get the death sentence commuted for a Native American, exploring disparities in justice for colonized people.

Initially focusing his talent on the Japanese form of poetry known as haiku in works such as *Raising the Moon Vines* (1964), *Seventeen Chips* (1965), *Slight Abrasions* (1966), and *Empty Swings* (1967), Vizenor subsequently wrote in a variety of genres, including novels and short stories as well as nonfiction works. He is an advocate of the oral Native American tradition as a method for keeping the memory of Indians alive—their survival and sustainability in times that challenge the present and future of Indians.

One of his main themes is the interrelationship between tribal and nontribal worlds, and he is a master at developing a bond between the real and imaginary worlds of tribal and secular society. As an enrolled member of the Ojibwe Nation, much of his work explores the interaction between Native Americans and White society using a variety of mythological techniques that focus on ethical and moral themes frequently pitting Native heroes and tricksters against villains, all the while under the overarching influence of nature and a benevolent environment.

Vizenor was an opponent of the American Indian Movement (AIM) and viewed one of its founders, Dennis Banks (also Ojibwe), as a fraudulent trickster, believing that Native Americans would be better served if they focused their energies more on the conflict between Native and dominant culture, and less on the cult of personality surrounding Banks and his colleagues.

Vizenor has won numerous awards for his writing including a Lifetime Achievement Award (2011) of MELUS (Society for the Study of Multi-Ethnic Literature of the United States); an American Book Award in 1998 bestowed by the Before Columbus Foundation for *Griever: An American Monkey in China*; an American Book Award in 2011 for *Shrouds of White Earth*; a 2005 Distinguished Achievement Award from the Western Literature Association; a PEN Excellence Award in 1996; and the Film-in-the-Cities Award of the Sundance Film Festival in 1983 for his screenplay for the film *Harold of Orange*.[35]

Native American writer and philosopher Gerald Vizenor (Chris Felver, Premium Archive, Getty Images).

The Native American literary renaissance had a significant social and philosophical influence on subsequent generations of Indigenous people in the Americas and around the world. A burgeoning array of literary works by Native Americans, from short stories and poetry to fiction and nonfictional contributions, demonstrate the folly of stereotypical generalizations depicting them as ignorant vagabonds. The contributions they are making to our culture range from the award-winning poetry of Duane Niaum (Klallum) and Louise Erdrich (Chippewa) to the American and National Book Awards and Pulitzer Awards and nominations for novels by Janet Campbell Hale (Coeur d'Alene/Cree), Leslie Marmon Silko (Leguna Pueblo), and Sherman Alexie (Spokane/Coeur d'Alene).

The renaissance in Native American writing began in the late 1960s. Prior to that, according to the late Choctaw and Cherokee novelist Louis Owens, only nine novels by Native American authors had been published by 1968.[36] Since then, there has been a profusion of works by Indians who have distinguished themselves in the literary world and the academy. American culture would be much poorer without the contributions of Native Americans who have described their personal experiences living on reservations and told stories that ignite the imagination of readers around the world.[37]

Native American Media

Accompanying the resurgence of Native American art, music, and literature has been an explosion of local and national media outlets emphasizing Native American issues. Technological innovations have facilitated print and online outlets of information related to Indians. As anthropologist David Trueur has noted, online communications and social media are bringing heretofore disparate individuals and groups closer together to pursue common agendas. And a multitude of tribal newsletters across North America recap court decisions affecting tribes and Indian Country as well as offer advice and comments about issues relevant to Indigenous people. Until recently, *Indian Country Today*, one of the leading publications of this genre, appeared in online and hard copy magazine format, but financial problems led the owner, Ray Halbritter, the CEO of the Oneida Nation and a graduate of Harvard Law School, to collaborate with the National Congress of American Indians, which now offers weekly and special features online. Tim Giago (Lakota), editor of the Rapid City *Native Sun*, was the founder and editor of *Indian Country Today*, running it for nearly two decades before it was sold to Halbritter. In an interview he told me he was heartbroken by the demise of the original format, but accepted the reality of the situation.[38]

A growing movement in telecommunications affecting Native Americans is the *Native American Calling* radio program that was, as of 2019, broadcast on about seventy community and tribal stations in the United States and Canada. Produced by the Koahnic Broadcasting Corporation in Anchorage, Alaska, live shows feature issues concerning Native Americans and link listeners with radio stations and the internet in an attempt to improve the quality of life for Native Americans.

And there are other vibrant and refreshing sources of information about Indigenous people in North America. *Turtle Talk*[39] is a source of current information about developments concerning Indigenous people in North America, and so is Native American Indians Online.[40] A decade ago, librarians Erica Swenson Danowitz and Carol Videon compiled an extensive bibliography of references about Native Americans in various media, "Native American Resources: Sites for Online Research."[41] Red-face.us can be found online and contains a history of the stereotypes about Native Americans. Of course, the National Congress of American Indians website has valuable information about issues concerning Native Americans.

A refreshing and perspicacious website about Native American affairs is Lastrealindians.com. Founded in 2012 by Matt Remle (Lakota) and Chase Iron Eyes (Oglala), the site is at times informative and iconoclastic.

For an up-to-date account of Native American issues see *Indian Country Today* online.[42] *Indian Country Today* also has a daily twenty-six-minute radio program carried by seventy stations, including some PBS affiliates, which reaches an estimated seventy-five million households. The NDN Collective, a nonprofit founded by Nick Tilsen (Oglala Lakota), seeks to develop interconnections among Indigenous groups of people and publishes information and news stories about Native American and Indigenous people. Tilson brings youthful exuberance to Native American issues and is a force for climate resiliency, sustainable housing, and equitable communities. His movement for decolonization and self-determination for Native Americans has brought him into conflict with the law as a strident advocate for Indian rights.

Another youthful advocate for Native Americans is Crystal Echo Hawk (Pawnee), founder of IllumiNative and CEO of Echo Hawk Consulting, which had a major role in producing the study *Reclaiming Native Truth*, the largest public opinion research project about Native Americans ever done. IllumiNative is a nonprofit committed to increasing the visibility of Indigenous people in the Americas by challenging stereotypes about them and providing tools far Native advocates to develop accurate representations of them.

Writing in the *New York Times*, Phoebe Lett summarized noteworthy podcasts that highlight Native American culture and issues.[43]

The Struggle to Maintain Identity

Aside from the contemporary profusion of Native American art, music, and literature, there has been a dramatic resurgence in Native American cultural activities designed to rekindle awareness by Indians, especially youth, and the general public in Native American traditions. This phenomenon is most apparent in the proliferation of Indian powwows and jamborees that are held around the United States each year, estimated at over one thousand in 2019.[44] Historian Philip Deloria contends that the origins of the powwow phenomenon are obscure, and he cites several doctoral dissertations to provide information about this.[45] The tradition of intertribal competition in dance and other activities may have paved the way for contemporary powwows. Some of the impetus for this movement may also have come from Captain (later General) Richard Henry Pratt, the founder of the Carlisle Indian School in Pennsylvania, who was obsessed with the goal of assimilating Native Americans into the dominant White society. By developing a pan–Indian stereotype that drew heavily on images of Plains Indians, Pratt hoped to use Indians as mascots and promoted the concept of powwows to eradicate diversity among Native Americans and eliminate their individuality. Depriving Indians of their religion, language, and customs would, he believed, replace their "backward," "uncivilized" nature with White (Anglo) tendencies that would enable them to adapt to modern society.[46] Ironically, the resurgence in powwows may be a reaction to Pratt's attempt to extinguish Native American customs.

There is a paradox in this movement to reclaim Native American identity. On the one hand, the renewed interest in learning about Indian languages and traditions is bolstered by the proliferation of powwows that educate and inform Native Americans as well as the general public. However, the presentation of Indians in traditional garb, dancing to the beat of drums, runs the risk of rekindling and reinforcing negative stereotypes about Indians as uncivilized savages.

The Native American struggle to maintain the viability of their traditions in the face of the all-encompassing dominant White culture, and the fight to keep ancient cultures vibrant, is a common theme among the Native Americans I interviewed. Every one of them—from Dr. Thomas Short Bull (Teton Sioux), the president of Oglala Lakota College in Kyle, South Dakota, to activist Suzan Shown Harjo (Cheyenne/Hodulgee Muscogee); Paul Chaat Smith (Comanche), a curator at the National Museum of the American Indian; attorney Mario Gonzalez (Lakota Sioux); Marilyn Pourier (Lakota Sioux), director of development at Oglala Lakota College; Jennifer Martel (Lakota Sioux), head of the Visitor's Bureau at Sitting Bull College in Fort Yates, North Dakota; Tim Giago (Lakota Sioux), editor of the *Native Sun* newspaper in Rapid City, South Dakota; Jacqueline Pata (Tlingit), former executive director of the National Congress of American Indians; Erin Weldon (Navajo/Diné), director of communications for the National Congress of American Indians; Lynn White (Lakota Sioux), holder of five college degrees and an adviser at Oglala Lakota College; and others—were uniform in their support of powwows as a method of teaching and reinforcing Native American values and traditions for Indians and the general public. They were not apprehensive about the possibility of these activities perpetuating stereotypes about Native Americans and welcomed the contribution powwows make to enriching and perpetuating Native American culture.

In recent years there has been an explosion in the field of multicultural education. This phenomenon now includes the promulgation of accurate (not revisionist) information about Native Americans. One of the first and most comprehensive online multicultural education sites continues to be provided through the Southern Poverty Law Center's website, Tolerance.org. The site provides lesson plans and advice for teachers, promoting understanding and inclusion, primarily in elementary and middle schools. Teachers are encouraged to contribute to an ongoing blog, and educators contribute articles in the center's flagship magazine *Teaching Tolerance*, published three times a year. The center also provides tool kits, posters, films, and other resources to over three hundred thousand people who participate in its crusade for social justice.

The Public Broadcasting System (PBS) has been producing a variety of shows that emphasize multicultural education, respect, and tolerance of various ethnic groups for decades. Materials are aired on television stations around the nation, and resources can be found on the PBS Kids website. The precursor of PBS multicultural education programs is Sesame Street, which resided in the PBS fold from 1969 until 2015. Formerly produced as the Children's Television Workshop, the show has thirty-five new episodes (compared to eighteen previously) in its new home on HBO. In the half century that the show has aired, there have been dozens of movies and special events designed to promote tolerance, understanding, and inclusivity among children.

In conjunction with the movement to promote multicultural education, the National Museum of the American Indian (NMAI) under the aegis of the Smithsonian Museum headquartered in Washington, D.C., with a branch in New York City, has developed and promotes a program for schools throughout the nation, NK360°. The program, managed by Edwin Schupman (Muscogee), is designed to give elementary through high school students an authentic perspective about the connections that Native Americans have with the United States. Launched in February 2018, the program provides teachers with more than thirty resources that are downloadable from the NK360° website (americanindian.si.edu/nk360). Supplementary workshops and other training opportunities for teachers are also offered by NMAI to assist them in their instruction and using the materials.

Although many states have standards that mandate educational programs about Native Americans, information about them is often sketchy and inaccurate. As the recent national survey *Reclaiming Native Truth*[47] reported, most people believe that their education about Native Americans was deficient. State standards vary widely across the nation. A 2015 study of state curricula concerning Native Americans by Sarah Shear, Ryan T. Knowles, Gregory J. Soden, and Antonio J. Castro found that they were uneven, often flawed, and overwhelmingly presented Indigenous peoples in a pre–1900 context, relegating them to the distant past.[48] Stoking Indians' fears about erasure, these curricula minimized the role of Indigenous people prior to settlement by Europeans, avoided discussions of violence perpetrated against them, and generalized about Indigenous perspectives regarding colonization. Only 13.3 percent of state standards related to Indigenous history or culture, or issues occurring after 1900. The authors concluded that "Indigenous Peoples are left in the shadows of Euro-American destiny."[49]

After conducting a review of elementary, middle, and high school textbooks, the NK360° staff at the NMAI concluded that the materials were incomplete and generally deficient, and launched their program to provide students with a broader and deeper understanding of Native Americans. This project represents a trend in American schools to provide students with accurate information that reflects the complex relationships that exist between Native Americans and White people from historical and contemporary lenses.[50]

There is also increasing interest in Native American cuisine, and foremost among the proponents of this trend are Sean Sherman, the Sioux Chef who is Oglala Lakota and the founder of the nonprofit North American Traditional Indigenous Food Systems, and Andi Murphy (Navajo). Murphy anchors the podcast "toastedsister," which began in 2017 and airs on public radio stations with the tagline "Radio about Native American Food."[51]

Despite the trend of Native Americans not living on reservations, many Indians retain warm feelings about their tribal homelands, even though they are frequently not in their nation's original territory. The growth of the powwow movement is being accompanied by an increase in tribal programs that recognize the importance of keeping the bonds vibrant between Indians and tribal reservations. Such programs draw on the diverse skills of nonreservation Indians, such as the Comanche Nation's outreach centers (e.g., in Dallas, Texas) and programs for tribal members in urban areas like the Menominee tribe in Chicago. Such programs are an effort to maintain cultural identity in the face of increasing threats of assimilation.

Even more consequential for preserving Native American culture is the renewal of interest in Indian traditions and spirituality. One of the most important figures in this movement is Oren R. Lyons, Jr. (1930). Raised in upstate New York, this renaissance man helped found the Faithkeepers movement and the Traditional Circle of Indian Elders and Youth. These organizations promote the history, customs, legends, and prophesies of his people.

A member of the Seneca and Onondaga nations, Lyons attended Syracuse University and was an all-American on its undefeated 1957 lacrosse team that featured NFL star running back Jim Brown. Lyons, an outstanding goalie, was later inducted into the Lacrosse Hall of Fame. After graduating from Syracuse University in 1958 with a bachelor's in fine arts, he became a successful commercial artist in New York City. His personal paintings are vivid and colorful. One of his most notable, the *Tree of Peace*, presents a variety of Native American clans interspersed among the leaves and branches of a large tree, the base standing on the back of a turtle, which symbolizes the United States. The protective branches of the great tree are presumed to create a place of peace where people can grow and renew themselves.

Lyons eventually abandoned New York City and commercial art for the life of an advocate for Native Americans and later broadened his activism on behalf of Indigenous people around the world. "At first, I wanted to defend the Iroquois. Then my sights broadened to embrace other Indians. Then I saw this had to include defending Indigenous peoples all over the world." He was a member of the Haudenosaunee (Iroquois Nations) delegation to the first World Conference on Racism in Geneva in 1978, and addressed the United Nations General Assembly in 1992, where he focused on the importance of preserving the environment of our planet. "The issue of energy is a global problem, and therefore it requires global solutions.... [W]e must think beyond our national borders and self-interests," he noted in remarks he made in 2001 before the U.S. Department of Energy's Tribal Summit.

He was an ardent supporter of the Red Power movement in the 1960s and '70s, even traveling to Washington, D.C., with a caravan to protest the Trail of Broken Treaties that occupied the Bureau of Indian Affairs. As a Faithkeeper, Lyons has responsibility for preserving and passing on the traditions of his people. He believes that the foundation of democracy of our nation was based on the advice and knowledge of the Six Nations Confederacy. Above all, people must respect one another and the environment. "We're [Native Americans] still here. The story is not over. If anything, I see the roots [of the *Tree of Peace*] still growing."[52]

Motion Pictures

A trend was set with the iconic Native American film *Smoke Signals*, directed by Chris Eyre (Cheyenne/Arapaho) and written by Sherman Alexie (Spokane/Coeur d'Alene) in 1998. The first major motion picture written and directed by Native Americans, with a budget of just $2 million, it won a dozen awards for best film, direction, writing, and acting, and grossed over $7.5 million worldwide. This film provided the impetus for other aspiring Native American filmmakers to forge ahead, and the trend was captured by Beverly Singer (Tewa/Diné) in *Wiping the War Paint off the Lens*.[53] But the dearth of Indigenous actors, directors, and producers has been perennially documented by industry analysts.[54] As we have seen, even more balanced contemporary films and television productions still proffer stereotypical impressions about Native Americans and use Native Americans sparsely in their casts (e.g., the HBO hit series *Westworld* featured Lakota Zahn McClarnon in period dress and face paint as Akecheta, but at least a Native American was used for the part).

Although there has been a precipitous decline in the number of Hollywood blockbusters and television shows with Native American themes since the latter part of the twentieth century and during the early decades of the twenty-first, there has been a virtual cornucopia of Native American films produced, especially documentaries and shorts, by Native American and Alaska Natives in recent years. With the help of numerous festivals like the imagineNative Film and Media Arts Festival in Toronto, Canada, which is approaching two decades of promoting Indigenous productions, the burgeoning works of Indigenous artists are being seen by eager audiences more than ever before in North America. At the 2017 festival in Toronto, more than

Native American writer, artist, and philosopher Oren Lyons (Charley Gallay, Getty Images Entertainment).

115 film and video works from 16 countries were presented during 5 days in October. The wide variation in content enabled viewers to get information on the current and future status of Indigenous people, but as Jason Ryle (Salteaux), the artistic director, noted, "These works need to be seen, and oftentimes our festivals are really the only one presenting this work."[55]

Despite the love and energy that goes into making these works of art, a relatively small segment of the general public is aware of them. For example, Alanis Obomsawim (Abenaki), regarded as one of the most influential Indigenous filmmakers of our time, has directed over fifty films with the National Film Board of Canada, but few people outside those attending the festivals have seen her work. Yet such film festivals have been increasing along with the appetite for these works among Indigenous people and the non–Indian public. Writing in a recent issue of the *National Museum of the American Indian*, Cynthia Benitez noted that the contemporary profusion of Indigenous film festivals might be traced to when the Sundance Institute added its Native American and Indigenous Program in 1994.[56]

An especially appealing genre prevalent among Native American and other Indigenous filmmakers has been storytelling. This approach helps build bridges between Indigenous people and the public by creating awareness and empathy about the lives of Native peoples. Such work enhances the public's attitudes about environmentalism and contributes to the preservation of Indigenous cultures, building support for their causes. But while the Native Cinema Showcase of the National Museum of the American Indian drew more than 2,700 people during its 17th annual event in 2017, these numbers pale in comparison to the feature film blockbusters that are seen by millions of viewers on an average weekend across the country.

The Political Struggle for Native American Rights

Paul Chaat Smith (Comanche) and Robert Allen Warrior (Osage) present a troubling narrative recounting the twists and turns of the founders of the Red Power movement that arose during the tumultuous civil rights era in the United States. From the seizure of Alcatraz by a disparate band of seventy-eight Indians on November 20, 1969, and the arrest by federal agents of the remaining fifteen holdouts on June 11, 1971, to the rise and dissolution of the American Indian Movement (AIM) in the following few years, their analysis reveals a litany of bad decisions and missed opportunities by youthful Native American leaders who put rebellion against the White dominant society before accommodation.[57]

Smith and Warrior review numerous incidents of Indian political actions, noting that many of their targets were government installations and sites of historical significance to Native Americans and dominant White people (e.g., an abortive attempt to "liberate" Ellis Island, the brief occupation of Mt. Rushmore in the sacred Black Hills of South Dakota, a Thanksgiving protest at Plymouth Rock, as well as numerous protests across the country at offices of the Bureau of Indian Affairs). The death knell for AIM came following the surrender of Native Americans at Wounded Knee on May 8, 1973, after a seventy-one-day occupation at the site of the massacre of Lakota Sioux on December 29, 1890.

Following intense negotiations with representatives of President Nixon, the Bureau of Indian Affairs, the FBI, and federal marshals, the tattered remnants of the All Indian Tribes occupying force, whose numbers fluctuated but rarely reached above the initial two hundred Oglala Lakota who seized the site on February 27, 1973, surrendered to a technologically superior force of federal, state, and local law enforcement agents. While Russell Means, one of the charismatic founders of AIM, was not present, Dennis Banks was, and AIM's troubles with the establishment were just beginning. After the end of the siege, a series of trials were conducted with the occupiers of Wounded Knee and the Lakota, who had declared the reservation a sovereign Independent Oglala Nation. Even before that, as Smith and Warrior noted, "During the seven weeks of the Wounded Knee occupation, the federal government arrested 562 people on charges directly connected to the siege. Dozens more were arrested in riot conspiracy charges across the country."[58]

The legal strategy of the federal government was to bring to trial every possible case it could, although it lost over 90 percent of them, but the expense of the litigation financially destroyed AIM. As Smith and Warrior noted: "It [the federal government] recognized that immobilizing AIM was more important than putting any individual behind bars. Even a well-organized and financially stable group would have withered under the pressure and expense of defending so many of its members; for AIM the task was overwhelming."[59] The movement was bankrupted, and with it went the ardor and confrontational strategy of AIM that gave way to today's legal pursuit of Native American rights.

The attractive and flamboyant spokesmen of AIM, Russell Means and Dennis Banks, survived numerous legal battles with various government entities over the years, although Banks served fourteen months in prison for riot and assault after being a fugitive for nine years. Both were popular lecturers. Means even starred as Chingachgook in the 1992 remake of the *Last of the Mohicans*, and Banks also had a role in the movie as well as many others. Means died in 2012 and Banks passed away in 2017, but their flair for rhetoric and confrontation made an indelible mark on relationships between the White and Native American societies in this country. As Smith and Warrior concluded: "Wounded Knee proved to be the final performance of AIM's daring brand of political theater. As quickly as Indian radicalism had exploded on the national stage, it faded, disintegrating under the weight of its own internal contradictions and divisions, and relentless legal assault by federal and state governments. In the months and years following the dissolution of the Independent Oglala Nation, Indians once again became a flickering, intermittent presence in the public affairs of the United States."[60]

Another account of Native American political contretemps was documented by Mario Gonzalez (Oglala Lakota) and Elizabeth Cook-Lynn (Santee/Yankton). They traced the effort by disparate groups of Native Americans, descendants of survivors of the Wounded Knee massacre in 1890 and other concerned and committed people, to establish a monument and memorial museum commemorating the event. After years of begging and cajoling elected officials to introduce legislation authorizing the appropriation of federal funds for the project, it seemed that the path had been cleared and the project would pass through Congress. Sadly, despite the valiant efforts by volunteers like attorney Gonzalez and Sam Eaglestaff (Lakota Sioux), the project drifted into oblivion as competing groups of Native Americans politicized it and withdrew their support, rejecting opposing proposals by the National Park Service and survivors' groups.

The fractious infighting among the Native Americans chronicled by Gonzalez and Cook-Lynn is disconcerting, but it is emblematic of contentious behavior that sometimes characterizes and sidetracks Native American efforts to achieve the goals of sovereignty and equity. Gonzalez and Cook-Lynn attribute some of this dissension to underdeveloped governing systems in Native American communities, vestiges of colonialism and federal paternalism.[61]

Reading about the many ill-fated attempts to create a memorial at the site of the 1890 massacre of Sioux (mostly women, children and elderly),[62] it became clear that there was deep-seated distrust of government (local, state, and national) by Native Americans, no doubt stemming from centuries of deceit, perfidy, abuse, and neglect. At times the democratic process embraced by Native Americans reinforced the cliché "analysis/paralysis"—some people focused more on the process and methodology than the goal.

There continues to be widespread friction among Native American tribes and organizations as they vie for a piece of the American pie. But nearly half a century after the second Wounded Knee debacle, there are indications that Native Americans have learned to become a more effective political force in the United States. Many of the tribes actively lobby for Native American and Alaska Native rights, at times creating confederations with like-minded tribes to strengthen their message.

More Indians ran for office in the 2018 elections than ever before—over sixty Native Americans currently hold local and state offices around the country. A record number of Indigenous people ran for office in 2020. Six were elected to the U.S. House of Representatives, including the reelection of Congresswomen Deb Haaland and Sharice Davids, as well as Congressmen Markwayne Mullen (Cherokee from Oklahoma) and Tom Cole (Cherokee from Oklahoma) and freshmen Congresspeople Yvette Harrell (Cherokee from New Mexico) and Kaiali'i Kahale (Native Hawaiian). Sharice Davids (D–Kansas) and Debra Haaland (D–New Mexico) served in Congress as the first female Native Americans elected to the U.S. House of Representatives; as of 2021, Haaland is serving as the first Native American cabinet secretary and the first Native Secretary of the Interior. Peggy Flanagan (Democratic Farm Labor Party and Ojibwe) is serving as the lieutenant governor of Minnesota, while Kevin Stitt (Republican and Cherokee) was elected governor of Oklahoma. The current principal chief of the Cherokee Nation, Chuck Hoskin, Jr., appointed Kimberly Teehee as the tribe's first delegate to the U.S. House of Representatives, a position guaranteed the Cherokee Nation in two treaties with the United States.[63]

Along with the growing awareness and appreciation of Native American culture in the United States, there has been growth of organizations, public, private, and governmental, that advocate for improvements in Native American life. Paramount among these are the National Congress of American Indians (est. 1944), headquartered in Washington, D.C., and the Americans for Indian Opportunities organization founded by La Donna Harris (Comanche) in 1970 to advance the cultural, political, and economic opportunities of Indigenous people in the United States and the world. Together with the Association on American Indian Affairs (est. 1922), these organizations are committed to protecting the sovereignty and culture of Native Americans.

Some of the most important work to improve the lives of Native Americans and

Alaska Natives is being done in the realm of the law. The Native American Rights Fund (est. 1971) provides legal assistance to Indian tribes (over 250 thus far), organizations, and individuals who can't afford representation. The Indian Law Resource Center, a nonprofit law and advocacy organization founded in 1983 by attorney Robert Coulter (Potawatomi), works on human rights and sovereignty issues and policies affecting Native Americans and Alaska Natives. The Native American Law Society is headquartered at Loyola University in New Orleans. It was founded in 1993 to promote the study of American Indian law. And the Native American Bar Association, founded in 1973, is headquartered in Tempe, Arizona.

Recognizing the importance of receiving a quality education, a number of organizations have been formed to promote that goal for Indians. The National Indian Education Association was founded in 1970 in Minneapolis, Minnesota, to convene educators to explore ways of improving the educational system for Native American, Alaska Native, and Indigenous Hawaiian children, and to promote Indigenous culture, languages, and policies at the local, state, and national level that benefit Indigenous education.

The American Indian Higher Education Consortium (est. 1972) works to strengthen tribally and federally funded chartered educational institutions so they can make a lasting difference in the lives of American Indians and Alaska Natives. The American Indian College Fund has given more than $100 million to assist Native American students to obtain a college education since its founding in 1989.

Native Americans recognize the importance of having a vibrant economy for Indians on and off reservations. The Native American Finance Officers Association, headquartered in Washington, D.C., was founded in 1988 to develop the financial capacity of tribal nations through training and policies that build economic skills. The American Indian Policy Institute at Arizona State University in Tempe is a think tank that focuses on public policy analysis and research to assist tribes. It is known for its Leadership Program and entrepreneurial classes.

The health of Native Americans has been the focus of many local, state, and federal programs, paramount among them is the Association of American Indian Physicians (est. 1971) to improve the health of Native Americans and Alaska Natives through education, while honoring traditional healing disciplines and principles to restore the balance of mind, body, and spirit. It is headquartered in Oklahoma City. The National Alaska Native American Indian Nurses Association is part of a coalition of minority nurses' associations (NCEMNA or the National Coalition of Ethnic Minority Nurse Associations) and was formed in 1998 to improve the health and well-being of minorities using traditional and innovative approaches for Indigenous people.

The National Council of Urban Indian Health is a 501(c)(3) organization that coordinates the work of forty-one urban centers around the nation that provide programs to improve the health and well-being of Native Americans and Alaska Natives living in urban areas. Through culturally competent programs, this organization facilitates grants, conducts conferences, and holds webinars to improve the health care delivery system to Indigenous people in the United States. It is headquartered in Washington, D.C., and has created a Youth Council responsible for inspiring Native youth to live healthy lives by investing in positive mental, physical, emotional, and spiritual health activities that promote resiliency and wellness among AI/AN youth.

The Alaska Native Tribal Health Consortium is a nonprofit organization based in Anchorage, Alaska, that provides direct health services to more than 160,000 Indigenous people. Established in 1997, the consortium of tribal organizations is the largest of its kind in the United States, employing 2,800 people. It delivers wellness programs, disease research and prevention projects, rural provider training, and rural water and sanitation system construction.

The federal government provides numerous resources for Indigenous peoples' health from physicians and nurses, to grants for research, service delivery, and facilities. The Administration for Native Americans was established in 1974 as part of the Native American Programs Act and is part of the Department of Health and Human Services. It promotes self-sufficiency for all Indigenous people in the United States, including American Samoa, Guam, and the Commonwealth of the Northern Mariana Islands by providing grants and training for projects as well as technical assistance.

The National Indian Child Welfare Association (NICWA), a private nonprofit established in 1987 to prevent child abuse with state, federal, and tribal assistance, is the most comprehensive source of information about American Indian and Alaska Native child welfare in the United States. NICWA works to eliminate child abuse and neglect by strengthening families, tribes, and laws that protect Indigenous children by building capacity in tribes and families to prevent child abuse. The organization faced an existential challenge because of a recent (October 2018) U.S. district court decision in Texas (*Brackeen v. Zinke*) that invalidated the 1978 Indian Child Welfare Act, but that decision was later vacated by the Fifth Circuit Court of Appeals (*Brackeen v. Bernhardt*, August 9, 2019).

A promising development is the creation of the Center for Native American Youth, founded by former U.S. Senator Byron Dorgan (D–North Dakota), which is affiliated with the think tank Aspen Institute and is headquartered in Washington, D.C., with a mission to improve the health, safety, and well-being of Native American youth twenty-four years old and younger. Hopefully, this organization, along with the movement to create a new narrative about Native Americans and Alaska Natives in the *Reclaiming Native Truth* movement, will produce further accomplishments among Indigenous people in this country and inform the non–Native public of the will and desire of Native Americans to participate as full partners in our society while preserving their culture and sovereignty.

The Doctrine of American Exceptionalism

The esteemed Seneca Chief Cornplanter recognized the White Europeans' insatiable desire for Native American land in 1790 when he noted in a letter to President Washington, "The land we live on our fathers received from God, and they transmitted it to us for our children, and we cannot part with it." Despite his misgivings about the new nation's policy of driving Indians further west to displace them for White settlers, the next century heightened White people's westward expansion, pushing Indians further from their homelands. The common belief among White people was that European/White civilization was superior to that of Indigenous people.

As Robert A. Williams, Jr. (Lumbee), pointed out in his incisive treatise on the evolution of Western conceptions of "savage" people, Indian civilization in North

America was doomed from its first contact with Europeans who embarked on a policy of displacement and compulsory assimilation that left Indians either dead or superfluous appendages to White civilization. "In the language of savagery embedded by the Founders into the United States' first Indian policy, this great American creation myth tells the story of Indian tribalism's ultimate doomed fate when confronted by an expansion-minded form of civilization."[64] The late Paul Bernal, a noted Pueblo Indian elder, once said: "The white man will not let the Indian live as he wishes. He should have died, the white man thinks. Then there would be no Indian problem."[65]

Contempt for Native American ventures to capitalize on White vices such as gambling and tobacco can be viewed as illustrations of White envy, and the incentive for eliminating and dispossessing Native Americans of their resources as invaders' acquisitive desires to control them and their property. Under the imperialist credo of "Manifest Destiny," a wave of White settlers and land speculators surged across Native American lands pushing Indians further and further into narrow isthmuses surrounded by hostile, acquisitive strangers. As the late Indian activist and one of the founders of the National Indian Youth Council, Clyde Warrior (Ponca), said, "All this country has meant to us is exploitation and watching greedy people come in and take advantage of inarticulate and inexperienced Indians. I despise what the white man has done to us."[66]

The depiction of White people as exceptional superior beings relegated the Indigenous people here and elsewhere into a subservient class of renegades without Christianity and its associated value system. The settlers' spirit of triumphalism along with the doctrine of American exceptionalism not only fueled the engine that devoured Indian lands, it consumed the Indigenous occupants as well.[67] This sentiment was succinctly expressed by the iconic Hollywood cowboy and Indian fighter, John Wayne, in a 1971 *Playboy* interview: "I don't feel we did wrong in taking this great country away from them.... Our so-called stealing of this country from them was just a matter of survival. There were great numbers of people who needed new land, and the Indians were selfishly trying to keep it for themselves."[68]

In reality, there were 370 federal treaties with Indians between 1778 and 1868 designed to take their land.[69] While Native Americans possessed nearly two billion acres before the European conquest, that amount was reduced to less than sixty million acres by 1968 and currently stands at around one hundred million. It would have been even less if not for an aggressive buy-back plan launched under the Obama administration, but threatened by cutbacks under President Trump. Much of Native American land is poor quality—unsuitable for farming, for the most part devoid of natural resources. As writer Steiner noted: "The land of the Indians has been dammed up, bled dry, eroded and flooded and stripped, leased out, wasted, and legally stolen. On the reservations are pockets of poverty and erosion of hopes, the reminders of defeat and degradation, where the poorest of the poor subsist on one-third to one-half the poverty level income, in substandard huts and shacks, beset by the highest disease and youngest death-age rates in the whole country."[70] This situation remains over half a century later.

Historian Slotkin demonstrated the important role that historian Frederick Jackson Turner and the nation's twenty-sixth president, Theodore Roosevelt, had in the formulation of the concept of the American Frontier and the doctrine of American exceptionalism. Basing their views of Indigenous people on derogatory racial stereotypes, their writing influenced the tenor of early twentieth-century thinking about Native Americans and their inability or unwillingness to assimilate into American society.

> The language and conceptual categories of the Frontier Myth were particularly important during the formative period of counterinsurgency doctrine. That myth taught us that historical progress is achieved only by the advance of White European racial cultures into and against the terrain of primitive, non–White "natives." The native races are inherently lacking in the capacity to generate "progress." The best of them are seen as passively willing to subordinate themselves to the progressive Whites. The worst are seen as savagely opposed to progress, preferring extermination to either civilization or subjugation.[71]

Roosevelt, like Turner, was a social Darwinist and frequently depicted Indians in derogatory terms. He was enamored by early American Anglo frontiersmen and even founded the Boone and Crockett Club to hunt, conserve, and preserve frontier American values. Together, they attributed the domination of Native Americans to what they believed to be the genetic superiority of White people. From their perspective, the wars against Native Americans were for ultimate supremacy and control of North American lands. It was a zero-sum game that justified barbaric savage acts like massacres and the killing of women and children. This perspective had its counterpart in the Nazi attempt to exterminate Jews, Gypsies, and homosexuals in the 1930s and '40s, the "ethnic cleansing" in the Balkan Wars of the early 1990s, and the massacre of Tutsis by the Hutus in Rwanda in 1994.

Slotkin apprehended this racist theme about Indian inferiority in American foreign wars, especially Vietnam, where special fighting units of scouts, Green Berets, commandos, and rangers used "savage" types of warfare as political and strategic methods for involving Indigenous people in a popular uprising against aggressive forces (e.g., communists), as well as utilizing methods that were designed to terrorize and demoralize the enemy—tactics that were originally used by Indian fighters and Indian haters, and later adopted during the Civil War by Lincoln and Grant. Although this strategy failed in Vietnam, it evoked memories of the Indian hater mythology that he described as "the evil twin of Cooper's Hawkeye."[72]

The defeat of the Native Americans and seizure of their lands changed the focus of writing and filmmaking in the United States. While the Frontier Myth extolling the virtue of American exceptionalism and Manifest Destiny reigned from colonial times through the twentieth century, it evolved from the early heroes Daniel Boone and Davy Crockett to crusading social reformers, as the struggle for social sanity and tranquility moved from the domination and exploitation of Native Americans to democratic representation and fair labor standards. As Slotkin noted, the frontiersman/hero was supplanted in this new industrial public relations and mass communications world by the hip private eye who comingled with the working class in a battle against the robber barons and captains of industry whose disregard for the safety and well-being of workers lagged behind their love of money and greed.[73]

The message of economic inequality was bolstered by social Darwinist ideology espoused by early twentieth-century academics such as sociologist E. A. Ross and historians John Commons, Frederick Jackson Turner, and Teddy Roosevelt. This ideology pitted the purportedly racially inferior Indians, Black people, immigrants, and working-class ethnic and religious minorities against the supposedly divinely inspired superior Anglo-Saxon class of natural leaders and protectors of the politically and economically imbalanced social order.

For Indians, their sense of time and present orientation was in conflict with the White European preoccupation with the future and ascetic Christian beliefs in deferred gratification and industriousness.[74] It has been said that "[t]he Indian lives within himself, but not for himself,"[75] in what may be considered a form of Indian humanism. The Council for Christian Social Action of the United Church of Christ once sought to distinguish between the Native American and Western philosophies of life: The "basic difference in cultures ... is in our value concepts. We [White people] memorialize 'rugged individualism' and free enterprise. The more we get the better we are. Materialism is our way of life. For the American Indian (and many other 'folk' cultures) the opposite is the highest value. The only reason for having something is to give it away."[76]

Paul Chatt Smith (Comanche) believes too much emphasis is placed on what Indians look like and their assimilation into American (White-dominated) society. Prevalent stereotypes depicting precontact Indian society as idyllic overlook many of the negative elements endured by Indigenous people on this continent: hunger, violence, and poverty. Instead of romanticizing about Native Americans, we should recognize that Indians live among us and they represent a broad spectrum of colors and behaviors. The assimilation argument is overblown. Indians, like everyone else, are struggling to survive in our competitive society—to work, pay bills, raise families, and enjoy their lives. "Ninety-nine percent of Indians in the United States live like the rest of the people. Most are Christian. Assimilation is problematic."[77] In other words, from his perspective, assimilation has already happened. Yet he acknowledged that stereotypes about Indians are not the same as those about Black people—they're not as pernicious, but, nevertheless, still detrimental and demeaning.

The proponents of American exceptionalism undergirded their writing with a plethora of pseudoscientific racial theories propounded by the progenitors of the twentieth-century eugenics movement that culminated in the mass exterminations of the Holocaust in the Second World War. Paramount among these false prophets were Houston Stuart Chamberlain, Madison Grant, and Lothrop Stoddard. Chamberlain, born in England, later became a resident of Germany and married the daughter of the famed German composer Richard Wagner. As a reporter prior to the entry of the United States in World War II, Stoddard actually observed the administration of Nazi Health Court sterilization proceedings and consulted with high Nazi officials.[78]

A logical extension of these perspectives is the denigration of non–White ethnic groups. Throughout the twentieth century, wars were waged in defense of the Fatherland and Motherland in the misguided ethnocentric belief that one ethnic, religious, or economic group was morally superior to others. The twenty-first century has been paralleling this disastrous phenomenon, and the "America First" slogan of President Trump, gleefully chanted by his uninformed, uneducated followers, is all too familiar. There is nothing wrong in being patriotic, but imagining that White people were divinely predestined to rule North America and the world is eerily reminiscent of beliefs that precipitated monumental human catastrophes. The antidote to fascism and eugenics is knowledge and the assiduous application of understanding and tolerance for the Other. Would that our forefathers had employed that principle in their treatment of Native Americans instead of Manifest Destiny and American exceptionalism.

A Final Word about Racist Stereotypes

The pages of this book have revealed the origin and application of racist stereotypes about Native Americans and other Indigenous people, and the detrimental ways these attitudes have affected their lives, even today. It is not difficult to understand why negative stereotypes about Native Americans and other Indigenous people persist. They flourish in situations and societies that cultivate anxiety and fear—fear about economic insecurity and fear of "the Other." When people in dominant majority groups feel threatened or insecure about their social or economic well-being, they turn to minorities—out groups—to denigrate and disparage them, blaming them for their problems. We have documented this behavior in films, television, art, literature, and the prevailing mythology that is used to rationalize and justify discrimination against Indians in our society.

Stereotypical representations of out-group members become more visible and frequent when members of the dominant group experience anxiety and frustration about their status in society, making Indians, for example, visible targets of racist characterizations. As one might expect, the existence of out-group members like Indians makes them more likely victims of discrimination—targets of opportunity—because of their very presence, much like the Jews were persecuted in Germany and Eastern Europe before and during World War II. Like attitudes toward the Jews, our research has revealed a strong and persistent strain of anti–Indianness that courses through the artistic and literary veins of our social system, a fact substantiated by the data collected in the *Reclaiming Native Truth* study, which surveyed over ten thousand people around this nation.

We have tried to demonstrate the scope and persistence of this attitudinal orientation as it manifests itself in the way Native Americans are depicted in our culture. Even though most people in the United States may be unfamiliar with the genesis of racial stereotypes about Native Americans, we have demonstrated how contemporary depictions of Indians perpetuate negative impressions about them as they conform to centuries-old mythological conceptions of Indigenous people in North America and around the world.

As long as our society is predicated on competition to secure necessary goods and services like food, housing, health care, and education, the motivation for dehumanizing people who look or behave differently from the dominant group will persist as it draws energy from the threat to the social and economic well-being of the dominant group. The Native American ethic of collaboration and sharing was used as a cudgel against them by the dominant White society that desired their land *and* feared the threat the Indians' value system posed to the capitalist ethic with its privatization of land and commodification of natural resources.

As we have seen, assimilation, long resisted and anathema to many Native Americans, is, in fact, progressing. But trends among Native Americans designed to celebrate their ancient cultures and sovereignty may help preserve their heritage and prevent their assimilation into the dominant materialist juggernaut that devours people and ideas while perpetuating social inequality. The recent efflorescence of interest in and reproduction of Indigenous culture is a promising development, bolstered by a renewed interest in the well-being of Native Americans and court decisions supporting their causes. Hopefully, this will eventuate in a new wave of cultural awareness and respect for Native Americans as they struggle to navigate through the challenges of stereotypes and the COVID-19 pandemic that is ravaging their communities.

David Treuer (Ojibwe) points out that Indians are becoming more entrepreneurial thanks in part to casino revenues (which might be in jeopardy because of internet gambling and the legalization of sports betting). But Treuer's interviews with industrious and successful Native American small businessmen and women reveals the fortitude of many Indians as well as their educational and occupational achievements. Indians are learning how to compete in and with the larger society. He also notes that technological innovations like the cell phone and internet are facilitating the creation of Native American communities based on their shared challenges and interests. Rivalries and blood feuds are being abandoned as Indians pool knowledge and resources to promote their traditions and culture, and assure their future.

The future of Native Americans is made brighter through their commitment to maintain their identity while their sovereignty is threatened. The challenge they face will be to continue the process of promoting their cultural efflorescence in the face of the dominant White civilization that moves like a giant amoeba over competing countercultures, oozing over and assimilating divergent lifestyles, modifying and devouring them in the process of furthering materialism and conformity. But as long as members of the dominant society find elements of Native American culture useful and attractive, and defenders of Native American culture exist and persist, the spirit of Native America will survive. As Treuer notes, "Whether we are urban or reservation, our story—the story of 'the Indian'—has been a story of loss: loss of land, loss of culture, loss of a way of life. Yes, Indians remain—we remain across the country, as modern Americans and modern Indians."[79]

So what are the lessons from the "clash of civilizations" between dominant White Europeans and Indigenous Native Americans? Not only is the number of Native Americans dramatically increasing in the United States, but so is the respect for their traditions. From the hundreds of powwows and the teaching of Native languages, to the increasing numbers of Native Americans obtaining college education and entering into professions such as medicine, law, and academia, as well as the interest in Indigenous customs, music, and art—all augurs well for the persistence of Native Americans in the face of pressures to conform and assimilate into the dominant materialistic ethos of American society.

From first contact with Europeans, Indians have been faced with unintentional and intentional genocide—infectious and communicable diseases ravaged tribes and laid waste to populations that previously coexisted with their environment. The onslaught of the colonizers introduced greed, avarice, and brutality as the invaders sought land, natural resources, and souls. Treaties with the Indians that were associated with the colonization stage left them without their land, impoverished and neglected. The allotment phase of this story was an attempt to seize vast Indian land holdings, but it gave way to a policy of resettlement—the relocation of Indians from reservations to urban areas. A misguided federal policy of termination from 1953 to 1968 was another attempt to grab their land, but since then the resurgence in Indian culture and pride have invigorated their quest for sovereignty.

Like the proverbial inaccurate obituary, the demise of the Indians is erroneous. They are gaining in numbers, and interest in their customs and traditions is flourishing. Worldwide we are witnessing a similar phenomenon with the resurgence of interest in populism, ethnocentrism, even, at times, tribalism. A fascination is occurring with discovering one's roots and preserving one's heritage. The phenomenal preoccupation with tracing our biological past through DNA assessment, though not in favor among many Native Americans, demonstrates the reluctance of many people to resist being totally assimilated by the corporate juggernaut that threatens to envelop the world in a standardized model of consumption. Racist stereotypes die hard, but the people of the United States and the world can learn from the resiliency of Indians—a valiant people who have defied attempts to marginalize them and turn them into "the vanishing American."

Epilogue

When the U.S. Supreme Court overturned the Professional and Amateur Sports Protection Act in August 2018, allowing sports betting, the National Football League amended its rules to allow teams to develop partnerships with casinos. In a televised ceremony on September 16, 2018, the Dallas Cowboys' owner of "America's Team," president and general manager Jerry Jones exuberantly announced a deal with the Chickasaw Nation's WinStar World Casino, on the border of north Texas and Oklahoma. The partnership will allow the casino to use Dallas Cowboys logos and gives the casino an official designation as the exclusive partner of the team. Said Jones: "It's very fitting that the great branding of WinStar be associated with us every day."

The governor of the Chickasaw Nation, Bill Anoatubby, exclaimed, "While this partnership is a great business deal, that is only one of the reasons we are excited to be involved in the Dallas Cowboys and the Jones family. Jerry Jones is committed to enhancing the quality of life of Arlington youth and others in the community which aligns closely with our mission to enhance the overall quality of life of the Chickasaw people."[1] Jack Robinson, the general manager of WinStar and a White male native of Zimbabwe, was equally effusive, but perhaps not as much as Roger Goodell, the CEO of the National Football League, which, according to the American Gaming Association, stands to gain $2.3 billion in extra revenue from legalized sports betting. Leading the way to these new riches is the landmark deal that brings together the Cowboys and the Indians!

On October 2, 2018, then U.S. Secretary of the Interior Ryan Zinke officially welcomed seven Native American nations into the fold of federally recognized tribes (Chickahominy, Eastern Division Chickahominy, Monacan, Pamunkey, Rappahannock, Upper Mattaponi, and Nansemond) at an event in Werowocomoco in Gloucester, Virginia, where Captain John Smith met Chief Powhatan in 1607. In December 2019, the Little Shell Tribe of Chippewa, a group of 5,400 people located primarily in the Great Falls, Montana, area, became the 574th federally recognized Indian tribe in the United States.

In December 2018 the U.S. Commission on Civil Rights report *Broken Promises: Continuing Federal Funding Shortfall for Native Americans* concluded: "Our nation has broken its promises to Native Americans for too long. The United States government must rededicate itself to working with tribal governments to tackle the crisis in Indian Country, including through living up to treaty obligations.... The federal government should provide steady, equitable, and non-discretionary funding directly to tribal nations to support the public safety, health care, education, housing, and economic development of Native tribes and people."[2]

In June 2019, Joy Harjo (Muscogee) was named the twenty-third poet laureate of the United States—the first Native American to hold that position. This good news was overshadowed by President Donald Trump's attempt to rebrand Native American Heritage Month (November) as National American History and Founders Month, fostering fears among Native Americans of erasing them and their history by changing the focus of the event. In the face of Native American opposition, the president reversed his decision. On March 11, 2020, the U.S. Senate passed two bills (Savanna's Act and the Not Invisible Act) to combat the epidemic of violence against Indigenous women and coordinate efforts between the secretary of the interior and victims' services organizations as well as establishing a joint advisory commission to make recommendations for reducing violent crimes against Native people. The House passed Savanna's Act in September 2020. Native American organizations were also lobbying society to promote October as Domestic Violence Awareness Month and to utilize the Stronghearts Native Helpline: 800–762–8483.

On July 6, 2020, a U.S. district court vacated the Army Corps of Engineers' Lake Oahe easement for the Dakotas Access Pipeline and ordered the removal of all oil from the pipeline by August 3, 2020, to ensure the treaty rights of the plaintiffs (Cheyenne River Sioux, Yankton Sioux, and Oglala Sioux) and protect the natural resources of the region, ordering a thorough environmental review. And on July 9, 2020, the U.S. Supreme Court ruled in *McGirt v. Oklahoma* that the treaty-defined boundaries of the Muscogee (Creek) Nation were valid and guaranteed through treaties between the tribe and the federal government going back to 1832, 1833, and 1866. The decision recognized Native American ownership of the eastern half of Oklahoma. "In holding the federal government to its treaty obligations, the U.S. Supreme Court put to rest what should never have been in question," said John Echohawk, executive director of the Native American Rights Fund. In September 2020, for the first time in its 150-year history, the Metropolitan Museum of Art in New York City hired Dr. Patricia Marroquin Norby (Pure'pecha) as an associate curator of Native American Art.

Debra Haaland, February 24, 2021 (Sarah Silbiger/ Getty Images News).

As the coronavirus ravaged Native American communities in the fall of 2020, President-Elect Joe Biden appointed Diné (Navajo) Jill Jim, the executive director of the Navajo Nation's Department of Health, to his COVID-19 Task Force Advisory Board on November 28, 2020. On December 17, 2020, President-Elect Biden selected U.S. Congresswoman Deb Haaland (Laguna Pueblo) for the position of secretary of the interior. Not since Hoover vice president Charles Curtis (Kaw Nation) has a Native American served in a Cabinet position. Judging by the Trump administration's scramble to open up sacred Indian lands for the exploitation of natural resources before the end of its term, she will be very busy.[3] The $1.9 trillion COVID-19 Relief Package signed by President Biden in March 2021 contained $6 billion for the Indian Health Service.

Appendix

List of Federal and State Recognized Tribes[1]

Federally Recognized Tribes

Alabama

- Poarch Band of Creeks

Alaska

- Native Village of Afognak (formerly the Village of Afognak)
- Agdaagux Tribe of King Cove
- Native Village of Akhiok
- Akiachak Native Community
- Akiak Native Community
- Native Village of Akutan
- Village of Alakanuk
- Alatna Village
- Native Village of Aleknagik
- Algaaciq Native Village (St. Mary's)
- Allakaket Village
- Native Village of Ambler
- Village of Anaktuvuk Pass
- Yupiit of Andreafski
- Angoon Community Association
- Village of Aniak
- Anvik Village
- Arctic Village (See Native Village of Venetie Tribal Government)
- Asa'carsarmiut Tribe
- Native Village of Atka
- Village of Atmautluak
- Atqasuk Village (Atkasook)
- Native Village of Barrow Inupiat Traditional Government
- Beaver Village

- Native Village of Belkofski
- Village of Bill Moore's Slough
- Birch Creek Tribe
- Native Village of Brevig Mission
- Native Village of Buckland
- Native Village of Cantwell
- Native Village of Chenega (a.k.a. Chanega)
- Chalkyitsik Village
- Cheesh-Na Tribe (formerly the Native Village of Chistochina)
- Village of Chefornak
- Chevak Native Village
- Chickaloon Native Village
- Chignik Bay Tribal Council (formerly the Native Village of Chignik)
- Native Village of Chignik Lagoon
- Chignik Lake Village
- Chilkat Indian Village (Klukwan)
- Chilkoot Indian Association (Haines)
- Chinik Eskimo Community (Golovin)
- Native Village of Chitina
- Native Village of Chuathbaluk (Russian Mission, Kuskokwim)
- Chuloonawick Native Village
- Circle Native Community
- Village of Clarks Point
- Native Village of Council
- Craig Community Association
- Village of Crooked Creek

- Curyung Tribal Council
- Native Village of Deering
- Native Village of Diomede (a.k.a. Inalik)
- Village of Dot Lake
- Douglas Indian Association
- Native Village of Eagle
- Native Village of Eek
- Egegik Village
- Eklutna Native Village
- Native Village of Ekuk
- Ekwok Village
- Native Village of Elim
- Emmonak Village
- Evansville Village (a.k.a. Bettles Field)
- Native Village of Eyak (Cordova)
- Native Village of False Pass
- Native Village of Fort Yukon
- Native Village of Gakona
- Galena Village (a.k.a. Louden Village)
- Native Village of Gambell
- Native Village of Georgetown
- Native Village of Goodnews Bay
- Organized Village of Grayling (a.k.a. Holikachuk)
- Gulkana Village
- Native Village of Hamilton
- Healy Lake Village
- Holy Cross Village
- Hoonah Indian Association
- Native Village of Hooper Bay
- Hughes Village
- Huslia Village
- Hydaburg Cooperative Association
- Igiugig Village
- Village of Iliamna
- Inupiat Community of the Arctic Slope
- Iqurmuit Traditional Council (formerly the Native Village of Russian Mission)
- Ivanoff Bay Village
- Kaguyak Village
- Organized Village of Kake
- Kaktovik Village (a.k.a. Barter Island)
- Village of Kalskag
- Village of Kaltag
- Native Village of Kanatak
- Native Village of Karluk
- Organized Village of Kasaan
- Kasigluk Traditional Elders Council (formerly the Native Village of Kasigluk)
- Kenaitze Indian Tribe
- Ketchikan Indian Corporation
- Native Village of Kiana
- King Island Native Community
- King Salmon Tribe
- Native Village of Kipnuk
- Native Village of Kivalina
- Klawock Cooperative Association
- Native Village of Kluti Kaah (a.k.a. Copper Center)
- Knik Tribe
- Native Village of Kobuk
- Kokhanok Village
- Native Village of Kongiganak
- Village of Kotlik
- Native Village of Kotzebue
- Native Village of Koyuk
- Koyukuk Native Village
- Organized Village of Kwethluk
- Native Village of Kwigillingok
- Native Village of Kwinhagak (a.k.a. Quinhagak)
- Native Village of Larsen Bay
- Levelock Village
- Lime Village
- Village of Lower Kalskag
- Manley Hot Springs Village
- Manokotak Village
- Native Village of Marshall (a.k.a. Fortuna Ledge)
- Native Village of Mary's Igloo
- McGrath Native Village
- Native Village of Mekoryuk
- Mentasta Traditional Council
- Metlakatla Indian Community, Annette Island Reserve
- Native Village of Minto
- Naknek Native Village
- Native Village of Nanwalek (a.k.a. English Bay)

- Native Village of Napaimute
- Native Village of Napakiak
- Native Village of Napaskiak
- Native Village of Nelson Lagoon
- Nenana Native Association
- New Koliganek Village Council
- New Stuyahok Village
- Newhalen Village
- Newtok Village
- Native Village of Nightmute
- Nikolai Village
- Native Village of Nikolski
- Ninilchik Village
- Native Village of Noatak
- Nome Eskimo Community
- Nondalton Village
- Noorvik Native Community
- Northway Village
- Native Village of Nuiqsut (a.k.a. Nooiksut)
- Nulato Village
- Nunakauyarmiut Tribe (formerly the Native Village of Toksook Bay)
- Native Village of Nunam Iqua (formerly the Native Village of Sheldon's Point)
- Native Village of Nunapitchuk
- Village of Ohogamiut
- Village of Old Harbor
- Orutsararmuit Native Village (a.k.a. Bethel)
- Oscarville Traditional Village
- Native Village of Ouzinkie
- Native Village of Paimiut
- Pauloff Harbor Village
- Pedro Bay Village
- Native Village of Perryville
- Petersburg Indian Association
- Native Village of Pilot Point
- Pilot Station Traditional Village
- Native Village of Pitka's Point
- Platinum Traditional Village
- Native Village of Point Hope
- Native Village of Point Lay
- Native Village of Port Graham
- Native Village of Port Heiden
- Native Village of Port Lions
- Portage Creek Village (a.k.a. Ohgsenakale)
- Pribilof Islands Aleut Communities of St. Paul and St. George Islands
- Qagan Tayagungin Tribe of Sand Point Village
- Qawalangin Tribe of Unalaska
- Rampart Village
- Village of Red Devil
- Native Village of Ruby
- Saint George Island (See Pribilof Islands Aleut Communities of St. Paul and St. George Islands)
- Native Village of Saint Michael
- Saint Paul Island (See Pribilof Islands Aleut Communities of St. Paul and St. George Islands)
- Village of Salamatoff
- Native Village of Savoonga
- Organized Village of Saxman
- Native Village of Scammon Bay
- Native Village of Selawik
- Seldovia Village Tribe
- Shageluk Native Village
- Native Village of Shaktoolik
- Native Village of Shishmaref
- Native Village of Shungnak
- Sitka Tribe of Alaska
- Skagway Village
- Village of Sleetmute
- Village of Solomon
- South Naknek Village
- Stebbins Community Association
- Native Village of Stevens
- Village of Stony River
- Sun'aq Tribe of Kodiak (formerly the Shoonaq' Tribe of Kodiak)
- Takotna Village
- Native Village of Tanacross
- Native Village of Tanana
- Tangirnaq Native Village (formerly Lesnoi Village)
- Native Village of Tatitlek
- Native Village of Tazlina
- Telida Village
- Native Village of Teller
- Native Village of Tetlin

- Central Council of the Tlingit and Haida Indian Tribes
- Traditional Village of Togiak
- Tuluksak Native Community
- Native Village of Tuntutuliak
- Native Village of Tununak
- Twin Hills Village
- Native Village of Tyonek
- Ugashik Village
- Umkumiute Native Village
- Native Village of Unalakleet
- Native Village of Unga
- Village of Venetie (See Native Village of Venetie Tribal Government)
- Native Village of Venetie Tribal Government (Arctic Village and Village of Venetie)
- Village of Wainwright
- Native Village of Wales
- Native Village of White Mountain
- Wrangell Cooperative Association
- Yakutat Tlingit Tribe

Arizona

- Ak Chin Indian Community of the Maricopa (Ak Chin) Indian Reservation
- Cocopah Tribe of Arizona
- Colorado River Indian Tribes of the Colorado River Indian Reservation (Arizona and California)
- Fort McDowell Yavapai Nation
- Fort Mojave Indian Tribe (Arizona, California, and Nevada)
- Gila River Indian Community of the Gila River Indian Reservation
- Havasupai Tribe of the Havasupai Reservation
- Hopi Tribe of Arizona
- Hualapai Indian Tribe of the Hualapai Indian Reservation
- Kaibab Band of Paiute Indians of the Kaibab Indian Reservation
- Navajo Nation (Arizona, New Mexico, and Utah)
- Pascua Yaqui Tribe of Arizona

- Quechan Tribe of the Fort Yuma Indian Reservation (Arizona and California)
- Salt River Pima-Maricopa Indian Community of the Salt River Reservation
- San Carlos Apache Tribe of the San Carlos Reservation
- San Juan Southern Paiute Tribe of Arizona
- Tohono O'odham Nation of Arizona
- Tonto Apache Tribe of Arizona
- White Mountain Apache Tribe of the Fort Apache Reservation
- Yavapai-Apache Nation of the Camp Verde Indian Reservation
- Yavapai-Prescott Indian Tribe

California

- Agua Caliente Band of Cahuilla Indians of the Agua Caliente Indian Reservation
- Alturas Indian Rancheria
- Augustine Band of Cahuilla Indians
- Bear River Band of the Rohnerville Rancheria
- Berry Creek Rancheria of Maidu Indians of California
- Big Lagoon Rancheria
- Big Pine Band Paiute Tribe of the Owens Valley
- Big Sandy Rancheria of Western Mono Indians of California
- Big Valley Band of Pomo Indians of the Big Valley Rancheria
- Bishop Paiute Tribe (previously listed as Paiute-Shoshone Indians of the Bishop Community of the Bishop Colony)
- Blue Lake Rancheria
- Bridgeport Indian Colony
- Buena Vista Rancheria of Me-Wuk Indians of California
- Cabazon Band of Mission Indians
- Cachil DeHe Band of Wintun Indians of the Colusa Indian Community of the Colusa Rancheria

- Cahuilla Band of Mission Indians of the Cahuilla Reservation
- Cahto Indian Tribe of the Laytonville Rancheria
- California Valley Miwok Tribe
- Campo Band of Diegueño Mission Indians of the Campo Indian Reservation
- Capitan Grande Band of Diegueño Mission Indians of California: Barona Group of Capitan Grande Band of Mission Indians of the Barona Reservation; Viejas (Baron Long) Group of Capitan Grande Band of Mission Indians of the Viejas Reservation
- Cedarville Rancheria
- Chemehuevi Indian Tribe of the Chemehuevi Reservation
- Cher-Ae Heights Indian Community of the Trinidad Rancheria
- Chicken Ranch Rancheria of Me-Wuk Indians of California
- Cloverdale Rancheria of Pomo Indians of California
- Cold Springs Rancheria of Mono Indians of California
- Colorado River Indian Tribes of the Colorado River Indian Reservation (Arizona and California)
- Cortina Indian Rancheria of Wintun Indians of California
- Coyote Valley Band of Pomo Indians of California
- Death Valley Timbi-Sha Shoshone Tribe
- Dry Creek Rancheria of Pomo Indians
- Elem Indian Colony of Pomo Indians of the Sulphur Bank Rancheria
- Elk Valley Rancheria
- Enterprise Rancheria of Maidu Indians of California
- Ewiiaapaayp Band of Kumeyaay Indians
- Federated Indians of Graton Rancheria
- Fort Bidwell Indian Community of the Fort Bidwell Reservation of California
- Fort Independence Indian Community of Paiute Indians of the Fort Independence Reservation
- Fort Mojave Indian Tribe (Arizona, California, and Nevada)
- Greenville Rancheria
- Grindstone Indian Rancheria of Wintun-Wailaki Indians of California
- Guidiville Rancheria of California
- Habematolel Pomo of Upper Lake
- Hoopa Valley Tribe
- Hopland Band of Pomo Indians
- Inaja Band of Diegueño Mission Indians of the Inaja and Cosmit Reservation
- Ione Band of Miwok Indians of California
- Jackson Band of Miwuk Indians
- Jamul Indian Village of California
- Karuk Tribe
- Kashia Band of Pomo Indians of the Stewart's Point Rancheria
- Koi Nation of Northern California
- La Jolla Band of Luiseño Indians
- La Posta Band of Diegueño Mission Indians of the La Posta Indian Reservation
- Lone Pine Paiute-Shoshone Tribe
- Los Coyotes Band of Cahuilla & Cupeno Indians
- Lytton Rancheria of California
- Manchester Band of Pomo Indians of the Manchester Rancheria
- Manzanita Band of Diegueño Mission Indians of the Manzanita Reservation
- Mechoopda Indian Tribe of Chico Rancheria
- Mesa Grande Band of Diegueño Mission Indians of the Mesa Grande Reservation

- Middletown Rancheria of Pomo Indians of California
- Mooretown Rancheria of Maidu Indians of California
- Morongo Band of Cahuilla Mission Indians
- Northfork Rancheria of Mono Indians of California
- Pala Band of Luiseño Mission Indians of the Pala Reservation
- Paskenta Band of Nomlaki Indians of California
- Pauma Band of Luiseño Mission Indians of the Pauma & Yuima Reservation
- Pechanga Band of Luiseño Mission Indians of the Pechanga Reservation
- Picayune Rancheria of Chukchansi Indians of California
- Pinoleville Pomo Nation (formerly the Pinoleville Rancheria of Pomo Indians of California)
- Pit River Tribe (includes XL Ranch, Big Bend, Likely, Lookout, Montgomery Creek, and Roaring Creek Rancherias)
- Potter Valley Tribe (formerly the Potter Valley Rancheria of Pomo Indians of California)
- Quartz Valley Indian Community of the Quartz Valley Reservation of California
- Quechan Tribe of the Fort Yuma Indian Reservation (Arizona and California)
- Ramona Band of Cahuilla
- Redding Rancheria
- Redwood Valley or Little River Band of Pomo Indians of the Redwood Valley Rancheria California
- Resighini Rancheria
- Rincon Band of Luiseño Mission Indians of the Rincon Reservation
- Robinson Rancheria
- Round Valley Indian Tribes, Round Valley Reservation
- San Manual Band of Serrano
- Mission Indians of the San Maual Reservation
- San Pasqual Band of Diegueño Mission Indians of California
- Santa Rosa Indian Community of the Santa Rosa Rancheria
- Santa Rosa Band of Cahuilla Indians (formerly the Santa Rosa Band of Cahuilla Mission Indians of the Santa Rosa Reservation)
- Santa Ynez Band of Chumash Mission Indians of the Santa Ynez Reservation
- Lipay Nation of Santa Ysabel (previously listed as the Santa Ysabel Band of Diegueño Mission Indians of the Santa Ysabel Reservation)
- Scotts Valley Band of Pomo Indians of California
- Sheep Ranch Rancheria of Me-Wuk Indians
- Sherwood Valley Rancheria of Pomo Indians of California
- Shingle Springs Band of Miwok Indians, Shingle Springs Rancheria (Verona Tract)
- Soboba Band of Luiseño Indians
- Susanville Indian Rancheria
- Sycuan Band of the Kumeyaay Nation (formerly the Sycuan Band of Diegueno Mission Indians of California)
- Table Mountain Rancheria of California
- Tejon Indian Tribe
- Tolowa Dee-ni' Nation
- Torres-Martinez Desert Cahuilla Indians
- Tule River Indian Tribe of the Tule River Reservation
- Tuolumne Band of Me-Wuk Indians of the Tuolumne Rancheria of California
- Twenty-Nine Palms Band of Mission Indians of California
- United Auburn Indian Community

of the Auburn Rancheria of California
- Upper Lake Band of Pomo Indians
- Utu Utu Gwaitu Paiute Tribe of the Benton Paiute Reservation
- Washoe Tribe (Carson Colony, Dresslerville Colony, Woodfords Community, Stewart Community, and Washoe Ranches) (California and Nevada)
- Wilton Rancheria
- Wiyot Tribe (formerly the Table Bluff Reservation-Wiyot Tribe)
- Yocha Dehe Wintun Nation
- Yurok Tribe of the Yurok Reservation

Colorado

- Southern Ute Indian Tribe of the Southern Ute Reservation
- Ute Mountain Tribe of the Ute Mountain Reservation (Colorado, New Mexico, and Utah)

Connecticut

- Mashantucket Pequot Tribe
- Mohegan Tribe of Indians of Connecticut

Florida

- Miccosukee Tribe of Indians of Florida
- Seminole Tribe of Florida (Dania, Big Cypress, Brighton, Hollywood, and Tampa Reservations)

Idaho

- Coeur D'Alene Tribe
- Kootenai Tribe of Idaho
- Nez Perce Tribe
- Shoshone-Bannock Tribes of the Fort Hall Reservation of Idaho

Indiana

- Pokagon Band of Potawatomi Indians (Michigan and Indiana)

Iowa

- Sac and Fox Tribe of the Mississippi in Iowa

Kansas

- Iowa Tribe of Kansas and Nebraska
- Kickapoo Tribe of Indians of the Kickapoo Reservation in Kansas
- Prairie Band Potawatomi Nation
- Sac and Fox Nation of Missouri (Kansas and Nebraska)

Louisiana

- Chitimacha Tribe of Louisiana
- Coushatta Tribe of Louisiana
- Jena Band of Choctaw Indians
- Tunica-Biloxi Indian Tribe of Louisiana

Maine

- Aroostook Band of Micmac Indians
- Houlton Band of Maliseet Indians
- Passamaquoddy Tribe
- Penobscot Nation

Massachusetts

- Mashpee Wampanoag Tribe
- Wampanoag Tribe of Gay Head (Aquinnah) of Massachusetts

Michigan

- Bay Mills Indian Community
- Grand Traverse Band of Ottawa and Chippewa Indians
- Hannahville Indian Community
- Nottawaseppi Huron Band of the Potawatomi
- Keweenaw Bay Indian Community
- Lac Vieux Desert Band of Lake Superior Chippewa Indians of Michigan
- Little River Band of Ottawa Indians
- Little Traverse Bay Bands of Odawa Indians
- Match-e-be-nash-she-wish Band of Pottawatomi Indians of Michigan

- Pokagon Band of Potawatomi Indians (Michigan and Indiana)
- Saginaw Chippewa Indian Tribe of Michigan
- Sault Ste. Marie Tribe of Chippewa Indians of Michigan

Minnesota

- Lower Sioux Indian Community in the State of Minnesota
- Mdewakanton Sioux Indians
- Minnesota Chippewa Tribe (Six component reservations: Bois Forte Band (Nett Lake); Fond du Lac Band; Grand Portage Band; Leech Lake Band; Mille Lacs Ban; White Earth Band)
- Prairie Island Indian Community in the State of Minnesota
- Mdewakanton Sioux Indians
- Red Lake Band of Chippewa Indians
- Shakopee Mdewakanton Sioux Community of Minnesota
- Upper Sioux Community

Mississippi

- Mississippi Band of Choctaw Indians

Montana

- Assiniboine and Sioux Tribes of the Fort Peck Indian Reservation
- Blackfeet Tribe of the Blackfeet Indian Reservation of Montana
- Chippewa-Cree Indians of the Rocky Boy's Reservation
- Confederated Salish and Kootenai Tribes of the Flathead Reservation
- Crow Tribe of Montana
- Fort Belknap Indian Community of the Fort Belknap Reservation of Montana
- Little Shell
- Northern Cheyenne Tribe of the Northern Cheyenne Indian Reservation

Nebraska

- Iowa Tribe of Kansas and Nebraska
- Omaha Tribe of Nebraska
- Ponca Tribe of Nebraska
- Sac and Fox Nation of Missouri (Kansas and Nebraska)
- Santee Sioux Nation
- Winnebago Tribe of Nebraska

Nevada

- Confederated Tribes of the Goshute Reservation (Nevada and Utah)
- Duckwater Shoshone Tribe of the Duckwater Reservation
- Ely Shoshone Tribe of Nevada
- Fort McDermitt Paiute and Shoshone Tribes of the Fort McDermitt Indian Reservation (Nevada and Oregon)
- Fort Mojave Indian Tribe (Arizona, California, and Nevada)
- Las Vegas Tribe of Paiute Indians of the Las Vegas Indian Colony
- Lovelock Paiute Tribe of the Lovelock Indian Colony
- Moapa Band of Paiute Indians of the Moapa River Indian Reservation
- Paiute-Shoshone Tribe of the Fallon Reservation and Colony
- Pyramid Lake Paiute Tribe of the Pyramid Lake Reservation
- Reno-Sparks Indian Colony
- Shoshone-Paiute Tribes of the Duck Valley Reservation
- Summit Lake Paiute Tribe of Nevada
- Te-Moak Tribe of Western Shoshone Indians of Nevada (Four constituent bands: Battle Mountain Band; Elko Band; South Fork Band; Wells Band)
- Walker River Paiute Tribe of the Walker River Reservation
- Washoe Tribe (Nevada and California) (Carson Colony, Dresslerville Colony, Woodfords

Community, Stewart Community, and Washoe Ranches)
- Winnemucca Indian Colony of Nevada
- Yerington Paiute Tribe of the Yerington Colony and Campbell Ranch
- Yomba Shoshone Tribe of the Yomba Reservation

New Mexico

- Jicarilla Apache Nation
- Mescalero Apache Tribe of the Mescalero Reservation
- Navajo Nation (Arizona, New Mexico, and Utah)
- Ohkay Owingeh (formerly the Pueblo of San Juan)
- Pueblo of Acoma
- Pueblo of Cochiti
- Pueblo of Jemez
- Pueblo of Isleta
- Pueblo of Laguna
- Pueblo of Nambe
- Pueblo of Picuris
- Pueblo of Pojoaque
- Pueblo of San Felipe
- Pueblo of San Ildefonso
- Pueblo of Sandia
- Pueblo of Santa Ana
- Pueblo of Santa Clara
- Kewa Pueblo
- Pueblo of Taos
- Pueblo of Tesuque
- Pueblo of Zia
- Ute Mountain Tribe of the Ute Mountain Reservation (Colorado, New Mexico, and Utah)
- Zuni Tribe of the Zuni Reservation

New York

- Cayuga Nation
- Oneida Nation of New York
- Onondaga Nation
- Saint Regis Mohawk Tribe (formerly the St. Regis Band of Mohawk Indians of New York)

- Seneca Nation of Indians
- Shinnecock Indian Nation
- Tonawanda Band of Seneca
- Tuscarora Nation of New York

North Carolina

- Eastern Band of Cherokee Indians

North Dakota

- Spirit Lake Tribe
- Standing Rock Sioux Tribe (North Dakota and South Dakota)
- Three Affiliated Tribes of the Fort Berthold Reservation
- Turtle Mountain Band of Chippewa Indians of North Dakota

Oklahoma

- Absentee-Shawnee Tribe of Indians
- Alabama-Quassarte Tribal Town
- Apache Tribe of Oklahoma
- Caddo Nation of Oklahoma
- Cherokee Nation
- Cheyenne and Arapaho Tribes
- Citizen Potawatomi Nation
- Comanche Nation
- Delaware Nation
- Delaware Tribe of Indians
- Eastern Shawnee Tribe of Oklahoma
- Fort Sill Apache Tribe of Oklahoma
- Iowa Tribe of Oklahoma
- Kaw Nation
- Kialegee Tribal Town
- Kickapoo Tribe of Oklahoma
- Kiowa Indian Tribe of Oklahoma
- Miami Tribe of Oklahoma
- Modoc Tribe of Oklahoma
- Muscogee (Creek) Nation
- Ottawa Tribe of Oklahoma
- Otoe-Missouria Tribe of Indians
- Pawnee Nation of Oklahoma
- Peoria Tribe of Indians of Oklahoma
- Ponca Tribe of Indians of Oklahoma
- Quapaw Tribe of Indians
- Sac and Fox Nation

- Seminole Nation of Oklahoma
- Seneca-Cayuga Nation
- Shawnee Tribe
- The Chickasaw Nation
- The Choctaw Nation of Oklahoma
- The Osage Nation
- Thlopthlocco Tribal Town
- Tonkawa Tribe of Indians of Oklahoma
- United Keetoowah Band of Cherokee Indians in Oklahoma
- Wichita and Affiliated Tribes (Wichita, Keechi, Waco, and Tawakonie)
- Wyandotte Nation

Oregon

- Burns Paiute Tribe
- Confederated Tribes of the Coos, Lower Umpqua, and Siuslaw Indians of Oregon
- Confederated Tribes of the Grand Ronde Community of Oregon
- Confederated Tribes of the Siletz Reservation
- Confederated Tribes of the Umatilla Indian Reservation
- Confederated Tribes of the Warm Springs Reservation of Oregon
- Coquille Indian Tribe
- Cow Creek Band of Umpqua Tribe of Indians
- Fort McDermitt Paiute and Shoshone Tribes of the Fort McDermitt Indian Reservation (Nevada and Oregon)
- Klamath Tribes

Rhode Island

- Narragansett Indian Tribe

South Carolina

- Catawba Indian Nation (Catawba Tribe of South Carolina)

South Dakota

- Cheyenne River Sioux Tribe of the Cheyenne River Reservation

- Crow Creek Sioux Tribe of the Crow Creek Reservation
- Flandreau Santee Sioux Tribe of South Dakota
- Lower Brule Sioux Tribe of the Lower Brule Reservation
- Oglala Sioux Tribe (previously listed as Oglala Sioux Tribe of the Pine Ridge Reservation)
- Rosebud Sioux Tribe of the Rosebud Indian Reservation
- Sisseton-Wahpeton Oyate of the Lake Traverse Reservation
- Standing Rock Sioux Tribe (North Dakota and South Dakota)
- Yankton Sioux Tribe of South Dakota

Texas

- Alabama-Coushatta Tribe of Texas
- Kickapoo Traditional Tribe of Texas
- Ysleta Del Sur Pueblo

Utah

- Confederated Tribes of the Goshute Reservation (Nevada and Utah)
- Navajo Nation (Arizona, New Mexico, and Utah)
- Northwestern Band of Shoshoni Nation
- Paiute Indian Tribe of Utah (Cedar Band of Paiutes, Kanosh Band of Paiutes, Koosharem Band of Paiutes, Indian Peaks Band of Paiutes, and Shivwits Band of Paiutes)
- Skull Valley Band of Goshute Indians of Utah
- Ute Indian Tribe of the Uintah and Ouray Reservation
- Ute Mountain Ute Tribe (Colorado, New Mexico, and Utah)

Virginia

- Pamunkey Indian Tribe
- Chickahominy Indian Tribe
- Chickahominy Indian Tribe–Eastern Division

- Upper Mattaponi Tribe
- Rappahannock Tribe, Inc.
- Monacan Indian Nation
- Nansemond Indian Tribe

Washington

- Confederated Tribes of the Chehalis Reservation
- Confederated Tribes of the Colville Reservation
- Confederated Tribes and Bands of the Yakama Nation
- Cowlitz Indian Tribe
- Hoh Indian Tribe
- Jamestown S'Klallam Tribe
- Kalispel Indian Community of the Kalispel Reservation
- Lower Elwha Tribal Community
- Lummi Tribe of the Lummi Reservation
- Makah Indian Tribe of the Makah Indian Reservation
- Muckleshoot Indian Tribe
- Nisqually Indian Tribe
- Nooksack Indian Tribe of Washington
- Port Gamble S'Klallam Tribe
- Puyallup Tribe of the Puyallup Reservation
- Quileute Tribe of the Quileute Reservation
- Quinault Indian Nation
- Samish Indian Nation
- Sauk-Suiattle Indian Tribe of Washington
- Shoalwater Bay Indian Tribe of the Shoalwater Bay Indian Reservation
- Skokomish Indian Tribe
- Snoqualmie Indian Tribe
- Spokane Tribe of the Spokane Reservation
- Squaxin Island Tribe of the Squaxin Island Reservation
- Stillaguamish Tribe of Indians of Washington
- Suquamish Indian Tribe of the Port Madison Reservation

- Swinomish Indian Tribal Community
- Tulalip Tribes of Washington
- Upper Skagit Indian Tribe of Washington

Wisconsin

- Bad River Band of the Lake Superior Tribe of Chippewa Indians of the Bad River Reservation
- Forest County Potawatomi Community
- Ho-Chunk Nation of Wisconsin
- Lac Courte Oreilles Band of Lake Superior Chippewa Indians of Wisconsin
- Lac du Flambeau Band of Lake Superior Chippewa Indians of the Lac du Flambeau Reservation of Wisconsin
- Menominee Indian Tribe of Wisconsin
- Oneida Tribe of Indians of Wisconsin
- Red Cliff Band of Lake Superior Chippewa Indians of Wisconsin
- St. Croix Chippewa Indians of Wisconsin
- Sokaogon Chippewa Community
- Stockbridge Munsee Community

Wyoming

- Arapaho Tribe of the Wind River Reservation
- Shoshone Tribe of the Wind River Reservation

State Recognized Tribes

Alabama

- Cher-O-Creek Intra Tribal Indians
- Cherokee Tribe of Northeast Alabama
- Cherokees of Southeast Alabama
- Echota Cherokee Tribe of Alabama
- Ma-Chis Lower Creek Indian Tribe of Alabama

- Mowa Band of Choctaw Indians
- Piqua Shawnee Tribe
- Star Clan of Muscogee Creeks
- United Cherokee Ani-Yun-Wiya Nation

Connecticut

- Eastern Pequot Tribal Nation
- The Golden Hill Paugussett
- Schaghticoke Tribal Nation

Delaware

- Lenape Indian Tribe of Delaware
- Nanticoke Indian Tribe

Georgia

- Cherokee of Georgia Tribal Council
- Georgia Tribe of Eastern Cherokee
- Lower Muskogee Creek Tribe

Louisiana

- Addai Caddo Tribe
- Biloxi-Chitimacha Confederation of Muskogee
- Choctaw-Apache Community of Ebarb
- Clifton Choctaw
- Four Winds Tribe Louisiana Cherokee Confederacy
- Grand Caillou/Dulac Band
- Isle de Jean Charles Band
- Louisiana Choctaw Tribe
- Natchitoches Tribe of Louisiana
- Pointe-Au-Chien Indian Tribe
- United Houma Nation

Maryland

- Piscataway Indian Nation
- Piscataway Conoy Tribe

Massachusetts

- Nipmuc Nation

New Jersey

- Nanticoke Lenni-Lenape Tribal Nation
- Ramapough Lenape Nation
- The Powhatan Renape Nation

New York

- Tonawada Band of Seneca
- Tuscarora Nation
- Unkechaug Nation

North Carolina

- Cohaire Intra-Tribal Council, Inc.
- Haliwa-Saponi Indian Tribe
- Lumbee Tribe
- Meherrin Nation
- Occaneechi Band of the Saponi Nation
- Sappony
- Waccamaw-Siouan Tribe

South Carolina

- Beaver Creek Indians
- Edisto Natchez Kusso Tribe of South Carolina
- Pee Dee Indian Nation of Upper South Carolina
- Pee Dee Indian Tribe of South Carolina
- Santee Indian Organization
- The Waccamaw Indian People
- Wassamasaw Tribe of Varnertown Indians

Vermont

- Elnu Abenaki Tribe
- Nulhegan Band of the Coosuk Abenaki Nation
- Koasek Abenaki Tribe
- Mississquoi Abenaki Tribe

Virginia

- Cheroenhaka (Nottoway)
- Chickahominy Tribe
- Eastern Chickahominy Tribe
- Mattaponi
- Monacan Nation
- Nansemond
- Nottoway of Virginia
- Pamunkey
- Pattawomeck
- Rappahannock
- Upper Mattaponi Tribe

Chapter Notes

Preface

1. First Nations Development Institute and Echo Hawk Consulting, *Reclaiming Native Truth: A Project to Dispel America's Myths and Misconceptions*, June 2018, https://www.reclaimingnativetruth.com.

2. Claude Steele and Joshua Aronson, "Stereotype Threat and the Intellectual Test Performance of African Americans," *Journal of Personality and Social Psychology* 65, no. 5 (November 1995); Claude Steele, "Thin Ice: 'Stereotype Threat' and Black College Students," *The Atlantic Monthly*, August 1999, 44–54.

Introduction

1. Dennis Zotigh, "Many Roads to Tribal Rights," *National Museum of the American Indian* 19, no. 1 (Spring 2018): 30.

2. Interview with Jennifer Martel (Lakota), Visitor Center coordinator, Sitting Bull College, Fort Yates, North Dakota, September 6, 2018.

3. First Nations Development Institute and Echo Hawk Consulting, *Reclaiming Native Truth*.

4. United Nations Human Rights, Office of the High Commissioner, "Native Americans Facing Excessive Force in North Dakota Pipeline Protests—UN Expert," November 15, 2016, https://www.ohchr.org/EN/NewsEvents/Pages/DisplayNews.aspx?NewsID=20868&LangID=E.

5. Joe Heim, "Showdown Over Oil Pipeline Becomes a National Movement for Native Americans," *Washington Post*, September 7, 2016.

6. See the "Construction of the Dakota Access Pipeline: Memorandum of the Secretary of the Army," *Federal Register*, January 24, 2017, allowing Energy Transfer Partners to complete the project, https://www.federalregister.gov/documents/2017/02/17/R1-2017-02032/construction-of-the-dakota-access-pipeline.

7. Joe Heim, "Showdown Over Oil Pipeline Becomes a National Movement for Native Americans," *Washington Post*, September 7, 2016.

8. This discussion drew on reports from the following sources: Joe Heim, "Showdown Over Oil Pipeline Becomes a National Movement for Native Americans," *Washington Post*, September 7, 2016; Justin Worland, "What to Know about the Dakota Access Pipeline Protests," *Time*, October 28, 2016, Time.com/4548566/Dakota-access-pipeline-standing-rock-sioux/;Blake Nicholson, "Dakota Access Developer Granted Hearing Delay in Dispute," *Associated Press*, August 15, 2017, https://apnews.com/article/57082a415dce40879c3ba333b21c4600; "Dakota Access Pipeline: The Who, What and Why of the Standing Rock Protests," *The Guardian*, November 3, 2016, https://www.theguardian.com/us-news/2016/nov/03/north-dakota-access-oil-pipeline-protests-explainer; Eric Wolff, "Obama Administration Blocks Dakota Pipeline, Angering Trump Allies," *Politico*, December 4, 2016, https://www.politico.com/story/2016/12/us-army-corps-blocks-dakota-access-pipeline-232172. For an analysis of the events surrounding the protest, see First Nations Development Institute and Echo Hawk Consulting, *Reclaiming Native Truth*, 34–40. For a review of legal maneuvers of this event, see U.S. Commission on Civil Rights, *Broken Promises: Continuing Federal Funding Shortfall for Native Americans* (Washington, D.C.: U.S. Government Printing Office, December 2018), https://www.usccr.gov/files/pubs/2018/12-20-Broken-Promises.pdf, 184–87. David Treuer (Ojibwe) offers an account of the events at Standing Rock that is more sympathetic to the Army Corps of Engineers and government, noting that records indicate government officials unsuccessfully attempted to meet with key tribal representatives to discuss the proposed pipeline, and they secured required permits; see David Treuer, *The Heartbeat of Wounded Knee: Native America from 1890 to the Present* (New York: Riverside Press, 2019), 432–38.

9. Stacy L. Smith, *Report on Diversity (CARD)*, Annenberg Foundation, February 22, 2016, Annenberg.usc.edu/news/faculty-research/c-suite-characters-screen-how-inclusive-entertainment-industry; Stacy L. Smith and the Media, Diversity and Social Change Initiative, "Inequality in 900 Popular Films," Annenberg Foundation, July 2017, Annenberg.usc.edu/research/mdsci.

Chapter 1

1. Perhaps someday, White Americans will be just as eager to claim their African genes. Witness the political flap between Massachusetts Senator Elizabeth Warren and President Donald Trump over her claim to be part Native American. One wonders whether this debate would have occurred if the dispute was over African lineage.

2. Wendy Wang, "Interracial Marriage: Who Is 'Marrying Out'?" *PEW Research Center*, June 12, 2015, www.pewresearch.org/fact-tank/2015/06/12/interracial-marriage-who-is-marrying-out/.

3. Journalist Laurie White listed twenty-one celebrities who claim Native American heritage. See "21 Celebrities You Didn't Know Were Native American," *B-Babble* (Disney Corp.), November 15, 2013.

4. The form is available at https://www.bia.gov/sites/bia.gov/files/assets/public/raca/online_forms/pdf/Certificate_of_Degree_of_Indian_Blood_1076-0153_Exp3-31-21_508.pdf.

5. Eva Marie Garroutte, *Real Indians: Identity and the Survival of Native Americans* (Berkeley: University of California Press, 2003), 15.

6. Richard Monette, "Blood Quantum: Fractionated Land, Fractionated People," in *The Great Vanishing Act: Blood Quantum and the Future of Native Nations*, ed. Kathleen Ratteree and Norbert Hill (Golden, CO: Fulcrum, 2017), 246–49. See also the essay on this topic by Jessica Kolopenuk (Lyiniw), "NDN DNA," in *The Great Vanishing Act*, ed. Ratteree and Hill, 159–72.

7. Garroutte, *Real Indians*, 42.

8. Keene, "Love in the Time of Blood Quantum," in *The Great Vanishing Act*, ed. Ratteree and Hill, 9.

9. Suzan Shown Harjo, "Vampire Policy Is Bleeding Us Dry—Blood Quantum, Be Gone!" in *The Great Vanishing Act*, ed. Ratteree and Hill, 79.

10. See Ratteree and Hill, *The Great Vanishing Act*, for articles about this issue.

11. Telephone interview with Suzan Shown Harjo, August 3, 2018.

12. Shawn Boburg, "Donald Trump's Long History of Clashes with Native Americans," *Washington Post*, July 25, 2016.

13. The outcome of this internal conflict has ramifications for the other four "civilized tribes" (so called because of their propensity to adopt Western/European/White culture: Choctaw, Chickasaw, Seminoles, and Creek. There were twenty thousand Freedmen in these five tribes).

14. Scott Malcomson, *One Drop of Blood: The American Misadventure of Race* (New York: Farrar, Straus and Giroux, 2000), 89.

15. *Ibid.*, 90.

16. An alternative explanation of the motivation of the Cherokee Nation can be found in Julia Coates (Cherokee), "Race and Sovereignty," in *The Great Vanishing Act*, ed. Ratteree and Hill, 111–24.

17. Information for the summary of the conflict in the Cherokee Nation was obtained from Ellen Knickmeyer, "Cherokee Nation to Vote on Expelling Slaves' Descendants," *Washington Post*, March 3, 2007; Jenni Monet, "Linking Arms, Marching Forward: Cherokee Nation Accepts Ruling on Freedmen," *Indian Country Today*, September 1, 2017. For another dispute about the legitimacy of Native American ancestry and qualification for tribal status, see Brooke Jarvis, "Who Decides Who Counts as Native American?" *New York Times Magazine*, January 18, 2017, 53–60.

18. See, for example, Doug Kiel's (Oneida) discussion of intermarriage among the French and Indians. Doug Kiel, "Bleeding Out: Histories and Legacies of 'Indian Blood,'" in *The Great Vanishing Act*, ed. Ratteree and Hill, 80–97. Historian Brian Dippie also addressed this phenomenon in his analysis of changing policies and attitudes toward Native Americans in *The Vanishing American: White Attitudes and U.S. Indian Policy* (Lawrence: University of Kansas Press, 1982), 250–62.

19. Lizzie Wade, "Genetic Study Reveals Surprising Ancestry of Many Americans," *Science*, December 18, 2014, www.sciencemag.org/news/2014/12/genetic-study-reveals-surprising-ancestry-many-americans.

20. Wang, "Interracial Marriage."

21. Mrs. Mary Rowlandson, *The Narrative of the Captivity and Restoration of Mrs. Mary Rowlandson* (Project Gutenberg, 2009), Gutenberg.org/files/851/851-h/851-h.htm.

22. Another famous female captive story concerns Hannah Duston, taken captive along with neighbors in March 1697 by Abenaki Indians in Haverhill, Massachusetts. Her infant child was reportedly murdered by the marauding Indians during the attack. Duston, the mother of nine, and Mary Neff, a neighbor, along with a young boy seized in an earlier Indian raid, were staying unbound at the lodging of their captors two weeks after the raid when they tomahawked and scalped ten sleeping members of the Indian family, including six children, canoed down the Merrimack River with the ten scalps, and were presented with a 50-pound reward by the General Assembly of Massachusetts. Three monuments were later erected in her honor. See Barbara Cutter, "The Gruesome Story of Hannah Duston, Whose Slaying of Indians Made Her an American Folk 'Hero,'" *Smithsonian Magazine*, April 9, 2018, https://www.smithsonianmag.com/history/gruesome-story-hannah-duston-american-colonist-whose-slaying-indians-made-her-folk-hero-180968721/. This story reverberates throughout literary critic Leslie Fiedler's analysis of the condition of Native Americans in his *Return of the Vanishing American* (New York: Stein and Day, 1968).

23. Frederick Drimmer, ed., *Captured by the Indians: 15 Firsthand Accounts, 1750–1870* (New York: Dover Publications Inc., 1961).

24. For a summary of Mary Rowlandson's experiences, see her account, *The Narrative of the Captivity and Restoration of Mrs. Mary Rowlandson.*

Information about Herman Lehmann is available at "Indian Captives," *Texas State Historical Association*, https://tshaonline.org/handbook/online/articles/bxiol. A summary of Mary Jemison's experiences are in James E. Seaver, *A Narrative of the Life of Mrs. Mary Jemison* (Whitefish, MT: Kessinger Publishing, LLC, 2010). Kathryn O'Hara's analysis of White female captive narratives reveals that many of the women's stories were written by White males who distorted the events for the purpose of developing religious/evangelical themes. See Kathryn O'Hara, "Female Captive Narratives in Colonial America," *The Gettysburg Historical Journal* 8 (2009): 34–52.

25. Cited in Thomas C. Leonard, "The Reluctant Conquerors," *American Heritage* 27, no. 5 (August 1976): 36.

26. *Ibid.*

27. See Peter Cozzens, *The Earth Is Weeping: The Epic Story of the Indian Wars for the American West* (New York: Vintage Books, 2016), 337–441, for a summary of Sitting Bull's last hours.

28. For a summary of Indian wars in the American West, see *ibid.* A summary of earlier wars fought against Native Americans can be found in Alan Axelrod, *Chronicle of the Indian Wars: From Colonial Times to Wounded Knee* (New York: Konecky and Konecky, 1993).

29. Grey's *Riders of the Purple Sage* (New York: Grosset and Dunlap, 1912) was vehemently anti–Mormon and was made into four motion pictures (two without sound), and a television version was released in 1996.

30. Zane Grey, *The Vanishing American* (New York: Harper and Brothers, 1925; Project Gutenberg, 2013), 108, https://gutenberg.net.au/ebooks13/1304581h.html.

31. *Ibid.*, 129.

32. *Ibid.*, 153.

33. *Ibid.*

34. *Ibid.*, 225.

35. *Ibid.*, 205.

36. *Ibid.*, 265.

37. *Ibid.*, 266.

38. *Ibid.*, 27.

39. *Ibid.*, Mrs. Withers to Marian, 38.

40. *Ibid.*, 56.

41. *Ibid.*, 113–14.

42. *Ibid.*, 294.

Chapter 2

1. For a comprehensive overview of structural racism, see the Anti-Poverty Network of New Jersey's study *The Uncomfortable Truth: Racism, Injustice and Poverty*. A summary can be found at https://2750d32d-03da-445f-8576-8ae3f5da7b2f.filesusr.com/ugd/14a332_15c12850391c4e679068dace44768bdf.pdf. For an analysis of the effects of racism on contemporary Native Americans, see U.S. Commission on Civil Rights, *Broken Promises*.

2. The following discussion emphasizes the adverse social, political, economic, and health situation of Native Americans in our society. This so-called deficit position has been criticized for its lopsided depiction of the status of Indians, but the facts speak for themselves. A precondition for social change is the acknowledgment of inequality, and in the case of Native Americans, they have managed to survive centuries of disrespect and inhumane treatment by Euro-Americans.

3. For an analysis of recent shootings and violence against African Americans in the United States, see Marc Lamont Hill, *Nobody: Casualties of America's War on the Vulnerable, from Ferguson to Flint and Beyond* (New York: Atria, 2016).

4. For examples of this, see the Stormfront website, the oldest hate website in the United States, launched in 1996 by former Klansman Don Black, https://www.stormfront.org/forum, or newer online versions such as the alt-right equivalent of Twitter, Gab, 4Chan, and 8Chan and the messenger site Discord.

5. "On Views of Race and Inequality, Blacks and Whites Are Worlds Apart," *PEW Research Center*, June 27, 2016, www.pewsocialtrends.org/2016/06/27/on-views-of-race-and-inequality-blacks-and-whites-are-worlds-.

6. Information about the poll can be found at "White and Black Americans Far Apart on Racial Issues," *Ipsos*, August 27, 2020, https://www.ipsos.com/en-us/news-polls/npr-racial-inequality-issues. For a perceptive article about the ephemeral commitment of White people to eradicating systemic racism, see Kali Holloway, "The Whitelash Next Time," *The Nation*, September 21–28, 2020, 10–11.

7. Robert Wood Johnson Foundation, National Public Radio, and the T. H. Chan School of Public Health at Harvard University, *Discrimination in America: Experiences and Views of Native Americans*, November 2017, https://legacy.npr.org/documents/2017/nov/NPR-discrimination-native-americans-final.pdf. Bold added.

8. *Ibid.*

9. "The Partisan Divide on Political Values Grows Even Wider," *PEW Research Center*, October 5, 2017, www.people-press.org/2017/10/05/4-race-immigration-and-discrimination; Samantha Neal, "Views of Racism as a Major Problem Increase Sharply, Especially among Democrats," *PEW Research Center*, August 29, 2017, www.pewresearch.org/fact-tank/2017/08/29/views-of-racism-as-a-major-problem-increase-sharply-esp.

10. Results of the poll can be found at "Protestors' Anger Justified Even If Actions May Not Be," Monmouth University Polling Institute, June 2, 2020, https://www.monmouth.edu/polling-institute/reports/monmouthpoll_us_060220.

11. See National Public Radio media critic Eric Deggans's perceptive analysis of right-wing talk radio in his book *Race-Baiter* (New York: Palgrave

Macmillan, 2012). For an analysis of hate on the internet, see Jesse Daniels, *Cyber Racism: White Supremacy and the New Attack on Civil Rights* (Lanham, MD: Rowman and Littlefield, 2009). The Southern Poverty Law Center has linked one hundred murders to people who utilized the White supremacist, racist Stormfront website.

12. Ruha Benjamin, *Race after Technology: Abolitionist Tools for the New Jim Code* (Medford, MA: Polity Press, 2019).

13. See U.S. Commission on Civil Rights, *Broken Promises*, for an analysis of federal budget cuts to Native American programs proposed by the Trump administration.

14. For a review of this research, see Project Implicit, https://implicit.harvard.edu/implicit/education.html.

15. U.S. Commission on Civil Rights, *Broken Promises*, 155.

16. *Ibid.*, 158.

17. *Ibid.*, 183.

18. U.S. Commission on Civil Rights, *A Quiet Crisis: Federal Funding and Unmet Needs in Indian Country*, July 2003, https://www.usccr.gov/pubs/na0703/na0204.pdf.

19. *Ibid.*, ix.

20. *Ibid.*

21. *Ibid.*, xii.

22. U.S. Commission on Civil Rights, *Broken Promises*.

23. *Ibid.*, Letter of Transmittal by Catherine E. Lhamon, Chair of the Commission.

24. *Ibid.*, 6.

25. Cited in U.S. Commission on Civil Rights, *Broken Promises*, 136.

26. *Ibid.*

27. *Ibid.*

28. *Ibid.*, 137.

29. Terry Anderson, "The Wealth of (Indian) Nations," *Defining Ideas: A Hoover Institution Journal* (October 25, 2016), https://www.hoover.org/research/wealth-indian-nations-1.

30. Nancy Pindus, G. Thomas Kingsley, Jennifer Biess, Diane Levy, Jasmine Simington, and Christopher Hayes, *Housing Needs of American Indians and Alaskan Natives in Tribal Areas: A Report from the Assessment of American Indian, Alaska Native, and Native Hawaiian Housing Needs*, Office of Policy Development and Research, U.S. Department of Housing and Urban Development, January 19, 2017, https://www.huduser.gov/portal/publications/HNAIHousingNeeds.html.

Additionally, there is a curious disclaimer at the beginning of the HUD report on the housing needs of Native Americans: "The contents of this report are the views of the authors and do not necessarily reflect the views or policies of the U.S. Department of Housing and Urban Development or the U.S. government." It did not augur well for the future support of Native American projects under the Trump administration.

31. Craig Harris and Dennis Wagner, "HUD: Housing Conditions for Native Americans Much Worse than Rest of U.S.," The Republic, *AZ Central*, January 19, 2017, https://www.azcentral.com/story/news/local/arizona-investigations/2017/01/19/new-hud-reports-find-housing-conditions-worse-among-native-americans/96783368/.

32. Vijaya Ramachandran and Julie Walz, "Is Haiti Doomed to Be the Republic of NGOs?" *Center for Global Development*, January 9, 2012, https://www.cgdev.org/blog/haiti-doomed-be-republic-ngos.

33. For an account of the Shoney's case, see Steve Watkins, *The Black O* (Athens: University of Georgia Press, 1997).

34. U.S. Department of Equal Employment Opportunity, "Charge Statistics (Charges Filed with EEOC) FY 1997 through FY 2020," http://www.eeoc.gov/eeoc/statistics/enforcement/charges.cfm.

35. Kevin McCoy, "Honda to Pay $25M," *Asbury Park Press*, July 15, 2015, 4B.

36. Nearly four in ten Native Americans reported experiencing racial slurs or offensive comments in the NPR/Harvard/Robert Wood Johnson study *Discrimination in America: Experiences and Views of Native Americans*, and nearly a quarter were told that they were unwelcome in a neighborhood because of their ethnicity. Robert Wood Johnson Foundation, National Public Radio, and the T. H. Chan School of Public Health at Harvard University, *Discrimination in America*.

37. *Ibid.*, 8–11.

38. Stacy Jones, "White Men Account for 72 percent of Corporate Leadership at 16 of the Fortune 500 Companies," *Fortune*, June 9, 2017, fortune.com/2017/06/09/white-men-senior-executives-fortune-500-companies-diversity-data.

39. U.S. Commission on Civil Rights, *Broken Promises*, 114–15.

40. Government Accounting Office, *Indian Affairs: Better Management and Accountability Needed to Improve Indian Education*, Report to the Chairman, Subcommittee on Interior, Environment, and Related Agencies, Committee on Appropriations, House of Representatives, September 24, 2013, https://www.gao.gov/assets/gao-13-774.pdf.

41. Helen Olife, "Graduation Rates and American Indian Education," *Partnership with Native Americans* (blog), May 16, 2017, blog.nativepartnership.org/graduation-rates-american-indian-education.

42. U.S. Commission on Civil Rights, *Broken Promises*, 119.

43. One of the most famous and significant projects confirming the importance of early childhood education was the HighScope project, https://highscope.org/perry-preschool-project/.

44. U.S. Commission on Civil Rights, *Broken Promises*, 118.

45. *Ibid.*, 108–09.

46. The letter is available at https://www2.ed.gov/about/offices/list/ocr/letters/colleague-201401-title-vi.html.

47. Dylan Scott, "Covid-19's Devastating Toll on Black and Latino Americans, in One Chart," *Vox*, April 14, 2020, https://www.vox.com/2020/4/17/21225610/us-coronavirus-death-rates-blacks-latinos-whites.

48. Dr. Michelle Tom interview with Meghna Chakrabarti on NPR's *On Point*, May 26, 2020, https://www.wbur.org/onpoint/2020/05/26/native-american-communities-coronavirus.

49. A particularly touching act of kindness was recorded during the pandemic. Money was being received (over $500,000) by Native Americans from unknown people in Ireland. The gifts were given to the Navajo and Hopi tribes as a thank you for the generosity of the Choctaw people who donated $170 in 1847 (equal to $5,000 today) to assist the Irish people during their struggle for survival in the potato famine. The original gift was particularly poignant because it came from Indians who had recently survived the infamous "Trail of Tears." See Ed O'Loughlin and Mihir Zaveri, "Irish Return Old Favor, Helping Native Americans Battling the Virus," *New York Times*, May 5, 2020, https://www.nytimes.com/2020/05/05/world/coronavirus-ireland-native-american-tribes.html.

50. Institute of Medicine Committee on Understanding and Eliminating Racial and Ethnic Disparities in Health Care, *Unequal Treatment: Confronting Racial and Ethnic Disparities in Health Care*, ed. Brian D. Smedley, Adrienne Y. Smith, and Alan R. Nelson (Washington, D.C.: National Academies Press, 2003), 1.

51. Carmen R. Green, S. Khady Ndao-Brumblay, Brady West, and Tamika Washington, "Differences in Prescription Opioid Analgesic Availability: Comparing Minority and White Pharmacies across Michigan," *The Journal of Pain* 6, no. 10 (October 2005): 689–99.

52. U.S. Department of Health and Human Services, "Disparities," Indian Health Service, October 2019, https://www.ihs.gov/newsroom/factsheets/disparities/.

53. U.S. Commission on Civil Rights, *Broken Promises*, 62.

54. *Ibid.*, 73.

55. U.S. Commission on Civil Rights, *Broken Promises*, 66.

56. National Council of Urban Indian Health, "NCUIH's Response to President Trump's FY 20 Budget Request," Press Release, March 3, 2019. The Biden Administration provided an additional $31 billion for COVID-19 relief to the Indian Health Service.

57. See the discussion of this in Tim Wise, *Color-Blind* (San Francisco: City Lights Books, 2010).

58. Audrey Smedley, *Race in North America: Origin and Evolution of a Worldview*, 2nd ed. (Boulder, CO: Westview Press, 1999), 330.

59. One expert noted that Native American children have rates of post-traumatic stress disorder as high as returning veterans from Iraq and Afghanistan and triple the rate of the general population in the United States. U.S. Commission on Civil Rights, *Broken Promises*, 76.

60. For a fascinating summary of this proposition, see Mary Annette Pember, *Intergenerational Trauma: Understanding Natives' Inherited Pain* (Indian Country Today Media Network, 2016), https://amber-ic.org/wp-content/uploads/2017/01/ICMN-All-About-Generations-Trauma.pdf. To understand the mechanics of epimutations that may occur from environmental stressors and the science of epigenetics, see the article by biologist Michael K. Skinner, "A New Kind of Inheritance," *Scientific American* 311, no. 2 (August 2014): 44–51.

61. See the review of the founding of our society in Joe R. Feagin, *White Party, White Government* (New York: Routledge, 2012).

62. As we noted earlier, Senator Elizabeth Warren (D–Massachusetts) claimed to have Native American ancestry, but it is an infinitesimal amount, and she has apologized for overstating her claim, yet President Trump continued to ridicule her about this, pejoratively referring to her as Pocahontas.

63. William Julius Wilson, *More than Just Race: Being Black and Poor in the Inner City* (New York: W. W. Norton and Company, 2009).

64. One of the most shocking illustrations of this belief was the cruel treatment of Black women who underwent gynecological procedures *without anesthesia* by the so-called founder of gynecology, J. Marion Sims, in the mid–1800s. See Barron H. Lerner, "Scholars Argue Over Legacy of Surgeon Who Was Lionized, Then Vilified," *New York Times*, October 28, 2003, https://www.nytimes.com/2003/10/28/health/scholars-argue-over-legacy-of-surgeon-who-was-lionized-then-vilified.html. A statue of him was removed from Central Park in New York City in April 2017.

65. John Strausbaugh, *Black Like You* (New York: Jeremy P. Tarcher/Penguin, 2006), 10.

66. Joe R. Feagin, *The White Racial Frame* (New York: Routledge, 2010).

Chapter 3

1. Ivan Hannaford, *Race: The History of an Idea in the West* (Baltimore: The Johns Hopkins University Press, 1996).

2. Thomas F. Gossett, *Race: The History of an Idea in America*, new ed. (New York: Oxford University Press, 1997). Ibram X. Kendi, in his award-winning analysis of the history of racist ideas in America, attempts to link the origin of racism to the writing of a Portuguese biographer, Gomes Eanes de Zurara, who defended slave trading through anti-Black, racist concepts. The issue is not whether his ideas provided the

underpinning of modern racism, but how such values and sentiments were infused and continue to surface in contemporary Western society, even when purveyors of these stereotypes *have not read or seen the primordial source*. See Ibram X. Kendi, *Stamped from the Beginning: The Definitive History of Racist Ideas in America* (New York: Nation Books, 2016), 22–30.

3. Hannaford, *Race*, 80.

4. Donald G. McNeil, Jr. "Finding a Scapegoat When Epidemics Strike," *New York Times*, August 31, 2009.

5. Oliver Goldsmith, *A History of the Earth and Animated Nature*, vol. 1 (York: Thomas Wilson and Son, 1808), 346–56.

6. For an elaboration of this point, see Adrian Desmond and James Moore, *Darwin's Sacred Cause* (Boston: Houghton Mifflin Harcourt, 2009).

7. See Gallup, "Poll: Evolution, Creationism, Intelligent Design," 2019, https://news.gallup.com/poll/21814/evolution-creationism-intelligent-design.aspx; Ed Stoddard, "Poll Finds More Americans Believe in Devil than Darwin," *Reuters*, November 29, 2007, https://www.reuters.com/article/us-usa-religion-beliefs/poll-finds-more-americans-believe-in-devil-than-darwin-idUSN2922875820071129.

8. Francois Leguat, *The Voyage of Francois Leguat (1708)*, 2 vols. (London: Pasfield Oliver, 1891); Daniel Beeckman, *A Voyage to and From the Island of Borneo* (London: T. Warneretal, 1719); Thomas Herbert, *Some Years Travels into Divers Parts of Asia and Africa* (London: Jacob Blome and Richard Bishop, 1638; Internet Archive, 2020). https://archive.org/details/dli.venugopal.476.

9. Francois Leguat, quoted in Francis Moran III, "Between Primates and Primitives: Natural Man as the Missing Link in Rousseau's *Second Discourse*," in *Philosophers on Race*, ed. Julie K. Ward and Tommy L. Lott (Oxford: Blackwell Publishers, 2002), 132.

10. *Ibid.*, 139. See the excellent summary of European conceptions of Indigenous peoples by Guido Abbattista, "European Encounters in the Age of Expansion," *European History Online*, January 24, 2011, http://ieg-ego.eu/en/threads/backgrounds/european-encounters/guido-abbattista-european-encounters-in-the-age-of-expansion.

11. John Block Friedman, *The Monstrous Races in Medieval Art and Thought* (Cambridge, MA: Harvard University Press, 1981), 207.

12. Hannaford, *Race*, 91.

13. For an elaboration of these themes, see David Goldenberg, *The Curse of Ham: Race and Slavery in Early Judaism, Christianity, and Islam* (Princeton, NJ: Princeton University Press, 2005); Stephen R. Haynes, *The Curse of Noah: The Biblical Justification for American Slavery* (New York: Oxford University Press, 2002).

14. Hannaford, *Race*, 91.

15. See Cotton Mather's *Decennium Luctuosum: An History of Remarkable Occurrences, In the Long War....*where he labels Indians as sorcerers and "hellish conjurers, and such as conversed with demons" (Boston: B. Green and J. Allen, 1699), https://quod.lib.umich.edu/e/evans/N00725.0001.001?view=toc.

16. See Zvi Ben-Dor Benite, "Mormon Scripture and the Lost Tribes of Israel," *Bible Odyssey*, https://www.bibleodyssey.org/en/places/related-articles/mormon-scripture-and-the-lost-tribes-of-israel. Theology professor Stephen Haynes also raised the possibility that other Protestant religions might have embraced the lost tribe argument to explain the presence of Native Americans. See Haynes, *The Curse of Noah*, 144–45.

17. Hannaford, *Race*, 167.

18. Nancy Shoemaker, "How Indians Got to Be Red," *The American Historical Review* 102, no. 3 (June 1997): 625–44.

19. Beeckman, cited in Moran, "Between Primates and Primitives," 131.

20. Cited in Moran, "Between Primates and Primitives," 131.

21. Goldsmith, *A History of the Earth and Animated Nature*, vol. 1, 356.

22. Henry Home, *Sketches of the History of Man*, vol. 1, "Preliminary Discourse, Concerning the Origin of Men and Languages" (Dublin: James Williams, no. 21, 1779), 13.

23. *Ibid.*, 14.

24. Roxanne Dunbar-Ortiz, "The Grid of History: Cowboys and Indians," *Monthly Review*, March 27, 2003, ouleft.sp-mesolite.tilted.net/?p=1295.

25. Friedman, *The Monstrous Races*, 30.

26. James H. Merrell, *Into the American Woods: Negotiators on the Pennsylvania Frontier* (New York: W. W. Norton, 1999), 20–23.

27. Robert A. Williams, Jr., *Savage Anxieties: The Invention of Western Civilization* (New York: St. Martin's Press, 2012).

28. *Ibid.*, 156.

29. "The Bull *Inter Caetera* (Alexander VI), May 4, 1493," http://www.nativeweb.org/pages/legal/indig-inter-caetera.html.

30. Bartolomé de Las Casas, *A Brief Account of the Destruction of the Indies*, https://manybooks.net/titles/casasb2032120321-8.html; David E. Stannard, *American Holocaust: The Conquest of the New World* (New York: Oxford University Press, 1992).

31. "Papal Bull *Sublimus Dei*: On the Enslavement and Evangelization of Indians," Pope Paul III, 1537, https://www.papalencyclicals.net/paul03/p3subli.htm.

32. See an excerpt of the English writer and historian Richard Hakluyt that represents these sentiments, "Reasons for Colonization, 1585," http:11therailsplitter.wikispaces.com/file/view/Ch.+2+Hakluyt+and+Frethorne.pdf.

33. See, for example, his *The Principal Navigations, Voyages, Traffiques and Discoveries of the*

English Nation, ed. and abridged by Jack Beeching (New York: Penguin Classics, 1972), and an analysis of his writing in *Richard Hakluyt and Travel Writing in Early Modern Europe*, ed. Claire Jowitt and Daniel Carey (Surrey, UK: Ashgate, 2012).

34. Richard Hakluyt, "The Second Voyage to Guinea Set Out by Sir George Barne, Sir John Yorke, Thomas Lok, Anthonie Hickman and Edward Castelin, in the year 1554," in Richard Hakluyt, *The Principal Navigations, Voyages, Traffiques and Discoveries of the English Nation*, ed. Edmund Goldsmid (Adelaide: University of Adelaide, 2012, originally published 1598–1600).

35. *Ibid.*

36. This letter was written by Sir George Peckham pertaining to Sir Humphrey Gilbert's expedition to Newfoundland in 1583 for England. It was published in Richard Hakluyt's *The Principal Navigations, Voyages, Traffiques, and Discoveries of the English Nation*, vol. XIII, America, Part II, ebooks.adelaide.edu.au/h/Hakluyt/voyages/index.htm.

37. Originally appeared in Arthur Helps, *The Spanish Conquest in America*, cited in Stannard, *American Holocaust*, 66.

38. Russell Thornton, *American Indian Holocaust and Survival: A Population History since 1492* (Norman: University of Oklahoma Press, 1987).

39. Roxanne Dunbar-Ortiz and Dina Gilio-Whitaker, *"All the Real Indians Died Off" and 20 Other Myths about Native Americans* (Boston: Beacon Press, 2016), 29.

40. "The Bull *Romanus Pontifex* (Nicholas V), January 8, 1455," https://www.nativeweb.org/pages/legal/indig-romanus-pontifex.html.

41. For examples of this behavior, see David A. Price, *Love and Hate in Jamestown* (New York: Alfred A. Knopf, 2007), 19, 272–73n8.

42. Dunbar-Ortiz and Gilio-Whitaker, *"All the Real Indians Died Off,"* 51–57.

43. Stephen Jay Gould, *The Mismeasure of Man* (New York: Norton, 1996).

44. Cited in William Blanton, *The Leopard's Spots: Scientific Attitudes toward Race in America, 1815–1859* (Chicago: University of Chicago Press, 1960), 41. See this book for an extended discussion of Morton's work and the endeavors of nineteenth-century scientists before Darwin to delineate the origin and varieties of humans.

45. Desmond and Moore, *Darwin's Sacred Cause.*

46. Charles Darwin, *On the Origin of the Species* (London: Murray, 1859); Charles Darwin, *The Descent of Man*, 2 vols. (London: Murray, 1871).

47. See Riazat Butt, "Half of Britons Do Not Believe in Evolution, Survey Finds," *The Guardian*, February 1, 2009. See also David Quammen, "Was Darwin Wrong?" *National Geographic Magazine*, November 2014, https://www.nationalgeographic.com/magazine/article/was-darwin-wrong.

48. Joseph-Arthur Comte de Gobineau, *The Moral and Intellectual Diversity of Races* (Philadelphia: J. B. Lippincott, 1856).

49. Joseph-Arthur Comte de Gobineau, *The Inequality of Human Races*, trans. Adrian Collins (London: William Heinemann, 1915), xiii. Originally published in 1854, https://archive.org/stream/inequalityofhuma00gobi/inequalityofhuma00gobi_djvu.txt.

50. *Ibid.*, 9.

51. *Ibid.*, 25.

52. *Ibid.*, 53.

53. *Ibid.*, 75.

54. *Ibid.*, 85.

55. *Ibid.*, 107.

56. *Ibid.*, 107.

57. *Ibid.*, 36–37.

58. *Ibid.*, 45.

59. *Ibid.*, 149.

60. *Ibid.*, 173.

61. *Ibid.*, 150.

62. *Ibid.*, 207.

63. *Ibid.*

64. *Ibid.*, 210.

65. Lothrop Stoddard, *The Revolt of Civilization: The Menace of the Underman* (New York: Charles Scribner's Sons, 1922), 223.

66. Madison Grant, *The Passing of the Great Race: Or the Racial Basis of European History*, 4th ed. (New York: Charles Scribner's Sons, 1921), xix. Originally published in 1914.

67. Associated Press, "What Did Donald Trump Say about Immigrants?" *Boston Globe*, June 29, 2015, https://www.bostonglobe.com/arts/television/2015/06/29/what-did-donald-trump-say-about-immigrants/Foraqp QHjwgeKRdVUdYrdM/story.html.

68. Haeyoun Park and Larry Buchanan, "Why It Takes Two Years for Syrian Refugees to Enter the U.S.," *New York Times*, November 20, 2015, https://www.nytimes.com/interactive/2015/11/20/us/why-it-takes-two-years-for-syrian-refugees-to-apply-to-enter-the-united-states.html?m&mtrref=undefined&gwh=5BDDC B04EA1FE43BF3A4C6B7EF208C88&gwt=regi&a ssetType=REGIWALL.

69. Michael Denning, *Mechanic Accents: Dime Novels and Working-Class Culture in America* (New York: Verso, 1987), 50–51.

70. Auguste Comte, *A General View of Positivism*, trans. J. H. Bridges (1865; Cambridge, UK: Cambridge University Press, 2009; Project Gutenberg, 2016), https://www.gutenberg.org/ebooks/53799; Herbert Spencer, *Social Statics* (London: John Chapman, 1851; Online Library of Liberty), https://oll.libertyfund.org/titles/spencer-social-statics-1851.

71. "Trump's Aide's Son Denounces Obama Comments," *Tampa Bay Times*, December 26, 2017, 8A.

72. "Active Hate Groups in the United States," Southern Poverty Law Center. This organization is currently tracking nearly 1,900 far-right extremist

groups in the United States. For more information on hate groups, go to https://www.splcenter.org.

73. "The Writings of George Washington," 392, https://babel.hathitrust.org/cgi/pt?num=393&seq=445&view=image&size=100&id=msu.312931045. Nevertheless, when four of the five Haudenosaunee (Iroquois) tribes sided with the British in the American Revolution, Washington ordered General John Sullivan to destroy forty of their towns and crops in 1779. Washington is still referred to as "Hanadahqoyus" (town destroyer) by them.

74. Levi Rickert, "U.S. Presidents in Their Own Words Concerning American Indians," *Native News Online*, February 19, 2018, https://nativenewsonline.net/currents/us-presidents-in-their-own-words-concerning-american-indians.

75. Thomas Jefferson, *Notes on the State of Virginia*, 150–51 (Chapel Hill, NC: Documenting the American South, University of North Carolina at Chapel Hill, 1785), https://docsouth.unc.edu/southlit/jefferson/jefferson.html.

76. *Ibid.*, 151–52.

77. *Ibid.*, 154–55.

78. Henry Wiencek, "Master of Monticello," *Smithsonian* Magazine, October 2012, 47.

79. Jefferson in a letter to John Eppes, 1820, cited in Kendi, *Stamped from the Beginning*, 136.

80. Thomas Jefferson, *Autobiography of Thomas Jefferson 1743–1790* (New York: G. P. Putnam's Sons, 1914), 77.

81. Material on Sacagawea was derived from: "Sacagawea," *History.com*, https://www.history.com/topics/native-american-history/sacagawea; "Sacagawea Biography," *Biography*, https://www.biography.com/people/sacagawea-9468731; PBS, "Sacagawea," *Lewis and Clark: The Journey of the Corps of Discovery*, www.pbs.org/lewisandclark/inside/saca.html.

82. April White, "Written Out of History," *Smithsonian* Magazine, March 2019, 14.

83. "From James Madison to the Delegations of Several Indian Nations, [ca. August 22] 1812," *Founders Online*, National Archives, founders.archives.gov/documents/Madison/03-05-02-0137.

84. Cited in "The Madison Administration," Lumen, Boundless US History, courses.lumenlearning.com/boundless-ushistory/chapter/the-madison-administration.

85. In his *Notes on the History of Virginia*, Jefferson wrongly concluded that the "aborigines [Indians] never submitted themselves to any laws, any coercive power, any shadow of government."

86. See Las Casas, *A Brief Account of the Destruction of the Indies*, for descriptions of their depredations.

87. "U.S. Presidents in Their Own Words Concerning American Indians," *Native News Online*, February 19, 2018, https://nativenewsonline.net/currents/us-presidents-in-their-own-words-concerning-american-indians.

88. Kendi, *Stamped from the Beginning*, 161–260.

89. Roy P. Basler, ed., "Fourth Debate with Stephen A. Douglas at Charleston, Illinois, September 18, 1858," in *The Collected Works of Abraham Lincoln*, vol. 3 (New Brunswick, NJ: Rutgers University Press, 1953), 145–46.

90. See chapter 15 for a fuller discussion of these events.

91. Christopher W. Anderson, "Native Americans and the Origin of Abraham Lincoln's Views on Race," *Journal of the Abraham Lincoln Association* 37, no. 1 (Winter 2016): 11–29.

92. W. Dale Mason, "The Indian Policy of Abraham Lincoln," *Indigenous Policy Journal*, December 16, 2009, https://ipjournal.wordpress.com/2009/12/16/the-indian-policy-of-abraham-lincoln/.

93. "The Pacific Railway: A Brief History of Building the Transcontinental Railroad," *The Transcontinental Railroad: Bridges, Tunnels, Rails, Rail Cars, Locomotives, Landmarks, Maps, Explosives, & More*, https://railroad.lindahall.org/essays/brief-history.html.

Chapter 4

1. For a summary of this case, see Rose Eveleth, "Genetic Testing and Tribal Identity," *The Atlantic*, January 26, 2015, https://www.theatlantic.com/technology/archive/2015/01/the-cultural-limitations-of-genetic-testing/384740/. A theatrical play, *Informed Consent*, by Deborah Zoe Laufer, was written about this case. Some skeptics question the validity of the Bering Strait theory as it pertains to the origin of Native Americans. A critique of the theory was written by Alex Ewen in which he methodically debunks the accuracy of and motivation for promoting it. Ewen reviewed studies that traced the ancestors of modern Indians in the continental United States over thirty thousand years, more than twice the time that the Clovis people were thought to occupy these lands. Linguistic diversity and DNA research also point to the possibility that ancient ancestors of modern Native Americans came to this continent earlier and through other means than walking across the purported trans–Siberian land bridge, an area known as Beringia. See Alex Ewen, *The Bering Strait Theory* (Phoenix, AZ: Indian Country Media Network, April 25, 2017) (ebook).

On the other hand, scientists at the University of Michigan analyzed genetic variation among 29 Native populations in 678 locations in North, Central, and South America and found evidence that supports the land bridge theory by demonstrating a genetic similarity between two Siberian groups and Native Americans. The similarity decreased the further a Native population was from the Bering Strait. They concluded that the first Americans came from a single source in a single or multiple migrations. See University of Michigan

Health System, "Gene Study Supports Single Main Migration Across Bering Strait," *Science Daily*, November 28, 2017, https://www.sciencedaily.com/releases/2007/11/071126170543.htm. Bolstering the Bering Strait migration theory is a recent scientific report that identified a gene linking East Asians and Native Americans more than twenty thousand years ago. The growth of shovel-shaped incisors and breast duct formation was found to be identical in all Native Americans and 40 percent of Asians studied. See "Surviving the Bering Strait," *American History* 53, no. 4 (October 2018): 10.

2. The Dawes Act led to fractionated tribal lands throughout the country until a Department of the Interior buy-back program was initiated in 2013. Funded with nearly $2 billion, 105 locations were identified as candidates for the buy-back consolidation program. Over two million acres from 680,000 fractionated landowners were donated to tribes by 2017, but the Trump administration sought drastic cuts to funds allocated for the repurchase of Native American lands. See Rob Capriccioso, "Trump Budget Serves Deep Cuts in Many Indian Areas," *Indian Country Today*, June 6, 2017; Renae Ditmer, "Will President Trump Eliminate the BIA?" *Indian Country Today*, June 9, 2017.

3. Eveleth, "Genetic Testing and Tribal Identity."

4. *Ibid.*

5. *Ibid.* Also, see her book *Native American DNA: Tribal Belonging and the False Promise of Genetic Science* (Minneapolis: University of Minnesota Press, 2013).

6. Cited in Stan Steiner, *The New Indians* (New York: Harper and Row, 1968), 77.

7. *Ibid.*

8. For an analysis of the historical demographic trends concerning the decline of Indigenous people in the Americas, see Stannard, *American Holocaust*; Michael R. Haines and Richard H. Steckel, *A Population History of North America* (New York: Cambridge University Press, 2000); Thornton, *American Indian Holocaust and Survival*. Thornton attributed the dramatic decline of the Indigenous population primarily to the lack of resistance that Native people had to infectious and communicable diseases introduced by Europeans, especially smallpox. Other pernicious diseases not found on the North American continent at the time of first contact were cholera, measles, pleurisy, whooping cough, scarlet fever, mumps, gonorrhea, diphtheria, malaria, the bubonic plague, some strains of influenza, typhoid fever, and alcoholism. Thornton claimed that Native Americans were relatively healthy prior to first contact and stated: "The European conquest of the American Indian was initially a medical conquest, one that paved the way for the more well known and glorified military conquests and colonizations" (47). And Stannard noted that Native Americans experienced ninety-three serious

epidemics and pandemics brought over from the Old World from the early sixteenth century until the early part of the twentieth century (45). On the other hand, Stannard accentuated the savagery of the Spaniards' military exploits and their impact on the Indigenous population. See, especially, chapters 3 and 4 in Stannard, *American Holocaust*. See also Dean R. Snow, Nancy Gonlin, and Peter S. Siegel, *Archaeology of Native North America*, 2nd ed. (Milton Park, UK: Taylor and Francis, 2019).

9. Alexander Koch, Chris Brienley, Mark M. Maslin, and Simon Lewis, "Earth System Impacts of the European Arrival and Great Dying in the Americas after 1492," *Quaternary Science Reviews* 207 (March 1, 2019): 13–36.

10. For further information about the sordid side of Columbus, see Ed Burmila, "The Invention of Christopher Columbus, American Hero," *The Nation*, October 9, 2017, https://www.thenation.com/article/the-invention-of-christopher-columbus-american-hero.

11. For a summary of this issue, see Katie Mettler, "Vermont to Abolish Columbus Day in Favor of Indigenous Peoples' Day," *Tampa Bay Times*, April 21, 2019, 6A.

12. For a description of events that unfolded in the early years of the Jamestown colony, see Price, *Love and Hate in Jamestown*.

13. This event supports evidence of cannibalism among Jamestown colonists noted later in this text as well as Price's version of the events that led to this behavior. Price, *Love and Hate in Jamestown*, chapter 9.

14. John Smith, *The General Historie of Virginia, New England, and the Summer Isles: With the Names* (London: I. D. and I. H. for Michael Sparks, 1624; Documenting the American South, University of North Carolina at Chapel Hill), https://docsouth.unc.edu/southlit/smith/menu.html.

15. This information was gathered from the following sources as well as John Smith's journal cited above: "A History of Jamestown," Jamestown Settlement & American Revolution Museum at Yorktown, www.historyisfun.org/jamestown-settlement/history-jamestown/; "Pocahontas," *History.com*, www.history.com/topics/native-american-history/pocahontas; "The True Story of Pocahontas as Not Told by Disney," *Ancient Origins*, www.ancient-origins.net/history-famous-people/true-story-pocahontas-not-told-disney-002285; "Pocahontas," *Biography*, https://www.biography.com/people/pocahontas-9443116; Vincent Schilling, "The True Story of Pocahontas: Historical Myths versus Sad Reality," *Indian Country Today*, March 21, 2017, https://indiancountrytoday.com/archive/true-story-pocahontas-historical-myths-versus-sad-reality. For a dramatic recreation of Smith's near-death encounter, see Price, *Love and Hate in Jamestown*, chapter 5. A more benign and traditional version of the life of Pocahontas and her relationships

with John Smith and the English colonists can be found in Price, *Love and Hate in Jamestown*.

16. Price, *Love and Hate in Jamestown*, 215.

17. Information about Squanto was obtained from: "Squanto 1580–1622," *Biography*, https://www.biography.com/political-figure/squanto; "Squanto: Native American Interpreter and Guide," *Britannica*, https://www.britannica.com/biography/squanto; "Squanto: The Former Slave," *History of Massachusetts Blog*, https://historyofmassachusetts.org/squanto-the-former-slave/; "Tisquantum ('Squanto')," *Mayflower-History.com*, http://mayflowerhistory.com/tisquantum.

18. Information about the sale of Manhattan was gathered from: Matt Soniak, "Was Manhattan Really Bought for $24?" *Mental Floss*, October 2, 2012, mentalfloss.com/article/12657/was-manhattan-really-bought-24; Janos Marton, "Today in NYC History: How the Dutch Actually Bought Manhattan (The Long Version)," *Untapped New York*, https://untappedcities.com/2015/05/06/today-in-nyc-history-how-the-dutch-actually-bought-manhattan-the-long-version/.

Chapter 5

1. Jared Diamond, *Guns, Germs and Steel: The Fates of Human Societies* (New York: W. W. Norton and Co., 1999), 67–68.

2. Las Casas, *A Brief Account of the Destruction of the Indies*.

3. *Ibid.*

4. Stannard, *American Holocaust*, 95.

5. Enrique Dussel, "Bartolomé de Las Casas," *Encyclopedia Britannica*, www.britannica.com/EBchecked/topic/330804/Bartolome-de-Las-Casas.

6. Diamond, *Guns, Germs and Steel*, 78.

7. "Trebuchet," www.lordsandladies.org/trebuchet.htm.

8. Smith, *The General Historie of Virginia*, 9.

9. Quoted in Charles Francis Adams, *Three Episodes of Massachusetts History* (Boston: Houghton Mifflin Company, 1892), 132–33.

10. Peter d'Errico, "Jeffrey Amherst and Smallpox Blankets: Germ Warfare Against American Indians," http://www.nativeweb.org/pages/legal/amherst/lord_jeff.html.

11. Frederick Zackel, "Robinson Crusoe and the Ethnic Sidekick," *Bright Lights Film Journal*, October 1, 2000, https://brightlightsfilm.com/robinson-crusoe-ethnic-sidekick/#.Yd29JRPMLxs.

12. See *ibid.*, and Ian Watt, "Robinson Crusoe as a Myth," *Essays in Criticism* 1, no. 2 (1951): 95–119.

13. Cited in Zackel, "Robinson Crusoe and the Ethnic Sidekick."

14. Watt, "Robinson Crusoe as a Myth."

15. Daniel Defoe, *The Life and Strange Surprising Adventures of Robinson Crusoe of York, Mariner* (eBooks@Adelaide), http://ebooks.adelaide.edu.au/d/defoe/Daniel/d31r/, 139.

16. *Ibid.*, 140.

17. *Ibid.*, 212.

18. *Ibid.*, 216.

19. *Ibid.*, 220.

20. *Ibid.*

21. *Ibid.*, 220–21.

22. *Ibid.*, 257.

23. Compare the comments of Donald Sterling, former owner of the Los Angeles Clippers basketball team, and his revulsion at seeing his girlfriend appearing with African Americans.

24. Defoe, *The Life and Strange Surprising Adventures of Robinson Crusoe*, 263.

25. *Ibid.*, 265.

26. *Ibid.*, 265–66.

27. *Ibid.*, 276.

28. *Ibid.*, 268.

29. *Ibid.*, 269.

30. Peter Martyr d'Anghiera, *De Orbe Novo, The First Decade*, book 1, trans. Francis Augustus Mac Nutt (1516; Project Gutenberg, 2004), www.gutenberg.org/files/12425/12425-h/12425-h.htm.

31. W. Arens, *The Man-Eating Myth* (New York: Oxford University Press, 1979), 182.

32. *Ibid.*, 139.

33. Crusoe was thought to inhabit an island off Trinidad near the Orinoco River.

34. Basil A. Reid, *Myths and Realities of Caribbean History* (Tuscaloosa: University of Alabama Press, 2009), 88.

35. Sarah Everts, "Europe's Hypocritical History of Cannibalism," *Smithsonian* Magazine, April 24, 2013, https://www.smithsonianmag.com/history/europes-hypocritical-history-of-cannibalism-42642371/. Evidence of cannibalism in the Jamestown settlement is also presented in this issue. For more information about cannibalism in the Jamestown colony, see the description of the "Starving Time" (1609–10) in the colony by George Percy, "Jamestown: 1609–10: 'Starving Time,'" National Humanities Center, nationalhumanitiescenter.org/pds/amerbegin/settlement/text2/jamestownpercyrelation.pdf, and George Percy, Journal Entry about Jamestown, Virtual Jamestown, etext.lib.virginia.edu/etcbin/Jamestown-browsemod?id=J1063.

36. Bill Schutt, *Cannibalism: A Perfectly Natural History* (Chapel Hill, NC: Algonquin Books, 2017), 108.

37. *Ibid.*, 119.

Chapter 6

1. Gobineau, *The Inequality of Human Races*, 173.

2. Cited in Robert F. Berkhofer, Jr., *The White Man's Indian: Images of the American Indian from Columbus to the Present* (New York: Vintage Books, 1978), 7.

3. *Ibid.*, 8–9.

4. *Ibid.*, 36–37.

5. *Ibid.*, xv.

6. Smedley, *Race in North America*, 54.

7. *Ibid.*, 61. Mohamed M. Keshavjee also discusses the English penchant for demonizing people of color in South Africa in *Into That Heaven of Freedom* (Toronto: Mawenzi House Publishers, Ltd., 2015).

8. Mark Twain, "Fenimore Cooper's Literary Offenses" (1895), http://twain.lib.virginia.edu/projects/rissetto/offense.html.

9. Leslie A. Fiedler, "James Fenimore Cooper: The Problem of the Good Bad Writer," Paper Presented at the Second Cooper Seminar, *James Fenimore Cooper: His Country and His Art*, State University of New York College at Oneonta, July 1979.

10. *Ibid.*

11. Robert M. Bird, *Nick of the Woods: Or, Adventures of Prairie Life* (Project Gutenberg, 2004), https://www.gutenberg.org/ebooks/13970, chapter 34.

12. Richard Slotkin, *Regeneration through Violence: The Mythology of the American Frontier* (Middletown, CT: Wesleyan University Press, 1973).

13. For example, Magua, the archetypical villain of his tale *The Last of the Mohicans*, delivers an impassioned address to a band of Delawares he is trying to enlist: "The Spirit that made men colored them differently. Some are blacker than the sluggish bear. These He said should be slaves, and he ordered them to work forever, like the beaver. You may hear them groan, when the south wind blows, louder than the howling buffaloes, along the shores of the great salt lake, where the big canoes come and go with them in droves. Some he made with faces paler than the ermine of the forests; and these he ordered to be traders; dogs to their women, and wolves to their slaves. He gave this people the nature of the pigeon; wings that never tire; young more plentiful than the leaves on the trees, and appetites to devour the earth. He gave them tongues like the false call of the wildcat; hearts like rabbits; the winning of the hog (but none of the fox), and arms longer than the legs of the moose. With his tongue he stops the ears of the Indians; his heart teaches him to pay warriors to fight his battles; his winning tells him to get together the goods of the earth; and his arms enclose the land from the shores of the salt-water to the islands of the great lake. His gluttony makes him sick. God gave him enough, and yet he wants all. Such are the pale-faces." James Fenimore Cooper, *The Leatherstocking Tales*, vol. 1, *The Last of the Mohicans*, chapter 29, 819–20 (New York: The Library of America, 1985).

14. *Ibid.*, chapter 25, 766.

15. Kennedy Williams, Jr., "Cooper's Use of American History," Paper Presented at the First Cooper Seminar, *James Fenimore Cooper: His Country and His Art*, State University of New York College at Oneonta, July 1978.

16. Cooper, *The Last of the Mohicans*, chapter 17, 672.

17. Benjamin Trumbull, *A General History of the United States of America* (Boston: Farrand, Mallory and Co., 1810), 372–73.

18. Jonathan Carver, *Travels Through the Interior Parts of North America in the Years 1766–1767* (London: C. Dilly, H. Payne and J. Phillips, 1781).

19. *Ibid.*, 309.

20. *Ibid.*, 320.

21. *Ibid.*, 324.

22. *Adventures in the Wilderness: The American Journals of Louis Antoine de Bougainville, 1756–1760*, trans. and ed. Edward P. Hamilton (Norman: University of Oklahoma Press, 1964), 121–22. Archaeologist David Starbuck concluded after investigating Fort William Henry that we can't be certain how many British and American fighters were killed, but probably around 185. David R. Starbuck, "The 'Massacre' at Fort William Henry," *Penn Museum* 50, no.1 (March 2008), www.penn.museum/sites/expedition/the-massacre-at-fort-william-henry/.

23. James H. Merrell, *Into the American Woods*, 26–27.

24. Bougainville, *Adventures in the Wilderness*, 332.

25. James Fenimore Cooper, *The Leatherstocking Tales, The Prairie*, chapter 24, 1171.

26. *Ibid.*, chapter 6, 950.

27. *Ibid.*, chapter 26, 1204–05.

28. *Ibid.*, 1207.

29. James Fenimore Cooper, *The Leatherstocking Tales*, vol. 1, *The Pioneers*, 84–85.

30. Oliver Edwards speaking to Louisa Grant in *The Pioneers*, chapter 12, 140.

31. Natty Bumppo speaking to a group in a tavern in *The Pioneers*, chapter 13, 156.

32. *Ibid.*, chapter 12, 143.

33. *Ibid.*

34. Richard to Elizabeth, *ibid.*, chapter 18, 202.

35. Richard to Judge Templeton and Elizabeth, *ibid.*, 204.

36. *Ibid.*, chapters 38–39.

37. See, e.g., the Christmas turkey shoot scene in chapter 17 at *ibid.*

38. *Ibid.*, chapter 18, 204.

39. *Ibid.*, chapter 41, 461.

Chapter 7

1. James Fenimore Cooper, *The Leatherstocking Tales*, vol. 2, *The Pathfinder, or The Inland Sea*, chapter 5, 79.

2. See, for example, comments made by Natty Bumppo about the exploits of Chingachgook in chapters 1, 13, and 41 of *The Pioneers* and numerous other references to scalping in *The Pathfinder*.

3. *The Pathfinder*, chapter 6, 91.

4. *Ibid.*, chapter 19, 318.

5. *Ibid.*, chapter 21, 353.

6. James Fenimore Cooper, *The Leatherstocking Tales*, vol. 1, *The Deerslayer*, chapter 21, 836.

7. See Drimmer, *Captured by the Indians*, 1961.

8. Juha Hiltunen, "Spiritual and Religious Aspects of Torture and Scalping among Indian Cultures in Eastern North America from Ancient to Colonial Times," *Religion and the Body* 23 (2011): 115–28, https://journal.fi/scripta/article/view/67402.

9. Dunbar-Ortiz, "The Grid of History."

10. For a discussion of this practice, see George A. Bray III, etc., http://www.aics.org/mascot/redskins.html. See also George A. Bray III, "Scalping during the French and Indian War," www.earlyamerica.com/review/1998/scalping.html; Roxanne Dunbar-Ortiz's discussion of terroristic warfare practiced by Europeans against Native Americans in *An Indigenous Peoples' History of the United States* (Boston: Beacon Press, 2014), 58 ff.

11. "The Scalp Industry," xroads.virginia.edu/~HYPER/HNS/scalping/oldfolks.html.

12. George Franklin Feldman, *Cannibalism, Headhunting and Human Sacrifice in North America: A History Forgotten* (Chambersburg, PA: Alan C. Hood and Company, 2008), 178–93.

13. Fiedler, "James Fenimore Cooper: The Problem of the Good Bad Writer."

14. Slotkin, *Regeneration through Violence*, 20.

15. Martin Barker and Roger Sabin, *The Lasting of the Mohicans: History of an American Myth* (Jackson: University of Mississippi Press, 1995).

16. *Ibid.*, 12.

17. *Ibid.*, 15.

18. Natty Bumppo in *The Pathfinder*, chapter 27, 445–46.

19. Slotkin, *Regeneration through Violence*, 34.

20. See Richard Slotkin, *Gunfighter Nation: The Myth of the Frontier in Twentieth-Century America* (New York: Atheneum, 1992).

21. *Ibid.*, 88.

22. "Transcript of the Northwest Ordinance of 1787," Article 3, https:www.ourdocuments.gov/doc.php?&lash=trie&doc=8&page=transcript.

23. There are eight references to cannibalism in Drimmer's (*Captured by the Indians*) captive anthology.

24. Slotkin, *Gunfighter Nation*, 145. For a review of the treatment of California Indians see: Damon B. Aikins and William J. Bauer, Jr., *We are the Land: A History of Native California*. Berkeley: University of California Press, 2021.

25. *Ibid.*, 162.

26. For an extended discussion of this phenomenon, see Feldman, *Cannibalism, Headhunting and Human Sacrifice in North America*. Feldman presents firsthand historical accounts of these practices among various Native American groups, but his narrative jumps across centuries and juxtaposes events as if they were contiguous and contemporary. Nevertheless, the stories and eyewitness accounts are persuasive.

27. See Richard A. Marlar, et al., "Biochemical Evidence of Cannibalism at a Prehistoric Puebloan Site in Southwestern Colorado," *Nature* 407 (September 7, 2000): 74–78, for the results of a forensic analysis of Indigenous remains that yielded evidence of cannibalism.

Chapter 8

1. From the log of Christopher Columbus, October11, 1492, www.franciscan-archive.org/columbus/opera/exerpts.html.

2. For accounts of these eventualities, see Diamond, *Guns, Germs and Steel*; Las Casas, *A Brief Account of the Destruction of the Indies*.

3. For a review of treaties between states, the federal government, and Native Americans, visit the site of the National Archives Records Administration, https://www.archives.gov.

4. Information about King Philip's War was obtained from: "The Grizzly Death of King Philip: Beheaded and Quartered, Body Tied in Trees for the Birds to Pluck," *Beyond the Bridgewater Triangle: History, Mysteries, Curiosities and Crimes*, https://beforeitsnews.com/alternative/2010/12/the-grizzly-death-of-king-philip-beheaded-and-quartered-body-tied-in-trees-for-the-birds-to-pluck-316398.html; "1675—King Philip's War," *The Society of Colonial Wars in the State of Connecticut*, Colonialwar-sct.org/1675.htm; Michael Tougias, "King Philip's War in New England," *The History Place*, www.historyplace.com/specials/writers/kingphilip.htm; Anthony Brandt, "Blood and Betrayal: King Philip's War," *HistoryNet*, https://www.historynet.com/blood-and-betrayal-king-philips-war.htm.

5. Gus Wiencke, "Chief Tamanend," ustwp.org/government/boards-commissions/historical-advisory-board/chief-tamanend/.

6. Information about Tamanend was derived from: Dennis Maurizi, "Un-Erasing Tammany," *American History* (February 2016): 50–55; Gus Wiencke, "Chief Tamanend," Upper Southampton Township, https://www.ustwp.org/government/boards-commissions/historical-advisory-board/chief-tamanend/.

7. For a summary of this battle, see Leeane Root, "A New Nation's Forgotten Indian Allies," *Indian Country Today*, Issue 2, June/July 2017, 32–34. The Oneida Nation donated $10 million to the new Museum of the American Revolution in Philadelphia, which has an exhibit about this battle.

8. Cited in Frederick Turner III, *The Portable North American Indian Reader* (New York: Penguin Books, 1973), 245–46.

9. Information about Tecumseh was gathered from: John Sugden, *Tecumseh: A Life* (New York: Henry Holt, 1998); "Tecumseh: Facts, Information and Articles about Tecumseh, a Native American Chief from the Wild West," *HistoryNet*, www.historynet.com/tecumseh.

10. Information pertaining to Cochise was gathered from: Kathy Weiser, "Legends of America: Cochise—Strong Apache Leader," *Legends of America*, http://www.legendsofamerica.com/na-cochise/; Edwin R. Sweeney, "Chiricahua Chief Cochise," *HistoryNet*, www.historynet.com/cochise#articles; "June 8, 1874: Apache Chief Cochise Dies," *History.com*, https://www.history.com/this-day-in-history/apache-chief-cochise-dies#:~:text=Apache%20chief%20Cochise%20dies%20Chief%20Cochise%2C%20one%20of,Arizona.%20Little%20is%20known%20of%20Cochise%E2%80%99s%20early%20life.

11. Information about Geronimo was gathered from: "Geronimo," *History.com*, www.history.com/topics/native-american-history/geronimo; "Geronimo," *Biography*, https://www.biography.com/political-figure/geronimo; Alysa Landry, "Native History: Geronimo Is Last Native Warrior to Surrender," *Indian Country Today*, September 4, 2013. See also, Stephen Melvil Barrett, *Geronimo's Story of His Life* (New York: Duffield and Company, 1906); Angie Debo, *Geronimo, The Man, His Time, His Place* (Norman: University of Oklahoma Press, 1996).

12. Sources used for the narrative on Sitting Bull include: "Wounded Knee," *History.com*, www.history.com/topics/nativeamerican-history/sitting-bull; "Sitting Bull," *Biography*, https://www.biography.com/people/sitting-bull-9485326; also see Gary C. Anderson, *Sitting Bull and the Paradox of Lakota Nationhood*, 2nd ed. (Upper Saddle River, NJ: Pearson, 2006); Ernie La Pointe, *Sitting Bull: His Life and Legacy* (Layton, UT: Gibbs Smith, 2009).

13. Information about Red Cloud was derived from the following sources: Cozzens, *The Earth Is Weeping*, 32–46; PBS, "Red Cloud," *Ken Burns Presents the West*, www.pbs.org/weta/thewest/people/i_r/redcloud.htm.; "Red Cloud, 1820–1909," *Partnership with Native Americans* (blog), www.nativepartnership.org/site/PageServer?pagename=PWNA_Native_Biography_redcloud. See also Charles Wesley Allen and Sam Deon, *Autobiography of Red Cloud: War Leader of the Oglalas*, ed. R. Eli Paul (Helena, : Montana Historical Society Press, 1997); Bob Drury and Tom Clavin, *The Heart of Everything that Is: The Untold Story of Red Cloud, An American Legend* (New York: Simon and Schuster, 2014). A less flattering view of Chief Red Cloud is offered in Mario Gonzalez and Elizabeth Cook-Lynn, *The Politics of Hallowed Ground: Wounded Knee and the Struggle for Indian Sovereignty* (Urbana: University of Illinois Press, 1999). They contend that Red Cloud was not revered as a leader among the Sioux and chose not to come to the aid of Chief Big Foot to prevent the massacre at Wounded Knee in 1890.

14. For a detailed discussion of his death, see Thomas Powers, *The Killing of Crazy Horse* (New York: Vintage, 2011).

15. Quoted in Kat Eschner, "The Memorial to Crazy Horse Has Been Under Construction for Almost 70 Years," Smart News, *Smithsonian* Magazine, December 4, 2017, https://www.smithsonianmag.com/smart-news/memorial-crazy-horse-has-been-under-construction-almost-70years-180967377/.

16. Sources used for this summary about Crazy Horse include: "Crazy Horse," *History.com*, www.history.com/topics/native-americanhistory/crazy-horse; "Crazy Horse," *Biography*, https://www.biography.com/people/crazy-horse-9261082. For more information on Crazy Horse, see William Matson and Mark Frethem (producers), *The Authorized Biography of Crazy Horse and His Family*, DVD released by Reelcontact.com (2006).

17. "I said in my heart that, rather than have war, I would give up my country. I would rather give up my father's grave. I would rather give up everything than have the blood of the white men upon the hands of my people." Cited in "Chief Joseph," History Link.org, www.historylink.org/File/8975.

18. Material for Chief Joseph was gathered from: Cozzens, *The Earth Is Weeping*, 315–40; "Chief Joseph," *Biography*, https://www.biography.com/people/chief-joseph-9358227; PBS, "Chief Joseph," *Ken Burns Presents the West*, https://www.pbs.org/weta/thewest/people/a_c/chiefjoseph.htm; Jim Kershner, "Chief Joseph (1840–1904)," *HistoryLink.org*, www.historylink.org/File/8975.

19. Material about Quanah Parker was derived from: "Quanah Parker," *Britannica*, https://www.britannica.com/biography/Quanah-Parker; Brian C. Hosmer, "Quanah Parker," *Handbook of Texas*, Texas State Historical Association, https://www.tshaonline.org/handbook/entries/parker-quanah. For an in-depth analysis of his life, see William T. Hagan, *Quanah Parker: Last Comanche Chief* (Norman: Oklahoma University Press, 1993).

20. For a discussion of current the status of the Navajo, see Jennifer Nez Denetdale, "Naal Tsoos Sani (The Old Paper)," *National Museum of the American Indian* 19, no. 2 (Summer 2018): 24–31. For a discussion of "the long walk," see Jennifer Nez Denetdale, *The Long Walk: The Forced Navajo Exile* (New York: Chelsea House, 2007).

21. See Steve Inskeep, *Jacksonland: President Andrew Jackson, Cherokee Chief John Ross, and A Great American Land Grab* (New York: Penguin Press, 2015), for a discussion of this issue.

22. Material on Sequoyah was derived from: "Sequoyah," *Britannica*, https://www.britannica.com/biography/sequoyah; "A Brief Biography of Sequoyah," The Sequoyah Birthplace Museum, www.sequoyahmuseum.org/index.cfm/m/5; "Sequoyah," www.powersource.com/gallery/people/sequoyah.html; Susan M. Abram, "Sequoyah," in *The Encyclopedia of Alabama*, www.encyclopediaofalabama.org/article/h-2159; "Sequoyah," *National Geographic*, https://www.nationalgeographic.

org/article/sequoyah-and-creation-cherokee-syllabary/; "Sequoyah and the Creation of the Cherokee Syllabary," National Geographic Society, https://www.nationalgeographic.org/article/sequoyah-and-creation-cherokee-syllabary/. For an in-depth look at Sequoyah's life, see Grant Foreman, *Sequoyah* (Norman: University of Oklahoma Press, 1938); Jack F. Kilpatrick, *Sequoyah of Earth and Intellect* (Austin, TX: Encino Press, 1965).

23. Material about Osceola was gathered from: Kathy Weiser, "Seminole Chief Osceola," *Legends of America*, https://www.legendsofamerica.com/na-osceola/; "The Seminole Wars," *Exploring Florida*, https://fcit.usf.edu/florida/lessons/sem_war/sem_war1.htm.

24. Information about the Modocs was obtained from Cozzens, *The Earth Is Weeping*, chapter 8; "How the West was Lost: Modoc Death Will Come Soon Enough," *History Channel*, March 4, 2017; "Captain Jack," *Encyclopedia.com*, https://www.encyclopedia.com/people/history/north-american-indigenous-peoples-biographies/captain-jack.

25. Cozzens discusses the notable exception of the professionalism and commitment of the segregated Black units of the U.S. infantry and cavalry, known as the Buffalo Soldiers, who fought with distinction during this time. See Cozzens, *The Earth Is Weeping*, 60–61.

26. General William T. Sherman is reported to have told his brother, Senator John Sherman, "The more I see of these Indians, the more I become convinced that they all have to be killed or be maintained as paupers. Their attempts at civilization are simply ridiculous." Cited in Cozzens, *The Earth Is Weeping*, 91.

27. The U.S. Army was also using the lever-action repeating Spencer rifle in the 1860s. It was designed by Christopher Spencer and considered the world's first military repeating rifle. Over two hundred thousand were produced in the United States between 1860 and 1869. It was capable of firing twenty rounds a minute compared to muzzle-loading rifles that discharged two to three rounds per minute, although the weapon had to be cocked before each firing. Spencer rifles held seven rounds in a tube in the buttstock and could hold up to thirteen cartridges. They were used by the Union Army at Gettysburg much to the Confederate troops' chagrin.

28. Peter Cozzens, *The Earth is Weeping*, 6. The quote was attributed to Col. John Chivington who was also responsible for the Sand Creek Massacre. Readers might wish to go to "The Sand Creek Massacre" to read the testimony of Col. Chivington in a federal inquiry of his actions at: Kclonewolf.com/History/SandCreek/sc-documents/sc-chivington-testimony.html.

29. Information about this event was obtained from Gina Dimuro, "The Forgotten Bear River Massacre May Be the Deadliest Native American Slaughter Ever," *ATI*, January 30, 2019, https://allthatsinteresting.com/bear-river-massacre.

30. The U.S. House Committee on the Conduct of the War (Plains Indians) concluded that Col. Chivington had "deliberately planned and executed a foul and dastardly massacre which would have disgraced the varied and savage among those who were the victims of his cruelty." Cited in J. Jay Myers, "Sand Creek Massacre," *HistoryNet*, https://www.historynet.com/sand-creek-massacre.

31. Material for the discussion of the Sand Creek Massacre was gathered from: Cozzens, *The Earth Is Weeping*; Myers, "Sand Creek Massacre"; Stan Hoig, *The Sand Creek Massacre* (Norman: University of Oklahoma Press, 1974).

32. Material for the Washita River Massacre was gathered from "Custer Massacres Cheyenne on Washita River," *History.com*, https://www.history.com/this-day-in-history/custer-massacres-cheyenne-on-washita-river.

33. Material about the Marias River Massacre was gathered from: "Soldiers Massacre Sleeping Camp of Native Americans," *History.com*, https://www.history.com/this-day-in-history/soldiers-massacre-the-wrong-camp-of-indians; Kathy Weiser, "The Marias Massacre of Montana," *Legends of America*, https://www.legendsofamerica.com/na-mariasmassacre/.

34. Alexandria.gov, "We Are All Americans," City of Alexandria, Virginia, https://www.alexandriava.gov/historic/fortward/default.aspx?id=40164. Material for this section was derived from this source.

35. Ruth Quinn, "Native American Scouts," U.S. Army, November 7, 2013, https://www.army.mil/article/114646/Native_American_Scouts.

36. *Ibid.*

37. *Ibid.*

38. One of the heroes of that battle was a young Native American Pima Indian, Ira Hayes, who was born in Sacaton, Arizona, in 1923. After being trained as a Marine parachutist, Hayes was sent into the battle for Iwo Jima and was one of six people who hoisted the American flag on Mount Suribachi after days of bloody warfare on the island. The picture by photographer Joe Rosenthal was immortalized and made Hayes a sought-after celebrity. He received a Marine commendation for his service and adulation from strangers around the country. Several motion pictures were made about him, including the 1961 film *The Outsider*, where he was portrayed by actor Tony Curtis. Prior to that John Wayne starred in a 1949 film about the events of the battle in *Sands of Iwo Jima*, and Clint Eastwood's 2006 film, *Flags of Our Fathers*, also explored the event. Sadly, Hayes was found dead from exposure and acute alcohol poisoning not far from his birthplace in Arizona on January 24, 1955. He was buried with full military honors at Arlington National Cemetery on February 2, 1955.

39. Material for this section on code talkers is derived from "Native Words, Native Warriors," National Museum of the American Indian,

www.nmai.si.edu/education/codetalkers/html/chapter7.html.

40. "The Thunderbird Division," *American Indian* 19, no. 1 (Spring 2018): 22–23. See also Laurence M. Hauptman, "Fighting the Nazis: A Creek Indian Wins the Congressional Medal of Honor," in *ibid.*, 17–20, about the military accomplishments of Ernest Childers.

41. For a visual summary of Native American contributions to the U.S. military, see the film *The Warrior Tradition*, released in 2019, directed by Lawrence Hott.

Chapter 9

1. Written by the Moravian missionary Heckewelder in 1818 quoting the chief. Cited in Helen Hunt Jackson, *A Century of Dishonor* (1881), 34, http://ia600506.us.archive.org/22/items/centuryofdishonor005246mbp/centuryofdishono005246mbp.pdf.

2. Barker and Sabin, *The Lasting of the Mohicans*.

3. David Sterritt, "Review of *The Last of the Mohicans*," *TCM Film*, www.tcm.com/Thismonth/article/480649/480765/The-last-of-the-mohicans.html

4. For a partial enumeration of works based on Cooper's writing, see Barker and Sabin, *The Lasting of the Mohicans*, 205–11.

5. David Tatara, "*The Last of the Mohicans*, 1936," *TCM Film*, www.tcm.com/thismonth/article/1608191/111463/The-last-of-the-mohicans.html.

6. "Michael Mann Looks Back on 'The Last of the Mohicans' 20 Years Later," *Uproxx*, May 12, 2012, https://uproxx.com/hitfix/michael-mann-looks-back-on-the-last-of-the-mohicans-20-years-later/.

7. Jeffrey Walker, "Deconstructing an American Myth: Hollywood and *The Last of the Mohicans*," Presented at the Tenth Cooper Seminar, *James Fenimore Cooper: His Country and His Art*, State University of New York College at Oneonta, July 1995, https://www.jfcoopersociety.org/articles/SUNY/1995SUNY-WALKER.HTML.

8. Las Casas, *A Brief Account of the Destruction of the Indies*; Vine Deloria, Jr., *Custer Died for Your Sins: An Indian Manifesto* (New York: Macmillan, 1969); Dee Brown, *Bury My Heart at Wounded Knee* (New York: Washington Square Press, 1970). This book remains one of the twentieth century's most critical indictments of White depredations of Native Americans.

9. A particularly incisive and acerbic analysis of the depredations of Native Americans is Dunbar-Ortiz's *An Indigenous Peoples' History of the United States*. Dunbar-Ortiz denounces the exploitation of Indigenous people, especially in North America, from colonial times to the present. The subsequent book by Dunbar-Ortiz and her collaborator, Dina Gilio-Whitaker, *"All the Real Indians Died Off,"* provides further historical

and current insight into U.S. governmental legal, cultural, and political policies that disadvantaged Native Americans in the United States.

10. Quoted from the U.S. Secretary of the Interior's Annual Report, 1876, cited in Jackson, *A Century of Dishonor*, 247.

11. Brown, *Bury My Heart at Wounded Knee*, 77.

12. From the Annual Report of the Secretary of the Interior, cited in Jackson, *A Century of Dishonor*, 217.

13. *Ibid.*, 339.

14. Brown, *Bury My Heart at Wounded Knee*, 379.

15. For a further discussion of this point, see Brown, *Bury My Heart at Wounded Knee*, 6.

16. Malcomson, *One Drop of Blood*, 108.

17. Jackson, *A Century of Dishonor*, 272.

18. Inskeep, *Jacksonland*.

19. *Ibid.*, 8.

20. *Ibid.*, 91.

21. *Ibid.*, 64.

22. *Ibid.*, 90.

23. *Ibid.*, 281.

24. Museum of the Cherokee Indian, "The Trail of Tears," www.cherokeeheritage.org/attractions/trail-of-tears.

25. Jackson, *A Century of Dishonor*, 288.

26. Inskeep, *Jacksonland*, 238.

27. *Ibid.*, 306.

28. This summary is taken from Jeffrey Steele, "Reduced to Images: American Indians in Nineteenth-Century Advertising," in *Dressing in Feathers: The Construction of the Indian in Popular Culture*, ed. S. Elizabeth Bird (Boulder, CO: Westview Press, 1996), 61–62.

29. Two of Custer's brothers, a cousin, and a brother-in-law were also killed during the battle. The summary of the Battle of the Little Bighorn was derived from: "The Battle of the Little Bighorn, 1876," *Eyewitness to History*, www.eyewitnesstohistory.com/custer.htm; "Custer's Last Stand, June 25, 1876," *America's Story from America's Library*, Library of Congress, www.americaslibrary.gov/jb/recon/jb_recon_custer_1.html; "Battle of the Little Bighorn," *History.com*, www.history.com/topics/native-american-history/battle-of-the-little-bighorn; "Custer's Last Stand, 1876, Dead and Wounded," *USGenWeb Archives*,http://files.usgwarchives.net/sd/military/big-horn.txt.

30. C. Richard King, "Segregated Stories: The Colonial Contours of the Little Bighorn Battlefield National Monument," in *Dressing in Feathers*, ed. Bird, 173.

31. *Ibid.*, 175.

32. In 2001 the National Congress of American Indians called for rescinding these medals. For a discussion of this issue, see Dana Lone Hill, "The Wounded Knee Medals of Honor Should be Rescinded," *The Guardian*, February 18, 2013. On June 25, 2019, a bill was introduced in the U.S. Congress ("Remove the Stain Act") by Reps. Denny Heck (D–Washington),

Deb Haaland (D–New Mexico and a Laguna Pueblo), and Paul Cook (R–California) to rescind the medals of honor awarded at the Wounded Knee Massacre. See Brian Mackley, "Lawmakers Introduce Bill to Rescind 20 Medals of Honor Issued in Connection with a Massacre of Native Americans," *Military Times*, June 25, 2019, https://www.militarytimes.com/news/pentagon-congress/2019/06/25/lawmakers-introduce-bill-to-rescind-20-medals-of-honor-issued-in-connection-with-a-massacre-of-native-americans/.

33. For a discussion of his attempts, see Mario Gonzalez and Elizabeth Cook-Lynn, *The Politics of Hallowed Ground: Wounded Knee and the Struggle for Indian Sovereignty* (Urbana and Chicago: University of Illinois Press, 1999).

34. For a fuller discussion of this siege, see Paul Chaat Smith and Robert Allen Warrior, *Like a Hurricane: The Indian Movement from Alcatraz to Wounded Knee* (New York: The New Press, 1996). Also see chapter 20 in this book for a discussion of the implications of Native American political movements.

35. Cited in Malcomson, *One Drop of Blood*, 15. For information about the commission and its classificatory scheme, see "Five Civilized Tribes—Cherokee, Chickasaw, Choctaw, Creek, and Seminole Tribes in Oklahoma: Dawes Records," National Archives, www.archives.gov/research/native-americans/dawes/.

36. Cited in Jacquelyn Kilpatrick, *Celluloid Indians: Native Americans and Film* (Lincoln: University of Nebraska Press, 1999), 10.

Chapter 10

1. Cited in Denise Oliver Velez, "Native Schools and Stolen Generations: U.S. and Canada," *Daily Kos*, April 14, 2013, https://www.dailykos.com/stories/2013/4/14/1200994/-Native-schools-and-stolen-generations-U-S-and-Canada.

2. Maureen Smith, "Forever Changed: Boarding School Narratives of American Indian Identity in the U.S. and Canada," *Indigenous Nations Studies Journal*, no. 2 (Fall 2001): 58.

3. *Ibid.*

4. Northern Plains Reservation Aid (formerly American Indian Relief Council), "History and Culture: Boarding Schools," http://www.nativepartnership.org/site/PageServer?pagename=airc_hist_boardingschools.

5. For a treatment of this theme in the United States, see Slotkin, *Regeneration through Violence*, chapter 7. A review of the Australian case can be found in the film *Rabbit Proof Fence* (2002).

6. Northern Plains Reservation Aid, "History and Culture: Boarding Schools."

7. Institute for Government Research, *The Problem of Indian Administration: Report of a Survey Made at the Request of Honorable Hubert Work, Secretary of the Interior* (Baltimore: The Johns Hopkins Press, 1928; Hathi Trust Digital Library, 2019), 3, https://babel.hathitrust.org/cgi/pt?id=coo.31924014526150&view=1up&seq=9.

8. *Ibid.*, 392–93.

9. *Ibid.*, 393.

10. You can read the act at http://aghca.org/wp-content/uploads/2012/07/indianreorganizationact.pdf.

11. Pember, *Intergenerational Trauma*. See also the play written about the boarding school abuses by Carl Gawboy (Chippewa), *The Great Hurt*, written in 1972 but only recently gaining in popularity.

12. Brian Dippie, *The Vanishing American: White Attitudes and U.S. Indian Policy* (Lawrence: University of Kansas Press, 1982), chapter 8.

13. *Ibid.*, 120.

14. Suzette Brewer, "Protect the Children, Preserve the Tribe," *Stand* (Summer 2015): 24–28. In their essay on Native American child welfare, Miriam Jorgensen, Adrian T. Smith, Terry Cross, and Sarah Kostelic note there was a long history of placing Native American children in adoptive and foster White homes in the United States. They cite a congressional committee report in 1974 that found 25–35 percent of Native American children were removed from their homes by the child welfare system, and 90 percent of the adoptions of Native children went to non–Native parents. In South Dakota, Indian children were sixteen times more likely to be placed in foster care than non–Indian children, and in Washington state the rate of foster care placements for Indian children was nineteen times greater than for non–Indian children. The report found that many decisions to place these children were based on the biases of child welfare personnel who lacked knowledge and understanding about Indian culture. See their essay, "What Can Tribal Child Welfare Policy Teach Us About Tribal Citizenship?" in *The Great Vanishing Act*, ed. Ratteree and Hill, 159–72.

Garroutte, *Real Indians*, 229–30 and note 3. Such practices were targeted by the Indian Child Welfare Act passed in 1978, which sought to prevent the excessive placement of Indian children in White homes.

15. See Prime Minister Harper's apology, "Statement of Apology to Former Students of Indian Residential Schools," *Facing History and Ourselves*, https://www.facinghistory.org/stolen-lives-indigenous-peoples-canada-and-indian-residential-schools/historical-background/prime-minister-harpers-apology.

16. See Nick Robins-Early, "Report Says Canada's Residential Schools Committed 'Cultural Genocide' against Aboriginals," *Huffington Post*, June 4, 2016, https://www.huffpost.com/entry/canada-residential-schools_n_7504016.

17. Commonwealth of Australia, *Bringing Them Home: Report of the National Inquiry into the Separation of Aboriginal and Torres Strait Islander Children from Their Families*, Canberra, April 1997, https://humanrights.

gov.au/our-work/bringing-them-home-report-1997. For a critique of the report, see "The Stolen Generations," *Australians Together*, https://australianstogether.org.au/discover/australian-history/stolen-generations.

18. Alice Bidwell, "Are American Indian Students the Least Prepared for College?" *U.S. News and World Report*, March 13, 2014, https://www.usnews.com/news/blogs/data-mine/2014/03/13/are-american-indian-students-the-least-prepared-for-college.

19. Kimberly Hefling, "GAO: Oversight Needed of Native American Schools," *Associated Press*, November 13, 2014, https://apnews.com/article/6fbc104627044ab792d165955e39bd26.

20. For more on the Wheeler-Howard Act, see David Wilma, "Wheeler-Howard Act (Indian Reorganization Act) Shifts U.S. Policy toward Native American Right to Self-Determination on June 18, 1934," *HistoryLink.org*, www.historylink.org/index.cfm?displaypage=output.cfm&file_id=2599.

21. Dean Chavers, "A History of Indian Voting Rights and Why It's Important to Vote," *Indian Country Today*, October 29, 2012, https://indiancountrytoday.com/archive/a-history-of-indian-voting-rights-and-why-its-important-to-vote. See also Willard Hughes Rollings, "Citizenship and Suffrage: The Native American Struggle for Civil Rights in the American West, 1830–1965," *University of Nevada Law Review* (Fall 2004), scholars.law.unlv.edu/cgi/viewcontent.cgi?article=1311&context=nlj. Dunbar-Ortiz provides a different perspective about the issue of conferring citizenship on Native Americans. She contends that the action of conferring citizenship on Native Americans by the U.S. government in 1924 was unsolicited and unwanted by them and was another attempt to assimilate them and annex their lands. See Dunbar-Ortiz, *An Indigenous Peoples' History of the United States*, 169. A recent report reveals the extent of impediments Native Americans currently face to secure their voting rights. See *Obstacles at Every Turn: Barriers to Political Participation Faced by Native American Voters* (Boulder, CO: Native American Rights Fund, 2020).

22. Noah Berman, "Pope Francis Canonizes Father Junipero Serra, Saying He Defended Native Americans," *Los Angeles Times*, September 23, 2015, www.latimes.com/nation/la-na-pope-visit-serra-20150923-story.html; PBS, "Junipero Serra," *Ken Burns Presents the West*, https://www.pbs.org/weta/thewest/people/S-z/serra.htm. See also Steven W. Hackel's biography of Serra, *California's Founding Father* (New York: Hill and Wang, 2013); Dunbar-Ortiz, *An Indigenous Peoples' History of the United States*, 125–29; Robert H. Jackson and Edward Castillo, *Indians, Franciscans, and Spanish Colonization: The Impact of the Mission System on California Indians* (Albuquerque: University of New Mexico Press, 1995). The destruction of Native Americans and their culture by the Spaniards pales in comparison to the genocide perpetrated against California Indians by U.S. governmental authorities, according to historian Benjamin Madley in his book *An American Genocide: The United States and the California Indian Catastrophe* (New Haven, CT: Yale University Press, 2016). See also the searing account of the Catholic missions movement on California Indians in Elias Castillo's *Cross of Thorns: The Enslavement of California's Indians by the Spanish Missions* (Fresno, CA: Craven Street Books, 2015) and the campaign waged against the Modocs by the federal government in Cozzens, *The Earth Is Weeping*, chapter 8.

23. Berman, "Pope Francis Canonizes Father Junipero Serra."

Chapter 11

1. Frank Woodworth Pine, ed., *Autobiography of Benjamin Franklin* (New York: Henry Holt, 1916; Project Gutenberg, 2006), chapter 13, https://www.gutenberg.org/files/20203/20203-h/20203-h.htm.

2. Cf. Friedman's characterization of "monstrous races." Friedman, *The Monstrous Races*.

3. Bonnie Duran, "Indigenous versus Colonial Discourse: Alcohol and American Indian Identity," in *Dressing in Feathers*, ed. Bird, 111–28.

4. Craig MacAndrew and Robert B. Edgerton, *Drunken Comportment: A Social Explanation* (Chicago: Aldine Publishing Company, 1969).

5. Cited in *ibid.*, 101.

6. Duran, "Indigenous versus Colonial Discourse," 117.

7. MacAndrew and Edgerton, *Drunken Comportment*, 106. They contend that "the Indians of what is now the United States and Canada had no alcoholic beverages before the coming of the white man" (110).

8. *Ibid.*, 114.

9. See Duran, "Indigenous versus Colonial Discourse," 119–23.

10. Quoted in Mc Andrew and Edgerton, *Drunken Comportment*, 143.

11. *Ibid.*, 143–44.

12. *Ibid.*, 122.

13. Duran, "Indigenous versus Colonial Discourse," 123.

14. MacAndrew and Edgerton, *Drunken Comportment*, 143.

15. Dunbar-Ortiz and Gilio-Whitaker, *"All the Real Indians Died Off,"* 136.

16. See his *Culture and Experience* (Philadelphia: University of Pennsylvania Press, 1955).

17. James K. Cunningham, Teshia A. Solomon, and Myra L. Muramoto, "Alcohol Use Among Native Americans Compared to Whites: Examining the Veracity of the 'Native American Elevated Alcohol Consumption' Belief," *Drug and Alcohol Dependence* 160 (March 1, 2016): 65–75.

18. Cindy L. Ehlers and Ian R. Gizer, "Evidence

for a Genetic Component for Substance Dependence in Native Americans," *American Journal of Psychiatry* 170, no. 2 (February 2014): 154–64.

19. Fred Beauvais, "American Indians and Alcohol," *National Institute on Alcohol Abuse*, Spotlight on Special Problems 22, no. 4 (1998): 253–59.

20. See Caroline Jiang et al., "Racial Gender Disparities in Suicide among Young Adults Aged 18–24: United States, 2009–2013," National Center for Health Statistics, Centers for Disease Control and Prevention, www.cdc.gov/nchs/data/hestat/suicide/racial_and_gender_2009_2013.htm.

21. Christopher Doering, "Thune Legislation Targets Suicide by Native American Youth," *Argus Leader* (*USA Today*), July 16, 2015, https://www.argusleader.com/story/news/politics/2015/07/16/thune-legislation-targets-suicide-native-american-youth/30256783/.

22. *Ibid.* See also Regina Garcia Cano, "Tribe Struggles to Stop Surge in Teen Suicides," *Associated Press*, April 13, 2015, https://apnews.com/e9fabe4378354aba82b2e96a88e4a790.

23. Sari Horwitz, "The Hard Lives—and High Suicide Rate—of Native American Children on Reservations," *Washington Post*, March 9, 2014, https://www.washingtonpost.com/world/national-security/the-hard-lives—and-high-suicide-rate—of-native-american-children/2014/03/09/6e0ad9b2-9f03-11e3-b8d8-94577ff66b28_story.html.

24. *Ibid.* For more information on the role of violence in Indigenous children's lives, see *Ending Violence so Children Can Thrive*, Report of the U.S. Attorney General's Advisory Committee on American Indian and Alaska Native Children Exposed to Violence, November, 2014, https://www.justice.gov/sites/default/files/defendingchildhood/pages/attachments/2015/03/23/ending_violence_so_children_can_thrive.pdf.

25. *Ibid.*

26. Joe Flood, "What's Lurking Behind the Suicides?" *New York Times*, May 16, 2015, http://www.nytimes.com/2015/05/17/opinion/sunday/whats-lurking-behind-the-suicides.html.

27. The 2016 chilling motion picture *Wind River*, directed by Taylor Sheridan, graphically depicted sexual violence experienced by Native American women victimized by White men on reservations.

28. André B. Rosay, *Violence against American Indian and Alaska Native Women and Men: 2010 Findings from the National Intimate Partner and Sexual Violence Survey*, National Institute of Justice Research Report, U.S. Department of Justice, May 2016, https://www.ncjrs.gov/pdffiles1/nij/249736.pdf.

29. Garet Bleir and Anya Zoledziowski, "Hate in America: Native Women are 10 Times More Likely to be Murdered," *Indian Country Today*, August 25, 2018. The article originally appeared in *News 21.*

30. "Ending Violence against Native Women," *Indian Law Resource Center*, indianlaw.org/issue/ending-violence-against-native-women.

31. "Missing and Murdered Indigenous Women and Girls: A Snapshot of Data From 71 Urban Cities in the United States," Urban Indian Health Institute, Seattle, 2018, 20.

32. Bleir and Zoledziowski, "Hate in America." On October 5, 2018, the Inter-American Commission on Human Rights held a public hearing at the law school of the University of Colorado, Boulder, to look into the nature and extent of rampant violence committed against Indigenous women in the United States. The commission is part of the Organization of American States, a group of thirty-five countries, including the United States, that promotes respect for human rights and holds hearings to investigate human rights concerns. In 2019 a definitive study of violence against Indigenous women and girls in Canada was released, which meticulously documented "acts of genocide against First Nations, Inuit and Métis women, and girls, and 2SLGBTQQIA people." The report concluded, "This violence amounts to a race-based genocide of Indigenous Peoples..." and that it "has been empowered by colonial structures," and other callous and insensitive governmental actions that have led to the "current increased rates of violence, death, and suicide in Indigenous populations." Privy Council Office, *Reclaiming Power and Place*, National Inquiry into Missing and Murdered Indigenous Women and Girls, Vancouver, Executive Summary, 2, https://www.mmiwg-ffada.ca/final-report/.

33. For more on this issue, see Brittney Bennett, "Law Was Meant to Let American Indians Prosecute Violence; Is It Working?" *USA Today*, March 25, 2017, https://indianlaw.org/safewomen/law-was-meant-let-american-indians-prosecute-violence-it-working. See also National Institute of Justice, "Five Things about Violence Against American Indians and Alaska Native Women and Men," U.S. Department of Justice, May 2016, https://www.ncjrs.gov/pdffiles1/nij/249815.pdf.

34. James Gray, *The Illinois* (New York: Henry Holt and Co. Inc., 1940), 12.

Chapter 12

1. National Indian Gaming Association Annual Report, 2019, https://online.flippingbook.com/view/317287/.

2. This figure includes Classes I, II, and III forms of gambling, not just casinos (Class III). For a discussion of Indian gambling and the fallacy of Native American wealth generated by it, see Dwanna L. Robertson, "The Myth of Indian Casino Riches," *Indian Country Media Network*, April 19, 2017. For a list of Indian gaming compacts with states, see https://www.bia.gov/as-ia/oig/gaming-compacts. For a recent review of the

economics of Indian gaming, see Vincent Schilling, "Tribal Gaming Is a $32 Billion Business: NIGC Releases Annual Revenue Figures," *Indian Country Today*, June 26, 2018.

3. National Indian Gaming Association Annual Report, 2019, 31–32.

4. See the Indian Gaming Tradeshow and Convention website for examples of contemporary activity, https://www.indiangamingtradeshow.com/510/indian-gaming-tradeshow-home.htm, and the website of the National Indian Gaming Association for upcoming events, https://www.indiangaming.org/about.

The NIGA was founded in 1985 "to protect and preserve the general welfare of the Tribes striving for self-sufficiency through gaming enterprises in Indian Country."

5. Rebecca Piccardo and Dan Sweeney, "Seminole Tribe Chairman Billie Ousted from Office by Unanimous Vote," *Florida Sun-Sentinel*, September 28, 2016, www.Sun-sentinel.com/local/broward/fl-seminole-chairman-removed-from-office-20160928-story.html.

6. Robertson, "The Myth of Indian Casino Riches."

7. For more information on the Blue Lake Rancheria tribe, see https://bluelakerancheria-nsn.gov.

8. Timothy Williams, "1 Million Each Year for All, as Long as Tribe's Luck Holds," *New York Times*, August 9, 2012, https://www.nytimes.com/2012/08/09/us/more-casinos-and-internet-gambling-threaten-shakopee-tribe.html.

9. It is noteworthy that data about per capita distribution of gaming revenues by tribes/nations is regarded as proprietary and not published by the Bureau of Indian Affairs, nor is it available through Freedom of Information inquiries as I was advised in a telephone interview with Debra DeLeon (Menominee) of the BIA on April 13, 2018. When I spoke with a representative of the Seminole Nation in August 2018 to ascertain the current per capita amount distributed to tribal members she replied, "We don't give out that information," and hung up on me.

10. For a discussion of these struggles and the legal implications of per capita disbursements for tribes, see Gabriel S. Galanda, "Tribal Per Capitas and Self-Termination," *Indian Country Today*, August 13, 2014. See also James Dao, "In California, Indian Tribes with Casino Money Cast Off Members," *New York Times*, December 12, 2011. Dao reports on the disenrolling of tribal members in nations flush with casino revenue. Focusing on the Chukchansi in California, whose casino is near Yosemite National Park, he pointed out that the tribe eliminated four hundred members between 2006 and 2011. At the time of writing, the tribe was disbursing $300 per person per month.

11. Brian Hallenbeck, "Foxwoods' Future Again Clouded by Debt," *The Day*, January 1, 2015.

12. Telephone interview with Lori Potter, Foxwoods Casino, August 17, 2018.

13. Brian Hallenbeck, "Foxwoods' Revenues Down Nearly 8 Percent in Latest Quarter," *The Day*, August 27, 2019, https://www.theday.com/article/20190827/Biz02/190829551.

14. Telephone interview with Brian Hallenback, September 3, 2019.

15. Brian Hallenbeck, "Tribes Unwilling to Withdraw from East Windsor Casino," *The Day*, August 5, 2019, https://www.theday.com/article/20190805/NWS01/190809697.

16. Competition for gamblers' dollars led to the layoff of ninety-five casino workers at the Twin River Casino in Lincoln, Rhode Island, shortly after a new casino, the Encore Boston Harbor, was opened in Everett, Massachusetts. Declines in slot machine revenue at Foxwoods and Mohegan Sun were also attributable to the presence of the new casino after its first full month of operation in July 2019. See Brian Hallenbeck, "Casinos in Connecticut, Elsewhere Already Feeling Encore's Impact," *The Day*, August 19, 2019.

17. There can be little doubt that Foxwoods has become a legitimate institution since the highly critical treatise about the origins of the tribe by Jeff Benedict, *Without Reservation: The Making of America's Most Powerful Indian Tribe and Foxwoods, the World's Largest Casino* (New York: Harper and Collins, 2000).

18. See the series by Jeff Testerman and Brad Goldstein, "Seminole Gambling: A Trail of Millions," *St. Petersburg Times*, December 20, 1997. The Seminole tribe later unsuccessfully sued the *St. Petersburg Times* for publishing "proprietary" information and defaming the tribe. See https://caselaw.findlaw.com/fl-district-court-of-appeal/1134254.html.

19. For a summary of the impact of the recession on Las Vegas and southern Nevada, see Jan Hogan, "Strip Left Reeling: Picking Up the Pieces after the Great Recession," *Las Vegas Review-Journal*, March 27, 2016, https://www.reviewjournal.com/news/special-features/neon-rebirth/strip-left-reeling-picking-up-the-pieces.

20. This section drew on the works of: Eve Darian-Smith, "Indian Gaming," *Britannica*, https://www.Britannica.com/topic/indian-gaming; Robertson, "The Myth of Indian Casino Riches"; Native American Rights Fund, *The NARF Legal Review* (Fall 1985), https://www.Yumpu.com/en/document/read/27906426/indian-gaming-law-and-legislation-native-american-rights-fund; the U.S. Department of the Interior, Indian Affairs, Office of Indian Gaming, https://www.bia.gov/as-ia/oig.

21. Celeste Lacroix, "High-Stakes Stereotypes: The Emergence of the 'Casino Indian' Trope in Television Depictions of Contemporary Native Americans," *Howard Journal of Communications* 22, no. 1 (2011): 1–23; Jeffrey Hawkins, "Smoke Signals, Sitting Bulls, and Slot Machines: A New Stereotype of Native Americans?" *Multicultural Perspectives* 7, no. 3 (2005): 51–54.

22. See First Nations Development Institute

and Echo Hawk Consulting, *Reclaiming Native Truth*.

23. Cited in Boburg, "Donald Trump's Long History of Clashes with Native Americans."

24. Aired on PBS *NewsHour* on August 13, 2019.

Chapter 13

1. John M. Coward, *The Newspaper Indian* (Urbana: University of Illinois Press, 1999), 81. Cf. today's slogan, "If it bleeds, it leads."

2. *Ibid.*, 127.

3. *Ibid.*, 128.

4. Cited in *ibid.*, 170.

5. *New York Times*, December 16, 1890, 1, cited in *ibid.*, 186.

6. Boston *Daily Globe*, December 16, 1890, 4, and December 17, 4, 1890, cited in *ibid.*, 188.

7. Chicago *Tribune*, May 19, 1879, 4, cited in *ibid.*, 208. For a history of the Poncas, who were terminated as a tribe by the U.S. government in 1962 and then reinstated in 1990, see "Ponca History," Ponca Tribe of Indians of Oklahoma, ponca.com/ponca-history.

8. *Daily Rocky Mountain News*, May 17, 1879, 2, cited in Coward, *The Newspaper Indian*, 210.

9. *Ibid.*, 233–34.

10. Mary Ann Weston, *Native Americans in the News: Images of Indians in the Twentieth-Century Press* (Westport, CT: Greenwood Press, 1996).

11. For a further discussion of Collier, see chapter 18.

12. *New York Times*, January 15, 1923, 28, cited in Weston, *Native Americans in the News*, 27.

13. Weston, *Native Americans in the News*, 28.

14. *Saturday Evening Post*, May 31, 1924, 27, 92, cited in *ibid.*, 33.

15. See the characterization of Native American dances such as these in the *New York Times* as "weird," "savage," and "barbaric" in 1926, in Weston, *Native Americans in the News*, 36.

16. For a review of laws affecting Native American religious practices, see Michael P. Gueno, "Native Americans, Law and Religion in America," *Oxford Research Encyclopedias*, November 2017, Religion.oxfordre.com/view/10.1093/acrefore/9780199340378.001.0001.acrefore-9780199340378-e-.

17. Weston, *Native Americans in the News*, 42.

18. *Ibid.*, 56.

19. *Time*, November 11, 1935, 11, cited in *ibid.*, 58.

20. *Ibid.*, 59.

21. *Scientific American*, January 1933, 22–24, cited in *ibid.*, 65.

22. First Nations Development Institute and Echo Hawk Consulting, *Reclaiming Native Truth*.

23. Ruth Mulvey Harmer, "Uprooting the Indians," *Atlantic Monthly*, March 1956, 54, cited in Weston, *Native Americans in the News*, 118.

24. Weston, *Native Americans in the News*, 133.

25. See the Introduction for a review of articles about Standing Rock.

26. One Native American tribe that grapples with these issues is the Ramapoughs of New Jersey. See Noah Remnick, "The Ramapoughs vs. the World," *New York Times*, April 14, 2017, https://www.nytimes.com/2017/04/14/nyregion/ramapough-tribe-fights-pipeline.html.

27. For an interesting glimpse at how these issues played out in Donald Trump's business ventures prior to his presidency, see Boburg, "Donald Trump's Long History of Clashes with Native Americans."

28. Weston, *Native Americans in the News*, 164.

29. A history of this publishing house and the phenomenon of the dime novel can be found in Albert Johannsen, *The House of Beadle and Adams*, vol. 1 (Norman: University of Oklahoma Press, 1950), xxiii.

30. Michael Denning, *Mechanic Accents: Dime Novels and Working-Class Culture in America* (New York: Verso, 1987).

31. For an analysis of the authors' writing process in dime novels, see Christine Bold, "The Voices of the Fiction Factory in Dime and Pulp Westerns," *Journal of American Studies* 17, no. 1 (April 1983): 29–46.

32. Vine Deloria, Jr., "The Indians," in *Buffalo Bill and the Wild West*, ed. David H. Katzive (New York: Brooklyn Museum, 1981), 55.

33. For an analysis of this trend, see Slotkin, *Gunfighter Nation*, chapters 5 and 6.

34. Owen Wister, *The Virginian* (New York: Gramercy Books, 1902).

35. For a review of Faust's works, see William F. Nolan, *Max Brand: Western Giant* (Bowling Green, OH: Bowling Green State University Press, 1985).

36. *Ibid.*, 2.

37. William A. Bloodworth, Jr., *Max Brand* (New York: Twayne Publishers, 1993), 72.

38. Robert Easton, *Max Brand the Big "Westerner"* (Norman: University of Oklahoma Press, 1970), 68. Easton was an actor, author, and educator and the son-in-law of Faust.

39. Edgar L. Chapman, "The Image of the Indian in Max Brand's Pulp Western Novels," *Heritage of Kansas* 2 (Spring 1978): 39.

40. Bloodworth, *Max Brand*, 46.

41. Cited in *ibid.*, 53.

42. Easton, *Max Brand the Big "Westerner,"* 64.

43. Whether for glory or purported religious beliefs, Brand (Faust) portrayed Indians as obsessed with garnering the scalps of their enemies. See Max Brand, *Thunder Moon* (New York: Street and Smith Publications, 1927). The edition referred to was published by Thorndike Press, large print edition, in 1983. See also Max Brand, *The Rescue of Broken Arrow* (New York: Street and Smith Publication, Inc., 1929, 1930), large print

edition by Center Point Publishing, Thorndike, Maine.

44. "[T]he men [Pawnees] had gone to pick Cheyenne scalps like daisies on the bloody slope of Bald Hill." Brand, *The Rescue of Broken Arrow*, 150.

45. Max Brand, *Farewell, Thunder Moon* (Lincoln: University of Nebraska Press, 1995), 49. Faust used this same theme in his Red Hawk series, where the hero, Rusty Sabin, was also captured as a child and grew up among the Cheyenne. And, not coincidentally, both Sutton and Sabin failed the painful Cheyenne initiation rite, forcing them to find heroic alternative actions to diminish their shame. Cf. Max Brand, *Cheyenne Gold* (New York: Frank A. Munsey Company, 1935), Reprinted by Hodder and Stoughton, London, 1973.

46. Brand, *Farewell Thunder Moon*, 24. The plot in *The Rescue of Broken Arrow* also revolves around White characters who become leaders of Pawnee and Cheyenne tribes—one a thief and the other a vain egomaniac.

47. Brand, *Farewell Thunder Moon*, 25.

48. *Ibid.*, 17.

49. *Ibid.*, 196.

50. *Ibid.*, 213.

51. Brand, *The Rescue of Broken Arrow*, 11.

52. *Ibid.*, 167.

53. *Ibid.*, 159.

54. *Ibid.*, 92.

55. *Ibid.*, 165.

56. *Ibid.*, 105.

57. Bloodworth, *Max Brand*, 162.

58. Compare Sheyahshe's observation with this passage from Max Brand's (Frederick Faust) book *Vengeance Trail* (New York: Dodd, Mead and Company, 1941): "When he came up to the boy, he rode straight in upon him with the expression of one about to strike a blow, but when he was close enough he checked his war pony and extended his hand with a gruff 'How!' No one has ever been able to pronounce that word exactly as the Indians did. It was partly nasal. It was partly guttural. It was partly a cry and partly a grunt. It could be spelled 'How!' or 'Ough' or 'Ugh' and has been given all of these meanings" (165).

59. For a discussion of Native Americans in comic books, see the analysis of Michael A. Sheyahshe, *Native Americans in Comic Books: A Critical Study* (Jefferson, NC: McFarland & Company, 2008).

60. Jon Proudstar as quoted in Sheyahshe, *Native Americans in Comic Books*, 192.

61. Anne Bolen, "Of Gods and Heroes," *National Museum of the American Indian* 20, no. 2 (Summer 2019): 34–41.

62. Go to ahcomics.com for information about this genre.

63. *National Museum of the American Indian* 20, no. 4 (Winter 2019).

64. Rebecca Roanhorse, cited in *ibid.*, 10.

65. John Seven, "Interview: Lee Francis Talks Native American Comics, Indigipop X and the Rise of the Indiginerd," *The Beat*, July 19, 2019, https://www.comicsbeat.com/interview-lee-francis-talks-native-american-comics-indigipop-x.

66. Jeffrey Steele, "Reduced to Images: American Indians in Nineteenth-Century Advertising," in *Dressing in Feathers*, ed. Bird, 45–64.

67. *Ibid.*, 147.

68. See Brian D. Behnken and Gregory D. Smithers, *Racism in American Popular Media: From Aunt Jemima to the Frito Bandito* (Santa Barbara, CA: Praeger, 2015), for a discussion of cigar store Indians. For more pictures of cigar store Indians, see Evan Schuman, "From the Sidewalk to Sotheby's, the Cigar Store Indian Is a Piece of American Tobacco History," *Cigar Magazine*, Winter, 2004–05, https://www.yumpu.com/en/document/view/11307103/the-cigar-store-indian-evan-schuman.

69. For a review of this issue and statements of professional associations opposed to the use of Indians as mascots, see "Understanding the American Indian Mascot Issue: A Collection of Writings on Team Names and Logos," *Students and Teachers Against Racism*, www.racismagainstindians.org/understandingmascots.htm.

70. C. Richard King, *Redskins: Insult and Brand* (Lincoln: University of Nebraska Press, 2016), 33.

71. Stephanie A. Fryberg, Hazel R. Markus, Daphna Oyserman, and Joseph M. Stone, "Of Warriors, Chiefs and Indian Princesses: The Psychological Consequences of American Indian Mascots," *Basic and Applied Social Psychology* 30 (2008): 216.

72. Interview with Tim Giago, Rapid City, September 7, 2018.

73. Ben Nuckols, "U.S. Poll Finds Widespread Support for Redskins Name," *AP The Big Story*, May 2, 2013, www.bigstory.ap.org/article/us-poll-finds-widespread-support-redskins-name.

74. King, *Redskins*, 34.

75. For a review of the decision, see Doug Mataconis, "Federal Judge Upholds Revocation of Redskins Trademark," *Outside the Beltway*, July 9, 2015, www.outsidethebeltway.com/federal-judge-upholds-revocation-of-redskins-trademarks/.

76. Michael McCann, "Why the Redskins Scored a Victory in the Supreme Court's Ruling in Favor of The Slants," *Sports Illustrated*, June 19, 2017, https://www.si.com/nfl/2017/06/19/washington-redskins-name-slants-trademark-supreme-court. See a summary of the ruling by Danielle Weitzman, "Washington Redskins U.S. Trademark Registrations Reinstated by Fourth Circuit," Ladas & Parry, https://ladas.com/education-center/Washington-redskins-us-trademark-registrations.

77. Mark Judge, "*Washington Post* Poll: 9 in 10 Native Americans Aren't Offended by Redskins' Name," May 19, 2016. In January 2018, Major

League Baseball announced that the logo for the Cleveland Indians, a stereotypical image called Chief Wahoo that was used since 1948, would no longer be on their uniforms beginning in 2019. The name, also a subject of controversy, will, however, remain. See David Waldstein, "Cleveland Indians Will Abandon Chief Wahoo Logo Next Year," *New York Times*, January 29, 2018, https://www.nytimes.com/2018/01/29/sports/baseball/cleveland-indians-chief-wahoo-logo.html.

78. Richard E. Besser, "Robert Wood Johnson Foundation: We Honored Sports Teams With Racist Mascots. Not Anymore," *USA Today*, May 7, 2018.

Chapter 14

1. Robert L. Gale, *Louis L'Amour* (New York: Twayne Publishers, 1992), 8.

2. Louis L'Amour, *Education of a Wandering Man* (New York: Bantam Books, 1989), 12.

3. "Louis L'Amour," biography.yourdictionary.com/louis-l-amour.

4. "Louis L'Amour," biography.yourdictionary.com/louis-l-amour.

5. The Official Louis L'Amour Website can be found at www.louislamour.com/aboutlouis/biography6.htm; Gale, *Louis L'Amour*.

6. Louis L'Amour, *The Sackett Companion: A Guide to the Sackett Novels* (New York: Bantam Books, 1988).

7. Louis L'Amour, *Down the Long Hill* (New York: Thorndike Press, 2008), 152.

8. *Ibid.*, 151.

9. L'Amour, *Education of a Wandering Man*, 14.

10. *Ibid.*, 172.

11. *Ibid.*, 175.

12. Louis L'Amour, *The Lonesome Gods* (New York: Bantam Books, 1983), 116.

13. *Ibid.*, 176. This may seem a somewhat outmoded perspective given today's mass shootings.

14. Louis L'Amour, "Sackett's Land," *Saturday Review Press*, 1974, v–vi.

15. *Ibid.*, 14.

16. *Ibid.*, 72.

17. Louis L'Amour, *Kiowa Trail* (New York: Thorndike Press, 1998), 21.

18. *Ibid.*, 58.

19. L'Amour, *Down the Long Hills*, 52.

20. L'Amour, *The Lonesome Gods*, 128.

21. *Ibid.*, 183.

22. L'Amour, *Kiowa Trail*, 59.

23. L'Amour, *Down the Long Hills*, 15.

24. L'Amour, *Kiowa Trail*, 13.

25. Louis L'Amour, *Last of the Bree* (New York: Thorndike Press, 1987), 328.

26. *Ibid.*, 482.

27. *Ibid.*, 279.

28. *Ibid.*, 253.

29. *Ibid.*, 256.

30. *Ibid.*, 91.

31. Louis L'Amour, *The Sackett Companion: A Personal Guide to the Sackett Novels* (New York: Bantam, 1988).

32. L'Amour, *The Sackett Companion*, 194.

33. *Ibid.*

34. Gale, *Louis L'Amour*, 114.

35. Easton, *Max Brand the Big "Westerner,"* 123.

Chapter 15

1. Francis M. Nevins, Jr., *Bar-20: The Life of Clarence E. Mulford* (Jefferson, NC: McFarland & Company, 1993), 72.

2. *Ibid.*

3. William A. Bloodworth, Jr., "Mulford and Bower: Myth and History in the Early Western," *Great Plains Quarterly* (Spring 1981): 102.

4. See Nevins, *Bar-20*, 121, for a review of Mulford's estate. From his will dated July 27, 1954: "I thoroughly believe our country has so far progressed through the personal initiative of its citizens. Such estate as I now possess I have acquired through my own industry and endeavors, despite persistent legislative handicaps tending toward involuntary distribution of my earnings, and I am quite out of sympathy with many of the apparent objects of the so-called 'welfare state' towards which for some years the predominant trend of legislation seems to be moving, as I sincerely believe this makes for the destruction of personal initiative, lays too much emphasis on so-called 'security' rather than thrift and enterprise, destroys the incentive of personal gain and venture, makes for remote control and raises up a multitude of public office holders" (*ibid.*, 121). Perhaps his belief in the value of individual initiative was linked to his ancestors who arrived in the colonies in 1643, with twenty of them fighting in the American Revolution. For an inventory of Mulford's written and film credits, see Nevins, *Bar-20*, 211–37.

5. *Ibid.*, 120.

6. Beau L'Amour, "About the Hopalong Cassidy Novels by Louis L'Amour," http://www.louislamour.com/novels/hopalong4byLouis.htm.

7. *Ibid.*

8. *O Pioneers!* (1913), *The Song of the Lark* (1915), and *My Antonia* (1918).

9. Latrobe Carroll, "Willa Sibert Cather," cather.unl.edu/writings/bohlke/interviews/bohlke.i.15#:~:text=Mencken%3A%20"There%20is%20no%20other,reputation%20is%20of%20recent%20growth.

10. William Holtz, *The Ghost in the Little House* (Columbia: University of Missouri Press, 1995). However, there is contradictory evidence. See the discussion on the evolution of Wilder's early writing in Pamela Smith Hill, ed., *Pioneer Girl: The Annotated Bibliography* (Pierre: South Dakota State Historical Society Press, 2014), xv–lxiv. Hill devoted more space to this issue in her interesting biography of Wilder, *Laura Ingalls Wilder: A Writer's Life* (Pierre: South Dakota State

Historical Society Press, 2007), especially chapters 10–13.

11. Caroline Fraser, *Prairie Fires: The American Dreams of Laura Ingalls Wilder* (New York: Metropolitan Books, 2017), 315.

12. Hill, *Laura Ingalls Wilder*, 7.

13. *Ibid.*, 3.

14. *Ibid.*, 42.

15. *Ibid.*, 51.

16. William Anderson, *Laura Ingalls Wilder: A Biography* (New York: HarperCollins, 1992), 13.

17. Hill, *Laura Ingalls Wilder*, 8.

18. *Ibid.*, 4.

19. *Ibid.*, 5.

20. Quoted in Anderson, *Laura Ingalls Wilder*, 14.

21. Max Weber, *The Protestant Ethic and the Spirit of Capitalism* (New York: Penguin Twentieth Century Classics, 2002).

22. Quoted in Anderson, *Laura Ingalls Wilder*, 35.

23. *Ibid.*, 52.

24. *Ibid.*, 85.

25. Laura Ingalls Wilder, *Little House on the Prairie* (New York: Harper and Row, 1935), 241. These sentiments also occur in Wilder's other books (e.g., in *Little House in the Big Woods* (set in Wisconsin), she recalled that at Christmas dinner the children in her family sat silently around the dinner table "for they knew that children should be seen and not heard"; Laura Ingalls Wilder, *Little House in the Big Woods* (New York: Harper and Brothers, 1953), 80).

26. *Ibid.*, 320.

27. *Ibid.*, 31.

28. *Ibid.*, 24–25.

29. *Ibid.*, 126.

30. *Ibid.*, 142.

31. *Ibid.*, 215.

32. *Ibid.*, 236.

33. Laura Ingalls Wilder, *Little House on the Prairie* (New York: Harper and Row, 1935), 316.

34. *Ibid.*, 237.

35. "Aftermath," *The US–Dakota War of 1862*, Minnesota Historical Society, www.usdakotawar.org/history/aftermath.

36. Cited at "The Trials & Hanging," *The US–Dakota War of 1862*, Minnesota Historical Society, https://usdakotawar.org/history/aftermath/trials-hanging.

37. *Ibid.*

38. For a summary of the principal battles in the 1862 Sioux Uprising, see Eric Niderost, "The Great Sioux Uprising of 1862," *Warfare History Network*, https://warfarehistorynetwork.com/daily/civil-war/the-great-sioux-uprising-of-1862.

39. By 1934, 1.6 million homestead applications had been processed by the federal government for more than 270 million acres of land (10 percent of the U.S. land mass). The Federal Land Policy and Management Act of 1976 repealed the Homestead Act in the forty-eight contiguous states. See "The Homestead Act," http://www.archives.gov/education/lessons/homestead-act.

40. See a discussion of this in Fraser, *Prairie Fires*, 154, 169, and 372, and compare Koch et al., "Earth System Impacts," with human interventions that led to climatic cooling in the seventeenth century.

41. For a fuller discussion of the mythological basis and impact of these themes, see Richard Slotkin's works on this topic.

42. Cited in Anderson, *Laura Ingalls Wilder*, 4.

43. Wilder, *Little House on the Prairie*, 211.

44. Cf. Friedman, *The Monstrous Races*.

45. Wilder, *Little House on the Prairie*, 47.

46. *Ibid.*, 56.

47. *Ibid.*, 135–36.

48. *Ibid.*, 140.

49. *Ibid.*, 144.

50. *Ibid.*, 265.

51. *Ibid.*, 284.

52. *Ibid.*, 286.

53. *Ibid.*, 287.

54. *Ibid.*, 310.

55. Frances W. Kaye, "Little Squatter on the Osage Diminished Reserve: Reading Laura Ingalls Wilder's Kansas Indians," *Great Plains Quarterly* 20, no. 2 (May 2000): 123–40.

56. Wilder, *Little House on the Prairie*, 191.

57. Laura Ingalls Wilder, *Little House in the Big Woods* (New York: Harper and Brothers, 1932), 161.

58. Laura was jealous of her older sister, "And Mary was a very good little girl who always did exactly as she was told" (182), but revered her and wound up caring for her after Mary lost her vision, purportedly from scarlet fever, at age fourteen in 1879.

59. See Fraser, *Prairie Fires*, 163–66.

60. *Ibid.*, 6.

61. *Ibid.*, 11.

62. See Kaye, "Little Squatter on the Osage Diminished Reserve."

63. Laura Ingalls Wilder, *On the Way Home* (New York: Harper and Row, 1962), 24.

64. Kaye, "Little Squatter on the Osage Diminished Reserve."

65. *Ibid.*, 125–26.

66. Eighth: Thou shall not steal. Tenth: You should not be envious of your neighbor's goods.

67. American Library Association, "ALA, ALSC Response to Wilder Medal Name Change," *ALA News*, June 25, 2018, www.ala.org/news/press-releases/2018/06/ala-alsc-respond-wilder-medal-name-change.

68. For a discussion of how teachers can effectively use Wilder's works with their students, see Laura McLemore, "Historical Perspective or Racism on the Prairie?" *LittleHouseOnThePrairie.com*, December 7, 2018, https://littlehouseontheprairie.com/historical-perspective-or-racism-in-little-house-on-the-prairie/.

69. John Price, "The Stereotyping of North American Indians in Motion Pictures," in *The*

Pretend Indians: Images of Native Americans in the Movies, eds. Gretchen M. Bataille and Charles L. P. Silet (Ames: Iowa State University, 1980), 85.

70. The Special Collection at the State University at Buffalo houses much of Striker's work but did not reveal how the terms *Kemo Sabe* and *Tonto* were conceived.

71. John C. Ewers, "The Static Images," in *The Pretend Indians*, ed. Bataille and Silet, 20.

72. Taylor, *Dressing in Feathers*, 242.

73. A rising Native American actor and stand-up comedian is Tatanka Means (Oglala Lakota, Omaha, Diné), who recently appeared in the HBO series *I Know This Much Is True* and the feature film *Once Upon a River*. For an interview with him, see "Healing through Humor with Tatanka Means," *Indian Country Today*, August 11, 2020.

74. The National Museum of the American Indian in Washington, D.C., has an exhibit focusing on stereotypes about Native Americans, including contemporary military appellations for hardware indicative of purported Native American savagery, e.g., the Apache helicopter, https://americanindian.si.edu.

Chapter 16

1. John E. O'Connor, "The White Man's Indian: An Institutional Approach," in *Hollywood's Indian: The Portrayal of the Native American in Film*, ed. Peter C. Rollins and John E. O'Connor (Lexington: University of Kentucky Press, 1998), 37.

2. For more information on Forrest and *Metamora*, see Sally L. Jones, "The First But Not the Last of the 'Vanishing Indians': Edwin Forrest and Mythic Re-Creation of the Native Population," in *Dressing in Feathers*, ed. Bird, 13–28. See also Deborah Boyer, "Edwin Forrest: A Legend of American Theater," *The Philly History Blog*, March 14, 2009, https://www.phillyhistory.org/blog/index.php/2009/03/edwin-forrest-a-legend-of-american-theater/.

3. Richard Slotkin, "The Wild West," in David H. Katzive, *Buffalo Bill and the Wild West* (New York: Brooklyn Museum, 1981), 37.

4. Vine Deloria, Jr., "The Indians," in Katzive, *Buffalo Bill and the Wild West*, 55.

5. *Ibid.*, 56.

6. Katzive, *Buffalo Bill and the Wild West*, 9.

7. "1885–1930: The Wild West Show," *HistoryNet*, https://www.historynet.com/how-the-west-was-spun-buffalo-bill-codys-wild-west-show.htm.

8. Quoted from Peter Carlson, "Buffalo Bill at Queen Victoria's Command," *American History* 50, no. 5 (December 2015): 17.

9. R. L. Wilson, *Buffalo Bill's Wild West: An American Legend* (New York: Random House, 1988), 316.

10. Deloria, "The Indians," in Katzive, *Buffalo Bill and the Wild West*, 55.

11. George Catlin, *Letters and Notes on the Manners, Customs, and Conditions of the North American Indians*, 2nd ed. (London: Self-published at The Egyptian Hall, Piccadilly, 1842).

12. *Ibid.*, vol. 1, 20–21.

13. *Ibid.*, 48.

14. *Ibid.*, 141.

15. *Ibid.*, 143.

16. *Ibid.*, 169.

17. *Ibid.*, 29.

18. *Ibid.*, 76.

19. *Ibid.*, 46.

20. *Ibid.*, vol. 2, 6.

21. *Ibid.*, vol. 1, 156.

22. Bruce Watson, "George Catlin's Obsession," *Smithsonian* Magazine, December 2002, https://www.smithsonianmag.com/arts-culture/george-catlins-obsession-72840046/.

23. Richard H. Ribb, "Colony of Kent," Texas State Historical Association, tshaonline.org/handbook/entries/colony-of-kent.

24. Material on Frederic Remington was gathered from: "Frederic Remington," *Frederic Remington Art Museum*, https://fredericremington.org/frederic-remington-c4.php; Thayer Tolles, "Frederic Remington (1861–1909)," The Met, https://www.metmusem.org/toah/hd/rem. See also Alexander Nemerov, *Frederic Remington and Turn-of-the-Century America* (New Haven, CT: Yale University Press, 1995).

25. This synopsis is primarily derived from Brian W. Dippie, "Charlie Russell's Lost West," *American Heritage Magazine* 24, no. 3 (April 1973): 5–21, 89. See also Harold McCracken, *The Charles M. Russell Book* (Garden City, NY: Doubleday and Company, 1957).

26. Edward S. Curtis, Foreword by Theodore Roosevelt, *The North American Indian*, vol. 1 (Project Gutenberg, 2006), www.gutenberg.org/ebooks/19449.

27. Material about Edward Curtis was derived from: Gilbert King, "Edward Curtis' Epic Project to Photograph Native Americans," *Smithsonian* Magazine, March 21, 2012, https://www.smithsonianmag.com/history/edward-curtis-epic-project-to-photograph-native-americans-162523282/; George H. Capture, "Edward Curtis: Coming to Light—Shadow Catcher," *American Masters*, April 23, 2001, www.pbs.org/wnet/americanmasters/edward-curtis-shadow-catcher/5681; Pedro Ponce, "The Imperfect Eye of Edward Curtis," *Humanities* 21, no. 3 (May–June 2000); Valerie Daniels, "Promoting Edward Curtis, 1907–1916," *Selling the North American Indian: The Work of Edward Curtis*, June 2002, https://xroads.virginia.edu/~MA02/daniels/curtis/promoting.html. Also see the documentary on Edward Curtis produced by Anne Makepeace, *Coming to Light: Edward Curtis and the North American Indians*, PBS Documentary, 2000; Laurie Lawlor, *Shadow Catcher: The Life and Work of Edward S. Curtis* (Lincoln, NE: Bison Books, 2005); Mick Gidley, *Edward S. Curtis and the North American Indian Incorporated* (New York: Cambridge University Press, 2000).

28. Historian Philip Deloria presents an interesting analysis of the composition of Native American music, a topic that has not been developed in this book. Deloria demonstrates the unique characteristics of the music as well as Native American performers and writers who, along with non–Native Americans, helped define the genre of Native American music in the early part of the twentieth century. He adroitly debunks myths about the "primitive" antimodern quality of the music while demonstrating the prevalence, to this day, of pejorative stereotypes about Native American music that evoke elements of the primitive, aggressive, and violent to the exclusion of unique, creative, and aesthetic qualities. See Philip Deloria, *Indians in Unexpected Places* (Lawrence: University of Kansas Press, 2004), 183–223.

Chapter 17

1. Michelle H. Raheja, *Reservation Reelism: Redfacing, Visual Sovereignty, and Representations of Native Americans in Film* (Lincoln: University of Nebraska Press, 2010), 32.
2. Kilpatrick, *Celluloid Indians*, 233.
3. Gretchen M. Bataille and Charles L. P. Silet, *The Pretend Indians: Images of Native Americans in the Movies* (Ames: Iowa State University, 1980), xxii.
4. See Deloria, *Indians in Unexpected Places*, 52–108, for a discussion of thematic material in early motion pictures.
5. *Moving Picture World*, March 11, 1911, 58. See the discussion of this incident in Raheja, *Reservation Reelism*, 42.
6. Ward Churchill, Mary Anne Hill, and Norbert S. Hill, Jr., "Examination of Stereotyping: An Analytical Survey of Twentieth-Century Indian Entertainers," in *The Pretend Indians*, ed. Bataille and Silet, 36.
7. Kilpatrick, *Celluloid Indians*, 51.
8. Leslie A. Fiedler, *The Return of the Vanishing America* (New York: Stein and Day, 1968).
9. Allison Griffiths, "Science and Spectacle: Native American Presentations in Early Cinema," in *Dressing in Feathers*, ed. Bird, 91.
10. Bataille and Silet, *The Pretend Indians*, xxiii.
11. Kilpatrick, *Celluloid Indians*, 18. Raheja discusses the futile attempt of Hollywood Indians in 1940 to become a recognized tribe known as De Mille Indians under the leadership of Chief Thundercloud (Victor Daniels) because they comprised a group of actors who were underrepresented and often abused in motion pictures and on sets. Raheja, *Reservation Reelism*, 1–2.
12. Churchill, Hill, and Hill, "Examination of Stereotyping," 39.
13. Bataille and Silet, *The Pretend Indians*, xxvii.
14. This fact was pointed out to me in an interview with Kyle White, a Lakota Sioux, who was indignant about it. Telephone interview conducted on September 4, 2018, in Rapid City, South Dakota.
15. Raymond William Stedman, *Shadows of the Indian: Stereotypes in American Culture* (Norman: University of Oklahoma Press, 1982), chapter 4.
16. Ralph E. Friar and Natasha A. Friar, "White Man Speaks with Split Tongue, Forked Tongue, Tongue of Snake," in *The Pretend Indians*, ed. Bataille and Silet, 95.
17. See Raheja, *Reservation Reelism*, 21.
18. See Slotkin, *Gunfighter Nation*, chapters 8–9, for a review of this phenomenon.
19. *Ibid.*, 718n7.
20. Frank Manchel, "Cultural Confusion: Broken Arrow," in *Hollywood's Indian: The Portrayal of the Native American in Film*, ed. Peter C. Rollins and John E. O'Connor (Lexington: University of Kentucky Press, 2003), 92.
21. Ken Nolley, "The Representation of Conquest: John Ford and the Hollywood Indian: 1939–1964," in *Hollywood's Indian*, ed. Rollins and O'Connor, 82.
22. John O'Connor, "The White Man's Indian: An Institutional Approach," in *Hollywood's Indian*, ed. Rollins and O'Connor, 32.
23. Cited in Kilpatrick, *Celluloid Indians*, 26–27.
24. Slotkin, *Gunfighter Nation*, 376.
25. Amanda Cobb, "This Is What It Means to Say Smoke Signals: Native American Cultural Sovereignty," in *Hollywood's Indian*, ed. Rollins and O'Connor, 206.
26. Annette M. Taylor, "Cultural Heritage in Northern Exposure," in *Dressing in Feathers*, ed. Bird, 231.
27. Kilpatrick, *Celluloid Indians*, 37.
28. *Ibid.*, 129.
29. John A. Price, "The Stereotyping of North American Indians in Motion Pictures," in *The Pretend Indians*, ed. Bataille and Silet, 81–82.
30. Stedman, *Shadows of the Indian*, 113.
31. For a historical account of this incident, see Cozzens, *The Earth Is Weeping*, 291–98.
32. Summarized in Stedman, *Shadows of the Indian*, 75.
33. *Ibid.*, 164.
34. See Deloria, *Indians in Unexpected Places*, 52–108, for his discussion of the evolution of stereotypes from Wild West shows through the early years of the cinema.
35. *Ibid.*, 73.

Chapter 18

1. Las Casas, *A Brief Account of the Destruction of the Indies*, 6–10.
2. *Ibid.*
3. For a discussion of the lurid details of his work, see Castillo, *A Cross of Thorns*. Social geographer Jared Diamond, *Guns, Germs and Steel*,

and historian David Stannard, *American Holocaust*, provide further examples of the decimation of Indigenous populations in the Americas.

4. Robert P. Jones, founder of the Public Religion Research Institute and holder of a PhD in religion from Emory University and a master's of divinity from Southwestern Baptist Theological Seminary, demonstrated the long tradition of White supremacy that undergirds Christian traditions and theology in the United States, especially among Evangelical Christians before and after the Civil War. See his *White Too Long: The Legacy of White Supremacy in American Christianity* (New York: Simon and Schuster, 2020).

5. One of the largest and most contentious claims relates to the Black Hills in South Dakota, a verdant territory 165 miles long and 65 miles wide, sacred to the area's Lakota, Cheyenne, Arapaho, Kiowa, and Apaches. It was taken from them by the federal government through a series of treaty violations in the late 1800s. A $17.5 million award from the federal government in a 1979 court decision (with interest amounting to $105 million) was rejected by Native Americans. Lakota tribal attorney Mario Gonzalez then sought an $11 billion award and the return of 7,300,000 acres of land in the designated area, but this claim was denied by the U.S. Supreme Court. The struggle over ownership and compensation for the area is still being contested.

6. Eveleth, "Genetic Testing and Tribal Identity."

7. "Frequently Asked Questions," National Park Service, https://www.nps.gov/nagpra/FAQ/INDEX.HTM.

8. Treuer, *The Heartbeat of Wounded Knee*.

9. Laurence Hauptman, *The Iroquois and the New Deal* (Syracuse, NY: Syracuse University Press, 1988), 28.

10. Treuer, *The Heartbeat of Wounded Knee*, 207.

11. Material on John Collier was gathered from Treuer, *The Heartbeat of Wounded Knee*, 204–09; "John Collier, 1884–1968," *The Living New Deal*, https://livingnewdeal.org/glossary/john-collier-1884-1968/#:~:text=Collier%20was%20also%20the%20prime,returning%20tribal%20lands%20to%20%5B2%5D. Also see a discussion of Collier's works at Dippie, *The Vanishing American*, 275–76, 294–95, 297–321, 322–44.

12. Friedman, *The Monstrous Races*.

13. Derek Freeman, *The Making of an Anthropological Myth* (Cambridge, MA: Harvard University Press, 1983).

14. Margaret Mead, *The Changing Culture of an Indian Tribe* (New York: AMS Press, 1969), originally published in 1932.

15. Thomas Biolsi and Larry J. Zimmerman, eds., *Indians and Anthropologists: Vine Deloria, Jr., and the Critique of Anthropology* (Tucson: The University of Arizona Press, 1997), 6.

16. For further information on the Tuskegee experiment, see Fred D. Gray, *The Tuskegee Syphilis Study: The Real Story Beyond Montgomery, Alabama* (Montgomery, AL: NewSouth Press, 1998); Susan M. Reverby, *Examining Tuskegee: The Infamous Study and Its Legacy* (Chapel Hill: University of North Carolina Press, 2009); Mary Kaplan, *The Tuskegee Veterans Hospital and Its Black Physicians* (Jefferson, NC: McFarland & Company, 2016), 89–122.

17. Deloria, *Custer Died for Your Sins*, 78.

18. *Ibid.*, 79.

19. *Ibid.*

20. *Ibid.*

21. Vine Deloria, Jr., "Anthros, Indians, and Planetary Reality," in *Indians and Anthropologists*, ed. Biolsi and Zimmerman, 209–21.

22. See the statement on ethics by the American Anthropological Association and related links at "AAA Ethics Forum," ethics.americananthro.org/category/statement/.

23. For more information, see their website at aia.americananthro.org.

24. Email communication from Daniel Ginsberg, manager of education, research, and professional development for the American Anthropological Association, August 19, 2019.

25. Collections pertaining to Native Americans can be found at many colleges and universities around the nation. Here are a few that deserve further attention: The University of California, Berkeley's collection, https.://guides.lib.berkeley.edu/c.ph?g=527365&p=4028861; the University of Southern California's collection, usc.edu/nativeamericanstudies/articles; Columbia Basin College has a collection "Native American Culture and History Resources" section, https://cbc.instructure.com/courses/804034/pages/native-american-culture-and-history-resources; New York University's library has a collection "Native American and Indigenous Studies Research Guide: Digital Research."

26. This legislation requires institutions that receive federal funding to inventory their collections, consult with federally recognized Native American tribes about research objectives, and repatriate human remains and/or cultural items that have a "reasonable relationship" between a Native American group and contemporary federally funded tribes. However, a study done by the U.S. Government Accountability Office found that Native American art and sacred relics were being auctioned overseas and no existing federal law prevented this practice. An analysis of auctions conducted in Paris, France, between 2012 and 2017 found that nearly one thousand pieces from Native Americans in the Southwest were offered for sale at principally five French auction houses during this time period. Of 1,400 items sold, half had a value of nearly $7 million. Yet many Native Americans view these items as priceless because of their tribal cultural heritage and religious or healing significance. The report concluded that federal agencies have not adopted leading collaboration practices to assist tribes in their quest to

repatriate sacred objects. See the report *Native American Cultural Property: Report to Congressional Requesters*, U.S. Government Accountability Office, August 2018, https://www.gao.gov/assets/700/693809.pdf. Further information on Native American artifacts in museums is available from the Peabody Museum of Archaeology and Ethnology at Harvard University, https:www.peabody.harvard.edu/node/310.

27. Deloria, "Anthros, Indians, and Planetary Reality," 220–21.

28. Peter Whiteley, "The End of Anthropology (at Hopi)?" *Journal of the Southwest* 35 (Summer 1993): 125–57.

29. Gail Landsman, "Informant as Critic: Conducting Research on a Dispute Between Iroquoianist Scholars and Traditional Iroquois," in *Indians and Anthropologists*, ed. Biolsi and Zimmerman, 160–76.

Chapter 19

1. Kim Baca, "Zinke Recommends Reducing Bears Ears," *Indian Country Today*, August 29, 2017.

2. *Ibid.*

3. First Nations Development Institute and Echo Hawk Consulting, *Reclaiming Native Truth*.

4. "15 Indian Tribes Have Unemployment Rates Over 80%," *AAANativeArts.com*, August 30, 2013, https://www.aaanativearts.com/?s=15+tribes+have+unemployment+rates+over+80%25.

5. Algernon Austin, "Native Americans and Jobs: The Challenge and the Promise," Economic Policy Institute, December 17, 2013, https://www.epi.org/publication/native-americans-and-jobs/.

6. See Robert Williams, Jr., *Like a Loaded Weapon: The Rehnquist Court, Indian Rights, and the Legal History of Racism in America* (Minneapolis: University of Minnesota Press, 2005), 223–25. Jackson, *A Century of Dishonor*, also has an extended discussion about the Doctrine of Discovery.

7. Telephone interview conducted with John Dawson, former legal counsel with the National Congress of American Indians, on July 31, 2018.

8. See Williams's discussion of this case in *Like a Loaded Weapon*, 152–157.

9. Treuer, *The Heartbeat of Wounded Knee*, 385.

10. For a discussion of this decision, see Hal Bernton, "Tied United States Supreme Court Decision Means Washington Must Remove Barriers to Salmon Migration," *Seattle Times*, June 11, 2018. For more, see "Supreme Court's Order Forces Washington to Continue Costly Culvert Replacement," *MYNorthwest*, June 12, 2018, https://mynorthwest.com/1016868/supreme-courts-order-forces-washington-to-continue-costly-culvert-replacement.

11. For an interesting review of Cobell's work, see the documentary film *100 Years* (Fire in the Belly Productions, 2016). For a review of Native American successes in the U.S. House of Representatives in 2020, see Dalton Walker, "U.S. House Candidates Make History," *Indian Country Today*, November 4, 2020.

12. For a review of Native Americans who ran for public office in the 2018 election, see Mark Trahant, "Meet the Native Americans Running for Office in 2018," *High Country News*, August 3, 2018, https://www.hcn.org/articles/election-2018-here-are-the-native-americans-running-for-office-2018; Leila Fadel and Talia Wiener, "Record Number of Native Americans Running for Office in Midterms," National Public Radio, *Morning Edition*, July 4, 2018, https://www.npr.org/2018/07/04/625425037/record-number-of-native-americans-running-for-office-in-midterms. For a summary about some contemporary Native American leaders, see Vincent Schilling, "Fight the Power: 8 Contemporary Heroes and Leaders of Native Resistance," *Indian Country Today*, October 20, 2014.

13. Berkhofer, *The White Man's Indian*, 71.

14. Kilpatrick, *Celluloid Indians*, 233.

15. Paul Chaat Smith, *Everything You Know about Indians Is Wrong* (Minneapolis: University of Minnesota Press, 2009), 71.

16. Joel M. Martin, "'My Grandmother Was a Cherokee Princess': Representations of Indians in Southern History," in *Dressing in Feathers*, ed. Bird, 138.

17. Shawn Regan, "Unlocking the Wealth of Indian Nations: Overcoming Obstacles to Tribal Energy Development," *PERC Policy Perspective*, February 2014, https://www.perc.org/2014/02/18/unlocking-the-wealth-of-indian-nations-overcoming-obstacles-to-tribal-energy-development/.

18. See, for example, *Broken Promises* for discussion of federal problems in funding Native American claims.

19. Deloria, *Custer Died for Your Sins*, 6.

20. *Ibid.*, 9.

21. *Ibid.*, 144.

22. Telephone interview with Suzan Shown Harjo, August 3, 2018.

23. Debra Utacia Krol, "Telling Our Own Story," *Indian Country Today*, no. 2 (June–July 2017) 38–41.

24. For example, see Phil Dierking, "Educators Try New Methods to Save American Indian Languages," *VOA: Learning English*, October 24, 2017, https://learningenglish.voanews.com/a/-american-indian-tribes-trying-new-methods-to-increase-language-speakers/4068111.html.

25. For more information on this activity, see Alex Jacobs, "On the Market: Santa Fe's Annual Indian Market," *Indian Country Today*, June–July 2017, 43. See also the recent discussion about and collection of Native American art in Adriana Greci Green and Tricia Laughlin Bloom, *Native Artists of North America* (New Brunswick, NJ: Rutgers University Press, 2019).

26. For a review of some contemporary Native American artists and recent exhibitions, see the Winter 2019 edition of the *National Museum of the American Indian* 20, no. 4.

27. For a review of this case, see Maraya Cornell, "Biggest Fake Native American Art Conspiracy Revealed," *National Geographic*, March 15, 2018, https://news.nationalgeographic.com/2018/03/native-american-indian-art-fake-forgery-hopi-zuni0/.

28. See the American Public Television film *Native Art Now!* for a portrayal of the evolution of Native art in the last twenty-five years.

29. For more on the Dream Warriors, see dreamwarriors.co/about/; for an interview with Taboo, see Vincent Schilling, "Grammy Winner Taboo from the Black Eyed Peas: An *Indian Country Today* Interview," *Indian Country Today*, https://indiancountrytoday.com/news/grammy-winner-taboo-from-the-black-eyed-peas-an-indian-country-today-interview-AbvhwGLFZU6riFbMKgj3Dw.

30. Deloria, *Indians in Unexpected Places*, 183–223.

31. For example, see the ranking of Native American bands by Kaluyuti, "Best Native American Rock Bands," *The Top Tens*, https://www.thetoptens.com/native-american-rock-bands/.

32. For more on this topic, see Felix Contreras, "American Indian Composers Go Classical," National Public Radio, *All Things Considered*, January 1, 2009, https://www.npr.org/templates/story/story.php?storyId=98884176. See the award-winning documentary film *Rumble: The Indians Who Rocked the World* for a review of Native American influence on contemporary music.

33. Cf. Deloria's critique of anthropologists in *Custer Died for Your Sins*.

34. Cf. W. E. B. Du Bois's "double consciousness" in *The Souls of Black Folk* (New York: Penguin, 1903).

35. Information for the discussion of Gerald Vizenor was obtained from: A. La Vonne Brown Ruoff and Gerald Vizenor, "Woodland Word Warrior: An Introduction to the Works of Gerald Vizenor," *MELUS* 3 (Spring–Summer 1986): 13–43; the official Gerald Vizenor website, www.hanksville.org/storytellers/vizenor/; "Gerald Vizenor," Poetry Foundation, https://www.PoetryFoundation.org/poets/Gerald-vizenor.

36. Louis Owens, *Other Destines: Understanding the American Indian Novel* (Norman: University of Oklahoma Press, 1992), 24.

37. For a synopsis of twenty distinguished Native American writers and their works, see "20 Native American Authors You Need to Read," Open Education Data Base, https://oedb.org/ilibrarian/20-native-american-authors-you-need-to-read/. For reviews of Native American literature, see Margo Lukens, "Native American Literature," in the *Oxford Handbook of Indigenous American Literature*, ed. James H. Cox and Daniel Heath Justice (New York: Oxford

University Press, 2014); Tara Ann Carter, "First and Second Wave Native American Literature," teachers.yale.edu/curriculum/viewer/initiative_16.01.03_u; James H. Cox and Heath Justice (Cherokee), eds., *The Oxford Handbook of Indigenous American Literature* (New York: Oxford University Press, 2014). On a lighter note, Alyssa London (Tlinglit, Czech, Norwegian), former Miss Alaska (2017), is garnering a following through her children's books, such as *Journey of a Freckled Indian*, and work on PBS.

38. Interview with Tim Giago, September 7, 2018, Rapid City, South Dakota.

39. Turtle Talk (blog), http://turtletalk.wordpress.com/category/news/.

40. Native American Culture, https://www.native-americans-online.com/native-american-culture.html.

41. *College and Resource Library News* 71, no. 8 (2010).

42. A number of media outlets exist that provide information about specific Native American nations. The Navajo, the largest Native American group, publishes the *Navajo Times*, which can be found at https://navajotimes.com. The second largest group, the Cherokee Nation, publishes *The Cherokee Phoenix* found at https://www.cherokeephoenix.org. *Indian Time News* (https://www.indiantime.net/section/news) provides information primarily about the Akwesasne (Mohawk) Nation.

43. For a review of Phoebe Lett's summary, see "Turn an Ear to Native Stories," *New York Times*, November 29, 2020, D4.

44. For a list and map of these events, see https://calendar.powwows.com/pow-wows-map/.

45. Deloria, *Indians in Unexpected Places*, 270–71n39.

46. I would like to thank Suzan Shown Harjo for providing me with this perspective in an interview on August 3, 2018.

47. First Nations Development Institute and Echo Hawk Consulting, Reclaiming Native Truth.

48. Sarah Shear, Ryan T. Knowles, Gregory J. Soden, and Antonio J. Castro, "Manifesting Destiny: Re/presentations of Indigenous Peoples in K–12 U.S. History Standards," *Theory and Research in Social Education* 43, no.1 (2015): 68–101.

49. Ibid., 90.

50. For a fuller discussion about the NK360° project, see Richard Walker, "Native History is American History," *National Museum of the American Indian* 21, no. 1 (Spring 2020): 28–33. An initiative borne out of the necessity to teach students virtually because of the COVID-19 pandemic was the creation of Lesson Plans for Remote Learning for teachers and students. It is a joint venture of IllumiNative, Amplifier, and the National Indian Education Association for the purpose of providing resources about Native American art, culture, history, and contemporary

life to more than one million students. For the materials, see https://illuminatives.org.

51. See Robin Babb, "Toasted Sister, 'Radio about Native American Food,'" *Alibi* 27, no. 46 (November 15–21, 2018), https://alibi.com/food/57410/toasted-sister-radio-about-native-american-food.html.

52. For an insightful overview of Lyons's perspective, see the July 3, 1991, PBS documentary *Oren Lyons the Faithkeeper*, featuring Bill Moyers and Lyons, https://billmoyers.com/content/oren-lyons-the-faithkeeper.

53. Beverly A. Singer, *Wiping the War Paint Off the Lens* (Minneapolis: University of Minnesota Press, 2001).

54. See the report from the Annenberg Foundation authored by Smith, *Report on Diversity* (CARD).

55. Cynthia Benitez, "Storytelling in Film: Convening an Industry," *National Museum of the American Indian* 18, no. 6 (Winter 2017): 7.

56. Ibid., 6–11.

57. Smith and Warrior, *Like a Hurricane.*

58. Ibid., 270.

59. Ibid.

60. Ibid., 269.

61. See Gonzalez and Cook-Lynn, *The Politics of Hallowed Ground.*

62. The exact number of Native Americans killed is in still in question, ranging from 150 to 300. Twenty-five U.S. soldiers died in the action.

63. Sean Murphy, "Cherokee Nation Seeks Congressional Delegate," *Asbury Park Press*, August 18, 2019, 21A.

64. Williams, *Savage Anxieties*, 217.

65. Quoted in Steiner, *The New Indians*, 89.

66. Ibid., 92.

67. One of the most erudite explorations of the mythological origins of the American conceptualization of Native Americans was compiled by Slotkin in *Regeneration through Violence* and *Gunfighter Nation*; however, his reliance on Freudian and Jungian insights might be off-putting for some readers.

68. John Wayne interview in *Playboy* magazine, May 1971, https://pages.shanti.virginia.edu/wild_wild_cold_war/files/2011/11/John_wayne_playboy_Int2.pdf.

69. Steiner, *The New Indians*, 161.

70. Ibid., 164.

71. See Slotkin, *Gunfighter Nation*, 446.

72. Ibid., 462.

73. Ibid.

74. For a discussion of this perspective, see Max Weber, *The Protestant Ethic and the Spirit of Capitalism with Other Writings on the Rise of the West*, 4th ed., trans. Stephen Kalberg (New York: Oxford University Press, 2008).

75. Steiner, *The New Indians*, 140.

76. Quoted in Steiner, *The New Indians*, 153.

77. Telephone interview with Paul Chaat Smith, August 3, 2018.

78. For a sampling of their writing, see Houston Stewart Chamberlain, *Foundations of the Nineteenth Century*, trans. John Lees (London: John Lane, 1911); Grant, The Passing of the Great Race; Stoddard, The Revolt of Civilization.

79. Treuer, *The Heartbeat of Wounded Knee*, 416.

Epilogue

1. Joss Wood, "Dallas Cowboys Teams Up with WinStar World in First Official NFL Casino Partnership," *Legal Sports Report*, September 6, 2018, http://www.legalsportsreport.com/23697/dallas-cowboys-winstar-casino-deal/.

2. U.S. Commission on Civil Rights, *Broken Promises*, 11.

3. See Eric Lipton, "Trump Unlocks Federal Lands in a Final Rush," *New York Times*, December 20, 2020, 1, 22.

Appendix

1. See National Conference of State Legislatures, https://www.ncsl.org/research/state-tribal-institute/list-of-federal-and-state-recognized-tribes.aspx#federal.

Bibliography

*Online citations were correct at the time of retrieval and have been updated, but they may have changed over time. Associated information for references has been provided when possible.

Abbattista, Guido. "European Encounters in the Age of Expansion." *European History Online*, January 24, 2011. http://ieg-ego.eu/en/threads/ backgrounds/european-encounters/guido-abbattista-european-encounters-in-the-age-of-expansion.

Abram, Susan. "Sequoyah." *The Encyclopedia of Alabama*. www.encyclopediaofalabama.org/ article/h-2159.

Adams, Charles Francis. *Three Episodes of Massachusetts*. Boston: Houghton Mifflin Company, 1892.

"Aftermath." *The US–Dakota War of 1862*. Minnesota Historical Society. www.usdakotawar.org/ history/aftermath.

Alexandria.gov. "We Are All Americans." City of Alexandria, Virginia. https://www. alexandriava.gov/historic/fortward/default. aspx?id=40164.

Allen, Charles Wesley, Sam Deon, and Red Cloud. *Autobiography of Red Cloud: War Leader of the Oglalas*. Edited by R. Eli Paul. Helena: Montana Historical Society Press, 1997.

American Library Association. "ALA, ALSC Response to Wilder Medal Name Change." *ALA News*, June 25, 2018. www.ala.org/news/press-releases/2018/06/ala-alsc-respond-wilder-medal-name-change.

Anderson, Christopher W. "Native Americans and the Origin of Abraham Lincoln's Views on Race." *Journal of the Abraham Lincoln Association* 37, no. 1 (Winter 2016): 11–29.

Anderson, Gary C. *Sitting Bull and the Paradox of Lakota Nationhood*, 2nd ed. Upper Saddle River, NJ: Pearson, 2006.

Anderson, Terry. "The Wealth of (Indian) Nations." *Defining Ideas: A Hoover Institution Journal* (October 25, 2016). https://www. hoover.org/research/wealth-indian-nations-1.

Anderson, William. *Laura Ingalls Wilder: A Biography*. New York: HarperCollins, 1992.

Anti-Poverty Network of New Jersey. *The Uncomfortable Truth: Racism, Injustice, and Poverty*. September 2017. https://2750d32d-03da-445f-8576-8ae3f5da7b2f.filesusr.com/ ugd/14a332_15c12850391c4e679068dace4476 8bdf.pdf.

"Apache Chief Cochise Dies." This Day in History, *History.com*. https://www.history.com/this-day-in-history/apache-chief-cochise-dies.

Arens, William. *The Man-Eating Myth*. New York: Oxford University Press, 1979.

Associated Press. "What Did Donald Trump Say About Immigrants?" *Boston Globe*, June, 29, 2015. https://www.bostonglobe.com/arts/ television/2015/06/29/what-did-donald-trump-say-about-immigrants/ForaqpQ HjwgeKRdVUdYrdM/story.html.

Austin, Algernon. "Native Americans and Jobs: The Challenge and the Promise." *Economic Policy Institute*, December 17, 2013. https://www.epi.org/publication/native-americans-and-jobs/.

Axelrod, Alan. *Chronicle of the Indian Wars from Colonial Times to Wounded Knee*. New York: Konecky and Konecky, 1993.

Babb, Robin. "'Toasted Sister,' Radio about Native American Food.'" *Alibi* 27, no. 46 (November 15–21, 2018). https://alibi.com/food/57410/ toasted-sister-radio-about-native-american-food.html.

Baca, Kim. "Zinke Recommends Reducing Bears Ears." *Indian Country Today*, August 29, 2017.

Barker, Martin, and Roger Sabin. *The Lasting of the Mohicans: History of an American Myth*. Jackson: University of Mississippi Press, 1995.

Barrett, Stephen M. *Geronimo's Story of His Life*. New York: Duffield and Company, 1906.

Basler, Roy P., ed. "Fourth Debate with Stephen A. Douglas." In *The Selected Works of Abraham Lincoln*, vol. 3. New Brunswick, NJ: Rutgers University Press, 1953.

Bataille, Gretchen, and Charles L. P. Silet. *The Pretend Indians: Images of Native Americans in the Movies*. Ames: Iowa State University Press, 1980.

"Battle of the Little Big Horn." *History.com*. www. history.com/topics/native-american-history/ battle-of-the-little-bighorn.

"The Battle of the Little Big Horn, 1876." *Eyewitness to History*. www.eyewitnesstohistory.com/ custer.htm.

Beauvis, Fred. "American Indians and Alcohol." *National Institute on Alcohol Abuse* 22, no. 4 (1998): 253–59.

Beeckman, Daniel. *A Voyage to and from the Island of Borneo*. London: T. Warneretal, 1719.

Behnken, Brian D., and Gregory D. Smithers. *Racism in American Popular Media: From Aunt Jemima to the Frito Bandito*. Santa Barbara, CA: Praeger, 2015.

Benedict, Jeff. *Without Reservation: The Making of America's Most Powerful Indian Tribe and Foxwoods, the World's Largest Casino*. New York: HarperCollins, 2000.

Benite, Zivi Ben-Dor. "Mormon Scripture and the Lost Tribes of Israel." *Bible Odyssey*. https://www.bibleodyssey.org/en/places/related-articles/mormon-scripture-and-the-lost-tribes-of-israel/.

Benitez, Cynthia. "Storytelling in Film: Convening an Industry." *National Museum of the American Indian* 18, no. 6 (Winter 2017): 6–11.

Bennett, Brittney. "Law Was Meant to Let American Indians Prosecute Violence: Is It Working? *USA Today*, March 25, 2017.

Berkhofer, Jr., Robert F. *The White Man's Indian: Images of the American Indian from Columbus to the Present*. New York: Vintage Books, 1978.

Berman, Noah. "Pope Francis Canonizes Father Junipero Serra, Saying He Defended Native Americans." *Los Angeles Times*, September 23, 2015. www.latimes.com/nation/la-na-pope-visit-serra-20150923-story.html.

Bernton, Hal. "Tied United States Supreme Court Decision Means Washington Must Remove Barriers to Salmon Migration." *Seattle Times*, June 11, 2018.

Besser, Richard E. "Robert Wood Johnson Foundation: We Honored Sports Teams with Racist Mascots. Not Anymore." *USA Today*, May 7, 2018.

Bidwell, Alice. "Are American Indian Students the Least Prepared for College?" *U.S. News and World Report*, March 13, 2014. https://www.usnews.com/news/blogs/data-mine/2014/03/13/are-american-indian-students-the-least-prepared-for-college.

Biolsi, Thomas, and Larry J. Zimmerman. *Indians and Anthropologists*. Tucson: University of Arizona Press, 1997.

Bird, Robert M. *Nick of the Woods: Or, Adventures of Prairie Life*. 1837; Project Gutenberg, 2004. www.gutenberg.org/ebooks/13970.

Black, Don. *Stormfront*. https://www.stormfront.org/forum (shut down in 2017).

Blanton, William. *The Leopard's Spots: Scientific Attitudes toward Race in America, 1815–1859*. Chicago: University of Chicago Press, 1960.

Bleir, Garet, and Anya Zoledziowski. "Hate in America: Native Women Are 10 Times More Likely to Be Murdered." *Indian Country Today*, August 25, 2018.

Bloodworth, Jr., William A. *Max Brand*. New York: Twayne Publishers, 1993.

_____. "Mulford and Bower: Myth and History in the Early Western." *Great Plains Quarterly* 1, no. 2 (Spring 1981): 95–104.

Blue Lake Rancheria Tribe. https://bluelakerancheria-nsn.gov.

Boburg, Shawn. "Donald Trump's Long History of Clashes with Native Americans." *Washington Post*, July 25, 2016.

Bold, Christine. "The Voices of the Fiction Factory in Dime and Pulp Westerns." *Journal of American Studies* 17, no. 1 (April 1983): 29–46.

Bolen, Anne. "Of Gods and Heroes." *National Museum of the American Indian* 20, no. 20 (Summer 2019): 34–41.

Boyer, Deborah. "Edwin Forrest: A Legend of American Theater." *The Philly History Blog*, March 14, 2009. https://www.phillyhistory.org/blog/index.php/2009/03/edwin-forrest-a-legend-of-american-theater/.

Brand, Max. *Cheyenne Gold*. New York: Frank A. Munsey Company, 1935.

_____. *Farewell, Thunder Moon*. Lincoln: University of Nebraska Press, 1995.

_____. *The Rescue of Broken Arrow*. New York: Street and Smith Publications, 1929.

_____. *Thunder Moon*. New York: Street and Smith Publications, 1927.

_____. *Vengeance Trail*. New York: Dodd, Mead and Company, 1941.

Brandt, Anthony. "Blood and Betrayal: King Philip's War." *HistoryNet*. https:www.historynet.com/blood-and-betrayal-king-philips-war.htm.

Bray III, George A. "Scalping during the French and Indian War." www.earlyamerica.com/review/1998/scalping.html.

Brewer, Susan. "Protect the Children, Preserve the Tribe." *Stand* (Summer 2015): 24–28.

"The Bull *Inter Caetera* (Alexander VI), May 4, 1493." http://www.nativeweb.org/pages/legal/indig-inter-caetera.html.

"The Bull *Romanus Pontifex* (Nicholas V), January 8, 1455." https://www.nativeweb.org/pages/legal/indig-romanus-pontifex.html.

Burmila, Ed. "The Invention of Christopher Columbus, American Hero." *The Nation*, October 9, 2017. https://www.thenation.com/article/the-invention-of-christopher-columbus-american-hero.

Butt, Riazat. "Half of Britons Do Not Believe in Evolution, Survey Finds." *The Guardian*, February 1, 2009. http://www.guardian.co.uk/science/2009/feb/01/evolution-darwin-survey-creationism.

Cano, Regina Garcia. "Impoverished Tribe Struggles to Stop Surge in Teen Suicides." *Associated Press*, April 13, 2015. https://apnews.com/e9fabe4378354aba82b2e96a88e4a790.

Capriccioso, Rob. "Trump Budget Serves Deep Cuts in Many Indian Areas." *Indian Country Today*, June 6, 2017.

Capture, George H. "Edward Curtis: Coming to Light—Shadow Catcher." *American Masters*,

April 23, 2001. www.pbs.org/wnet/american masters/edward-curtis-shadow-catcher/5681.

Carlson, Peter. "Buffalo Bill at Queen Victoria's Command." *American History* 50, no. 5 (December 2015).

Carter, Tara Ann. "First and Second Wave Native American Literature." https://teachers.yale.edu/curriculum/viewer/initiative_16.01.03_u.

Carver, Jonathan. *Travels through Interior Parts of North America in the Years 1766–1767*. London: C. Dilly, H. Payne and J. Phillips, 1781.

Castillo, Elias. *Cross of Thorns: The Enslavement of California's Indians by the Spanish Missions*. Fresno, CA: Craven Street Books, 2015.

Cather, Willa. *My Ántonia*. Boston: Houghton Mifflin, 1918.

_____. *O Pioneers!* Boston: Houghton Mifflin, 1913.

_____. *The Song of the Lark*. Boston: Houghton Mifflin, 1915.

Catlin, George. *Letters and Notes on the Manners, Customs, and Conditions of the North American Indians*, 2nd ed. London: Self-published at the Egyptian Hall, Piccadilly, 1842.

Chamberlain, Houston Stewart. *Foundations of the Nineteenth Century*. Translated by John Lees. London: John Lane, 1911.

Chapman, Edgar L. "The Images of the Indian in Max Brand's Pulp Western Novels." *Heritage of Kansas* 2 (Spring 1978).

Chavers, Dean. "A History of Indian Voting Rights and Why It's Important to Vote." *Indian Country Media Network*, October 29, 2012.

Cherokee Nation. "Sequoyah and the Cherokee Syllabary." Cherokee.org. https://www.cherokee.org/search?term=sequoyah&searchRoot=1088.

Cherokee Phoenix. https://www.cherokeephoenix.org.

"Chief Joseph." *Biography*. https://www.biography.com/people/chief-joseph.9358227.

Churchill, Ward, Mary Anne Hill, and Norbert S. Hill, Jr. "Examination of Stereotyping: An Analytical Survey of Twentieth-Century Indian Entertainers." In *The Pretend Indians: Images of Native Americans in the Movies*, edited by Gretchen Bataille and Charles L. P. Silet, 35–48. Ames: Iowa State University Press, 1980.

Clavin, Tom. *The Heart of Everything that Is: The Untold Story of Red Cloud, an American Legend*. New York: Simon & Schuster, 2014.

Cobb, Amanda. "This Is What It Means to Say Smoke Signals: Native American Cultural Sovereignty." In *Hollywood's Indian: The Portrayal of the Native American in Film*, edited by Peter C. Rollins and John E. O'Connor, chapter 14. Lexington: University of Kentucky Press, 1998.

"Colonel George Custer Massacres Cheyenne on Washita River." This Day in History, *History.com*. https://www.history.com/this-day-in-history/custer-massacres-cheyenne-on-washita-river.

Columbus, Christopher. *Log*. Franciscan-archives.org/Columbus/opera/excerpts.html.

Commonwealth of Australia. *Bringing Them Home: Report of the National Inquiry into the Separation of Aboriginal and Torres Strait Islander Children From Their Families*. Canberra, April 1997. https://humanrights.gov.au/our-work/bringing-them-home-report-1997.

Comte, Auguste. *A General View of Positivism*. Translated by J. H. Bridges. 1865; Cambridge, UK: Cambridge University Press, 2009; Project Gutenberg, 2016. https://www.gutenberg.org/ebooks/53799.

"Construction of the Dakota Access Pipeline: Memorandum of the Secretary of the Army." *Federal Register*, January 24, 2017. https://www.federalregister.gov/documents/2017/02/17/R1-2017-02032/construction-of-the-dakota-access-pipeline.

Contreras, Felix. "American Indian Composers Go Classical." National Public Radio, *All Things Considered*, January 1, 2009. https://www.npr.org/templates/story/story.php?storyid=98884176.

Cooper, James Fenimore. *The Leatherstocking Tales*. New York: The Library of America, 1985.

Cornell, Maraya. "Biggest Fake Native American Art Conspiracy Revealed." *National Geographic*, March 15, 2018. https://www.nationalgeographic.com/history/article/native-american-indian-art-fake-forgery-hopi-zuni0.

Coward, John. *The Newspaper Indian*. Urbana: University of Illinois Press, 1999.

Cox, James H., and Heath Justice, eds. *The Oxford Handbook of Indigenous American Literature*. New York: Oxford University Press, 2014.

Cozzens, Peter. *The Earth Is Weeping: The Epic Story of the Indian Wars for the American West*. New York: Vintage Books, 2016.

"Crazy Horse." *Biography*. https://www.biography.com/people/crazy-horse-9261082.

"Crazy Horse." *History.com*. www.history.com/topics/native-americanhistory/crazy-horse.

Cunningham, James, Teshia A. Solomon, and Myre L. Muramoto. "Alcohol Use among Native Americans Compared to Whites: Examining the Veracity of the 'Native American Elevated Alcohol Consumption' Belief." *Drug and Alcohol Dependence* 160 (March 1 2016): 65–75.

Curtis, Edward S. *The North American Indian*, vol. 1. Project Gutenberg, 2006. www.gutenberg.org/ebooks/19449.

"Custer's Last Stand, 1876, Dead and Wounded." *USGenWeb Archives*. https://www.files.usgwararchives.net/sd/military/big-horn.txt

"Custer's Last Stand, June 25, 1876." *America's Story from America's Library*, Library of Congress. www.americaslibrary.gov/jb/recon/jb_recon_custer_1.html.

Cutter, Barbara. "The Gruesome Story of Hannah Duston, Whose Slaying of Indians Made Her an American Folk 'Hero.'" *Smithsonian* Magazine, April 9, 2018.

"Dakota Access Pipeline: The Who, What and Why of the Standing Rock Protests." *The Guardian,* November 3, 2016. https://www.theguardian.com/us-news/2016/nov/03/north-dakota-access-oil-pipeline-protests-explainer.

Daniels, Jesse. *Cyber Racism: White Supremacy and the New Attack on Civil Rights.* Lanham, MD: Rowman and Littlefield, 2009.

Daniels, Valerie. "Promoting Edward Curtis, 1907–1916." *Selling the North American Indian: The Work of Edward Curtis,* June 2002. xroads.virginia.edu/~ma02/daniels/Curtis/promoting.html.

Danowitz, Erica S., and Carol Videon. "Native American Resources: Sites for Online Research." *College and Resource Library News* 71, no. 8 (2010).

Dao, James. "In California, Indian Tribes with Casino Money Cast Off Members." *New York Times,* December 11, 2011.

Darian-Smith, Eve. "Indian Gaming." *Britannica.* www.britannica.com/topic/indian-gaming.

Darwin, Charles. *On the Descent of Man,* 2 vols. London: Murray, 1871.

_____. *The Moral and Intellectual Diversity of Races.* Philadelphia: J. B. Lippincott, 1856.

_____. *On the Origin of the Species.* London: Murray, 1859.

Debo, Angie. *Geronimo: The Man, His Time, His Place.* Norman: University of Oklahoma Press, 1996.

Defoe, Daniel. *The Life and Strange Adventures of Robinson Crusoe of York, Mariner.* eBooks@Adelaide. http://ebooks.adelaide.edu.au/d/defoe/Daniel/d31r/.

Deggans, Eric. *Race Baiter.* New York: Palgrave Macmillan, 2012.

Deloria, Jr., Vine. *Custer Died for Your Sins: An Indian Manifesto.* New York: Macmillan, 1969.

_____. *Indians in Unexpected Places.* Lawrence: University of Kansas Press, 2004.

_____. "The Indians." In *Buffalo Bill and the Wild West,* edited by David H. Katzive, 56–58. New York: Brooklyn Museum, 1981.

Denetdale, Jennifer Nez. *The Long Walk: The Forced Navajo Exile.* New York: Chelsea House, 2007.

_____. "Naal Taoos Sani (The Old Paper)." *National Museum of the American Indian* 19, no 2 (Summer 2018): 24–31.

Denning, Michael. *Mechanic Accents: Dime Novels and Working Class Culture in America.* New York: Verso, 1987.

d'Errico, Peter. "Jeffrey Amherst and Smallpox Blankets: Germ Warfare Against the Indians." http://www.nativeweb.org/pages/legal/amherst/lord_jeff.html.

Desmond, Adrian, and James Moore. *Darwin's Sacred Cause.* Boston: Houghton Mifflin Harcourt, 2009.

Diamond, Jared. *Guns, Germs and Steel: The Fates of Human Societies.* New York: W. W. Norton and Company, 1999.

Dierking, Phil. "Educators Try New Methods to Save American Indian Languages." *VOA: Learning English,* October 24, 2017. https://learningenglish.voanews.com/a/american-indian-tribes-trying-new-methods-to-increase-language-speakers/4068111.html.

Dimuro, Gina. "The Forgotten Bear River Massacre May Be the Deadliest Native American Slaughter Ever." *ATI,* January 30, 2019. https://allthatsinteresting.com/bear-river-massacre.

Dippie, Brian. "Charlie Russell's Lost West." *American Heritage Magazine* 24, no. 3 (April 1973): 5–21, 89.

_____. *The Vanishing American: White Attitudes and U.S. Indian Policy.* Lawrence: University of Kansas Press, 1982.

Ditmer, Renae. "Will President Trump Eliminate the BIA?" *Indian Country Today,* June 9, 2017.

Doering, Christopher. "Thune Legislation Targets Suicide by Native American Youth." *Argus Leader (USA Today),* July 16, 2015. https://www.argusleader.com/story/news/politics/2015/07/16/thune-legislation-targets-suicide-native-american-youth/30256783/.

Drimmer, Frederick, ed. *Captured by the Indians: 15 Firsthand Accounts 1750–1870.* New York: Dover Publications Inc., 1961.

Du Bois, W. E. B. *The Souls of Black Folk.* New York: Penguin, 1903.

Dunbar-Ortiz, Roxanne. "The Grid of History: Cowboys and Indians." *Monthly Review,* March 27, 2003. ouleft.sp-mesolite.tilted.net/?p=1295.

_____. *An Indigenous Peoples' History of the United States.* Boston: Beacon Press, 2014.

Dunbar-Ortiz, Roxanne, and Dina Gilio-Whitaker. *"All the Real Indians Died Off" and 20 Other Myths about Native Americans.* Boston: Beacon Press, 2016.

Duran, Bonnie. "Indigenous versus Colonial Discourse: Alcohol and American Indian Identity." In *Dressing in Feathers: The Construction of the Indian in American Popular Culture,* edited by S. Elizabeth Bird, 111–28. Boulder, CO: Westview Press, 1996.

Dussel, Enrique. "Bartolomé de Las Casas." *Britannica.* www.britannica.com/EBchecked/topic/330804/Bartolome-de-Las-casas.

Easton, Robert. *Max Brand the Big "Westerner."* Norman: University of Oklahoma Press, 1970.

Editors. "The Thunderbird Division." *American Indian* 19, no. 1 (Spring 2018): 22–23.

Ehlers, Cindy L., and Ian R. Gizer. "Evidence for a Genetic Component for Substance Dependence in Native Americans." *American Journal of Psychiatry* 170, no. 2 (February 2014): 154–64.

Ending Violence so Children Can Thrive. Attorney General's Advisory Committee on American Indian/Alaska Native Children Exposed to Violence, November 2014. https://www.justice.gov/sites/default/files/defendingchildhood/pages/attachments/2015/03/23/ending_violence_so_children_can_thrive.pdf.

Eschner, Kat. "The Memorial to Crazy Horse Has Been Under Construction for Almost 70 Years." Smart News, *Smithsonian* Magazine, December 4, 2017. https://www.smithsonianmag.com/smart-news/memorial-crazy-horse-has-been-under-construction-almost-70years-180 967377/.

Eveleth, Rose. "Genetic Testing and Tribal Identity." *The Atlantic*, January 26, 2015. https://www.theatlantic.com/technology/archive/2015/01/the-cultural-limitations-of-genetic-testing/384740/.

Everts, Sarah. "Europe's Hypocritical History of Cannibalism." *Smithsonian* Magazine, April 25, 2014. https://www.Smithsonianmag.com/history/europes-hypocritical-history-of-cannibalism-42642371/.

Ewen, Alex. *The Bering Strait Theory*. Phoenix, AZ: Indian Country Media Network, April 25, 2017, ebook.

Ewers, John C. "The Static Images." In *The Pretend Indians: Images of Native Americans in the Movies*, edited by Gretchen M. Bataille and Charles L. P. Silet. Ames: Iowa State University Press, 1980.

Fadel, Leila, and Talia Wiener. "Record Number of Native Americans Running for Office in Midterms." National Public Radio, *Morning Edition*, July 4, 2018. https://www.npr.org/2018/07/04/625425037/record-number-of-native-americans-running-for-office-in-midterms.

Feagin, Joe R. *White Party, White Government*. New York: Routledge, 2012.

_____. *The White Racial Frame*. New York: Routledge, 2010.

Feldman, George F. *Cannibalism, Headhunting and Human Sacrifice in North America: A History Forgotten*. Chambersburg, PA: Alan C. Hood and Company, 2008.

Fiedler, Leslie A. "James Fenimore Cooper: The Problem of the Good Bad Writer." Paper Presented at the Second James Fenimore Cooper Symposium, *James Fenimore Cooper: His Country and His Art*, State University of New York College at Oneonta, July 1979.

_____. *Return of the Vanishing American*. New York: Stein and Day, 1968.

"15 Indian Tribes Have Unemployment Rates Over 80%." *AAANativeArts.com*, August 30, 2013. https://www.aaanativearts.com/?s=15+tribes+have+unemployment+rates+over+80%25.

"Five Civilized Tribes—Cherokee, Chickasaw, Choctaw, Creek and Seminole Tribes in Oklahoma: Dawes Records." National Archives. www.archives.gov/research/native-americans/dawes/.

Flood, Joe. "What's Lurking Behind the Suicides?" *New York Times*, May 6, 2015.

Foreman, Grant. *Sequoyah*. Norman: University of Oklahoma Press, 1938.

Fraser, Caroline. *Prairie Fires: The American Dreams of Laura Ingalls Wilder*. New York: Metropolitan Books, 2017.

"Frederic Remington." Frederic Remington Art Museum. https://fredericremington.org/frederic-remington-c4.php.

Freeman, Derek. *The Making of an Anthropological Myth*. Cambridge, MA: Harvard University Press, 1983.

Friar, Ralph E., and Natasha A. Friar. "White Man Speaks with Split Tongue, Forked Tongue, Tongue of Snake." In *The Pretend Indians: Images of Native Americans in the Movies*, edited by Gretchen Bataille and Charles L. P. Silet. Ames: Iowa State University Press, 1980.

Friedman, John B. *The Monstrous Races in Medieval Art and Thought*. Cambridge, MA: Harvard University Press, 1981.

Fryberg, Stephanie A., Hazel R. Markus, Daphna Oyserman, and Joseph M. Stone. "Of Warriors, Chiefs and Indian Princesses: The Psychological Consequences of American Indian Mascots." *Basic and Applied Social Psychology* 30 (2008): 208–16.

Galanda, Gabriel S. "Tribal Per Capitas and Self-Termination." *Indian Country Today*, August 14, 2014.

Gale, Robert. *Louis L'Amour*. New York: Twayne Publishers, 1992.

Gallup. "Poll: Evolution, Creationism, Intelligent Design." 2019. https://news.gallup.com/poll/21814/evolution-creationism-intelligent-design.aspx.

Garroutte, Eva M. *Real Indians: Identity and the Survival of Native Americans*. Berkeley: University of California Press, 2003.

"Gerald Vizenor." Poetry Foundation. https://www.PoetryFoundation.org/poets/gerald-vizenor.

Gerald Vizenor Website. www.hanksville.org/storytellers/vizenor/.

"Geronimo." *Biography*. https://www.biography.com/political-figure/geronimo.

"Geronimo." *History.com*. www.history.com/topics/native-american-history/geronimo.

Gidley, Mick. *Edward S. Curtis and the North American Indian Incorporated*. New York: Cambridge University Press, 2000.

Gobineau, Joseph-Arthur (Comte) de. *The Inequality of Human Races*. Translated by Adrian Collins. London: William Heinemann, 1915.

Goldenberg, David. *The Curse of Ham: Race and Slavery in Early Judaism, Christianity, and Islam*. Princeton, NJ: Princeton University Press, 2005.

Goldsmith, Oliver. *A History of the Earth and Animated Nature*, vol. 1. York: Thomas Wilson and Son, 1808.

Gonzales, Mario, and Elizabeth Cook-Lynn. *The Politics of Hallowed Ground: Wounded Knee and the Struggle for Indian Sovereignty*. Urbana: University of Illinois Press, 1999.

Google. "Louis L'Amour." https://www.google.

com/search?q=biography.yourdictionary. louis+l'amour+facts&ie=utf-8&client,and

Gossett, Thomas F. *Race: The History of an Idea in America*. New York: Oxford University Press, 1997.

Gould, Stephen J. *The Mismeasure of Man*. New York: W. W. Norton, 1981.

Government Accounting Office. *Indian Affairs: Better Management and Accountability Needed to Improve Indian Education*. Report to the Chairman, Subcommittee on Interior, Environment, and Related Agencies, Committee on Appropriations, House of Representatives, September 24, 2013. https://www.gao.gov/assets/gao-13-774.pdf.

Gray, Fred D. *The Tuskegee Syphilis Study: The Road Beyond Montgomery, Alabama*. Montgomery, AL: NewSouth Press, 1998.

Gray, James. *The Illinois*. New York: Henry Holt and Company, 1940.

Green, Adriana Greci, and Tricia L. Bloom. *Native Artists of North America*. New Brunswick, NJ: Rutgers University Press, 2019.

Green, Carmen R., et al. "Differences in Prescription Opioid Analgesic Availability: Comparing Minority and White Pharmacies Across Michigan." *The Journal of Pain* 6, no. 10 (October 2005): 689–99.

Grey, Zane. *Riders of the Purple Sage*. New York: Grosset and Dunlap, 1912.

_____. *The Vanishing American*. New York: Harper and Brothers, 1925.

Griffiths, Allison. "Science and Spectacle: Native American Presentations in Early Cinema." In *Dressing in Feathers: The Construction of the Indian in American Popular Culture*, edited by S. Elizabeth Bird, chapter 6. Boulder, CO: Westview Press, 1996.

"The Grizzly Death of King Philip: Beheaded and Quartered, Body Tied to Trees for the Birds to Pluck." *Beyond the Bridgewater Triangle: History, Mysteries, Curiosities and Crimes*. https://www.thebridgewatertriangle.net/2010/11/the-grizzly-death-of-king-philip.html.

Gueno, Michael P. "Native Americans, Law and Religion in America." *Oxford Research Encyclopedias*, November 2017. Religion.oxfordre.com/view/10.1093/acrefore/9780199340378.001.0001. acrefore-9780199340378-e-.

Hackel, Steven W. *California's Founding Father*. New York: Hill and Wang, 2013.

Hagan, William T. *Quanah Parker: Last Comanche Chief*. Norman: University of Oklahoma Press, 1993.

Haines, Michael, and Richard H. Steckel. *A Population History of North America*. New York: Cambridge University Press, 2000.

Hakluyt, Richard. *The Principal Navigations, Voyages, Traffiques, and Discoveries of the English Nation*. Edited by Jack Beeching. New York: Penguin Classics, 1972.

_____. *The Principal Navigations, Voyages, Traffiques, and Discoveries of the English Nation*. Edited by Edmund Goldsmid. (Adelaide: University of Adelaide, 2012).

_____. "Richard Hakluyt Makes the Case for English Colonization, 1584." *The American Yawp Reader*. https:www.americanyawp.com/reader/colliding-cultures/Richard-hakluyt-makes-the-case-for-english-colonization-1584.

Hallenbeck, Brian. "Casinos in Connecticut, Elsewhere Already Feeling Encore's Impact." *The Day*, August 19, 2019. https://www.theday.com/article/20190819/NWS01/190819419.

_____. "Foxwoods' Revenues Down Nearly 8 Percent in Latest Quarter." *The Day*, August 27, 2019. https://www.theday.com/article/20190827/Biz02/190829551.

_____. "Tribes Unwilling to Withdraw from East Windsor Casino." *The Day*, August 5, 2019. https://www.theday.com/article/20190805/NWS01/190809697.

Hallowell, A. I. *Culture and Experience*. Philadelphia: University of Pennsylvania Press, 1955.

Hamilton, Edward P., trans. and ed. *Adventures in the Wilderness: The American Journals of Louis Antoine de Bougainville 1756–1760*. Norman: University of Oklahoma Press, 1964.

Hannaford, Ivan. *Race: A History of an Idea in the West*. Baltimore: Johns Hopkins University Press, 1996.

Harjo, Suzan S. "Vampire Policy Is Bleeding Us Dry—Blood Quantum Be Gone!" In *The Great Vanishing Act: Blood Quantum and the Future of Native Nations*, edited by Kathleen Ratteree and Norbert Hill, 77–79. Wheat Ridge, CO: Fulcrum Publishers, 2017.

Harper, Stephen. "Statement of Apology to Former Students of Indian Residential Schools." June 11, 2008. *Facing History and Ourselves*. https://www.facinghistory.org/stolen-lives-indigenous-peoples-canada-and-indian-residential-schools/historical-background/prime-minister-harpers-apology.

Harris, Craig, and Dennis Wagner. "HUD Housing Conditions for Native Americans Much Worse than Rest of U.S." The Republic, *AZ Central*, January 19, 2017. https://www.azcentral.com/story/news/local/arizona-investigations/2017/01/19/new-hud-reports-find-housing-conditions-worse-among-native-americans/96783368/.

Institute of Government Research. *The Problem of Indian Administration: Report of a Survey Made at the Request of Honorable Hubert Work, Secretary of the Interior*. Baltimore: The Johns Hopkins Press, 1928; Hathi Trust Digital Library, 2019. https://babel.hathitrust.org/cgi/pt?id=coo.31924014526150&view=1up&seq=9.

HathiTrust.org. "The Writings of George Washington." https://catalog.hathitrust.org/record/000366819

Hauptman, Lawrence M. "Fighting the Nazis: A Creek Indian Wins the Congressional Medal of Honor." *American Indian* 19, no. 1 (Spring 2018): 17–20.

_____. *The Iroquois and the New Deal.* Syracuse, NY: Syracuse University Press, 1988.

Hawkins, Jeffrey. "Smoke Signals, Sitting Bulls, and Slot Machines: A New Stereotype of Native Americans?" *Multicultural Perspectives* 7, no. 3 (2005): 51–54.

Haynes, Stephen R. *The Curse of Noah: The Biblical Justification for American Slavery.* New York: Oxford University Press, 2002.

Hefling, Kimberly. "GAO: Oversight Needed of Native Schools." *Associated Press*, November 13. 2014, https://apnews.com/article/6fbc1046 27044ab792d165955e39bd26.

Heim, Joe. "Showdown Over Oil Pipeline Becomes a National Movement for Native Americans." *Washington Post*, September 7, 2016.

Herbert, Thomas. *Some Years and Travels into Divers Parts of Asia and Afrique.* London: Jacob Blome and Richard Bishop, 1638; Internet Archive, 2020. https://archive.org/details/dli.venugopal.476.

HighScope Project. https://highscope.org/perry-preschool-project.

Hill, Marc L. *Nobody: Casualties of America's War on the Vulnerable, from Ferguson to Flint and Beyond.* New York: Simon and Schuster, 2016.

Hill, Pamela S. *Laura Ingalls Wilder: A Writer's Life.* Pierre: South Dakota State Historical Society Press, 2007.

_____. *Pioneer Girl: The Annotated Bibliography.* Pierre: South Dakota State Historical Society Press, 2014.

Hiltunen, Juha. "Spiritual and Religious Aspects of Torture and Scalping among Indian Cultures in Eastern North America from Ancient to Colonial Times." *Religion and the Body* 23 (2011): 115–28. https://journal.fi/scripta/article/view/67402.

"A History of Jamestown." Jamestown Settlement & American Revolution Museum at Yorktown. www.historyisfun.org/jamestown-settlement/history-jamestown/.

Hogan, Jan. "Strip Left Reeling: Picking Up the Pieces after the Great Recession." *Las Vegas Review-Journal*, March 27, 2016. https://www.reviewjournal.com/news/special-features/neon-rebirth/strip-left-reeling-picking-up-the-pieces.

Hoig, Stan. *The Sand Creek Massacre.* Norman: University of Oklahoma Press, 1974.

Holloway, Kali. "The Whitelash Next Time." *The Nation*, September 21–28, 2020, 10–11.

Holtz, William. *The Ghost in the Little House.* Columbia: University of Missouri Press, 1995.

Home, Henry. "Preliminary Discourse Concerning the Origins of Man and Languages." In *Sketches of the History of Man*, vol. 1. Dublin: James Williams, Number 21, 1779.

"Homestead Act." *History.com.* https://www.history.com/topics/american-civil-war/homestead-act.

Horowitz, Sari. "The Hard Lives—and High Suicide Rate—of Native American Children on Reservations." *Washington Post*, March 9. 2014.

Hosmer, Brian C. "Quanah Parker." https://www.tshonline.org/handbook/entries/parker-quanah.

How the West was Lost: Modoc Death Will Come Soon Enough. History Channel, March 4, 2017.

Hyslop, Stephen G. "How the West Was Spun—Buffalo Bill Cody's Wild West Show." *History Net.* https://www.historynet.com/how-the-west-was-spun-buffalo-bill-codys-wild-west-show.htm.

Indian Gaming Compacts. U.S. Department of the Interior, Indian Affairs. https://www.bia.gov/as-ia/oig/gaming-compacts.

Indian Gaming Tradeshow and Convention. https://www.indiangamingtradeshow.com/510/indian-gaming-tradeshow-home.htm.

Indian Law Resource Center. "Ending Violence Against Native Women." indianlaw.org/issue/ending-violence-against-native-women.

Indian Reorganization Act. 1934. https:www.uaf.edu/tribal/112/unit_2/indianreorganizationact1934.php.

Inskeep, Steve. *Jacksonland: President Andrew Jackson, Cherokee Chief John Ross, and a Great American Land Grab.* New York: Penguin Press, 2015.

Institute of Government Research. *The Problem of Indian Administration: Report of a Survey Made at the Request of Honorable Hubert Work, Secretary of the Interior.* Baltimore: The Johns Hopkins Press, 1928; Hathi Trust Digital Library, 2019. https://babel.hathitrust.org/cgi/pt?id=coo.31924014526150&view=1up&seq=9.

Institute of Medicine Committee on Understanding and Eliminating Racial and Ethnic Disparities in Health Care. *Unequal Treatment: Confronting Racial and Ethnic Disparities in Health Care.* Edited by Brian D. Smedley, Adrienne Y. Smith, and Alan R. Nelson. Washington, D.C.: National Academies Press, 2003.

Jackson, Helen Hunt. *A Century of Dishonor, 1881.* Project Gutenberg, 2015. www.gutenberg.org/ebooks/50560.

Jackson, Robert H., and Edward Castillo. *Indians, Franciscans, and Spanish Colonization: The Impact of the Mission System on California Indians.* Albuquerque: University of New Mexico Press, 1995.

Jacobs, Alex. "On the Market: Santa Fe's Annual Indian Market." *Indian Country Today*, June–July, 2017.

"From James Madison to the Delegations of Several Indian Nations, [ca. 22 August] 1812." *Founders Online*, National Archives, August 22, 1812. https://founders.archives.gov/documents/Madison/03-05-02-0137.

Janko, Melinda, dir. and prod. *100 Years: One Woman's Fight for Justice.* Fire in the Belly Productions, 2016.

Jarvis, Brooke. "Who Decides Who Counts as Native American?" *New York Times Magazine*, January 18, 2017, 53–60.

Jefferson, Thomas. *Autobiography of Thomas Jefferson, 1743–1790.* New York: G. P. Putnam's Sons, 1914.

_____. *Notes on the State of Virginia.* Chapel Hill, NC: Documenting the American South, University of North Carolina at Chapel Hill, 1785. https://docsouth.unc.edu/southlit/jefferson/jefferson.html.

Jiang, Caroline, et al. "Racial Gender Disparities in Suicide among Young Adults Aged 18–24: United States, 2009–2013." National Center for Health Statistics, Centers for Disease Control and Prevention. www.cdc.gov/nchs/data/hestat/suicide/racial_and_gender_2009_2013.htm.

Johannsen, Albert. *The House of Beadle and Adams,* two vols. Norman: University of Oklahoma Press, 1950.

"John Collier (1884–1968)." *The Living New Deal.* https://livingnewdeal.org/glossary/john-collier-1884-1968.

Jones, Robert P. *White Too Long: The Legacy of White Supremacy in American Christianity.* New York: Simon and Schuster, 2020.

Jones, Sally L. "The First But Not the Last of the 'Vanishing Indians': Edwin Forrest and Mythic Re-Creation of the Native Population." In *Dressing in Feathers: The Construction of the Indian in American Popular Culture,* edited by S. Elizabeth Bird, chapter 2. Boulder, CO: Westview Press, 1996.

Jones, Stacy. "White Men Account for 72 Percent of Corporate Leadership at 16 of the Fortune 500 Companies." *Fortune,* June 9, 2017. https://fortune.com/2017/06/09/white-men-senior-executives-fortune-500-companies-diversity-data/.

Jorgensen, Miriam, et al. "What Can Tribal Child Welfare Policy Teach Us about Tribal Citizenship?" In *The Great Vanishing Act: Blood Quantum and the Future of Native Nations,* edited by Kathleen Ratteree and Norbert Hill, 228–45. Ann Arbor, MI: Fulcrum Publishing, 2017.

Jowitt, Claire, and Daniel Carey, eds. *Richard Hakluyt and Travel Writings in Early Modern Europe.* Surrey, UK: Ashgate, 2012.

Judge, Mark. "Washington Post Poll: '9 in 10 Native Americans Aren't Offended by Redskins' Name." *Washington Post,* May 19, 2016.

Kaluyuti. "Best Native American Rock Bands." *The Top Tens.* https://www.thetoptens.com/native-american-rock-bands/.

Kaplan, H. Roy. *The Myth of Post-Racial America.* Lanham, MD: Rowman and Littlefield, 2011.

Kaplan, Mary. *The Tuskegee Veterans Hospital and Its Black Physicians.* Jefferson, NC: McFarland & Company, 2016.

Kaye, Frances W. "Little Squatter on the Osage Diminished Reserve: Reading Laura Ingalls Wilder's Kansas Indians." *Great Plains Quarterly* 20, no. 2 (May 2000): 123–40.

Keene, Adrienne. "Love in the Time of Blood Quantum." In *Great Vanishing Act: Blood Quantum and the Future of Native Nations,* edited by Kathleen Ratteree and Norbert Hill, 3–13. The Wheat Ridge, CO: Fulcrum Publishers, 2017.

Kendi, Ibram X. *Stamped from the Beginning: The Definitive History of Racist Ideas in America.* New York: Nation Books, 2016.

Kershner, Jim. "Chief Joseph (1840–1904)." *HistoryLink.org.* www.historylink.org/File/8975.

Keshavjee, Mohamed M. *Into That Haven of Freedom.* Toronto: Mawenzi House Publishers, Ltd., 2015.

Kiel, Doug. "Bleeding Out: Histories and Legacies of 'Indian Blood.'" In *The Great Vanishing Act: Blood Quantum and the Future of Native Nations,* edited by Kathleen Ratteree and Norbert Hill, 80–97. Wheat Ridge, CO: Fulcrum Publishers, 2017.

Kilpatrick, Jack F. *Sequoyah of Earth and Intellect.* Austin, TX: Encino Press, 1965.

Kilpatrick, Jacquelyn. *Celluloid Indians: Native Americans and Film.* Lincoln: University of Nebraska Press, 1999.

King, C. Richard. *Redskins: Insult and Brand.* Lincoln: University of Nebraska Press, 2016.

_____. "Segregated Stories: The Colonial Contours of the Little Bighorn Battlefield National Monument." In *Dressing in Feathers: The Construction of the Indian in Popular Culture,* edited by S. Elizabeth Bird, chapter 11. Boulder, CO: Westview Press, 1996.

King, Gilbert. "Edward Curtis' Epic Project to Photograph Native Americans." *Smithsonian* Magazine, March 21, 2012. https://www.smithsonianmag.com/history/edward-curtis-epic-project-to-photograph-native-americans-162523282/.

Knickmeyer, Ellen. "Cherokee Nation to Vote on Expelling Slaves' Descendants." *Washington Post,* March 3, 2007.

Koch, Alexander, et al. "Earth System Impacts of the European Arrival and Great Dying in America After 1492." *Quaternary Science Review* 297 (March 1, 2019): 13–36.

Kolopenuk, Jessica. "NDN DNA." In *The Great Vanishing Act: Blood Quantum and the Future of Native Nations,* edited by Kathleen Ratteree and Norbert Hill, 159–72. Wheat Ridge, CO: Fulcrum Publishers, 2017.

Krol, Debra Utacia. "Telling Your Own Story." *Indian Country Today,* no. 2 (June–July 2017): 38–41.

L'Amour, Beau. "About the Hopalong Cassidy Novels by Louis L'Amour." http://www.louislamour.com/novels/hopalong4byLouis.htm.

L'Amour, Louis. *Down the Long Hill.* New York: Thorndike Press, 2008.

_____. *Education of a Wandering Man.* New York: Bantam Books, 1989.

_____. *Kiowa Trail.* New York: Thorndike Press, 1998.

_____. *Last of the Breed.* New York: Thorndike Press, 1987.

_____. *The Lonesome Gods.* New York: Bantam Books, 1983.

_____. *The Sackett Companion: A Guide to the Sackett Novels.* New York: Bantam Books, 1988.

_____. *Sackett's Land.* New York: Saturday Review Press, 1974.

Landry, Alysa. "Native History: Geronimo is Last Native Warrior to Surrender." *Indian Country Today,* September 4, 2014.

Landsman, Gail. "Informant as Critic: Conducting Research on a Dispute Between Iroquoist Scholars and Traditional Iroquois." In *Indians and Anthropologists,* edited by Thomas Bilosi and Larry J. Zimmerman, 160–76. Tucson: University of Arizona Press, 1997.

La Pointe, Ernie. *Sitting Bull: His Life and Legacy.* Layton, UT: Gibbs Smith, 2009.

Las Casas, Bartolomé de. *A Brief History of the Destruction of the Indies.* Project Gutenberg, 2007. www.gutenberg.org/ebooks/20321.

Lawlor, Laurie. *Shadow Catcher: The Life and Work of Edward S. Curtis.* Lincoln, NE: Bison Books, 2005.

Lecroix, Celeste. "High Stakes Stereotypes: The Emergence of the Casino Indian Trope in Television Depictions of Contemporary Native Americans." *Howard Journal of Communications* 22, no. 1 (2011): 1–23.

Leguat, Francois. *The Voyage of Francois Leguat (1708),* 2 vols. London: Pasfield Oliver, 1891.

Leonard, Thomas C. "The Reluctant Conquerors." *American Heritage* 27, no. 5 (1976): 34–41.

Lerner, Barron H. "Scholars Argue Over Legacy of Surgeon Who Was Lionized, Then Vilified." *New York Times,* October 8, 2003. https://www.nytimes.com/2003/10/28/health/scholars-argue-over-legacy-of-surgeon-who-was-lionized-then-vilified.html.

Lone Hill, Dana. "The Wounded Knee Medals of Honor Should Be Rescinded." *The Guardian,* February 18, 2013.

"Louis L'Amour." *The Famous People.* https://www.thefamouspeople.com/profiles/louis-lamour-54697.php.

Louis L'Amour Website. www.louislamour.com/aboutlouis/biography6.htm.

Lukens, Margo. "Native American Literature." In *The Oxford Handbook of Indigenous American Literature,* edited by James H. Cox and Daniel Heath Justice. New York: Oxford University Press, 2014.

MacAndrew, Craig, and Robert B. Edgerton. *Drunken Comportment: A Social Explanation.* Chicago: Aldine Publishing Company, 1969.

Mackley, Brian. "Lawmakers Introduce Bill to Rescind 20 Medals of Honor Issued in Connection with a Massacre of Native Americans." *Military Times,* June 25, 2019. https://www.militarytimes.com/news/pentagon-congress/2019/06/25/lawmakers-introduce-bill-to-rescind-20-medals-of-honor-issued-in-connection-with-a-massacre-of-native-americans/.

Madley, Benjamin. *An American Genocide: The United States and the California Indian Catastrophe.* New Haven, CT: Yale University Press, 2016.

Malar, Richard, et al. "Biochemical Evidence of Cannibalism at a Prehistoric Puebloan Site in Southwestern Colorado." *Nature* 407 (September 7, 2000): 74–78.

Malcomson, Scott. *One Drop of Blood: The American Misadventure of Race.* New York: Farrar, Straus and Giroux, 2000.

Manchel, Frank. "Cultural Confusion: Broken Arrow." In *Hollywood's Indian: The Portrayal of the Native American in Film,* edited by Peter C. Rollins and John E. O'Connor, chapter 7. Lexington: University of Kentucky Press, 1998.

Marcia, Dan. "At a Navajo Veterans' Event Trump Makes 'Pocahontas' Crack." *CNN,* November 27, 2017. https://www.cnn.com/2017/11/27/politics/trump-pocahontas-navajo-code-talkers/index.html.

Martin, Joel M. "'My Grandmother Was a Cherokee Princess': Representations of Indians in Southern History." In *Dressing in Feathers: The Construction of the Indian in American Popular Culture,* edited by S. Elizabeth Bird, chapter 9. Boulder, CO: Westview Press, 1996.

Marton, Janos. "Today in NYC History: How the Dutch Actually Bought Manhattan (The Long Version)." *Untapped New York.* https://untappedcities.com/2015/05/06/today-in-nyc-history-how-the-dutch-actually-bought-manhattan-the-long-version/.

Martyr d'Anghiera, Peter. *De Orbe Novo, The First Decade,* book 1. Translated by Francis Augustus MacNutt. 1516; Project Gutenberg, 2004. www.gutenberg.org/files/12425/12425-h/12425-h.htm.

Mason, W. Dale. "The Indian Policy of Abraham Lincoln." *Indigenous Policy Journal* (Fall, December 16, 2009). https://ipjournal.wordpress.com/2009/12/16/the-indian-policy-of-abraham-lincoln/.

Mataconis, Doug. "Federal Judge Upholds Revocation of Redskins Trademark." *Outside the Beltway,* July 9, 2015. www.outsidethebeltway.com/federal-judge-upholds-revocation-of-redskins-trademark/.

Mather, Cotton. *Decennium Luctuosum: An History of Remarkable Occurrences, In the Long War....* Boston: B. Green and J. Allen, 1699; Ann Arbor: Evans Early American Imprint Collection. https://quod.lib.umich.edu/cgi/t/text/text-idx?c=evans;idno=N00725.0001.001.

Matson, William, and Mark Frethem, prods. *The Authorized Biography of Crazy Horse and His Family.* DVD released by Reelcontact.com, 2006.

Maurizi, Dennis. "Un-Erasing Tammany." *American History* (February 2016): 50–55.

McCann, Michael. "Why the Redskins Scored a Victory in the Supreme Court's Ruling in Favor of the Slants." *Sports Illustrated,* June 19, 2017.

McCoy, Kevin. "Honda to Pay $25M." *Asbury Park Press*, July 15, 2015, 4B.

McCracken, Harold. *The Charles M. Russell Book*. Garden City, NY: Doubleday and Company, 1957.

McLemore, Laura. "Historical Perspective or Racism on the Prairie?" *LittleHouseOnThe Prairie.com*, December 7, 2018. https://littlehouseontheprairie.com/historical-perspective-or-racism-in-little-house-on-the-prairie/.

Mead, Margaret. *The Changing Culture of an American Tribe*. New York: AMS Press, 1969. Originally published in 1932.

Merrell, James H. *Into the Woods: Negotiators on the Pennsylvania Frontier*. New York: W. W. Norton, 1999.

Mettler, Katie. "Vermont to Abolish Columbus Day in Favor of Indigenous Peoples' Day." *Tampa Bay Times*, April 21, 2019, 6A.

"Michael Mann Looks Back on 'The Last of the Mohicans' 20 Years Later." *Uproxx*, May 12, 2012. https://uproxx.com/hitfix/michael-mann-looks-back-on-the-last-of-the-mohicans-20-years-later/.

Midge, Tiffany. "Five Inspiring Native American Musical Artists Come Together as 'Dream Warriors.'"

"Missing and Murdered Indigenous Women and Girls: A Snapshot of Data From 71 Urban Cities in the United States." Urban Indian Health Institute, Seattle, 2018.

"Modoc War 1872–1873." *Encyclopedia.com*. https://www.encyclopedia.com/history/united-states-and-canada/us-history/modoc-war-1872-1873.

Monet, Jenni. "Linking Arms, Marching Forward: Cherokee Nation Accepts Ruling on Freedmen." *Indian Country Today*, September 1, 2017.

Monette, Richard. "Blood Quantum, Fractionated Land, Fractionated People." In *The Great Vanishing Act: Blood Quantum and the Future of Native Nations*, edited by Kathleen Ratteree and Norbert Hill, 246–59. Wheat Ridge, Colorado: Fulcrum Publishers.

Moran III, Francis. "Between Primates and Primitives: Natural Man as the Missing Link in Rousseau's Second Discourse." In *Philosophers on Race*, edited by Julie K. Ward and Tommy L. Lott, 125–44. Oxford: Blackwell Publishers, 2002.

Moyers, Bill, and Oren Lyons. *Oren Lyons the Faithkeeper*. Interview on PBS Television, July 3, 1991. https://billmoyers.com/content/oren-lyons-the-faithkeeper/.

Murphy, Sean. "Cherokee Nation Seeks Congressional Delegate." *Asbury Park Press*, August 18, 2019, 21A.

Myers, J. Jay. "Sand Creek Massacre." *HistoryNet*. https://www.historynet.com/sand-creek-massacre.

National Archives and Records Administration. https://www.archives.gov.

National Congress of American Indians Website. www.ncai.org.

National Council of Urban Indian Health. "NCUIH's Response to President Trump's FY 20 Budget Request." Press Release, March 3, 2019.

National Gaming Association Annual Report, 2019. https://online.flippingbook.com/view/317287.

National Indian Gaming Association. https://www.indiangaming.org/about.

National Institute of Justice. "Five Things about Violence Against American Indians and Alaska Native Women and Men." U.S. Department of Justice, May 2016. https://www.ncjrs.gov/pdffiles1/nij/249815.pdf.

National Museum of the American Indian 20, no. 4 (Winter 2019).

Nations Development Institute and Echo Hawk Consulting. *Reclaiming Native Truth: A Project to Dispel America's Myths and Misconceptions*. June 2018. https://www.reclaimingnativetruth.com.

Native American Rights Fund. https://www.narf.org.

"Native Words, Native Warriors." National Museum of the American Indian. www.nmai.si.edu/education/codetalkers/html/chapter7.html.

Navajo Times. https://navajotimes.com.

NDN Collective. https://ndncollective.org/who-we-are/.

Neal, Samantha. "Views of Racism as a Major Problem Increase Sharply, Especially among Democrats." *PEW Research Center*, August 29, 2017. www.pewresearch.org/fact-tank/2017/08/29/views-of-racism-as-a-major-problem-increase-sharply-esp.

Nemerov, Alexander. *Frederic Remington and Turn-of-the-Century America*. New Haven, CT: Yale University Press, 1995.

Nevins, Francis. *Bar-20: The Life of Clarence Mulford*. Jefferson, NC: McFarland & Company, 1993.

Nicholson, Blake. "Dakota Access Developer Granted Hearing Delay in Dispute." *Associated Press*, August 15, 2017. https://apnews.com/article/57082a415dce40879c3ba333b21c4600.

Niderost, Eric. "The Great Sioux Uprising of 1862." *Warfare History Network*. https://warfarehistorynetwork.com/daily/civil-war/the-great-sioux-uprising-of-1862.

NK 360°. https://americanindian.si.edu/nk360.

Nolan, William F. *Max Brand: Western Giant*. Bowling Green, OH: Bowling Green State University Press, 1985.

Noley, Ken. "The Representation of Conquest: John Ford and the Hollywood Indian: 1939–1964." In *Hollywood's Indian: The Portrayal of the Native American in Film*, edited by Peter C. Rollins and John E. O'Connor, chapter 6. Lexington: University of Kentucky Press, 1998.

Northern Plains Reservation Aid (formerly

American Indian Relief Council). "History and Culture: Boarding Schools." http://www.nativepartnership.org/site/PageServer?pagename=airc_hist_boardingschools.

Nuckols, Ben. "US Poll Finds Widespread Support for Redskins Name." *AP The Big Story*, May 2, 2013. www.bigstory.ap/org/article/us-poll-finds-widespread-support-redskins-name.

Obstacles at Every Turn: Barriers to Political Participation Faced by Native American Voters. Boulder, CO: Native American Rights Fund, 2020.

O'Connor, John E. "The White Man's Burden: An Institutional Approach." In *Hollywood's Indian: The Portrayal of the Native American in Film*, edited by Peter C. Rollins and John E. O'Connor. Lexington: University of Kentucky Press, 1998.

O'Hara, Kathryn. "Female Captive Narratives in Colonial America." *The Gettysburg Historical Journal* 8 (2009): 34–52.

O'Laughlin, Edward, and Mihir Zaveri. "Irish Return Old Favor, Helping Native Americans Battling the Virus." *New York Times*, May 5, 2020. https://www.nytimes.com/2020/05/05/world/coronavirus-ireland-native-american-tribes.html.

Olife, Helen. "Graduation Rates and American Indian Education." *Partnership with Native Americans* (blog), May 16, 2017. blog.native-partnership.org/graduation-rates-american-indian-education.

"On Views of Race and Inequality, Blacks and Whites are Worlds Apart." *PEW Research Center*, June 27, 2016. www.pewsocialtrends.org/2016/06/27/on-views-of-race-and-inequality-blacks-and-whites-are-worlds.

Owens, Louis. *Other Destinies: Understanding the American Indian Novel.* Norman: University of Oklahoma Press, 1992.

"The Pacific Railway: A Brief History of Building the Transcontinental Railroad." *The Transcontinental Railroad: Bridges, Tunnels, Rails, Rail Cars, Locomotives, Landmarks, Maps, Explosives, & More.* https://railroad.lindahall.org/essays/brief-history.html.

"Papal Bull *Sublimus Dei*: On the Enslavement and Evangelization of Indians." Pope Paul III, 1537. http://www.papalencyclicals.net/paul03/p3subli.htm.

Park, Haeyoun, and Larry Buchanan. "Why It Takes Two Years for Syrian Refugees to Enter the U.S." *New York Times*, November 20, 2015. https://www.nytimes.com/interactive/2015/11/20/us/why-it-takes-two-years-for-syrian-refugees-to-apply-to-enter-the-united-states.html?m.

"The Partisan Divide on Political Values Grows Even Wider." *PEW Research Center*, October 5, 2017. www.people-press.org/2017/10/05/4-race-immigration-and-discrimination.

PBS. "Chief Joseph." *Ken Burns Presents the West.* https://www.pbs.org/weta/thewest/people/a_chiefjoseph.htm.

_____. "Junipero Serra." *Ken Burns Presents the West.* https://www.pbs.org/weta/thewest/people/S-z/serra.htm.

_____. "Red Cloud." *Ken Burns Presents the West.* www.pbs.org/weta/thewest/people/i_r/redcloud.htm.

_____. "Sacagawea." *Lewis and Clark: The Journey of the Core of Discovery.* www.pbs.org/lewisandclark/inside/saca.html

Pember, Mary Annette. *Intergenerational Trauma: Understanding Natives' Inherited Pain.* Indian Country Media Network, 2016. https://amber-ic.org/wp-content/uploads/2017/01/ICMN-All-About-Generations-Trauma.pdf.

Percy, George. Journal Entry about Jamestown. Virtual Jamestown. extext.lib.virginia.edu/etcbin/Jamestown=browsemod?id=J1063.

_____. "Jamestown: 1609–10: 'Starving Time.'" National Humanities Center. nationalhumanitiescenter.org/pds/amerbegin/settlement/text2/Jamestownpercyrelation.pdf.

Piccardo, Rebecca, and Dan Sweeney. "Seminole Tribe Chairman Billie Ousted from Office by Unanimous Vote." *Florida Sun-Sentinel*, September 28, 2016. www.Sun-Sentinel.com/local/broward/fl-seminole-chairman-removed-from-office-20160928-story.html.

Pindus, Nancy G., et al. *Housing Needs of American Indians and Alaskan Natives in Tribal Areas: A Report from the Assessment of American Indian, Alaska Native, and Native Hawaiian Housing Needs.* Department of Housing and Urban Development, January 19, 2017. https://www.huduser.gov/portal/publications/HNAIHousingNeeds.html.

Pine, Frank W., ed. *Autobiography of Benjamin Franklin.* New York: Henry Holt, 1916; Project Gutenberg, 2006. https://www.gutenberg.org/files/20203/20203-h/20203-h.htm.

"Pocahontas." *Biography.* https://www.biography.com/people/pocahontas-9443116.

"Pocahontas." *History.com.* www.history.com/topics/native-american-history/pocahontas.

"Ponca History." Ponca Tribe of Indians of Oklahoma. ponca.com/ponca-history.

Ponce, Pedro. "Edward Curtis' Epic Project to Photograph Native Americans." *Humanities* 21, no. 3 (May/June 2000).

Powers, Thomas. *The Killing of Crazy Horse.* New York: Vintage Books, 2011.

Price, David A. *Love and Hate in Jamestown.* New York: Alfred A. Knopf, 2007.

Price, John. "The Stereotyping of North American Indians in Motion Pictures." In *The Pretend Indians: Images of Native Americans in the Movies*, edited by Gretchen M. Bataille and Charles L. P. Silet. Ames: Iowa State University Press, 1980.

Privy Council Office. *Reclaiming Power and Place: The Final Report of the National Inquiry into Missing and Murdered Indigenous Women and Girls.* National Inquiry into Missing and Murdered Indigenous Woman and Girls.

Vancouver: Privy Council Office, 2019. https://www.mmiwg-ffada.ca/final-report/.

Project Implicit. Harvard University. https://implicit.harvard.edu/implicit/education.html.

Quammen, David. "Was Darwin Wrong?" *National Geographic Magazine*, November 2004. https://www.nationalgeographic.com/magazine/article/was-darwin-wrong.

"Quanah Parker." *Britannica*. https://www.britannica.com/biography/Quanah-Parker.

Quinn, Ruth. "Native American Scouts." U.S. Army. November 7, 2013. https://www.army.mil/article/114646/Native_American_Scouts.

"Rabbit-Proof Fence." YouTube. https://www.youtube.com/watch?v=mNbPPvetL.Cw.

Raheja, Michelle H. *Reservation Reelism: Redfacing, Visual Sovereignty, and Representations of Native Americans in Films.* Lincoln: University of Nebraska Press, 1999.

Ramachandran, Vijaya, and Julie Walz. "Is Haiti Doomed to Be the Republic of NGOs?" *Center for Global Development*, January 9, 2012. https://www.cgdev.org/blog/haiti-doomed-be-republic-ngos.

Ratteree, Kathleen, and Norbert Hill, eds. *The Great Vanishing Act: Blood Quantum and the Future of Native Nations.* Wheat Ridge, CO: Fulcrum Publishers, 2017.

"Red Cloud, 1820–1909." *Partnership with Native Americans* (blog). www.nativepartnership.org/site/PageServer?pagename=PWNA_Native_Biography_redcloud.

Regan, Shawn. "Unlocking the Wealth of Indian Nations: Overcoming Obstacles to Tribal Energy Development." *PERC Perspective*, February 2014. https://www.perc.org/2014/02/18/unlocking-the-wealth-of-indian-nations-overcoming-obstacles-to-tribal-energy-development/.

Reid, Basil A. *Myths and Realities of Caribbean History.* Tuscaloosa: University of Alabama Press, 2009.

Remnick, Noah. "The Ramapoughs vs. the World." *New York Times*, April 14, 2017.

Reverby, Susan. *Examining Tuskegee: The Infamous Study and Its Legacy.* Chapel Hill: University of North Carolina Press, 2009.

Rickert, Levi. "U.S. Presidents in Their Own Words Concerning American Indians." *Native New Online*, February 19, 2018. https://nativenewsonline.net/currents/us-presidents-in-their-own-words-concerning-american-indians.

Robert Wood Johnson Foundation, National Public Radio, and the T. H. Chan School of Public Health at Harvard University. *Discrimination in America: Experiences and Views of Native Americans.* November 2017. https://legacy.npr.org/documents/2017/nov/NPR-discrimination-native-americans-final.pdf.

Robertson, Dwanna L. "The Myth of Indian Casino Riches." *Indian Country Media Network*, April 19, 2017.

Robins-Early, Nick. "Report Says Canada's Residential Schools Committed 'Cultural Genocide' against Aboriginals." *Huffington Post*, June 4, 2015. https://www.huffpost.com/entry/canada-residential-schools_n_7504016.

Rollings, William H. "Citizenship and Suffrage: The Native American Struggle for Civil Rights in the American West, 1830–1965." *University of Nevada Law Review* (Fall 2004). scholars.law.unlv.edu/cgi/viewcontent.cgi?article=1311&context=nlj.

Root, Leeane. "A New Nation's Forgotten Indian Allies." *Indian Country Today* 2 (June–July 2017): 32–34.

Rosay, André B. *Violence against American Indian and Alaska Native Women and Men: 2010 Findings from the National Intimate Partner and Sexual Violence Survey.* National Institute of Justice Research Report, U.S. Department of Justice, May 2016. https://www.ncjrs.gov/pdffiles1/nij/249736.pdf.

Rowlandson, Mary. *The Narrative of the Captivity and Restoration of Mrs. Mary Rowlandson.* Project Gutenberg, 2009. Gutenberg.org/files/851/851-h/851-h.htm.

Ruoff, A. LaVonne Brown, and Gerald Vizenor. "Woodland Word Warrior: An Introduction to the Works of Gerald Vizenor." *MELUS* 3 (Spring–Summer 1986): 13–43.

"Sacagawea." *Biography*. https://www.biography.com/people/sacagawea-9468731.

"Sacagawea." *History.com*. https://www.history.com/topics/native-american-history/sacagawea.

"Sand Creek Massacre." This Day in History, *History.com*. https://www.history.com/this-day-in-history/sand-creek-massacre.

"The Scalp Industry." xroads.virginia.edu/~Hyper/HNS/scalping/oldfolks.html.

Schilling, Vincent. "Fight the Power: 8 Contemporary Heroes and Leaders of Native Resistance." *Indian Country Today*, October 20, 2014.

_____. "Grammy Winner Taboo from the Black Eyed Peas: An *Indian Country Today* Interview." *Indian Country Today*. https://indiancountrytoday.com/news/grammy-winner-taboo-from-the-black-eyed-peas-an-indian-country-today-interview-AbvhwGLFZUbri

_____. "Tribal Gaming Is a $32 Billion Business: NIGC Releases Annual Revenue Figures." *Indian Country Today*, June 26, 2018.

_____. "The True Story of Pocahontas: Historical Myths Versus Sad Reality." *Indian Country Today*, March 21, 2017.

Schuman, Evan. "From the Sidewalk to Sotheby's, the Cigar Store Indian is a Piece of American Tobacco History." *Cigar Magazine* (Winter 2004–05): 78–88.

Scott, Dylan. "Covid-19's Devastating Toll on Black and Latino Americans in One Chart." *Vox*, April 14, 2020. https://www.vox.com/2020/4/17/21225610/us-coronavirus-death-rates-blacks-latinos-whites.

Seaver, James E. *A Narrative of the Life of Mary Jemison*. Whitefish, MT: Kessinger Publishing, LLC, 2010.

"The Seminole Wars." *Exploring Florida*. https://fcit.usf.edu/florida/lessons/sem_war/sem_war1.htm.

"Sequoyah." *Britannica*. https://www.britannica.com/biography/Sequoyah.

"Sequoyah and the Creation of the Cherokee Syllabary." National Geographic Society. https://www.nationalgeographic.org/article/sequoyah-and-creation-cherokee-syllabary/.

"Sequoyah's Syllabary: Overcoming Challenges." The Sequoyah Birthplace Museum. http://www.sequoyahmuseum.org/history/sequoyahs-syllabary/.

Seven, John. "Interview: Lee Francis Talks Native American Comics, Indigipop X and the Rise of the Indiginerd." *The Beat*, July 19, 2019.

Shear, Susan, Ryan T. Knowles, Gregory J. Soden, and Antonio J. Castro. "Manifesting Destiny: Re/presentations of Indigenous People in K–12 U.S. History Standards." *Theory and Research in Social Education* 43, no. 1 (2015): 68–101.

Sheyahshe, Michael A. *Native Americans in Comic Books: A Critical Study*. Jefferson, NC: McFarland & Company, 2008.

Shoemaker, Nancy. "How Indians Got to Be Red." *The American Historical Review* 102, no. 3 (June 1997): 625–644.

Shutt, Bill. *Cannibalism: A Perfectly Natural History*. Chapel Hill, NC: Algonquin Books, 2017.

Singer, Beverly A. *Wiping the War Paint Off the Lens*. Minneapolis: University of Minnesota Press, 2001.

"Sitting Bull." *Biography*. https://www.biography.com/people/sitting-bull-9485326.

"Sitting Bull." *History.com*. www.history.com/topics/nativeamerican-history/sitting-bull.

"1675—King Philip's War." The Society of Colonial Wars in the State of Connecticut. colonialwarsct.org/1675.htm.

Skinner, Michael R. "A New Kind of Inheritance." *Scientific American* 311, no. 2 (August 2014): 44–51.

Slotkin, Richard. *Gunfighter Nation: The Myth of the Frontier in Twentieth Century America*. New York: Atheneum, 1992.

_____. *Regeneration through Violence: The Mythology of the American Frontier*. Middletown, CT: Wesleyan University Press, 1973.

_____. "The Wild West." In *Buffalo Bill and the Wild West*, edited by David H. Katzive. New York: Brooklyn Museum, 1981.

Smedley, Audrey. *Race in North America: Origin and Evolution of a Worldview*. Boulder, CO: Westview Press, 1999.

Smith, John. *The General Historie of Virginia, New England, and the Summer Isles: With the Names*. London: I. D. and I. H. for Michael Sparks, 1624; Documenting the American South, University of North Carolina at Chapel Hill. https://docsouth.unc.edu/southlit/smith/menu.html.

Smith, Maureen. "Forever Changed: Boarding School Narratives of an Indian Identity in the U.S. and Canada." *Indigenous Nations Studies Journal* 2, no. 2 (Fall 2001): 57–82.

Smith, Paul C. *Everything You Know about Indians Is Wrong*. Minneapolis: University of Minnesota Press, 2009.

Smith, Paul C., and Robert Allen Warrior. *Like a Hurricane: The Indian Movement from Alcatraz to Wounded Knee*. New York: The New Press, 1996.

Smith, Stacy L. *Report on Diversity (CARD)*. Annenberg Foundation, February 22, 2016. Annenberg.USC.edu/news/faculty-research/c-suite-characters-screen-how-inclusive-entertainment-industry.

Smith, Stacy L., and the Media Diversity and Social Change Initiative. "Inequality in 900 Popular Films." Annenberg Foundation, July 2017. Annenberg.USC.edu/research/mdsc/.

Snow, Dean R., Nancy Gonlin, and Peter Siegel. *Archaeology of Native North America*, 2nd ed. Milton Park, UK: Taylor and Francis, 2019.

"Soldiers Massacre Sleeping Camp of Native Americans." This Day in History, *History.com*. https://www.history.com/this-day-in-history/soldiers-massacre-the-wrong-camp-of-indians.

Soniak, Matt. "Was Manhattan Really Bought for $24?" *Mental Floss*, October 2, 2012. mentalfloss.com/article/12657/was-manhattan-really-bought-24.

Southern Poverty Law Center. "Active Hate Groups in the United States." https://www.splcenter.org.

_____. "Extremist Files." https://www.splcenter.org/fighting-hate/extremist-files.

Spencer, Herbert. *Social Statics*. London: John Chapman, 1851; Online Library of Liberty. https://oll.libertyfund.org/titles/spencer-social-statics-1851.

"Squanto." *Biography*. https://www.biography.com/political-figure/squanto.

"Squanto." *Britannica*. https://www.britannica.com/biography/squanto.

"Squanto: The Former Slave." *History of Massachusetts Blog*. https://historyofmassachusetts.org/squanto-the-former-slave.

Starbuck, David R. "The 'Massacre' at Fort William Henry." *Penn Museum* 50, no. 1 (March 2008). www.penn.museum/sites/expedition/the-massacre-at-fort-william-henry/.

Stedman, Raymond William. *Shadows of the Indian: Stereotypes in American Culture*. Norman: University of Oklahoma Press, 1982.

Steele, Claude. "Thin Ice: 'Stereotype Threat' and Black College Students." *The Atlantic Monthly*, August 1999, 44–54.

Steele, Claude, and Joshua Aronson. "Stereotype Threat and the Intellectual Test Performance of African Americans." *Journal of Personality and*

Social Psychology 69, no. 5 (November 1995): 797–811.

Steele, Jeffrey. "Reduced to Images: American Indians in Nineteenth Century Advertising." In *Dressing in Feathers: The Construction of the Indian in American Popular Culture*, edited by S. Elizabeth Bird, 45–64. Boulder, CO: Westview Press, 1996.

Steiner, Stan. *The New Indians*. New York: Harper and Row, 1968.

Sterritt, David. "Review of *The Last of the Mohicans*." *TCM Film*. www.tem.com/This-month/article/480649/480765/The-Last-of-the-mohicans.html.

Stoddard, Ed. "Poll Finds More Americans Believe in Devil than Darwin." *Reuters*, November 29, 2007. https://www.reuters.com/article/us-usa-religion-beliefs/poll-finds-more-americans-believe-in-devil-than-darwin-idUSN2922875820071129.

Stoddard, Lothrop. *The Revolt of Civilization: The Menace of the Underman*. New York: Charles Scribner's Sons, 1921.

"The Stolen Generations." *Australians Together*. https://australianstogether.org.au/discover/australian-history/stolen-generations.

Strausbaugh, John. *Black Like You*. New York: Jeremy P. Tarcher/Penguin, 2006.

Sugden, John. *Tecumseh: A Life*. New York: Henry Holt, 1998.

"Surviving the Bering Strait." *American History* 53, no. 4 (October 2018).

Sweeney, Edwin R. "Chiricahua Chief Cochise." *HistoryNet*. www.historynet.com/cochise#articles.

Tallbear, Kim. *Native American DNA: Tribal Belonging and the False Promise of Genetic Sciences*. Minneapolis: University of Minnesota Press, 2013.

Tatara, Paul. "*The Last of the Mohicans*, 1936." *TCM Film*. www.tcm.com/tcmdb/title/80897/the-last-of-the-mohicans/articles.html.

Taylor, Annette M. "Cultural Heritage in Northern Exposure." In *Dressing in Feathers: The Construction of the Indian in American Popular Culture*, edited by S. Elizabeth Bird, chapter 15. Boulder, CO: Westview Press, 1996.

"Tecumseh: Facts, Information and Articles about Tecumseh, a Native American Chief from the Wild West." *HistoryNet*. https://www.historynet.com/tecumseh.

Testerman, Jeff, and Brad Goldstein. "Seminole Gambling: A Trail of Millions." *St. Petersburg Times*, December 20, 1997.

Texas State Historical Association. "Indian Captives." https://tshaonline.org/handbook/online/articles/bxiol.

Thornton, Russell. *American Indian Holocaust and Survival: A Population History since 1492*. Norman: University of Oklahoma Press, 1987.

"Tisquantum ('Squanto')." *MayflowerHistory.com*. Mayflowerhistory.com/tisquantum.

Tolles, Thayer. "Frederic Remington 1861–1909."

The Met. https://www.metmuseum.org/exhibitions/listings/2017/frederic-remington.

Tougias, Michael. "King Philip's War in New England." *The History Place*. www.historyplace.com/specials/writers/kingphilip.htm.

Trahant, Mark. "Meet the Native Americans Running for Office in 2018." *High Country News*, August 3, 2018.

"Trail of Tears Exhibit." Cherokee Heritage Center, Tahlequah, Oklahoma. www.cherokeeheritage.org/attractions/trail-of-tears.

Treuer, David. *The Heartbeat of Wounded Knee: Native America from 1890 to the Present*. New York: Riverhead Books, 2019.

"The Trials & Hangings." *The US–Dakota War of 1862*. Minnesota Historical Society. https://usdakotawar.org/history/aftermath/trials-hanging.

"The True Story of Pocahontas as Not Told by Disney." *Ancient Origins*, March 2, 2019. www.ancient-origins.net/history-famous-people/true-story-pocahontas-not-told-disney-002285.

Trumbull, Benjamin. *A General History of the United States of America*. Boston: Farrand, Mallory and Company, 1810.

"Trump's Aide's Son Denounces Obama Comments." *Tampa Bay Times*, December 26, 2017, 8A.

Turner III, Frederick Jackson. *The Portable North American Indian Reader*. New York: Penguin Books, 1973.

Twain, Mark. "Fenimore Cooper's Literary Offenses." 1895. https://twain.lib.virginia.edu/projects/rissetto/offense.html.

"20 Native American Authors You Need to Read." *Open Education Data Base*. http://oedb.org/ilibrarian/20-native-american-authors-you-need-to-read/.

"Understanding the American Indian Mascot Issue: A Collection of Writings on Team Names and Logos." *Students and Teachers Against Racism*. www.racismagainstindians.org/understandingmascots.htm.

United Nations Human Rights, Office of the High Commissioner. "Native Americans Facing Excessive Force in North Dakota Pipeline Protests—UN Expert," November 15, 2016. http://www.ohchr.org/EN/NewsEvents/Pages/DisplayNews.aspx?NewsID=20868&LangID=E.

University of Michigan Health System. "Gene Study Supports Single Main Migration Across Bering Strait." *ScienceDaily*, November 28, 2007. www.sciencedaily.com/releases/2007/11/071126170543.htm

U.S. Commission on Civil Rights. *Broken Promises: Continuing Federal Funding Shortfall for Native Americans*. Washington, D.C.: U.S. Government Printing Office, December 2018. https://www.usccr.gov/files/pubs/2018/12-20-Broken-Promises.pdf.

_____. *A Quiet Crisis: Federal Funding and Unmet*

Needs in Indian Country. July 2003. https://www.usccr.gov/pubs/na0703/na0204.pdf.

U.S. Department of Equal Employment Opportunity. "Charge Statistics (Charges Filed with EEOC) FY 1997 through FY 2020." https://www.eeoc.gov/statistics/charge-statistics-charges-filed-eeoc-fy-1997-through-fy-2020.

U.S. Department of Health and Human Services. "Disparities." Indian Health Service, October 2019. https://www.ihs.gov/newsroom/factsheets/disparities/.

U.S. Department of the Interior. Indian Affairs, Office of Indian Gaming. https://www.bia.gov/as-ia/oig.

U.S. Department of Justice and U.S. Department of Education. "Joint 'Dear Colleague' Letter." January 8, 2014. https://www2.ed.gov/about/offices/list/ocr/letters/colleague-201401-title-vi.html.

Velez, Denise Oliver. "Native Schools and Stolen Generations: U.S. and Canada." *Daily Kos,* April 14, 2013. https://www.dailykos.com/stories/2013/4/14/1200994/-Native-schools-and-stolen-generations-U-S-and-Canada.

Wade, Lizzie. "Genetic Study Reveals Surprising Ancestry of Many Americans." *Science,* December 18, 2014. https://www.sciencemag.org/news/2014/12/genetic-study-reveals-surprising-ancestry-many-americans.

Waldstein, David. "Cleveland Indians Will Abandon Chief Wahoo Logo Next Year." *New York Times,* January 29, 2018

Walker, Dalton. "US House Candidates Make History," *Indian Country Today,* November 4, 2020.

Walker, Jeffrey. "Deconstructing an American Myth: Hollywood and The Last of the Mohicans." Paper Presented at the Tenth Symposium on James Fenimore Cooper, *James Fenimore Cooper: His Country and His Art,* State University of New York College at Oneonta, July 1995. https://www.jfcoopersociety.org/articles/SUNY/1995SUNY-WALKER.HTML.

Walker, Richard. "Native History Is American History." *National Museum of the American Indian* 21, no. 1 (Spring 2020): 28–33.

Wang, Wendy. "Interracial Marriage: Who Is 'Marrying Out'?" *PEW Research Center,* June 12, 2015. www.PEWresearch.org/fact-tank/2015/06/12/interracial-marriage-who-is-marrying-out/.

Watkins, Steve. *The Black O.* Athens: University of Georgia Press, 1997.

Watson, Bruce. "George Caitlin's Obsession." *Smithsonian* Magazine, December 2002. https://www.smithsonianmag.com/arts-culture/george-caitlin-obsession-72840046.

Watt, Ian. "Robinson Crusoe as Myth." *Essays in Criticism* 1, no. 2 (1951): 95–119.

Wayne, John. Interview. *Playboy* Magazine, May 1971. https://pages.shanti.virginia.edu/wild_wild_cold_war/files/2011/11/John_wayne_playboy_Int2.pdf.

Weber, Max. *The Protestant Ethic and the Spirit of Capitalism.* New York: Penguin Twentieth Century Classics, 2002.

Weiser, Kathy. "Legends of America: Cochise—Strong Apache Leader." *Legends of America.* http://www.legendsofamerica.com/na-cochise.

_____. "The Marias Massacre of Montana." *Legends of America.* https://www.legendsofamerica.com/na-mariasmassacre/.

_____. "Seminole Chief Osceola." *Legends of America.* https://www.legendsofamerica.com/na-osceola/

Weitzman, Danielle. "Washington Redskins US Trademark Registrations Reinstated by Fourth Circuit." Ladas & Parry. https://ladas.com/education-center/Washington-redskins-us-trademark-registrations.

Weston, Mary Ann. *Native Americans in the News: Images of Indians in the Twentieth Century Press.* Westport, CT: Greenwood Press, 1996.

White, April. "Written Out of History." *Smithsonian* Magazine 49, no. 10 (March 2019): 14.

"White and Black Americans Far Apart on Racial Issues." *Ipsos,* August 27, 2020. https://www.ipsos.com/en-us/news-polls/npr-racial-inequality-issues.

White, Laurie. "21 Celebrities You Didn't Know Were Native American." *B-Babble* (Disney Corp.), November 15, 2013.

Whiteley, Peter. "The End of Anthropology (or Hopi)?" *Journal of the Southwest* 35 (Summer 1993): 125–57.

Wiencek, Henry. "The Dark Side of Thomas Jefferson." *Smithsonian* Magazine, October 2012. https://www.smithsonianmag.com/history/the-dark-side-of-thomas-jefferson-35976004.

Wiencke, Gus. "Chief Tamanend." Upper Southampton Township. https://www.ustwp.org/government/boards-commissions/historical-advisory-board/chief-tamanend/.

Wilder, Laura Ingalls. *Little House in the Big Woods.* New York: Harper and Brothers, 1932.

_____. *Little House on the Prairie.* New York: Harper and Row, 1935.

_____. *On the Way Home.* New York: Harper and Row, 1962.

Williams, Jr., Kennedy. "Cooper's Use of American History." Paper Presented at the First James Fenimore Cooper Symposium, *James Fenimore Cooper: His Country and His Art,* State University of New York College at Oneonta, July 1978.

Williams, Jr., Robert A. *Like a Loaded Weapon: The Rehnquist Court, Indian Rights, and the Legal History of Racism in America.* Minneapolis: University of Minnesota Press, 2005.

_____. *Savage Anxieties: The Invention of Western Civilization.* New York: St. Martin's Press, 2012.

Williams, Timothy. "1 Million Each Year for All, as Long as Tribe's Luck Holds Out." *New York Times,* August 4, 2012.

Wilma, David. "Wheeler-Howard Act (Indian Reorganization Act) Shifts U.S. Policy toward

Native American Right to Self-Determination on June 18, 1934." *HistoryLink.org*, August 12, 2020. www.historylink.org/index.cfm?display page=output.cfm&file_id=2599.

Wilson, R. L. *Buffalo Bill's Wild West: An American Legend*. New York: Random House, 1988.

Wilson, William J. *More than Just Race: Being Black and Poor in the Inner City*. New York: W. W. Norton and Company, 2009.

Wister, Owen. *The Virginian*. New York: Gramercy Books, 1902.

Wolff, Eric. "Obama Administration Blocks Dakota Pipeline, Angering Trump Allies." *Politico*, December 4, 2016. https://www.politico.com/story/2016/12/us-army-corps-blocks-dakota-access-pipeline-232172.

Wood, Joss. "Dallas Cowboys Team Up with WinStar World in First Official NFL Casino Partnership." *Legal Sports Report*, September 6, 2018. http://www.legalsportsreport.com/23697/dallas-cowboys-winstar-casino-deal/.

Worland, James. "What to Know about the Dakota Access Pipeline Protests." *Time*, October 28, 2016. https://time.com/4548566/dakota-access-pipeline-standing-rock-sioux/.

Zackel, Frederick. "Robinson Crusoe and the Ethnic Sidekick." *Bright Lights Film Journal*, October 1, 2000. https://brightlightsfilm.com/robinson-crusoe-ethnic-sidekick/#.YeCFcRPMLxt.

Index